UNDERSTANDING SURAH AL-BAQARAH

A Modern Interpretation of the Quran in the Light of the Quran

Sun Behind The Cloud

In the Name of Allah, the Beneficent, the Merciful

Published by Sun Behind The Cloud Publications

PO Box 15889, Birmingham, B16 6NZ

A CIP catalogue record of this book is available
from the British Library

ISBN (Print): 978-1-908110-72-5

ISBN (eBook): 978-1-908110-73-2

www.sunbehindthecloud.com

info@sunbehindthecloud.com

Contents

Author's Foreword 20

Editor's Introduction 22

Verse by Verse Tafsir 28

Verse 1-2 **28**

- Disjointed letters
- The Book of Guidance

Verse 3-7 **34**

- Description of The God Conscious
    - Belief in the Unseen
    - Belief in previous revelations
- The debate over the predeterminism of faith

Verse 8–16 **42**

- Description of the Hypocrites
    - Lack of Faith in God and the Last Day
    - Deceiving God
    - Sickness of the Soul
    - Corruption on the Earth
    - Deriding God
    - Types of Hypocrites

Verse 17-20 50

- The Parable of the Torch
- Spiritual Blindness
- The Parable of the Rainstorm

Verse 21-24 57

- The universal call
- Reasons to worship God
- The Quran's challenge
- The Fuel of the Fire

Verse 25-29 66

- Description of Paradise
- Drawing a Parable
- Is guidance predestined by God?
- A Covenant with God
- Lifeless to life to death
- The creation of the Earth
    - *For* humans?
    - Where did God turn?
    - The order of creation

Verse 30-34 83

- Creation of a vicegerent
    - Addressing the angels
    - *Nasnās*
- The knowledge of the names

- Prostration before Prophet Adam

Verse 35-39 **94**

- The nature of the Garden
- Satan's deception
- The meaning of *ẓulm*
- Descending to Earth
- Prophet Adam's repentance
- Getting down from the Garden
- Rejecting God's Signs

Verse 40-42 **105**

- The children of Israel
- Types of worshippers
- God's blessing on the Israelites
- Addressing the scholars and those in religious authority
    - Confirming what has been sent before
    - Selling signs for paltry gain
    - Mixing truth with falsehood

Verse 43-46 **111**

- The message is the same
- The command to bow
- The conditions of bidding others to piety
- Assistance through patience and prayer
- Humble hearts and certitude

Verse 47-54 **116**

- Blessings bestowed on the Israelites
- Intercession
- The blessings in detail
    - Delivery from the Pharoah
    - Two instances when the sons were killed
    - Parting the sea
    - The Torah
- Testing the Israelites
- Adopting the cattle
- *Kitāb, Zabūr* and *Furqān*
- The punishment for worshipping the cow

Verse 55-59 **133**

- The request to see God
- *Raj'a*
- More blessings on the Israelites
    - Shade
    - Food
- Attempting to wrong God
- Entering the town
- Changing God's words
- Plague

Verse 60-61 **144**

- The miracle of striking the rock

- The twelve springs
- The ungratefulness of the Israelites
    - Replacing the superior with the inferior
- The consequence of transgression
    - Defying the signs of God
    - Killing the Prophets

Verse 62-66 **153**

- The Sabeans
- Universal issues facing all communities
- Religious pluralism
- The pledge and the Mount
- Violating the Sabbath

Verse 67-73 **164**

- The command to slaughter a cow
    - The reason
    - Clarification
- Exposing the concealed
- Bringing the murdered man back to life
- Sacrificing the animalistic desires

Verse 74-75 **174**

- Hardening the heart
- Pure hearts
- Distorting the scripture

Verse 76-79 **184**

- A dialogue between the Jews of Medina and the Muslims
- Meaning of "God has opened for you"
- *ummīyūn*
- Following the clergymen
- Misleading commentaries

Verse 80-82 **193**

- Enduring the fire for a short time
- The universal rule about heaven and hell

Verse 83-84 **199**

- The pledge from the Children of Israel
    - Worship no one but God
    - Doing good to parents
    - Looking after the orphans and the needy
    - Speak kindly to people
    - Do not shed your blood
    - Do not remove people from their homes

Verse 85-86 **208**

- Believing in one part of the book and defying the other
- Sectarian conflict
- Punishment is not a static process
- Similarities between the Jews and the early Muslims

Verse 87-88 214

- Manifest proofs of Prophet Jesus
- The Holy Spirit
- Meaning of *ghulf*
- Curse of God

Verse 89-92 219

- A brief history of the Jews of Medina
- Cursing
- Rejecting God's message
- Envy
- Earning God's wrath
- Challenging prejudices

Verse 93-96 229

- Raising the mount
- Love for the calf
- Challenging the exclusivist view
- Longing for death

Verse 97-99 237

- The meaning and the context of "Gabriel is our enemy"
- Denying the signs

Verse 100-105 243

- Breaking covenants and treaties
- Denying the Prophet

- Magic
- Hārūt and Mārūt
- *īmān* and *taqwā*
- *ra'inā* and *unẓurnā*
- Jealous of blessings

Verse 106-109 **259**

- Abrogation
- Questioning the Prophet
- Turning away from the truth

Verse 110-113 **271**

- Being steadfast
- Meaning of "beside God"
- Who will enter Paradise?
- Hostility between Jews and Christians
- Safety of the mosques

Verse 114-123 **281**

- The East and The West
- The face of God
- God taking a son
- Process of creation "Be and it is"
- Bearer of Good News
- Divine Guidance
- Following the Quran
- Concluding the discussion on the Israelites

Verse 124-132 295

- The significance of the Kabah
- Prophet Abraham's tests
- Station of Abraham
- Imamate
- Prophet Abraham's requests
- The meaning of "*ummah*"
- The creed of Abraham
- Submission to God

Verse 133-141 315

- Following Prophet Abraham
- *ḥanīf*
- The tribes
- Defiance
- The *ṣibqa* of God
- Challenging sectarianism

Verse 142-150 325

- The change in the direction of prayer
    - As a test
    - The foolish people
    - The *badā'*
    - The middle nation
    - The meaning of *shahīd*
    - The aim of the change
    - The influence of Jews over Muslims in Medina

Verse 151-157 **338**

- Beautiful qualities of the holy Prophet
- Remembering God
- Preparing for war
- Patience and Prayer
    - Types of patience
- Belonging to God
- The meaning of *ṣalawāt*

Verse 158-162 **346**

- Ṣafā and Marwa
- *al-bayyināt* and *al-hudā*
- The cursers
    - An exception from the curse

Verse 163-167 **351**

- Monotheism
- God's signs in nature
- Equating others with God
- God is severe in punishment
- Regret and free will

Verse 168-170 **361**

- Eating the lawful
- Following in Satan's steps
- Blind following

Verse 171-176 **366**

- Life on different levels
- Thanksgiving
- Unlawful food
- A metaphor for concealing the truth
- Speaking to God on the Day of Judgment
- Purification

Verse 177-182 **376**

- A definition of the righteous people
    - Acting out of love for God
- Retribution
- Inheritance

Verse 183-185 **392**

- Fasting
    - Those who are exempted from fasting
- Theories on the revelation of the Quran

Verse 186-189 **399**

- Our relationship with God
    - The meaning of *qarīb*
    - Calling God
    - God's response
- Marital relations in the month of Ramadan
- Commencing the fast
- God's bounds

- Being litigious
- Crescent moon
- Entering houses from the rear

Verse 190-195 409

- Defensive War
    - Has this verse been abrogated?
    - Fighting the faithless?
    - Financing the army

Verse 196-203 420

- Hajj and Umrah
    - Acting *for God's sake*
    - Rules for performing hajj
    - Arafāt and Mash'ar
    - A lesson in what to ask God for
    - The appointed days

Verse 204-209 432

- Materialism
- Manipulative rhetoric
- Striving to serve God
- Wholehearted submission
- Stumbling

Verse 210-212 439

- Collective punishment

- Shades of clouds
- Blessings which lead to arrogance
- Reward without reckoning

Verse 213-215 **444**

- Single community
- The *fiṭra*
- Calamities
- Whom to spend on
- What to give

Verse 216-220 **452**

- The meaning of *qitāl*
- Repulsiveness of war
- Fighting in the holy months
    - A mistake and propaganda
- Apostasy (*irtidād*)
    - Invalidation of good deeds
- Gambling
- Alcohol
- Treatment of orphans

Verse 221-237 **463**

- Marrying idolators
- Intercourse during menses
- Treatment of women in a male dominated society
- *Īlā'*

- Divorce
    - Waiting period
    - Honourable norms
- A degree above women
- Suckling
- Widows
    - Waiting period
    - Proposing to widows
- Divorce and dowry
    - Suckling
    - Graciousness

Verse 238-239 **485**

- Prayer
    - The middle prayer
    - Establishing prayer

Verse 240-242 **487**

- Providing for widows
- Providing for divorcees

Verse 243-252 **489**

- Death is in God's hands
- Lending God a good loan
- The attitude of the Israelites towards jihad
- Prophet Saul
    - God's criteria for choosing a king
    - Ark of the covenant

    - Relics
    - The test of the stream
    - The prayer of the faithful
    - Prophet David and Goliath

Verse 253-254 **504**

- Degrees of the prophets
- Fighting amongst religious groups
- Spending in the way of God

Verse 255-257 **509**

- *Āyāt al-Kursī*
    - Merits of recitation
    - The names of God
    - The *kursī* and the *ʿarsh*
    - God's management of the universe
- No compulsion in religion
- Guardianship

Verse 258-260 **521**

- *Ṭāghūt* takes disbelievers from light into darkness
    - Prophet Abraham and King Nimrud
- God takes the faithful from darkness into light
    - Reviving the dead
    - Physical resurrection
        - Prophet Ezra
        - Prophet Abraham

Verse 261-276 **528**

- The parable of the grain
- Do not follow charity with reproach
- Honourable word
- The parable of the rock compared to the garden
- The quality of the charity
- Satan's tricks
- God gives to whoever he wants
- Private and public charity
- Whom to offer charity to
- The reward of charity

Verse 277-281 **547**

- The harms of usury
- Remaining in hell
- Effects of charity and usury
- Declaration of war on the usurers
- The ethics of financial matters
- The meaning of being "brought back" to God

Verse 282-284 **551**

- Contract law
    - o Eliminating sources of conflict
- Witnesses
    - o One man for two women?
- Contracts when travelling
- God is the true owner and knower of all

Verse 285-286 **558**

- A distinction between the Prophet and the faithful
- Tenets of faith
- Capacity and test
- A prayer taught to the believers

ENDNOTES 564

BIBLIOGRAPHY 582

Foreword

This book is the product of a partnership between Dr. Seyfeddin Kara, Sun Behind The Cloud Publications, and myself. It is the outcome of a rigorous and lengthy process after the transcription of my lectures on Surah al-Baqarah at the Shia Ithna-asheri Community of Middlesex (The Salaam Centre). It would have not taken the form of a book had it not been for Seyfeddin and Sun Behind The Cloud.

With his keen enthusiasm for the Quran, Dr. Seyfeddin Kara started to arrange the transcriptions in a creative manner, translating all the Arabic verses that I used in the lectures and giving my spoken word a written format. That was not all; by providing the references, adding footnotes, and enriching the contents in many areas, he has contributed greatly to the authorship of this book.

The work would have not been completed if it was not for Sun Behind The Cloud's scrupulous and steadfast efforts to edit the work in a way that makes it easy to read and understand. They helped me greatly by pointing out areas that needed to be explained further, the points that needed clarification and some very important issues that had been left out in the lectures. They painstakingly and meticulously examined the subject matters discussed in the book to produce the very helpful contents pages, which makes different sections of the huge text easily available to the reader.

Completion of this work is certainly a grace that God has bestowed upon us. However, the aim is not achieved without enthusiastic Quran lovers who go through the pages of this book in search of deeper meanings in the verses of the Holy Book.

As a small and insignificant servant of God, I pray that he extends his grace on us by granting us deeper knowledge of the Quran and to all those who read this book; he is the only bestower of knowledge.

سُبْحَانَكَ لَا عِلْمَ لَنَا إِلَّا مَا عَلَّمْتَنَا ۖ إِنَّكَ أَنتَ الْعَلِيمُ الْحَكِيمُ

Immaculate are You! We have no knowledge except what you have taught us. Indeed, you are the All-knowing, the All-wise.

Mohammad Saeed Bahmanpour

July 2021

INTRODUCTION

The practice of interpreting the Quran has been fundamental to the study of Islam from its very beginning. It is well-established among all Muslims that Imam Ali ibn Abi Talib was one of the first scribes of the Quran. He would write notes on the Prophet's commentary of the verses in the margins of his codex. This is known to be the first codex of the Quran, which he collated soon after the death of the Prophet.[1] Thus, Imam Ali is known to be the first to teach the interpretation of the Quran.

Imam Ali's method of the interpretation of the Quran is best described in a tradition where he says, "One part of the Quran explains another and one part witnesses to the other."[2] This is based on the teaching of the Prophet that, "The verses were revealed to confirm each other."[3] This is the method of interpreting the verses of the Quran in the light of the Quran.

The Shi'i Imams also adopted this method as well as some Muslim exegetes. One of the most important representatives of this method is Fakhr al-Din al-Razi (d. 606/1209) in his book *Mafātīh al-ghayb* which, aside from relying on rational arguments, also uses the method of interpretation of the Quran through the verses of the Quran to some extent.

Perhaps the most prominent commentary of the Quran which exclusively relies on this method is Mohammad Hossein Tabatabai's (d. 1981) *Tafsīr al-mīzān*. Through a detailed analysis of the verses of the Quran, Tabatabai developed a set of coherent concepts, and he interpreted the verses of the Quran based on these concepts, with remarkable skill.

Tabatabai's pioneering contribution to the field of *tafsir* studies has not only changed the trend in the field from a speculative intellectual exercise to well-grounded scientific research, but also made a long-lasting impact on the scholars and intellectuals of the Muslim world. His work and legacy have set a precedent about how God's revelation can be used as the only source of explaining complex religious concepts.

Instead of using the Quran to legitimise preconceived religious views and ideologies, Tabatabai used some verses to explain other verses in the Quran. In this way, he remained unprejudiced and independent from the influences of particular religious and cultural world-views, which meant that the explanations and conclusions he formed had universal appeal. [4]

This book follows the path that has been set by Tabatabai's methodology that places the revelation of God before anything else. It is based on Shaykh Muhammad Saeed Bahmanpour's extensive research and teaching of the Quran, including weekly *tafsir* lectures at the Shia Ithna-asheri Community of Middlesex (The Salaam Centre), since 2003. Bahmanpour extensively discusses Tabatabai's method in his *tafsir* to extract ideas from it and explain complex theological concepts. He also makes use of some of the prominent classical and contemporary Sunni and Shi'i commentators including: Fakhr al-Din al-Razi, Abū al-Qāsim al-Qushayrī, Abū al-Qāsim al-Balkhī, Jalāluddīn al-Suyūṭī, Muḥammad Jamāluddin al-Qāsimi, Muhammad Abduh, Fayḍ Kāshānī, al-Sharīf al-Murtaḍā, al-Faḍl b. al-Ḥasan Tabrisi, Shaykh Tusi, and al-Kalbī. This work extends beyond sectarian boundaries in the field of the interpretation of the Quran and makes use of the knowledge of great Shi'i and Sunni scholars of Quran.

Throughout this book, Bahmanpour critiques and elaborates on existing views on the interpretation of the verses of the Quran and he produces compelling alternatives and independent opinions in his work. He shows a remarkable ability to simplify complex and baffling religious concepts and make them accessible to the broader community. His style of the interpretation of the Quran is tailored explicitly for Muslims and non-Muslims who live in the West.

It gives great pleasure to me to be part of such an important project. I had the opportunity and privilege of attending Bahmanpour's *tafsir* classes in various venues since 2004, and from that time till now, they have been a constant source of knowledge for my spiritual and intellectual development. I have been transcribing and editing Bahmanpour's online *tafsir* lectures available on YouTube for the past two years. Further to this, I revised my notes from attending his more academic teachings at his daily *tafsir* classes at the Seminary and some of his courses at the Islamic College in London and incorporated them into the present book. I have also included some brief supplementary research to further explain some of the concepts, especially those related to the comparative study of the Quran and Bible. In the translation of the verses, I have mostly relied on Ali Quli Qara'i's *Phrase-by-Phrase English Translation*[5] but on some occasions, I have revised them based on Bahmanpour's interpretation. Bahmanpour read the final draft and made further revisions on it.

This book is intended to benefit those Muslim and non-Muslim readers who are interested in a comprehensive understanding of the Quran and Muslim faith. The *tafsir* also delves into some of the most complicated issues related to Muslim, Christian and Jewish relations, Muslims in the West, Islam and modernity, Islam and human rights, gender issues, Islamic eschatology, ethics, and law. Therefore, it will also be beneficial for junior and advanced academic researchers working on the Quran and Muslim societies.

***

Surah al-Baqarah is the longest chapter of the Quran and it was revealed entirely in Medina. The Prophet, along with his followers, escaped from the persecution of the Meccan polytheist establishment and settled in Medina in year 1/622. In this city, the Prophet and the emerging Muslim community also formed relationships with the existing polytheist and Jewish communities in Medina. The city had provided a perfect environment for Prophet Muhammad to spread his message to the surrounding areas in the Arabian Peninsula. Once the news of a charismatic Prophet preaching a new faith and his struggle with his own tribe spread across the Peninsula, people began to come to Medina, some out of spiritual urge and some out of curiosity, to listen and question the Prophet. In this way, the interaction of the Prophet with the hostile Meccans, sympathetic Medinan community, hypocritical figures, the curious visitors, and Medina's Jewish tribes triggered one of the greatest and longest conversations between God and his creation.

God conversed with the Prophet to warn people about the fleeting nature of this world and urge them to prepare for the next stage of the human journey towards God. Surah al-Baqarah includes detailed discussions on the origin of humankind, and the story of Adam and Eve. This story provides a unique insight into the main human weaknesses, as well as ways to remedying them. Iblis rebels against God due to his arrogance and instigates Adam and Eve to commit the first sin. This came about due to their lack of experience regarding the commands of God and the innate urge of man to have an immortal life in an ephemeral world. The three major sins are the foundations of human deceit and corruption in this world. Ernest Becker, in his Pulitzer Prize-winning, *The Denial of Death* elucidated the idea of his "immortality project" thesis based on the psychological and philosophical study of human behaviour. He concluded that the uncontrolled human drive to be immortal has been the leading cause of human corruption in terms of instigating wars, causing bigotry, genocide, and racism.

In the creation story narrated in this surah, God, out of his abundant mercy, provides a solution for humanity's impatience to attain immortality: humbleness and humility. These are the single most important qualities that can defuse the many vices that accumulate in the human soul. Humility was the paramount quality that saved Adam from God's wrath despite his disobedience to God. Conversely, Satan's flagrant arrogance was exposed when God asked him to respect Adam and prostrate to him.

Forgetfulness, anger, jealousy, greed and desires may lead humans and *jinn* to commit sin. This is not uncommon, in fact, it is expected that creatures make mistakes. However, the sheer insistence on repeating errors at the expense of accepting eternal damnation is what God finds abhorrent. The insistence on rebelling against God is a sign of deep-rooted and cultivated deformity of the soul.

The worst crime in the eyes of God is arrogance and not turning back from evident mistakes. Arrogance is a kind of virus that takes over the soul and changes its structure to turn it into a destructive force for itself and the others. This is why God would never allow the arrogant to enter into Paradise. Not because he is an unforgiving and sadistic Being who enjoys torturing those who are defiant to his commands. Rather, the arrogant deformed souls act like a virus and destroy everything good in Paradise. Therefore, the arrogant need to be isolated in the reformatory environment of Hell, with the effort and hope that they would be healed and eventually let into Paradise.

Of course, the process of recovery in Hell is a painful one; at this point of human progress, nothing but fire can heal deformed souls. In fact the fuel of this fire would emanate from the deformative part of the souls. In other words, the source of fire in Hell would be the arrogant soul itself, and so long as it is not healed, it would continue to cause distress for the guilty. But once the deformity is healed, the fire will be extinguished for the individual and it would then be possible to move onto Paradise.

The majority of verses in Surah al-Baqarah explain the trials and tribulations that the Israelites faced as well as the many mistakes they made. Many verses also detail the transgressions of the Jews in Medina at the time. This book takes care to convey the true meaning and reasons for narrating these stories in the Quran. By moving away from racist or antisemitic readings of the Quran, this work focuses on the lessons we can learn from their story as an excellent example of basic human deficiencies and strengths. Furthermore, the stories of the Israelites and the Jews in Medina were of particular relevance to the early Muslims who have been repeatedly reminded in this surah to obey God and his prophet. While some of the Israelites succumbed to their desires and blatantly disobeyed God, others such as Prophet Moses, David and Solomon glowed like the beacons of ultimate submission and dedication to God.

The surah also seeks to guide us to a pure understanding of religion through the verses which deal with the legislative rulings on different subjects such as the direction of prayer, inheritance, divorce, gambling, wine, and usury to stories of the past prophets including Adam, Abraham, Jacob, Moses and Jesus. The surah also deals with theological issues such as the oneness of God, entry into Heaven, the process of guidance and Imamate to name but a few. The verses also examine a wide variety of subjects that are of significant relevance to contemporary Muslim debates and concerns.

This *tafsir* work explains the context of the revelation of the verses and the attitudes of the early Muslims. Using reliable narrations, the stories of the prophets are also recounted in some depth and many relevant lessons are drawn. Furthermore, the book has not hesitated to discuss some controversial concepts such as male-dominated interpretation of the Quran, gender relations, the need to prefer the spirit of the law over the letter of the law, religious pluralism, Muslim sectarianism, anthropomorphic interpretations of the Quran, and the role of free will and determinism in the way God guides his creation.

Seyfeddin Kara

Toronto 2021

Verse by Verse Tafsir

بِسْمِ اللَّهِ الرَّحْمَٰنِ الرَّحِيمِ
الم ﴿١﴾

Alif, Lām, Mīm.

Alif, lām, mīm is an example of the disjointed letters (*ḥurūf muqaṭṭa*) in the Quran. The disjointed letters appear at the beginning of twenty-nine chapters and altogether there are fourteen letters. These letters appear in different numbers and different combinations. The shortest example is the use of a single letter, like *ṣād*, or *qāf* and the longest is composed of five letters: *kāf, hā, yā, ʿayn, ṣād.*

The disjointed letters are one of the most mysterious features of the Quran. There are more than twenty theories mentioned by exegetes regarding the interpretation of these letters, yet none of them can give assurance and confidence of heart. This being the case, some have concluded that the disjointed letters fall in the category of the equivocal verses (*mutashābihāt*). However, all equivocal verses of the Quran also have an apparent meaning. The equivocal verses are called equivocal because they imply more than one meaning and the intended meaning is unknown. That is why they can be interpreted in different ways and the Quran warns, *As for those in whose hearts is deviance, they pursue what is equivocal in it, courting temptation and courting its interpretation.* (Q. 3:7) The disjointed letters do not have any apparent meaning; they are not words to imply meanings, but they are letters placed beside each other. Therefore, the idea that the disjointed letters are from *mutashābihāt* is not completely accurate.

Mahmud b. Umar Zamakhsharī (d. 538/1143), who was arguably the greatest Mutazili exegete, believed that these letters are the names of the chapters of the Quran in which they appear. For example, *Alif lām mīm* is another name for Surah al-Baqarah and *Nūn* is another name for Surah al-Qalam. After all, there are numerous chapters in the Quran which have more than one name; for example, the Surah al-Mu'min (the Believer) is also known as Surah al-Ghāfir (the Forgiver), or Surah al-Dahar (Endless Time) is also called Surah Insān (Men). This view is also adopted by Tusi (d. 460/1067). However, this would mean that several chapters would then have the same name. Chapters 2, 3, 29, 30, 31, and 32 all begin with *alif lām mīm* and it would mean that six chapters have the same name. Tusi would not see any objection in this since the chapters can be distinguished from each other by a second qualifier.

A third common view regarding the disjointed letters is that they are abbreviations for the names of God. In other words, God starts these chapters with his own name, but in a condensed form. For example, *alif lām mīm* means "*Ana Allahu a'alamu*" (I am God and I know) which is not a combination of names *per se*, but a sentence describing God. This sentence is formed by taking the *alif* from the beginning of the first word, *lām* from the middle of the second word and *mīm* from the end of the last word, or, *alif lām mīm rā* means "*Ana Allahu a'alamu wa-arā*" (I am God, I know and see). The issue with this view is that the choice of letters from each word is so arbitrary that only someone with inspired knowledge would be able to recognise and decode these sentences.

A fourth opinion, which is related to the above view, is suggested by Sa'īd b. Jubayr (d. 95/714) who was one of the Successors (*Tābi'ūn*) and a great exegete. He believed that by putting these letters in the right order we can arrive at the names of God. For example, if we put *alif lām rā* before *hā mīm* and put *nūn* from Surah al-Qalam after them then we arrive at the name al-Raḥmān (The Most Merciful). Although attractive, not all these letters could be arranged together as smoothly as the quoted example.

Following this speculative method, Shi'i and Sunni commentators have tried to arrange these fourteen letters in ways to support their respective creeds. For example, some Shi'i interpreters have arranged them as صراط على حق نمسكه the path of Ali is right we grab to it) or علي صراط حق نمسكه (Ali is the right path we grab to him). On the other hand, some Sunni interpreters have arranged them as: كل سني معه صراط حق (with every Sunni there is a right path).

The fifth opinion is that these letters are oaths (*qasams*) through which God swears an oath to emphasise a point. God swears by his creation in many chapters of the Quran. These include swearing by the sun, the moon, the night, the day, fig, olive, and many more. In the same manner, some say these letters have also been used to swear an oath. However, the preposition of *qasam* is absent in all the cases, and secondly, what is sworn by is unknown to the audience. Usually, God swears by things that have some importance or value to the listeners in order to arouse a sense of acceptance in them. Taking an oath by something which is unknown to the audience would not illicit any impact from the audience.

Another view which is very common among exegetes of the Quran is that at the beginning of Islam, when the Prophet recited the Quran, the disbelievers used to listen to it. But after they understood the dangers those verses posed to their traditions, they tried to stop people listening to the verses and created noise and commotion whenever the Prophet started to recite: *The faithless say, 'Do not listen to this Quran and hoot it down so that you may prevail.'* (Q. 41:26) To overcome this stratagem, the style of the chapters was changed, to begin with the disjointed letters. This method confused the disbelievers, because they did not know what these letters meant, and they wanted to listen to see what followed. This view is allegedly based on a rare practice of Arab poets who used to attract the attention of their listeners by shouting a letter at the beginning of their poems. However, what significantly weakens this view is that these letters appear at the beginning of some chapters which were revealed in Medina, like Surah al-Baqarah and Surah Āl 'Imrān where the audience was exclusively Muslim.

These were just some of the views regarding the disjointed letters of the Quran and none of them are definitively convincing. There is another view mentioned by Mohammad Hossein Tabatabai (d. 1981) in his famous *Tafsīr al-mīzān* which is quite conceptual, although not conclusive. He initially concedes that the meaning and the purpose of these letters are unknown to ordinary believers, and they are like codes used between God and his messenger. However, after examining the chapters which begin with these letters, every letter used at the beginning of a chapter may be related to a set of concepts in that chapter; therefore, the chapters with common disjointed letters should cover shared concepts. In this way, every chapter starting with *alif lām rā* has a set of concepts related to it. With close study of these chapters and comparisons with other chapters beginning with the same letters these concepts can be formulated. A chapter starting with *alif lām mīm*, should still contain common concepts with other *alif lām rā* chapters, because some concepts are related to *alif*, some to *lām*, some to *mīm*, and others to *rā*, and between these two sets of chapters, concepts related to *alif* and *lām* must share a common trend. In the same way, Surah A'raf which begins with the letters *alif lām mīm ṣād* will comprise of concepts covered in Surah al-Baqarah, for example, and those covered in Surah Ṣād. This theory, as beautiful as it is, remains chiefly conceptual as Tabatabai has not delved into details of identifying those common concepts.

One final note on the subject, which is inspired by Tabatabai's theory, is that these letters certainly contained great association for the Prophet personally, to the extent that they may even be placed there exclusively for the Prophet. They may be like passwords by which the Prophet, and the infallible Imams as his heirs, could glean a totally different level of meaning which is not available to others. Thus, when *alif* or *ṣād* or *qāf* is mentioned at the beginning of a chapter, in addition to its apparent meanings, the Prophet and his heirs would have found access to a higher realm of meaning with the help of those passwords. In other words, we recite these chapters without knowing these keywords and without ever fully understanding their intended apparent meanings, but those who know the keywords would reach a depth of meaning which is not accessible without the password.

ذَٰلِكَ الْكِتَابُ لَا رَيْبَ ۛ فِيهِ ۛ هُدًى لِّلْمُتَّقِينَ ﴿2﴾

This is the Book, there is no doubt in it, a guidance to the Godwary.

This is the Book; The Arabic term used here for "this" is *dhālika* which is a demonstrative pronoun used to point to distant objects. Although the verse mentions *this* Book, *dhālika* is used to signify the elevated position of the Book being mentioned. Naturally, the structure of the sentence should have been "this is *a* Book" in which there is no doubt, however, the verse uses a definite article by saying, "this is *the* Book." This has led some of the commentators to think that this verse refers to the Book which the Jews were awaiting. Based on this, the verse would mean, "this is the awaited Book and there is no doubt in that." Al-Mubarrad (d. 285/ 898-899), a leading grammarian of his time, stated that the verse means, "This Quran is that Book that I promised to you (Muhammad) in the previous Books."[6] This meaning is corroborated by a report in the *Tafsīr* of the eleventh Imam Hasan al-Askari (d. 260/874) which explains that this verse means, "This is the Book that Moses and the prophets after him informed us about."[7]

It is a guide for the Godwary people. (*hudan lil-muttaqīn).* Exegetes have debated in detail about whether it is the Quran which makes people Godwary through its guidance or whether people need to be Godwary as a prerequisite to receiving its guidance. They have taken two main positions: one is held by Tabatabai who maintains that God-wariness (*taqwā*) in this instance is not acquired through religion. It is the type of God-wariness that is innate in a person and attracts people towards accepting religion.[8] To elaborate on this view, there are two groups of people in the face of divine revelation: one group rejects the revelation outright and the other group accepts it. What is the difference between these two groups? Why do some people accept the revelation, yet others reject it? There must be something innate within our souls that attracts us towards revelation. This is the God-wariness that is inbuilt in every human being, if they choose to listen to their nature (*fiṭra*).

Although well set out, this argument conflicts with the definition of Godwary people (*muttaqīn)* in the following verse: *Those who believe in the unseen, establish the prayer and give away of what We have provided for them.* (Q. 2:2) The Godwary believers are described in similar ways to this verse in other parts of the Quran; it is not a description of people who have a prior God-wariness as Tabatabai mentions. According to Tabatabai the five qualities mentioned in verses two and three are general qualities that everybody might have prior to accepting the faith. However, this argument is paradoxical. Why would someone need to accept faith if they already possess elements of faith? Also, there are some Muslims who do not have any of the qualities mentioned in these two verses (such as praying, giving charity). Would the Book be a guide for them as well?

The second explanation, which is held by the majority of exegetes, maintains that this type of God-wariness may only be acquired through religion and performing the five practices mentioned in the following verses. In this way, the Quran can be likened to an extremely sophisticated system which only works when a master knows how to operate it. If someone simply opens the Quran and starts reading, they should not expect to grasp its deeper meanings and to be guided instantly. There are procedures to be completed which then enable the Quran to guide people. Like driving a car. If you do not know how to drive a car; you cannot sit in the car and expect it to move. Therefore, the guidance of the Quran will not work for some people but will work for others. It only provides enlightenment when a person has the qualities mentioned in verses 3 and 4. This is clearly mentioned in Q. 17:82: *We send down in the Quran that which is a cure and mercy for the faithful; and it increases the wrongdoers only in loss.*

$$\text{الَّذِينَ يُؤْمِنُونَ بِالْغَيْبِ وَيُقِيمُونَ الصَّلَاةَ وَمِمَّا رَزَقْنَاهُمْ يُنفِقُونَ ﴿3﴾}$$

Who believe in the Unseen, and maintain the prayer, and spend out of what We have provided for them;

$$\text{وَالَّذِينَ يُؤْمِنُونَ بِمَا أُنزِلَ إِلَيْكَ وَمَا أُنزِلَ مِن قَبْلِكَ وَبِالْآخِرَةِ هُمْ يُوقِنُونَ ﴿4﴾}$$

And who believe in what has been sent down to you and what was sent down before you and are certain of the Hereafter.

Who believe in the Unseen; There are differing views regarding what "the unseen" (*ghayb*) refers to in this verse. Ibn Abbas (d. 68/687-8) describes the "unseen" as whatever knowledge comes from God. Ibn Masud (d. 32-3/652-4) believed that the "unseen" refers to whatever knowledge is hidden, such as the knowledge of Hell and Paradise, destinies and the like. Tusi (d. 460/1067) prefered the latter view because it is more general. He adds that it can include belief in the occultation and the advent of al-Mahdi.[9] It may also mean "those who believe with their heart" or "those who believe in private as well as public", thus excluding the hypocrites. This may be true for many. There may be certain aspects of faith that a person does not truly believe in the very depths of their hearts, but in front of people, they pretend to have faith in them.

"Those who believe in the unseen" also means "those who believe in things which exist but cannot be seen." This is what we call faith. The existence or non-existence of the unseen cannot be established by science or experiments; rather, believers and disbelievers alike have a conviction in the unseen. Their convictions are not based on any experience that they can demonstrate directly but instead they are based on faith. This faith can be demonstrated as being rational or irrational, possible or impossible, plausible or implausible. Belief in the unseen can lead to superstition at times. For this reason, superstitions can be found in almost all religions, and this poses a problem for the faithful. Razi clarifies this problem in the following way; he contends that there are two types of belief in the unseen:

The first type of faith in the unseen is that for which there is evidence; this includes faith in God. Of course, God can never be seen by anyone. Neither angels nor prophets can see him even in the Hereafter because he is beyond the grasp of any imagination. If one had been able to grasp God completely, God would have been limited and that is impossible. However, we do have rational evidence for his existence. God is beyond the sensual realm; thus, his presence is not demonstrable through the five senses. However, it is demonstrable through rational argument. The world with God is much more plausible than the world without God. But this needs faith too. Even the angels, despite their closeness, know him through faith: *Those [angels], at the closest point to God and those around it, exalt their Lord with praise and they have faith in Him...* (Q. 40:7) This means even the closest angels to God need to have faith in him and worship him through faith. For the angels, God is unseen in the same way as the angels are unseen to us. The only way to connect to God is through faith and faith comes from worship. This is explained by Imam Ali when he was asked if he had seen the Lord that he worships. He replied: "I have never worshipped a Lord that I have not seen. Although human eyes cannot see God, their hearts can grasp him by the truths of the faith."[10]

Since there is great evidence for the existence of God, believing in God is not classed as superstition. In contrast, atheism *is* based on superstition. Their arguments to explain the creation of man through "evolution" or the creation of the universe as a result of an "accident" are not based on substantial evidence. They may provide some scientific evidence for supporting their theories, but afterall what they produce is "theory" which is based on the interpretation of circumstantial evidence. Further, it falls far short of substantiating such grand and faith-based theories. There is also great evidence for Prophets receiving revelation from God, because of their miracles, teachings, and influences. The second type of the unseen is a means to explain those things which we have no evidence for or are based on very weak evidence; believing in such unseen is regarded as superstition.

This way of explaining the unseen has been practiced by Muslim scholars since the earliest periods of Islam. For example, if a tradition is reported from the Prophet, it is accepted as fact, but these traditions should be scrutinised and corroborated before taking them as evidence. According to Shi'i scholars, a tenet of faith cannot be based on one or two traditions (isolated traditions or *khabar al-wāḥid*) attributed to the Prophet. A tenet of faith may only be established based on overwhelming evidence. Therefore, only the Quran and *mutawātir* traditions (traditions which are reported numerously by various narrators and various chains of transmissions) are used to establish a tenet of faith.

One important matter to discuss at this point is that some Shi'i exegetes have argued that faith in the unseen, as stated in this verse, refers to the occultation and advent of the twelfth Shi'i Imam, al-Mahdi. They evidenced this with traditions narrated from the Ahl al-Bayt. However, it appears that these exegetes over emphasise this particular instance of faith as being included in the unseen. It is not correct to state that faith in the unseen is restricted to faith in Imam al-Mahdi alone. Criticising this position, Razi mentions that some Shi'is believe that this specific verse refers to the return of Imam al-Mahdi.[11] He acknowledges that there is great evidence from the Quran and the *hadith* of the Prophet that the Mahdi will come before the Day of the Judgment, but restricting this general verse to a specific issue is inaccurate.

Although what he says is true, the Shi'i position does not actually restrict the meaning of this verse to being related to the return of Imam al-Mahdi alone. Fayd Kashani (d. 1091/1680-1681) in his *Tafsīr al-ṣāfī*[12] states that faith in the unseen as mentioned in this verse refers to whatever is unseen, including God, angels, revelation, Paradise and Hell, as well as the coming of al-Mahdi. The verse mentions general instances of the unseen and believing in the Mahdi is one of these instances, but not the only instance. This is because there is great evidence about the coming of al-Mahdi mentioned in the Quran as well as Sunni and Shi'i *hadith*.

Those who believe in whatever has been revealed to you and whatever was revealed to people before you; Ibn Abbas and Ibn Masud, the two great experts of the Quran, decipher that this refers to those believers from the People of the Book. They argue that it is the People of the Book who believed in what was mentioned in previous Scriptures in detail, not Muslims. Muslims had no need for any books prior to the revelation of the Quran because the Quran contains everything that is needed. Of course, it is very difficult to oppose the views of such great scholars of the Quran, but it is questionable whether they really held this view, due to the plethora of fabricated traditions attributed to Ibn Abbas and Ibn Masud. If anybody wanted to promote a view regarding the interpretation of the Quran, they would attribute those views to Ibn Abbas and Ibn Masud to gain credibility. Although we do not question the authority of Ibn Abbas and Ibn Masud in their field, given this plethora of fabricated traditions attributed to them, doubts arise as to whether this view was originally held by them. It is clear from this verse that it refers to those who believe in the idea of revelation; and that God guides them and the nations before them. We know that God has guided people throughout history by sending many prophets.

They have certainty in the Hereafter; The verse starts with faith in the unseen and ends with certainty (*yūqinūna*). The reason that certainty is mentioned is because without certainty in the Hereafter it is almost impossible to have faith, or it will result in a weak standard of faith. A firm belief in the Hereafter gives substance to faith.

أُولَٰئِكَ عَلَىٰ هُدًى مِّن رَّبِّهِمْ ۖ وَأُولَٰئِكَ هُمُ الْمُفْلِحُونَ ﴿5﴾

Those follow their Lord's guidance, and it is they who are the felicitous.

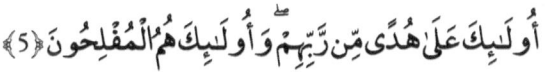

This verse is the continuation of the previous verses and addresses the Godwary people. The previous verses narrate five qualities of the Godwary people: believing in the unseen, establishing prayer, giving charity, belief in the revelations of God and certainty in the Day of Judgment. In this verse, the description is elaborated to include being guided by God Almighty. Furthermore, they are chosen to be guided by God.

The Asharites use this verse to reinforce their position on predeterminism, that only God can decide whom to guide and that everything is predetermined by our destiny and there is no free will. However, the response given by both Mutazilites and Shi'is who believe in free will, especially in terms of guidance of God Almighty, is that if anyone absorbs and implements those five qualities mentioned in the previous verses, the inner guidance of God Almighty will embrace them and lead them towards contentment. Therefore, those who do not perform these five acts of piety should not expect inner guidance from God and those who perform these five acts of piety will be blessed with guidance from God. This would be an inner guidance and light which would glow and expand gradually as God would guide them in their hearts. Thus, this verse is not concerned with predestination.

إِنَّ ٱلَّذِينَ كَفَرُوا۟ سَوَآءٌ عَلَيْهِمْ ءَأَنذَرْتَهُمْ أَمْ لَمْ تُنذِرْهُمْ لَا يُؤْمِنُونَ ﴿6﴾

As for those who have chosen not to believe, it is the same for them whether you warn them, or you do not warn them. They will not believe.

It is the same for them whether you warn them or do not warn them. They will not believe. Taken out of context, these verses can be used to promote the Asharite view of predetermination (*jabr*) by claiming that it is God who decides whether people are believers or non-believers and there is no free choice in the matter. However, this view does not consider the Quranic view in its entirety. A holistic approach to the verses is essential in order to truly understand any concept in the Quran. If we explore this verse in the light of other verses which explicitly express the free will of human beings in their actions, we understand that disbelief here refers to intentional rejection.

If this verse is rendered "those who do not believe" then it may give credibility to the idea of predeterminism held by the Asharites. However, if it is rendered "those who have *chosen* to reject" or "those who have *chosen* not to believe" then it no longer supports the Asharite view. This verse alludes to a person who has already made up their mind to the extent that it is impossible to change or correct their position. From the very beginning of the Prophet's mission, there were people who had made up their minds already and did not want to listen to the Prophet. Of course, there were others who listened to the Prophet and some of them accepted the message. For those who chose not to listen to the revelation it is the same whether they are warned or not, because they have already made up their minds.

Tabatabai notes this apparent problem with the translation "those who do not believe". He argues that if this was the case, it would be pointless to preach to disbelievers about Islam, because they would never be able to change their minds anyway.[13] To resolve this problem, he contends that the verse must refer exclusively to the disbelievers who lived at the time of the Prophet; it may not include other disbelievers. For Tabatabai this verse should be read in the context of its revelation and is a prophesy about the reaction of some disbelievers against the message of Islam, which later transpired to be true. The verse was revealed at the beginning of the Migration (*Hijra*) and before the Battle of Badr. At the Battle of Badr when Abū Jahl and the other leaders of the disbelievers, who had made up their minds not to believe, were killed, the foretelling of this verse came true. This exact phrasing also appears in Surah Yā-sin, verse 10 which was revealed in Mecca. To sum up, the Asharite argument would not hold if this verse were interpreted as a contextual statement, or if *kufr* is interpreted as optional rejection. This verse may be better understood in connection to the next verse.

خَتَمَ اللَّهُ عَلَىٰ قُلُوبِهِمْ وَعَلَىٰ سَمْعِهِمْ ۖ وَعَلَىٰ أَبْصَارِهِمْ غِشَاوَةٌ ۖ وَلَهُمْ عَذَابٌ عَظِيمٌ ﴿7﴾

God has set a seal on their hearts and their hearing, there is a blindfold on their sight and there is a great punishment for them.

God has set a seal on their hearts; This verse intially appears to reinforce the position of the Asharites by implying that it is God who sets a seal on a person's heart, not allowing them to believe. There might be an element of truth to this view, but it needs to be understood in its totality. These issues are very subtle and cannot be taken at face value. It is absolutely true that God Almighty has sealed their hearts and their ears but the issue is whether this is something God initiated or is a result of a course of events chosen by the individual, which led them towards being engulfed by absolute blindness and deafness. Verse 155 in Surah Nisā clarifies this matter: *Because of their disbelief, God set a seal [on their hearts]*. It is not the case that God first sealed their heart and therefore doomed them to be disbelievers.

This process may best be explained with the example of someone who wants to commit suicide by throwing themselves from the top of a building. Once the person jumps, they cannot change their mind midway; at this point, it is too late to reverse the situation. They must face the necessary outcome because of the voluntary act they chose to do beforehand. In the same manner, if somebody chooses disbelief then this sets into motion a compulsory series of events. God would take them into further darkness as mentioned in Q. 40:35: *As such, God seals every arrogant tyrant's heart,* or according to Q. 2:257 *...And those who disbelieve, their guardians are the evil rebel (Satan) who will take them from light to darkness...*

Another example is Q. 45:23: *Have you regarded someone who has taken his own desire as god. God misguided him despite the knowledge he had and sealed his ears and his heart and veiled his vision...* The common theme in these examples is that individuals make their own decisions about faith and, as a result of their own choices, they face certain consequences. Take the example of making a bad decision, such as lying. When a person starts lying, it is just an inclination, but if they continue it becomes a habit and finally it becomes part of their nature. At this stage it is difficult to change this disposition. This is how the sealing of the heart takes place: evil inclinations become habits and then they finally form a part in primary nature, which consequently seals the heart.

The prophets insisted on delivering their guidance to everyone in their community, regardless of whether they accepted or not, because at that point in their mission it was not certain who would choose to follow their guidance. It may be the case that for some people it is difficult for the message to penetrate their hearts and for other people this process is much easier. For companions like As'ad b. Zurāra (d. 1/623), Muṣ'ab b. 'Umayr (d. 3/625), Sa'd b. Mu'ādh (d. 5/627) and Usayd b. Ḥuḍayrit (d. 20/641) it was easy to become Muslim. As soon as they heard the Quran, they eagerly converted to Islam. Others took a long time to become Muslim, such as, Abbas b. Abd al-Muttalib (d. c. 32/653), the uncle of the Prophet.

In our aim to spread the religion and direct people towards good practice, we should also emulate the practice of the prophets. We should not be disheartened by some people's negative reactions. This is what Prophet Noah did; he preached for 950 years after which only a handful of people believed in him, but God told him to continue delivering his message to the people. There is always hope so long as a person is alive – we cannot determine if their hearts are sealed or open to guidance. Our duty is to keep conveying the message that the Prophet has conveyed to us.

وَمِنَ النَّاسِ مَن يَقُولُ آمَنَّا بِاللَّهِ وَبِالْيَوْمِ الْآخِرِ وَمَا هُم بِمُؤْمِنِينَ ﴿8﴾

And among the people are those who say, 'We have faith in God and the Last Day,' but they have no faith.

'We have faith in God and the Last Day,' Faith in God and the Day of Judgment are the two pillars of Islamic faith. One cannot survive without the other. The polytheists of Mecca believed in a sublime god, but they believe that he allocated his powers to the idols. They did not believe in the Day of Judgment or life after death; thus, devotion and faith were used as a bargaining tool rather than a path and this meant there was no sense of spirituality. Those who believe in God but do not believe in the Day of Judgment cannot be considered as believers as their way of thinking implies that God is void of wisdom and works in an unreasonable manner. It is an accusation against God to not believe in the Day of Judgment and continuation of life after this world. That is why in Surah Fuṣṣilat the polytheists are described as those who do not give charity and deny the Day of Judgment. This verse is describing the attitude of some of the people in Medina who claimed they were faithful and were following the Prophet, whilst in reality their faith was a pretence. The Quran calls these people the hypocrites (*al-munāfiqūn*).

يُخَادِعُونَ اللَّهَ وَالَّذِينَ آمَنُوا وَمَا يَخْدَعُونَ إِلَّا أَنفُسَهُمْ وَمَا يَشْعُرُونَ ﴿9﴾

They seek to deceive God and those who have faith, yet they deceive no one but themselves, but they are not aware.

They seek to deceive God; It is impossible to deceive God and therefore this verse refers to the attempted deception of the Prophet by the hypocrites. Some exegetes had the opinion that the Quran did not distinguish between God and his Prophet in terms of obedience and therefore "seek to deceive God" in reality means "seek to deceive the Prophet."

yet they deceive no one but themselves; Another opinion is that the hypocrites try to deceive God, thinking that they are achieving something good by their stratagem. By trying to deceive the Prophet and run away from the guidance he brings, they are actually deceiving themselves and losing the benefits which faith can provide. It is like someone trying to deceive a nurse by not taking their medication.

فِي قُلُوبِهِم مَّرَضٌ فَزَادَهُمُ اللَّهُ مَرَضًا وَلَهُمْ عَذَابٌ أَلِيمٌ بِمَا كَانُوا يَكْذِبُونَ ﴿10﴾

There is a sickness in their hearts; then God increased their sickness, and there is a painful punishment for them because of the lies they used to tell.

There is a sickness in their hearts; The heart is often used in the Quran as a metaphor for the human soul due to its life-giving function. "Sickness of the heart" alludes to the prevention of the soul from performing its normal function due to the influence of some vices (such as hypocrisy, greed, jealousy and the like). An important function of the soul is to comprehend realities which lie beyond the sensual realm, including faith in God. Sickness of the heart prevents people from acknowledging those realities and so the heart can not facilitate nearness to God. The drive of the soul is to achieve nearness to God, see beyond the physical realm and seek that connection between the physical realm and God. In the *Malakūt* (Higher Realm), God's creation is connected to God directly without the chain of cause and effect. However, in the *Mulk* (Lower Realm or this world) the creation of God is connected to God through the chain of cause and effect.

then God increased their sickness; If a disease in the heart is not cured, it spreads like physical illness. The increase of sickness in the heart is due to evil decisions resulting from a sick heart and the actions which follow. Therefore, this verse refers to the law that God has set to govern this world.

and there is a painful punishment for them because of the lies they used to tell; Finally, the verse states that there is a double punishment for the hypocrites, because not only do they deny God, but they also try to deceive others by claiming that they believe in him. Therefore, according to the Quran, the hypocrites will be in the lowest place of Hell, even lower than the disbelievers.

وَإِذَا قِيلَ لَهُمْ لَا تُفْسِدُوا فِي الْأَرْضِ قَالُوا إِنَّمَا نَحْنُ مُصْلِحُونَ ﴿11﴾

When they are told, 'Do not cause corruption on the earth,' they say, 'We are only reformers!'

This verse continues to describe the hypocrites and is a dialogue between them and the believers. During the time of the revelation, the believers and the hypocrites lived together as neighbours, relatives, and even friends. As such, they would engage in discussions about Islam and the Prophet. Of course, it was not easy to identify a hypocrite since they pretended to have faith and expressed views in opposition to the Prophet under the guise of well-intentioned suggestions. Their exact actions and intentions are not clear from this verse. Some commentators[14] have interpreted it as disbelief and discouraging others to believe. What we understand from this verse is that the Muslims who lived with them realised that the behaviour of the hypocrites was incorrect, and that it led to corruption and division amongst Muslims.

corruption on the earth; This concept has been mentioned in the Quran on numerous occasions. One verse states that when some people are given authority, they create corruption on the earth and destroy crops and stock (or culmination of human efforts) and human lives. (Q. 2:205) In other verses, the Quran describes corruption as the act of people who take up arms to fight against God and his apostle (Q. 5:33) and make factions and cause division among people to discriminate between them. (Q. 28:4) The Quran also discusses corruption in terms of polytheism and disbelief. (Q. 2:251) It is plausible that the corruption brought about by the hypocrites in Medina was creating disharmony in society, conspiring against the Prophet and disheartening Muslims.

"On the earth" (*al-arḍ*) may refer to the city of Medina or the world in general. A general meaning of *fasād* (corruption) is to bring about a situation that leads to disharmony, disunity and eventually the destruction of the crop, the stock and human lives (*harth* and *nasl).* Applying this historical lesson to our current situation, we can see that corruption may be caused by anyone, including Muslims. Present-day sectarianism is one of the most lethal forms of corruption. Therefore, anyone who is involved in harmful sectarian rhetoric could be thought of as a cause of corruption and disharmony.

أَلَآ إِنَّهُمۡ هُمُ ٱلۡمُفۡسِدُونَ وَلَٰكِن لَّا يَشۡعُرُونَ ﴿12﴾

Look! They are themselves the agents of corruption, but they are not aware.

---

but they are not aware; This verse shows that the hypocrites were so deeply deceived by their own corruption that they viewed their corruption as goodness. They believed that they were aiming to bring about righteousness. In their view, faith was useless and what the Prophet had brought for the people of Medina was to their detriment. Therefore, the hypocrites of Medina believed that they should collaborate with the Jews in Medina and the polytheists in Mecca to restore the way things were in the past. The same twisted mindset about causing corruption with the intention of "bring about good" is applicable to many contemporary problems too.

The current sectarian discourse is one of the starkest examples of it: those Shi'is who attack the sanctities of the Sunni Muslims or the Sunnis who excommunicate (*takfir*) Shi'i Muslims all think what they are doing is the right thing and their ultimate aim is to bring goodness to both religion and society. But in fact, what they do is senseless and un-Islamic.

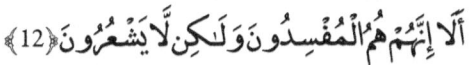

وَإِذَا قِيلَ لَهُمْ آمِنُوا كَمَا آمَنَ النَّاسُ قَالُوا أَنُؤْمِنُ كَمَا آمَنَ السُّفَهَاءُ ۗ أَلَا إِنَّهُمْ هُمُ السُّفَهَاءُ وَلَٰكِن لَّا يَعْلَمُونَ ﴿13﴾

And when they are told, 'Believe like the people who have believed,' they say, 'Shall we believe like the fools who have believed?' Look! They are themselves the fools, but they do not know.

Those who regard themselves to be the elite among the people often consider believers to be "fools" who believe in supernatural beings and vain promises about the afterlife. This verse states that in fact, it is *they* who are the real fools, because they assume that the world of existence must be confined to the five senses of a human being who is only a small part of all of existence. According to religious teachings, the afterlife is a definite reality, and so anyone who denies that and exhausts themselves in this transient life has fooled themselves. Exegetical works do not provide any information regarding the context of the conversation mentioned in this verse. However, we can say that this mindset is another quality of the hypocrites who regard themselves as being above others in terms of knowledge and understanding. Almost all the prophets faced strong resistance from these types of people. They would refer to the believers as simple-minded people, immature in their understanding and simpletons in accepting any view and idea.

A beautiful conversation is quoted in the Quran between Prophet Noah and the so-called elite in his community: *Certainly, We sent Noah to his people to declare: 'Indeed I am a manifest warner to you. Worship none but God. Indeed, I fear for you the punishment of a painful day.'* But the elite amongst the faithless from among his people said, *We do not see you to be anything but a human being like ourselves, and we do not see anyone following you except those who are simple-minded riffraff from our midst. Nor do we see that you have any merit over us. Rather we consider you to be liars.* (Q. 11:25-27) Prophet Noah's response to such arrogance is so beautiful. He said, *I do not say of those who are despicable in your eyes that God will not grant them any good. God knows the best what is in their hearts for then I would indeed be a wrongdoer.* (Q. 11:31)

وَإِذَا لَقُوا الَّذِينَ آمَنُوا قَالُوا آمَنَّا وَإِذَا خَلَوْا إِلَىٰ شَيَاطِينِهِمْ قَالُوا إِنَّا مَعَكُمْ إِنَّمَا نَحْنُ مُسْتَهْزِئُونَ ﴿14﴾

When they meet the faithful, they say, 'We believe,' but when they are alone with their devils, they say, 'We are with you; we were only deriding [them].'

Shayāṭīn is the plural of *shayṭān* or Satan, meaning devil. It is not a specific name but an attribute. Anyone who is evil or has evil intention in their heart is called *shayṭān*. Iblis is called *shayṭān* because of his evil deeds and intentions. Thus, *shayṭān* is a description that can be attributed to any being, including *jinn* and human beings. The Quran states *Thus, for every prophet We appointed as enemy the Satans (shayāṭīn) from among humans and jinn, who inspire each other with flashy words, deceptively.* (Q. 6:112) In this verse, "*shayāṭīn*" could refer to other hypocrites in Medina or the polytheists in Mecca. It may be that when some hypocrites visited the Prophet or his faithful companions, they confirmed their faith but when they returned to the other hypocrites or polytheists of Mecca they would say: "We are with you, we were just pretending and mocking them."

اللَّهُ يَسْتَهْزِئُ بِهِمْ وَيَمُدُّهُمْ فِي طُغْيَانِهِمْ يَعْمَهُونَ ﴿15﴾

It is God who derides them and leaves them bewildered in their rebellion.

It is God who derides them; The consequence of deriding the believers is that they will be derided by God. There is a tradition reported from the eighth Imam Rida (d. 202/818) in which he states that "God never derides, ridicules or deceives his creatures. Rather, he gives punishment as a result of their actions of deriding or ridiculing."[15] This means that God would punish them for their derision which some can perceive as God deriding them. Another interpretation is to take the second sentence of the verse as an explanation for the first. In other words, providing hypocrites with the means to continue in rebellion, bewildered and blindfolded, is in itself a derision for them. This is the same process mentioned in the Q. 2:10: *God increases the disease in their heart* by allowing and providing them to do more mischief.

and leaves them bewildered in their rebellion; The word used in this verse for blindness and bewilderment is *ya'mahūn* from the root verb *'amaha*. There are two words for blindness in Arabic, *'amaya* and *'amaha*. In general, *'amaya* means physical blindness and *'amaha* means spiritual blindness. Therefore, the exact meaning of the word *ya'mahūn* in this verse is that *God leaves them to transgress in their spiritual blindness*. Physical blindness is limited to this world, but the spiritual blindness will continue with us in the Hereafter. This is the meaning of *We will gather him on the Day of Resurrection blind* (Q. 20:124) and *Whoever is blind in this world will also be blind in Hereafter, and more astray in the path.* (Q. 17:72)

One might question why God allows the hypocrites to continue their rebellion. Would it not be more merciful to end their lives so that they cannot continue in their transgressions? Yet, God gives enough time to every human being to accomplish the necessary requirements to enter Paradise. On this path some may swerve and transgress, but they are being given time and a chance to repent and stop their transgression. Although this world is filled with wrongdoings and evil, from the perspective of the evil doers, they are being time to reform and repent. Should they not be given a second chance? Thus, no matter how evil people are, God continues to provide them with a chance to repent and reform themselves.

When God sent Prophet Moses and Prophet Aaron to the Pharaoh, he instructed them to *speak gently to him so that he may be reminded and fear [God].* (Q. 20:44) However, if wrongdoers do not take the merciful opportunity given to them to rectify their wrongs, they are as if derided by God. Put another way, the act of "mocking of God" changes how things end for an individual. If the transgressor repents in the end there is no derision, and they attain salvation. If the transgressor does not repent, then they will be as if derided.

أُولَـٰئِكَ الَّذِينَ اشْتَرَوُا الضَّلَالَةَ بِالْهُدَىٰ فَمَا رَبِحَت تِّجَارَتُهُمْ وَمَا كَانُوا مُهْتَدِينَ ﴿16﴾

They are the ones who bought error for guidance, so their trade did not profit them, nor were they guided.

There were different types of hypocrites at the time of the Prophet. Some never believed in the Prophet but pretended that they believed. Some of them believed in the Prophet initially, but then under the influence of others, changed their ranks and lost their faith. This group of hypocrites are mentioned in Surah al-Munafiqun, *Because they believed first and then disbelieved...* (Q. 63:4).

their trade did not profit them; They first received guidance from the Prophet, but then they sold this guidance for misguidance, because they received an offer from the other disbelievers in exchange for their faith in the Prophet. In the verse, *al-ḍalāla* (the error) is what the hypocrites were offered and sold in exchange for the Prophet and guidance from the Quran. They made a business deal which of course, it did not provide them with any profit. In the heat of the moment, they did not realise this, but in hindsight we can see that these hypocrites were the losers, and they did not benefit from their transaction.

nor were they guided. Fayd Kashani in *al-Ṣāfī* explains two meanings for the statement that *they were not guided (muhtadīn).* Firstly, they could not find guidance towards the truth; thus, they were blinded. Secondly, that the hypocrites could not decipher between profit and loss; they sold their capital because they thought they would receive something of higher value in return.[16] In other words, they wrongly believed that the worldly benefit would avail them.

مَثَلُهُمْ كَمَثَلِ الَّذِي اسْتَوْقَدَ نَارًا فَلَمَّا أَضَاءَتْ مَا حَوْلَهُ ذَهَبَ اللَّهُ بِنُورِهِمْ وَتَرَكَهُمْ فِي ظُلُمَاتٍ لَّا يُبْصِرُونَ ﴿17﴾

Their parable is that of one who lighted a torch, and when it had lit up all around him, God took away their light, and left them sightless in a manifold darkness.

God gives two striking parables here about the hypocrites. Parables are used to make conceptual matters tangible to our physically oriented minds. This parable explains the way faith enlightens the path and the darkness that follows if faith leaves the heart. This relates to those hypocrites who initially believed in the Prophet but lost their faith. By believing in the Prophet, it was as if they had lit a torch. By that torch they could see the path and understand the purpose of life, and how to conduct themselves. But as soon as their surroundings were lit and the fire of the torch glowed, their hearts wavered and denied. So, the light was put out and they plunged back into darkness once again.

God took away their light and left them sightless in a manifold darkness; Here, the act of taking the light away is attributed to God. This is one of the deepest concepts about faith which is repeatedly mentioned in the Quran. It is God that brings the light of guidance to hearts, and it is he who takes it away. *God leads astray whomever He wishes, and guides whomever He wishes.* (Q. 35:8) The initial guidance which comes through the Prophet brings light and brightness for all. Whoever believes and acknowledges that light would submit their hearts to God, and He would guide them and shine true light into their hearts. Whoever does not believe and declines to submit their heart, God would let their hearts linger in darkness.

This verse also shows that faith must not be taken for granted; if one does not protect it, faith may gradually leave the heart. The believers must be very careful and protective about their faith. In this regard, there are many traditions that warn that faith (*imān*) is sometimes *mustaqar* which is established faith, and sometimes *mustawda'a,*[17] a faith entrusted for a while. Sometimes certain desires, states of mind or lifestyles can drag a person away from faith and blind them spiritually; such a person may no longer be able to distinguish truth from falsehood and this process may eventually take a person's faith away. This is what happened to the hypocrites mentioned in this verse and this type of faith is described as faith entrusted for a while. We are warned that this temporary faith may continue to persist for some people until the end of their lives only to be taken away at the moment of death. This may be because the desires of this world have found a firm foothold in their hearts and when their souls are being taken away, they object to the wisdom of God and instead they resist his will.

A sermon in *Nahj al-balāgha* clearly explains the volatility of faith. Imam Ali says:

> Some belief is that which is firm and steadfast in hearts, and some is that which is endowed between the heart and the chest up to an appointed time. So, if you were to disown any person, you should wait till death approaches him, for that is the time limit for disowning.[18]

Everyone experiences fluctuations in faith and spirituality. Sometimes we feel spiritually uplifted and refreshed, and at other times we lose that spiritual elation and start to question God's grace and justice. In this way faith constantly commutes between the heart and the chest. This happens until an appointed time (time of death).

In the same way that a believer cannot take their faith for granted, those who commit sins have a chance to embrace faith up until the point of death. A disbeliever might depart this world with faith and a believer might depart this world without faith. It is not known until the time of death. A good example of this is the magicians of the Pharaoh. These magicians had been practicing magic all their lives. But as shown in the Quran, they were the first people who believed in Prophet Moses and broke away from the ranks of the Pharaoh. These magicians became so strong in their faith that it remained strong in their hearts, even when faced with the Pharoah's gruesome punishment. This is what Imam Ali states in his sermon. People's faith may change at any time, so no one must judge the faith of others until they depart this world. Only God knows about people's faith as he has knowledge of the past, present, and future. Therefore, the practice of *takfir* (excommunication) as exercised by some Muslim groups has no place in Islam.

Some of the parables in the Quran resemble the parables mentioned in the Gospels. As Muslims, we do not have certainty about the source of the Gospels as they were written long after the life of Jesus. However, there are certain sections of the Gospels that concur with the Quranic teachings, and we can be sure from their content that they were uttered by Jesus. One of them is the Parable of the Sower that is present in the three synoptic Gospels.[19]

> 1 On the same day Jesus went out of the house and sat by the sea. 2 And great multitudes were gathered together to Him, so that He got into a boat and sat; and the whole multitude stood on the shore.
>
> 3 Then He spoke many things to them in parables, saying: "Behold, a sower went out to sow. 4 And as he sowed, some seed fell by the wayside; and the birds came and devoured them. 5 Some fell on stony places, where they did not have much earth; and they immediately sprang up because they had no depth of earth. 6 But when the sun was up they were scorched, and because they had no root they withered away. 7 And some fell among thorns, and the thorns sprang up and choked them. 8 But others fell on good ground and yielded a crop: some a hundredfold, some sixty, some thirty. 9 He who has ears to hear, let him hear! ...

> 18 Therefore hear the parable of the sower:
> 19 When anyone hears the word of the kingdom, and does not understand it, then the wicked one comes and snatches away what was sown in his heart. This is he who received seed by the wayside. 20 But he who received the seed on stony places, this is he who hears the word and immediately receives it with joy; 21 yet he has no root in himself, but endures only for a while. For when tribulation or persecution arises because of the word, immediately he stumbles. 22 Now he who received seed among the thorns is he who hears the word, and the cares of this world and the deceitfulness of riches choke the word, and he becomes unfruitful. 23 But he who received seed on the good ground is he who hears the word and understands it, who indeed bears fruit and produces: some a hundredfold, some sixty, some thirty.[20]

Biblical scholars often remark that the parables are the most authentic parts of the Gospels, and it is almost certain that the Parable of the Sower can be traced back to the time of Jesus.[21] According to the Gospel of Mark, Jesus mentioned the parable in public but did not explain what he meant by it. This is the typical style of the parables in the Gospel; that Jesus mentions a parable in public, but the explanation of these parables was given to his Twelve Disciples in private. In public Jesus just said after the four types, "he who has ears let him hear." However, his close disciples privately asked him what he meant by the parable. He then explained the meaning of the Parable of the Sower. The metaphor of "*seed* fell by the wayside" refers to the disbelievers. The parable of "stony places" is the same as the verse at hand (Q. 2:16) and refers to the faith of the hypocrites. Faith comes to the heart quickly and departs from the heart quickly. The metaphor of "some fell among thorns" refers to many people with faith. The metaphor of "he who received seed on the good ground" is about true believers and is identical to the Quranic verse: *The good soil brings fruit with the permission of the Lord, and as for that which is bad, it does not come out except sparsely. Thus, do We paraphrase the signs variously for a people who give thanks.* (Q. 7:58)

صُمٌّ بُكْمٌ عُمْيٌ فَهُمْ لَا يَرْجِعُونَ ﴿18﴾

Deaf, dumb, and blind, they will not come back.

Deaf, dumb, and blind; This expression has been used in many places in the Quran; sometimes concerning the Hereafter and at other times it is used in relation to this world. As discussed in the previous verse, people who have the deficiency of spiritual blindness in this world will continue to have the same deficiency in the Hereafter. The "deafness, dumbness" mentioned in this verse can be seen as an extension of this spiritual blindness. There are several verses that mention that whoever is "deaf, dumb and blind" in this world will be raised in the Hereafter in the same way: *...We will raise them on the Day of Judgment on their faces – blind, dumb and deaf...* (Q. 17:97) These deficiencies are a direct result of an inability to see and hear the signs of God in this life and to acknowledge them; therefore, these verses do not refer to physical disabilities. They hear the verses of the Quran, but do not wish to understand its meaning. The revelation of truth that we will see in the Hereafter will worsen these deficiencies. This is because such a soul has developed certain deficiencies due to being in a constant state of transgression and, as a result, they are not able to process or understand goodness. Whatever enters their soul through the faculties of hearing and vision will be processed in the same way in which that soul is used to seeing and understanding the world. Similarly, they would be able to speak but they would be unable to speak Godly words as whatever comes from their hearts to their tongues is ungodly. For this reason, one of the requests that we make in the Supplication of Kumayl is "make my tongue flow with your remembrance..."

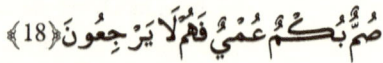

Abd al-Karim al-Qasim Qushayri (d. 465/1072-73), the famous Sunni mystic exegete, in his *Laṭā'if al-isharat bi-tafsīr al-qur'ān,*[22] made an interesting comment[23] about the expressions of "deaf, dumb and blind". He contends that those who are "deaf, dumb and blind" cannot hear the truth; in the physical sense they may hear the truth, but they perceive it as being the opposite of truth (*bāṭil*). In the same vein, they cannot see and perceive the truth by observing what is around them. Furthermore, the Quran (Q. 17:97) informs us that these deficiencies will continue in the Hereafter and the transgressors will not be able to perceive the magnificence of God. One important point regarding Q. 17:97 is the use of the term "*'alā wujūhihim*" (on their faces). The face here signifies the attention of the transgressors: we always turn our faces to give someone or something attention, thus the face is the focus of our attention. For the transgressors the point of attention has always been themselves as well as their physical or carnal satisfaction.

أَوْ كَصَيِّبٍ مِّنَ السَّمَاءِ فِيهِ ظُلُمَاتٌ وَرَعْدٌ وَبَرْقٌ يَجْعَلُونَ أَصَابِعَهُمْ فِي
آذَانِهِم مِّنَ الصَّوَاعِقِ حَذَرَ الْمَوْتِ وَاللَّهُ مُحِيطٌ بِالْكَافِرِينَ ﴿19﴾

Or that of a rainstorm from the sky, wherein is darkness, thunder, and lightning: they put their fingers in their ears due to the thunderclaps, apprehensive of death; and God besieges the faithless.

يَكَادُ الْبَرْقُ يَخْطَفُ أَبْصَارَهُمْ كُلَّمَا أَضَاءَ لَهُم مَّشَوْا فِيهِ وَإِذَا أَظْلَمَ عَلَيْهِمْ
قَامُوا وَلَوْ شَاءَ اللَّهُ لَذَهَبَ بِسَمْعِهِمْ وَأَبْصَارِهِمْ إِنَّ اللَّهَ عَلَىٰ كُلِّ شَيْءٍ قَدِيرٌ ﴿20﴾

for them, they walk in it, and when the darkness falls upon them, they stand. Had God willed, He would have taken away their hearing and their sight. Indeed, God has power over all things.

These verses deal with the second parable that speaks about people who never believed in the Prophet but pretended that they did.

These are the second type of hypocrites who lived within the Muslim community.

Or that of a rainstorm from the sky; Revelation would descend frequently, and these hypocrites perceived it to be like a "rainstorm" (*ṣayyib*). Paradoxically, rain is essential for human existence. However, due to their blindness to the truth, these hypocrites only saw the negative and terrifying features of a rainstorm, such as darkness and shock. This was especially so when the Prophet spoke about obedience to God, the Hereafter and the Day of Judgment, and related warnings and threats of retribution which were dark and gloomy subject for the hypocrites. They only perceived worldly and carnal subjects to be cheerful and bright. Traditions elaborate that if the transgressors had come out of Hell without completing their purification, they would not have seen anything but darkness. They are not able to endure life in Heaven which consists of pure light. Furthermore, they perceive the revelation like "thunder" (*ra'dun*) and "lightning" (*barqun*); because the Prophet through revelations informs them about the duties of Muslims which include praying, almsgiving, fasting and *jihad* to name a few. These are painful and burdensome instructions for the hypocrites who do not believe in God but try to pretend that they believe. Nevertheless, the verse states that God is in control of them.

Verse 20 mentions the other attitude of the hypocrites who never believed in the Prophet. There were occasions during the Prophet's mission when the hypocrites received guidance momentarily. When distributing war booties, the hypocrites would receive their share as established in the Quran and it would make them very pleased with the Prophet. However, if there was a difficult situation, they would quickly lose their state of happiness, and as a result they would lose the guidance again.

يَا أَيُّهَا النَّاسُ اعْبُدُوا رَبَّكُمُ الَّذِي خَلَقَكُمْ وَالَّذِينَ مِن قَبْلِكُمْ لَعَلَّكُمْ تَتَّقُونَ ﴿21﴾

O mankind! Worship your Lord, who created you and those who were before you, so that you may be Godwary.

O mankind! Up to verse 20, this surah has described three types of people: God-fearing (*Muttaqīn*), disbelievers (*kuffār*) and hypocrites (*munāfiqūn*). Verse 21 is the concluding statement to this discussion and addresses all three categories of people calling; "O people!" (*yā-ayyuhā al-nās*!). When God addresses all people, it is to convey a universal message to appeal to the *fiṭra* or conscience of all people as human beings.

Worship your Lord, who created you and those who were before you; This verse appeals to that innate understanding embedded in the soul of humankind, that they have been designed and created by a higher being and that it is impossible to come into existence without a maker and this is stated by the phrase "that he created you" (*alladhī khalaqakum*). Creation alone is not enough for persistence of a living being without providence. It is impossible to live unless we are provided the means of living, be it soil and sun, rain and suitable climate, or food and facilities. Thus, the creator is the provider as well, and this is highlighted by the term *rabbakkum* (your Lord and cherisher). Therefore, the verse addresses anyone who has the heart and mind to direct their attention towards the Sublime being and to establish a way of connecting with him through worship.

so that you may be Godwary. (*la-'allakum tattaqūn*) this is the goal of worshipping God. There are two interpretations to consider. Firstly, the previous statement, "that he created you", refers to the purpose of creation which is to be aware of God. This is also stated in the verse *I did not create the jinn and the humans except that they may worship Me.* (Q. 51:56) *Taqwā* (God-wariness) is the outcome of worship. The essence of worship is to create a bond between us and God. This bond is in addition to the bond of creation and the bond of provision; it is a heartfelt bond with God. This bond is the ladder that elevates a person in the spiritual realm and hence in our existence as he is *The Lord of the lofty stations,* (*min Allāh dhī al-ma'ārij*). (Q. 70:3) It is only through this bond of worship that we can ascend; thus, by linking these verses together, the meaning of worship becomes clear: God only created us to ascend towards him and this is the wisdom behind creation.

Secondly, an analysis of the phrase, "so that you may be Godwary" to "worship your Lord" (*u'budū rabbakum*), shows that worshipping God is a means to find God-wariness (*taqwā).* It means that sheer belief in God without worship would not bring about God-wariness. It is only through worship that we can become aware of him and invite him into our hearts and lives. In this sense, the verse can be read as "I have created you so that you may be my guest, or I become your guest." This is also mentioned in the verse regarding fasting: *O believers, fasting has been prescribed for you as it was prescribed for those who lived before you, so that you may be Godwary.* (Q. 2:183) Therefore, worship is a crucial part of faith. A religion without worship cannot fulfil the role described here, because without worship it is impossible to establish a bond between God and his creation.

An interesting point to mention here is recorded in the *Tafsīr* of Imam Hasan al-Askari. When asked about the meaning of this verse, he pointed out the two possibilities mentioned above.[24] One may wonder why the Imam gave two separate interpretations for one verse. Was the Imam uncertain about which of the two meanings were indicated by this verse? Tabatabai in *al-Mīzan* answers this question by stating that the Imam wanted to enlighten us about how verses of the Quran could carry layers of meaning if we reflect on them deeply.

الَّذِي جَعَلَ لَكُمُ الْأَرْضَ فِرَاشًا وَالسَّمَاءَ بِنَاءً وَأَنْزَلَ مِنَ السَّمَاءِ
مَاءً فَأَخْرَجَ بِهِ مِنَ الثَّمَرَاتِ رِزْقًا لَكُمْ فَلَا تَجْعَلُوا لِلَّهِ أَنْدَادًا وَأَنْتُمْ
تَعْلَمُونَ ﴿22﴾

He who made the earth a place of repose and rest for you, and the sky a canopy, and He sends down water from the sky and with it He brings forth crops for your sustenance. So, do not set up equals to God while you know.

This verse highlights further explanations about why we should worship God – his unlimited provision for us, which is often taken for granted, and his creation of the earth and its functions, which are in need of his constant attention to subsist. A tradition[25] reported from the fourth Imam Zayn al-Abidin (d. 95/713) elaborates on the phrase, *He who made the earth a place of repose and rest for you*. The Imam says that the earth is a pleasant place for human beings, with everything in perfect balance for our needs. The ambient temperature is just suitable for us, the ground is just soft enough to plant crops or bury the dead, the variety of plants and animals around us are perfect for our diet, and the list goes on. Imam Zayn al-ʻAbidin then mentions many other aspects to show that we take these blessings for granted and we assume that they are supposed to be there. Of course, these natural blessings are given to people collectively and do not include individual blessings.

the sky a canopy; There are several interpretations as the word "sky" is used in many ways in the Quran. One meaning includes all the galaxies, stars and planets, which are interwoven in such a way that if one of them is not there then the whole structure may collapse. As it is mentioned in the Quran *[I swear] by the sky which is knitted together.* (Q. 51:7) All these galaxies and the gravity that they create, are interwoven. The "sky" may also allude to the earth's atmosphere which is like a strong ceiling above us, protecting us from meteors and harmful celestial rays and objects.

We have oceans that are full of water, but we cannot use the water from the oceans; it is too salty and often far from human settlements. God purifies it by evaporation and brings it to our place of residence by sending it down as rain. There is a perfect and beautiful system at work, but we take it for granted. Imam Zayn al-'Abidin in the above narration states in relation to this verse that, God does not bring down the water all at once so that it may destroy what is underneath. Instead, it comes down in units and gradually so that we may benefit from it. However, at times there are droughts or floods and destruction. This is why in Surah Furqān, God says in relation to the rain *We alternate it between them so that they may take admonition. But most people are only intent on ingratitude.* (Q. 25:50) God sometimes pours rain down upon us and sometimes withholds it so that people do not take it for granted and this should be a point of reflection for us. However, in such instances, we often complain instead of taking notice of God's wisdom and mercy.

So, do not set up equals to God while you know. This verse further continues to elaborate on the blessings God has bestowed upon mankind and then concludes with this statement. The word *andād* (equals) is the plural of *nid* which means "an equal who is opposed to the other equal". It is not just any equal; but equals between whom there is a rivalry. One may say that no one assumes an equal to God Almighty. Even the polytheists who believed in idols did not believe that their idols were rival equals to God. They accepted that God was the creator of everything including the idols, but that God had delegated worldly affairs to the idols.

Yet, there is a more subtle meaning to be aware of. Assuming independent authority for anyone or anything in this world means setting up a rival to God's absolute authority. Appreciating the sun as a blessing from God which makes life possible on earth is an acknowledgement and appreciation of God's blessings but worshipping the sun as an independent agent with the same effect is to assume a rival for God's bounties and authority.

وَإِن كُنتُمْ فِي رَيْبٍ مِّمَّا نَزَّلْنَا عَلَىٰ عَبْدِنَا فَأْتُوا بِسُورَةٍ مِّن مِّثْلِهِ وَادْعُوا
شُهَدَاءَكُم مِّن دُونِ اللَّهِ إِن كُنتُمْ صَادِقِينَ ﴿23﴾

And if you are in doubt about what we have sent down to our servant (Muhammad), then bring a chapter like it, and invoke your helpers beside God, should you be truthful.

And if you are in doubt; In the present order of the Quran, this verse marks the first challenge (*taḥaddī*) regarding the inimitability of the Quran. If one doubts that it is from God, then let them produce something like it if they can. The word *rayb,* used for "doubt" in this verse, specifically refers to a doubt that agitates and shadows the comfort of the heart.

about what we have sent down to our servant (Muhammad); The verse clarifies the position of the Prophet; he says and does nothing of his own accord. He is a slave (*ʿabd*) doing and saying what God, his Lord has instructed from him. Secondly, the guidance has been sent down by God. It is something that has descended from a higher realm to our lower realm. Two different subjugates of the verbal noun *nuzūl* (descent) have been used for revelation in the Quran: *nazzalnā* and *anzalnā*. Exegetes usually state that these two terms refer to two different types of descent. *Anzalnā* refers to a sudden descent of the Quran from its higher realm, *al-Lawḥ al-Maḥfūẓ* (the Protected Book), to a lower realm which is known as *al-Bayt al-Maʿmūr*[26] (the Frequented House) where Angel Gabriel can receive it.[27] When it is at the higher realm with God Almighty, Gabriel cannot receive it. Therefore, it first descends from the highest realm to a lower realm from where Gabriel receives it and brings it to the Prophet gradually.[28] The second stage is when Gabriel brings it to the Prophet, and this is referred as *nazzalnā* (or *tanzīl*).

The point in this discussion is that the disbelievers questioned the Prophet about the way the Quran was revealed slowly and in parts. They would argue that it is people who need time to produce a book, not God; therefore, since this book is being made gradually, the author of the Quran must be a human being. This argument is also mentioned in Surah Isrā'. They said we will not believe in you until: *...you ascend into the sky and we will not believe your ascension until you bring down for us a book that we may read.* (Q. 17:93) To some extent this seems a valid argument by disbelievers and the Quran needed to address it. In several places in the Quran, God mentions that even if he had given these people a complete book, they would have still rejected it.[29] God goes so far as to say that even if the Prophet had ascended to the sky to bring them a sign, they would not have believed in him.[30]

Surah Isrā' addresses this question again in verse 32, where God gives another response: *In this way, we wanted to strengthen your heart.* This verse states the reason for the Quran being revealed gradually was due to the limitations of human nature and its capacity to absorb religious teachings. Consequently, the believers were able to absorb the guidance gradually. Another reason may be that the revelation was linked to events and circumstances during the lifetime of the Prophet and therefore poignant verses were revealed at the right times. The verses needed to come down to respond to the events and questions that occurred during the life of the Prophet so that the teachings could have been elaborated on and clarified by him. In this way the context of revelation is very important to the interpretation of verses. If the Quran had been revealed all at once, it would have been abstract and irrelevant to the needs of the time and would not have been understood by people. This verse challenges the disbelievers to produce a chapter like any chapter of the Quran and seek help in that from anyone they wished.

And invoke your helpers beside God, should you be truthful. The onus is on the disbelievers to call any mediator to judge whether their chapter is superior to the Quran. This challenge is rhetorical as the disbelievers knew that they could not rival the chapters of the Quran in terms of content or eloquence. They knew that these words were from God, but through engaging in such rhetoric, they aimed to discredit the Quran and hinder the Prophet's mission.

One might wonder why, when faced with such a challenge, the talented poets of the time could not compose a poetic couplet to rival the shorter surahs such as Surah Kawthar. This has been a point of discussion even for the early commentators of the Quran.

There were some who tried and failed, such as Musaylima, the false prophet, who attempted to produce some chapters similar to the chapters of the Quran after the death of the Prophet. However, due to the bizarre style of his fabricated chapters, he made a mockery of himself. One could argue that Musaylima was not a man of literature, however the exegetes insist no one has been able to do so. In fact, the disbelievers who were being directly challenged by this verse at the time of the Prophet, despite their strong hostility against Islam, never tried to respond to the challenge as they were mesmerised with the style and beauty of the Quran.

Some Shi'i scholars such as al-Sharif al-Murtada (also known as A'lām al-Hudā) (d. 463/1044) and many Mutazili scholars in the Sunni world maintained that it is theoretically impossible for anyone, including talented people of literature to produce chapters that may be similar to the chapters of the Quran, especially the short chapters. This is because God would not allow anyone to seriously attempt it due to the theory of prevention (*al-ṣarfa*). They say that this is a miracle that God distracts those people who intend to produce something similar to the Quran. However, most scholars in this field do not accept this theory. They say that, bearing in mind all aspects of the Quran in both form and content, it is actually not possible for a human mind to produce something like it.

Another view which is mentioned in many commentaries is that *fa'tū bi sūratin min mithlihi* does not mean, "bring a chapter like it," but it means "bring a chapter from *someone* like *him*."[31] That means the pronoun in *mithlihi* does not refer to the Quran, but to the Prophet. They argue that it may be possible for a practicing poet and a man of letter and literature to produce something like the Quran, but it is not possible from a man like the Prophet with no background in literature and poetry to produce something like that. Thus, the challenge is to find someone with the same background and see if he or she can compose literature like the Quran. Although this view may be plausible and intended in this verse, other verses imply different meanings. For example, *Do they say, 'He has fabricated it?' Say, 'Then bring a surah like it, and invoke whomever you can, besides God, should you be truthful.'* (Q. 10:38) Or, *Do they say, 'He has fabricated it?' Say, 'Then bring ten surahs like it, fabricated, and invoke whomever you can, besides God, should you be truthful.'* (Q. 11:13) In the syntax of these verses the pronoun cannot refer to the Prophet.

فَإِن لَّمْ تَفْعَلُوا وَلَن تَفْعَلُوا فَاتَّقُوا النَّارَ الَّتِي وَقُودُهَا النَّاسُ وَالْحِجَارَةُ أُعِدَّتْ لِلْكَافِرِينَ ﴿24﴾

And if you do not, and you will never be able to do it, then beware of the Fire its fuel is men and stones, prepared for the disbelievers.

The first part of this verse is self-explanatory and was covered in the discussion of the previous verse. It reaffirms the inimitability of the Quran, in the past and future.

you will never be able to do it; This verse can be taken as one of the predictions of the Quran which has come true. No one in the history of Islam to the present day has produced something equal to the Quran it its form and context. On the contrary, every expert in Arabic literature has acknowledged its superior nature. There are three further matters to be discussed in this verse. Firstly, the meaning of "the Fire its fuel is men and stones". Secondly, the meaning of "prepared for the disbelievers". Thirdly, how stones can be the fuel of Hell.

the Fire its fuel is men and stones; The punishment in the Hereafter does not follow the conventions of this world. There is no courtroom and judge who decides a person's fate based on reasonable evidence. Rather, a person's fate in the Hereafter is a direct consequence of their actions in this world. In other words, the actions that are committed in this world come back to people on the Day of Judgment. That is why everyone has a "book", and this book is the book of actions which is given back to them on the Day of Judgment. *Every nation will be summoned to its book: Today you will be requited for what you used to do. This is Our book, which speaks truly against you. Indeed, We used to record what you used to do.* (Q. 46:28-29) And *We have attached every person's omen to his neck, and We shall bring it out for him on the Day of Resurrection as a wide-open book that he will encounter.* (Q. 17:13)

The Fire that this verse mentions is not like the fire that we experience in this world. It may seem from this verse that there would be bodies of people as fuel, burning to create fire so that other people would be thrown into it, but this explanation is not reasonable. The fire of Hell is that fire which *overspread the hearts.* (Q. 104:7) It is the evil soul and heart of the vicious which create that fire and burns anyone who has been associated to them and has followed them.

Furthermore, there are different views on the nature of the stones mentioned in this verse. Some exegetes argue that they may be brimstones. Others suggest that stone is mentioned to emphasise the ferocity of the Hellfire as stones are hard to burn and Hellfire must be ferocious enough to set the stones on fire. A group have suggested that they refer to the stone idols which will be burned in Hell alongside the idol worshippers. However, this explanation does not corroborate with other relevant verses of the Quran, such as in Surah Taḥrīm: *O you who believe! protect yourselves and your families from a fire that its fuel is men and stones.* (Q. 66:6) This verse addresses the believers, so the stone here cannot allude to idols. Hence, verse 66:6 further explains verse 2:24 by implying that it is the actual people who will turn into fire - regardless of whether they are Muslims or disbelievers, they may end up in Hellfire as a result of their actions. A person's actions are more important that their religious affiliations or labels – it is what people do, not what people say, that matters to God.

In summary, Hell is not simply a place people are thrown into and then set ablaze. The fire is not always external from the person; it flares from within their hearts, soul and minds. People themselves, their concepts, ideas and beliefs will be the fuel of the fire too. Of course, a stone is a stone – it cannot be good or bad in itself, but if people start worshipping stones, they become a concept and this concept will be the fuel of the fire along with the people who create these God-defying concepts. These concepts are not limited to idol worship, and may be in various forms. In this respect, Tabatabai, states that verse 2:24 is a clear indication that human actions will be brought to life in the Hereafter.[32] People are burnt from within themselves, by their misdeeds; therefore, the fire originates from people themselves. If they live and transgress, they accumulate fuel for themselves, which will then be set on fire on the Day of Judgment, although if they reform themselves while they are alive, then this process will be reversed. This interpretation of the verse is further supported by other verses, such as *The day when every soul will find present whatever good it has done; and as to whatever evil it has done it will wish there were a far distance between it and itself.* (Q. 3:30) and *On that day, mankind will issue forth in various groups to be shown their deeds. So whoever does an atom's weight of good will see it, and whoever does an atom's weight of evil will see it.* (Q. 99:6-8)

prepared for the disbelievers. Qushayri states that the final phrase of this verse is a relief for the believers.[33] Up until this final section, the verse expresses terrifying threats but then expresses that these threats are only for the disbelievers and the believers have nothing to worry about. At first glance, Qushayri's interpretation of the verse sounds promising. However, Surah Taḥrīm, verse 6, addresses the believers as well. Thus, it appears that as opposed to Qushayri's interpretation, the above-mentioned threats may also be addressed the believers. Combining the interpretation of these two verses, we may arrive at a third explanation that the "disbelievers" mentioned in this verse may refer not only to those who deny God, but also those who are ungrateful towards him and deny the injunctions of God or refuse to perform these injunctions.

وَبَشِّرِ الَّذِينَ آمَنُوا وَعَمِلُوا الصَّالِحَاتِ أَنَّ لَهُمْ جَنَّاتٍ تَجْرِي مِن تَحْتِهَا الْأَنْهَارُ كُلَّمَا رُزِقُوا مِنْهَا مِن ثَمَرَةٍ رِّزْقًا قَالُوا هَٰذَا الَّذِي رُزِقْنَا مِن قَبْلُ وَأُتُوا بِهِ مُتَشَابِهًا وَلَهُمْ فِيهَا أَزْوَاجٌ مُّطَهَّرَةٌ وَهُمْ فِيهَا خَالِدُونَ ﴿25﴾

And give good tidings to those who have faith and do righteous deeds that for them there shall be gardens; streams running in them. Whenever they are provided with fruits for nourishments they will say, 'This is what we were provided with before.' And they are given something resembling to it. Therein they will have purified mates for them, and they will remain in it forever.

This verse renders a beautiful description and a deeper understanding of Paradise. As humans, we divest our concepts of Paradise and Hell from what we understand from pain and pleasure in this world. The previous verse, which describes Hell, rendered a deeper understanding of Hell; it is not a place where God has merely set a fire and throws people in it, but the fire originates from people and their vices.

Whenever they are provided with fruits for nourishments they will say, 'This is what we were provided with before.' If "fruits" are interpreted in a literal sense, it may mean that the fruits we eat in Heaven will be very similar to the fruits available in this world. But the explanation of this verse cannot be limited to saying that the dwellers of Heaven eat fruit similar to apples and pears. For this reason, most commentators have not taken this comparison to be between the fruits of this world and those found in the Hereafter. For example, Yahya b. Abi Kathir (d. 132/747-50) said that whenever the fruits of Paradise are picked they are renewed in their place, so when people pick them again they say this is what we were provided with before.[34] Or it is reported from Hasan al-Basri (d. 110/728) that since the fruits of Paradise are all similar in taste and fineness, they will say this is what we were provided with before, although they know it is different.[35] However, Ibn Abbas gives a different meaning to the sentence. He says, whatever they are given in Paradise, they will say this is what we were given in the world (*dunyā*).[36] This is a much deeper meaning. It means whatever is given in Paradise is the fruit of an achievement in this world.

This meaning is further explained by Tabatabai who maintains that the word "fruit" here is used figuratively and not literally. His argument is based on evidence derived from the Quran and not based on speculation or imagination. For example, we may ask someone "what is the fruit of your life? Or what is the fruit of your studies?" These are commonly used expressions in which the word fruit is used figuratively to mean the result, outcome or consequence of a person's effort. Therefore, in this verse the word fruit refers to the fruit of their deeds that they performed in the previous world (*dunya*). In this vein, the word *ruziqū* (they are provided) does not only mean food or fruit but includes all kinds of blessings bestowed upon people including knowledge, good character, and happiness. In the Hereafter, these blessings which were attained through the actions in this world (such as prayer, fasting, giving charity, being humble) will be presented to them in terms of physical and spiritual provisions and when people see these provisions, they will say *this is the result of a certain deed that I committed in the previous world and this reward is the consequence of it.* The intensity of the taste of these fruits will be in direct correlation to their commitment and connection to God Almighty in this world.

It is also important to know that people cannot take credit for the good deeds they do. Rather, they perform these actions by the power and permission of God, so they are blessings of God upon them. Their only contribution is having the will to perform these good deeds. In turn, these good deeds produce fruits for eternity in the Hereafter as it is mentioned in the Quran: ... *the example of a good word [or good concept/belief] is like a good tree which is so high its roots are firmly fixed and its branches [reach high] in the sky. It bears fruit constantly with the permission of its Lord.* (Q. 14:25-26)

Therein they will have purified mates for them; the description "purified" (*muṭahhara*) for mates (*azwāj)* is a universal description for all mates in Paradise. The literal meaning of the word *muṭahhara* alludes to physical purity, however, this word is used in the Quran to denote both physical and spiritual purity. The spiritually pure ones are those who can access sublime spiritual concepts and meanings due to the purity of their hearts. As it is mentioned in the Quran: *None shall be able to touch it [the concepts given in the Quran] except the purified ones (al-muṭahharūn).* (Q. 56:79) With this verse, we can conclude that the "purified spouses" referred to in this verse are spouses who have no restriction in their experience of God Almighty as a result of their pure souls and lack of evil in their hearts.[37] By the time people arrive in Heaven everyone will be purified from their evil deeds. Hence, the term "purified spouses" may be interpreted as "matching spouses" as everyone will be purified before they arrive in Heaven.

and they will remain in it forever. the word *khālidūn* (they will remain therein eternally) refers to the eternal life of human beings. As soon as people are created, they are eternal beings. They may change form and move from one dimension to another and then finally move to Heaven or Hell, but they never cease to exist.

إِنَّ اللَّهَ لَا يَسْتَحْيِي أَنْ يَضْرِبَ مَثَلًا مَا بَعُوضَةً فَمَا فَوْقَهَا ۚ فَأَمَّا الَّذِينَ
آمَنُوا فَيَعْلَمُونَ أَنَّهُ الْحَقُّ مِنْ رَبِّهِمْ ۖ وَأَمَّا الَّذِينَ كَفَرُوا فَيَقُولُونَ مَاذَا
أَرَادَ اللَّهُ بِهَٰذَا مَثَلًا ۘ يُضِلُّ بِهِ كَثِيرًا وَيَهْدِي بِهِ كَثِيرًا ۚ وَمَا يُضِلُّ بِهِ إِلَّا
الْفَاسِقِينَ ﴿26﴾

Indeed, God is not ashamed to draw a parable whether it is that of a gnat or something above it [in smallness]. As for those who have faith, they know it is the truth from their Lord. As for the faithless, they would say 'what did God mean by this parable?' Thereby He leads many astray and He guides many. And He leads no one astray except the transgressors.

This verse is connected to the previous verses regarding the inimitability of the Quran. (Q. 2:23) Some may have argued that there is no value in parables, such as the parable about the gnat[38] or spider web[39] if this Book is from God. It is not clear from the sources which people presented such arguments. Some say it was the Jews, others say it was the hypocrites and some say it was the polytheists. Regardless of the identity of those who formed this argument, the verse generally presents an eloquent answer.

The verse answers that a mosquito may seem a tiny creature, yet it is an extremely sophisticated being and hence God is not ashamed to bring an example of a mosquito or anything smaller than it. The sophistication and wonders of such tiny units of life is something that has become manifest through the advancement of modern technology and insight into the life of smaller creatures. There is a fascinating tradition in Ibn al-Fadl Tabrisi's (d. 548/1153-54) *Majma' al-bayān* attributed to the sixth Imam Jafar al-Sadiq (d. 148/765). He states that: "God has given this parable of a gnat because, despite its minute size, everything that is found in an elephant is also found in a gnat with the addition of two extra limbs."[40] This means that those who wanted to defeat the arguments presented by way of parables in the end defeated their own counterargument since, despite their minute size, gnats are immensely complex creatures. This is the position of the disbelievers. As for the believers, they acknowledge the truth of whatever they see in the world, and whatever they hear from the Book of God Almighty and from the Prophet.

Thereby He leads many astray and He guides many. And He leads no one to astray except the transgressors. This part of the verse has played an important role in theological debates. As discussed previously, these types of verses are the basis of theological schools in Islam such as the Asharites and Mutazilis. The Asharites advocated the idea that guidance and misguidance are predestined by God alone and in this world he either guides or misguides people based on his initial decision. The Mutazilis, on the other hand, would not negate God's justice and human's free will and responsibility. They considered it unjust if God guides some and misguides others based on his own will and then rewards or punishes them for deeds they have no control over.

It is counter-intuitive to accept the former view that guidance and misguidance are only decided by God and people do not have any influence in the matter. Moreover, the last part of the verse makes it clear that *He leads no one astray except the transgressors* (*al-fāsiqīn*, sing. *fāsiq*). Thus, misguidance is a direct result of an individual's choices and deeds. As a result of their actions, a habitual sinner will deviate from the right path and will be misguided. The word *fāsiq* (transgressor) is derived from the verbal noun *fusuq*, which means "to come out", thus the word *fāsiq* means someone who comes out of faith by sinning.

By sinning, people abandon the faith, because committing sins is contradictory to faith. This idea is mentioned in the Quran multiple times, for example, in Surah Ibrāhīm: *God misleads the oppressors and God does whatever He wants.* (Q. 14:27)

Considering this discussion, there are two important questions to be answered: if someone is already a habitual sinner (*fāsiq*) or disbeliever or oppressor, how can they be misguided? And are there different types of misguidances? To answer these questions, we must first elaborate on the concept of *zīna* (adornment) in the Quran. The Quran talks about two types of adornment; adornment of God and adornment of Satan. The adornment of God is whatever is made attractive for people in this world to make their life continue, including the taste of food, wealth, opposite gender and other desires. These are positive adornments as they make continuation of life possible in this world. They also give people an opportunity to display and develop their inner qualities, such as patience, generosity, honour, self-restraint and integrity of character. By controlling their desires towards these adornments, people increase the quality of their souls.

Conversely, the adornment of Satan embellishes the same desires in such a way that it leads to transgression – to negatively desire what does not belong to us or is not honourable. In the same way, there are the concepts of the misguidance (*iḍlāl*) of God and the misguidance of Satan. The misguidance of Satan means that he calls upon us to disobey God and deviate from His path as it is mentioned in the Quran: *I (Satan) will lead them astray, I will make them to have false desires in life...* (Q. 4:119) and *He (Satan) leads a great many of you astray. Do you not ponder?* (Q. 36:62)

God would not lead people astray in this way. He always calls people to the straight path and does not want them to deviate from it. Therefore, it is the misguidance of Satan that makes people disbelievers, sinners or oppressors; this is what people choose to do when they succumb to the manipulation of Satan. It is entirely based on people's choices and deeds, but it is difficult to understand the reasons and process that lead them to such deviation as they happen in the deep level of the human soul which is a complicated entity. Yet people are in this world to manifest what is hidden in their souls and need provocations to good and evil.

The misguidance of God sets in after this stage. Once people have already deviated from the straight path and have followed Satan, then God shows them his signs which are found inherently within their souls and are abundantly available around them. If, however, they deny and deride these signs, reject their creator, and accuse him of injustice and evil they are misguided even further. Therefore, there is a clear distinction between the misguidance of God and misguidance of Satan: the misguidance of Satan leads people to commit evil, but the misguidance of God manifests the extent of evil in the human soul. This is clearly explained in Surah An'ām; *Whomever God desires to guide, He opens his breast to islām, and whomever He desires to lead astray, He makes his breast narrow and straitened as if he were climbing to a height. Thus, does God lay [spiritual] defilement on those who do not have faith.* (Q. 6:125)

A person needs to have a good character in order to open their heart to submission to God. If the person is good, then the heart accepts submission (*islām*). If the person is bad, the heart will never be open to submission, because of their evil doings. In this case, God tightens their heart so that they never become attracted to anything related to God. Therefore, the guidance and misguidance of God are rewards or punishments based on the deeds of individuals. In the same manner, this verse refers to a particular type of people, whose hearts have been tightened due to their own transgressions and therefore they respond to the example of the gnat by deriding and dismissing it.

الَّذِينَ يَنقُضُونَ عَهْدَ اللَّهِ مِن بَعْدِ مِيثَاقِهِ وَيَقْطَعُونَ مَا أَمَرَ اللَّهُ بِهِ أَن
يُوصَلَ وَيُفْسِدُونَ فِي الْأَرْضِ أُولَٰئِكَ هُمُ الْخَاسِرُونَ ﴿27﴾

Those who break the covenant made with God after having pleaded it solemnly and severed what God has commanded to be joined and caused corruption on the earth; it is they who are the losers.

This verse is a description of the habitual sinners (*fāsiqūn*) mentioned in the previous verse. They derided the parable of the gnat and were misguided by God Almighty as a result of their misdeed. The concept of having a covenant with God has been repeatedly mentioned in the Quran. Tabrisi in *Majma' al-bayān* puts forward four possible meanings for this covenant.[41]

Firstly, that the covenant is rooted in human intellect and a means to discover *tawḥīd* (oneness of God), the veracity of the messengers of God, the justice of God and similar universal religious concepts. Disregarding these is a violation of the covenant.

Secondly, the covenant is the set of instructions that God has sent to people through his messengers. Defying these instructions break his covenant. This may include what is mentioned in Surah Yāsīn, *Did I not exhort you, O children of Adam, saying, 'Do not worship Satan. He is indeed your manifest enemy, and worship Me. That is a straight path'?* (Q. 36:60-61)

According to Ṭabarī, the third possibility is that this verse addresses the People of the Book. The covenant was taken from them in the Torah that when Prophet Muhammad arrives, they should believe in him and support him. But *when there came to them an apostle from God, confirming that which is with them, a part of those who were given the Book cast the Book of God behind their back, as if they did not know.* (Q. 2:101)

Lastly, it is possible that the covenant is the pledge humankind made before coming into this world in *'ālam al-dhar* (the World of Atoms), the story of which is mentioned in detail in some narrations. However, Tabrisi rejects this view stating that people cannot be held accountable for a pledge that they do not remember. Discussing the same verse, Razi also rejects that the pledge refers to *'ālam al-dhar.* He maintained that this covenant is embedded in our nature and has been taken from every person individually. As such, this view is the same as the first meaning mentioned by Tabrisi.

The first view is the most appealing. In fact, if it were not for this innate covenant, people would not have the capacity to understand the messengers as they have been sent to remind us of this knowledge. In *Nahj al-balāgha,* Imam Ali states:

> From Adam's progeny God chose prophets and took their pledge for his revelation and for carrying His message as their trust. In the course of time many people perverted God's covenant with them and ignored His position and took compeers along with Him. The devils turned them away from knowing Him and kept them aloof from His worship. Then God sent His Messengers and series of His prophets towards them to get them to fulfil the covenant of His creation, to recall to them His bounties, to exhort them by preaching, to unveil before them the hidden virtues of intellect and show them the signs of His Omnipotence.[42]

They severed what God has commanded to be joined; Breaking the covenant of God is the first quality of the habitual sinners (*fāsiqūn*). This verse mentions their second quality as severing what God has commanded to be joined. The most general definition of what God has commanded to be joined is the bond between men and God. However, the process of breaking bonds with God Almighty can also be subdivided into smaller categories. These categories are explained in the clearest way in Muhsin Fayd Kashani's (d. 1091/1680-81) *Tafsīr al-ṣāfī.* Kashani states that there are instances in a person's life that represent cutting the bond with the Almighty. These instances are:[43]

1. Severing relations with relatives and not looking after their needs. In this respect he states that the Prophet and his family are spiritual relatives of Muslims and therefore Muslims need to honour their rights more than the rights of our biological relatives.

2. To discriminate between the prophets and their books in confirmation of their messages. God has commanded us to confirm all the prophets and their messages; therefore, rejecting some or undervaluing others is deemed as cutting the bonds with the Almighty.

3. Deserting friendships with believers. Believers must be friends with each other and support each other. Failure to do so is considered one of the instances of cutting the bonds with the Almighty.

4. Abandoning the Friday prayers and congregational prayers.

5. Anything that is deemed to be a rejection of good and an implementation of evil.

Based on this explanation, cutting the bonds with God takes place as a result of certain deeds. It is not simply professing disbelief. The third aspect of habitual sinning is to cause corruption on the earth, as discussed in depth under verse 11.

it is they who are the losers. means, in committing any corruption, the real loser is the perpetrator. Of course, others may be harmed as a result of their corruption too, but the one who carries out the corruption will be harmed the most. This harm manifests itself as misguidance and blackening of the heart in this world, and Hellfire and other forms of punishment in the next.

كَيْفَ تَكْفُرُونَ بِاللَّهِ وَكُنتُمْ أَمْوَاتًا فَأَحْيَاكُمْ ۖ ثُمَّ يُمِيتُكُمْ ثُمَّ يُحْيِيكُمْ ثُمَّ إِلَيْهِ تُرْجَعُونَ ﴿28﴾

How can you be unfaithful to God? Knowing that you were lifeless, and He gave you life and He will make you die. Then He shall bring you back to life again and then you will be brought back to Him.

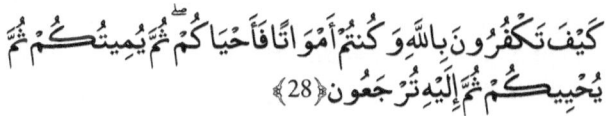

This verse asks a fundamental question that speaks to the core of the human soul. Seriously contemplating on this verse leads to the realisation that drifting away from God will result in becoming lost. This verse mentions the cycle of human existence from lifelessness to coming to life and then dying and returning to life again to go back to God Almighty. This verse considers these stages of a human's journey towards God a blessing. Specifically, it considers death to be a blessing.

The exegetes have discussed the meaning of lifelessness as referring to the stage of creation when an embryo is in the womb while the soul has not yet been blown into it. After God blows life into us, people grow and enter this world full of life and continue in our lives until we reach the peak of our abilities. Gradually our bodies begin to decline, people grow infirm, and life takes back all its blessings. At this point, people begin to wish to die; death becomes a blessing for the feeble towards the end of our journey in this world. But *No soul can die unless with the permission of God* (Q. 4:166) and without a new favour and relief from him to "make you die".

He will make you die; If we consider death from the perspective of human life in this world, it is the loss of human life and destruction. However, seen from the other side, it is rebirth into a higher realm of existence. Death is not a loss of life; rather it is the upgrade of life. That is why it is counted in this verse as a blessing. If we consider death from the perspective of a human soul's journey towards God which will never end, then we can see death as a natural station in the direction of our destination. It is the beginning of the new phase of human life or the transfer of our human soul to another dimension.

then He shall bring you back to life again; Returning to life is an expression used to describe the transfer of the soul from the intermediate world of *barzakh* to the eternal abode of the Hereafter. Fayd Kashani explains this journey by stating that the verse first mentions the creation of the human soul in the womb where God grants life to a person for the first time. Then people go from this dimension and find life in another dimension – the intermediate realm (*barzakh*). Death is the name given to describe this transfer of the soul and the separation of the soul from the body. In the intermediate realm the believers will be blessed by the grace of God Almighty and the disbelievers will be punished. After that, the souls will be transferred to another world on the Day of Judgment. God will destroy the entire Universe and recreate it in the form of Heaven and Hell. This transfer is the second death of the soul.

Then you will be brought back to Him. Kashani states that this phrase refers "to return to God's reward or God's punishment", which is a common explanation for the verse held by many exegetes. Although this is true, it is not completely accurate; to return to God's reward or punishment is not the same as returning to God himself. This verse refers to the destination when people are given life and a new body after resurrection. The whole purpose of life is that people go through these stages so that they develop sufficiently to be able to go towards him and live in his proximity. But this is a spiritual proximity and so cannot be described as going back to his reward or punishment. People will have their physical environment and location, but the proximity will be spiritual. Living with God may be very pleasant for people who are in Paradise and may be very unpleasant for people who live in Hell. Nevertheless, everyone is destined to go back to God, whether they are believers or disbelievers.

هُوَ الَّذِي خَلَقَ لَكُم مَّا فِي الْأَرْضِ جَمِيعًا ثُمَّ اسْتَوَىٰ إِلَى السَّمَاءِ فَسَوَّاهُنَّ
سَبْعَ سَمَاوَاتٍ وَهُوَ بِكُلِّ شَيْءٍ عَلِيمٌ ﴿29﴾

He is the one who has created for you (or because of you) all that is on the earth. He then turned to the heaven and fashioned it into seven heavens and He has knowledge of all things.

He is the one who has created for you; the expression used in this verse, *khalaqa lakum*, may mean "created *for* you" or "created *because of* you", meaning that God provides a suitable environment for humankind to live on the earth. This idea is mentioned many times in the Quran, for example, *And the grazing livestock He has created for you; in them is warmth and [numerous] benefits, and from them you eat.* (Q. 16:5)

It is problematic to assume that everything on the earth is created for humankind; it is improbable that every animal on the earth or every fish in the unfathomable depths of the oceans is created purely for human beings and their comfort. Unless we say that it means human beings collectively can own anything on the earth. However, interpreting the verse to mean "He created all that is on the earth because of you," we acknowledge that there is an independent purpose for each and every single creation, while the ultimate purpose is that it all should lead to the creation of man.

In other words, this verse indicates that human beings are the elite of all creation and everything else is created to bring about the creation of mankind. That means man is created for a sublime purpose which excels the purpose of all other creations on the earth. However, we need to be mindful not to misuse blessings that God has bestowed upon humankind. Alluding to this point, Imam Ali is reported to have said, "He created [everything] for you so that you reflect in it and seek his pleasure by it and protect yourself from the punishment of his fire."[44]

One interesting point of discussion is that God often states in the Quran that everything on the earth is created because of you (or for you), however when referring to the heavens and the earth the Quran states that *everything in the heavens and the earth is controlled for you* ... (Q. 45:13) This may direct us to the idea that not all of the universe with its width and breadth and with its two trillion galaxies is created "for us" or "because of us" while part of it, namely our solar system, may have been created because of us.

Furthermore, "created for you" collectively addresses all human beings. Hence, it implies that the wealth of the earth is the property of all and so must be distributed fairly, based on justice and benevolence. It is therefore not permissible for some to monopolise the wealth created for human beings on the earth at the expense of depriving others from benefiting from this. No matter how much people try to earn their wealth, part of it should go to the deprived in the form of zakat and other dues.

He then turned to the heaven; Exegetes have given different meanings for *istawā* (He turned).[45] The first meaning is to turn to something. According to this view, *istawā* may be translated as, "He then *turned* towards the heavens", meaning that God attended to the creation of the heavens.

The second meaning which is more popular is "to exert power over". According to this view, *istawā* may be translated as "He *started to exert his power* in the heavens."

The third meaning, which is mostly held by the literalists, is "to elevate over", thus the meaning becomes "He *elevated* to the heavens." This meaning is also mentioned in *Ṣaḥiḥ al-bukhārī* in a report narrated by Rabī' b. Anas.[46] It means that God created everything on the earth, he then left the world and went to the heavens and stayed there. The Salafi scholar, Muḥammad Jamāl al-Dīn al-Qāsimī (d. 1914), contends in *Maḥāsin al-ta'wīl*[47] that "all traditions prove that God is in the heaven" and there are many verses that support this view such as: *When God said: 'O Jesus, I will elevate you to Myself and purify you...'* (Q. 3:55) According to his interpretation of the verse, God is in the heavens and elevated Jesus to the heavens as well. Al-Qāsimī states that all the *Salaf* (pious ancestors) believed in the view that God is in the heavens and refers to Imam al-Dhahabī's (d. 748/1348) work *al-'Ulūw lil-'alī al-ghaffār* saying "all people of sharia (all Muslims) have confirmed that God has direction, and he is up there (in the heavens)."[48]

This view was apparently prevalent among Sunni scholars until the Mutazilite school developed and refuted the idea of a direction for God. Some later Asharites such as Razi and Ghazali (d. 505/1111) also agreed with Mutazilites on this issue that God has no direction; thus, al-Dhahabī's argument is left unsubstantiated. Throughout history, many Mutazilite scholars who wanted to speak of God more rationally, were ostracised, persecuted, or even killed. In conclusion, due to the preposition *ilā* (towards) the best meaning for *istawā* would render "He *turned* to." This gives rise to another question: if we read the verse as "God first created the earth and then *turned to* the heaven to create it," does that mean the earth was created before the skies? This is counterintuitive and does not conform with our knowledge of the formation of the universe.

There are two sets of seemingly opposing verses in the Quran: one set of verses state that God first created the earth and then turned towards the heaven. The other set of verses state that he created the heaven and then expanded the earth. The verse at hand is an example of the first set of verses. The verses in Surah Fuṣṣilat may also be included in the first set of the verses:

> Say, 'Do you really disbelieve in Him who created the earth in two days, and ascribe partners to Him? That is the Lord of all the worlds!' He set in it firm mountains [rising] above it, and blessed it and ordained therein its [various] means of sustenance in four days, alike for all the seekers [of the means of sustenance]. Then He turned to the heaven, and it was smoke, and He said to it and to the earth, 'Come! Willingly or unwillingly!' They said, 'We come heartily.' Then He set them up as seven heavens in two days, and revealed in each heaven its ordinance. We have adorned the lowest heaven with lamps, and guarded them. That is the ordaining of the All-mighty, the All-knowing. (Q. 41:9-12)

On the other hand, in Surah Nāzi'āt there is an opposite account of the order of creation:

> Is it you whose creation is more prodigious or the sky which He has built? He raised its vault, and fashioned it, and darkened its night, and brought forth its day; and after that He spread out the earth. (Q. 79:27-30)

The difficulty of reconciling these opposing sets of verses has been a long-standing issue to the extent that Razi mentions that some atheists and followers of other religions have used these two ostensibly opposing sets of verses together to claim that there is a contradiction in the Quran.

To address this apparent contradiction, a distinction needs to be made between the creation of the earth (*khalq al-arḍ)* and the expansion of the earth (*daḥwa al-arḍ).* The latter signifies the emergence of the land from the sea and the verse above (Q. 79:30) refers to this phenomenon. The whole earth was initially covered by water and the first piece of land which emerged from the water was the land underneath the Holy Kabah. Clearly, the expansion of the earth (*daḥwa al-arḍ)* must have happened after the creation of the heavens. Other verses talk about the creation of the earth before the heavens, which is different from the expansion of the earth, therefore this cannot be seen as a contradiction.

Regarding the first set of verses, they indicate, in their apparent meaning, that the heavens were created *after* the earth. The meaning of heavens here is not explained. Whether it refers to the heavens immediately above the earth, or to the heavens of the solar system, or to the galaxy of the milky way, or to other galaxies, is a question yet to be answered. Bearing in mind the wider connotations of the word "heavens," it is impossible to determine the stages of creation. Even if the Big Bang theory is deemed plausible, the details of the formation of the universe remain unknown. Rather, it is more plausible that parts of the earth were being formed while the heavens were still being created. Based on these verses, although we cannot determine the stages of creation, we may gather that God Almighty created the heavens and the earth in stages, and these stages somehow developed simultaneously and were interwoven.

Another compelling concept in this verse is that of the seven heavens *(sab'a samawāt*). The prevalent astronomical theory at the time of revelation was Ptolemaic astronomy. According to Ptolemy's theory, the Earth was the centre of the universe around which nine spheres rotated. These were the sun and the moon, the five known planets of the solar system at that time, the stellar sphere of the fixed stars and the empyrean. Taking his theory as fact, many commentators of the Quran tried to accommodate the Seven Heavens of the Quran within the nine spheres of Ptolemy, and since their numbers did not tally, they added the Throne (*arsh*) and the Footstool (*kursī*) as the eighth and ninth spheres. However, the concept of the Seven Heavens cannot be farther from the Ptolemaic theory. It is clearly stated in Q. 67:5 that, *We have beautified the first heaven with the planets and stars*, something which is quite alien to Ptolemy's astronomy.

It is clear from this verse that all the planets and stars are located in the first heaven (*al-Samā'a al-Dunyā*) and then there are other heavens that we are unaware of. Tabatabai held this view,[49] and stated that all of the known universe consists of the first heaven. According to the Quran, there are other heavens beyond the first heaven, but human discovery has not been able to detect them. Beyond that there are six other heavens which are all parts of the material world. Potentially, humankind may be able to discover these heavens, but currently they have not been able to make the necessary scientific and technological tools to be able to detect them. God informs us about them but does not explain what they are. Connected to seven material heavens there are seven spiritual heavens which are mentioned in the Quran, where the angels reside. God *has created seven heavens, and of the earth [a number] similar to them. The command gradually descends through them, God is Who created seven heavens and [seven] corresponding earth. God sends down the command through these [layers]...* (Q. 65:12).

According to Tabatabai, this verse points out that there are seven layers or dimensions for creation and God's command reaches to the earth through these layers or dimensions. Each dimension is an abode for different types of angels who receive the command of God and pass it down to the angels of the lower heaven. The world of angels is different from the material world and is from *malakūt*. However, the layers of *malakūt* in which they reside are called heavens because they surround the material world in the same way as the heaven surrounds the earth.

and He has knowledge of all things. Finally, the verse highlights that despite the enormous measures of the creation, God is aware of everything from the most minuscule particle to the biggest of creation.

وَإِذْ قَالَ رَبُّكَ لِلْمَلَائِكَةِ إِنِّي جَاعِلٌ فِي الْأَرْضِ خَلِيفَةً قَالُوا أَتَجْعَلُ فِيهَا مَنْ يُفْسِدُ فِيهَا وَيَسْفِكُ الدِّمَاءَ وَنَحْنُ نُسَبِّحُ بِحَمْدِكَ وَنُقَدِّسُ لَكَ قَالَ إِنِّي أَعْلَمُ مَا لَا تَعْلَمُونَ ﴿30﴾

When your Lord said to the angels, 'indeed I am going to set a vicegerent on the earth." They (angels) said: 'Will you set someone [as vicegerent] on it who will cause corruption and shed blood on it, while we praise and glorify your sanctity?' God said: 'I know that which you do not know.

This verse is a concise summary of the events prior to the creation of Adam and Eve and its juxtaposition to verse 29 is of great significance. God first describes the sophisticated nature of the creation of the universe and then mentions the creation of human beings as his vicegerent, thus highlighting that the universe is created for the spiritual nourishment of human beings to enable them to reach this level of being a vicegerent of God. It is unlikely that God is addressing all angels in this verse. In fact, there are "the absorbed angels" (*malā'ikat al-muḥayyamūn*); who are so deeply engrossed in God's grandeur that they are oblivious to anything else that God has created. Rather, it is more likely here, that God is addressing a select group.

Furthermore, from a linguistic perspective, the phrase, "he told people" is a common linguistic expression that may mean only a group of people is being addressed and not the entire population who live on earth. In this way "he told people" can mean "he told *some* people." Such expressions are mentioned in the Quran abundantly; for example, "*did you (Jesus) say to people*" (Q. 5:116) does not refer to all people but to *some* people who were his audience. Prophetic traditions confirm this idea that God did not speak to all the angels universally, rather he spoke to a specific group of angels who had already been on the earth for a mission, and were aware of what was happening on the earth.

Razi[50] mentions two different views on this verse; the first view he attributes to Ibn Abbas who has reportedly said that this is addressed to the angels who were fighting under Iblis or Satan. He says that before humans, God had made the jinn reside on the earth, but they were the cause of corruption, murder, and bloodshed, and as a result God sent a group of angels led by Iblis to defeat them and expel them to remote islands. Then God announced that he would set a vicegerent on the earth. The second view, which he attributes to most of the Companions and the Successors, was that the verse was an address to all the angels without exception.

Whichever the case, this verse indicates that when the news of the creation of Adam broke, the angels debated this decision in order to understand God's wisdom. This debate was not intended to disobey or undermine God, but to understand his reasons for creating another being as his vicegerent on the earth, while the angels were more qualified for that position and were praising and glorifying their Lord constantly and continuously. The verse in Surah Ṣād which says, *I (Muhammad) had no knowledge of the Highest Angels (Mala'i al-A'lā) when they were disputing among themselves* (Q. 38:69), shows that the Higher Angels were the ones who debated the issue, but it does not negate the idea that other angels also discussed the matter.

In a compelling parallel, the Old Testament also refers to the existence of a "Divine Council" where God discusses various matters with a group of divine beings: "God presides in the Divine Council; he renders judgment among the 'gods.'"(Psalm 82:1) Due to the influence of pagan culture from the Greco-Roman world on Judaism, some elements of paganism may have infiltrated the Old Testament and this verse of Psalms is an indication of it.[51] In the Divine Council, God discusses some matters with other divine beings who are named as "the gods". However, it is possible that these were the Highest Angels that the Quran mentions, with whom God held the discussion on the creation of Adam.

Concerning the creation of Adam, the Old Testament narrates, "Then God said, 'Let us make mankind in our image,'" (Genesis, 1:26), the use of "let us" indicates that, in accordance with the Quran, God Almighty informs an audience about his plan. The idea of referring to the Archangels as "the gods" is the influence of the pagan faith which was predominant during that era. According to the pagan faith of the time, there was a main God who shared his powers with smaller gods. The notion of monotheism is prominent elsewhere in the Old Testament that talks of an All-sovereign God, who has power over everything. Thus, it is plausible to assume that this idea permeated the Old Testament. Nevertheless, the idea of the Divine Council seems to be concurrent within the monotheistic religions where God reveals certain matters to the Archangels.

According to some narrations, prior to the creation of human beings the inhabitants of the earth were called *nasnās* and were created seven thousand years before the creation of man.[52] In their composition and appearance, they looked like human beings, but they were extremely vicious and evil as they had none of the humane characteristics which Adam and his children were granted. They shed blood and spread corruption on the earth.[53]

Current scientific speculations account for two distinct human species: Neanderthals and Homo sapiens. According to one theory, Homo sapiens, a more intelligent species, destroyed Neanderthals and replaced them, causing Neanderthals to become extinct. If Neanderthals correspond to *nasnās*, then according to the traditions, these human-like creatures were not destroyed by the presence of a more intelligent kind; rather they were destroyed by angels who were fulfilling God's command. God erased them from the face of the earth due to their corrupt nature. According to some traditions, God destroyed these primitive humans and the jinn who were living with them through the angels and Iblis (Satan) was one of the jinn who ruled over the world. When the angels came and destroyed these primitive humans along with other vicious creatures, they captured Iblis and took him to the heavens. Iblis grew there and worshipped God with the angels and excelled in his worship and devotion to God to the extent that angels who were created after this incident thought that Iblis was an angel too.[54] According to the same traditions, here, God is addressing the angels who destroyed the primitive semi-humans along with other vicious creatures. They were surprised that God still intended to create human beings as His vicegerent on the earth, despite witnessing their corruption on the earth. This was the reason for their objection to God's announcement.

Shi'i commentators have suggested three different viewpoints on this subject. These views were represented by three different scholars: Kashani, Tusi and Tabatabai. Kashani's interpretation of this verse is similar to the first view held by Sunni scholars detailed earlier. In *al-Ṣāfī*, Kashani states that God addressed a specific group of angels who came to the earth to destroy the human-like creatures and the jinn because of the great corruption that they had caused. He presents the Shi'i traditions on the subject which support the view that before the creation of Adam, there were jinn and primitive vicious creatures similar in their appearance to human beings on the earth. They inhabited the earth for a long time and caused great corruption and havoc. He then presents several traditions to support his view, including a tradition[55] from *Tafsir Qummī* attributed to the sixth Imam Jafar al-Sadiq.

Despite being aware of these traditions, Tusi disregards them completely. He was adamant that Iblis was an angel (not a jinn) and that angels have free will and consequently the potential to disobey God. He followed the ideas of his teacher Mufid (d. 413/1022) who, in his famous work *Awā'il al-maqālāt*[56] developed the idea that angels are fallible creatures due their free will, and it is possible for them to disobey God and commit sin, but due to their lack of lowly desires they rarely realise this potential. Tusi also held this view and argued that Iblis was an angel who disobeyed God.

Tabatabai's *al-Mīzān* applies a different methodology to the interpretation of the Quran. After discussing a verse, Tabatabai includes all the relevant traditions, even those he disregards and interprets differently. When discussing this verse, Tabatabai first deals with the question of the angels' objection towards the creation of Adam.

He notes that the angels immediately understood that God was not referring to angels when he said, *indeed I am going to set a vicegerent on the earth*. He goes on to suggests that it is wrong to assume that the angels made a direct comparison between the *nasnās* and the creation of Adam. Such a comparison would have been an analogy and angels never use analogies, in the way Iblis did (see Q. 7:12). Thus, it is improbable that the angels made a comparison between the reported events of the past and the future.

Tabatabai also presents a lengthy discussion on the meaning of "*khalifa*" rendered here as "vicegerent". He concludes that a vicegerent is someone who is capable of manifesting the names (*asmā'*) of God. The angels were aware of the fact that corruption is a fundamental part of life on earth and saw an apparent contradiction in creating an earthly creature with unlimited and manifold desires to represent God. Rather than negating the accusation that humans will cause corruption and shed blood, God responds with the phrase, "*I know that which you do not know*." The angels were right; human beings have constantly been the source of corruption on the earth. However, despite the inevitability of bloodshed and corruption, the ultimate achievement of the creation of human beings would compensate for these negative effects and the outcome would be much greater than the suffering and evil that have been caused by some human beings.

I know that which you do not know. God silences their argument with these words. This statement means that although there is some truth in the angels' assessment of human creation, there are certain aspects of it that the angels are unaware of.

وَعَلَّمَ آدَمَ الْأَسْمَاءَ كُلَّهَا ثُمَّ عَرَضَهُمْ عَلَى الْمَلَائِكَةِ فَقَالَ أَنبِئُونِي بِأَسْمَاءِ
هَٰؤُلَاءِ إِن كُنتُمْ صَادِقِينَ ﴿31﴾

He taught all the names to Adam and He then presented them to the angels and asked, 'inform Me the names of these, if you are the truthful.'

The knowledge of the names (*asmā'*) made Adam and, by extension, potentially his descendants, superior to the angels. In this way, every human being is *potentially* superior to angels due to their inherent ability to know these names. The angels were bewildered with this demonstration of God's names. They knew nothing of these names, yet they were taken aback that there was something in the creation of God Almighty which was completely beyond the scope of their knowledge. The reason for their lack of knowledge was not that God wanted to withhold knowledge (the names) from them, but that they were innately incapable of grasping it. Even after Adam informed them about the names, they still could not learn them; they then realised that Adam had a knowledge that went beyond their capacity.

inform Me the names of these, if you are truthful. In the light of the previous verse, it seems the reason that angels are not capable of being a vicegerent of God is due to their lack of knowledge. Instead of rebuking the angels for their questioning, God shows them the reality of his creation.

قَالُوا سُبْحَانَكَ لَا عِلْمَ لَنَا إِلَّا مَا عَلَّمْتَنَا ۖ إِنَّكَ أَنتَ الْعَلِيمُ الْحَكِيمُ ﴿32﴾

They replied: 'Immaculate are You, we have no knowledge except what you have taught us. Indeed, You are the all Knowing and all Wise.'

قَالَ يَا آدَمُ أَنبِئْهُم بِأَسْمَائِهِمْ ۖ فَلَمَّا أَنبَأَهُم بِأَسْمَائِهِمْ قَالَ أَلَمْ أَقُل لَّكُمْ إِنِّي أَعْلَمُ غَيْبَ السَّمَاوَاتِ وَالْأَرْضِ وَأَعْلَمُ مَا تُبْدُونَ وَمَا كُنتُمْ تَكْتُمُونَ ﴿33﴾

"Then He said: 'O Adam inform them about their names.' When he then informed them about their names, He said: 'Did I not tell you that I indeed know the unseen in the heavens and earth and whatever you disclose and whatever you have concealed?'

These two verses continue to mention the bounties that God has granted human beings from the very beginning. He first created the heavens and the earth and made the earth a habitable place; then he created Adam out of clay in the best fashion, which is in itself a great blessing. After the creation, he granted humankind the highest level of bounty by teaching Adam the names. Adam represents humanity, as the knowledge of the names is inherited by his progeny and the rest of humanity. The names are the culmination of all bounties that God granted human beings. Understanding the meaning of these names entails grasping a type of knowledge that the angels are not capable of reaching.

In general, exegetes have taken three main views regarding the nature of the names. The view of the majority of exegetes is represented by renowned exegete Jalaladdin al-Suyuti (d. 911/1505) in *Tafsīr al-jalālayn.*[57] He purported that the names were the names of everything in the world. Therefore, the names could include examples such as: this is a table, this is a tree, this is a stone and so on. Razi states that this is the view of the majority.[58] This is not a special knowledge, and it is almost certain that the angels would have known these names. The other problem with this view is that there is no mention of the language in which these names were taught to Adam.

Puzzled with the same question, Razi tries to solve the problem by arguing that God taught the names to Adam in *all* languages.[59] This is a rather strange attempt by Razi, as there are thousands of existing and extinct languages in the world. Razi's theory implies that God must have taught all these languages to Adam and the children of Adam must also have knowledge of all these languages. This interpretation is not plausible as this ability is beyond human capability and inconsistent with the way in which God operates. Furthermore, such an ability is not something that would make a great distinction between the angels and human beings. Angels have far greater communication skills than human beings as they do not even need language to communicate. Human beings will attain this ability only after death. Moreover, this idea undermines our knowledge about how languages develop, as it concedes that all languages in the human world have been developed from one language.

Though Razi goes to great lengths to justify the commonly held view on the names, he is not satisfied with it himself. He, therefore, presents an original alternative to the common interpretation. He argues that the Arabic word *ism* (pl. *asmā'*; names) can sometimes mean *ṣiffa* (quality).[60] If we are to apply this meaning to the verse; the meaning becomes "God Almighty taught Adam qualities of everything." The qualities may mean the knowledge of the actual potential of the things; how to bring them about, how they operate, how to change, improve or destroy them. Human beings through their knowledge and experience can acquire knowledge of things. Such knowledge is highly advanced. This is of course one aspect of the knowledge granted to Adam and his progeny. Although Razi's argument is more plausible than the mainstream view, it still leaves unanswered questions: would the angels be satisfied with the explanation that Adam is superior due to his knowledge of the quality of creation? Misusing such vast knowledge leads to corruption, so this explanation reinforces the case of the angels who initially objected to the creation of Adam on the same grounds. Therefore, this is also not a very convincing interpretation.

The third view is held by Tabatabai who rejects the previous explanations for the names that God taught Adam. Remarking that if the names were languages, then Adam would have taught these languages to the angels when God Almighty asked him to inform the angels about the names. Thus, they would have attained the same knowledge, thereby eliminating the knowledge gap between Adam and the angels. This criticism would also apply to Razi's view; once Adam taught the angels about the qualities of things, the angels would have the same knowledge as him, and Adam and his progeny would no longer be considered superior to the angels. On the contrary, the angels also had knowledge of many things that Adam did not know; with the addition of this new knowledge, they would have become superior to Adam. Angels are extremely intelligent creatures who can understand complicated concepts and carry out monumental tasks.

On these grounds, Tabatabai rejects the previous ideas and argues that there was a deeper knowledge that Adam attained that is inaccessible to angels. He then references the following verse: *When he then informed them about their names, He said: 'Did I not tell you that I indeed know the unseen in the heavens and earth and whatever you disclose and whatever you have concealed?'* Based on this, Tabatabai suggests that the knowledge must have been related to the unseen of the heavens and earth. "The unseen of the heavens and earth" is that knowledge which is *beyond* "the heavens and earth." It appears that in this verse God manifested this unknown knowledge to the angels, who then realised their ignorance and confirmed the superiority of Adam and his progeny. However, referring to a verse in Surah Ḥijr, *There is not a thing, but that its sources are with Us, and We do not send it down except in a known measure.* (Q. 15:21), Tabatabai states that there is also a type of knowledge that God keeps only for himself.

Based on this verse, Tabatabai argues that every creation has a source which remains with the presence of God. This source has no limit or measure. When God decides to create things from these sources, he gives them measures and limits. Creation takes places in lower levels of the presence of God and this is what is described in the Quran as the process of "sending down". When God creates, he sends down things from that unlimited, uncountable origin; and it is this process that gives them limit and measure. In the proximity of God, they are in their sources which have no limit, and they are out of the reach of causality. For example, when God wanted to create Adam, he first had the source for it in his presence and the source is kept hidden from everything in the heavens and earth as he states in the verse "with us" (*'indanā*). According to Tabatabai, the names mentioned in the verse refer to the source of the things from which everything was created, including the angels. In other words, by teaching the names to Adam, God shared the secret knowledge of the source of creation with humans and elevated them to the highest station among His creations. Such knowledge is not accessible to the angels.

Of course, this knowledge is not attainable by every human being in this world; only the purest ones can attain it by accessing those treasures and knowing why and how things were created. Only the most elite amongst the human race can achieve such spiritual growth in this world. However, during a person's journey in the Hereafter, a great majority of people will attain this knowledge in heaven. Adam had attained this knowledge from the beginning before he was sent down to this world and when he was in his purest state.[61]

Reflecting on these verses brings about a deep sense of gratitude that God Almighty has bestowed the potential for great knowledge to human beings alone. In this group of verses, the Arabic pronouns used for "the names" (in verse 31, *'araḍahum* and in verse 33, *bi-asmā'ihim*) are used for intelligent beings. Exegetes have attempted to explain this by saying that when Adam was taught the names of things, he was also taught the names of human beings (either their names in different languages or their qualities). Tabatabai objects and argues that the reason for using these pronouns is that the treasures (or sources) that these verses refer to are alive and have intelligence.[62]

whatever you disclose and whatever you have concealed; addresses Iblis, not the angels, because it was Iblis who was hiding his *kufr* (disbelief). This disbelief had already penetrated his heart and it was only manifested when he was asked to prostrate before Adam.

وَإِذْ قُلْنَا لِلْمَلَائِكَةِ اسْجُدُوا لِآدَمَ فَسَجَدُوا إِلَّا إِبْلِيسَ أَبَىٰ وَاسْتَكْبَرَ
وَكَانَ مِنَ الْكَافِرِينَ ﴿34﴾

And when We said to the Angels to prostrate before Adam, they prostrated but not Iblis (Satan). He refused and acted arrogantly, and he was one of the faithless.

The nature of this prostration has been widely debated by exegetes,[63] who have questioned the permissibility of prostrating before anything except God. However, such a debate is redundant – angels have no form, and their prostration is different to the physical prostration of our prayers. Instead, the angel's prostration was an acknowledgment of the status of Adam – it was a process of their acknowledgment of the hierarchy of God's creations. Initially, the angels thought that they were superior to Adam. They could not make sense of God's plan to make Adam his vicegerent on the earth. Once God Almighty demonstrated Adam's status, he asked them to humble themselves before him and they complied.

they prostrated but not Iblis; Amongst the angels it was only Iblis who refused to prostrate before Adam, arguing that because he was created from fire, he was superior to Adam, who was created from clay. This verse states that his actions were caused by his arrogance.

he was one of the faithless. This indicates thar he was a disbeliever due to his *kufr* even before this event took place. It is clear from this that arrogance is a direct result of *kufr* to God Almighty. The term *kufr* signifies both disbelief and ungratefulness. It is ungratefulness that leads to disbelief in the creator. Iblis was already a disbeliever, but he had not been put in any situation where this disbelief had the potential to be manifested. This verse also indicates that, aside from Iblis, there were other creatures who were also disbelievers: "he was *one of* the faithless". The jinn were created before Adam and many of them were ungrateful to God and may therefore be among the faithless the verse refers to.

The experience of Iblis teaches an important lesson: we may seem amicable, grateful and humble people for a long period of time, but when we are faced with a great test, the true state of our hearts will manifest and, in that moment, we may act in a way which is contrary to our previous character, just as Iblis did. The Quran (175:7) mentions the example of Bal'am Bā'ūrā who was one the greatest puritans amongst the Jews. He had been given a very high status by God before Prophet Moses came and when Moses came, he was expected to follow him as a prophet. This was the greatest test for Bal'am as Moses was given a higher status than him and he was not willing to accept it; therefore, he turned against Prophet Moses and fell from grace. Therefore, it is not only Iblis who lapsed in this way; some human beings have also followed his corrupt example. We may then understand that God's method of testing is the same for human beings, jinn and angels.

وَقُلْنَا يَا آدَمُ اسْكُنْ أَنتَ وَزَوْجُكَ الْجَنَّةَ وَكُلَا مِنْهَا رَغَدًا حَيْثُ شِئْتُمَا
وَلَا تَقْرَبَا هَٰذِهِ الشَّجَرَةَ فَتَكُونَا مِنَ الظَّالِمِينَ ﴿35﴾

O Adam dwell with your mate in Paradise and eat thereof freely whencesoever you wish but do not approach this tree lest you be among the wrongdoers.

O Adam dwell with your mate in Paradise; Unlike the account of creation in the Old Testament, the Quran does not provide many details about the location of the garden where Prophet Adam lived, or the details of the creation of Eve. Exegetes have developed different views on these details. Some of them are not relevant to this discussion, for example, how soon Eve was created or whether she was sent to the garden together with Adam or if she joined him later.

However, it is important to know the *nature* of the garden that Adam was sent to. Exegetes have expressed various views on this subject. Tusi in his *Tafsīr*[64] simply presents the views of other commentators without providing any opinion himself. He explains that some say the garden refers to the eternal Paradise, whilst others say it was a garden on the earth. He refers to the renowned Mutazilite theologian and exegete Abū al-Qāsim al-Balkhī (d. 319/931) whom Tusi quotes often in his *Tafsīr*. Al-Balkhī believes that the place Adam was sent was not the Paradise, as it will be the final abode for people who were tested on the earth and earn entrance to. Tusi further explains that Hasan al-Basri (d. 110/728), one of the most prominent exegetes of the Tābiʿūn (Successors), ʿAmr b. ʿUbayd (d. 144/761), Wāṣil b. ʿAṭā (d. 130/748), and the majority of the Mutazilites believed that the garden refers to the eternal Paradise.

Razi states that two prominent Mutazilites disagreed with this view: al-Balkhī and Abū Muslim Iṣfahānī (d. 322/934).[65] Both stated several reasons in support of their position on the subject: first, Iblis cannot enter the eternal Paradise, as it is stated in the Quran in many places that evil is barred from entering Paradise, and Iblis (or Satan) represents the worst form of evil. Secondly, the Quran states in several places that whoever enters the eternal Paradise would not come out of it. Therefore, Adam and Eve could not be expelled from it. Thirdly, the right to enter Paradise is only granted as a reward for people's deeds which are done in accordance with free will. The nature of the heaven is that it is created by our deeds; therefore, without action Paradise would not be real paradise. On the other hand, one might argue that the word *janna* accompanied by the definite article, *al,* cannot refer to anything but the eternal Paradise.[66]

Tabatabai takes the view that the garden was on the earth where Adam and Eve were created, but they were blessed with the fruits and bounties of the intermediary world called Barzakh. They could eat, drink, and enjoy that environment by their ability to access the intermediary world. The awareness of the intermediary world usually happens after death, however, occasionally some special people become aware of it while they are still in this world. With this interpretation, relegation to the earth meant a disappearance of the awareness and accessibility to the intermediary world and instead they had to face the toil and struggle on earth for making a livelihood.

do not approach this tree; Tusi quotes different views about the nature of the tree that Adam and Eve were forbidden from approaching.[67] Ibn Abbas states that the verse refers to wheat, but wheat does not grow on trees. Ibn Jurayj (d. 150/768), an exegete of the early second century, states that it was a fig tree. There is a report from Ibn Masud that it was vine and grapes. There is also a weak report[68] attributed to Imam Ali which states that it was the tree of Camphor. Lastly, the famous Shi'i commentator al-Kalbī (d. 146/764) suggested that it was the tree of knowledge of good and evil.

Perhaps the reason why the type of tree is not mentioned is because it is of little importance. Instead, the Quran focuses on the consequences of eating from the tree and how Satan deceived Adam and Eve into eating from it. They did not eat because Satan told them that "it was the most delicious tree", rather it was because he told them "it was the tree of eternality, and this is the reason God does not want them to eat from it; he does not want you to have an eternal life." They were deceived for the sake of eternality, not for the sake of the fruit: they wanted to stay in the garden forever and the idea of death and leaving the garden scared them. The very fact they knew they would die at some point indicates that the garden was not the eternal Paradise but was somewhere on the earth, because in Paradise no one dies. Satan continues to make use of the same arguments to deceive mankind. He makes death seem grim and scary, so people strive to escape death by false conceptions of power, wealth, family and lust.

In the discussion of the story of Adam and Eve in Surah A'raf, God gives four pieces of advice to the children of Adam to help us avoid making the same mistake and to allow us to escape the temptations of Satan. *O children of Adam beware so that Satan would not deceive you in the same way that made your parent come out of the garden.* (Q. 7:27) This verse alludes to the promise of eternality and the desire to be immortal which Satan exploited. This idea is explicitly highlighted in two verses of the Quran. The first verse is in Surah Ṭaha: *Then Satan tempted him. He said, 'O Adam! Shall I show you the tree of immortality, and an imperishable kingdom.'* (Q. 20:120) When Adam eventually agreed to go to the tree and saw that it was the same forbidden tree and objected to Satan's temptation, he was told, *Your Lord has only forbidden you from this tree lest you should become angels, or lest you become immortal.* (Q. 7:20)

The incentive for Prophet Adam eating from the tree is clarified in these verses. It is a weakness that exists in every human being. In order to overcome this weakness, we need to remind ourselves that we will eventually become immortal when we reach Paradise. This world is full of evils, deficiencies, stress and distress, and it does not make sense to try to remain in this world forever. Immortality is only worthwhile when we reach our destination.

God described Adam and Eve as good and upright, and taught Adam all the names, however at the same time they ate from the fruit and consequently they became "wrongdoers" (*al-ẓālimīn*), and according to Q. 7:44, God curses wrongdoers who are described as evil people. How can we reconcile this apparent conflict? Furthermore, being a wrongdoer (*ẓālim*) is worse than being a sinner; by eating from the forbidden tree, Adam and Eve not only became sinners, but they also became wrongdoers. This is difficult to come to terms with as Adam was a prophet of God. The explanation for this is found in the origin of the word *ẓulm* (wrongdoing), which is to fall short of the due right of something. The exact meaning of the word is found in Surah Kahf, verse 33: "Both of two gardens were yielding their products and it did not fall short of (*taẓlim*) anything...". In the case of *ẓulm* of a human being it may have different meanings. One of the meanings is to do injustice and be evil. This cannot be attributed to messengers of God, and this is the meaning of wrongdoing when it is mentioned in Q. 7:44. The other meaning is to commit sin, which is to act unjustly regarding our relationship with God.

The Mutazilites believed that a prophet may commit minor sins and be considered a wrongdoer (*ẓālim*). However, all Shi'i scholars reject the idea that prophets commit minor sins because, as Tusi states, "for us there is no difference between minor and major sins." He argued that in comparison to our position with God, every sin is major, especially in the case of the messengers of God. Since they have greater knowledge and understanding, even the smallest sin for them becomes a major sin.

If it is not possible for prophets to commit sins, how is it possible to explain that Prophet Adam was a wrongdoer (*ẓālim*) as he has been described in the Quran? Tusi explains that another meaning for *ẓulm* is to lose some reward, in other words wronging yourself.[69] This meaning has been used in the Quran for prophets too, for example in case of Prophet Moses when he killed the Egyptian man, he said: *My Lord, indeed I wronged myself (ẓalamtu) so forgive me...* (Q. 28:16) In this verse, it was not a sin to kill the Egyptian man, an oppressor who was about to kill an innocent man – Prophet Moses was simply preventing the person from killing another person, inadvertently leading to the death of the assailant. Yet Prophet Moses said he had wronged himself because he had to leave his plans of bringing reform in Egypt and improving the situation of the Israelites, instead having to flee to a faraway land.

It was Prophet Jonah who said: *There is no deity except You; exalted You are. I was from the wrongdoers.* (Q. 21:87) This is not the kind of wrongdoing that God curses; Prophet Jonah expresses his regret in the sense that he lost the great reward of God and put himself in great difficulty. Therefore, Tusi argues that the word *ẓulm*, when used to describe actions of the prophets, means losing the great reward of God or putting oneself in difficulty. This latter meaning is explicitly mentioned about Prophet Adam in *Surah Ṭaha*: *We said, 'O Adam! This is indeed an enemy of yours and your mate's. So do not let him expel you from Paradise, or you will be miserable.'* (Q. 20:120) It does not mean that by minor or major sins we bring about punishment. As a matter of fact, for every sin we commit we lose reward, but some sins bring punishments too. Considering Tusi's argument, we may re-translate the last section of the verse as: "But do not get close to this tree [if you do so], you will lose great reward."

فَأَزَلَّهُمَا الشَّيْطَانُ عَنْهَا فَأَخْرَجَهُمَا مِمَّا كَانَا فِيهِ ۖ وَقُلْنَا اهْبِطُوا
بَعْضُكُمْ لِبَعْضٍ عَدُوٌّ ۖ وَلَكُمْ فِي الْأَرْضِ مُسْتَقَرٌّ وَمَتَاعٌ إِلَىٰ حِينٍ
﴿36﴾

Then Satan caused them to stumble from it, and he dislodged them from what they were in; and We said, 'Go down, being enemies of one another! On the earth shall be your abode and sustenance for a time.'

We said, 'Go down, being enemies of one another! Here "*ihbitū*" (sin. *ihbāt*) means "descent from a higher place to a lower place." Assuming the garden was situated in Paradise, it would be plausible to say they were sent down from Paradise to the earth. However, it may also have the meaning of descending from one's spiritual position or station. For example, when the Israelites were in the desert, they were given a special kind of food from God every morning, without making any effort. Yet they protested that they could not live on such food and demanded *green herbs, cucumbers, garlic, lentils and onions* (Q. 2:61), then God Almighty commanded them "*ihbiṭū miṣran*" (go down to a city). Even though a city is considered to be superior to the desert where the Israelites had been living, God instructed them to "go down" (*ihbiṭū)* to the city. The phrase "go down" here means to descend from a high position with God, where worldly benefits such as food are directly provided, to a city without such benefits where they will have to work and find their own provisions.

There is a striking similarity between the story of the Israelites in the desert and the story of Prophet Adam and Eve. Adam and Eve were given food without any effort in the garden and the Israelites were given food without effort in the desert. When they were not satisfied with what God had provided for them, they were both sent down to a lower station where they were made to work for their food. Therefore, it is plausible to suggest that Prophet Adam and Eve resided somewhere on the earth and when they were "sent down", they downgraded to a lower position and were no longer able to enjoy some of the special blessings of God, just as was the case with the Israelites.

being enemies of one another; Many exegetes argued that this verse refers to the enmity between human beings and Satan. However, connecting all the verses in this context, a more fitting explanation would be, "some of you humans would be enemies of some others." In other words, this verse refers to the choices people make; some would be believers, and others would be disbelievers. *It is He who created you. Then some of you are faithless and some of you are faithful, and God watches what you do.* (Q. 64:2) It is inevitable that there will be enmity between the two groups: in this setting, disbelievers would not be able to control their greed which is the fuel of every war, and believers would try to defend themselves and the rights of the oppressed. Of course, there would be other reasons for war; ignorance, prejudice, arrogance, self-conceit and the like, which makes this animosity more manifest. With this explanation, the addressees of the word "*ihbitū*" (descend) are Adam and Eve and their children.

On the earth shall be your abode and sustenance for a time; This sentence makes two things clear. Firstly, that man will not live on earth forever. It is only an abode "for a time." It will come to an end when all the children of Prophet Adam have lived and been tried within it. Then there will be a new phase of human life in a new abode. Secondly, sustenance will be provided for humankind for as long we live on earth. The sustenance in the Garden was described as *You will neither be hungry in it nor naked. You will neither be thirsty in it, nor suffer from the sun.* (Q. 20:118-119) However, it would not be like that on the earth – on earth, people must struggle for their provisions.

فَتَلَقَّىٰ آدَمُ مِن رَّبِّهِ كَلِمَاتٍ فَتَابَ عَلَيْهِ ۚ إِنَّهُ هُوَ التَّوَّابُ الرَّحِيمُ ﴿37﴾

Then Adam received certain words from his Lord, and God accepted Adam's repentance, indeed He is all Clement and all Merciful.

Then Adam received certain words from his Lord; Prophet Adam did not remain in a state of disobedience for long; he quickly repented to God. There are many traditions describing the extent of Prophet Adam's regret and remorse for disobeying God and God's acceptance of his repentance. Regret is an essential component of repentance and, whilst this was deeply felt by Prophet Adam and Eve after their expulsion, they were not aware of the method of repentance and returning to God. This is an interesting phenomenon; we disobey and sin, and then it is God Almighty who teaches us how to return to him through repentance. In this specific case, Prophet Adam was given certain words by God to repent with. The word *talaqqā* is translated "learned," this term is used in the same meaning in other places in the Quran: *Indeed, you are learning (tulaqqā) this Quran from the Wise and Knowledgeable.* (Q. 27:6)

The most significant view concerning the nature of the *kalimāt* (words) is put forward by Hasan al-Basri (d. 110/728), Mujahid b. Jabr[70] (d. 102/722), Qatada b. Diama (d. 118/736) and some other exegetes from among the Tābiʿūn (Successors; the second generation of followers of the Prophet). They state that God taught Prophet Adam the following verse of the Quran: *Both of them said: 'Our Lord! We have wronged ourselves and if you do not have mercy on us, we will be among the losers.'* (Q. 7:23) Thus, God taught them to seek forgiveness through these words. God does not want his servants to lose out, and if by mistake or ignorance or negligence they do something which makes them of the losers, he would be more than willing to teach them the way back to righteousness.

The "words" taught to Adam, Eve and their progeny give us insight into to the method of repentance. Firstly, a person needs to confess that they have done wrong (*Our Lord! We have wronged ourselves)*; they must not act like Iblis who never confessed that he was in the wrong. Iblis blamed God saying, *You have made me slip...* (Q. 7:16) God would never wrong anyone – it is individuals who wrong themselves due to their greed, arrogance, lust, negligence, and other personal defects, and recognising this is the first step towards true repentance. Secondly, to be able to return to the right path, the person needs to genuinely regret what they have done. Thirdly, they need to compensate for what they have done. This incident holds a very important lesson for all of humanity. If Adam and Eve had not committed that mistake, and God had not taught them the way to repent and return, no one would have known how to return to God after committing a misdeed.

It is mentioned in Shi'i traditions that in addition to the contents of the above-mentioned verse, God also taught Adam the method of *tawassul* (seeking a means to God) through the names of Prophet Muhammad, Imam Ali, Imam Hasan, Imam Husayn and Lady Fatima. Both views are mentioned by Tusi in *Tibyān*[71] where he states that both are correct and there is no contradiction between them. Tabrisi reports a hadith from the Ahlul Bayt regarding this *tawassul*:[72] "Adam saw honourable and dignified names written on the *'arsh*. When he enquired about them, he was told that these are the names of those who have the highest position with God. The names were Muhammad, Ali, Hasan, Husayn and Fatima. Prophet Adam requested God to accept his repentance and elevate his position by the honour of those names." This is the meaning of *tawassul*.

This verse demonstrates that repentance is a two-way process; first God returns (*tāba 'alayhi*) to us with mercy when he sees our regret and remorse over the sin we have committed. Then from that attention of God we can return to him, and then God accepts our repentance. That is why Kashani mentions that the *tawba* of the servant is always between two *tawba* from God.[73] When the Arabic word *tāba* is accompanied by the preposition *'alā* (on, above) it refers to God, and when it is accompanied by the preposition *ilā* (to), it refers to people;

this is because God is at a higher position and when he wants to return to his servant, "He returns to them from above" and, since we are at a lower status, when we want to repent, "we return to him or go up to him." Therefore, this verse shows that people cannot repent unless God first returns to them and after their repentance, he must return a second time to accept it. When somebody wants to repent and go back to God, their broken heart and feelings of remorse spark the mercy of God on them. Consequently, God returns to the person, which makes it possible for the remorseful person to return to God and his repentance to be accepted.

A narration from Imam Rida[74] clarifies the issues well. He says,

> God the Glorified and Mighty created Adam as a proof (*hujja*) on his earth and a vicegerent in His lands. He did not create him for the Garden. The disobedience of Adam was in the Garden to realise the destinies of God's decree. However, when he was sent down to earth and God made him a proof and a vicegerent, he was kept from sin by his word, 'Indeed God chose Adam and Noah, and the progeny of Abraham and the progeny of Imran above all the nations.' (Q. 3:33)

قُلْنَا اهْبِطُوا مِنْهَا جَمِيعًا ۖ فَإِمَّا يَأْتِيَنَّكُم مِّنِّي هُدًى فَمَن تَبِعَ هُدَايَ فَلَا خَوْفٌ عَلَيْهِمْ وَلَا هُمْ يَحْزَنُونَ ﴿38﴾

We said, 'Get down from it, all together! Yet, should any guidance come to you from Me, those who follow My guidance shall have no fear, nor shall they grieve.'

Despite God's acceptance of Adam and Eve's repentance, they were no longer permitted to live in the Garden. Although Adam and Eve would not sin again, their children would certainly commit sin, and they would have to be evicted from the Garden as it is a protected environment. Therefore, the move was not a simple consequence of their actions – it concerned their progeny too. The protected state in the Garden came to an end and they were given the opportunity to make a fresh start on the earth. This second chance, however, does *not* carry the burden of "the original sin" as the repentance of Adam and Eve was accepted, and this is the difference between the Christian theology and Islam; the children of Adam do not carry the burden of the original sin.

'Get down from it, all together!' The command "Get down from it" appears in verses 36 and 38. However, as Tabatabai explains, these expressions refer to two different commands or decrees from God. The first decree was: *Get down, being enemies of one another! On the earth shall be your abode and sustenance for a time*. This command was a decree from God banishing man to earth to be enemies of one another and to struggle for their sustenance. This is the same miserable life that he had warned Prophet Adam about when he said, *O Adam! This is indeed an enemy of yours and your mate's. So do not let him expel you from the Garden, or you will be miserable.* (Q. 20:117) However, this was rectified by the repentance of Prophet Adam and Eve. There was now a second decree, to go down with guidance. *Get down from it, all together! Yet, should any guidance come to you from Me, those who follow My guidance shall have no fear, nor shall they grieve.* The tone of the command after the repentance is very different from before. Here, God honours Adam and his progeny with guidance, reassuring them with absence of fear and sorrow.

'...those who follow My guidance shall have no fear, nor shall they grieve.' Prophet Adam experienced "fear" and "sorrow" when he was expelled from his previous station – sorrow about the past and fear for the future. He was deeply troubled with his and Eve's future as well as the future of his progeny. Therefore, God reassured Adam that so long as they follow the guidance, they should not have any sorrow or fear and eventually they will be placed in the eternal Paradise, which is superior to the initial garden they were placed in.

وَالَّذِينَ كَفَرُوا وَكَذَّبُوا بِآيَاتِنَا أُولَٰئِكَ أَصْحَابُ النَّارِ ۖ هُمْ فِيهَا خَالِدُونَ ﴿39﴾

But those who are faithless and deny Our signs, they shall be the inmates of the Fire and they shall remain in it forever.

This verse makes a clear distinction between those who follow the guidance and choose to become good, and those who deny the guidance and chose to become evil. Tusi has argued that, based on this verse, whoever dies insisting on disbelief and rejecting the signs of God without repenting, will be eternally in fire.[75] He also mentions that *khulūd* in the common usage means "eternal stay", but in the original coinage of the term it alluded to "detention".[76] The signs of God referred to in this verse include his communications through his messengers and the evidence of his creation which guide us to his qualities.

يَا بَنِي إِسْرَائِيلَ اذْكُرُوا نِعْمَتِيَ الَّتِي أَنْعَمْتُ عَلَيْكُمْ وَأَوْفُوا بِعَهْدِي أُوفِ بِعَهْدِكُمْ وَإِيَّايَ فَارْهَبُونِ ﴿40﴾

O children of Israel! Remember my blessings which I gave you and fulfil your promise to me, I will fulfil my promise to you and be afraid of me alone.

Razi provides a beautiful justification for the order of the verses leading to this conversation and the way in which the conversation flows.[77] He says, after God provides the arguments for monotheism (*tawḥīd*), prophethood and the resurrection, he mentions his favours to human beings in general, then specifically the bounties he gave to the former generations of Jews and reminds them that they should display their gratitude for those favours by believing in the last Prophet. *And believe in that which I have sent down confirming that which is with you, and do not be the first ones to defy it, and do not sell My signs for a paltry gain and be wary of Me alone.* (Q. 2:41) He then reminds them of certain qualities that prevent them from belief in the Prophet. This is followed by a concise account of those favours saying, *O Children of Israel, remember My blessing which I bestowed upon you*, encouraging them by the statement, *and I gave you an advantage over all the nations.* (Q. 2:47) This is followed by the strong warning, *Beware of the day when no soul shall compensate for another, neither any intercession shall be accepted from it, nor any ransom shall be received from it, nor will they be helped.* (Q. 2:48) Then the verses start counting those favours in detail up to the verse 74 followed by an account of their misdeeds until verse 123.

O children of Israel! God's address to the "children of Israel" begins with this verse. There were many Jews living in Medina at the time of revelation. They rejected the message of the Prophet, even though his coming was foretold in their Book. This conversation spans more than a hundred verses. Israel (*Isrā'īl*) is an epithet for Prophet Jacob. The word *Isrā* can mean "worshipper" or "power", thus Israel can mean "servant of God" or "power of God" (that manifested itself in Jacob). Israelites are all the descendants of Jacob, hence in the Quran they are often referred to as the "children of Israel."

Although there is a seemingly abrupt change of topic within the chapter, the story of the Israelites is connected to the story of Adam. The Israelites thought they were the chosen nation and the only people who were given guidance and blessed with a Book. The story of Adam, on the other hand, zooms out of the specific situation to speak to humanity in general, declaring that anyone who follows God's guidance will be successful regardless of race or heritage. God told Prophet Adam, *Should any guidance come to you from Me, those who follow My guidance shall have no fear, nor shall they grieve.* (Q. 2:38) – this covenant is between God and all of humanity. The verses that follow call into question whether the Israelites had been faithful to that original covenant (*'ahd*).

Remember my blessings which I gave you; According to Tabrisi, Tusi and Ibn Abbas,[78] the blessing (*ni'ma*) on the Israelites referred to in this verse is Prophet Muhammad. They suggest that the Torah mentioned the coming of Prophet Muhammad and this was the reason why some Jews had settled in that area. In this verse, therefore, God reminds the Israelites about this blessing and urges them to fulfil the promise (*'ahd*). Whoever follows Prophet Muhammad will be saved and enter Paradise. So the verse should be read, "If you fulfil your promise by following Prophet Muhammad, I will then fulfil my promise and let you in to Paradise."

This idea can be corroborated by the verses in Surah A'rāf where Prophet Moses prayed to God: *And appoint goodness for us in this world and the Hereafter, for indeed we have turned back to You...* God replied by the following verses which allude to Prophet Muhammad:

> And appoint goodness for us in this world and the Hereafter, for indeed we have come back to You. Said He, 'I visit My punishment on whomever I wish, but My mercy embraces all things. Soon I shall appoint it for those who are Godwary and give the *zakat* (alms) and those who believe in Our signs, – those who follow the Apostle, the uninstructed prophet, whose mention they find written with them in the Torah and the Evangel, who bids them to do what is right and forbids them from what is wrong, makes lawful to them all the good things and forbids them from all vicious things, and relieves them of their burdens and the shackles that were upon them – those who believe in him, honour him, and help him and follow the light that has been sent down with him, they are the felicitous.' (Q. 7:156-157)

and be afraid of me alone. This fear is in regard to breaching this covenant, in other words, "fear me in breaking your covenant and do not fear anyone or anything else in keeping it."

وَآمِنُوا بِمَا أَنزَلْتُ مُصَدِّقًا لِّمَا مَعَكُمْ وَلَا تَكُونُوا أَوَّلَ كَافِرٍ بِهِ وَلَا تَشْتَرُوا بِآيَاتِي ثَمَنًا قَلِيلًا وَإِيَّايَ فَاتَّقُونِ ﴿41﴾

And believe in that which I have sent down confirming that which is with you, and do not be the first ones to defy it, and do not sell My signs for a paltry gain and be wary of Me alone.

This type of verse addresses scholars and those in religious authority (due to their influence and responsibility) to guide the general population. The argument follows that if the Jewish scholars had confirmed the prophethood of Muhammad, the Jewish congregation of Medina would have converted to Islam all together. This assumption is valid for every religion. Therefore, the most severe condemnation in these verses is directed towards scholars of every faith. Although the religious scholars are praised and commended by God in all scriptures, they also carry the burden of responsibility. If they follow their desires and make decisions based on vested interests, and knowingly mislead people, their punishment would be much more severe than the punishment received by an ordinary person.

Confirming the revelation that you already have; There are two possible meanings in this verse.[79] Firstly, the Quran confirms Moses and Jesus as prophets and the Torah and the New Testament as true revelations, so belief in the Quran reaffirms the belief in those Books. Secondly, because it was written in the Torah and Gospel that Prophet Muhammad, the Messenger of God, would come and guide everyone to salvation, his arrival confirms the truth of the Torah and Gospel and his denial is the denial of those Books.

The second view is favoured by most exegetes. Kashani mentions from *Tafsīr al-imām al-askarī* that the Jews of Medina denied the prophethood of Muhammad *despite* their knowledge about him. They betrayed him saying, "We know that Muhammad is a prophet and Ali is his successor, but you are not that Muhammad, and this is not that Ali. They will come in the future, in five hundred years' time."[80] This is corroborated by Q. 2:89: *And when there came to them a Book from God, confirming that which is with them and earlier they would pray for victory over the pagans; when there came to them what they recognised, they defied it. So may the curse of God be on the faithless!* The verse indicates that in their fights and disputes with the pagans of Medina, the Jews used to threaten them with the advent of Prophet Muhammad for whom they had settled in Medina, awaiting his arrival. Even though *They would pray for victory over the pagans*, when he arrived, they rejected the Prophet despite recognising his signs.

do not be the first ones to reject it; Some exegetes[81] have explained that this command refers to not being "the first amongst the Jews" to reject the Prophet. However, since the Prophet had begun his mission in Mecca, and the Jews were not the first to reject his message, a better interpretation of the verse could be that it refers to rejecting what was written in the Torah about the Prophet. As mentioned, the coming of the promised prophet was written in the Torah and the Jews of Medina were aware of it. By rejecting the Prophet, the Jews of Medina were also rejecting their own sacred Book and they became *the first* ones to reject their own book.

And do not sell My signs for a paltry gain and be wary of Me alone. This is a warning mainly addressed to the Jewish scholars. They were the main beneficiaries of an established and lucrative economic-religious system. Jewish scholars would receive alms, religious taxes, and other fees from their followers and instead of spending it in the legislated manner, they often spent these funds on maintaining their temples and on themselves. Obviously, it was not easy to let go of such benefits, and by confirming the mission of the Prophet they would have lost all of them. Thus, they sold the revelation of God in exchange for the paltry gain of their material benefits. "Paltry gain" may also refer to their prejudice concerning the superiority of their lineage. They did not believe in the Prophet because he was a gentile (*ummī*) and it was humbling for them to believe in a non-Jew prophet. In fact, this was one of the main reasons for their rejection of Prophet Muhammad. That is why God emphasises in Surah Jum'ah that prophethood is a grace from God and he gives it to whomever he wishes: *It is He who sent to the people with no Scripture an apostle from among themselves, to recite to them His signs, to purify them, and to teach them the Book and wisdom, and earlier they had indeed been in manifest error.* (Q. 62:2) *That is God's grace which He grants to whomever He wishes, and God is dispenser of a great grace.* (Q. 62:4)

وَلَا تَلْبِسُوا الْحَقَّ بِالْبَاطِلِ وَتَكْتُمُوا الْحَقَّ وَأَنْتُمْ تَعْلَمُونَ﴿42﴾

And do not mix the truth with falsehood, nor conceal the truth while you know.

This verse begins with the condemnation of the Jewish scholars of Medina, exposing their deceptive mindset. As mentioned in the previous verse, the Jewish scholars of Medina did not deny the coming of an awaited prophet, rather they claimed he would not arrive for another five hundred years. Thus, they acknowledged the truth but mixed it with falsehood to deny the prophethood of Muhammad. The Jewish scholars of Jerusalem rejected Prophet Jesus in the same way. They had been expecting the arrival of Messiah for a long time, but when he arrived, they said, "the time is not right for his arrival," and denounced him.[82]

People inherently want to follow the truth. Complete falsehood is often immediately rejected, and covering the truth often leads to exposure, but when truth is mixed or manipulated with falsehood, confusion often follows, and people can be misled. There is a tradition reported from Imam Ali saying: "If wrong had been pure and unmixed it would not be hidden from those who are in search of it. And if right had been pure without a mixture of wrong those who bare hatred towards it would have been silenced."[83]

while you know; This phrase alludes to the fact that the Jewish scholars of Medina pursued wrong *knowingly* to preserve their vested interests and maintain their prejudices. Religious scholars have a great responsibility; they constantly need to search for the truth and inform and educate the public even when there is a conflict of interest. Of course, they may make mistakes and may misinform the public inadvertently. That is forgiveable provided they take the utmost care to sincerely establish the truth. However, if they mislead people deliberately, that is unforgivable. According to the Quran, the Jewish scholars of Medina deliberately misled their own people in an attempt to sabotage the mission of Prophet Muhammad, while knowing that he was truthful. Therefore, the Jewish scholars of Medina will bear the responsibility of misleading their people in the Hereafter.

وَأَقِيمُوا الصَّلَاةَ وَآتُوا الزَّكَاةَ وَارْكَعُوا مَعَ الرَّاكِعِينَ﴿43﴾

Establish prayer, give charity and bow with those who bow.

Establish prayer, give charity; These rituals are part of the foundations of every religion. Although in Islam praying takes on a different form to Christianity or Judaism, prayer is the basis of every monotheistic religion as it establishes a connection with God.

The same is true for giving charity: all the monotheistic religions require their followers to give charity in different forms and it serves to establish connections between people. Based on this verse, we may argue that the connections between people are two essential connections in all monotheistic religions: the connection with God and the connection with his creation. It is the duty of the followers of all monotheistic faiths to establish and uphold these connections and the ultimate purpose of prayer and giving charity is to achieve this. Through expressing this basic principle, God is reminding the Jews of Medina that Prophet Muhammad is delivering the same message, which was already included in the Torah.

and bow with those who bow. Bowing (*ruku'*) establishes a part of the prayer. However, preferring this meaning would indicate repetition in the verse, as there is already a call to establishing prayer. For this reason, some exegetes maintain that "bow with those who bow" is a command to attend congregational prayers. They argued that "establish the prayer" is the injunction to pray in private and "bow with those who bow" is a specific instruction to attend the congregational prayers to strengthen the communal bonds between Muslims.

Some other exegetes have suggested that instead bowing (*ruku'*) is used in the literal sense as opposed to its technical meaning. The literal meaning of *ruku'* is to humble oneself. In the context of this verse, the meaning then becomes "humble yourself [to the Prophet] as all others have humbled themselves", referring to the people of Medina, including the pagans, who had humbled themselves before the Prophet. The pagans of Medina had a sophisticated system of law and theology and a strong sense of tribal pride. They regarded themselves as the leaders and chieftains of the Arabs, yet they humbled themselves before the Prophet. Hence, according to this interpretation, God urges the Jews of Medina to humble themselves before the Prophet like all the other people of Medina.

أَتَأْمُرُونَ النَّاسَ بِالْبِرِّ وَتَنسَوْنَ أَنفُسَكُمْ وَأَنتُمْ تَتْلُونَ الْكِتَابَ
أَفَلَا تَعْقِلُونَ ﴿44﴾

Will you bid others to piety and forget yourselves, while you recite the Book? Do you not apply reason?

The Jews of Medina were regarded as ethical role models. They had Scripture and law, claimed proximity to God, and boasted that they were the children of Abraham. The rest of the people of Medina, who were mostly pagan, had no such claims to blessed heritage, scripture or written laws. Therefore, God reminds them that, although they had always advised people to be ethical, they had forgotten themselves and were acting against their ethical teachings by denying the awaited Prophet. Similarly, there are crucial moments in our life where we need to practice what we preach; words are not enough, and action is required. These moments can be challenging; we may forget ourselves and act against the very ethical values that we had been defending and teaching throughout our lives.

Similarly, there are many traditions reported from the Imams, especially from Imam Ali mentioned in *Nahj al-balāgha,* that if someone advises others to do good and avoid evil, they must first practice it themselves: "O people! By God, I do not impel you to any obedience unless I practise it before you and do not restrain you from any disobedience unless I desist from it before you."[84] The only way that advice may take effect on people's heart is if it is supported by action. The reason that Imam Ali's admonitions still have the same influence over people is because he was deeply committed to his own preaching. Consequently, when he advised people, he made a great impact on their heart and this influence has stood the test of time.

While you recite the Book; is a reminder to the Jews of Medina, that they have all the necessary means at their disposal to acknowledge the Prophethood of Muhammad. The pagans of Medina did not have anything aside from their intellect to lead them to follow the Prophet, yet the Jews had a Scripture which had described the Prophet clearly for them and had a tradition which had made them await his arrival, yet they were the ones who denied him.

وَاسْتَعِينُوا بِالصَّبْرِ وَالصَّلَاةِ ۚ وَإِنَّهَا لَكَبِيرَةٌ إِلَّا عَلَى الْخَاشِعِينَ ﴿45﴾

And seek help through patience and prayer, and it is certainly hard [to do that] except for the humble.

And seek help through patience and prayer; Converting to another faith has always been a difficult challenge because those who convert are expected to go against the traditions which they have been brought up with. In the same manner, it was a great challenge for the Jews to convert to Islam and follow the instructions of the Prophet. To overcome this great challenge, they needed to seek help through patience and prayer. The act of seeking help through patience and prayer is recommended for every believer when they face a difficulty or go through hardship. However, this verse directly addresses the Jews of Medina.

Based on the traditions and interpretations suggested for this verse, we understand that there is a great emphasis placed on the instances of patience mentioned in this verse. In verse 40, they were asked to "fulfil your promise", which, as discussed, referred to believing in Prophet Muhammad. Here they are advised that in order to be able to believe they should seek help through prayer and patience.

In *al-Kāfī*, *Man lā yaḥḍuruhu al-faqīh* and other Shi'i books, there are reports attributed to the Imams about the explanations of this verse. One of the reports attributed to Imam Jafar al-Sadiq states that: "Patience mentioned in this verse is fasting."[85] Fasting is one of the instances of practising patience. What the Imam may mean by giving the example of fasting is that sometimes to display patience, one needs certain physical exercises and fasting is an excellent exercise to practice patience. Moreover, Imam Jafar al-Sadiq is reported to have said: "When a hard calamity hits a person, he should fast. God Almighty says: 'seek help through prayer and patience', which means fasting."[86] Another narration from Imam Jafar al-Sadiq states that: "When a hard calamity fell upon Imam Ali, he sought help from prayer and then he recited this verse."[87]

Remembrance of God through prayer and fasting will bring tranquillity and comfort to the heart. Therefore, faithful people should remember these two things to alleviate every hardship: to preserve their connection with God as these would. Similarly, when a person experiences success in their lives, they must never abandon these two qualities. Some can persevere but have no connection to God. Some people have a connection with God but have no perseverance. Of course, it is difficult to obtain the two together and therefore the verse immediately states that **"it is certainly hard [to do that] except for the humble."** The next verse goes on to describe those who do not find it difficult to seek help through patience.

الَّذِينَ يَظُنُّونَ أَنَّهُم مُّلَاقُو رَبِّهِمْ وَأَنَّهُمْ إِلَيْهِ رَاجِعُونَ ﴿46﴾

Those who are certain that they will meet their Lord, and they will return to Him.

Those who are certain; This refers to those "the humble" mentioned in the previous verse. They are certain that they will encounter God's judgment and subsequently his reward or punishment. Such certainty about the Day of Judgment is crucial for any heart to become humble. In the Arabic language the word *ẓann* has two opposing meanings: one meaning is certainty or having certain knowledge about something. The second meaning is to have uncertain knowledge. According to Arabic linguists, there is a clear way to differentiate which meaning of the word *ẓann* is intended. When used in the context of worldly affairs, its meaning is uncertainty and whenever it is used in the context of the Hereafter its meaning is certainty. Therefore, in the context of this verse, its meaning must be certainty.

that they will meet their Lord, and they will return to Him. For a person to be regarded by God as humble, this certainty must be established in their heart. It should be noted that humbleness in this context is not limited to your attitude towards people. Rather, it is a state of heart which makes a person meek and submissive to their Lord. If a person's heart is not humble, they must seek the origin of this lack of humility which is often linked to a lack of certitude in what is going to happen to us after death, especially encountering God. If there is certainty on both accounts, then the natural consequence is humility of the heart. Conviction is not achieved through certain practices like praying; rather, it is a state of mind and heart, and if this state is achieved then submitting yourself to God's guardianship and overcoming difficulties becomes a smooth and painless task.

يَا بَنِي إِسْرَائِيلَ اذْكُرُوا نِعْمَتِيَ الَّتِي أَنْعَمْتُ عَلَيْكُمْ وَأَنِّي
فَضَّلْتُكُمْ عَلَى الْعَالَمِينَ (47)

O children of Israel, remember My blessings which I bestowed upon you, and that I gave you an advantage over all [other] nations.

Initially this verse seems to be a repetition of verse 40. However, verse 40 refers to fulfilling the promise, and this verse refers to the other blessings that God granted to the Israelites. It informs us about God's favours on the Israelites which were incomparable to any other nation. Not only did he grant them guidance and a great number of prophets, but God also saved them from Pharaoh, split the sea for them, gave them the most delicious foods when they had to wander in the desert and gave them the Torah and many other miracles. However, the Quran reports that throughout history, the Israelites have not received such favours with gratefulness; instead, they harmed themselves and those around them.

وَاتَّقُوا يَوْمًا لَا تَجْزِي نَفْسٌ عَنْ نَفْسٍ شَيْئًا وَلَا يُقْبَلُ مِنْهَا شَفَاعَةٌ وَلَا
يُؤْخَذُ مِنْهَا عَدْلٌ وَلَا هُمْ يُنْصَرُونَ (48)

Beware of the day when no soul shall compensate for another soul, neither any intercession shall be accepted from it, nor any ransom shall be received from it, nor they shall be helped.

This verse continues to criticise the Israelites by directly tackling four different aspects of Jewish theological doctrines about the Hereafter. One of the beliefs of the Jews in Medina was that if they did something wrong, their family members or acquaintances have the ability to set it right in the Hereafter through intercession (*Beware of the day when no soul shall compensate for another soul).* The second belief was that regardless of their actions, they would be able to pay compensation for their wrong acts (*Neither any intercession shall be accepted from it).* Thirdly, they believed in the idea of ransom, which was a belief distinctly attributed to the Jews, that they would be able to pay a ransom to save themselves from punishment *(nor any ransom shall be received from it)*; and fourthly, they believed they could receive help from others on Judgment Day (*nor they shall be helped*).

The rejection of intercession (*shafā'a*) on the Day of Judgment in this verse needs to be understood within its context. There are many other verses[88] in the Quran which confirm the existence of intercession on the Day of Judgment – with certain conditions – and it is a well-established concept in Islamic theology. Therefore, the exegetes have tried to reconcile this verse with other, supposedly contradictory, verses. Before proceeding with the discussion about intercession in the Quran, a definition of the term is required. Intercession comes into effect if somebody has a certain level of faith, but this level of faith is not sufficient for them to enter Paradise. In such a situation, God Almighty or some of his privileged agents can intermediate and boost the individual's level of faith with extra blessings which then enables the person to enter Paradise. This is related to the mercy of God, as he wants people with faith to enter Paradise.

One way of explaining this apparent contradiction is mentioned in Kashani 's *al-Ṣāfi.*[89] He states that "the day" mentioned in this verse refers to the day of individual deaths, not to the Day of Judgment. In this way, the verse alludes to when a person's life comes to an end, and nobody can intercede or give ransom to postpone their death. A similar view is argued by Jamāl al-Dīn al-Qāsimī who states that there are different stations and stages on the Day of Judgment and that in some of these stages, intercession will be accepted whilst at other stages it will not.[90]

A third way of explaining this verse is mentioned by Tusi, who says that rejection of intercession is restricted to the disbelievers; and the Prophet will intercede for the believers.[91] In other words, intercession is only accepted through certain conditions and one of the most important conditions of the recipient is to have faith. If someone rejects part of the faith by rejecting some parts of the Book they are regarded as faithless. This is how the Quran describes the Jews of Medina, since they did not accept the parts of the Torah that described the coming of the Prophet; *Do you believe in part of the Book and defy another part?* (Q. 2:85)

The verses that are mentioned in the Quran about intercession are of three types: first are the group of verses that categorically deny the existence of intercession (for example, Q. 2:254, 44:41). The second group of verses explain that certain mediums or agents will attempt to intercede on the Day of Judgment, but it will not be accepted. For example, some verses inform us that there are intercessors, but their intercession will not avail (for example, Q. 2:48, 2:123, 26:98-101, 74:46-48). These verses indicate that there are agents of intercession (*al-shāfiʿīn*) but their attempt to intercede will be refused (*lā yuqbalu*) by God. This basis for the rejection of intercession is that the recipients do not have a minimum required level of faith in their hearts and so they would never be allowed to enter Paradise.

The third group of verses further clarify the concept of intercession. They say that only God can grant permission for intercession and through his permission some selected agents can intercede on behalf of the needy who have the minimum required faith in their hearts (for example, Q. 10:3,19:87, 20:109, 21:28, 34:23, 39:44, 44:40-42, 53:26). The agents of intercession are mentioned in the third group of verses. God states in verse 34:23: *The intercession does not benefit except for those whom He permits [to intercede or to receive intercession]* ... Verse 21:28 mentions the condition of being the recipient of intercession: *They cannot intercede except on behalf of those whom God is pleased with.*

In summary, based on the analysis of these three groups of verses of the Quran, the authority of intercession is with God alone. He may delegate this authority to some of his selected agents on the condition that those who receive it have the minimum level of required faith in their heart. Consequently, when we say that the Prophet, the Imams and even a pious good friend can intercede for us, it means that our shortcoming in obedience to God is redeemed by the greatness of their soul and their high spiritual station. In support of this view, the Quran states: *Those whom they invoke beside him, they would not possess intercession, except those who are witnesses of the truth.* (Q. 43:86)

The concept of intercession has been misunderstood throughout history by believing that the prophets and saints have the independent or unchecked power to intercede on behalf of people on the Day of Judgment. Thus, people began to worship the prophets and saints. In contrast, others have completely rejected the existence of intercession and consider it to be a form of polytheism, on the grounds that people who believe in the intercession ascribe partners to God. As discussed above, the ability to intercede may only be granted by God and can be done under his supervision and may take place within the procedures that he has set. Furthermore, recipients of the intercession must have the required amount of faith in their heart so that intercession may work for them. It is not a simple act of favouritism or nepotism as critics of the concept have argued. It is a systematic process and fully dependent on the receivers' level of faith and their deeds.

وَإِذْ نَجَّيْنَاكُم مِّنْ آلِ فِرْعَوْنَ يَسُومُونَكُمْ سُوءَ الْعَذَابِ يُذَبِّحُونَ
أَبْنَاءَكُمْ وَيَسْتَحْيُونَ نِسَاءَكُمْ وَفِي ذَٰلِكُم بَلَاءٌ مِّن رَّبِّكُمْ
عَظِيمٌ ﴿49﴾

And when We delivered you from the Pharaoh's clan, who inflicted a terrible torment upon you, slaughtering your sons and sparing your women. And in that there was a great trial from your Lord.

From verse 47 (*O children of Israel, remember My blessings which I bestowed upon you...*) onwards, God begins to recount the nature of these blessings in detail.

And when We delivered you from the Pharaoh's clan who inflicted a terrible torment upon you, slaughtering your sons and sparing your women. The first blessing of God upon the Jews was that he saved them from slavery, oppression and torture at the hands of the Pharaoh and his people. One of these torments was the murder of their new-born sons whilst sparing the lives of their women. Of course, the verses do not mention the extent of the torment that the Pharaoh and his people inflicted upon the Jews in Egypt. The Jews were enslaved by the Pharaoh and were subject to abuse and heavy labour. This verse implies that in comparison to killing the baby boys and exploiting their women, heavy labour was less significant. The verb *yudhabbiḥūna,* mentioned in this verse, is an exaggerated form of the verb *yadhbahūna* which means "slaughtering", thus *yudhabbiḥūna* means "slaughtering with terrible pain". Another verse refers to the same subject of oppression that the Jews suffered under the Pharaoh by using the verb *yuqattilūna abnā'akum, killing your sons with great pain.* (Q. 7:141) Therefore, the same Arabic form is used to emphasise the great extent of suffering that the little boys and their parents had endured at the time.

It is worth noting that killing the sons of the Israelites occurred twice. The first time was before Prophet Moses was born, when the Pharaoh had a dream about Moses and ordered all the new-born Jewish boys to be killed. The second time occurred after Prophet Moses defeated the magicians and they accepted the faith of Moses and Aaron. (Q. 7:120-122) After this great event, people began to convert en masse to the religion of Moses, including some Egyptians. The most heinous forms of killing and slaughtering of the Jewish young males took place at this juncture in order to punish and prevent people from following Moses: The leaders among the people of the Pharaoh said: '*Will you leave Moses and his people to cause corruption in the land, forsake you and your gods?' [Pharaoh] replied: 'We will kill painfully their sons and spare their women, and we are subjugators over them.*' (Q. 7:127) Although they brutally killed the Jewish young males, the Pharaoh did not dare to kill Prophet Moses himself, as he feared the consequences of this murder, especially after Prophet Moses defeated the magicians in a public display of power. Thus, Prophet Moses was free to preach his religion publicly, but people were not allowed to follow him. In order to prevent people from following Moses, Pharaoh took an extreme measure which was to kill all the male children of anyone who followed Moses. The Arabic word *yastaḥyūna* could originate from two words: either from *ḥayāt* (to live) or *ḥayā'* (modesty). If it is from the first root, it would mean: "they sought to keep your women alive", so that they can used for labour or as concubines. If the verb is derived from the second root, it may mean "they sought to remove the modesty from your women" by taking them as concubines and exchanging them amongst themselves, thus stripping away the modesty of the Israelite women.

Such a terrible torment prevented almost everyone from following Prophet Moses: *But none believed in Moses except some youths from among his people, for the fear of the Pharaoh and his elite that he would persecute them. For the Pharaoh was indeed a tyrant in the land, and indeed he was an unrestrained despot.* (Q. 10:83) In such a difficult time, Prophet Moses urged his followers to show patience and perseverance. *Moses said to his people, 'turn to God for help and be patient. The earth indeed belongs to God, and He gives its inheritance to whomever He wishes of His servants, and the outcome will be in favour of the Godwary.'* (Q. 7:128) Despite the presence of a prophet, the support and deliverance of God arrived at the appropriate time and not a moment sooner. Therefore, time and patience are needed so that due process can take place through which the good are purified and those who are astray are given an opportunity to find the right path. Only when the process is completed does the support of God arrive.

And in that there was a great trial (balā') from your Lord. The use of the word *balā'* in the last part of the verse is interesting. In this verse, the term is used to mean "trial." Trials can take place in pleasant and unpleasant circumstances. The Quran uses the word in both meanings: ... we inflicted them (*balawnāhum*) with what *was pleasant and what was unpleasant...* (Q. 7:168) This word is deliberately used in this verse to indicate that the process of God's trial can take place in the form of calamity or blessing. Therefore, the precise meaning would be: "And in that there was a great calamity from your Lord."

One might wonder why God tested the Jews in such a horrifying way, the murder of their male offspring and the exploitation of their women. It begs the broader question of why God tests people to the extremes of their capabilities. In fact, God's tests stem from his desire to grant us salvation and redemption from past transgressions. Through tests and trials, God awakens the souls and re-opens the channels of communication with God. The Jews had adopted many of the sinful practices of the Egyptians, such as the use of magic, immoral lifestyles, and even worshipping Egyptian gods. Therefore, their hearts needed an intensive level of purification in order to wash away all the past sins, to be able to receive the blessings from God. It was a terrible test, but the Jews at that time had to endure it for the sake of their own salvation.

This interpretation assumes that the demonstrative pronoun *dhālikum* (that was) refers to the "trial" (*balā'*). It could refer to *najjaynākum* (we saved you) and *balā'* could be rendered as a blessing, instead of calamity. This meaning is also plausible. In fact, both meanings support the notion that God delivered the Jews from the Pharaoh's oppression.

وَإِذْ فَرَقْنَا بِكُمُ الْبَحْرَ فَأَنجَيْنَاكُمْ وَأَغْرَقْنَا آلَ فِرْعَوْنَ وَأَنتُمْ تَنظُرُونَ

﴿50﴾

And when We parted the sea for you, and We delivered you and drowned Pharaoh's clan while you were looking on.

This verse mentions the second great blessing that God Almighty bestowed on the Jews, the like of which had never happened in the history of humankind. In order to save the Jews from the Pharaoh, God split the sea to allow the Israelites to pass through it. When the

Pharaoh and his army tried to follow them, the sea was folded in, and they were all drowned, thus God destroyed the enemy of the Israelites.

Furthermore, God did not simply save the Jews from Pharaoh; he also destroyed their enemies before their eyes. Surah Shu'arā gives a detailed account of the episode: God gathered a huge army of all the Egyptian elites and their auxiliaries who had been instrumental in the oppression exerted by Pharaoh and made them follow Prophet Moses and the Israelites in an unjust rage of anger and tyranny. By the order of God, Prophet Moses guided his followers to the shores of the Red Sea from where they were expected to cross over to Arabian Peninsula, an unusual route from Egypt to Palestine. However, arriving at the seashore, there was no sign that they could possibly cross the sea; God made Prophet Moses and his followers wait for several days on the shores, while knowing that the massive army of Pharaoh was approaching. The pursuit reached its most dramatic moment when the army of Pharaoh was detected on the horizon and the hearts of the Israelites were filled with horror. At that moment God guided Prophet Moses to strike the sea with his staff, causing the sea to split and allowing the Jews to pass through safely. Pharaoh and his army, who were captivated by the delirium of hot pursuit, without carefully contemplating the situation, followed then and fell into the trap set for them by God Almighty. When the last Israelite set foot on the other side of the sea and the last Egyptian set foot inside the sea, the sea re-joined, and Pharaoh and his army perished, as the verses explain:

> We revealed to Moses, 'Take My servants on a journey by night, and you will be pursued.' Then Pharaoh sent heralds to the cities, announcing: 'These are indeed a small gang. They have surely aroused our wrath, and indeed we are all on our guard.' So, We expelled them from gardens and springs, and from treasures and splendid places. So it was; and We bequeathed them to the Children of Israel. Then they pursued them at sunrise. When the two hosts sighted each

> other, the companions of Moses said, 'Indeed we have been caught up.' He said, 'Certainly not! Indeed, my Lord is with me. He will guide me.' Thereupon We revealed to Moses: 'Strike the sea with your staff!' Whereupon it parted, and each part was as if it were a great mountain. There, We brought the others near. And We delivered Moses and all those who were with him. Then We drowned the others. There is indeed a sign in that, but most of them do not have faith. (Q. 26:52-67)

In all this, God's plan was not only to save the Jews from Pharaoh, but also to destroy their enemies who had tortured and tormented them. By drowning them in the sea, they witnessed that justice had been fulfilled. This was indeed a great sign and a huge favour that should have reinforced their faith in their creator.

وَإِذْ وَاعَدْنَا مُوسَىٰ أَرْبَعِينَ لَيْلَةً ثُمَّ اتَّخَذْتُمُ الْعِجْلَ مِن بَعْدِهِ وَأَنتُمْ ظَالِمُونَ
﴿51﴾

When we made an appointment with Moses for forty nights [to give him the Torah] you took up the Calf [for worship] in his absence and you were wrongdoers.

This verse recognises that the third blessing given to the Jews was to grant them the Torah. In order to receive the Torah, Prophet Moses needed an extensive spiritual purification exercise. This extensive training programme as mentioned in the verse took place for forty days or nights. During this period, Prophet Moses fasted, prayed, and kept night vigils for contemplation. Of course, the Torah was a guidance and blessing for the Israelites, but they reciprocated this favour with ingratitude and disloyalty. As soon as Prophet Moses went to meet his

Lord to receive the Torah, the Israelites betrayed him by taking the calf for worship. Thus, God, in this verse, reminds them of another of his great favours and yet another of their misdeeds.

When we made an appointment with Moses for forty nights; The Quran states that God initially made Prophet Moses' appointment for thirty days and nights but then added another ten more days and nights to complete the number to forty. (Q. 7:142) The addition of ten more nights was a test for the Israelites. They had become dependent on Prophet Moses instead of being dependent on their Lord, and they feared Prophet Moses more than they feared their Lord. This was because they had witnessed what Prophet Moses was capable of: defeating the magicians, splitting the sea and destroying the mighty army of Pharaoh and many other examples. They assumed Prophet Moses was the source of these miracles, and consequently the very presence of Prophet Moses was enough for them to follow his instruction. When Prophet Moses did not return, after he had promised that he would return in thirty nights due to God's extension of the appointment, they decided to forgo their promise to Prophet Moses and break their covenant with God.

you took up the Calf [for worship] in his absence and you were wrongdoers; In order to understand how the Israelites quickly adopted the cattle-god in the absence of Prophet Moses, we need to briefly examine the roots of the practice. There was a special bull which was the greatest manifestation of the god-kings in Egypt, and the Israelites worshipped this cattle god when they lived under the slavery of the Pharaoh in Egypt, after 1750 BC. When Prophet Moses returned to Egypt, he outlawed this practice, but when he went to meet his Lord, the Jews returned to their old habit of worshipping the cattle. Cattle worshipping was a well-established faith in ancient Egypt and there were three major bulls: Mnevis, Buchis and Apis. Apis (in Egyptian Api, Hapi or Hep) the bull was the most important deity for the ancient Egyptians. They had worshipped Apis since 3000 BC, during the era of the First Dynasty. In brief, Apis was believed to be an intermediary deity between humans and more powerful deities such as Ra, Ptah, Osiris and Atum. Ptah and Atum were the creator-gods in different parts of Egypt and therefore the most powerful gods.[92] It is difficult to overlook the connection; as soon as Prophet Moses's return was delayed, the Jews wanted to replace Prophet Moses with an intermediator like Apis who would keep the communication between the Israelites and the Creator God of Moses. It was Samiri who made the bull out of gold in the absence of Prophet Moses and he was a great believer of Apis in Egypt. The absence of Prophet Moses demonstrated that faith in true monotheism had not penetrated their hearts. By following Prophet Moses, they were in fact imitating monotheism rather than understanding it. This was also shown by another incident that happened soon after they crossed the sea as mentioned in Surah A'rāf:

> We carried the Children of Israel across the sea, whereat they came upon a people cleaving to certain idols that they had. They said, 'O Moses, make for us a god like the gods that they have.' He said, 'You are indeed an ignorant lot. What they are engaged in is indeed bound to perish, and what they have been doing shall come to naught.' He said, 'Shall I find you a god other than God, while He has graced you over all the nations?' (Q. 7:138-140)

ثُمَّ عَفَوْنَا عَنكُم مِّن بَعْدِ ذَٰلِكَ لَعَلَّكُمْ تَشْكُرُونَ ﴿52﴾

Then we forgave you after that so that you may give thanks.

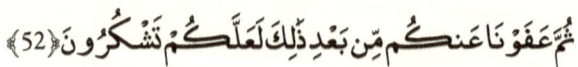

Although the Jews failed the test, God opened the way for their forgiveness. This opportunity occurred whilst the Jews had exceeded all limits of ingratitude and insolence. Thus, it is another great blessing for the Jews. Of course, accepting their repentance on such a dramatic deviation had its conditions that will be discussed later in verse 54.

وَإِذْ آتَيْنَا مُوسَى الْكِتَابَ وَالْفُرْقَانَ لَعَلَّكُمْ تَهْتَدُونَ ﴿53﴾

And when we gave Moses the Book and the Criterion (*furqān*) so that you may be guided.

Here, God mentions another blessing that he granted to the children of Israel: the Book. The Book (*Kitāb*) mentioned in this verse refers to the Torah that was written by God on the Tablets and contained guidance and instructions for the children of Israel. As mentioned in the Quran, the Books given to the prophets were of two types. *But if they deny you, then before you other apostles have been denied, who came with manifest signs, holy writs (zabūrs), and an illuminating scripture (kitāb).* (Q. 3:184) *Kitāb* is a book which contains laws in addition to wisdom and enlightenment, while *zabūr* is a book containing only wisdom and enlightenment without laws. *Kitāb* was revealed to only five messengers: Noah, Abraham, Moses, Jesus and Muhammad, whilst *zabūr* was given to many prophets. As an example, Prophet David's Psalms was a *zabūr* while the Torah given to Moses was a *Kitab*.

Israelite prophets had various different *zabūrs* but they all followed one *Kitāb* and that was the Torah. Aside from being a *Kitāb*, the Torah and the Quran are also *Furqān* (Criterion); they enable people to distinguish between right and wrong. Another important meaning of *Furqān* is to distinguish the true believers from the false believers. In the example of the Israelites, the true followers of Prophet Moses were those who followed the injunctions of the Torah. In this way the Torah acted as a *Furqān* by distinguishing the true believers among the Israelites from the false ones. The Quran does the same; there are certain injunctions in the Quran that true believers accept and observe whilst the hypocrites refuse to follow them.

وَإِذْ قَالَ مُوسَىٰ لِقَوْمِهِ يَا قَوْمِ إِنَّكُمْ ظَلَمْتُمْ أَنفُسَكُم بِاتِّخَاذِكُمُ الْعِجْلَ فَتُوبُوا إِلَىٰ بَارِئِكُمْ فَاقْتُلُوا أَنفُسَكُمْ ذَٰلِكُمْ خَيْرٌ لَّكُمْ عِندَ بَارِئِكُمْ فَتَابَ عَلَيْكُمْ إِنَّهُ هُوَ التَّوَّابُ الرَّحِيمُ ﴿54﴾

And [recall] when Moses said to his people 'O my people, you have indeed wronged yourselves by taking of the cow [for worship]. Now turn penitently to your Maker, and slay yourselves. That will be better for you with your Maker.' Then He turned to you clemently, indeed He is the all Clement, all Merciful.

Now turn penitently to your Maker, and slay yourselves; This verse details one of the most outstanding events in the history of the Israelites. After worshipping the calf, they realised their transgression when Prophet Moses returned, and God set a condition for accepting their repentance. *But when they became remorseful and realised they had gone astray, they said, 'Should our Lord have no mercy on us, and forgive us, we will be surely among the losers.'* (Q. 7:149) The condition was that those who did not worship the calf were to take the lives of those who did worship the cow even if they were their fathers and brothers. The condition seems to be extremely harsh and gruesome, and incompatible with the mercy of God. However, this verse highlights the mercy of God and corrects misconceptions about his forgiveness. By regarding certain misdeeds as trivial, we expect God to forgive them without any condition or act of repentance. But, as the verse demonstrates, this is a delusion and a failure to realise our responsibilities towards God. Moreover, by such a harsh condition for repentance, God wanted to obliterate the desire to worship the cow-god Apis and remove all remnants of polytheism from their hearts.

Prophet Moses had a dominant role, and the Jews were heavily dependent on him. As soon as they lost sight of him, they broke their promise and worshipped another God and, when he returned, without any resistance, they again obeyed him as their leader and without any resistance accepted the gruesome punishment of killing their dearest ones. An examination into how the story is narrated in the Bible will prove useful before delving into this discussion further from the Muslim perspective. The story is mentioned in Exodus 32:

> When the people saw that Moses was so long in coming down from the mountain, they gathered around Aaron and said, "Come, make us gods who will go before us.[1] As for this fellow Moses who brought us up out of Egypt, we don't know what has happened to him." [2] Aaron answered them, "Take off the gold earrings that your wives, your sons and your daughters are wearing, and bring them to me." [3] So all the people took off their earrings and brought them to Aaron. [4] He took what they handed him and made it into an idol cast in the shape of a calf, fashioning it with a tool. Then they said, "These are your gods, Israel, who brought you up out of Egypt." [5] When Aaron saw this, he built an altar in front of the calf and announced, "Tomorrow there will be a festival to the Lord." [6] So the next day the people rose early and sacrificed burnt offerings and presented fellowship offerings. Afterward they sat down to eat and drink and got up to indulge in revelry.
>
> [7] Then the Lord said to Moses, "Go down, because your people, whom you brought up out of Egypt, have become corrupt. [8] They have been quick to turn away from what I commanded them and have made themselves an idol cast in the shape of a calf. They have bowed down to it and sacrificed to it and have said,

'These are your gods, Israel, who brought you
up out of Egypt.' 9 "I have seen these people,"
the Lord said to Moses, "and they are a stiff-
necked people..."

19 When Moses approached the camp and saw
the calf and the dancing, his anger burned and
he threw the tablets out of his hands, breaking them to pieces at the foot of the mountain. 20 And he took the calf the people had
made and burned it in the fire; then he ground
it to powder, scattered it on the water and
made the Israelites drink it. 21 He said to Aaron, "What did these people do to you, that you
led them into such great sin?" 22 "Do not be angry, my lord," Aaron answered. "You know how
prone these people are to evil. 23 They said to me,
'Make us gods who will go before us. As for this
fellow Moses who brought us up out of Egypt,
we don't know what has happened to him.' 24 So
I told them, 'Whoever has any gold jewellery,
take it off.' Then they gave me the gold, and I
threw it into the fire, and out came this calf!"
25 Moses saw that the people were running wild
and that Aaron had let them get out of control
and so become a laughingstock to their enemies. 26 So he stood at the entrance to the camp
and said, "Whoever is for the Lord, come to
me." And all the Levites rallied to him. 27 Then
he said to them, "This is what the Lord, the God
of Israel, says: 'Each man strap a sword to his
side. Go back and forth through the camp from
one end to the other, each killing his brother

> and friend and neighbour.'" [28] The Levites did as Moses commanded, and that day about three thousand of the people died.[29]

In this account, it is Prophet Aaron who makes the golden calf for them, while in the account of the Quran it is Samiri, and the Israelites overpower Aaron and his followers in the absence of Prophet Moses.

O my people, you have indeed wronged yourselves by taking of the cow [for worship]. Continuing with the study of the verse, when Prophet Moses returned from his appointment with God, he found some of his people worshipping the calf and he admonishes them. The wrong must be set right by the mass killing of those who worshipped the calf. However, despite this dramatic instruction, most of those who worshipped the calf were spared by the grace of God. According to sources, there were approximately 600,000 Jews at the time and most of them had worshipped the calf.[93]

This gruesome event, in which at least 3,000 (12,000 according to Muslim sources) Jews were killed, is regarded as the fifth favour that God bestowed on the Jews. It is a blessing because God guided them to correct their mistake instead of leaving the Jews to continue their transgression by worshipping the calf. This verse states that even when the Jews worshipped the calf, God did not abandon them when they showed signs of remorse and regret. Instead, God accepted their repentance, and they were guided back to the right path. It was also a blessing in the sense that after a limited number of them were killed, God accepted their collective repentance and instructed them to stop the killing, otherwise tens of thousands more would have been killed or destroyed.

The harrowing nature of this event has led some exegetes[94] to raise the possibility of an alternative interpretation, although they themselves suggest it to be improbable. The alternative interpretation is that "slay yourselves" may mean kill your lower self[95] (*nafs al-ammāra*). Thus, the injunction did not command physically killing each other, but a command to repent and return to God by killing the lower self. This is an implausible interpretation of the verse. The event clearly refers to an actual command of killing, the Bible refers to the event, and many traditions refer to the event in the same manner. Furthermore, there is reference in the Quran to killing (*qatl*) used to denote suppressing the lower self (*nafs*) and it is therefore clear that the killing mentioned in the verse cannot be understood figuratively.

From a worldly perspective, the simple act of worshipping a cow does not warrant such a severe punishment from God. However, from a spiritual perspective worshipping objects other than God is a serious offence due to the destructive effect it has on the soul. In this specific case, worshipping the calf was a significant transgression as it highlighted the deviated state of some individuals. Furthermore, as noted above, this calf was not an ordinary calf; it was one of the most revered gods of Egypt at the time. When the Israelites lived in Egypt under Pharaoh's rule, they worshipped it and took its love and reverence with them beyond the sea. Therefore, when they began to worship it again, in the absence of Prophet Moses, it transpired that they were longing for their previous ungodly life, and they were not truly committed to believing in God. As the Quran states, *their hearts had been imbued with the love of the calf, due to their faithlessness.* (Q. 2:93) Something was fundamentally misguided in their minds and hearts, and it was impossible to set it right without subjecting them to a drastic cleansing. God Almighty wanted to remove this disease from their hearts once and for all so that they may never return to it. Hence from the wider perspective it was a blessing.

Overall, the message of this verse is that we should not expect unqualified mercy from God, as this would not be instrumental to our growth. He is not a miser in extending his mercy, but that mercy sometimes reaches us in strange and unexpected ways. His mercy is measured and dispensed according to the broad view of creation and not by the short-sighted understanding of hasty people. God's compassion for us is not to provide us with unqualified mercy and pardon; his aim is to help us to purify ourselves from the vices of the soul so that we may attain eternal bliss in the Hereafter. Forgiving such a great sin, without treating the actual cause of it, would have been equal to a doctor treating a symptom instead of a patient's underlying condition.

وَإِذْ قُلْتُمْ يَا مُوسَىٰ لَن نُّؤْمِنَ لَكَ حَتَّىٰ نَرَى اللَّهَ جَهْرَةً فَأَخَذَتْكُمُ
الصَّاعِقَةُ وَأَنتُمْ تَنظُرُونَ ﴿55﴾

And when you said, 'O Moses, we will not believe you, until we see God visibly', thereupon a thunderbolt seized you while you were looking on.

Shi'i and Sunni traditions report that Prophet Moses was requested to take representatives from the Israelites to God in order to thank him for his forgiveness following the incident with the calf.

According to the report from al-Suddi,[96] seventy[97] people from the Israelites were chosen by Prophet Moses to journey with him to Mount Sinai to repent to God for worshipping the calf. These were the seventy most pious people of the Israelites.

'O Moses, we will not believe you, until we see God visibly' When they arrived at Mount Sinai, these people demanded to hear the Lord in the same way that Moses heard him, and God then allowed them to hear him. Despite this miracle they said: *O Moses, we will not believe you, until we see God visibly.* It is obvious that the Israelites confused hearing and seeing God. As mentioned in Surah al-Shūrā: *It is not possible for a man that God speaks to him except through revelation [signalling in the heart] or from behind a veil...* (Q. 42:51) This confusion is also evident in the Jewish account mentioned in the Hebrew Bible:

> Moses and Aaron, Nadab and Abihu, and the seventy elders of Israel went up and saw the God of Israel. Under his feet was something like a pavement made of lapis lazuli, as bright blue as the sky. But God did not raise his hand

> against these leaders of the Israelites; they saw God, and they ate and drank. (Exodus, 24:9-10)

The verse clearly states that Prophet Moses and the Jewish leaders saw God at Mount Sinai, yet another verse in the same chapter states: "you cannot see my face, for no one may see me and live." (Exodus, 33:19) This contradiction between these two Biblical verses explains the confusion caused to the later writers of the Hebrew Bible regarding the visibility of God.[98] Comparing these Biblical accounts with the Quranic account, Exodus, 33:19 is the true statement of God, and the Biblical account of the meeting with God at Mount Sinai has been distorted. Further, the statement that "you cannot see my face, for no one may see me and live" supports the Quranic account that when these seventy Jewish leaders insisted on seeing God with their own eyes, God Almighty caused them to die, supporting the idea that it is impossible to see God and remain alive. To ask to see God is a pure confusion. There are many veils between God and his creation, and it is not possible to see God at all even from behind those veils. The narration continues that due to their unrealistic demands, the Lord takes their lives through a thunder strike.

Ibn Babawayh (d. 381/991) (aka al-Shaykh al-Saduq) narrated a similar tradition in *'Uyūn akhbār al-riḍā* from Imam al-Rida which states that Prophet Moses chose seventy people who were the elite of the Israelites in terms of reliability, piety and manners and took them to Mount Sinai. When they arrived, these Israelites demanded that since Prophet Moses saw God, they should also see God. Prophet Moses told them that he had never seen God, but the Israelites then responded that they "do not care and would not believe in him until they see God."[99] They were expecting to see God on Mount Sinai and therefore continued to insist on their demand. If these Israelites had gone back to their people and told them they had not seen God, and that they no longer believe in Prophet Moses, it would have had a detrimental effect on their already tenuous faith. Therefore, God seized them by a thunder strike, and they all died.

Prophet Moses began to pray to God to bring them back to life as he knew that if he went back to the Israelites without their representatives, they would have blamed him and turned against him and the Lord. God answered his prayer and brought them back to life. In this way, the representatives knew that they had died and been brought back to life. This was a miracle and although they did not see God as they had wished, they were pleased with experiencing this miracle and went back to their people to inform them about their experience, which strengthened their faith. Therefore, this episode was also another blessing of God Almighty, as he had mercy on them instead of making them perish for making unreasonable and foolish demands. As Prophet Moses says in Q. 7:155:

> My Lord, had You wished, You would have destroyed them and me before. Will You destroy us because of what the fools amongst us have done? It is only Your test by which You lead astray whomever You wish and guide whomever You wish. You are our master, so forgive us and have mercy on us, for You are the best of those who forgive.

Thus, instead God made them experience death and brought them back to life.

while you were looking on. Some exegetes state that there were additional people present when the miracle took place and they themselves saw what had happened to the seventy people. Others argue that "while you were looking on" is in reference to "whilst you were waiting to see God." The main point of the verse is the criticism of the corporeal attitude of the Israelites and God's constant favours over the Israelites. Their simplistic attitude continued until the time of Prophet Muhammad. Surah Nisā informs the Prophet about the materialistic character of the Israelites: *The People of the Book ask you to bring down for them a Book from the sky. Certainly, they asked Moses for something greater than that, for they said, 'Show us God visibly.'* (Q. 4:153) They demanded a Book from the Prophet like the Tablets of Moses. One might wonder why Prophet Moses was given written Tablets while Prophet Muhammad was not given a written book. The history of the Israelites indicates that they would not have believed in Prophet Moses, until they had seen a Book written and signed by God Almighty and, in the same way, the Jews of Medina expected the equivalent from Prophet Muhammad.

ثُمَّ بَعَثْنَاكُم مِّن بَعْدِ مَوْتِكُمْ لَعَلَّكُمْ تَشْكُرُونَ ﴿56﴾

Then we raised you after your death, so that you may give thanks (shukr).

Then we raised you after your death, Some Shi'i commentators have regarded this verse among others in the Quran as proof of the possibility of *raj'a*, the ideology that some of the dead will return to life during or after the reappearance of the Mahdi. According to Kashani, Imam Ali referred to this verse when the Kharijite leader Ibn al-Kawwā'(d. unknown) denied *raj'a.*[100] Also, Ali b. Ibrahim Qummi states that, "this verse is a proof for the occurrence of *raj'a* in the umma (followers) of Muhammad, because he said, 'nothing happened to the Israelites unless the likes of it also happens in my umma.'"

so that you may give thanks (*shukr*). Razi made an insightful observation about this verse. The word "thanks" refers not only to a literal thanks, but it includes all acts of worship and obedience.[101] This ideology is supported in Q. 34:13: *O House of David, observe thanksgiving, and few of My servants are grateful,* in which the expression "observe thanksgiving" is used rather than "give thanks". Therefore, the verse may be interpreted as *so that you may give thanks* and return to your previous state of faith and obey Prophet Moses in all aspects of religion.

وَظَلَّلْنَا عَلَيْكُمُ الْغَمَامَ وَأَنزَلْنَا عَلَيْكُمُ الْمَنَّ وَالسَّلْوَىٰ كُلُوا مِن
طَيِّبَاتِ مَا رَزَقْنَاكُمْ وَمَا ظَلَمُونَا وَلَٰكِن كَانُوا أَنفُسَهُمْ يَظْلِمُونَ ﴿57﴾

And we shaded you with clouds, and we sent down to you manna and quails, 'Eat from the purest things we have provided for you.' And they did not wrong us, but they used to wrong themselves.

This is the eighth blessing that God recounts for the Israelites. These favours had also been granted to the forefathers of the Jews of Medina at the time of the Prophet. Evidence in the Quran suggests that they saw themselves as a close-knit community with ancient roots. They regularly boasted about their heritage and their lineage. Therefore, God reminds them of the blessings that had been granted to them in the past.

And we shaded you with clouds; This refers to the period after the Israelites crossed the sea when they were lost in the desert for forty years because they refused to fight their way into Jericho. According to the Old Testament, the Jews feared the children of Anak (Anakim) whose fierce warriors were stronger than the Jews (Numbers 13: 28-31). The Quran gives a similar account of their refusal to fight:

> When Moses said to his people, 'O my people, remember God's blessing upon you when He appointed prophets among you, and made you kings, and gave you what none of the nations were given. O my people, enter the Holy Land which God has ordained for you, and do not turn your backs or you will become losers.' They said, 'O Moses, they are a tyrannical people in it. We will not enter it until they leave it. But once they leave it, we will go in.' Said two men

> from among those who were Godfearing and whom God had blessed: 'Go at them by the gate! For once you have entered it, you will be victors. Put your trust in God, should you be faithful.' They said, 'O Moses, we will never enter it so long as they remain in it. Go ahead, you and your Lord, and fight! We will be sitting right here.' He said, 'My Lord! I have no power over anyone except myself and my brother, so part us from the transgressing lot.' He said, 'It shall be forbidden to them for forty years: they shall wander about in the earth. So do not grieve for the transgressing lot.' (Q. 5:21-26)

Despite their disobedience, God did not stop shading them from the sun and providing them their daily food by sending them "manna and quails," as he was doing before their disobedience.

and we sent down to you manna and quails; Manna was a food similar to honey, provided for them every morning. It may have oozed out of the harsh plants where the Israelites dwelled in the desert or appeared on them like dews. Manna would keep them satiated until evening when God provided them with quails. According to some commentators, quails were travelling from North Africa to the area where the Israelites resided in the desert. By the time these birds reached this area, they were so tired, that they could not move any more, hence the Israelites could easily catch them with their own hands[102] every day to provide a meal for themselves. For something like this to happen every day in the correct measure to satiate the Israelites was a great miracle.

God showered the Israelites with so many miraculous blessings, yet they were still ungrateful and disobedient. They took these blessings for granted and became desensitised to the fact that they were receiving these miracles from God. People today also suffer from the same desensitisation; from the moment we are born, nature provides everything for us, and if we truly contemplated on it, we would realise that this happens in a miraculous way. Yet we take this for granted and perceive it as an ordinary occurrence. Although these verses appear to be reprimanding the Israelites, in reality, they draw attention to one of the inherent weaknesses in human nature: ungratefulness towards the creator.

'Eat from the purest things we have provided for you.' Purity has literal and figurative meanings in this verse. Literally the foods God provided were wholesome, nutritious and beneficial for the Israelites. Figuratively, the Israelites did not need to engage in business or transaction to earn and struggle for their provisions. The struggle to earn and compete over limited resources can often lead to cheating and deception. The Israelites received their food directly from God and thus it was in its purest form. Despite all these blessings, a feeling of rejection, hatred and jealousy towards Prophet Moses grew in their hearts. They were afraid of Prophet Moses after having witnessed these miracles, but they certainly did not love him. These bitter feelings were holding them back from submitting themselves to God, which is why God mentions at the end of this verse *and they did not wrong us, but they used to wrong themselves.*

and they did not wrong us, but they used to wrong themselves (*wa-mā ẓalam-nā*). The use of the pronoun "us" (*nā*) refers to God. Numerous times in the Quran, God refers to himself as "we" or "us" which is used in the Arabic language to emphasise the majestic position of God. However, at other times in the Quran "we" or "us" may refer to God and other pure beings whose will is merged with God's will. For example, Surah Kahf, verses 60-82, narrate the story of Prophet Moses wishing to learn wisdom from "a servant" of God as part of his prophetical training. Prophet Moses accompanies the servant of God in three events during which he tests Prophet Moses. Upon seeing a lack of patience in Moses, he explains the wisdom behind these three events. Interestingly, he uses pronouns interchangeably: in verse 79, he uses the pronoun "I", in verse 80, he uses the pronoun "we" (the servant and God) and in verse 82, he uses he (the Lord). In other words, the servant is not only the executer of God's will due to his purity and wisdom, but his will is merged with the will of God and he is acting as the true agent of God on earth. This illustrates how the pronouns are used to describe merging the will of pure and wise human beings with the will of God.

The verse states there was a clear and continuous effort by some Israelites to undermine Prophet Moses's attempt to establish the true religion among the Israelites. But these efforts neither harmed God nor Prophet Moses; they only harmed the perpetrators of the plots as they deprived themselves from guidance and salvation and served to prolong their punishment.

وَإِذْ قُلْنَا ادْخُلُوا هَٰذِهِ الْقَرْيَةَ فَكُلُوا مِنْهَا حَيْثُ شِئْتُمْ رَغَدًا وَادْخُلُوا الْبَابَ سُجَّدًا وَقُولُوا حِطَّةٌ نَغْفِرْ لَكُمْ خَطَايَاكُمْ وَسَنَزِيدُ الْمُحْسِنِينَ ﴿58﴾

And when we said: 'Enter this town and eat there freely, whatever you want and enter prostrating at the gate and say, 'relieve us of the burdens of our sins' that we may forgive your inequities and soon we will enhance the virtuous.'

This verse recounts the ninth blessing that God bestowed upon the Israelites.

Enter this town; Most exegetes believe that the town referred to here is Jerusalem; however, based on historical accounts, after their escape from Egypt, the city that the Israelites were asked to enter was Jericho. They refused to do so due to their fear of the strong warriors of the city, namely the Anakim or Amalekites.

According to sources, the Amalekites were the oppressive rulers of the land of Canaan. They needed to be punished for their oppression and transgression, thus God wanted the Israelites to punish the oppressors by removing them from Jericho and settle down there as their reward. The Biblical account of the event suggests that God expected the Jews to massacre all the inhabitants, including women, children, and animals (1 Sam 15:1-3). However, the aforementioned Quranic verse undermines this account, although it refers to a city other than Jericho.

enter prostrating at the gate; This order from God suggests that the Israelites were to enter the city with humility and humbleness of the heart (*sujjadan*). Some commentators have interpreted the term *sujjadan* literally, indicating that the gates of Jericho were too low, thus people needed to bow down when they were entering the city. Even if we take this account to be true, God still demands humility from them; Zamakhshari in his *al-Kashshāf*[103] says that prostrating means to bow their heads so that their entrance would be with meekness and humbleness of the heart. Tabrisi reports a view which discards the physical sense altogether; he interprets *sujjadan* as humbleness and submissiveness.[104] Although the Israelites were victorious, they needed to be humble towards the inhabitants of the city while seeking forgiveness from God. However, some accounts report that they did not have humility in their hearts, and they did not want to physically bow their heads and instead sat on their rumps and dragged themselves backwards into the low gate.[105]

Most commentators have identified this verse either regarding relation to the conquest of Jericho at the time of Joshua or with their refusal to enter the city at the time of Moses. However, some commentators have raised the possibility[106] that the city mentioned here is neither Jerusalem nor Jericho but another city they passed by during their journey. There are two compelling reasons for this; firstly, the Quran speaks of Jericho with respect calling it *"the Holy Land which God has ordained for you"* (Q. 5:21), or "*the land which We had blessed*". (Q. 7:137) In contrast, a much more casual expression is used here.

The second reason is that assuming "this city" refers to Jericho would take the whole verse out of context and would go against the chronological order of events. This series of verses deal with what happened to the children of Israel after deliverance from Egypt, while travelling with Prophet Moses towards the holy land. Verses 49 to 56 mention the story from the crossing of the sea to receiving of the Torah and verses 57 to 61 give an account of what happened on the way. Therefore, it is not logical for verses 58 and 59 to suddenly jump to the time of Joshua and go back to the time of Moses again. Hence, 'the city' here is most probably neither Jericho nor Jerusalem.

Say, 'relieve (*ḥiṭṭa*) us of the burdens of our sins'; as in the case of *sujjadan*, this phrase is a command that should not be considered in a literal sense. The verse does not indicate that when the Israelites enter the city, they should simply utter this expression with their tongues. Rather, it urges the Israelites to ask for true forgiveness from God and wash away their previous sins. Thus, the verse warns them not to be arrogant with their victory and not to be complacent. Instead, the verse encourages the Israelites to ask forgiveness for the sins they committed from the time they escaped from Egypt. By uttering *ḥiṭṭatan* they were expected to be humble and conscious of their past in order to appreciate the blessings of God and make a fresh start after that.

enhance the virtuous; The end of this verse implies that those who comply with the command of God by asking forgiveness while entering the city with humbleness will be branded as the virtuous and God will grant them further blessings. The increase in blessings is applicable to both this world and the next world. According to Razi, this statement may have another interpretation too.[107] It may mean that if sinners entered with humility while asking forgiveness they would remove the burden of their sins, but for the virtuous (*muḥsinīn*) who were obedient before and did not have a burden of sins, the same act would increase their blessings and enhance their position in the Hereafter.

فَبَدَّلَ الَّذِينَ ظَلَمُوا قَوْلًا غَيْرَ الَّذِي قِيلَ لَهُمْ فَأَنزَلْنَا عَلَى الَّذِينَ ظَلَمُوا رِجْزًا مِّنَ السَّمَاءِ بِمَا كَانُوا يَفْسُقُونَ (59)

But the wrongdoers changed the saying with other than what they were told, so we sent down upon those who were wrongdoers a plague from the sky because of the transgressions they used to commit.

The exegetes are divided about the interpretation of this verse. One group have a very literal understanding; they argue that instead of saying, forgive us (*ḥiṭṭa*), the Israelites uttered a similar word *ḥinṭa,* which means [give us] wheat. They said this in order to ridicule Prophet Moses and God, showing what they really believed in. For them, seeking forgiveness did not have any use; and they only valued actual worldly gains. However, the problem with this interpretation is that *ḥiṭṭa* is an Arabic word, it is the translation of what God told them in Hebrew. We know that God speaks with many prophets in different languages and reports these conversations in the Quran in Arabic; he gives us the translations of these conversations. Therefore, both *ḥiṭṭa* and *ḥinṭa* are translations and in their original Hebrew the two words may not sound similar. Thus, such interpretation of the verse does not seem to be plausible. However, one may still argue that the sentiment of this interpretation may be valid on the grounds that the actual words were not uttered, but they valued wheat as the symbol of food and material benefit more that forgiveness and being relieved from the burdens of sins.

The second view is held by many Mutazilite commentators inlcuding the famous Abu Muslim Isfahani (d. 322/934). According to this view, changing God's word alludes to changing his commands. This meaning is used in Q. 48:15 when the hypocrites wanted to follow the Prophet to Khaybar. "*They want to change the word of God. Say, 'You shall never follow us! Thus, has God said beforehand,'*" which means they intended to change the command of God that had been revealed to the Prophet. In the case of this verse, the injunction was "Enter this town," however they changed that command and said, "*O Moses, we will never enter it so long as they remain in it. Go ahead, you and your Lord, and fight! We will be sitting right here.*" (Q. 7:32) Although this interpretation is correct in essence, from the previous conclusion that the town mentioned here is not Jericho, Q. 7:32 cannot apply to it.

So, we sent down upon those who were wrongdoers a plague (*rijz*) from the sky; the word translated as plague is *rijz* which means punishment. This is translated as plague based on the views which regard this specific punishment to be a plague. According to Ibn Zayd, God sent them a plague that killed 25,000 people in one day.[108] However, the nature of the punishment is not stated in the verse. Some commentators say that the *rijz* refers to their wandering in the desert for forty years,[109] however, this wandering was due to their refusal to enter Jericho and we have concluded this verse is not referring to that. Moreover, the wandering was not restricted to the wrongdoers alone. The expression "from the sky," refers to the decree of God which is sent from his high position and does not mean the punishment literally came from the sky above. As Tabrisi states, it means God had decreed it from heaven.[110]

وَإِذِ اسْتَسْقَىٰ مُوسَىٰ لِقَوْمِهِ فَقُلْنَا اضْرِب بِّعَصَاكَ الْحَجَرَ ۖ فَانفَجَرَتْ مِنْهُ
اثْنَتَا عَشْرَةَ عَيْنًا ۖ قَدْ عَلِمَ كُلُّ أُنَاسٍ مَّشْرَبَهُمْ ۖ كُلُوا وَاشْرَبُوا مِن رِّزْقِ
اللَّهِ وَلَا تَعْثَوْا فِي الْأَرْضِ مُفْسِدِينَ ﴿60﴾

When Moses prayed for water for his people, We said 'strike the rock with your staff.' Twelve springs gushed out of this rock and every tribe knew of their watering place. 'Eat and drink from God's provisions but do not cause grave corruption on the earth.'

This verse details the tenth blessing that God bestowed on the Israelites. This miracle took place after crossing the river on their way to Canaan and after they were sent manna and quails. Both blessings continued when they were camping by Mount Sinai and during the desert period. Finding water for such a huge number of people during the journey was one of the greatest challenges for Prophet Moses. There was no regular source of water on the way and most of the water was owned by other people. The Israelites used to carry water, but it was not sufficient. Hence, when they were inflicted with severe thirst and were on the verge of dying, Prophet Moses prayed for rain. It is highly probable that the companions of Prophet Moses also joined in the prayer. Nevertheless, God's focus in this story is Prophet Moses, so only his name is mentioned here.

We said 'strike the rock with your staff.' This was God's response, instructing Prophet Moses to hit a specific rock with his staff, and water gushed forth from it. This rock was then taken by the Israelites on their journey, and they set it down at the centre of their camps wherever they stopped. In this way, they always had access to water. It is interesting to note that this episode is the opposite of what Prophet Moses did with his staff at the Red Sea. With the command of God, he used the same staff to hit the sea and the sea split apart, creating a dry corridor for Moses and his followers to pass. This time, he used the same staff to bring forth water from a rock. On one occasion the staff dried out water and, in another, it made water gush out.

Twelve springs gushed out of one rock. It could have been either a huge rock so that twelve springs could come out of it at once or the water could have come from one spot initially at a low intensity which then enlarged and spread to twelve springs. It is said that the rock was a cubic stone with four sides and three streams flew from each side.[111] It was sized in a way that could be carried on a camel. There were twelve Israelite tribes, and each tribe was under the command of its own chiefs.[112] On their long journey, the tribal hierarchy was pragmatic; Prophet Moses would inform the tribal chiefs about the plan and then they would convey the message to their people and make sure they move or camp in an orderly manner. To keep the order and efficiency, when they stopped, the members of every tribe camped in a specific area. Hence, when the water gushed out from the rock, each spring found their way through the camping area of each tribe. This was another miracle in addition to the water gushing out of the rock itself.

Razi[113] suggests that there are five specific aspects of this incident, every one of which is a miracle in itself: the appearance of water by hitting the stone with a staff; flowing water from the stone; gushing water in abundance from a small stone; providing the exact amount of water that they needed; and the ceasing of water when the need was over. He then compares this with a miracle of Prophet Muhammad where, during a battle, his army ran out of water; the Prophet put his hand in the bowl in which he used to make ablution and water gushed out from between his fingers.[114]

The event of the miracle of the stone is mentioned in the Bible in Exodus, 17:

> 3 But the people were thirsty for water there, and they grumbled against Moses. They said, "Why did you bring us up out of Egypt to make us and our children and livestock die of thirst?"
> 4 Then Moses cried out to the Lord, "What am I to do with these people? They are almost ready to stone me."
> 5 The LORD answered Moses, "Go out in front of the people. Take with you some of the elders of Israel and take in your hand the staff with which you struck the Nile and go.
> 6 I will stand there before you by the rock at Horeb. Strike the rock, and water will come out of it for the people to drink." So, Moses did this in the sight of the elders of Israel.
> 7 And he called the place Massah and Meribah because the Israelites quarrelled and because they tested the Lord saying, "Is the Lord among us or not?"[115]

The water gushed from the rock in such an amazing way that "Every tribe knew of their watering place," and each stream went into the encampment of each of the tribes, so every tribe knew where their watering place was. The miraculous distribution of water was a much-needed blessing, especially considering the large number of the Israelites at the time, which most sources put at about 600,000.

eat and drink from God's provisions; This is a command to the Israelites to combine God's two blessings on the Israelites long journey. Eat may refer to "manna and quails" mentioned in verse 57 and drink may refer to the water that gushed out of the rock. This can also be taken in general terms permitting the usage of the "provisions" of God for all human beings. However, the condition for enjoying these blessing is not to "cause grave corruption on the earth."

وَإِذْ قُلْتُمْ يَا مُوسَىٰ لَن نَّصْبِرَ عَلَىٰ طَعَامٍ وَاحِدٍ فَادْعُ لَنَا رَبَّكَ يُخْرِجْ لَنَا
مِمَّا تُنبِتُ الْأَرْضُ مِن بَقْلِهَا وَقِثَّائِهَا وَفُومِهَا وَعَدَسِهَا وَبَصَلِهَا قَالَ
أَتَسْتَبْدِلُونَ الَّذِي هُوَ أَدْنَىٰ بِالَّذِي هُوَ خَيْرٌ اهْبِطُوا مِصْرًا فَإِنَّ لَكُم مَّا
سَأَلْتُمْ وَضُرِبَتْ عَلَيْهِمُ الذِّلَّةُ وَالْمَسْكَنَةُ وَبَاءُوا بِغَضَبٍ مِّنَ اللَّهِ ذَٰلِكَ
بِأَنَّهُمْ كَانُوا يَكْفُرُونَ بِآيَاتِ اللَّهِ وَيَقْتُلُونَ النَّبِيِّينَ بِغَيْرِ الْحَقِّ ذَٰلِكَ بِمَا
عَصَوا وَّكَانُوا يَعْتَدُونَ ﴿61﴾

When you said 'O Moses! We will not put up with one kind of food, so invoke your Lord for us that He may bring forth for us of that which earth grows, its greens and its cucumbers and its garlic and its lentils and its onions.' Moses said: 'Do you seek to replace what is superior with that which is inferior? Go down to any town (or Egypt), and you will get what you ask for.' So, they were struck with abasement and poverty, and they earned God's wrath. That was because they defied the signs of God, and killed the prophets unjustly, that because they would disobey and used to commit transgression.

This is a relatively long verse of the Quran. It is does not follow the pattern of the previous set of verses mentioning the bounties of God. Instead, this verse addresses the ungratefulness of the Israelites towards

God's blessings and the consequence of their ungratefulness. We do not know when this conversation between Prophet Moses and his people took place. We are also not informed about the context; of course, for the Quran the context is not important. The Quranic emphasis here is on the *attitude* of the people and the lessons that we can learn from them.

'O Moses! We will not put up with one kind of food,' Although the Israelites received all the blessings mentioned in the previous verses, they continued to complain about the limited selection of food available. They questioned why God would not send them a variety of foods and urged Prophet Moses to ask God to provide them with ingredients like greens, cucumbers, garlic, lentils, and onions. The extent of their ungratefulness demonstrates the warped mindset of some of those people who were not satisfied with the unprecedented blessings which God bestowed upon them.

Do you seek to replace what is superior with that which is inferior? Furthermore, the Israelites did not only criticise Prophet Moses for the limited variety of foods, but they also criticised God himself as he was the one providing them with those foods. Prophet Moses, in return, posed this question to them. The superiority mentioned here may relate to the nutritional value of the foods. The verse reminds the Israelites that what God is giving them is sufficient in its nourishment and wholesomeness. The verse is telling them that what God has granted them is superior and contains all the vitamins and minerals they need; in fact, they are more nutritious than the foods the Israelites were demanding. Thus, they were seeking to replace the superior foods with lower quality foods. The second meaning is related to the superior status of the food, which was a gift from God. The food came to the Israelites directly from God and they wished to replace it with food which was cultivated by people. Undoubtedly, food from God is superior in all ways to the food that people cultivate.

go down to any town (or down to Egypt); Here, Prophet Moses tells the Israelites to go after what they seek. The literal translation of "*Miṣran*" is "city" or "town". Egypt was called *Miṣra*, because the cities in Egypt were the most magnificent cities in the ancient world. If *Miṣran* alludes to Egypt, the verse may be a command to return to Egypt; in Egypt the Israelites partook in all these foods and more, yet they were slaves who were oppressed by the brutal ruler, Pharaoh. Thus, God instructs the Israelites to return to Egypt to that humiliating state, if they would like to return to eating those foods.

In the discussion concerning the Surah al-Baqarah, verse 36, the word "*ihbitū*" (go down) referred to Adam and Eve's descent from the garden to the earth, from a higher place to a lower place, and the same can be applied here with the story of the Israelites.

Some commentators state that "*miṣran*" refers to any city. If this is the case, then the verse means they did not deserve to continue the journey with Prophet Moses, and that they should go and settle in a city to partake of their insignificant demands. Some commentators have suggested that "*miṣran*" may refer to Jericho. However, it does not seem plausible since Jericho was the Holy Land and the destination set for them by God.

So they were struck with abasement and poverty; Almost all commentators agree that the continuation of the verse, is an independent statement explaining the ill fate of the transgressing Jews throughout history. It refers to the consequences of their transgression and disobedience which led them to not only disbelieve but also to murder the prophets after Prophet Moses.

The "poverty" mentioned in the verse may not mean lack of wealth but may also describe their insatiable appetite for worldly possessions. They had a constant desire for more and that meant that they were always in need; their calamity was greed. Tabrisi refers to this as the "poverty of the heart", citing a hadith from the Prophet that "the real affluence is the affluence of the soul."[116] Just like the example above, they were given manna and quails, but they were not satisfied with it and wanted more. As a result, this attitude turned into a character trait for them.

This "abasement" or humiliation did not leave the Israelites after their rebellion against God and Prophet Moses. Following that event, the Israelites were repeatedly enslaved, massacred, exiled and raided by other empires. Of course, these actions against the Israelites were heinous crimes often committed by oppressive states or groups. Yet this points to a general rule of the world that insatiable greed and unrestrained ambition often leads to conflict of interest and invasion of rights and wealth. This would inevitably trigger dreadful consequences including conflict, war and destruction. Although the Quran mentions the Israelites by name, this example can be applied as a general rule concerning all of mankind. Other nations,[117] groups and individuals who might suffer from the same kind of insatiable greed and unrestrained ambition would eventually face the same consequences and many others have suffered from a similar ill-fate due to their actions. Therefore, mankind must all stay vigilant against adopting these self-destructive traits.

As stated in the next verse, not all Israelites shared these qualities. Rather, the consequences of evil are evil for everyone, and the next verse tells us that the consequences of good are good for everyone. The Quran always distinguishes between good and evil in every nation and, here, it excludes some members of the Israelites from this trait and its ill-consequences. This is another sign that certain characteristics are not exclusive to a specific nation, and it is possible to remain free of such characteristics despite the dominant surrounding toxic culture of uncontrolled greed and ambition.

and they earned God's wrath; the verse continues by acknowledging the consequences of adopting these ill-traits. The Israelites earned nothing as a result of their transgressions and greed except the wrath of God and "abasement and poverty". They spent most of their life in slavery and as soon as they were delivered from it, they were stricken with an insatiable greed and ambition, thus they never achieved inner peace and finally were only left with distressing responses from God. In other words, they wasted their lives and never achieved material or spiritual satisfaction and will receive a painful punishment in the Hereafter.

That was because they defied the signs of God and killed the prophets unjustly; The following section of the verse is very important not only in terms of commentary of the Quran, but also for its theological implications. The verse rejects the idea of fatalism in Islam and emphasises how human fate is a consequence of a person's own actions. The Israelites were belittled and stricken by poverty of heart and earned the wrath of God because they rejected the communications of God and murdered the prophets; this was the result of choosing disobedience and exceeding the limits.

Furthermore, this phrase indicates that the subjects of the verse are not only the Jews who followed Prophet Moses but the Israelites in general, and all other nations who may adopt similar traits and commit similar transgressions.

The Israelites who followed Moses in the desert did not kill their prophets. Killing the prophets took place in later generations when prophets were sent to them to rectify their understanding of the Book. It is reported from the Prophet Muhammad that, "The Israelites killed forty-three prophets in one morning and killed another hundred and twelve people who rose and advised them towards goodness in the evening."[118] Their last attempt according to the Quran was to kill Jesus, who escaped death by divine intervention. God blessed the children of Israel with the Torah that included divine instruction, but they wilfully interpreted these instructions in a way that would serve their own worldly interests rather than serving the will of God. These prophets did not bring new books or instructions, instead they attempted to rectify the twisted interpretations of the Torah which were provided by some rabbis, who had vested interests in their role as custodians of divine instructions. This inevitably led to a conflict between those rabbis and the prophets of God which culminated in the murder of the prophets.

Similarly, there is a striking tradition from the Prophet which provides a similar perspective about the Muslim nation. According to Shi'i belief, the Imams of the Ahl al-Bayt have the same role as the prophets sent to the Israelites. They are the custodians of faith and interpreters of the Quran and the *Sunna* (Prophetic tradition). The Prophet said: "The scholars (*'ulamā'*) of my umma (community) are like the prophets of the Israelites."[119] This tradition tells us two things: firstly, the prophets of the Israelites who were killed while discharging their duties were giving the correct interpretation of the Torah; they were not tasked with bringing anything new. Similarly, this was the task of the scholars of the community of Prophet Muhammad. Secondly, in the Muslim community there have been some people who have always been able to correctly interpret the Quran, yet Muslims treated them in the same way as the Israelites treated their prophets. These scholars are the Imams, who were tasked to provide a correct interpretation of the Quran. The tradition does not refer to any regular scholar who learns the religion and teaches it to others. The knowledge of these scholars is based on opinion whilst the knowledge of the Imams is God-given. The Imams have explicitly mentioned that "*naḥnu al-'ulamā'*"[120] (we are the scholars), the scholars that the Prophet mentions in the above hadith, are the Imams – they are the scholars who correctly interpret the religion for people in the same way that the prophets of the Israelites came to correctly interpret the Torah.

Ironically, as a result of their efforts, like the Jewish prophets, the Imams were rejected and killed by their own people. Therefore, as Muslims we need to be very careful, and must not expect God to grant us glory and superiority over other religious communities just because we have called ourselves Muslims. The Quran teaches us that superiority is not about being given the correct guidance or having the right faith, instead superiority is attained by always being committed to correct teachings. We must remain faithful to guidance at any cost and always strive to achieve the correct interpretations of religion. Only by maintaining this state of mind through continuous effort can superiority be granted to people.

that, because they would disobey and used to commit transgression. Here, the reason behind the Israelites defiance of the signs of God and rejection and killing of their prophets is revealed: they disobeyed and committed transgressions. The verse also points out important correlations between human traits and their consequences;

the outcome of certain attitudes will lead to certain actions. Before committing an unjust act, a negative change must have occurred in the heart. In other words, unjust acts are not independent from the state of a person's heart; injustice is a symptom of a corrupt heart. Therefore, when people commit an injustice, it comes about as the consequence of the disease in their heart. This disease is as a result of the disobedience and transgression that people themselves commit over a period of time. In this way, the verse rejects fatalism, and instead tells us that people are not born as criminals or oppressors; we develop or earn these traits gradually, as a result of our habitual misdeeds which then lead us to commit heinous crimes. In the same way, when spirituality is gradually developed and cultivated in a person's heart, it leads to habitual good deeds which in turn make a person attain higher spiritual stations in the long term.

إِنَّ الَّذِينَ آمَنُوا وَالَّذِينَ هَادُوا وَالنَّصَارَىٰ وَالصَّابِئِينَ مَنْ آمَنَ بِاللَّهِ
وَالْيَوْمِ الْآخِرِ وَعَمِلَ صَالِحًا فَلَهُمْ أَجْرُهُمْ عِندَ رَبِّهِمْ وَلَا خَوْفٌ عَلَيْهِمْ
وَلَا هُمْ يَحْزَنُونَ ﴿62﴾

Indeed, the faithful (Muslims), the Jews, the Christians, the Sabeans, those of them who have faith in God and the last day and act righteously, they shall have their reward near their Lord, and they will have no fear and nor will they grieve.

This verse is interestingly and very suitably placed here as it emphasises the universality of the issues facing all communities. It is not only the Israelites who need to be vigilant against committing these same mistakes; rather, it is every community. Guidance and reward may be given to any community or nation. Oblivious to this understanding of the verse, some exegetes have questioned the suitability of the verse in its current order.

Indeed, the faithful (Muslims), the Jews, the Christians, the Sabeans; This verse mentions four religious communities: Muslims,

Jews, Christians and Sabeans. All these groups are well known, established communities, apart from the Sabeans. They are reported to be a group of Semites who lived in Southern Arabia. Since they are mentioned three times in the Quran (2:62, 5:69 and 22:17), the Arabs at the time of the Prophet would have been aware of them. However, evidence suggests that their connection was lost over time, and later exegetes did not have much knowledge of this community. For this reason, there has been much debate among the second-generation Muslims about the identity of the Sabeans and their religion. It is strange that a religion which is not well-known and followed by a small number of people is mentioned in this verse alongside great religions like Islam, Judaism and Christianity. Therefore, it is important to know why the Sabeans were mentioned in the verse.

Some of the second-generation exegetes such as Qatada said the Sabeans were a group of people who worshipped angels and prayed to the sun five times a day.[121] A different report from Qatada suggests that they worshipped the stars whilst, also acknowledging the creator, the Judgment Day, and some of the prophets. Hasan al-Basri and Mujahid believed they did not have a distinct faith and categorised them as somewhere between Judaism and Zoroastrianism. Al-Suddi classified them as the People of the Book reading the Psalms (Zabūr).[122] *Tafsīr Qummī* states that they were not from the People of the Book, and they worshipped stars and other planets.[123] The existence of such diverse opinions suggests that the second-generation exegetes did not know much about the Sabeans.

The suggestion that they worshipped angels, stars or two deities is absurd because the verse gives the Sabeans the status of those who believed in God and the Day of Judgment; and that is why most Sunni jurists have categorised them as the People of the Book,[124] and regarded them as monotheists. The reason why Mujahid and Qatada mentioned such views may have been that they were in the opinion that the Sabeans were initially among the People of the Book, but they later became polytheists. Recent scholarship[125] suggests that the Sabeans are the Mandaeans, a gnostic religion who followed John the Baptist (Prophet Yahya). We can also conclude that they follow a sacred Book;

otherwise, they would not have been mentioned alongside Islam, Judaism and Christianity. They have always lived close to rivers due to their religious teachings that gives great significance to running water. They need to baptise themselves (or *ghusl* in Islamic tradition) every week. Therefore, they mostly settled beside the rivers of Tigris and Euphrates and their numbers were around 100,000 and 150,000.

Given that their numbers were small, one might wonder why they were included alongside other great religions. There may be two explanations for their inclusion in this verse: one may be that the pagans of Medina and later Muslims used to travel to Syria in the summer in order to conduct their business affairs. Along the way, they would have come across the Sabeans who lived by Tigris and Euphrates and would have become familiar with the Sabeans and their faith. It is possible that they appreciated these people and their gnostic lifestyle. However, they had not been mentioned among the People of the Book in the early years of the mission of the Prophet, thus God mentioned this group of people in the later periods as an example of those who were faithful and sincere but not from the faith of the great religions.

The second possibility is that since the Sabeans were a small faith community, God wanted to mention that any faith community who are sincere, devoted and following a Book of God, as the Sabeans did, would be regarded among the People of the Book.

Interestingly, there is a current debate among the Shi'i religious scholars about the status of Buddhists. Some Shi'i scholars argue that if the book they follow was a Book of God, regardless of whether it has been distorted, we may still regard them as the People of Book, despite a lack of knowledge about their prophets.

those of them who have faith in God and the last day and act righteously, they shall have their reward near their Lord, and they will have no fear and nor will they grieve. The implications of this verse are far reaching and it is often discussed in contemporary debates about religious pluralism. By mentioning the Sabeans alongside the great religions, one might question whether the name and description of your faith really matters, or whether sincerity of your faith would be sufficient for reward in the Hereafter. If the verse implies that sincerity is what is most important, there may be no need to invite people to Islam.

Pure sincerity is not sufficient as a religion. History is witness to many sincere people who created great corruption based on their sincere faith. People have sacrificed their children before idols out of sincerity. Sincerity cannot be a singular guide, rather, it needs to be guided. Therefore, the verse cannot be interpreted to mean that believing in any faith would lead to success in the Hereafter. First, because such an interpretation would contradict several other verses that clearly identify the religion with God to be Islam (Q. 3:19), and that *should anyone seek a religion other than Islam, it shall never be accepted from him, and he will be among the losers in the Hereafter.* (Q. 3:85) Although Islam in these verses refer to the religion expressed most brilliantly by Prophet Abraham, as it has been established elsewhere, it also shows that there is a criterion for the correct faith *They say, 'Be either Jews or Christians, that you may be guided.' Say, 'Rather [we will follow] the creed of Abraham, a hanif, and he was not one of the polytheists'.* (Q. 2:135) *Then We revealed to you [saying], 'Follow the creed of Abraham, a hanif, and he was not one of the polytheists'* (Q. 16:123).

Second, the Quran calls the People of the Book to embrace Islam. There would be no call to Islam if this verse was acknowledging their present faith as an alternative way to salvation. *So if they believe in the like of what you believe in, then they are certainly guided; and if they turn away, then they are only [steeped] in defiance. God shall suffice you against them, and He is the All-hearing, the All-knowing.* (Q. 2:137) Furthermore, Muslims are warned not to follow the Jewish or Christian religion. *Never will the Jews be pleased with you, nor the Christians, unless you follow their creed. Say, 'Indeed it is the guidance of God which is the [true] guidance.' And should you follow their desires after the knowledge that has come to you, you will not have against God any guardian nor any helper.* (Q. 2:120)

This verse should be understood in the context of Q. 5:68, *Say,*

"O People of the Book! You do not stand on anything until you observe the Torah and the Evangel and what was sent down to you from your Lord." The good tiding of the coming of the last Messenger of God was revealed in the Torah and the Evangel. *And when Jesus son of Mary said, "O Children of Israel! Indeed, I am the apostle of God to you, to confirm what is before me of the Torah, and to give the good news of an apostle who will come after me, whose name is Aḥmad."* (Q. 61:6) The Jews in Medina knew Prophet Muhammad through the descriptions given in the Torah as well as they knew their own sons. *Those whom We have given the Book recognize him just as they recognize their sons, but a part of them indeed conceal the truth while they know.* (Q. 2:146) Thus, not believing in Prophet Muhammad amounted to rejecting the Torah and the Evangel, and they did not stand on anything until they observed the Torah and the Evangel.

In conclusion, this verse refers to those People of the Book who lived before the advent of Islam, or those who lived during the time of the Prophet and acknowledged him and believed in him in. The verse says their actions before converting to Islam will receive their due reward.

وَإِذْ أَخَذْنَا مِيثَاقَكُمْ وَرَفَعْنَا فَوْقَكُمُ الطُّورَ خُذُوا مَا آتَيْنَاكُمْ بِقُوَّةٍ وَاذْكُرُوا مَا فِيهِ لَعَلَّكُمْ تَتَّقُونَ ﴿63﴾

And when We took a pledge from you, and raised the Mount above you [declaring], 'Hold on with power to what We have given you, and remember that which is in it, so that you may be Godwary.'

And when we took a pledge from you; This pledge is different from the pledge mentioned in Q. 2:83-84. That pledge or *'ahd* describes the instructions that the Israelites had been waiting for and came to them through the revelation of the Torah. However, after the Torah was revealed and they were informed of its contents, some of them refused to accept and practice it, claiming that its instructions were too hard to follow. They asked Prophet Moses to go back and ask God to change those instructions and give them easier duties. They compared the act of God to the decisions of human beings which may be taken spontaneously and without wisdom and consideration.

and raised the Mount above you [declaring]; In an awe-inspiring display of God's power, he miraculously raised the mount by which they had gathered to complain until it hung over their heads and covered the entire Israelite nation: *And when we plucked the mountain [and held it] above them as if it were a canopy and they thought it was about to fall on them...* (Q. 7:171) Threatened with its crushing fall over them, they submitted and pledged to obey and follow. *And We raised the Mount above them for the sake of their covenant... and We took from them a solemn covenant.* (Q. 4:154)

The Torah does not explicitly refer to this event. Exodus 19:17 only states that "the Jews stood under the mountain", an expression which is alternatively translated as "at the foot of the mountain" or "at the bottom of the mountain". However, this vague reference in the Torah is interpreted explicitly in the Talmud. In Tractate Shabbos, the Talmud explains that God literally placed the Jews under the mountain by lifting the mount above them like a giant pot and declared, "If you will accept the Torah, fine, but you do not accept the Torah, this will become your final resting place." Therefore, the midrashic interpretation of Exodus 19:17 is that the mountain was uprooted from its place and turned over them like a vat.[126]

'Hold on with power to what We have given you, and remember that which is in it;' Holding to the Scripture with power is mentioned more than once in the Quran: *O John! [We said,] 'Hold on with power to the Book!' And We gave him judgment while still a child* (Q. 19:12); *And We wrote for him in the Tablets advice concerning all things and an elaboration of all things, [and We said], 'Hold on to them with power.'* (Q. 7:145)

"Holding to the Book with power" means to intimately following its instructions with deep understanding, devotion and determination. Despite this command, the Jews, in due course, broke their covenant and defied God's signs, and even killing his prophets. (Q. 4:155) One might wonder why God chose to answer the Israelites with a threatening display of his power while *there is no compulsion is religion.* (Q. 2:256) However, this was not coercion or compulsion. The fact that they were not all chastised and destroyed after they turned away and broke the covenant, as mentioned in the next verse, proves that even the raising of the mount over their heads was not to coerce them to submit. It was to subdue the mischief makers in their midst and give the rest a chance to experience obedience and live by God's laws. According to Tabatabai, compelling the Israelites to accept the pledge with God does not go against verses like *there is no compulsion in religion* (Q. 2:256) and *will you then force men until they become believers?* (Q. 10:99) If this was the case then other miracles (such as seeing the staff change to a serpent, the plagues to the Pharaoh, being struck by lightning, and so on) can also be said to "compel" people as they would have been frightened at witnessing them.[127] Being scared or warned is not the same as being compelled.

'so that you may be Godwary.' This is also proof that this display off power was to give them a chance to recognise God, rather than being coercion. The raising of the mount despite knowing they would disobey later, was to show God's compassion to guide after all other means had failed, and to exhaust all excuses against them.

ثُمَّ تَوَلَّيْتُم مِّن بَعْدِ ذَٰلِكَ ۖ فَلَوْلَا فَضْلُ اللَّهِ عَلَيْكُمْ وَرَحْمَتُهُ لَكُنتُم مِّنَ الْخَاسِرِينَ ﴿64﴾

Then after that you turned away; and were it not for God's grace on you and His mercy, you would surely have been among the losers.

Then after that you turned away; means "then you returned to disobedience after witnessing the signs with your own eyes." If not for his decree in granting respite and his forbearance in acts of grace, God would punish without delay and cause a great misfortune to descend and all transaction would be entirely a loss.[128]

Razi, quoting al-Qaffāl[129] (d. 365/976), lists[130] the matters they turned away from: they altered the Torah, forsook acting on it, killed prophets, disbelieved in them, and opposed their commands. Some of this was done by the former generations and some by the later ones. Although they witnessed miracles continuously in the desert, day and night, they still opposed Prophet Moses, objecting to everything he asked of them, causing him hardship, annoying him and troubling him.

And were it not for God's grace on you and His mercy, you would surely have been among the losers. Had God not given them respite and delayed chastisement so that they may repent, they would have all *been among the losers*. This teaches us that God's grace and mercy is not only to guide the faithful, but also to rescue those who have gone astray so that they are not *among the losers*.

وَلَقَدْ عَلِمْتُمُ الَّذِينَ اعْتَدَوْا مِنكُمْ فِي السَّبْتِ فَقُلْنَا لَهُمْ كُونُوا قِرَدَةً خَاسِئِينَ ﴿65﴾

And certainly you know those of you who violated the Sabbath, whereupon We said to them, 'Be you spurned apes.'

The incident in this verse occurred at the time of Prophet David in the fishing village of Ayla, which is probably the present day Eilat on the Red Sea. The story is told in detail in Surah al-Aʿrāf:

> Ask them about the town that was situated on the seaside, when they violated the Sabbath, when their fish would come to them on the Sabbath day, visibly on the shore, but on days when they were not keeping Sabbath they would not come to them. Thus, did We test them because of the transgressions they used to commit. When a group of them said, 'Why do you advise a people whom God will destroy or

> punish with a severe punishment?' They said, 'As an excuse before your Lord, and [with the hope] that they may be Godwary.' So when they forgot what they had been reminded of, we delivered those who forbade evil [conduct] and seized the wrongdoers with a terrible punishment because of the transgressions they used to commit. And when they defied [the command pertaining to] what they were forbidden from, we said to them, 'Be you spurned apes.' (7:163-6:)

those of you who violated the Sabbath; In Arabic the word *sabt* means "to cut off".[131] The same meaning is intended in Hebrew by Sabbath. Therefore, Sabbath is a day in which working must be ceased or cut off. Abandoning working on Sabbath was one of the fundamental instructions of the Torah. It was a day in which the workers should have rested and attended to devotional acts of worship.

We said to them, 'Be you spurned apes.' this was a decree from God. It does not mean God "said" it rather that "he willed it". This is a figure of speech to signify ease and immediacy. There is no gap between God's decree and its fulfillment. *All that We say to a thing, when We will it, is to say to it, 'Be!' and it is* (Q. 16:40). So *be you spurned apes* means they instantaneously changed their appearances to resemble apes. Most exegetes quote a report from Ibn Abbas that those who were thus punished did not reproduce and all perished within three days of their transfiguration.[132]

Most exegetes also agree that this verse speaks of a deformation (*maskh*) that was physical and literal and not an analogy expressing their inner state of being. However, a few like Ahmad b. Mustafa al-Maraghi (d. 1952), a contemporary Egyptian scholar of Quran, likened this transformation to verses comparing people to *an ass* (Q. 62:5) or like *cattle.* (Q. 7:179)[133] This interpretation is unnecessary here: firstly, because in the other verses there is a clear mention of "the example of... is like..." Secondly, it is established amongst Muslim scholars that the miracles mentioned regarding the Children of Israel in particular were all literal and not metaphors. However, Mujahid is reported to have said that their character and traits turned to monkey-like traits and they only imitated the letter of the law instead of keeping its spirit.

The word *khāsīn* (sing. *khāsi*, "spurned") means despised, belittled distanced and rejected. For example, when a dog comes near people they say to it in Arabic, *ikhsā* meaning "be gone!" It is used in Q 67:4 with the meaning of "humbled". In this verse, it is used as an adjective for the apes as a reminder that apes, as animals and creatures of God, are not distant from God's mercy in themselves. It is the humans who behave like animals and transform into apes that are removed from God's mercy and *spurned* or despised.

Qushayri has a very insightful comment:

> When [the Children of Israel] abandoned [God's] command and disdained what was imposed on them from the law, the punishments came quickly in their disgrace, metamorphosis, and the other things which are included in the text. In a similar way, the community [of Muḥammad] was punished because of their violation of the Covenant and rejection of the limit [imposed by God], but [their punishment] was in the metamorphosis of their hearts and the alteration of their states. [God] Most High said, '*And We shall confound their hearts and their eyes; just as they did not believe the first time*' [6:110]. The punishments of hearts are far worse than the punishments of the bodily selves.[134]

فَجَعَلْنَاهَا نَكَالًا لِّمَا بَيْنَ يَدَيْهَا وَمَا خَلْفَهَا وَمَوْعِظَةً لِّلْمُتَّقِينَ

﴿66﴾

So We made it an exemplary punishment for the present and the succeeding [generations], and an advice to the Godwary.

So We made it an exemplary punishment; *Nakālan* is translated as "an exemplary punishment." The effects of this punishment remain for others to witness and learn from. It is meant to deter others from the temptation to commit the same crimes. The pronoun "it" (*hā*) in *so We made it (ja'alnāhā)* could refer to the Israelites who were transformed to apes or could refer to the transformation itself. Some exegetes like Razi and Tha'labī (d. 427/1035), have said it could also refer to the village where the divine punishment descended or the chastisement in general.[135]

for the present and the succeeding [generations]; a tradition reported from the fifth Imam Muhammad Baqir (d. 114/732) and Imam Jafar says, "*the present* refers to the generation of that time whereas *the succeeding [generations]* refers to the later generations including us (Muslims) and therefore it is an admonition."[136]

and an advice to the Godwary; The Godwary do not need to witness an *exemplary punishment* as an admonition to keep away from transgression like the rest of the people do, rather they benefit from the story as *an advice.*

وَإِذْ قَالَ مُوسَىٰ لِقَوْمِهِ إِنَّ اللَّهَ يَأْمُرُكُمْ أَنْ تَذْبَحُوا بَقَرَةً ۖ قَالُوا أَتَتَّخِذُنَا هُزُوًا ۖ قَالَ أَعُوذُ بِاللَّهِ أَنْ أَكُونَ مِنَ الْجَاهِلِينَ ﴿67﴾

Remember when Moses said to his people, 'Indeed God commands you to slaughter a cow.' They said, 'Do you take us in derision?' He said, 'I seek God's protection from being one of the senseless.'

This verse marks the beginning of the main story in Surah Baqarah, the Story of the cow from which the surah derives its name. The Israelites were ordered to slaughter a cow to solve a mysterious murder. By way of summary, the incident begins with the murder of a man from one of the Israeli tribes, either before or after the episode of the Golden Calf. One may argue that the incident took place when the Israelites were still in Egypt, but this would have been an impossible as Prophet Moses did not have any authority to resolve legal or criminal disputes at that time.

When they were camping by Mount Sinai, the Israelites had their own fortified encampments in their allocated places according to their tribal affiliations. There are two accounts of the episode. The first account states that two cousins wanted to marry the same girl, and the girl's family had chosen the better man, so his cousin killed him out of jealousy. According to another account, there was a very old and rich man whose nephew was anticipating his death in order to inherent his wealth. So his nephew killed him out of impatience. In both accounts, they threw the corpse of the murdered man near the encampment of another tribe in an attempt to accuse them of the murder.

Thus, the accused tribe and the family of the murdered man began to quarrel, which soon escalated into a tribal conflict. They then escalated the matter to Prophet Moses and asked him to mediate. Initially, Moses asked for proofs for their accusations, but this was unavailable, so he asked for mutual oathing, but they rejected that too. So, to prevent tribal war, Moses decided to resolve the matter in an unorthodox way. He asked the parties to slaughter a cow. This was such a strange suggestion that the leaders of the tribes were taken aback and questioned the wisdom of Moses's judgment. This was the second time that a matter regarding a cow is related to an incident with the Israelites. As previously discussed, the cow was amongst the greatest Egyptian gods and when the Israelites were in Egypt, they had begun to worship some of these gods beside God. They especially believed in the cow-god, thinking that it would grant them blessing and prosperity. This is why Samiri made the Golden Calf in the absence of Prophet Moses and told the Israelites that "this is your god and the god of Moses." They readily accepted his call and started to worship the cow because it invoked the love they had for the cow-god in Egypt.

In this verse, Prophet Moses asked the members of the two disputing tribes to slaughter a cow for the trial. Moses's request went against the sanctity that the Israelites had placed in the cow. Therefore, they reacted strongly against his request. However, the account in the Old Testament, Deuteronomy 21:1-9 states that this is a general rule of collective oathing, whilst the Quran relates the incident as a special case judged by Prophet Moses:

> [1] If someone is found slain, lying in a field in the land the Lord your God is giving you to possess, and it is not known who the killer was, [2] your elders and judges shall go out and measure the distance from the body to the neighbouring towns. [3] Then the elders of the town nearest the body shall take a heifer (a female cow) that has never been worked and has never worn a yoke [4] and lead it down to a valley that has not been ploughed or planted and where there is a flowing stream. There in the valley they are to break the heifer's neck. [5] The Levitical priests shall step forward, for the Lord your God has chosen them to minister and to pronounce

> blessings in the name of the Lord and to decide all cases of dispute and assault. [6] Then all the elders of the town nearest the body shall wash their hands over the heifer whose neck was broken in the valley, [7] and they shall declare: 'Our hands did not shed this blood, nor did our eyes see it done. [8] Accept this atonement for your people Israel, whom you have redeemed, Lord, and do not hold your people guilty of the blood of an innocent person.' Then the bloodshed will be atoned for, [9] and you will have purged from yourselves the guilt of shedding innocent blood, since you have done what is right in the eyes of the Lord.

Remarkably, this story is reported in reverse order in the Quran. It does not mention the murder but skips the initial events and continues to the injunction regarding slaughtering the cow. The initial events are mentioned towards the end of the relevant verses. This style of writing makes the story more compelling by shifting the focus of the story from the murder, to how the Israelites treated Prophet Moses when he informed them about God's instruction to kill the cow. Notably, the focus is also about the love of cattle which was deeply rooted in the hearts of the Israelites. Again, the style of the Quran is unique. As stated earlier, God's focus is always on the individuals representing his teachings and executing his orders on the earth. The others are insignificant, and only mentioned in their relation to the chosen servants of God Almighty. In this story, the focus is Prophet Moses, and the Israelites are mentioned only because of their disobedience and ill treatment towards him.

They said, 'Do you take us in derision?' This question shows that regardless of being in Moses's presence for several years, the Israelites still did not respect Moses in the way he deserved. Although Prophet Moses's request to kill the cow may have been surprising, they should have known by now that he was not like any other man and would not ridicule such serious matters. What makes their statement even more absurd is that Prophet Moses told them that this is the command of God: *Indeed, God commands you to slaughter a cow.* Yet, they did not accept it from Prophet Moses and thought that he was mocking them.

He said, 'I seek God's protection lest I should be one of the senseless!' Here, Prophet Moses means that ridiculing people is a sign of ignorance and senselessness and certainly the messengers of God are far from being senseless. Tabrisi provides a good explanation here.[137] He says derision is either about a person's natural constitution or about their voluntary actions. In the first case, derision is not justified because it is an act of creation, and in the second case, if the action is unseemly, the person should not be derided and instead, they must be reminded to refrain from it. Hence, in both cases derision is a sin which only arises in senseless people.

قَالُوا ادْعُ لَنَا رَبَّكَ يُبَيِّن لَّنَا مَا هِيَ ۚ قَالَ إِنَّهُ يَقُولُ إِنَّهَا بَقَرَةٌ لَّا فَارِضٌ وَلَا بِكْرٌ عَوَانٌ بَيْنَ ذَٰلِكَ ۖ فَافْعَلُوا مَا تُؤْمَرُونَ ﴿68﴾

They said, 'Invoke your Lord for us, that He may clarify for us what [sort of cow] she may be.' He said, 'He says, she is a cow, neither old nor young, of a middle age. Now do what you are commanded.'

After the initial rejection and rebuke from Prophet Moses, the Israelites finally succumbed to his judgment. But first, they questioned him about the identity of the cow. Perhaps they thought that if the cow will be used to identify the murderer, then it must not be an ordinary cow. They thought Prophet Moses was unaware of the gravity of the situation and that the cow must be explained in detail. Thus, they began asking him questions which made finding the cow increasingly difficult for them.

This story reminds us of how some individuals quibble over unnecessary details of religious rulings and reminds us that at times it would be better for us to do what we are told instead of questioning unnecessary particulars which may have been left to our discretion. Some people do this very often, taking pleasure in analysing the minute details and asking different *Marāji'*[138] about it; comparing various views, which in return make life more difficult for those following the ruling. This verse addresses these types of people who, instead of focusing on the essence of the ruling, ask unnecessary questions which show their hearts are not intent on implementing the ruling but in finding an excuse to evade it.

In connection to this concept, there is a verse in the Quran which stresses the hollowness of unnecessary questions about particulars: *O you who believed, do not ask about things that if the answer comes to you, it would place you in hardship.* (Q. 5:101) This was the trouble that the Israelites brought upon themselves in the story of the cow.

'Now do what you are commanded.' Prophet Moses then advised the people to stop asking for further details and find any cow of that quality and slaughter it. However, they regarded themselves holier, and argued that this is a religious ruling that cannot be taken lightly and must be clarified to the minutest detail. Another possibility is that they really did not want to do it and were making excuses, but Prophet Moses advises them to do what they are told by God.

قَالُوا ادْعُ لَنَا رَبَّكَ يُبَيِّن لَّنَا مَا لَوْنُهَا ۚ قَالَ إِنَّهُ يَقُولُ إِنَّهَا بَقَرَةٌ صَفْرَاءُ فَاقِعٌ
لَّوْنُهَا تَسُرُّ النَّاظِرِينَ ﴿69﴾

They said, 'Invoke your Lord for us, that He may clarify for us what her colour may be.' He said, 'He says, she is a cow that is yellow, of a bright hue, pleasing to the onlookers.'

قَالُوا ادْعُ لَنَا رَبَّكَ يُبَيِّن لَّنَا مَا هِيَ إِنَّ الْبَقَرَ تَشَابَهَ عَلَيْنَا وَإِنَّا إِن شَاءَ اللَّهُ لَمُهْتَدُونَ ﴿70﴾

They said, 'Invoke your Lord for us, that He may clarify for us what she may be. Indeed, all cows are much alike to us, and, if God wishes, we will surely be guided.'

In the verse 69, the Israelites concoct additional questions, and in return they received a more specific description. In verse 70, they ask further questions about the cow's appearance. These questions are insincere and show their unwillingness to cooperate with Prophet Moses and carry out God's injunction. God told the Jews to slaughter a cow – they did not need to ask numerous questions about the particulars of the cow. They only needed to slaughter a cow to fulfil God's injunction. It is reported from Imam al-Rida that, "Had they chosen any cow it would have sufficed them, but they pressed, and God pressed on them."[139]

'We will surely be guided.' Razi quotes from al-Qaffāl who offers different meanings to interpret the last section of verse 70. Firstly, by the Israelites saying, "we hope we may be guided", they are trying to show that they are not opposing God's instructions but are simply asking for more detail. They sincerely wanted to be precise about the request. Secondly, they hoped to be guided so that they can reveal the identity of the murderer.[140]

قَالَ إِنَّهُ يَقُولُ إِنَّهَا بَقَرَةٌ لَّا ذَلُولٌ تُثِيرُ الْأَرْضَ وَلَا تَسْقِي الْحَرْثَ مُسَلَّمَةٌ لَّا شِيَةَ فِيهَا قَالُوا الْآنَ جِئْتَ بِالْحَقِّ فَذَبَحُوهَا وَمَا كَادُوا يَفْعَلُونَ ﴿71﴾

He said, 'He says, She is a cow not broken to till the earth or to water the tillage, sound and without blemish.' They said, 'Now have you come up with the truth!' And they slaughtered it, though they were about not to do it.

'Now have you come up with the truth!' is an insolent statement to the messenger of God, implying that he was not talking sense until that point. The questions leading to such a rude statement indicates a collective character of mistrust and misjudgment towards Moses.

And they slaughtered it, though they were about not to do it. could be understood in three ways. Firstly, it may indicate their intention behind asking about minute details of the cow was to make it impossible to find the right cow to slaughter. Secondly, their reluctance may have gone back to their great reverence for cattle that they considered cows as divine. Or it may indicate the difficulty of finding a cow with all those very specific qualities. A yellow cow of a bright hue, sound and without blemish, pleasing to the onlooker, which is neither old nor young, not broken to till the earth or to water the tillage, was very difficult to find, if not impossible. Narrations say that there was only one cow in all the Israelites' camps matching this description, which belonged to a young man who only agreed to sell it for a very high price. Qummī reports[141] that the cow belonged to a young man who was extremely kind and benevolent to his father and the price paid for it was a reward for his benevolence. The third possibility is that they were about not to do it because of the high price demanded by the owner of the cow.

وَإِذْ قَتَلْتُمْ نَفْسًا فَادَّارَأْتُمْ فِيهَا ۖ وَاللَّهُ مُخْرِجٌ مَا كُنْتُمْ تَكْتُمُونَ ﴿72﴾

And when you killed a soul and accused one another about it and God was to expose whatever you were concealing.

After elaborating on the non-compliant attitude of the Israelites concerning the cow, the verse then deals with the murder, which is of secondary importance in this story. Interestingly, the episode of the cow is juxtaposed to the verses condemning the previous history of the Israelites. Here, the Jews of Medina are reprimanded for the behaviour of their forefathers, because they boasted about the history and traditions of their past generations.

For a better perspective, imagine if some Muslims boasted about the Umayyads and what they did in the history of Islam. They may be challenged and reprimanded on the grounds that taking pride in the actions of the Umayyads, who murdered the grandson of the Prophet and committed many other atrocities, is reprehensible. However, if Muslims denounce the transgressions of the Umayyads, then there is no blame on them. In the same vein, if the Jews of Medina had denounced the transgressions of their forefathers, they would not have received such harsh reprimand. However, they were complacent with the misdeeds of their past generations, and they used their history to oppose the new revelations and the Messenger of God. Therefore, they continued with their heritage which was full of misdeeds and transgression and created obstacles for the Prophet.

and God was to expose whatever you were concealing; One important issue here is the use of the word "*mukhrijun*" (to expose) which is in the present tense, even though this event took place in the past. Some exegetes argue that this is because the verse does not refer solely to the Israelites and to this incident. Rather, it should be treated as a general ruling according to which no good or bad deed will remain concealed; of course, on the Day of Judgment, everything will be exposed, but even in this world, concealed things will be exposed at some point.[142] However, the universality of this is disputable since God covers many sins that his servants commit because he is *Sattār* (The One who Covers). This may be true for good deeds only as the narration says, "If a person worships behind seventy veils (so that no one knows about it), God will reveal it one day."[143]

Imam Ali is a very good example of this tradition. For sixty years, he was cursed from the pulpits throughout the Muslim lands and was the subject of numerous accusations against him. The accusations went as far as to claim that he was not even a Muslim, and he did not pray. Finally, when he was assassinated in a mosque, the propaganda against him in Syria was so revolting that some people asked, "what was Ali doing in the mosque?" However, we are all witness to how God Almighty exposed his merits. This is also the case about many past prophets and pious individuals, sometimes long after their death.

God discloses the true nature either of vicious and oppressive people, during their lifetime or afterwards, for example in the cases of Pharaoh or Yazid b. Muawiya.

فَقُلْنَا اضْرِبُوهُ بِبَعْضِهَا ۚ كَذَٰلِكَ يُحْيِي اللَّهُ الْمَوْتَىٰ وَيُرِيكُمْ آيَاتِهِ لَعَلَّكُمْ تَعْقِلُونَ ﴿73﴾

We said, 'Strike him with a piece of it' thus does God revive the dead, and He shows you His signs so that you may apply reason.

We said, 'Strike him with a piece of it,' According to the instructions set by God Almighty, they were told to strike the corpse of the murdered man with a part of the slaughtered cow. The early commentators have speculated widely about the particular part of the animal which they used to strike the corpse. Some said it was its tail, others said its tongue, others said it was its round, and some said it was a bone of it,[144] but these are all merely speculation. The *Tafsīr* attributed to Imam Askari says it was the tailbone, known as the coccyx in human beings, the small triangular bone at the base of the spinal column. It is reported from the Prophet that "All human parts will decay [after death] except one bone, the coccyx, from which the people are recreated on the Day of Resurrection."[145]

When they made contact, the murdered man was brought back to life and informed them who had killed him. Some say he lived, whilst some say he died again, as his time had come to an end; however, he was given the opportunity to name his killer.

thus does God revive the dead; There is a great sign in this verse. When someone is dead and the soul has departed from his body, it is possible that the soul may return to the body with the permission of God. Bringing the dead back to life, in this episode, seems to be limited to fresh corpses which remain intact. Nevertheless, God Almighty made the Israelites witness one of his greatest miracles and made them witness how he can bring the dead back to life. The verse indicates that if it is possible to resurrect freshly dead corpses, then it is also possible to resurrect corpses that are completely decomposed. Thus, God demonstrated a glimpse of what will happen when we are resurrected on the Day of Judgment.

However, this was not the first-time he made the Israelites witness resurrection. As previously discussed, when Prophet Moses took the seventy leaders of the Israelites to Mount Sinai, and they insisted on seeing God with their eyes, he made them die and then brought them back to life. The Israelites were fortunate (or unfortunate) to witness one of the greatest miracles of God Almighty twice in their lifetime. Witnessing such resurrection is indeed a blessing for the believers as it would increase their faith; however, it is yet another unfortunate event for the faithless, as even witnessing the miracle of resurrection failed to turn their hearts towards God, thus increasing the extent of their transgression.

Qushayri provides some interesting comments regarding this verse. He says that the Quran is based on four layers of meaning. The first layer is *al-ibāra* (the expression) – this is what we try to understand by analysing the text. Almost all commentaries and interpretations are attempts to explain the expressions of the Quran. The second layer is *al-ishāra* (the hidden allusion), the hidden meaning of all the expressions which can only be understood by the elite of the believers. The third layer is *al-latā'if* (the subtle meanings), the personal and private meanings given to those who are pure of heart such as the *awlīyā'* (saints). These meanings are not something that could be conveyed to others as their meanings are based on concepts which are not known to the general public. The fourth layer is *al-ḥaqā'iq* (the realities), which is the realities of what is conveyed by the Quran, which according to the hadith are only given to the prophets.

Mystical interpretations usually try to find *the ishārāt* hidden under the first layer of meanings. *Al-latā'if* and *al-ḥaqā'iq* cannot be captured and expressed in words. However, Qushayri, in the title of his book combines the names of the second and third layers of the meaning of the

Quran and calls it *Laṭā'if al-ishārāt.* Regarding this verse, he states that "God instructed the Israelites to slaughter an animal for the revival of the murdered man". The *ishāra* (allusion) here is that in order to revive the life of the heart, the animalistic lower self must be sacrificed.[146] The resemblance of the lower self to an animal is eloquent; the lower self, similar to animals, is always pursuing material pleasure and disregards spiritual satisfaction. The "life of heart" signifies the unveiled exposure of the heart to the divine revelation, the fulfilment of the true human purpose in this world. Qushayri then continues to say that "if you kill the animal of the heart (the lower self), it will then give life to your heart".[147]

He concludes the hidden meaning of the verse is that "anyone who wants to revive the life of their heart, can only do so once they destroy their lower self. For those who achieve this, their heart would be able to see things that others cannot. Additionally, if God wants to make someone's name known for eternity, the person should first kill his own desire for fame in this world."[148] History testifies to the truth of this; many great saints, mystics and common people who worshipped in isolation, were made famous in Christianity, Judaism and Islam. These are some deeper lessons found within the verse.

ثُمَّ قَسَتْ قُلُوبُكُم مِّنۢ بَعْدِ ذَٰلِكَ فَهِيَ كَٱلْحِجَارَةِ أَوْ أَشَدُّ قَسْوَةً ۚ وَإِنَّ مِنَ
ٱلْحِجَارَةِ لَمَا يَتَفَجَّرُ مِنْهُ ٱلْأَنْهَٰرُ ۚ وَإِنَّ مِنْهَا لَمَا يَشَّقَّقُ فَيَخْرُجُ مِنْهُ ٱلْمَآءُ ۚ
وَإِنَّ مِنْهَا لَمَا يَهْبِطُ مِنْ خَشْيَةِ ٱللَّهِ ۗ وَمَا ٱللَّهُ بِغَٰفِلٍ عَمَّا تَعْمَلُونَ ﴿74﴾

Then your hearts are hardened after that, so they are like stones or even harder. For indeed there are some stones, from which streams gush forth and indeed there are some of them that split and water issues from them and indeed there are some of them that fall for the fear of God. God is not oblivious of what you do.

Then your hearts are hardened after that; may address the Israelites who lived at the time of Prophet Moses or the Jews who lived at time of Prophet Muhammad. If it refers to the Israelites at the time of Prophet Moses, it may indicate that after God's revival of the murdered man, one of the greatest miracles of God, the hearts of the Israelites initially softened. But, then when the inspiration from this moment passed, their hearts returned to their hardened state, indicating that became disobedient and stubborn in accepting the commands of God.

However, if it refers to the Jews of Medina, it may mean upon hearing about God's abundant blessings on their forefathers, their hearts were initially softened. They then became receptive to the divine message presented by Prophet Muhammad. However, soon after, their hearts became hardened again, and they continued to reject the divine revelation.

Despite the nuance, both interpretations carry the same meaning. As noted above, if a group of people boast about their ancestors' transgressions in the eyes of God, there is no difference between the transgressors who committed the actual transgressions and their descendants who are pleased and accepting of their heritage.

It is said that the heart moves between two qualities in relation to its reaction to divine guidance: hardness (*qaswa*) and softness (*riqqa*). Hardness may also be indicated by the word "tightness" (*ḍīyq*), or the heart being closed. As the Quran mentions: *...Whoever God wishes to misguide, He hardens the heart and closes it completely...* (Q. 6:125) The closing of the heart is probably the worst punishment that one can suffer. Of course, this happens due to an individual's actions. When a heart is hardened, a person is prevented from remembering God; thus, the person cannot see or remember anything beyond this world.

There are a couple of traditions mentioned in relation to the following verse: *...Woe to those whose hearts are hard when God is mentioned...* (Q. 39:22) One tradition attributed to the Prophet, reported by both Sunni and Shi'i narrators, is mentioned in *Rawḍāt al-wā'iẓīn* by Muḥammad b. al-Ḥasan al-Fattāl al-Nīshābūrī (d. 508/1114-1115) and the Sunni version is reported by Aḥmad b. Mūsā b. Mardawayh al-Isfahanī (d. 410/1019) from Ibn Masud. The tradition reads:

> The Prophet recited this verse and said, 'when the light of guidance falls into the heart, the heart expands and opens up.' His companions said, 'is there a sign for the falling of light into the heart?' The Prophet said, 'yes, rising above the deceptive world, turning towards the eternal world, and preparing for death before it arrives.' This is the attitude of the person whose heart is open and the remembrance of God goes into his heart.[149]

The tradition articulates a sense of heightened spirituality that we may feel when we really ponder over the temporary nature of this world, and we internalise the imminence of death. In those moments, when we recite the Quran, perform our prayers and supplicate, our heart is open. Whatever worship we do is absorbed by the heart in its entirety. Conversely, the closure of the heart occurs when we are absorbed with the "needs" and pleasures of this world. If our minds are occupied in this way, then our prayers, fasting and supplications cannot penetrate our hearts. This is the hardening of the heart. Therefore, hardness of the heart occurs when the heart turns away from God towards this world. This makes the heart unreceptive to the remembrance of God. The hardness and softness of the heart are not associated with cruelty or politeness; it is concerned with the scope of understanding the purpose of life.

This tradition mentioned by Ibn Mardawayh has a similar meaning:

> When this verse was recited, we (the Companions) asked the Prophet of God how the heart opens? The Prophet replied: 'If the light enters into the heart, it opens and expands.' We asked, 'what is the sign of it?' He replied, 'Turning towards the eternal life, rising up from this deceptive world and preparation for death before its arrival.'[150]

Here, the world is described as deceptive because it tricks people into thinking that it will never end. However, this world is the means to the end, a diving board to the eternal abode. These teachings of the Prophet were echoed in the supplications of his Holy Family. The supplication of Imam Zayn al-Abidin that he recited on the night of the 27th of Ramadan includes the exact content of these two traditions. It is reported that the Imam continuously recited this supplication from sunset to sunrise: "O God, I ask you to rise above the deceptive world, and to turn towards the eternal abode, and preparation for death before it arrives."[151]

Returning to the discussion concerning the Jews addressed in this verse, God conveys to them that their hearts have completely turned towards this world, forgetting the eternal abode. They implemented the laws mentioned in the Torah scrupulously and were proud of the legacy of their forefathers and their religion, yet they were completely absorbed with love of this material world. According to a verse of the Quran, their love of the material world was so great that it even exceeded that of the polytheists who did not believe in a Hereafter at all. *You will find them the greediest for life, of all people even the idolaters. Each of them is eager to live a thousand years.* (Q. 2:96)

That is why the Quran addresses this quality in Surah Jum'ah: *Say to the Jews, if you claim that you are the friend of God, then wish for death, if you are the truthful.* (Q. 62:6) The verse clearly draws attention to their deep attachment to the material world; despite boasting that they were the friends of God and the chosen people. Therefore, there is a direct relation between the hardening of the heart and attachment to this world. Conversely, there is a direct correlation between softening of the heart and detachment from the material world.

like stone or even harder; Stone is regarded as one of the hardest substances, yet when the heart is hardened its hardness exceeds even that of stone. The way God perceives the solidity of stone is superior and more insightful to how people perceive it; the degree of hardness depends on their purpose and how they are of benefit to man. Stones, like all of God's creation, operate within a great design that God has put in place, and they execute the will of God. Hence, despite their hardness, they are extremely obedient to God. Some of them submit and let streams gush forth from them. Some are cleaved to allow water to spring from them, whereas others move and fall from their place to another appointed place. Yet the hardened hearts neither give way nor move as they are not submissive or obedient to God the way a stone is.

Just as there are different degrees of hardness of the heart, there are different degrees of softness too. There are those who are hesitant in their faith; and others whose strong faith opens their hearts to all signs of God.

The third group are those whose hearts prostrate from the fear of God; these are those pure hearts whose purity spreads to others. They are extremely pure and strongly connected to God and therefore the hearts of other believers are pulled towards them. Prophet Abraham is a very good example of such a person. The Quran describes him in the following manner:

> And [remember] when We made the House a place of reward for mankind and a sanctuary, [declaring], 'Take the venue of prayer from Abraham's Station.' We charged Abraham and Ishmael [with its upkeep, saying], 'Purify My House for those who go around it, [for] those who make it a retreat and [for] those who bow and prostrate.' (Q. 2:125)

The House was purified by the pure hearts of Prophet Abraham and Prophet Ishmael. Anyone can build a mosque, including kings and dictators. They can instruct their subordinates to build a magnificent mosque embellished with gold and silver. But that is not what God regards as a spiritual place. Prophet Abraham was instructed to build the Kabah with his own hands. Prophet Abraham was a wealthy man and could have easily employed servants to build the Kabah. Yet he came all the way from Palestine to Arabia to build the House, because it was to become a place of pure worship. A meeting place between man and God, and this required pure hands to make it. Prophet Abraham built the Kabah as a small cubic house. Since then, others have expanded it making an even greater mosque. However, that mosque continues to derive its holiness from that small house made by the hands of Prophet Abraham.

Prophet Abraham and Prophet Ishmael's hearts were pure, which made the House pure and therefore it deserved to be called The House of God. The verses of the Quran concerning this are remarkable. The call for Hajj is a call to go to Prophet Abraham rather than to the Kabah: *And proclaim the Hajj to people: they shall come to you on foot and on lean camels coming from distant places.* (Q. 22:27) This is extraordinary. The Quran describes Hajj as a call to go to Abraham. It does not call us to pray beside the Kabah, but specifically to pray where Prophet Abraham stood. *And when We made the House a place of reward for mankind and a sanctuary,* declaring, *Take the venue of prayer from Abraham's Station.* This is because *We charged Abraham and Ishmael [with its upkeep, saying], purify My House for those who come from afar and those who reside by it and for those who bow and prostrate.* (Q. 2:125) This demonstrates how pure hearts live on throughout history.

And indeed, there are some of them that fall for the fear of God. The description of stone in the next part of the verse is compelling. Do stones or mountains fear God as some human beings fear him? Some reputable modern exegetes, such as 'Alī Akbar Qurashī[152] have provided a possible natural explanation to clarify this verse, although he personally does not agree with it. He states that when water from rain and snow freeze into the grooves in rocks and stones, their volume expands and widens the grooves. Repetition of this process gradually makes the rocks shatter and fall. Fear of God here may mean submitting to the laws of nature put in place by God.

Relating this natural phenomenon to fear of God is unusual. Based on different verses of the Quran, we understand that there are aspects of nature which are hidden from us and our understanding of science. In that hidden aspect, everything has an intelligence and understanding of God. The evidence for the universal comprehension of God is found in many verses of the Quran. For example, *The seven heavens glorify Him, and the earth too, and whoever is in them. There is not a thing but celebrates His praise, but you do not understand their glorification. Indeed, He is All-forbearing, All-forgiving.* (Q. 17:44) Or regarding how rocks and mountains also fear God, the Quran states, *Had We sent down this Quran upon a mountain, you would have surely seen it humbled and go to pieces with the fear of God.* (Q. 57:21) Furthermore, it specially talks about mountains praising God with David: *Indeed, We disposed the mountains to glorify God with him at evening and dawn.* (Q. 38:18)

Prophet David's soul affected the environment around him when he was worshipping his Lord, vibrating and reverberating in such a way that the hidden aspect of these mountains was revealed, and they manifested their praise of God.[153] We also have traditions narrated in both Sunni and Shi'i sources that Prophet Muhammad was greeted by the trees, rocks and stones on his way to his seclusion in the Cave Ḥirā three years prior to becoming a Prophet. These verses and narrations make it clear that objects such as stones, mountains and all of God's creation are able to understand, praise and fear God.

أَفَتَطْمَعُونَ أَن يُؤْمِنُوا لَكُمْ وَقَدْ كَانَ فَرِيقٌ مِّنْهُمْ يَسْمَعُونَ كَلَامَ اللَّهِ ثُمَّ يُحَرِّفُونَهُ مِن بَعْدِ مَا عَقَلُوهُ وَهُمْ يَعْلَمُونَ ﴿75﴾

Are you then eager that they should believe you, though a part of them would hear the word of God and then they would distort it, after they had understood it and they knew what they were doing.

Are you then eager that they should believe you; After describing the uncompromising state of the Jews of Medina, God now addresses the believers, who were ex-pagans who always held the Jews in high regard. One of the most disheartening occurrences in Medina during the revelation, was that after the expectation that they would precede others in joining the Prophet, the Jews turned away from the Prophet despite their knowledge of the scripture. Prophet Muhammad preached that Islam was not a new religion, but a continuation of the Abrahamic religions, displaying the strong link between Islam and Judaism. Nevertheless, the Jews of Medina continued to show staunch opposition to the Prophet and his message. Furthermore, the Prophet had told his followers that he had been described in the Jewish scriptures and the Jews knew about him; therefore, the Jewish hostility against the Prophet hampered the mission of the Prophet in Medina. The previous verse described the stiffness of their hearts and how they were harder than rocks, implying that they would never accept the message. The believers had an inaccurate expectation of them, because in the past they had committed crimes which were more heinous than rejecting a new prophet.

though a part of them would hear the word of God and then they would distort it; The verse accuses the Jews of distorting the word of God while being aware of what they were doing, in order to receive meagre gain. Distorting the scripture can happen two ways – the text itself can be distorted or the *meaning* behind the scripture can be distorted. All exegetes agree that the distortion referred to in this verse is the distortion of the text within the scripture; however, they disagree about the identity of the culprits. A group of early commentators, including Ibn Abbas, Ibn Ishaq (d. 150/767) and the Mutazilite scholar Abū al-Qāsim Balkhī, believe that the accusation refers to the seventy elites of the Israelites who were chosen to go with Prophet Moses to Mount Sinai to hear the Word of God when the Torah was being revealed, and bear testimony that they heard the word of God. *Moses chose seventy men from his people for Our tryst.* (Q. 7:155) However, on their return, they changed parts of the revelation to suit their own wishes and said they had heard something different from what Prophet Moses claimed. Tusi prefers this view because the verse talks about those who *heard* the word of God and changed it, and the only people who literally *heard* the word of God were those seventy Israeli elites.[154]

However, this view is undermined by the fact that hearing the Word of God may be interpreted as indirect hearing, which could mean understanding or comprehending the word of God. Also, the verb used for "hear" is in the present tense (*yasmaʿūn*) which signifies a continuous practice. A second group of commentators including Mujahid and Suddi, believe that this is a general statement that includes all Jewish scholars who changed the text of the Bible throughout history for their own vested interests or after being bribed.[155] A third group believe that the verse refers to the Jewish scholars of Medina who had read the descriptions of Prophet Muhammad in the Torah but instead of believing in him, they distorted the text to prevent the Jews attaching themselves to him.[156] Whichever interpretation is correct, the verse is telling Muslims that they should not expect the Jews in Medina to submit to Islam while they have distorted their own Scripture, especially those parts that describe the Prophet.

after they had understood it and they knew what they were doing. This phrase clearly shows that the Israelites made deliberate decisions when they distorted the meaning and wording of the Old Testament. This was not done out of negligence, misunderstanding or ignorance.

When it comes to distorting the scripture of the Quran, Muslim scholars unanimously believe that the text of the Quran is unchanged and has been protected from distortion. This view is supported by overwhelming historical evidence. However, there have always been some marginal groups among both Shi'i and Sunni schools who have referred to some false and weak narrations or misunderstood some other traditions and have claimed alteration of the text of the Quran. There are certain narrations from Shi'i Imams who have acknowledged *taḥrīf* (distortion or falsification) of the Quran. However, *taḥrīf* does not always mean distortion of the text. In fact, the original meaning of *taḥrīf* is distortion of the meaning and this sense of the word is also used in the Quran. The *taḥrīf* in the Quran does not merely refer to changing the actual Words of God. It also refers to changing the meaning or the interpretation of the text while knowing its true meaning and interpretation. This is probably what is meant by *taḥrīf* in verses like, *Among the Jews are those who pervert words from their meanings* (Q. 4:46) and *Then, because of their breaking their covenant, We cursed them and made their hearts hard: they pervert words from their meanings and have forgotten a part of what they were reminded.* (Q. 5:13)

In this way, some Shi'is believe that some Sunnis committed *taḥrīf* of the meaning of the verses of the Quran. For example, they believe that they committed *taḥrīf* regarding the verse, *Indeed God desires to repel all impurity from you, O People of the Household, and purify you with a thorough purification.* (Q. 33:33) by changing the meaning of the "People of the Household," by also including the wives and other relatives of the Prophet to the Prophet 's own definition which limited the People of the House to his daughter Fatima, her husband Ali and their children Hasan and Husayn.

Another example is the verse *Your guardian is only God, His Apostle, and the faithful who maintain the prayer and give the zakat while bowing down,* (Q. 5:55) which was revealed about Imam Ali, but the meaning was changed and extended to all the believers. There are other similar verses of the Quran whose meaning has been changed and these changes have been considered as *taḥrīf* of the Quran by the Imams and Shi'i scholars. They believe that the reason for this distortion was to support the Sunni version of Islamic history and theology.

However, it is important to note that the Imams always rejected the idea of literal distortion of the Quran. According to Shi'i Imams and scholars, the wording of the Quran is preserved verbatim as it was revealed to the Prophet. There is no distortion in relation to its wording; the distortion is related to the *meaning* of the verses of the Quran. Those who attributed the concept of the literal distortion of the Quran to Shi'is justified it by citing the views of some of the marginal heretical groups within Shi'ism who have misunderstood the narrations of *taḥrīf*. But from the very early periods, Shi'i scholars, especially after Mufid, denounced such tendencies and considered these beliefs and groups un-Islamic.[157] However, according to the Quran, in the case of the Bible, there has been a distortion of the meaning of the verses, as well as a distortion in the literal sense by omitting and inserting words or verses into the Bible.

وَإِذَا لَقُوا الَّذِينَ آمَنُوا قَالُوا آمَنَّا وَإِذَا خَلَا بَعْضُهُمْ إِلَىٰ بَعْضٍ قَالُوا أَتُحَدِّثُونَهُم بِمَا فَتَحَ اللَّهُ عَلَيْكُمْ لِيُحَاجُّوكُم بِهِ عِندَ رَبِّكُمْ أَفَلَا تَعْقِلُونَ ﴿76﴾

When they meet the faithful they say, 'we believe,' and when they are alone with one another, they say, 'do you recount to them what God has revealed (*fataḥa*) to you, so that they may argue with you therewith before your Lord?' Do you not apply reason?

A group of people who lived in 7th century Arabia do not represent the Jews of our time, who maintain a variety of backgrounds and religious views. The Jews of Arabia who lived at the time of the Prophet tried to disrupt the Prophet of Islam and interfere with his mission. It is inaccurate and unfair to imagine that the Jews that live today, or any other religious group, would think or act in a similar way.

According to this verse, the Jews of Medina believed that because they were able to hide their true feelings and beliefs from the people, this meant they could also hide their true beliefs from God Almighty.

It may be possible that because of their isolated lifestyle around Medina, the Jews had turned into a close-knit community and were under the strong influence of tribalism. They did not seem to consider accepting Prophet Muhammad's message as a religious decision, rather for them it was a tribal and cultural matter. They believed that the Jews were a superior race, religion and culture over the Arabs and therefore did not pay serious attention to the message of the Prophet. However, some of the Jews did embrace Islam. Here, the verse rebukes the ignorant ideas of the Jews of Medina who thought that they could conceal the truth from God.

In addition to the communications that took place between the Jews and the Prophet, there was an ongoing dialogue between the Jews and ordinary Muslims. There were different alliances between the Jewish tribes and the two main Arab tribes of Aws and Khazraj as they had many economic, social and cultural ties with each other. It was natural for an ongoing dialogue to occur between them. At the time of the Prophet, the dialogue between the Jews and Muslims was taking place at different levels. The Prophet discussed with the rabbis, those who were well-educated from both sides often debated, and at a third level, the common people regularly interacted with each other and discussed current issues. Through these conversations, some of the Jews who were more sincere or open minded used to tell Muslims that "it is written in our books that a prophet will migrate to this city, and we would have liked to believe in him, but our rabbis say Muhammad is not that awaited Prophet."[158]

This acknowledgement offered the ordinary Muslims ideological support. They were reassured by the fact that *even* the Jews agreed that a prophet would migrate to Medina. Therefore, this verse refers to the dialogue between the ordinary Jewish and Muslim people. When these dialogues eventually flared up and attracted greater public attention, the rabbis condemned their people saying that they should not have informed Muslims about this knowledge in Jewish scriptures, because the rabbis considered it as exposing the Jews to criticism and questioning their integrity and honesty. They thought by revealing this information, Muslims may have an argument against them on the Day of Judgment; that they did not follow the Prophet despite their firm knowledge about the coming of a prophet. They held that if they could withhold such information from Muslims, they could dodge their responsibility of following the Prophet and, on the Day of Judgment, they would not have been held responsible for it.

what God has opened (*fataḥa*) to you; (*fataḥa Allāhu ʿalaykum);* This expression could have three possible meanings. The first meaning is "taught" (*ʿallama*), because by teaching something you open the doors to its knowledge. The second and more popular meaning is "judged" (*ḥakama*), because by judging, you unravel the hidden aspects of a case that has been complicated. In the Quran the word *fataḥa* is used mainly in this second meaning. The following verses present clear examples of the usage the word *fataḥa* to mean judgment. When Surah al-Anfāl was revealed after the Battle of Badr, the pagans were told: *If you sought a judgment [from God], the judgment (fatḥ) has certainly come to you...* (Q. 8:19) The same root word is used in Surah A'rāf... *Our Lord judge! (iftaḥ) Judge justly between us and our people! You are the best of judges.* (Q. 7:89) Therefore, if *fataḥa* means judgment, the verse renders, "Do you recount to them what God has *judged against you* (regarding Prophet Muhammad), so that they may argue with you therewith before your Lord?"

The third meaning of *fataḥa* is "*anzala*" (revealed). In this case the verse would read "do you recount to them what God has revealed to you (regarding Prophet Muhammad), so that they may argue with you therewith before your Lord?" In all cases, the verse would refer to the rabbis rebuking the ordinary Jews for informing Muslims about what God had revealed to them in the Torah about the coming of a prophet.

أَوَلَا يَعْلَمُونَ أَنَّ اللَّهَ يَعْلَمُ مَا يُسِرُّونَ وَمَا يُعْلِنُونَ ﴿77﴾

Do they not know that God knows whatever they hide and whatever they disclose?

In combination with the previous verse, this verse exposes the warped theology of the Jewish rabbis of Medina at the time of the Prophet. They seriously thought that they were able to hide things from God by not uttering them in public. This is a strange view of God, and it is not clear how they came to accept this understanding. Jewish theology is very complex, and it is beyond the scope of this book to understand the origins of such a farfetched view about God. Certainly, the Jews of the time had a different theology to Jews today or the Jews who lived in different geographical locations.

وَمِنْهُمْ أُمِّيُّونَ لَا يَعْلَمُونَ الْكِتَابَ إِلَّا أَمَانِيَّ وَإِنْ هُمْ إِلَّا يَظُنُّونَ ﴿78﴾

Among them are the ignorant (ummiyyūn) who know nothing of the Book except hearsay, and they only make conjectures.

According to Tusi most of the exegetes believe that *ummiyyūn* refers to someone who is illiterate. However, he reports another meaning from Ibn Abbas and contends that this meaning is more favourable. Ibn Abbas states that "*ummiyyūn* are a group of people who did not have a heavenly Book"; therefore, the word in this verse refers to some of the Jews with little or no knowledge of the scriptures. They were ignorant of the true teachings of the Torah and the book they read was written with their own hands, as mentioned in the next verse.[159] In general, the word *ummī* does not mean "illiterate" in the Quran, but as supported by many verses, it can mean a group of people who have not been given a scripture. For example, in the verse *Those who follow the Apostle, the uninstructed (ummī) prophet, whose mention they find written with them in the Torah and the Evangel, who bids them to do what is right and forbids them from what is wrong...* (Q. 7:157)

Prophet Muhammad was referred to as *ummī,* a title by which he was also referred in the Bible. The word *ummī* mentioned in the Bible would certainly not mean "illiterate," yet this translation has become almost standard. Being illiterate is usually a negative characteristic and God would not describe his messenger with this terminology.

A more accurate interpretation of the word *ummī* is a non-Jew or gentile. Up to the time of the Prophet, the Jews considered all the other nations as *ummī* because they did not receive a divine scripture. Muslims also believe that prophethood was placed in the progeny of Prophet Abraham. However, his progeny was not restricted to Prophet Isaac's line of descent. Ishmael was also from the progeny of Prophet Abraham. Yet, the Jews believed that Prophet Abraham's bloodline only continued through Isaac and therefore considered Ishmael's bloodline as gentiles. Prophet Muhammad is a descendant of Prophet Ishmael and so he was also referred to as a gentile. A further verse to evidence this argument is: ... *And say to those who were given the Book and those who were not given a book (ummiyyūn)...* (Q. 3:20) Here, people are divided into two categories: those who were given a scripture and those were not. *Ummiyyūn* (plural of *ummī*) refers to those who were not given a scripture, who were called gentiles.

The third example is in Surah Āl 'Imrān:

> Among the People of the Book is he who if you entrust him with a quintal will repay it to you, and among them is who, if you entrust him with a dinar will not repay it to you unless you persist over him. That is because they say, 'We have no obligation to non-Jews (*ummiyyūn*).' But they attribute lies to God, and they know [it]. (Q. 3:75)

In this verse, *ummiyyūn* does not mean illiterate, but refers to gentiles. As they were gifted with Scripture, the Jews believed that they were superior to gentiles and entitled to do anything to them, such as cheating, stealing, usurping, taking them as slaves and killing them.[160]

However, in this verse the word *ummī* is used to refer to ignorant people or those Jews with little or no understanding of the teachings of the Torah. They were only aware of the lies that they were told by those who fabricated parts of the book themselves, which led them to believe that all Jews will end up in Paradise regardless of their deeds. Having made this comment about a group of common Jews who lived in Medina, it may be important to discuss the position of the common people in every faith who may be considered in the category of *ummī* mentioned in this verse.

In every religion there are scholars, whose role is to define the theology, law and ethics of the religion. If they are responsible scholars, the common people who follow them would be guided; if not, then they would be misguided. There is a remarkable conversation between Imam Jafar al-Sadiq and one of his followers who rightly points out what this verse is really implying.

The follower asks the Imam, if it is the case that in every religion the masses follow the judgments and interpretations of clergymen, what is the difference between common Muslims and common followers of other religions? We follow our clergymen, and they follow theirs – in the end it seems that we are sheep who follow the instructions of the shepherd. God criticises such blind following of the scholars, so what is the difference? In a long and well-known tradition[161] the Imam acknowledges that there is a similarity as well as difference between Islam and the other faiths in this regard. The tradition is mentioned in the *tafsīr* of Imam Hasan al-Askari and does not have a sound chain (*mursal*). It is also mentioned in Tabrisi's *al-Iḥtijāj* without any chain of narration; thus, it is probable that the author copied it from *tafsīr* of Imam Hasan al-Askari without the chain of narration. Nevertheless, all scholars have regarded the content of this tradition credible, especially prominent scholar al-Hurr al-Amili (d. 1033/1624), who mentioned this tradition in his *Wasā'il al-shi'i*, one of the most reliable books of Shi'i jurisprudence, which makes the content of the tradition credible. The exact question which was put to Imam Jafar al-Sadiq is this:

> O son of God's Messenger, what is the reason that God flays the Jews that they cannot recognise the divine Book without hearing it from their scholars? They have no other option. Why are they censured for following the scholars in their precepts and practices? Their people are like our people who follow their learned men. If they are not allowed to accept the sayings of their learned, why is it permissible for Muslims to accept the words of their learned?

Imam Jafar al-Sadiq responds:

> Between our people and our learned and their

people and their learned there is a difference from one aspect and a similarity in another aspect. As for the similarity, God has also condemned our community in following the learned like he condemned those people but, in the instance when there is difference, there is no condemnation of people following our learned.

The man said: 'please tell me what is the reason for this?' The Imam said:

The Jew populace knew that their learned were clearly lying, consuming unlawful wealth and accepting bribes. Upon recommendation by others and through bribes they made changes in divine commands. They knew that their scholars were bigoted and because of this they even abandoned faith; when they became prejudiced against someone, they trespassed their rights and when they sanctioned support to someone, they gave away riches unjustly to outsiders and oppressed the rightful persons on his behalf.

Thus, the people knew that their scholars were guilty. But in spite of knowing that they continued to follow them. For this reason, God has censured them. Because they followed those whom they knew were corrupt. The same order is applicable to the Muslim community also that when they realise that their learned are openly involved in sins and debauchery and guilty of bigotry and greed for worldly riches

> and that they oppress those they are prejudiced against and unduly favourable to those whom they like, it becomes unlawful to follow such scholars and those who continue to follow such scholars will be like those Jews whom the Almighty God has condemned for following their learned.
>
> But those scholars who protect themselves and guard their faith, who oppose their unduly desires and who are obedient of their Lord, then the populace is obliged to follow them. And these attributes are only found in some Shiʿi scholars and not in all of them...[162]

As the tradition attributed to Imam Jafar al-Sadiq elaborates, when we read any verses of the Quran that mention previous nations such as Jews and Christians, we must question whether we are falling into the same transgressions ourselves. There is no difference in God's ruling between different nations or religious groups. Being a Muslim does not give us any privilege in the court of God. This is a great delusion and there is no support for it in the Quran or from the traditions of the Prophet. God does not have any chosen nation and does not discriminate between people and nations – he is just in all cases. Therefore, if we as Muslims commit the mistakes of the previous nations, we will also be held accountable.

فَوَيْلٌ لِّلَّذِينَ يَكْتُبُونَ الْكِتَابَ بِأَيْدِيهِمْ ثُمَّ يَقُولُونَ هَٰذَا مِنْ عِندِ
اللَّهِ لِيَشْتَرُوا بِهِ ثَمَنًا قَلِيلًا فَوَيْلٌ لَّهُم مِّمَّا كَتَبَتْ أَيْدِيهِمْ وَوَيْلٌ لَّهُم مِّمَّا
يَكْسِبُونَ ﴿79﴾

So, woe to those who write the Book with their hands and then say, 'This is from God,' that they may sell it for a paltry gain. So, woe to them for what their hands have written, and woe to them for what they earn!

The previous verse discussed the situation of the common people of the Israelites who were ignorant of the true teachings of the Torah and blindly followed their religious leaders. However, in this verse, God informs us that these common people do not bear the responsibility for their deeds. They will only be held responsible for following their scholars while knowing that they are grave sinners. The real culprits are those who distort the Book of God with their own hands, specifically those tasked with teaching and preaching the Scriptures. This verse, as well as many similar verses in the Quran, makes clear that some sections of the Old Testament were distorted.

This distortion is not exclusively in the form of physically inserting and omitting sections of the Bible. It also includes confusion between the text and the notes in the margin. Some scholars might have explained the Bible in the margins and then these explanations might have gradually been incorporated in the text.

So, woe to those who write the Book with their hands; In general, the word *wayl* (woe) carries the meaning of strong condemnation. However, some exegetes have suggested that *wayl* is a pit in Hell. When God mentions *wayl* in this verse it refers to those "who write the Book with their hands" will go to the pit of *wayl* in Hell. Razi mentions a report attributed to the Prophet about the pit of *wayl*: "It is a valley in Hell, into which the disbelievers fall, and it takes forty years for them to fall before reaching its bottom."[163]

Some exegetes have suggested that "those who write the Book with their hands," refers to those Jewish scholars who wrote commentaries on the description of the Prophet which were deliberately misleading. Their descriptions intentionally did not match Prophet Muhammad. However, they would present these commentaries as God's word and part of the original Book. They would deny that they had inserted these comments in the Book themselves.

that they may sell it for a paltry gain; The "paltry gain" referred to here is the leadership role in society which provided them with benefits such as religious alms. The arrival of the new Prophet would have certainly stripped them of these privileges. However, in the eyes of God these worldly gains and positions have no value and are insignificant in comparison to the reward and punishment of the Hereafter.

and woe to them for what they earn! may either refer generally to the sin earned through their distortion or it could refer to the religious taxes, alms, prestige, bribes or other benefits that they gathered because of their preservation of their religious leadership roles.

وَقَالُوا لَن تَمَسَّنَا النَّارُ إِلَّا أَيَّامًا مَّعْدُودَةً ۚ قُلْ أَتَّخَذْتُمْ عِندَ اللَّهِ عَهْدًا فَلَن يُخْلِفَ اللَّهُ عَهْدَهُ ۖ أَمْ تَقُولُونَ عَلَى اللَّهِ مَا لَا تَعْلَمُونَ ﴿80﴾

And they say, 'The Fire shall not touch us except for a number of days.' Say, 'Have you taken a promise from God? If so, God shall never break His promise. Or do you ascribe to God what you do not know?'

And they say, 'The Fire shall not touch us except for a number of days.' According to Fayd Kashani,[164] while some of the Jewish religious leaders were preaching their distorted description of the awaited prophet and claimed its origin was from the Torah, some other erudite Jews protested, claiming that the leaders were misleading people. In response, the Jewish religious leaders claimed that they were aware that what they were doing was wrong, but it was necessary in order to preserve their faith. The means justified the end. They perceived the Prophet and Islam as a threat to their established religion. They understood that they may have to endure fire as a result of their misdeeds, but their actions were necessary for the longevity of the Jewish community. They believed that as they were the chosen people of God their punishment would be for a limited time and they would not stay in Hell more than a few days.

As previously noted, this mentality is common in all religions. Some Muslims have the same mindset that Muslims are the chosen people and therefore, regardless of their deeds, they will avoid Hellfire. We understand that the believers will eventually receive intercession and leave Hell, but the length of time before we are released is not clear. It may take several million years before some sins are forgiven depending on their gravity. Also, it is not something guaranteed as some sins may strip a person of their faith altogether.

Further, there is a difference between knowing for certain that one would remain in Hell only for a few days and between believing in intercession. Razi reports[165] that the famous Mutazilite scholar, al-Jubbā'i, has taken this verse as evidence that God has not promised the followers of Prophet Moses that they will be able to leave Hell once they have entered within it. If this is the case, then the same must follow for Muslims as well. Al-Jubbā'i rejects that the Muslim sinners who enter Hell would come out of it by receiving intercession.

However, Razi disagrees with this view: firstly, just as the sinners from our umma are promised intercession, the sinners from other ummas are also promised intercession; what is rejected in this verse is their claim for staying only for a few days, while depending on the nature of the sin, the purification of the soul may take many thousands of years. Secondly, although we believe in intercession, it can never be *guaranteed* for any specific person. Thirdly, the people who commit enormous misdeeds cannot be regarded as believers. They believed that in the worst-case scenario, they would remain in Hell only for a few days and then they would receive intercession and would come out of it. This mindset is erroneous and self-destructive and may lead to eternal damnation regardless of religious affiliation.

The subject matter of this verse is those who completely rejected the revelation by distorting it. This distortion of revelation indicates that they deny it in its essence. This is an extreme form of sin, and the perpetrators are expected to be punished in Hell for a long time. However, those who sin on smaller scales would not be subjected to such a prolonged punishment.

When the Jewish scholars accepted that they would be punished for their actions, they were sure that it would only be for "for a number of days," simply because they were followers of Prophet Moses. According to a number of exegetes, the Jews of Medina believed that if they end up in Hell, it would be for a maximum of seven days.[166] This idea stems back to how their forefathers worshipped the cow for seven days, and thus the Jews would never be punished for more than seven days, or because the duration of creation was seven thousand years and God would punish them only one day for each thousand years.

Say, 'Have you taken a promise from God?' God asks why they think he will not punish you for more than these few days? If so, how did they receive that promise? If it was through revelation, then *God shall never break His promise*. But God never sent such a revelation, and *you ascribe to God what you do not know.*

بَلَىٰ مَن كَسَبَ سَيِّئَةً وَأَحَاطَتْ بِهِ خَطِيئَتُهُ فَأُولَٰئِكَ أَصْحَابُ النَّارِ هُمْ فِيهَا خَالِدُونَ﴿81﴾

No, it is not the case. Whoever earns evil and his sins beset him on every side, these are the inmates of the Fire, and they shall remain in it [forever].

Whoever earns evil and his sins beset him on every side, these are the inmates of the Fire; This verse is one of the outstanding verses of the Quran that sets a universal standard for entry into Heaven and Hell that governs everybody regardless of their religious affiliation. It establishes one of the fundamental principles of Islamic eschatology. The context of the verse is the evil deeds of those Jews who distorted the Torah while assuming that they were being faithful to their religion.

and they shall remain in it [forever]. The verse implies that those who commit sins but are not besieged by their evil may eventually leave Hell. In other words, the verse makes two statements about the destiny of the inhabitants of Hell: some people would remain there eternally, and others would eventually be released.

This verse introduces two key attributes that would entrap sinners in Hell eternally. The first is "earning evil". The second condition is that the earned evil must be so grave that "sin bests them on every side." Their souls are surrounded by the evil of the sin in such a manner that there would be no room for mercy to penetrate their souls.

Misdeeds and sins are actions; however, actions by themselves are not enough to keep someone in Hell eternally. Rather, it is the quality of a person's soul that matters as it has been shaped as a result of the accumulation of misdeeds that surrounded the soul and become its primary feature. Thus, if someone commits misdeeds habitually, the evil consequences of their sins gradually surround the soul and become part of its nature. They can never get rid of the confinement of evil that they have brought upon themselves and consequently will remain in Hell eternally.

Many verses of the Quran speak about the severe consequence of evil deeds which impact people even in this world. *So they were hit by the evil consequences of what they did...* (Q. 16:34) *Whatever affliction that may visit you is because of what your hands have earned, and He excuses many an offense.* (Q. 42:30) This is a general rule in this world and in the next. If we carry evil deeds with us, they become ingrained in our souls and, consequently, keep us away from God and inflict punishment upon us in this world and the next. As far as the next world is concerned, God states that when the sinners see Hell, *the evil consequences of what they used to do appears before them...* (Q. 39:48) In this world, we do not always see it, although sometimes people commit evil deeds and see the consequences of it in this world.

This process also takes place when a person commits minor sins. We may commit a sin and regard it as insignificant and by repetition it is normalised. This becomes so deeply rooted in our soul that we no longer consider it a sin and may even begin to see it as positive behaviour. For example, if a person embezzles small amounts of money from a company through some mistruths, they may over time come to the conclusion that embezzling money from large companies is harmless or even a just way to behave, because the large corporations are wealthy and do not pay their employees fairly. Therefore, a person may begin to justify their actions by believing that they are merely taking back their rightful money. The Quran describes this as a decoration of Satan, ... *Satan decorates for them what they do.* (Q. 6:43) This process eventually leads to muting of the human conscience, and it may advance to God and the Hereafter: *Then the fate of those who committed misdeeds was that they denied the signs of God and they deride them.* (Q. 30:10) This is how evil besieges a person. However, sometimes people commit misdeeds and are hit by the evil consequences of those deeds, but the evil does not take over or besiege their hearts. In other words, the misdeeds they commit are not habitual or have not yet become an attribute of the soul. In such cases, purification of the soul might be easier, and God may cleanse their heart out of his grace in this world through tests and tribulations. If it is not possible to clean the sick heart in this world, he might purify a person's heart in *barzakh* (intermediary world). Finally, if *barzakh* is also not successful, then a period of stay in Hell would purify a sick heart.

The suffering endured from a stay in Hell will break the confinement of evil. When this confinement is broken, then the person may leave.

Surah Zukhruf alludes to a test for the people of Hell to enable them to come out of Hell:

> [The people of Hell] will call, O Mālik (Manager of Hell) now ask your Lord to finish us off! He will say: No, you will remain here. However, we brought you the truth [once again] but most of you had reluctance towards it. (Q. 43:77-78)

Due to the intensity of the punishment, the people of Hell will beg

Mālik, the Manager angel of Hell, to mediate between them and God so that God may end their existence. However, God never withdraws existence after he has granted it. Instead, they are given an opportunity to leave Hell by accepting the truth that is presented to them. However, they show unwillingness to accept it, and for this reason most of them remain in Hell eternally. One may question why they would rather cease to exist than accept the truth. Denying the truth has become part of their nature and they cannot deny their nature, even if they wished to do so. It is not possible to lie or cheat in Hell. Therefore, the only way to come out of Hell is to overcome their unwillingness to accept the truth.

God is not a guard who puts people into prison at will and releases them at will. Rather, entering and leaving Hell are results of a necessary process. People enter Hell due to the consequences of their evil actions and in order to leave Hell they need to be prepared to accept the truth from God. This process is applicable regardless of a person's religious affiliation.

وَالَّذِينَ آمَنُوا وَعَمِلُوا الصَّالِحَاتِ أُولَـٰئِكَ أَصْحَابُ الْجَنَّةِ ۖ هُمْ فِيهَا خَالِدُونَ ﴿82﴾

And those who have faith and do righteous deeds – they shall be the inhabitants of Paradise; they shall remain in it [forever].

This verse confirms to the believers that so long as they have faith and perform good deeds, they will enter Paradise and remain there eternally. Unlike Hell, people do not leave Paradise; once they are entitled to enter Paradise, they would remain there forever. However, although faith and righteous deeds are mentioned here as qualifiers to enter Paradise, people must bear in mind that they are only necessary causes and not the sufficient cause. They become the sufficient cause only after they are matched by the mercy of God.

In relation to this verse, there is a long narration known as the

Questions of 'Abdullāh b. Salām. There are two prominent figures named 'Abdullāh b. Salām in Islamic history. One is the famous 'Abdullāh b. Salām from the Jewish tribe of Banu Qaynuqā, whose original name was Ḥuṣayn and who is usually mentioned in narrations. He converted to Islam in the first year of Hijra. He was promoted by the Umayyads later on because he supported Muawiya over Imam Ali. In Islamic traditions, he asks some questions from the Prophet, but the questions he asks are not significant here.

The other 'Abdullāh b. Salām was a Jewish scholar who lived in Khaybar and his original name was Ismā'īl, but the Prophet called him 'Abdullāh. He was the chief Rabbi in Khaybar, and all the other rabbis were his students. When he considered visiting the Prophet, he extracted 1404 questions from the Torah and came to Medina to scrutinize the Prophet. Most of these questions are mentioned in *Bihār al-anwār* in the section titled "Masā'il 'Abdullāh b. Salām" (the Questions of 'Abdullāh b. Salām).[167] The narration at hand shows that this man was deeply rooted in knowledge and faith. One of his questions, which is related to these verses, was regarding the necessary qualification to enter Paradise.

He asked, "What makes people deserve entering into Paradise; is it Islam, or *īmān* (faith), or their actions?" The Prophet replied, "They gain necessary [but not sufficient] qualification by faith, they enter due to the mercy of God, and they distribute it among themselves by their actions." Everyone who enters Paradise does so by the mercy of God; however, what qualifies people to receive the mercy of God in order to enter Paradise is their faith.

وَإِذْ أَخَذْنَا مِيثَاقَ بَنِي إِسْرَائِيلَ لَا تَعْبُدُونَ إِلَّا اللَّهَ وَبِالْوَالِدَيْنِ إِحْسَانًا
وَذِي الْقُرْبَىٰ وَالْيَتَامَىٰ وَالْمَسَاكِينِ وَقُولُوا لِلنَّاسِ حُسْنًا وَأَقِيمُوا
الصَّلَاةَ وَآتُوا الزَّكَاةَ ثُمَّ تَوَلَّيْتُمْ إِلَّا قَلِيلًا مِنْكُمْ وَأَنْتُمْ مُعْرِضُونَ ﴿83﴾

And when We took a pledge from the Children of Israel: 'Worship no one but God, do good to parents, relatives, orphans, and the needy, and speak kindly to people, and maintain the prayer, and give the charity,' you turned away, except a few of you, and you were disregardful.

This verse highlights the eight pledges or covenants (*mīthāq*) taken by the Children of Israel. There are two other pledges which are mentioned in the following verse that amount to ten covenants in total that the Jews were obliged to fulfil. They mostly correlate to the Ten Commandments mentioned in the Bible. However, the verses themselves do not mention these ten principles as the Ten Commandments mentioned in the Bible. The Ten Jewish Commandments which are mentioned in the Book of Exodus are as follows:

> And God spoke all these words:
>
> 2 I am the Lord your God, who brought you out of Egypt, out of the land of slavery.
>
> 3 You shall have no other gods before me.
>
> 4 You shall not make for yourself an image in the form of anything in heaven above or on the earth beneath or in the waters below. 5 You shall not bow down to them or worship them; for I, the Lord your God, am a jealous God, punishing the children for the sin of the parents to the third and fourth generation of those who hate me, 6 but showing love to a thousand generations of those who love me and keep my commandments.
>
> 7 You shall not misuse the name of

> the Lord your God, for the Lord will not hold anyone guiltless who misuses his name.
>
> 8 Remember the Sabbath day by keeping it holy. 9 Six days you shall labour and do all your work, 10 but the seventh day is a sabbath to the Lord your God. On it you shall not do any work, neither you, nor your son or daughter, nor your male or female servant, nor your animals, nor any foreigner residing in your towns. 11 For in six days the Lord made the heavens and the earth, the sea, and all that is in them, but he rested on the seventh day. Therefore, the Lord blessed the Sabbath day and made it holy.
>
> 12 Honour your father and your mother, so that you may live long in the land the Lord your God is giving you.
>
> 13 You shall not murder.
>
> 14 You shall not commit adultery.
>
> 15 You shall not steal.
>
> 16 You shall not give false testimony against your neighbour.
>
> 17 You shall not covet your neighbour's house. You shall not covet your neighbour's wife, or his male or female servant, his ox or donkey, or anything that belongs to your neighbour.168

By extending the meaning of the principles mentioned in the verses at hand, it may be possible to include the Ten Commandments as a more comprehensive approach.

The word used in the verse for pledge is *mīthāq*, which has a stronger meaning than a covenant – it is a promise taken from people which is linked to consequences of reward and punishment.

Worship no one but God; The idea of worship is one of those concepts that is easy to understand but very difficult to define. What is the meaning of worshipping God? Why is it stressed so much that you should not worship anything but God? It may be useful to discuss these questions in the light of both the Quranic and Biblical verses comparatively. Three of the Ten Commandments specifically address the issue of worshipping one God. In short, these commands state, "you shall have no other gods before me, you shall not make idols and you shall not take the name of your Lord in vain." The first two commands are self-explanatory, and "not taking the name of your Lord in vain" can alludes to sincerely following God's injunctions with actions and not just words. Readers may refer to the commentaries from Biblical scholars for interpretations of these commandments.[169]

Regarding the Quranic injunction, Razi contends that the command to worship God and none but him assumes knowledge of God and all his attributes, knowing his unicity, and impossibility of him having any equal or opposite or any children. It also presupposes knowledge of how worship should be performed, which is only known through revelation. In short, it includes everything contained in theology and Islamic law, since worship cannot be correctly established without this knowledge.[170] Although Razi is correct in principle, for an ordinary person to be aware of this knowledge in detail before starting to worship God is neither required nor possible. The essence of worship is submission to God as outlined in this verse.

There is a tradition attributed to Imam al-Baqir that explains a different aspect to the essence of worship: "God does not require anything from his servants, except two qualities; that they acknowledge his bounties so that he multiplies them and acknowledge their sins so that he forgives them."[171] The first part of the tradition mentions the ideological aspect of worship, that everything is from God Almighty and no one else. The second part focuses on the obedience through worship and practice. Kashani also eloquently defines worship. He says that worship means that you "do not compare him and his creatures, do not deviate from his commands, and do not do things that must be done for him for the sake of others."[172] He again draws attention to the two aspects of worship: ideological and practical. Kashani then mentions a tradition attributed to Imam Jafar al-Sadiq: "God has never given anything more precious to a servant than the quality that there be nothing in their heart beside God."[173]

In conclusion, the first three commandments mentioned in the Bible and the commandment mentioned in the Quran suggest that there are two aspects to worship: firstly, that you should know God ideologically and acknowledge that everything belongs to him. Secondly, that you must obey him by following his commands and avoid committing sins.

In the Ten Commandments and in the Quran, doing good to parents is mentioned immediately after worshipping God. Therefore, it is placed above every other command that God has given. For example, in Surah Isrā': *Your Lord has decreed that you would not worship anything besides Him and do good to parents.* (Q. 17:23) Doing good (*iḥsān*) to parents is a comprehensive concept which includes benevolent acts, such as giving financial and emotional support if they need it, obeying them (in anything that is not against the will of God), respecting them, and looking after them in their old age. Kulayni reports a tradition from Imam Jafar al-Sadiq regarding the meaning of doing good (*iḥsān*):

> Imam Jafar was asked, 'what is the meaning of this *iḥsān*?' He replied, 'That you be a nice company to them, and to provide for them before making them ask for it even if they are not in need. Is it not that God says, *You will never attain piety until you spend out of what you hold dear?*' (Q. 3:92)[174]

relatives, the orphans and the needy. The Quran commands that we extend doing good to these groups of people. The idea of having good relationships with blood relatives is heavily emphasised in the

Quran. If one has the means, they should look after their relatives in the same way as they would look after their parents. These acts are mentioned as part of the covenants because they are of vital importance for social cohesion. Orphans and the needy are the most vulnerable members of society. They are especially vulnerable to abuse in terms of financial matters. The Quran therefore commands us to take care of them.

It is not sufficient to simply give charity (*zakat*) or pay *khums* (payment of a fifth of acquired wealth) and consider that our obligations as Muslims have been discharged towards society. We must also implement social justice and protect the rights of the vulnerable. These covenants are universal to every Abrahamic religion; they are the building blocks of a healthy and just society where God's religion can flourish. If these principles were properly implemented, there would be a revolution in society. If Muslims fail to achieve social justice within Muslim societies, it is not due to the religion of Islam lacking in its principles. Rather, it is an indication of how Muslims are failing in our duty and responsibility towards society and evidence of how we are deviating from our faith and the guidelines God has set for us.

speak kindly to people; To "speak" is not simply a verbal action, it also includes one's behaviour, attitude and disposition. The word "people" (*nās*) in this verse is not restricted to people of a certain faith alone, but refers to people in general regardless of their faith, race and colour.

The verse at hand has an interesting structure and provides a unique insight into how God prioritises social cohesion. The main priority is to worship God, followed by social obligations prioritised in the order of parents, relatives, orphans and the needy and then finally establishing prayer and giving alms. We often do not consider social obligations as part of faith, but this verse teaches otherwise. Prayer and almsgiving have been manifested in different forms in Judaism, Christianity and in other faiths, but the core component of prayer and almsgiving is common in all monotheistic religions. This is because, for God, there is only one religion, and all the prophets have preached only that one religion, but people were unable to preserve that unity and created different faiths.

In the same way that Muslims are instructed to perform prayer and give *zakat*, the Quran quotes Jesus saying *...and God has enjoined upon me to perform prayer and give zakat as long as I remain alive.* (Q. 19:31) This was the same instruction given to Noah, Abraham and Moses; *Nothing is said to you except what has already been said earlier to the messengers before you.* (Q. 41:43)

Then you turned away, except a few of you; So far, the verse established eight principles, and there are two more principles which will be mentioned in the following verse, making ten in total. Before turning to the other two, a strong rebuke is addressed to them at the end of this verse. This draws attention to the treacherous nature of most people who first accepted the covenant, but later on, when made to choose between their own base desires and the commands from God, chose their desires over *taqwā* (Godwary-ness). However, God always acknowledges the good practice of those few who comply and excludes them from the condemned ones; "except a few of you". This is the general style of the Quran that, if there are positive examples, regardless of their numbers, their good deeds are acknowledged, and they are excluded from the condemnation of the majority.

and were disregardful. There is a beautiful emphasis within this verse. People may disobey God impulsively. However, they may return to God again and compensate for the mistake. Often, turning away from God is not a permanent state of the heart; it is as a result of a momentary decision dictated by some abnormal circumstances. However, in this case, the verse states that they "turned away" because they "were disregardful" of God and his instructions. They intentionally and wholeheartedly distanced themselves from the covenant that they had made with God and did not regard the commands of the covenant as part of their duty to him. In other words, "you turned away" is speaking of their acts, and "you were disregardful" speaks of the state of their hearts. According to this interpretation, *tawallaytum* (you turned away) refers to the Jews at the time of Moses and *wa antum mu'riḍūn,* which also may mean you turn away, refers to the Jews of Medina.[175] Hence, the statement reads as "Then you turned back except a few of you, and you (now too) turn aside."

وَإِذْ أَخَذْنَا مِيثَاقَكُمْ لَا تَسْفِكُونَ دِمَاءَكُمْ وَلَا تُخْرِجُونَ أَنفُسَكُم مِّن دِيَارِكُمْ ثُمَّ أَقْرَرْتُمْ وَأَنتُمْ تَشْهَدُونَ ﴿84﴾

And when We took a pledge from you: 'You shall not shed your [own people's] blood, and you shall not expel your folks from your homes.' Then you confessed, and you testify [to this pledge of your ancestors].

This verse mentions the remaining two injunctions that, with the previous eight, make up a total of ten instructions of the covenant. The verses remind the Jews of Medina of the covenant of God with the Jews at the time of Moses so that they do not make the mistake their forefathers committed by disregarding their covenant.

'You shall not shed your [own people's] blood, and you shall not expel your folks from your homes.' These injunctions are mentioned separately because they are of greater importance than the previous eight. These two injunctions draw attention to sectarian conflicts and other types of inter-tribal wars between the Jewish tribes that resulted in shedding blood and removing people from their homes.

'You shall not shed your [own people's] blood,' Some argue that this is a general injunction that means faithful people need to be pacifists and not engage in any type of conflict which may result in bloodshed. However, this is not congruent with what we find in the Bible and the Quran about defensive wars that the faithful are urged to support and participate in. The following verses from the Quran are evidence for that:

> How many a prophet there has been beside whom a multitude of godly men fought. They

> did not falter for what befell them in the way of God, neither did they weaken, nor did they abase themselves; and God loves the steadfast. (Q. 3:146)

> Those who are fought against are permitted to fight because they have been wronged, and God is indeed able to help them. Those who were expelled from their homes unjustly, only because they said, "God is our Lord." Had not God repulsed the people from one another, ruin would have befallen the monasteries, churches, synagogues and mosques in which God's Name is mentioned greatly. God will surely help those who help Him. Indeed, God is All-strong, All-mighty. (Q. 22:39-40)

In fact, it is impossible for any religion or worldview to remain completely pacifist whilst protecting their members from aggression. Of course, allowing aggression and waging unprovoked wars is completely forbidden. God only allows defensive wars for the believers and shedding blood is only sanctioned in specific circumstances.

However, this verse is not a general statement. It addresses intra-religious wars and conflicts which mostly occurred as a result of sectarianism or tribalism. The Jews of Medina occasionally usurped each other's lands with the help of the pagan tribes of Medina when internal conflicts broke out. The verse reminds them that their ancestors took a covenant that internal wars should not be waged in order to take land from other Jewish tribes or groups. This verse indicates that they confessed and testified that this pledge had been taken from them. Although this verse is talking about the Jews, it can also logically be extended to Muslims. It can warn us about sectarian conflict in the Muslim world. God also took the same pledge from Muslims in the verse *The believers are brothers and so make peace between your brothers.*

(Q. 49:10) and *Hold firmly to the rope of God all of you, and do not become divided.* (Q. 3:103) Thus, it is a general injunction from God for the faithful, that they must not fight amongst themselves.

In conclusion, this series of verses challenges the view held by the Jews of Medina that they would only briefly stay in Hell regardless of their actions. In return, God reminds them of their forefathers' misdeeds and their disregard for the covenant, and that the Jews of Medina were following this path of their forefathers. However, as emphasised previously, it would be a mistake to assume that these verses only rebuke the Jews. The covenant is valid for all the faithful – including Muslims.

ثُمَّ أَنتُمْ هَٰؤُلَاءِ تَقْتُلُونَ أَنفُسَكُمْ وَتُخْرِجُونَ فَرِيقًا مِّنكُم مِّن
دِيَارِهِمْ تَظَاهَرُونَ عَلَيْهِم بِالْإِثْمِ وَالْعُدْوَانِ وَإِن يَأْتُوكُمْ أُسَارَىٰ
تُفَادُوهُمْ وَهُوَ مُحَرَّمٌ عَلَيْكُمْ إِخْرَاجُهُمْ أَفَتُؤْمِنُونَ بِبَعْضِ الْكِتَابِ
وَتَكْفُرُونَ بِبَعْضٍ فَمَا جَزَاءُ مَن يَفْعَلُ ذَٰلِكَ مِنكُمْ إِلَّا خِزْيٌ فِي الْحَيَاةِ
الدُّنْيَا وَيَوْمَ الْقِيَامَةِ يُرَدُّونَ إِلَىٰ أَشَدِّ الْعَذَابِ وَمَا اللَّهُ بِغَافِلٍ عَمَّا
تَعْمَلُونَ ﴿85﴾

Then there you were, killing your folks and expelling a part of your folks from their homes, backing one another against them in sin and aggression! And if they came to you as captives, you would ransom them, though their expulsion itself was forbidden to you. What! Do you believe in part of the Book and defy another part? So, what is the requital of those of you who do that except disgrace in the life of this world? And on the Day of Resurrection, they shall be consigned to the severest punishment. And God is not oblivious of what you do.

This verse refers to how the different Jewish tribes in Medina broke the covenant. Of course, the Quran refers to the Jews of Medina as an example for humanity to learn from and so the conclusions deduced from the verse are applicable to humanity in general.

There were three main Jewish tribes in Medina; *Banū Naḍīr, Banū Qurayẓa* and *Banū Qaynuqā'*. Each of these tribes had forged allegiances with the pagan Arab tribes in Medina, either with *Banū Aws* or *Banū Khazraj*. According to al-Suddi,[176] the famous exegete of the second generation of Muslims, one of the main alliances was between *Banū Qurayẓa* and *Banū Aws*. Another alliance was between *Banū Naḍīr* and *Banū Khazraj*. Whenever there was a war between *Banū Aws* or *Banū Khazraj*, their Jewish allies, *Banū Naḍīr* and *Banū Qurayẓa* also fought alongside with them. These wars were fierce and brutal and resulted in members of the Jewish tribes killing and capturing each other. Interestingly, if there were captives from one of these Jewish tribes in these wars, both tribes together raised ransom money to free the Jewish captives. This is because they believed that God told them in their Scripture that if there was a Jewish captive, they were obligated to free him, regardless of his tribal affiliation. This is a peculiar mindset, and this verse also considers it strange as it emphasises the irrational argument of the Jews. They saw no problem in breaching these covenants, but wanted to preserve the section of the covenant which instructs them to free the captives; this is inconsistent, *And if they came to you as captives, you would ransom them, though their expulsion itself was forbidden to you. What! Do you believe in part of the Book and defy another part?*

Early Muslim sources state that the people of Medina also found the practice of the Jews to be inconsistent, and they would deride them for it. "How is it that you fight them and then ransom them by your own money?" They would reply, "Because we are instructed to ransom them." They were then told, "Why then do you fight them in the first place?" They would say, "Because we feel embarrassed to despise our allies."[177] The wars that took place between *Banū Aws* and *Banū Khazraj* were related to power struggles, and they posed no threat to the Jewish tribes. Yet, the Jews participated in these wars for worldly gains and did not hesitate to kill their fellow Jews. Ironically they sought to free their captives.

Do you believe in part of the Book and defy another part? It may be difficult to understand the unusual practices of the Jewish tribes in Medina, but these examples highlight their belief in only parts of the Scripture and disbelief in other parts. Their religion was a cherry-picking process of accepting what was convenient and rejecting the rest. This verse suggests that the Jewish practice of striving hard to secure the release of Jewish captives was a matter of convenience and they would participate in these wars against their fellow Jewish tribes to gain further power in Medina - but it was not morally acceptable to do so ,because they were killing and driving out their fellow Jews. Therefore, they made an extraordinary effort to comply with some parts of their Scripture, at least. This partial belief has no value in the eyes of God and amounts to complete disbelief.

There is a tradition in *al-Kāfī* attributed to Imam Jafar al-Sadiq in which he defines different types of disbelief:

> The fourth type of disbelief is to abandon what God has enjoined. The evidence for that is the verse (he recited this verse). Then said: 'God attributed them to disbelief, because they did not follow what God had ordered them. Also, He attributed them to faith, but he did not accept this faith from them.'[178]

By making this statement, Imam Jafar al-Sadiq highlights a very important aspect of faith; that just because somebody *claims* that they are a Muslim, Jew or Christian, they may not be regarded as such in the eyes of God. This is especially so if the person disregards core injunctions of the Book for their own convenience. Therefore, there may be some who call themselves Muslims, Jews and Christians who are in reality disbelievers.

In the end, God alone will be the judge of who is a true believer; therefore, if certain people or groups identify themselves with Islam or other Abrahamic religions, we must accept their proclamation because they fulfil the legal requirement of embracing Abrahamic religions. Therefore, upon accepting Islam, regardless of how they practice their religion, regardless of what kind of faith they have, we have to consider them as Muslims; and the same is true for other faiths. This mindset should be sufficient to stop any sectarian and religious conflict and make social interaction between different followers of a faith smooth and easy. However, we should bear in mind that God will have his own judgment, which will be at a higher level to the basic legal rules set for worldly interactions to establish peace and harmony among people. On the Day of Judgment, God will reveal the true nature of people. Consequently, if some consider themselves Muslims and disregard God's injunctions for personal reasons, then they would be considered disbelievers and they will receive the appropriate treatment. It is not our place to judge people in this world, or to label certain individuals or groups as disbelievers due to their unconventional views and practices about religion.

So, what is the requital of those of you who do that except disgrace in the life of this world? Here it is clear that "disgrace" is the ultimate consequence of sectarian wars. Moreover, if members of a religion fight with each other for worldly gains, as with the Jews of Medina, they would receive the severest punishment on the Day of Judgment, as the verse states.

and on the Day of Resurrection, they shall be consigned to the severest punishment. When the Quran mentions forms of punishment, it uses certain expressions such as "severe punishment", "the severest punishment", "painful punishment". These expressions draw attention to the different degrees of punishment that are inflicted on people based upon the different types of evil they committed. The sectarian conflict described in this verse deserves "the severest punishment" even though perpetrators of these crimes are believers. Therefore, we may say that followers of the Abrahamic religions may face far greater punishments than those disbelievers who have not committed such crimes.

God is not oblivious of what you do. The verse ends with this concise and powerful line. It is not possible to trick God.

أُولَـٰئِكَ الَّذِينَ اشْتَرَوُا الْحَيَاةَ الدُّنْيَا بِالْآخِرَةِ ۖ فَلَا يُخَفَّفُ عَنْهُمُ الْعَذَابُ وَلَا هُمْ يُنصَرُونَ ﴿86﴾

They are the ones who bought the life of this world for the Hereafter; so their punishment shall not be lightened, nor will they be helped.

This verse recounts the misdeeds of the Israelites again in an effort to warn the Jews of Medina not to making the same mistakes that their forefathers made. But the greater implication of this verse is that it also warns *mankind* not to make these similar mistakes. This verse likens those Jews who killed and expelled their fellow brothers and sisters in religion as having sold their Hereafter in exchange for the life of this world, for wealth, money, power, and prejudice. They sold their Hereafter by disregarding the commands of God.

so, their punishment shall not be lightened; This verse suggests that it is possible for the punishment in Hell to be lightened for certain people after some time. The punishment in Hell is a cleansing process and needs to be endured to decrease the person's evil characteristics. Therefore, as their evil nature begins to diminish, the punishment they are subjected to will begin to lighten. The punishment in Hell is not a static process; it has a nature that corresponds to the depth of evil that is ingrained in the human soul. If there is no change in the attitude of the soul, then the punishment would remain the same.

However, this verse states that the punishment would not be lightened for those who commit the crime of sectarian violence for worldly gain. This is not because God wants to be harsh on them, rather it is an indication of how this act creates a deeply rooted and incurable illnesses in the hearts of people. They use faith as a pretext to commit evil acts and such vicious deeds would inevitably lead their soul to a terrible state. Thus, they would not be able to rid themselves of the evil, even through an extensive process of purging of their evil in Hell and so their punishment would remain the same.

There is a thought-provoking tradition in this regard, attributed to the Prophet, pointing out the parallels between the Jews and Muslims.

> When the verse Q. 2:87 was revealed about the Jews who broke their covenant with God, and denied and killed their prophets, the Messenger of God said, 'Should I not inform you about the people who are like the Jews in this nation (*umma*)?' His companions said, 'Yes, inform us O Messenger of God!' The Prophet said, 'A group of my nation claim that they are of my faith. Yet, they will kill the best of my progeny and change my law and my *Sunna*, and they will kill my sons Hasan and Husayn in the same way that predecessors of the Jews killed Prophets Zechariah and John the Baptist. God would curse them in the same way that he cursed Jews [who killed their prophets].'[179]

In this way, Yazid b. Muawiya (d. 25/646) and his cohorts ruled Muslims after his father's death for three years. During his short reign, in the first year he killed Imam Husayn, and the second year he attacked the city of Medina killing thousands of people, including 1,700 first- and second-generation Muslims. In the third year, he destroyed the Kabah, the House of God. Given these heinous crimes, how will God deal with them on the Day of Judgment?

If some Jews killed the prophets of God for their worldly gain and some Muslims killed the progeny of the Prophet for their worldly gains, why should God treat them differently? There is no reason that God would treat Muslims or any other nation with special favour. Therefore, Muslims always need to take lessons and take heed when we read verses regarding past nations. Muslims should not have the false impression that these verses are about the Jews alone and not also related to us.

وَلَقَدْ آتَيْنَا مُوسَى الْكِتَابَ وَقَفَّيْنَا مِن بَعْدِهِ بِالرُّسُلِ وَآتَيْنَا عِيسَى
ابْنَ مَرْيَمَ الْبَيِّنَاتِ وَأَيَّدْنَاهُ بِرُوحِ الْقُدُسِ أَفَكُلَّمَا جَاءَكُمْ رَسُولٌ بِمَا لَا
تَهْوَىٰ أَنفُسُكُمُ اسْتَكْبَرْتُمْ فَفَرِيقًا كَذَّبْتُمْ وَفَرِيقًا تَقْتُلُونَ ﴿87﴾

Certainly, We gave Moses the Book, and followed him with the apostles, and We gave Jesus, the son of Mary, manifest proofs, and confirmed him with the Holy Spirit. Is it not that whenever an apostle brought you (Jews) that which was not to your liking, you would act arrogantly; so, you would impugn a part [of them], and slay another part?

Certainly, We gave Moses the Book, and followed him with the apostles; God sent the prophets after Moses to protect the true interpretation and understanding of the Book. In the same way, Shi'is believe that after Prophet Muhammad, God appointed Imams with inspired knowledge to protect the true meaning of the Quran. Based on the previous examples, we understand that God does not send down a divine Book to people and then leave them to practice it in any way they want. The Imams were charged with the duty of explaining the Quran and teaching people how to practice it. The same was true for the prophets who came between Moses and Jesus.

and We gave Jesus, the son of Mary, manifest proofs; Amongst prophets that God sent to the Jews after Prophet Moses was Prophet Jesus, but he was not like other prophets. He was like Prophet Moses, who came with great miracles, proofs and, of course, a Book. God supported him with the Holy Spirit as well. 'Manifest proofs' describe the miracles given to Prophet Jesus:

> O Jesus son of Mary, remember My blessing upon you and upon your mother, when I strengthened you with the Holy Spirit, so you would speak to the people in the cradle and in adulthood, and when I taught you the Book

> and wisdom, the Torah and the Evangel, and when you would create from clay the form of a bird, with My leave, and you would breathe into it and it would become a bird, with My leave; and you would heal the blind and the leper, with My leave, and you would raise the dead, with My leave; and when I held off [the evil of] the Children of Israel from you when you brought them manifest proofs, whereat the faithless among them said, 'This is nothing but plain magic.' (Q. 5:110)

and confirmed him with the Holy Spirit. There are different views among Quranic commentators regarding the Holy Spirit.[180] The most plausible interpretation is that it refers to Angel Gabriel. This is confirmed when comparing the following two verses. The first is Q. 2:97: *Say, 'Whoever is an enemy of Gabriel [should know that] it is he who has brought it down on your heart with the will of God.'* The second is: Q. 16:102: *Say, the Holy Spirit has brought it (the Quran) down duly from your Lord to fortify those who have faith and as a guidance and good news for Muslims.* Angel Gabriel is also called the Trustworthy Spirit as in Q. 26:192-194: *This is indeed [a Book] sent down by the Lord of all the worlds, brought down by the Trustworthy Spirit upon your heart so that you may be one of the warners.*

The question that may arise here is that if the Holy Spirit is Angel Gabriel, then he was a messenger of God to many prophets. Yet Jesus is singled out as having been confirmed by the Holy Spirit. The explanation may be that Angel Gabriel not only brought the message of God to Jesus, but he also supported him in performing miracles and had a special connection to Jesus, the like of which was not found with any other prophet.

you would impugn a part [of them], and slay another part? God then asks the Jews of Medina to pass a judgment on their forefathers. Do they condone the behaviour of their ancestors who either denied the prophets or killed them when they did not like what they preached? This may also act as an indication to Muslims in Medina who always admired to the Jews and were now perplexed by their denial of the Prophet of Islam. This verse shows that this is not the first time the Jews had denied the truth of a prophet; their history is full of denial and murder of prophets.

وَقَالُوا قُلُوبُنَا غُلْفٌ ۚ بَل لَّعَنَهُمُ اللَّهُ بِكُفْرِهِمْ فَقَلِيلًا مَّا يُؤْمِنُونَ ﴿88﴾

And they say, 'Our hearts are uncircumcised (covered).' Rather God has cursed them for their unfaith, little do they believe.

And they say, 'Our hearts are uncircumcised (covered).' Here "uncircumcised (covered)" is rendered *ghulf* in Arabic. Depending on how *ghulf* is translated this verse can have one of three meanings.[181] The first meaning of ghulf is *ghilāf* which is to case or envelope. Therefore, they would have said, "our hearts are like an empty encasement; it is void of any knowledge that you are a prophet."

The second meaning is to take *ghulf* as the plural of *aghlaf*, meaning uncircumcised. All commentators have mentioned this meaning and Tabatabai has preferred it over other interpretations.[182] It simply means that "our hearts are covered from what you tell us, so, we cannot understand anything you say." It is like the statement of the pagans when they said to the Prophet, *'Our hearts are in veils [which shut them off] from what you invite us to, and there is a deafness in our ears, and there is a curtain between us and you. So, act [as your faith requires]; we too are acting [according to our own.]'* (Q. 41:5)

By claiming that God put their hearts under a covering, the Jews put the burden of responsibility for their rejection of the Prophet onto God himself. Like an uncircumcised person who has a cover on his flesh created by God, they wanted to argue that the cover on their hearts was created by God too and they could not hear any call except from Moses. They claimed that this was beyond their choice because their hearts were created uncircumcised. That is why God has refuted their control by saying: *Nay! Rather God has set a seal upon them owing to their disbelief, so they shall not believe except a little.* (Q 4:155)

The third meaning of the word was mentioned by Abū Bakr al-Aṣam (d. 220/843),[183] a prominent Mutazilite scholar and exegete of the Quran. Great Sunni and Shi'i exegetes such as Razi, Tabrisi and Tusi often referred to his views in their works. Al-Aṣam reads the word as "*ghulufun*" (sing. *ghilāf*) instead of "*ghulfun.*" *Ghilāf* in this sense means a filled encasement. Thus, the meaning would be "our heart is a container full of knowledge, thus how is it that we do not understand what you (the Prophet) say?" They are saying to the Prophet that his teachings are against their religious sources from where they had acquired their knowledge, and so it would be impossible to ever believe in him.

God has cursed them for their unfaith; that the phrase confirms that the reason their hearts could not accept the truth of the Prophet was due to God, but not in the way that they argued. Rather, God had cursed them for their unfaith, which meant that they were unable to believe. It is important to remember that this curse was due to their voluntary disbelief.

The curse of God is put on people as a punishment for those who do wicked acts – it is a natural consequence of their misdeeds. There are numerous examples of this in the Quran:

> Indeed, those who conceal what We have sent down of manifest proofs and guidance, after We have clarified it in the Book for mankind, they shall be cursed by God and cursed by the cursers. (Q. 2:159);

> How shall God guide a people who have disbelieved after their faith and after bearing witness that the Apostle is true, and after manifest proofs had come to them? God does not guide

> the wrongdoing lot. Their requital is that there shall be upon them the curse of God, the angels, and all mankind. (Q. 3: 86-87);
>
> Then, because of their breaking their covenant, We cursed them and made their hearts hard. (Q. 5:13)

These are but a few examples, and they are mainly about the Jews who denied the truth while they knew it was the truth and concealed it from their people.

A prominent practice amongst Shiʿi Muslims is to ritually curse the murderers of Imam Husayn,[184] however some people oppose this practice of cursing. Shiʿis argue that just as God curses the Jews who killed his messengers, it must be equally correct to curse the killers of Imam Husayn. His only aim was to preserve the true teachings of the Quran and the practices of his grandfather, Prophet Muhammad. Furthermore, God curses some believers of the scriptures who failed to follow what was written in their scripture when they were asked to do so.

little do they believe. (*fa qalīlan mā yuʾminūn*); This may mean that only a small number of them believed while the majority rejected the faith. Or it may mean faith does not enter their hearts except a minute amount; they reject the most important articles of faith and only believe in superficial aspects of religion. There may be many Muslims who also fall into this category of having little or superficial faith. Such people, whether they are Jews or Muslims, only believe and practice the cursory aspects of the religion and reject the more important and deeper aspects. This understanding of religion is not acceptable to God, and so they are treated as faithless on the Day of Judgment. However, it is important to note that legally they are regarded as Muslims, and they deserve to enjoy the full rights of a Muslim in society.

وَلَمَّا جَاءَهُمْ كِتَابٌ مِنْ عِنْدِ اللَّهِ مُصَدِّقٌ لِمَا مَعَهُمْ وَكَانُوا مِنْ قَبْلُ يَسْتَفْتِحُونَ عَلَى الَّذِينَ كَفَرُوا فَلَمَّا جَاءَهُمْ مَا عَرَفُوا كَفَرُوا بِهِ فَلَعْنَةُ اللَّهِ عَلَى الْكَافِرِينَ ﴿89﴾

And when there came to them a Book from God, confirming that which is with them – and earlier they would pray for victory over the pagans – so when there came to them what they recognised, they defied it. So may the curse of God be on the faithless!

Briefly covering the history of the Jews of Medina enables a greater understanding of this verse. In a tradition included in both *al-Kāfī*[185] and *Tafsīr al-ʿayyāshī,* Imam Jafar al-Sadiq presents one of the best accounts of the history of the Jews of Medina. He says that the Jews had read in their scriptures that the last Prophet will migrate to a place in northern Arabia between [the Mountains of] ʿAyr and Uḥud (the city of Medina). We do not know which one of the Jewish scriptures the tradition is referring to, but it is probable that these scriptures were lost over time. According to the same report, a large group of Jews were being oppressed in their cities. They were looking for a place to migrate to and moved to this area. The exact reason why these Jews abandoned their homeland is not known, but it is likely that they had already made their decision to leave their lands and it was appealing for them to move to the land where the appearance of the last prophet was promised. We also do not know when exactly this exodus occurred. It may have been after the massacre of Jews by Nebuchadnezzar around 600 BC or after the conquest of Jerusalem by the Romans about 70 CE.

When they arrived, they found a mountain called Ḥadād and assumed that this was the distorted name of Uḥud, the place mentioned in their scriptures. They decided to settle in different places around Mount Ḥadād and wait for the last promised prophet. Some of them camped at Taymā, which is between Khaybar and what later became Yathrib (Medina). By this time, they were still unsure of their location and had not yet found mount Uḥud. Some of them camped and built their town in Khaybar and others settled in Fadak, which is near Khaybar.

After their settlement, the group who were in Taymā decided to visit their fellow brethren in Khaybar. They hired some camels from a *badawī* (nomadic Arab). The nomadic Arab told them that there is only one way to get there and that was between [the Mountains of] 'Ayr and Uḥud. The name was immediately familiar: this was the place they had been searching for. They told the nomadic Arab that he should inform them when they arrive between the mountains of 'Ayr and Uḥud. When they arrived there, they decided to abandon their trip and settle there. They also sent letters out to other Jews who had scattered around the area to inform them that they have found the place they had been searching for. They then settled in the area and begin farming and trading, and they flourished, becoming significantly wealthier than the Jews of Khaybar.

At the time, the area belonged to the Kingdom of Yemen or *Qawmi Tubba'* as they are named in the Quran (Q. 44:37), which was one of the greatest kingdoms in the world. When the king of Yemen heard about the wealth of the Jews of Yathrib, he travelled there with his army to fight them. However, the Jews had built fortified castles which had strengthened their position. Their castles stood tall until the arrival of the Prophet, when they were conquered by the Muslims. Despite their strength, the Jews could not defeat the Yemeni army, and were besieged by them. The siege lasted a long time, and the Yemeni army ran out of food themselves. In addition to soldiers, there were women, children and some weak people who had scarce food supplies among the Yemeni army. The Jews were very soft hearted at the time. Sometimes at night they would throw food from the castles to the vulnerable people in the Yemeni army.

When the king of Yemen found out about these acts of kindness, he decided to negotiate with the Jews instead of fighting them. He told them, "I have heard you are kind-hearted people and I do not wish to fight with you, but this land is very rich and belongs to me. I would like to settle down here and exploit its wealth." The Jews replied that they came there to wait for the last Prophet, and in their scriptures, there is no information about a king settling down in the area, thus it may not be possible for him to do so. The king replied that, instead he would like to leave two of his trusted tribes, who were participating in the siege of the Jewish castles, so that they would help the Prophet whenever he arrives. He then lifted the siege and left the two Yemeni tribes, who came to be known as Banū Aws and Banū Khazraj in Yathrib.[186] Therefore, historically, both Banū Aws and Banū Khazraj originated in Yemen, but the Jews migrated there before the tribes of Banū Aws and Banū Khazraj.[187] There is conformity between the historical accounts and the account of Imam Jafar.

The Banū Aws and Banū Khazraj were intelligent and resourceful; they utilised the land and its assets to flourish rapidly. They quickly accumulated great wealth and soon overtook the Jews in the area. They began to exploit the Jews and fought over the control of resources around the city. During these tensions, the Jews kept reminding Banū Aws and Banū Khazraj that "we are here for the coming of our promised Prophet and we will be the victors when he comes." They prayed to God to send the Prophet sooner to give them victory over the pagans. This is the meaning mentioned in the verse: "and earlier they would pray for victory over the pagans."

What happened after the arrival of the Prophet is one of the greatest ironies in history. When the Prophet came, Banū Aws and Banū Khazraj quickly embraced Islam – they went to the Prophet themselves and invited him to the city of Yathrib, renaming it as Madīna al-Nabī (City of the Prophet) in his honour. They followed him with great passion, sacrificing everything they held dear in the way of Islam. On the other hand the Jews, whose very purpose of settling in the area was to wait for the Prophet, opposed him outright. They had been praying to God to expedite the coming of the Prophet so that he would lead them in victory over Banū Aws and Banū Khazraj, but "when there came to them what they recognised, they defied it."

The expectation of the Jews in Yathrib prior to the arrival of the Prophet indicates that the Jews had an incorrect ideology about the

Prophet. They wanted him to be someone who would serve their worldly ambitions, rather than a guide who would lead them to eternal salvation. They wanted a sectarian Prophet who would kill and destroy all the enemies of the Jews. They did not expect a prophet for all of humanity, who would not discriminate between Jews and non-Jews. When we read the verses in their historical context, the confrontation and hostility of the Jews towards the Prophet in Medina becomes illogical. Although the Jews had been well informed about the Prophet before his arrival to Medina, they resisted following him because he did not meet their warped expectation. Thus, the account of Imam Jafar al-Sadiq about the origins of the Jews of Medina is significant in this regard.

And when there came to them a Book from God, confirming that which is with them; Refers to the Torah and the confirmation of the Torah as a Book of God. The Quran does not confirm everything written in the Torah, especially the distorted stories about the previous prophets, as well as any statements that negate monotheism or promote the superiority of the Jews. Furthermore, there are some rulings in the Torah which the Quran then admonishes. In principle, the Quran confirms that the Jews received the scripture of the Torah which was sent to them by God.

Despite this, most exegetes have an alternative explanation. They have argued that the verse refers to the description of the Prophet given in the Torah, thus the Jews were familiar with the description of the Prophet. But they still rejected him because he was a gentile and wanted to redistribute their privileges and authority.

so may the curse of God be on the faithless! Here God shows a strong reaction to this rejection and disbelief. Curse (*la'na*) has been mentioned several times in the Surah. As it is explained by Razi, to curse is to remove the blessings of the Hereafter, as deprivation of blessings in this world alone cannot be called a curse.[188] A person may be blessed with all the amenities of this world, yet they may still be cursed.

There may be a number of reasons why the blessings of the Hereafter are taken away from someone; for example, in Surah Nūr, *Those who accuse chaste and unwary faithful women shall be cursed in this world and the Hereafter...* (Q. 24:23) Here a person can bring a curse upon themselves. This particular verse is about Muslims who make false allegations. The curse in this world refers to a loss of faith due to the gravity of their bad actions. In this case, they ruined the reputation of an innocent person and as a result, they evoke the curse of God. Even if Muslims fulfil their obligatory and recommended acts, making false accusations would result in God not accepting their prayers because they are cursed. Although the curse in this world is mentioned, its main consequences will be realised in the Hereafter.

In his commentary on the verse, Razi makes a compelling connection. He states that God mentions in the Quran, *...speak good to people...* (Q. 2:83), yet in this verse, he curses people and teaches us to also curse such people. God also mentions in the Quran, *Do not insult those whom they invoke besides God...* (Q. 6:108), thus clarifying that we are not even allowed to insult the false gods of the polytheists. Razi then questions whether there is any inconsistency in God's teachings. In response to his own query, Razi contends that there are general statements in the Quran which are qualified by other statements. In this case God qualifies the general statement of not insulting others by invoking a curse on those who commit these misdeeds. In such a case cursing becomes a recommended act due to the gravity of the act.

Ghazali in *Iḥyā' 'ulūm al-dīn* (The Revival of the Religious Sciences), in the section of *āfāt al-lisān* (Defects of the Tongue) notes that one of the defects of the tongue is cursing others. He goes as far as to say that although he does not approve of the deeds of Yazid b. Muawiya, nonetheless he does not like cursing him.[189] As we see, this is against Razi's position that when there is a matter of distortion of the faith, one should not simply remain indifferent. In this regard, Razi has a more tenable position than Ghazali. It is good to purify the tongue from all sorts of curse and insult, but there are exemptions to this rule. As the Quran states, for certain people, *Their requital is that there shall be upon them the curse of God, the angels, and all mankind.* (Q. 3:87) Another example of how some have been cursed by the prophets can be found in Surah Maidah, *The faithless among the Children of Israel were cursed on the tongue of David and Jesus son of Mary. That, because they would disobey, and they used to commit transgression.* (Q. 5:78)

It is interesting to note that Abu al-Qasim Khoei (d. 1992), one of the most prominent Shi'i scholars of the 20th century, has expressed his surprise that Ghazali permits cursing the *Rāfiḍa,*[190] the Khawārij and the Jews, but does not permit cursing Yazid.[191]

بِئْسَمَا اشْتَرَوْا بِهِ أَنفُسَهُمْ أَن يَكْفُرُوا بِمَا أَنزَلَ اللَّهُ بَغْيًا أَن يُنَزِّلَ اللَّهُ مِن
فَضْلِهِ عَلَىٰ مَن يَشَاءُ مِنْ عِبَادِهِ فَبَاءُوا بِغَضَبٍ عَلَىٰ غَضَبٍ وَلِلْكَافِرِينَ
عَذَابٌ مُّهِينٌ ﴿90﴾

Evil is that for which they have sold their souls, by defying what God has sent down, out of envy, that God should bestow His grace on any of His servants that He wishes. Thus, they earned wrath upon wrath, and there is a humiliating punishment for the faithless.

This verse continues with the description of the Jews of Medina who rejected the Prophet of Islam, despite his description being mentioned in their Book.

Evil is that for which they have sold their souls, by defying what God has sent down; This refers to the Jews' rejection of the Quran and equates this rejection to selling their souls for the transitory gains of this world. This is because by refusing to accept the message of God, they were able to continue their way of life which provided them with some worldly benefits, especially for the leaders and scholars of the Jewish community in Medina. But they sacrificed the eternal benefits of the Hereafter for this paltry gain.

Our souls are our capital, and there is a strong emphasis in the Quran and traditions that we should take great care of our souls and invest in them in the greatest way possible. This investment will lead to an abundance of spiritual and physical profit in the Hereafter. There is a narration attributed to Imam Ali that draws attention to the significance of this matter: "Beware that your souls have no price less than Paradise, so do not sell it cheaper."[192] Many times, we sell our souls for the price of a fleeting pleasure, worthless ambition, or futile aspiration. These might give us temporary pleasures and a sense of self-satisfaction, but ultimately these are the acts that may destroy our soul and bar us from entering Paradise and receiving eternal happiness and satisfaction.

Out of envy, that God should bestow His grace on any of His servants; Here, envy is mentioned as their motivation for rejecting God's Message. The Jews were aware that the Prophet was the awaited Messenger of God, yet they rejected him because he was not a Jew and because they were envious that someone from the children of Prophet Ishmael was given this grace. This jealousy may have been intensified by their assumption that a Jewish Prophet would have been more lenient on them, in the sense that he would not have interfered with the power of the existing Jewish leadership, nor would he have caused obstacles for their unscrupulous activities. It may be that they were longing for a Jewish prophet with nepotistic religious teachings.

Envy is one of the most dangerous human vices that can lead to the destruction of individuals, groups and entire nations. In Surah Shūrā, God states that envy is the main motivator behind most religious disputes and conflicts: *They [people of the previous faiths] did not become divided until after the knowledge had come to them, out of envy among themselves...* (Q. 42:14) Some people have ravenous ambitions which leads them to desire the positions that others (who may be more qualified than them) may occupy. Some people also desire to rule over others, which leads to a conflict of interest. Many times, religion is used as the pretext for these divisions and conflicts occurring. Sunnis and Shi'is have also acted wrongly under the influence of envy, even amongst those who are seemingly religious.

Aḥmad b. Hilāl al-Karkhī (d. 267/880) was a religious individual who was riddled with envy. He was a close companion of Imam al-Hadi and Imam al-Askari. He then became the companion of 'Uthmān b. Sa'īd al-'Amrī (d. circa 257/880), the first deputy of Imam al-Mahdi, but later denied the deputyship of his son Muḥammad b. 'Uthmān (d. 305/917). He was known to be a committed and pious person; he went to Pilgrimage fifty-four times; twenty times on foot. He even used to display some *karāmāt* (supernatural powers). However, when the second deputy was appointed, he thought that he was more deserving of the leadership position, so he rejected the deputyship of Muḥammad b. 'Uthmān and declared himself as the deputy without any mandate from the Imam.

Therefore, we should not assume that only people of weak faith are susceptible to envy; people of great position and commitment are also vulnerable if they lose control of their lower self. When such people slip from their elevated statuses, the consequences are extremely severe. Therefore, it is important to monitor ourselves with the contemplation of death and fear of God to ensure our intentions are sincere and that envy does not enter our hearts.

God bestows His grace on any of His servants that He wishes. God's response to the Jews of Medina and any other envious people is clear. It is not *people* who determine whom God should bestow his grace upon. God may grant his grace to people from different communities, social classes, races or genders. Sometimes he might grant his grace to the least expected person because of their spiritual capacity and achievements. People may be unaware of these qualities: only God knows our souls and we should not be surprised or be driven by envy.

thus, they earned wrath upon wrath; Muslim exegetes have expressed various ideas to explain the phrase; some have said the first wrath was due to their disbelief in the Torah and the second wrath was due to their rejection of the Quran.[193] Others have said that the first wrath was a result of their rejection of Jesus and the second was a result of their rejection of Prophet Muhammad. However, some have argued that earning wrath upon wrath alludes to the continuous misdeeds of the Jews, since the time of Moses until the time of Prophet Muhammad. It does not specifically refer to two individual wraths but instead indicates the continuous wrath of God upon the Jews because of their continuous misdeeds.[194]

and there is a humiliating punishment for the faithless. God promises them a humiliating punishment as a result of earning God's wrath. Interestingly, not all punishments are humiliating; for example, the punishment for greed is that people do not remember God and the Hereafter, but this is not an outwardly humiliating punishment. However, there are certain punishments, such as those mentioned in this verse, that would be humiliating on the Day of Judgment. Only God knows what those punishments will be.

In conclusion, all the verses that mention God's reprimand, wrath, punishment and humiliation were directed towards the Jews of Medina who were believers. Therefore, it is important to remember that Muslims who also call themselves believers will not be saved by the label they give themselves or by virtue of the fact that they call themselves followers of the Prophet. God is just and will judge people based on their merit. In the verses mentioned, God calls those Jews "disbelievers" and he may also call some Muslims the same if they commit the same mistakes and the same sins.

وَإِذَا قِيلَ لَهُمْ آمِنُوا بِمَا أَنزَلَ اللَّهُ قَالُوا نُؤْمِنُ بِمَا أُنزِلَ عَلَيْنَا وَيَكْفُرُونَ
بِمَا وَرَاءَهُ وَهُوَ الْحَقُّ مُصَدِّقًا لِّمَا مَعَهُمْ قُلْ فَلِمَ تَقْتُلُونَ أَنبِيَاءَ اللَّهِ مِن قَبْلُ
إِن كُنتُم مُّؤْمِنِينَ ﴿91﴾

When they are told, 'Believe in what God has sent down,' they say, 'We believe in what was sent down to us,' and they disbelieve what is besides it, though it is the truth confirming what is with them. Say, 'Then why would you kill the prophets of God formerly, should you be faithful?'

In this verse, God challenges the prejudices of the Jews of Medina again. They rejected the Prophet on the grounds that he was not a Jewish Prophet, even though the Prophet's message confirmed many teachings of the Torah.

'Then why would you kill the prophets of God formerly, should you be faithful?' Now God points out the lack of sincerity in their arguments. This accusation refers to their forefathers who killed many Jewish prophets sent after Moses. Therefore, their argument was simply an excuse to justify rejecting the Prophet. There is a tradition in *Tafsīr al-'ayyāshī* attributed to Imam Jafar al-Sadiq about this verse in which he states that:

> this verse was revealed about the Jews of Medina who lived at the time of the Prophet. They themselves did not kill any prophet; their forefathers killed the prophets. Yet they were held responsible for the actions of their forefathers and were rebuked for it. This is because by rejecting Prophet Muhammad, they followed the same path as their forefathers and were proud of their actions.[195]

The following two verses highlight the disobedience of the Jewish forefathers towards Moses, a Jewish prophet.

وَلَقَدْ جَاءَكُم مُّوسَىٰ بِالْبَيِّنَاتِ ثُمَّ اتَّخَذْتُمُ الْعِجْلَ مِن بَعْدِهِ وَأَنتُمْ ظَالِمُونَ ﴿92﴾

Certainly, Moses brought you manifest proofs, but then you took up the Calf in his absence, and you were wrongdoers.

These events have already been mentioned in this surah. In this case, the story is framed within a different context. The Jews claimed that they will only believe in their own prophets; therefore, God is reminding them of these two incidences which display how their forefathers disobeyed their own prophet. These episodes were first mentioned in relation to the ungratefulness of the Jews; however, this time it is mentioned to show their dishonesty. They killed most of their prophets and only believed in Prophet Moses. However, even in the case of Moses, when his meeting with God was prolonged for ten days, the Israelites ceased to believe in him and took the calf as their god instead.

وَإِذْ أَخَذْنَا مِيثَاقَكُمْ وَرَفَعْنَا فَوْقَكُمُ الطُّورَ خُذُوا مَا آتَيْنَاكُمْ
بِقُوَّةٍ وَاسْمَعُوا قَالُوا سَمِعْنَا وَعَصَيْنَا وَأُشْرِبُوا فِي قُلُوبِهِمُ الْعِجْلَ بِكُفْرِهِمْ
قُلْ بِئْسَمَا يَأْمُرُكُمْ بِهِ إِيمَانُكُمْ إِنْ كُنْتُمْ مُؤْمِنِينَ ﴿93﴾

And when We took covenant with you and raised the Mount above you [declaring], 'Hold on with power to what We have given you and listen!' They said, 'We hear, and disobey,' and their hearts had been imbued with [the love of] the Calf, due to their faithlessness. Say, 'Evil is that to which your faith prompts you, should you be faithful!'

And raised the Mount above you; This verse alludes to one of the most bizarre events in the history of religion. As it was discussed in the verse 63, when the followers of Moses did not comply with the injunction of their revealed Book, a mountain was raised above them. It is not clear when and where this incident happened, and which mount was raised above them. Apparently, after the Torah was revealed, many of the Israelites did not find its contents and injunctions desirable and asked Prophet Moses to change those rulings or bring another Book for them. This is similar to what the pagans of Mecca asked the Prophet: *When Our communications are recited to them, those who do not expect to encounter Us say, 'Bring a Quran other than this, or alter it.' Say, 'I may not alter it of my own accord. I follow only what is revealed to me.'* (Q. 10:15)

Prophet Moses asked God to help him against his disobedient followers, since they did not listen to any logic or argument.[196] God wanted to show them that they may not argue with the revelation, instead they must accept what has been revealed by the All-Powerful, All-Wise. Raising the mount on top of their heads was not meant to force them to believe unwillingly, as compulsion in faith is not possible (Q. 2:256), and as this verse testifies when they said, "we hear" but in their hearts they wanted to "disobey." Rather it was to stop them creating discord by continuously objecting to the Torah.

Commentators have expressed different views regarding the Mount. Some have said that it was Mount Sinai where Moses received revelation.[197] Others have said it was just a mount nearby.[198] Mullā Fatḥullāh Kāshānī (d. 988/1580), the famous Persian commentator of the 10th/16th century, names it as the Mount of Ibn Ismā'īl in Palestine.[199] Likewise, Muqātil b. Sulaymān said that it was a mount in the Holy Land.[200] However, what is important for the Quran is the event and its implications.

Hold on with power to what We have given you and listen! Taking the contents of the Book lightly means to act upon them in a way that makes a mockery of the commands narrated in the Book. This happens in every religion. Muslims also make the same mistake. Sometimes, the way in which they practice some rulings of our faith makes a mockery of them: Muslims search for loopholes in the laws of God and try to circumvent God's injunctions. Behaviour like this makes a mockery of God's instructions. For example, due to wisdom related to the overall good of society, God has placed the right of divorce in the hands of men. However, he warns to not practice this right in a manner which becomes a mockery of the law:

> When you divorce women and they complete their term, then either retain them honourably or release them honourably, and do not retain them maliciously in order that you may transgress; and whoever does that certainly wrongs himself. Do not take the communications of God for a mockery. (Q. 2:231)

This is when men use that right unduly, neither keeping nor

divorcing their wives, causing them to suffer.

They said, 'We hear, and disobey.' There are two views[201] regarding this statement. A group of commentators believe that these were the actual words said in mockery of Prophet Moses. Another group believe that they said, "we hear" out of fear as the mount was raised over their heads and it was about to fall on them, at the same time their hearts said "we disobey". The first view is improbable since in that moment of fear they would not have uttered a statement of disobedience. The verse is not referring to what they uttered with their mouth, but what they thought and believed in their minds and hearts. Their attitude was that "we hear but we will not follow the instructions."[202]

Sayyid Qutb (d. 1966) in *Fī ẓilāl al-qur'ān* provides a different view. He agrees that they said, "we hear," but argues that they neither said "we disobey" by their tongues nor in their hearts. Rather they *showed* that disobedience later through their actions. He contends that this expression articulates the principal foundation of Islam which gives value to actions over words.[203]

Their hearts had been imbued with [the love of] the Calf, due to their faithlessness. This statement draws attention to the Israelites' deep attachment to the love of the calf that they used to worship in Egypt and later in the absence of Moses. The attachment led them to disregard the instructions of God.

they were given to drink the love of the Calf; (*ushribū fī qulūbihum al-'ijla*). The Arabic expression used to describe the love of the calf is very distinct. Some exegetes[204] have highlighted that there is a subtle but important difference between the way the body absorbs what is eaten and drunk. When we eat, the food is not often completely absorbed by our body. Consequently, when we eat, some of the food may be expelled from the body as it is not fully absorbed. However, fluids are absorbed differently: when we drink something, it is absorbed by the deepest cells of our body. Similarly, the love for the calf had penetrated the deepest parts of the Israelites' minds and hearts in Egypt. Despite the fact that Prophet Moses forbade them from worshipping the calf, they still felt an attachment to it. Sayyid Qutb is fascinated by this expression. He writes,

> The sarcasm and the severity of the image are unmistakable. They were forcibly made to drink something nasty; but what is it? It is nothing other than the calf, which is shown to be forced into their hearts. It is easy to get carried away by this image so as to almost overlook the real significance of the metaphor used here. It shows their love and adoration for the calf to be so strong that it runs in their veins. Such powerful imagery is but one tool of the inimitable Quranic style.[205]

due to their faithlessness; This is the reason for their love of the calf. They did not sincerely believe in God as they should in a monotheistic framework. Instead, they believed in God's physical qualities but could not believe in a transcendent God. They also believed that worship could be offered to other than God.[206] That is why throughout history they also worshipped idols. The Quran refers to their adoration of Baal, the great deity of the Canaanites. *And Elijah was from among the messengers. When he said to his people, 'Will you not fear God? Do you call upon Baal and leave the best of creators?'* (Q. 37:123-125)

Say, 'Evil is that to which your faith prompts you, should you be faithful!' This refers to the instructions of their "evil faith" including – killing prophets, breaking God's covenant, outwardly believing by the tongue and rejecting by the heart and through action and worshipping other than God.

قُلْ إِن كَانَتْ لَكُمُ الدَّارُ الْآخِرَةُ عِندَ اللَّهِ خَالِصَةً مِّن دُونِ النَّاسِ فَتَمَنَّوُا الْمَوْتَ إِن كُنتُمْ صَادِقِينَ ﴿94﴾

Say, 'If the abode of Hereafter with God were exclusively for you, and not for other people, then long for death, should you be truthful.'

Say, 'If the abode of Hereafter with God were exclusively for you, and not for other people...' One of the false beliefs of the Israelites was that they had the exclusive right to enter Heaven. Christians also held the view that Christians alone would enter Heaven: *And they say, 'No one shall enter Paradise except one who is a Jew or a Christian.' Those are their [false] hopes! Say, 'Produce your evidence, should you be truthful.'* (Q. 2:111) Many Muslims fall into the same exclusivist trap by assuming that only Muslims would enter Heaven. The common view of these elitist ideas is that aside from the selected group, everyone else would go to Hell. However, Q. 2:111 clearly expresses that these views are misguided.

'...then long for death, should you be truthful.' Yet again, God challenges this misconception that only a select group of people will enter Heaven. The verse asks: if the Jews were so certain that only they would enter Heaven, why were they so attached to this world? Instead, they should long for death in order to reach their abode in Heaven. But they never wished for death because they would be made accountable for the sins that they have committed. By challenging their claims, God lays bare the deepest desires of their souls.

One may question the desirability of longing for death even if one is guaranteed a place in Paradise. It is reported from the Prophet that, "None of you should wish to die because of sufferings that visit them. Rather, they must say, 'my Lord keep me alive if life is better for me and make me die if death is better for me.'"[207] This is true; however, the verse is challenging the confused state of mind of the Jews of

Medina. On one hand, they believed that Heaven belonged to them exclusively, on the other hand they were afraid of the grave sins they were committing. This is also mentioned elsewhere in the Quran: *The Jews and the Christians say, 'We are God's children and His beloved ones.' Say, 'then why does He punish you for your sins?' Rather you are humans from among His creatures.* (Q. 5:18)

It is reported that in the Battle of Siffin, Imam Ali told his son Imam Hasan: "Your father does not care if death meets him, or he meets death."[208] This is the position of a true believer. A believer would not wish for death but would always be prepared and ready to embrace it. They would feel that this world is a prison for them and that they are waiting for their prison sentence to come to an end so that they can be set free.

The Jews of Medina feared death, and here God is challenging their twisted thinking by exposing that, deep down in their hearts, they do not truly believe in what they claim. If they had firmly believed in it, they would have overcome their fear of death and longed to meet God sooner.

وَلَن يَتَمَنَّوْهُ أَبَدًا بِمَا قَدَّمَتْ أَيْدِيهِمْ ۗ وَاللَّهُ عَلِيمٌ بِالظَّالِمِينَ ﴿95﴾

But they will not long for it ever because of what their hands have sent ahead, and God knows best the wrongdoers.

---

because of what their hands have sent ahead; This is a metaphorical reference to their deeds. According to Tabatabai, this sentence counts every deed as having been done by the hands; and it ascribes the action of "sending forth" to the hands while in fact it is the man who sends his deeds forth. The actions of a person, and especially habitual actions, are a clear mirror of s person's subconscious personality. Evil deeds expose the evil nature of the doer; and this nature does not look forward to meeting its Lord or staying in the abode of his friends.[209]

وَلَتَجِدَنَّهُمْ أَحْرَصَ النَّاسِ عَلَىٰ حَيَاةٍ وَمِنَ الَّذِينَ أَشْرَكُوا ۚ يَوَدُّ أَحَدُهُمْ لَوْ يُعَمَّرُ أَلْفَ سَنَةٍ وَمَا هُوَ بِمُزَحْزِحِهِ مِنَ الْعَذَابِ أَنْ يُعَمَّرَ ۗ وَاللَّهُ بَصِيرٌ بِمَا يَعْمَلُونَ ﴿96﴾

Surely, you will find them the greediest for life, of all people - even the idolaters. Each of them is eager to live a thousand years, though it would not deliver him from the punishment, were he to live [that long]. And God sees best what they do.

Surely, you will find them the greediest for life; In the verse at hand, God exposes their inner attitude to this world and the Hereafter. Based on the Arabic grammar, we understand that *ʿalā ḥayātin* "for any life" refers to any type of life in this world regardless of quality, honour, and dignity. Even though their tongues claim that they are friends of God, that they are loved by God, that they are his chosen people, and Paradise belongs to them exclusively; their hearts do not believe in what their tongues express.

of all people - even the idolaters; Therefore, they are greedy for any type of life to such an extent that this greed even surpasses the greed of the pagans who do not even believe in life after death. Understandably, someone who does not believe in the Hereafter clings to this life as much as they can. Yet the pagans were not as greedy for this world as the Jews of Medina. Such an insatiable greed for the world inevitably led some Jewish sects to completely deny the existence of the Hereafter, such as the Essenes and Sadducees. Sayyid Qutb writes,

> Besides being a belief in God's absolute justice and his most gracious reward, belief in the Hereafter is an expression of the value and vigour of life itself, not confined to, or restricted by, the limits of this world. It links man's existence to a life that goes far beyond this one, to

> reach spheres and realms the edges of which are known only to God Almighty.[210]

Each of them is eager to live a thousand years; This statement measures their greed for the life of this world. "A thousand years" refers to a great number and does not literally mean that they wished to live a thousand years. In Arabic, it is the highest denomination which is described by a single word. It indicates that they wished to live in this world forever, without any accountability.

though it would not deliver him from the punishment, were he to live [that long]; This reminds us that living longer does not ward off whatever is due and there is no escape from God's justice.

Tusi in *Tafsīr al-tibyān* questions the difference between those Jews who did not wish to die and Muslims who have the same attitude. Why does God only reprimand the Jews for not longing for death, while not saying anything about Muslims who have the same approach towards death? The answer Tusi gives to this question is that there is a difference between Muslim and Jewish attitudes towards death. Faithful Muslims do not believe that they have exclusive access to Heaven, and they do not believe that they will go to Heaven purely because they are Muslims.

According to faithful Muslims, it is their deeds which would take them to Heaven or Hell. Hence, they are always fearful of the Day of Judgment, not knowing what their destiny will be. They continually seek forgiveness and remain between hope and fear. This is alluded to in some verses in the Quran: *And those who give whatever they give while their hearts tremble with awe that they are going to return to their Lord.* (Q. 23:60) Furthermore, this verse describes those who have faith to be "apprehensive" of the Day of Judgment: those who do not believe in it (Day of Judgment) ask to hasten it, but those who have faith are apprehensive of it, while know that it is true. *Look! Indeed, those who are in doubt about the Hour are surely in extreme error.* (Q. 42:18)

Based on an examination of this verse and explanations from Tusi, we may conclude that if some Muslims believe that only Muslims would enter Heaven, regardless of their deeds, and become attached to the life of this world, they would be in the same position as the Jews of Medina. God is not interested in labels; calling yourself a Jew, Christian or Muslim does not change the reality. In the eyes of God, actions, thoughts, and intentions of individuals are important. What distinguishes Muslims from others is that they have believed in the last Prophet of God and follow him, while others have rejected him.

قُلْ مَن كَانَ عَدُوًّا لِّجِبْرِيلَ فَإِنَّهُ نَزَّلَهُ عَلَىٰ قَلْبِكَ بِإِذْنِ اللَّهِ مُصَدِّقًا لِّمَا بَيْنَ يَدَيْهِ وَهُدًى وَبُشْرَىٰ لِلْمُؤْمِنِينَ ﴿97﴾

Say, 'Whoever is an enemy of Gabriel [should know that] it is he who has brought it down on your heart with the will of God, confirming what has been [revealed] before it, and as a guidance and good news to the faithful.'

Initially, this verse seems to be out of context; the previous verses mention the defiance of the Israelites and Jews of Medina; their attitude towards worldly life and the Hereafter and their claims about their exclusive right to the grace of God and Heaven. This verse seems to suddenly shift attention to an enmity against Archangel Gabriel. However, this is in fact a continuation of the previous criticisms of the Israelites: that they would only accept faith based on their own terms and conditions. The Israelites has expected that their favourite archangel, Michael, and not Gabriel would bring the revelation to the awaited Prophet. It is this same mentality that made them long for a non-gentile prophet to deliver God's message and guide them.

Many exegetes in this regard accepted the *asbāb al-nuzūl* (the occasions, context, and cause of revelation) for this verse. These occasions of revelation are often problematic, as it is very difficult to establish the accuracy of the relevant traditions, but in this case, seeking a deeper understanding from the *asbāb al-nuzūl* may help to make better sense of the verse at hand.

According to tradition, there was a prominent Jewish scholar among the Jews of Fadak named ʿAbdullāh b. Ṣūriyā. He led a delegation of Jewish scholars from Fadak to meet the Prophet and question him about his religion to verify if he was the promised Prophet whom they had been awaiting. ʿAbdullāh b. Ṣūriyā asked the Prophet several questions. Those relevant to this discussion are mentioned below.

He asked the Prophet, "Tell us about your sleep; we have been informed about the sleep of the prophet who comes at the end of time." The Prophet replied: "My eyes sleep, but my heart is awake." The heart of the Prophet is not supposed to be sleeping, instead it is constantly engaging in the remembrance of God and may even receive revelation while sleeping. ʿAbdullāh b. Ṣūriyā and his companions were pleased with this answer because, reportedly, they had a similar description in their scriptures. After asking more questions, they asked about the description of God. "Tell us about your Lord," they said. In the answer, the Prophet recited Surah Ikhlas: *Say, 'He is God, the One. God is the All-embracing. He neither begat, nor was begotten, nor has He any equal.'* ʿAbdullāh b. Ṣūriyā and his companions were pleased again.[211]

He then told the Prophet they had only one more question to ask and if the Prophet gave them the "right" answer, they would believe in him. "Which angel brings you the revelation?" He asked. "Gabriel," the Prophet replied. ʿAbdullāh b. Ṣūriyā was displeased with this answer saying, "Gabriel is our enemy, he is the messenger of killing, fighting and ferocity, while Angel Michael descends with ease and prosperity. We would have believed in you if Michael would have brought you revelation."[212]

If this tradition is authentic, this is the most unacceptable pretext for refusing a prophet. It is preposterous to assume that the believers can determine which angel should bring revelations from God. Some exegetes[213] have argued that this belief exemplifies the influence of the Greco-Roman and Egyptian belief systems on the Jewish faith. According to these belief systems, some angels were deities and had independent agendas and ambitions. Therefore, the Jews of this time assumed that if Archangel Michael delivered the message to the

Prophet, it would have been more favourable for them.

The verse highlights the fact that Gabriel does not do anything of his own accord and the Prophet is not the one who decides which angel brings the revelation. Gabriel only executes the will of God. Therefore, it is not possible for believers to consider him as an enemy. In the Quran, Archangel Gabriel is known as *rūḥ al-amīn* (the Trustworthy Spirit) (Q. 26:193) and *rūḥ al-quds* (the Holy Spirit) (Q. 16:102).

It is he who has brought it down on your heart with the will of God; It is reported in traditions that Gabriel came to the Prophet with revelations in the form of a human being. This was a means to ease the burden of revelation for the Prophet. Sometimes he saw Gabriel in his angelic form, but this did not happen frequently; perhaps no more than twice, as mentioned in Q. 53:6-15. There were two other types of revelation received by the Prophet: direct revelation into his heart and hearing a voice from behind a veil. These three types are mentioned in Surah Shura: *It is not possible for any human that God should speak to him except through revelation or from behind a curtain or send a messenger who reveals by His permission whatever He wishes. Indeed, He is All-exalted, All-wise.* (Q. 42:51)

Direct revelation weighed heavily on the Prophet because it required an upliftment from his human realm to a higher realm. This is challenging given the restrictions of the physical body, and so the Prophet often fainted or showed signs of tension with this type of revelation. He also heard the speech of God from behind a veil, during the Ascension (*mi'rāj*). However, the easiest way to receive the revelation was the first method; instead of the Prophet moving up to the higher realms, Gabriel descended to a lower realm, appearing to the Prophet in human form. Even when Gabriel appeared in human form speaking the revelation to the Prophet, it was not received by his ears but into his heart. While Gabriel recited the verses of the Quran to the Prophet, he also embedded the depth of its meanings into his heart as the verse says, *It was brought down by the Trustworthy Spirit upon your heart so that you may be one of the warners.* (Q. 26:193-194) It is worth noting that "heart" is used in the Quran to indicate a non-physical part of the human personality that receives and understands. It does not refer to the physical human organ. The heart according to the Quran is the centre of human perception.[214]

confirming what has been [revealed] before it; The verse challenges, in passing, the criticism of the Jews of Medina against Gabriel whom they viewed as their enemy. God uses a simple yet effective second argument to refute their claim against his trusted Archangel. This revelation confirms and conforms with what was revealed before it in the Torah.

and as a guidance and good news to the faithful. The argument continues. According to Tabatabai, the verses contain four replies to their arrogance in denial of the Quran:

Firstly, Gabriel has revealed the Quran to the Prophet's heart by God's Command, not by Gabriel's own wish. Therefore, even if they feel enmity towards Gabriel, it should not prevent them from believing in the revelation. Secondly, the revelation confirms the Divine Book which was revealed before it and which they have in their hands. Thirdly, it is a guidance for those who believe in it. Lastly, it is also good news for the believers. Thus, how can a sane person turn his face away from guidance and good news, even if it is brought to him by a supposed enemy of his?[215]

مَن كَانَ عَدُوًّا لِّلَّهِ وَمَلَائِكَتِهِ وَرُسُلِهِ وَجِبْرِيلَ وَمِيكَالَ فَإِنَّ اللَّهَ عَدُوٌّ لِّلْكَافِرِينَ ﴿98﴾

Whoever is an enemy of God, His angels and His apostles, and Gabriel and Michael [let him know that], God is indeed the enemy of the faithless.

The Jews of Medina made it clear to the Prophet that Gabriel was their enemy. In response, God told them that Gabriel is purely the executer of his will; Gabriel has no free will of his own to convey the message of God.[216] If they believe that Gabriel was working for his own benefit and not acting on God's behalf, then they must have seen Gabriel as a deity. Of course, they knew that Gabriel was not a deity, but were using this issue to voice their disappointment with God's choice of a gentile prophet rather than a Jewish prophet. Gabriel was targeted because the message to a gentile Prophet was sent through him. They were jealous and bitter, and this clouded their judgment, which in turn led them to reject the Messenger of God.

This is a common human reaction - in the face of disappointment or calamity, we say things that show animosity towards the decisions of God; "Why did this happen to me?" or "Why did God let it to happen?" This attitude begins to generate a feeling of bitterness and animosity in our heart against God. In the same vein, the attitude of the Jews was a flagrant demonstration of their animosity towards God. Once a person harbours animosity towards God, they display this animosity towards the agents of God too.

and Gabriel and Michael [let him know that]; In return, of course, God and his agents would be their enemy too. Michael is mentioned specifically in the verse to draw attention to the claim of the Jews of Medina that if the angel Michael had brought the revelation, they would have believed in it. One might question how the Jews of Medina would have responded if Michael had brought down a revelation that was not to their liking.

God is indeed the enemy of the faithless. This seems to be a harsh statement. God being an enemy of someone is the greatest disaster that can befall a person. God creates an individual, nurtures, sustains and provides for them, but after investing so much in an individual, he can still become their enemy. This is because our relationship with God is reciprocal; once an individual becomes an enemy of God, they manifest animosity with their actions – it does not remain a mere feeling but advances into evil manifestations. As such, God, his agents and the believers becomes the enemy of these people. This is like what the Quran states: *O you who have faith! Be wary of God, and abandon [all claims to] what remains of usury, should you be faithful. And if you* *do not, then be informed of a war from God and His Apostle. And if you repent, then you will have your principal, neither harming others, nor suffering harm.* (Q. 2:278-279)

Here, the very act of taking interest makes one an enemy of God and at war with him.

وَلَقَدْ أَنزَلْنَا إِلَيْكَ آيَاتٍ بَيِّنَاتٍ ۖ وَمَا يَكْفُرُ بِهَا إِلَّا الْفَاسِقُونَ ﴿99﴾

We have certainly sent down manifest signs to you, and none disbelieves in them except transgressors.

We have certainly sent down manifest signs to you; This verse is the continuation of what was discussed earlier concerning the animosity of the Jews of Medina towards Gabriel. It mentions that God sent down "manifest signs" for people. In the Quran, this expression often refers to miracles, but in each case, the context of the verse needs to be taken into consideration. In some other verses, the phrase "manifest signs" may refer to clear rational arguments communicated to the people through the verses of the Quran. In this context, it seems the expression "manifest signs" means the signs or description about the Prophet Muhammad that had been revealed to the Jews in their scriptures. Given that the main argument of the Jews of Medina against the Prophet was that he was a gentile, these verses challenge that perception by emphasising that they had the clear description of the Prophet and that being a gentile is not a reason to reject him.

and none disbelieves in them except the transgressors. The verse then goes on to explain the cause of their disbelief. In this context, "transgressors" (*fāsiqūn*) refer to those who had strayed out of the Jewish faith. Anyone who was truly following the Jewish scripture would have accepted the promised Prophet and followed his instructions.

It is ironic how the most traditional Jews of the time were the transgressors. They had a keen interest in meticulously following the traditions of Judaism and for this very reason refused to believe in the promised Prophet. Consequently, God called them "transgressors." This is because if you reject one part of the faith, in essence, you have rejected all of it: you are discriminating between God's commands and therefore it is considered a rejection of the faith in its entirety. Consequently, this verse is a lesson for Muslims too. We may take some parts of the religion and reject parts; this is sufficient to qualify someone as among the transgressors. A transgressor often fails to pass God's test by rejecting certain parts of the faith, especially the ones that go against their interests or way of thinking.

أَوَكُلَّمَا عَاهَدُوا عَهْدًا نَّبَذَهُ فَرِيقٌ مِّنْهُم ۚ بَلْ أَكْثَرُهُمْ لَا يُؤْمِنُونَ ﴿100﴾

Is it not that whenever they made a covenant, a group of them would break it? Rather the majority of them do not have faith.

Is it not that whenever they made a covenant, a group of them would break it? This verse is related to the covenants and treaties that the Prophet made with the Jews, on his arrival in Medina. These treaties mandated peace between Muslims and Jews in Medina. One after another of the Jewish tribes violated this covenant; first *Banū Qaynuqa* then *Banū Naḍīr* and finally *Banū Qurayza*. They also violated the treaty which is often referred to as the Constitution of Medina, alongside numerous other pledges that were made to the Prophet. It may also refer to the history of Jews. This was evident when they broke the covenant they made with God on Mount Sinai, and the numerous withdrawn pledges with prophets and patriarchs, as well as in their breach of the treaty they had made with the Prophet.[217]

Honouring treaties and pledges is one of the core components of every religion. The first aspect is to honour the pledge or covenant one makes with God. The second aspect is related to social covenants and contracts that establish and control a person's status in society. The Jews in Medina, despite respecting their tribal treaties and alliances, did not respect their covenants with the Prophet. This mindset is not exclusive to the Jews of Medina; rather, people of every faith, have thought that they are entitled to break covenants and treaties that they make with people without faith. This is a flagrant violation of the teachings of the Abrahamic religions, and a clear example of the misuse of faith for personal gain. Thus, the Jews of Medina wanted to take advantage of their religion by breaking their covenants when it suited them. This was usually against people who they deemed to be of inferior faith. The following verse exposes them and portrays God's reaction to it:

> And among the People of the Book is he who, if you entrust him with a quintal will repay it to you, and among them is he who, if you entrust him with a dinar will not repay it to you unless you stand persistently over him. That is because they say, 'We have no obligation to the non-Jews.' But they attribute lies to God, and they know [it]. (Q. 3:75)

whenever they made a covenant, a group of them would break it? Here, "a group of them" is referred to because *the majority of them do not have faith*. The verse, therefore, draws attention to an important aspect of man's attitude towards faith. Although they superficially appear to believe in God and his injunctions, faith had not penetrated deep into their hearts. Following traditions and customs does not imply true faith. The Jews in Medina implemented the outward rituals of the faith meticulously, and even convinced themselves that they were the true followers of the faith. The corruption, superficiality and even the breaches in covenants became normalised in society.

وَلَمَّا جَاءَهُمْ رَسُولٌ مِّنْ عِندِ اللَّهِ مُصَدِّقٌ لِّمَا مَعَهُمْ نَبَذَ فَرِيقٌ مِّنَ الَّذِينَ
أُوتُوا الْكِتَابَ كِتَابَ اللَّهِ وَرَاءَ ظُهُورِهِمْ كَأَنَّهُمْ لَا يَعْلَمُونَ ﴿101﴾

> And when there came to them an apostle from God, confirming that which is with them, a part of those who were given the Book cast the Book of God behind their back, as if they did not know [that it is the Book of God].

And when there came to them an Apostle from God; The "apostle" here refers exclusively to Prophet Muhammad. The first section of the verse refers to the knowledge of the Jews about the promised prophet. However, when the Prophet arrived and matched the description of the promised prophet given in the Torah, they rejected him by casting the Book of God behind their back, ignoring what was said in it regarding the Prophet. They did not believe in him because he was not a Jew, and made ludicrous objections to avoid believing in what was written in their Book. They said, "we would have believed if it was revealed to you by Angel Michael rather than Angel Gabriel" and "God has pledged us not to believe in any apostle unless he brings us an offering consumed by fire," to which the Quran replied, *Say, 'Apostles before me certainly brought you manifest signs and what you speak of. Then why did you kill them, should you be truthful?'* (Q. 3:183) In another instance, they demanded a complete written book from heaven as a condition for their belief: *The People of the Book ask you to bring down for them a Book from the sky. Certainly, they asked Moses for something greater than that, for they said, 'show us God visibly.'* (Q. 4:153) Their demands had no end. Therefore, this verse refers to the attitude of the Jews towards the truth: they were so steeped in falsehood that they concealed the foretelling of the Prophet of Islam in the Torah and refused to believe in the Quran which verified that which was with them.

وَاتَّبَعُوا مَا تَتْلُو الشَّيَاطِينُ عَلَىٰ مُلْكِ سُلَيْمَانَ ۖ وَمَا كَفَرَ سُلَيْمَانُ وَلَٰكِنَّ
الشَّيَاطِينَ كَفَرُوا يُعَلِّمُونَ النَّاسَ السِّحْرَ وَمَا أُنزِلَ عَلَى الْمَلَكَيْنِ
بِبَابِلَ هَارُوتَ وَمَارُوتَ ۚ وَمَا يُعَلِّمَانِ مِنْ أَحَدٍ حَتَّىٰ يَقُولَا إِنَّمَا نَحْنُ
فِتْنَةٌ فَلَا تَكْفُرْ ۖ فَيَتَعَلَّمُونَ مِنْهُمَا مَا يُفَرِّقُونَ بِهِ بَيْنَ الْمَرْءِ وَزَوْجِهِ ۚ وَمَا هُم
بِضَارِّينَ بِهِ مِنْ أَحَدٍ إِلَّا بِإِذْنِ اللَّهِ ۚ وَيَتَعَلَّمُونَ مَا يَضُرُّهُمْ وَلَا يَنفَعُهُمْ ۚ وَلَقَدْ
عَلِمُوا لَمَنِ اشْتَرَاهُ مَا لَهُ فِي الْآخِرَةِ مِنْ خَلَاقٍ ۚ وَلَبِئْسَ مَا شَرَوْا بِهِ أَنفُسَهُمْ ۚ
لَوْ كَانُوا يَعْلَمُونَ ﴿102﴾

And they followed what the devils pursued during Solomon's reign – and Solomon did not turn faithless, but it was the devils who were faithless – teaching the people magic, and what was sent down to the two angels at Babylon, Hārūt and Mārūt, and they would not teach anyone without telling [him], 'We are only a test, so do not be faithless.' But they would learn from those two that with which they would cause a split between man and his wife – though they could not harm anyone with it except with God's leave. And they would learn that which would harm them and bring them no benefit; though they certainly knew that anyone who buys it has no share in the Hereafter. Surely, evil is that for which they sold their souls; had they known!

This verse continues to criticise the Jews of Medina who practiced magic. The verse refers to the reign of Prophet Solomon or shortly after. The focus of the verses is the use of magic, which is often practiced with the help of the *jinn*. Here, the *jinn* are referred to as the devils (*al-shayāṭīn*). After Solomon's death, some hostile people claimed that Prophet Solomon's ability to control the *jinn* was through magic. They used this as an excuse to learn and teach magic to control the *jinn* in order to fulfil their own personal ambitions. They produced some texts based on these methods and attributed these teachings to Prophet Solomon. Despite God's clear prohibition of magic, equating the practice of magic to disbelief, many Jews also learnt, taught and practiced it.

At the time of the Prophet, some Jews in Medina thought that they could overcome the Prophet using magic and assigned their most skilled magicians with the task of overcoming the Prophet and his efforts. By doing so, they achieved nothing but an increase in their disbelief. There is a relevant tradition from Imam Baqir explaining this verse:

> When Solomon died, Iblis invented sorcery and wrote it in a book; then folding it, wrote on its back: 'This is the valuable treasure of knowledge which 'Āṣif b. Barkhiyā[218] produced for the king Solomon. Whoever wanted such and such thing, should do so and so.' Then he buried it under Solomon's throne. Thereafter, he unearthed it for the Jews and recited it (before them). The Jews claimed than the Prophet 'gained supremacy over us but because of this.' And the believers said: 'Nay! He was a servant of God and his prophet.'[219]

This tradition says that it was Satan who invented, wrote and recited sorcery. One may think there is a discrepancy between this statement and the verse which ascribes these things to the devils (Satans from among the *jinn*). However, we should remember that all evil from *jinn* is ultimately attributed to Iblis or Satan, since he is the source of all that. Such usage is common in narrations, since it is Satan who instigates wickedness.[220]

The source of magic is often traced back to the *jinn,* and includes knowledge about the evil forces in this world and how to invoke these to bring about certain effects. This knowledge has accumulated over time. There is a tradition attributed to Imam Jafar al-Sadiq, when he was asked about how the *jinn* could acquire this knowledge. The Imam answered: "The way the physicians have found the knowledge of medicine, some by experiment and some by exploration and treatment."[221] They gradually found this knowledge and taught it to people.

Invoking the evil forces of the world through evil methods is possible, just as it is possible to invoke the benign forces of this world by good practise or calling God. The very fact that this practice is forbidden in religion is evidence that it is possible. According to Islamic teachings, anyone who practices black magic is deemed a disbeliever, regardless of whether they have faith or not.

The Jews of Medina knew about the horrors of practicing black magic, yet to defeat the Prophet's mission and oppose his authority in Medina, they tried to practice black magic on him. Therefore, this verse criticises them for resorting to a heinous practice. It is ironic that the Jews believed that Prophet Solomon turned faithless by practicing magic; that is why the verse rebuts this idea, saying "and Solomon did not turn faithless." However, despite that they did not hesitate to practice black magic themselves on the Prophet.

And what was sent down to the two angels at Babylon, Hārūt and Mārūt; Aside from practicing black magic which they had learnt from the devils, they also practiced another field of magic that they had learnt from another source: "the two angels at Babylon, Hārūt and Mārūt". The verse seems to be referring to the Babylonian Captivity era, when Nebuchadnezzar II (r. 605-562 BC) captured Jerusalem in circa 605 and exiled several Jewish elites and their families, including the King of Judea, from the Kingdom of Judah to Babylonia. The exiles lasted until the Persian king Cyrus the Great captured Babylon and permitted the Jews to return to Judah in 539 BC. During their stay in Babylonia, the Israelites learnt different types of magic, taught by Hārūt and Mārūt.

However, it is possible that the verse refers to a different time, long before the time of the Babylonian Captivity. Some narrations indicate that the two angels might have taught their magic to the Babylonians long before the Israelites' captivity and the Israelites may have learnt of this on their arrival. [222]

There are some mythical stories reported by Muslim sources, in both Shi'i and Sunni narrations regarding the two angels Hārūt and Mārūt.

These stories, which are similar to Greco-Roman mythologies, suggest that Hārūt and Mārūt were the angels most zealous against committing sins. When the angels witnessed the way humans spread corruption on the earth, the angels asked God why he permitted human beings to live such a sinful life. They implored "Our Lord! You have created them and asked us to prostrate before them and bestowed them with great blessings, so why do you not destroy them for being such ungrateful creatures?"[223] God told them to choose two angels among themselves whom he would grant what he had granted man and would place in them lust and human desires and send them to earth to see how they behave compared to humans. According to the story, they chose Hārūt and Mārūt. Before being sent to Earth, God warned them against committing four acts: fornication, intoxication, idolatry and murder.

The story continues that as soon as the two angels descended to Babylon, they encountered a beautiful woman. As they had been bestowed with human desire and lust, they both fell in love with her. Both angels approached the woman, whose name was Zuhra (Venus), to express their intention of having a relationship with her. She responded positively but set a condition that both angels should worship her idol. The angels refused to do so, stating that their God had forbidden idolatry. She then suggested that they should drink some wine which would help them make up their minds, but the angels again refused, saying their God forbids intoxication. Zuhra then said in that case she wanted nothing to do with them. In the end, as a result of Zuhra's deception both angels drank wine and worshipped her idol. Before satisfying their lust with her, a beggar came begging and saw the two angels with Zuhra and asked them what they were doing with this woman. Upon making the comment, the beggar immediately left the place. Zuhra told the angels that if this beggar reports that he saw her with two men, all of them would be in big trouble, thus they needed to kill him. The two angels then captured and murdered the beggar. They then came back and engaged in fornication with Zuhra. In the end they had committed all the four forbidden acts.

Consequently, God punished Zuhra (Venus) by banishing her to the sky and turning her into the star Venus. As for the two angels,

God asked them if they wanted the punishment of this world or the punishment of the Hereafter. The angels responded by saying that they wished to be punishment in this world as the punishment of the Hereafter is eternal. God then transformed them into two stars hanging in the sky until the Day of Judgment. [224]

As noted above, it is almost certain that this story was taken from Greco-Roman mythologies, yet they are also included in some of the Shi'i commentaries, such as *Tafsīr qummī, Tafsīral-'ayyāshī* and most of the classical Sunni commentaries of the Quran.[225] It is appropriate to quote Tabatabai's response to these narrations in *al-Mīzān*:

> These are fictitious stories, which collectively ascribe to the angels of God the worst type of polytheism and the most heinous sins, that is, idol-worship, murder, fornication and liquor-drinking. Could the angels indulge in such sins, when they are known to be the honoured servants of God who are purified from all sins and mistakes? And they accuse the planet Venus to be a woman of loose character, who was transformed into a luminary body – have you ever heard of such a punishment!! – while it is known to be a heavenly body, free from any defect in its creation or any flaw in its system; a planet by which God swears in the Quran: But nay! I swear by the stars that run their course (and) hide themselves. (81:15-16) Moreover, the astronomy has today unveiled its reality, and found out in detail the elements it is made of, as well as their quantity and combination – in short, all matters related to it. This story, like that given earlier (about Solomon and his ring), is in complete agreement with the leg-

> ends popular among the Jews. They remind one of the Greek mythologies related to the stars and the planets.[226]

In addition, there are traditions about these two angels that completely reject the mythical narrations. For example, it is reported that Imam al-Rida said in a discussion with the Abbasid Caliph al-Ma'mūn (d. 218/833):

> And as for Hārūt and Mārūt, they were two angels; they taught sorcery to the people in order that they could protect themselves from the enchantments of the sorcerers and could nullify their devices. And they did not teach any one any enchantment until they had said to him: 'Surely, we are only a trial, therefore do not be a disbeliever.' But a group became disbelievers by practising what they were warned against; and they caused separation between a man and his wife with their practice of sorcery. God has said: 'and they cannot hurt with it anyone except with God's permission.'[227]

There is a similar tradition reported from Imam Hasan Askari:

> Someone told Imam Hasan Askari that 'some people believe Hārūt and Mārūt were two angels that God chose when the sins of the children of Adam multiplied and sent both of them to this world. Zuhra misled the two angels and they committed fornication, drank wine, committed murder and taught black magic; thus God is punishing them.' Imam replied, 'I seek refuge in God for such a story. The angels are sinless, they are protected from disbelief and

> indecent acts. Does not God say in the Quran that the angels never disobey God? They only do what they were commanded to do. Does not God say in the Quran that "To Him belongs whoever is in the heavens and the earth and those who are near Him do not disdain to worship Him, nor do they become weary."' (Q. 21:19) Therefore, we cannot accept such mythological stories about the angels of God.

It is evident that these narrations, found in Shi'i sources, directly contradict the mythical story mentioned above. In order to resolve this contradiction, exegetes like Kashani sought a solution. He suggested that it may be possible that the mythical narrations were symbolic; they refer to the two angels as the soul and heart of mankind coming to this world to achieve the divine objective but fail due to worldly temptations. However, this allegorical interpretation of the verse is incoherent and is simply an attempt to justify doubtful traditions. It is more plausible to say that these myths were taken from the unauthentic sources placed in Muslim traditions with some false chains of narration.

At the time of Prophet Moses, practicing black magic was common. In fact, black magic was one of the most developed fields in ancient Egypt. The well-known encounter of Moses with the magicians of Pharaoh, mentioned in the Quran (Q. 7:103-137 and 7:159-166), is a fitting example which depicts the magicians' role in the society and at the court of Pharaoh. Furthermore, it is not difficult for angels to appear in human form and interact with people. Gabriel and some other angels went to Sodom, the city of Prophet Lot, and appeared to people in the form of human beings. (Q. 11:17) Therefore, the Quran demonstrates that this appearance is possible. It is also possible that the two angels were tasked with teaching the ways of black magic and how to counter it. As previously noted, this was a time when the use of black magic was widespread, and no one was immune to the adverse effects of it.

Finally, one might wonder why God Almighty allowed black magic to spread widely when it is such a practice which can destroy people's lives. The answer is that God has given the jinn and human beings free will as a test, to manifest the hidden qualities of their souls. Having free will to practise evil does not mean that God condones their behaviour.

God sent down instructions through the angels Hārūt and Mārūt, to human beings in order to defend themselves against black magic, but they used this ability to harm others rather than defend themselves. Hārūt and Mārūt's main objective was to teach people how to *repel* black magic, but in order to teach this they also needed to educate people about how black magic was being performed. It is like teaching onchologists about cancer before teaching them how to treat it. Further, when Hārūt and Mārūt taught the people about black magic, they warned people clearly that the knowledge of black magic is "only a test, so do not be faithless" by using magic to destroy the lives of people.

وَلَوْ أَنَّهُمْ آمَنُوا وَاتَّقَوْا لَمَثُوبَةٌ مِّنْ عِندِ اللَّهِ خَيْرٌ لَّوْ كَانُوا يَعْلَمُونَ ﴿103﴾

Had they believed and feared, the reward from God would have been better; had they known!

---

the reward from God would have been better; This verse draws attention to one of the most important and oft-repeated themes of the Quran: that God's reward supersedes all worldly gains and achievements. It may be true that the Jews of Medina gained some benefit and achieved some of their desires through practicing magic, but these gains are not comparable to the rewards that Godwary people will receive in this world and the Hereafter.

Had they believed and feared; It is interesting to note the juxtaposition of faithfulness (*imān*) and Godwariness (*taqwā*) as two separate phenomena. Usually, *īmān* and *taqwā* go hand in hand; if you have faith then as a result you would develop *taqwā*. This verse suggests otherwise; sometimes we have faith, but we do not have Godwariness. This internal conflict occurs when, despite having faith, we do not follow God's commands. Godwariness is a manifestation of faithfulness through our actions. Faithfulness is the cause and Godwariness is the effect. The verse indicates that had they believed (*īmān*) in the revelation and followed it in action (*taqwā*), they would have obtained the reward from God.

This relationship between *īmān* and *taqwā* is expressed repeatedly in the Quran: *if the people of the towns had been faithful and Godwary, We would have opened to them blessings from the heaven and the earth...* (Q. 7:96) Many of us call ourselves Muslims because we have faith in God, but we often fail to put this faith fully into practice. Thus, our *īmān* reaches a limited level of practice and that leads to a limited level of *taqwā*. Exercising faith through action would attain the special status of Godwaryness and, in such a case, as the verse states, God would grant us blessings from the Heavens and the Earth.

Most of the time, faith is practiced partially, and we are therefore unable to receive the maximum benefit of it, in this world and the Hereafter. The verse at hand refers to the worldly benefits because those Jews practicing black magic did so to gain worldly benefits. God states that by practicing magic, you may achieve some worldly gains, and take a shortcut for some goals. However, if you had both faith and Godwariness, the rewards would have been much more favourable to them. There are many other verses of the Quran that support this view that if you are virtuous and do good in this world, you would receive the benefits of it in this world as well as in the next world: *For those who do good in this world there will be a good [reward], and the abode of Hereafter is better, and the abode of the Godwary is surely excellent.* (Q. 16:30) In another verse: *Those who migrate for the sake of God after they have been wronged, We will surely settle them in a good place in the world, and the reward of Hereafter is surely greater, had they known.* (Q. 16:41)

In conclusion, this verse states that the Jews of Medina needed to practice their faith instead of practicing magic, so that they could receive the blessings of God both in this world and the Hereafter. Practicing magic may have provided them with some short-term benefits, but they lost their Hereafter, whilst the worldly benefits that they received were minimal in comparison to what they would have received through *taqwā*.

يَا أَيُّهَا الَّذِينَ آمَنُوا لَا تَقُولُوا رَاعِنَا وَقُولُوا انظُرْنَا وَاسْمَعُوا ۗ وَلِلْكَافِرِينَ عَذَابٌ أَلِيمٌ ﴿104﴾

'O you who believe! Do not say *ra'inā*, but say *unẓurnā*, and listen!' And there is a painful punishment for the faithless.

O you who believe! This is the first place in the Quran where the believers are addressed as *"O you who believe"* This type of address has been used 88 times in the Quran.

Do not say *ra'inā*, but say *unẓurnā*;"[228] The Jews were intent on continuously breaching the covenants and treaties they had made with the Prophet, and so they resorted to insult, derision and mockery. They sometimes used Hebrew words to mock the Prophet or whispered derogatory words behind his back. There is another verse in the Quran that mentions the way in which the Jews targeted the Prophet:

> Among the Jews are those who pervert words from their meanings and say, 'We hear and disobey' and 'Hear without listening!' and *'rā'inā'* twisting their tongues and reviling the faith. But had they said, 'We hear and obey' and 'Listen' and *'unẓurnā'* it would have been better for them, and more upright. But God has cursed them for their faithlessness, so they will not believe except a few. (Q. 4:46)

In Arabic the word *ra'inā* means "look after us" or "be patient with us." The early Muslims used this expression often when the Prophet delivered a speech to implore him to slow down so they could catch up with him. When Muslims said *ra'inā* to the Prophet, the Jews twisted the word by using a similar sounding word in Hebrew which meant "you stupid man!" to refer to the Prophet. They would resort to this cowardly form of abuse because they would not dare insult the Prophet openly. Therefore, in this verse God instructs Muslims to use the word *unẓurnā* which has the same meaning of "be patient with us" instead of the word *ra'inā*. The Jews of Medina were not able to distort the word *unẓurnā* in the same way as they did with *ra'inā* to deride the Prophet.

According to some sources, Muslims had already warned each other not to use the word *ra'inā* prior to the revelation of this verse that banned Muslims from using it, as they had realised that the Jews used this word to ridicule the Prophet. However, some Muslims rejected this ban and instead believed they should simply ignore the Jews and what they say. This debate continued until this verse was revealed to instruct Muslims to protect the dignity of the Prophet and not allow others to ridicule or degrade him.

This is an important lesson for contemporary Muslims as well; even if what they are doing is valid, they always need to protect the dignity of their faith if anti-Islamic individuals or groups use it as a pretext to attack Islam. In such cases it would be justified to choose an alternative course of action without compromising the essence of the faith.

and listen! This is God's command to those Muslims who were unwilling to change their use of expression. According to Sayyid Quṭb, this verse demonstrates the extent of Jewish resentment and envy towards Muslims at the time. It also represents how the Jews of the time were discourteous and underhanded.[229]

and there is a painful punishment for the faithless. This may refer to the Jews of the time who were using derogatory terms in relation to the Prophet, or it may refer to Muslims who rejected the command that they must stop using the word *ra'inā*. If the latter is the case, the verse indicates that if one does not obey the command of the Prophet and God, they would be punished. Using such a harsh warning for something which may seem trivial shows how protective God is regarding the dignity of his Prophet.

مَّا يَوَدُّ الَّذِينَ كَفَرُوا مِنْ أَهْلِ الْكِتَابِ وَلَا الْمُشْرِكِينَ أَن يُنَزَّلَ
عَلَيْكُم مِّنْ خَيْرٍ مِّن رَّبِّكُمْ وَاللَّهُ يَخْتَصُّ بِرَحْمَتِهِ مَن يَشَاءُ وَاللَّهُ ذُو
الْفَضْلِ الْعَظِيمِ ﴿105﴾

Neither the faithless from among the People of the Book, nor the idolaters, like that any good be showered on you from your Lord; but God singles out for His mercy whomever He wishes, and God is dispenser of a mighty grace.

The categorisation of "People of the Book" in this verse includes all the communities who had received Scripture from God. The Quran commonly uses this phrase to address the Jews and the Christians. However, here it refers exclusively to the Jews, as mentioned in the preceding verses. However, as Tabatabai writes,[230] the phrase here may include both the Jews and the Christians. Both groups shared many characteristics, especially their enmity towards Islam. Some later verses support this interpretation. For example: *And they say: 'None shall enter Paradise except he who is a Jew or a Christian.'* (Q. 2:111) Should that be the case, the verse speaks of Jews, Christians and idolaters, describing them as faithless because they denied God's final message to man, which he revealed to Prophet Muhammad.

faithless from among the People of the Book; The Quran uses this expression in several other places to associate them with the *mushrikūn* (the pagans). Being of the "faithless" does not mean that they did not believe in God or in their religion, rather, it refers to their rejection of some aspects of their faith. For example, as previously discussed, their Scriptures had mentioned the description of the promised prophet, but when he arrived, they did not accept him even after having verified these descriptions of him. In the Quran, the term "faithless" is also to describe Muslims (Q. 3:97) and refers to those Muslims who rejected some parts of the religion.

The Jews were not pleased to see the Quran being revealed to

Muslims, as this made them recipients of a Book too. This deprived them of their distinction as being the People of the Book. They wanted to stop that grace coming down, but they could not, so they stood against God by hiding the instructions of their own Book behind their back. This is what is referred to in the following part of the verse: *That any good be showered on you from your Lord.* The context of the verse is mostly about the Jews of Medina who did not wish to grant any rights to gentiles, and they did not want any good to come to the Muslims.

This is a reminder to us all. When we live harmoniously in a multicultural society, we assume people from all faiths have the same friendly attitude in their hearts towards us. This brings about a cohesive and peaceful community, especially if members of other faiths have the same non-judgmental attitude towards us. However, if there is a difference in the attitudes of Muslims and some members of other faiths, then that good heartedness may instead be damaging. This was the case with the Muslims in Medina – they did not harbour any ill-intentions towards other faiths groups, yet some of the Jews harboured hatred towards them. This verse refers to that hatred. The Jews did not reciprocate the love and kindness which Muslims displayed towards them, but showed jealousy and anger towards them.

but God singles out for His mercy whomever He wishes; God's wish is not arbitrary; it is only derived by knowledge and wisdom. He made the choice to bestow his mercy on Prophet Muhammad and his followers, who were not only not Jews but had previously been pagans. He made this decision because he knew that they were worthy of it. God decides to grant his blessings and mercy to whomever he sees fit. In our own lives too, we should not feel jealous of people who appear to have a better material or spiritual blessing. It is the grace of God, and he gives it to anyone he wishes. There is no use being jealous of others, as this jealousy would not change or remove God's blessings from them.

In this vein, there is a relevant supplication which is beneficial to recite after the morning and sunset prayers: "I praise God for every blessing he has given me and has given everyone from the beginning of the creation to the end."[231] Rather than thinking of ourselves, we should consider the whole of humanity. We are all connected to each other spiritually and if someone is given more blessings in one way or another, they share it with those who are receptive to it. For example, the prophets, and especially our Holy Prophet and his household, received great blessings from God, and they shared it. Their selfless efforts collectively uplifted the spiritual status of all humanity.

Furthermore, sometimes we may hear that people of other faiths have been blessed with spiritual grace, but we tend to be dismissive of such possibilities and assume that only the followers of our faith could be awarded such privileges. Of course, anyone who sincerely devotes themselves to God, despite not having received the full guidance, may be both spiritually and materially rewarded by God for their sincerity and effort. Therefore, we should not have the false perception that God's grace should only come to us because we have confessed the faith of Islam.

In conclusion, this verse highlights how the faithless among the People of the Book and pagans disliked the idea of Muslims receiving blessings from God. These blessings included economic prosperity, good health, a big family, victory in a battle or, above all, receiving guidance from God.

مَا نَنسَخْ مِنْ آيَةٍ أَوْ نُنسِهَا نَأْتِ بِخَيْرٍ مِّنْهَا أَوْ مِثْلِهَا أَلَمْ تَعْلَمْ أَنَّ اللَّهَ عَلَىٰ
كُلِّ شَيْءٍ قَدِيرٌ ﴿106﴾

For any sign that We abrogate or remove from memories, We bring another which is better than it, or similar to it. Do you not know that God has power over all things?

This verse addresses another objection of the Jews of Medina to the Prophet and his followers, which created much controversy regarding abrogation and its theological implications.

For any sign that We abrogate; The term "sign" (*āya*) used in the phrase may refer to a verse of the Quran which is a sign of God's communication, or it may mean a more general sign like a prophet, miracle or Scripture. Miracles are specifically referred to in the Quran as signs: *They say, 'Why have not some signs been sent down to him from his Lord?' Say, 'The signs are only with God, and I am only a manifest warner.'* (Q. 29:50) Depending on which meaning of *āya* is used, the understanding of this verse changes dramatically.

If the meaning of *āya* to is a verse of the Quran, then the discussion would centre around the abrogation of verses of the Quran by other verses. Or it may refer to the abrogation by verses of the Quran of rulings which, although not mentioned in the Quran, were practised by Muslims. For example, Muslims used to pray towards Jerusalem until this was later changed to praying towards the Kabah. *Naskh* technically means abrogation of a ruling by another ruling that was revealed after it. It has a specific meaning which refers only to rulings and legislation, since they originate from convention. There is no meaning for abrogation in existential matters like attributes of God or historical facts. Having said that, abrogation in the Quran is one of the most debated issues as it entails complex debates, including the motivation behind the abrogation (*mansūkh*) verses in the Quran, their benefit and their implications.

There are three main views regarding the concept of abrogation of the verses of the Quran. Some exegetes are of the opinion that even if they discover the slightest difference in the verses, or the tone used, the later verse abrogates the previous verse. Other exegetes completely rule out the existence of abrogation in the Quran altogether. A third group of exegetes hold a moderate position: they concede that there is evidence of abrogation in the Quran. However, they maintain that the number of abrogated verses is very limited. This is why the scholars greatly differ on the number of abrogating (*nāsikh)* and abrogated (*mansūkh)* verses in the Quran.

Abū Muslim Iṣfahānī (d. 322/935) raised objections concerning *naskh*. He believed that, while it is conceivable that *naskh* can occur in the Quran, there are no rulings to demonstrate it. According to Ibn al-Jawzī (d. 597/1201), Abū Muslim Iṣfahānī (d. 322/933) was the first scholar to go against the consensus (*ijmā'*) of all other scholars before him by rejecting the validity of abrogation.[232] On the other hand, Ibn al-Jawzī has cited 247 instances. Abū Ja'far al-Naḥḥās (d. 338/950) in *al-Nasīkh wa-al-mansūkh*[233] has recounted 138 instances of *naskh* in the Quran.

Khoei, in *Prolegomena to the Quran*, mentions 36 instances of the 138 and concludes that there is nothing to suggest that the number of verses that are thought to be abrogated should exceed this number. Having said that, he rejects *naskh* having taken place in any of them save for one.[234] Razi has also accepted Abū Muslim Iṣfahānī's view on *naskh,* while Suyuti accepted 20 instances. Based on Abū Muslim Iṣfahānī's understanding, some contemporary scholars, such as Muhammad Abduh (d. 1905), the Grand Mufti of Egypt, completely denied the possibility of *naskh* between verses of the Quran. Abduh's perspective was that those verses discussing *naskh* solely refer to the abrogation of laws from previous prophets or from the *sunnah* of Prophet Muhammad such as in the case of the change in *qibla* (direction of prayer).[235] The Lebanese scholar Subhi Salih (d. 1986) acknowledged only 10 abrogated verses and Muḥammad 'Abd al-'Aẓīm al-Zurqānī (d. 1948), a scholar of al-Azhar, in *Manāhil al-'irfān* accepted only seven instances.[236]

Such a vast discrepancy in the number of the abrogated verses stems from the definition of abrogation that each scholar has used. The most important condition for *naskh* to occur is that the two rulings in question must directly contradict each other, such that both rulings cannot be applied simultaneously, and there exists no way to reconcile them. Therefore, the following cannot be regarded as instances of *naskh*:

1 – one of the rulings applies to one case, and the other applies to a different case.

2 – one of the rulings specifies the other ruling.

3 – one of the rulings qualifies the other ruling.

Early scholars did not use the term *naskh* to refer to abrogation exclusively. They also used the term to apply to specification (*takhsīs*) and qualification (*taqyīd*). Most of the narrations regarding the importance of this knowledge would refer to this general meaning of *naskh*. Nowadays, *naskh* refers to the replacement of an old law (*mansūkh*) by a new law in the sense that the previous law is completely replaced by the abrogating (*nāsikh*) law.

All doubts and discussions centre on this recent meaning. It is said that the first person to limit the meaning of *naskh* to apply to abrogation exclusively was Imam Shafi (d. 204/820) in his famous treatise *al-Risāla*.[237] Therefore, accounts of abrogation from earlier scholars cannot be immediately taken as an example of *naskh* by this definition. It is this factor which has been one of the greatest causes of confusion with regards to the number of abrogated verses in the Quran.

Let us now discuss the single case conceded by Khoei to be a genuine case of abrogation, of two consecutive verses in Surah Mujādila:

> O you who have faith! When you wish to consult the Prophet in private, offer a charity before your consultation. That is better for you and purer. But if you cannot afford [to make the offering], then God is indeed All-forgiving, All-merciful. (Q. 58:12)

This ruling was legislated and remained in force for only a couple of days. It was then abrogated by its following verse, because people left the Prophet isolated, not willing to give charity:

> Were you apprehensive of offering charities before your private consultation [with the Prophet]? So, as you did not do it, and God was clement to you, maintain the prayer and pay the *zakat* and obey God and His Apostle. And God is well aware of what you do. (Q. 58:13)

Khoei states that this is the only verse within the Quran that is fully abrogated with its following verse. The other verses that are in question are not cases of true abrogation; rather they refer to different applications in different circumstances. However, although verse 58:13 abrogates 58:12, having them beside each other gives an insight into the attitude of those Companions of the Prophet who used to accompany and converse with him consistently. It shows that their conversations with the Prophet did not have any true benefit for them and only disturbed his peace. They might have wanted his attention or to boast to others about their company and conversation with the Prophet. Therefore, God tested their sincerity in having private consultations with the Prophet by introducing the condition that they must pay charity to the poor before conversing with the Prophet in private. The people who had a real purpose for conversing with the Prophet would pay the charity without hesitation. Since God did not specify an amount for the charity, it would have been easy to pay a small amount toward charity and gain access to the Prophet. However, Q. 58:12 proved that the Companions that sought the greatest number of private conversations with the Prophet had no real purpose to their discussions. From this perspective, it is more a case of explanation rather than abrogation. Although the limitation was lifted by 58:13, the Companions realised that they should not disturb the Prophet for trivial matters.

Interestingly, we know from the traditions that the only person who gave charity to the poor and visited the Prophet consistently was Imam Ali. He always had a serious matter to discuss with the Prophet. Suyuti reports from several sources that Imam Ali said:

> There is a verse in the Book of God that no one before me practised it and no one after me would ever practise it. That is 'O you who have faith! When you talk secretly to the Apostle, offer a charity before your secret talk.' I had one *dinār* which I sold for ten *dirhams*. So, whenever I had a secret talk to the Prophet, I preceded it by one dirham until it was abrogated.[238]

With regards to the other verses that Khoei examines, they suggest the changing of a ruling stipulated by some verses in specific situations. They do not mean that the rulings of such verses were abrogated; rather that one ruling was preferred over another in a specific situation, while in different circumstances the previous ruling may still be applicable.

or remove from memories; The verb used in the verse is *nunsihā* which means "remove it from memory." There is another mode of reciting the word as *nunsi'hā* which means "delay it."[239] Depending on which mode of recitation is preferred, the meaning would slightly change; however, in the printed Quran the reading found is the former. The Quran we read today is based on the recitation of Ḥafṣ b. Sulaymān from 'Āṣim b. Bahdala Abī al-Najūd al-Asadī from Abū 'Abd al-Raḥmān al-Sulamī from Imam Ali from the Prophet. Over the centuries it has been established as the most reliable recitation for both Sunni and Shi'i, although all the men in its chain were Shi'i scholars. However, despite having *nunsihā* (remove it from memory) in the Ḥafṣ recitation, some Shi'i commentators have opted for the other recitation,[240] *nunsi'hā* (delay it) for a reason discussed below.

If we take the term *āya* in the verse to mean a miracle or a prophet, or a Book revealed to him, the translation "remove it from memory" fits with the following verse. God has sent so many prophets, miracles and Books that have been forgotten or abrogated, yet they have been replaced by a similar or better sign. The ruling of the Torah regarding praying towards Jerusalem is now abrogated by a superior ruling. The Torah is now replaced by a superior Book and although Prophet Moses is no longer available, another sign of God, Prophet Muhammad, replaced him.

Based on the context, this verse is the continuation of the discussion and debate between the Jews of Medina and Muslims regarding their scriptures; therefore, it is related to the abrogation of previous scriptures and their rulings. Perhaps Jews argued that there was no need to abrogate some of the rulings of the Torah if the Prophet accepts the Torah as the Book of God and the Quran was simply referred to as the confirmation of the Torah. Or why did God have to send another Book to Prophet Muhammad when the Torah already existed?

However, if the verse refers to the abrogation of the verses of the Quran, then a suitable meaning must be found for *nunsihā*. Most exegetes would agree that it means, "We make the ruling of it to be forgotten, but not the recitation of it." However, we must remember the ruling in order to know that it has been abrogated. The Sunni scholars, based on some spurious narrations have extended the classification of abrogation into three types:

1 – The abrogation of the ruling of the verse without the abrogation of its recitation (*naskh al-ḥukm dūna al-tilāwa).* This is the standard type of *naskh*, as discussed above. Here the verse is recited in the Quran, but its ruling is removed such as Q. 58:12.

2 – The verse itself is abrogated and is no longer recited or written in the Quran, but its ruling persists (*naskh al-tilāwa dūna al-ḥukm*): the text of the verse is removed but the ruling remains, like what is attributed to the second caliph Umar b. al-Khattab (d. 23/644) insisting that the following was a verse of the Quran: "If a *shaykh* (old man) and *shaykhah* (old woman) commit adultery, you certainly stone them as a punishment from God. God is All-mighty, All-wise."[241] In the reports narrated through Ibn Abbas and Sa'īd b. al-Musayyab, the second caliph insisted that this sentence was part of the Quran. But Zayd b. Thabit failed to record it in the Quran. He maintained this belief until the last moment in his life, although none of the Companions ever accepted it.

3 – The abrogation of the ruling and the verse together (*naskh al-ḥukm wa-al-tilāwa*): both the ruling and the text of the verse are removed and abrogated, such as in the hadith attributed to Aisha (d. 58/678), the Mother of the Believers:

> Narrated to me on the authority of Mālik, on the authority of ʿAbdullāh b. Abī Bakr b. Ḥazm, on the authority of ʿAmra bint ʿAbd al-Raḥman, on the authority of ʿĀ'isha, the wife of the Apostle (ṣ) who said: the [verse about the] ten clear suckling making marriage unlawful, was among what was sent down of the

> Quran. It was later abrogated with the five clear [suckling]. When the Messenger of God (ṣ) passed away it was what recited of the Quran.
>
> Yaḥyā said that Mālik said, 'One does not act on this.'[242]

Here Aisha refers to a verse which she claimed was revealed regarding ten suckling. It was then abrogated by another verse making it five suckling. The text of the latter verse was removed from the Quran while the ruling remained. Hence, the verse regarding the ten suckling was abrogated both in its text and its ruling.

These two latter types of abrogation were devised to protect specific narrations reported in credible books. However, after the Quran was standardised at the time of the third caliph Uthman b. Affan (d. 36/656) these narrations must be disregarded. They should be regarded as narrations of *taḥrīf* or distortion and must be rejected. Otherwise, how could it be justified that the *tilāwa* (recitation) of a verse, which is the basis of a permanent ruling, be abrogated, but the ruling remains?

The motivation for the lengthy explanation of the Sunni interpretation of *nunsihā* (remove it from memory) refers to the third type of abrogation – that is the abrogation of the ruling and the text altogether. They even report from Abu Musa al-Ashari that, "A chapter was revealed at the time of the Prophet with the same length as Surah Tawba but was taken away!" Or more ludicrously, it is alleged that Abdullah b. Masud said, "A verse was revealed at the time of the Prophet, and I wrote it in my *muṣḥaf* (codex), however, when I woke up in the morning, it was blank. I informed the Prophet about it. He said, 'Did you not know that it was withdrawn last night?'"[243]

Do you not know that God has power over all things? The conclusion of the verse proves that the verse is not discussing the removal of rulings but of Books, miracles, or prophets. Abrogation of rulings requires other qualities of God to be invoked, like wisdom or knowledge.

أَلَمْ تَعْلَمْ أَنَّ اللَّهَ لَهُ مُلْكُ السَّمَاوَاتِ وَالْأَرْضِ ۗ وَمَا لَكُم مِّن دُونِ اللَّهِ مِن وَلِيٍّ وَلَا نَصِيرٍ ﴿107﴾

Do you not know that to God belongs the kingdom of the heavens and the earth? And besides God you do not have any guardian or any helper.

This verse points out the indefensibility of questioning the wisdom and power of God in abrogating the previous scriptures or replacing one sign with another.

Do you not know that to God belongs the kingdom of the heavens and the earth? God is the sole sovereign in the world and can do whatever he wishes based on his infinite wisdom. Consequently, he can abrogate a scripture with another scripture or, when past prophets and miracles are forgotten, he can replace them with new ones. When discussing the abrogation of a scripture with another scripture, in this case, the abrogation of the Torah with the Quran, the different communities and different living conditions and cultures must be considered, as these necessitate changes in the rulings of God.

And besides God you do not have any guardian or any helper. God provides everything for us because he is our kind and wise guardian. It is better to accept his ruling and submit to him because he only intends to look after us and to help us. Guardianship is from none but him.

أَمْ تُرِيدُونَ أَن تَسْأَلُوا رَسُولَكُمْ كَمَا سُئِلَ مُوسَىٰ مِن قَبْلُ ۗ وَمَن يَتَبَدَّلِ الْكُفْرَ بِالْإِيمَانِ فَقَدْ ضَلَّ سَوَاءَ السَّبِيلِ ﴿108﴾

Would you question your Apostle as Moses was questioned formerly? Whoever changes faith for unfaith certainly strays from the right way.

Based on the context, it appears that the Jews of Medina would instigate Muslims to ask certain questions from the Prophet or make certain demands from him. As previously mentioned, Muslims and Jews in Medina were often involved in debates. It is possible that the Jews attempted to manipulate Muslims by asking difficult questions about their faith, instigating them to put these questions to the Prophet.

Based on some traditions regarding the occasions of revelation, some exegetes, including Hasan al-Basri, stated that this verse refers to the polytheists of Mecca and their demands made to the Prophet, as mentioned in Surah Isra verses 90-93. Mujahid also expressed similar views.[244] However, this cannot be the case for several reasons. Firstly, the verses mentioned in Surah Isrā' were revealed in Mecca, but the verse at hand was revealed in Medina. Secondly, this interpretation does not fit with the context of the verse which is the debate with the Jews of Medina who staunchly opposed the mission of the Prophet.

Unfortunately, some Muslim exegetes fall into the comfortable trap of neglecting the context of the verse and relying on narrations about the occasions of revelation which do not match the context. From the context, it appears that the Jews questioned Muslims about theological debates such as why we cannot see God. In an attempt to confuse the Muslims, they instructed them to ask the Prophet to show them God. This was the same demands that the Israelites made of Prophet Moses: *And when you said, 'O Moses, we will not believe you until we see God visibly.'* (Q. 2:55) Therefore, the verse is referring to the Jews of Medina who asked the Muslims to make the same demands of the Prophet as their ancestors had asked of Prophet Moses.

Whoever changes faith for unfaith certainly strays from the right way; As discussed at the beginning of this book, Surah Baqarah is an extensive chapter of the Quran revealed over ten years when Muslims were in Medina. "Whoever changes faith" shows that by the time this verse was revealed, the main tenets of the faith had already been established and Muslims had been given an extensive education about matters of faith. If this is the case, the verse also informs us about an alarming problem amongst the early Muslims. Even when the Prophet's mission had been well established in Medina, some Companions were still ignorant about the most important tenets of Islam. Questioning the Prophet to see God with their own eyes is a strange request for a monotheist who had already been Muslim for a considerable length of time. Therefore, we understand that until the end of the Prophet's mission, there were still some people who were Muslims but did not have a deep understanding if the faith. God clearly stated it in the Quran:

> The Bedouins say, 'We have faith.' Say, 'You do not have faith yet; rather say, 'We have embraced Islam,' for faith has not yet entered into your hearts. Yet if you obey God and His Apostle, He will not stint anything of [the reward of] your works. Indeed, God is All-forgiving, All-merciful.' (Q. 49:14)

This also puts into contect the reasons for the confusion and civil strife after the death of the Prophet.

وَدَّ كَثِيرٌ مِّنْ أَهْلِ الْكِتَابِ لَوْ يَرُدُّونَكُم مِّن بَعْدِ إِيمَانِكُمْ كُفَّارًا حَسَدًا مِّنْ عِندِ أَنفُسِهِم مِّن بَعْدِ مَا تَبَيَّنَ لَهُمُ الْحَقُّ فَاعْفُوا وَاصْفَحُوا حَتَّىٰ يَأْتِيَ اللَّهُ بِأَمْرِهِ إِنَّ اللَّهَ عَلَىٰ كُلِّ شَيْءٍ قَدِيرٌ ﴿109﴾

Many of the People of the Book are eager to turn you into unbelievers after your faith, out of their inner envy, [and] after the truth had become manifest to them. Yet excuse [them] and forbear until God issues His edict. Indeed, God has power over all things.

This verse suggests that the Jews intended to confuse Muslims and turn them towards disbelief by posing questions and demanding from the Prophet what their forefathers had demanded from Prophet Moses.

out of their inner envy; Here the motivation for their desire to turn Muslims into disbelievers is exposed as envy.

after the truth had become manifest to them; Indicates that they knew that Prophet Muhammad was the true Messenger of God. However, out of jealousy they tried to turn Muslims away from him. Ibn Abbas states[245] that the verse refers to Ḥuyayy b. Akhṭab[246] (d. circa 7/628), the chief of Banū al-Naḍīr and his brother Abū Yāsir b. Akhṭab who staunchly rejected the Prophet. When the Prophet arrived in Medina, they went to visit him. On their return, Abū Yāsir asked Ḥuyayy if he believed that Muhammad was the promised Prophet; he replied affirmatively. He asked, "What will you do in this case?" He replied, "I will be his enemy until death." He was true to his word. Ḥuyayy was the one who broke Banū Naḍīr's treaty with the Prophet and later pressed Banū Qurayẓa to break their treaty and fight the Prophet. Some other traditions mention that the verse was revealed in relation to Ka'b b. Ashraf who was another Jewish leader from Banū Naḍr and was allegedly assassinated by the Muslims after the Battle of Badr.

many of the People of the Book; It is possible that the subject of this verse is not an individual but a group of people from the Jews of Medina. These people desired to turn Muslims away from their faith because Muhammad was a non-Jewish Prophet. It was their lower self (*nafs*) that prevented them from following a gentile Prophet. They were also jealous of the Prophet's popularity among his followers and their growing numbers. Rejection of the truth is more serious for people who know the truth yet choose to reject it; and this was the case with the group of people that this verse refers to.

These two groups are often both branded as disbelievers. However, this is not the way of the Quran. A person who commits a crime out of ignorance is not treated in the same way as someone who has full knowledge of the facts and consequences, yet continues to commit crimes out of envy, ambition, greed or lust. Certainly, even secular laws treat these two people differently. God also acknowledges this distinction and treats people according to what is truly in their hearts.

"Excuse [them] and forbear until God issues His edict." Some exegetes[247] have suggested that "until God issues his edict," indicates that the initial state of inaction may be abrogated when God's edict arrives. They strengthen their case with a report from Qatada[248] which says that in the end this ruling was abrogated by the verses that commanded the Prophet to fight the People of the Book until they believe or pay *jizya* (a yearly taxation that Muslims levied on non-Muslim subjects). (Q. 9:29)

However, as discussed earlier, we should not rush into a judgment regarding abrogation. The verses may address two different situations, and both may be applicable in their own circumstances rather than one abrogating the other.

وَأَقِيمُوا الصَّلَاةَ وَآتُوا الزَّكَاةَ ۚ وَمَا تُقَدِّمُوا لِأَنفُسِكُم مِّنْ خَيْرٍ
تَجِدُوهُ عِندَ اللَّهِ ۗ إِنَّ اللَّهَ بِمَا تَعْمَلُونَ بَصِيرٌ ﴿110﴾

And maintain the prayer and give the zakat (alms-giving). Any good that you send ahead for your souls, you shall find it with God. Indeed, God sees best what you do.

After a set of verses that mostly concern the Jews of Medina, the focus shifts from the Jews to the Muslims. While the verses condemn the Jews of Medina for their rejection of the revelation and plotting against the Prophet and Muslims, they also warn Muslims against the plots and instigations of some of the Jews and encourage Muslims to remain steadfast in the way of Islam. Therefore, the previous verse warned Muslims against some Jews who plotted to turn them away from Islam. This verse continues to encourage Muslims to remain steadfast in the way of Islam and seek help through prayer and almsgiving with a promise of success in the Hereafter.

Prayer and almsgiving purify the soul in preparation for the Hereafter. Almsgiving has two functions; one is to bring welfare to the poorer classes of society and the other is to purify one's own soul. This is clearly mentioned in Q. 9:103: *Take charity from their possessions to cleanse them and purify them thereby; and bless them.*

It is important to note that the two terms used in the Quran for charity both relate to the *person* performing the act. *Sadaqa* as charity refers to something that confirms the truth of a person's faith; whereas *zakat* is what purifies the person's soul and property. Thus, charity has a dual effect; it impacts the heart of the person who gives, and benefits those who receive the charity. Society also benefits from individuals who have purified themselves through giving.

According to Islam, by coming into this world, we start an endless journey towards God. This journey consists of different stages, such as the life in this world, death and the life in *barzakh*, and the life after the Day of Judgment. Certain parts of this journey, such as in *barzakh* and the life after the Day of Judgment, require provisions which can be acquired in this world. However, acquiring these provisions in the later stages of the journey would be extremely difficult, if not impossible. When we perform good deeds in this world, God with his power and kindness preserves these deeds; he would not let them be forgotten or disappear. The verse confirms this by stating: *Any good that you send ahead for your souls, you shall find it with God.*

you shall find it with God; The use of this phrase has often been interpreted by the exegetes as meaning "you shall find its reward with God." However, a group of exegetes, including Tabatabai, believe in the idea of the embodiment of deeds themselves, meaning that these deeds will find a physical form. They argue that it is that form which is returned to believers rather than the reward of the deed. Believers may also have a reward in addition to the deeds, but that will act as an additional blessing.

with God; This term is particularly important in the context of this verse and its meaning deserves a brief discussion. The realm to which people will be travelling to after death is very near to the realm of God. We do not really know much about these two realms; it is certainly not a physical place. In this place, our knowledge of God and his power will increase exponentially. This is the realm where everything exists in its source form. *There is not a thing but that its sources are with Us, and We do not send it down except in a known measure.* (Q. 15:21) With him is the source without measure, and when it is reduced to our world, measures are placed upon it. When God sends down his creation from its source to lower realms, such as to our world, we receive it in a diluted form, accompanied with measures and limitations. Therefore, when God mentions the rewards of Paradise, we need to be clear that Paradise will be near the realm of God and believers will be able to receive the rewards of Paradise in their source form, which would be limitless and unmeasured.

وَقَالُوا لَن يَدْخُلَ الْجَنَّةَ إِلَّا مَن كَانَ هُودًا أَوْ نَصَارَىٰ ۗ تِلْكَ أَمَانِيُّهُمْ ۗ قُلْ
هَاتُوا بُرْهَانَكُمْ إِن كُنتُمْ صَادِقِينَ ﴿111﴾

And they say, 'No one shall enter Paradise except one who is a Jew or a Christian.' Those are their [false] hopes! Say, 'Produce your evidence, should you be truthful.'

And they say, 'No one shall enter Paradise except one who is a Jew or a Christian.' The Jews and Christians did not collectively agree that: "No one shall enter Paradise except one who is a Jew or a Christian." Rather the Jews said, "only Jews will enter into Paradise" and Christians said, "only Christians will enter into Paradise." In this way, the verse highlights the prejudicial attitudes of people. In general, people of faith can often harbour the ambition that their faith is superior to the others' faith, and they are exclusively on the right path. This false believe is also held by many Muslims who purport that only Muslims will go to Paradise. Muslims then limit this to certain sects such as only Shi'is or only Sunnis would enter Paradise only. Of course, following certain tenets of a particular faith superficially, or simply observing some rituals is not sufficient to secure Paradise.

Those are their [false] hopes! Say, 'Produce your evidence, should you be truthful.' The verse clearly condemns these false beliefs. God challenges these people to bring forward their proof for it. Unconditional promises have not been made in the Books of God. In the case of the Quran, there are severe warnings addressed to the believers concerning their duties and responsibilities and failure to do so will result in Hellfire (no matter what religious label a person carries). The idea of exclusivity of Paradise to certain faith group is a manufactured theology created over centuries by misled religious scholars. It has been embraced by the common people wholeheartedly and has been turned into an instrument to fight against the Book of God, instead of serving it. The Books of God, in their original forms, reject exclusivist ideas categorically and this rejection inevitably leads to a conflict of ideas between the Book of God and the manufactured theology.

بَلَىٰ مَنْ أَسْلَمَ وَجْهَهُ لِلَّهِ وَهُوَ مُحْسِنٌ فَلَهُ أَجْرُهُ عِندَ رَبِّهِ وَلَا خَوْفٌ عَلَيْهِمْ
وَلَا هُمْ يَحْزَنُونَ ﴿112﴾

Certainly, whoever submits his will to God and is virtuous, he shall have his reward near his Lord, and they shall have no fear, nor shall they grieve.

Certainly, whoever submits his will to God and is virtuous; The verse highlights two criteria to enter Paradise: submitting your will to God and being virtuous. Submission to God may occur even with an incorrect understanding of religion. However, for God, this is not a significant problem. If one sect of Islam is proven to have a correct understanding, the other sect would not go to Hell. Rather, God will take believers to Paradise based on their level of submission to him and their effort to be virtuous.

Tabatabai mentions an interesting point regarding this verse. He notes that verses 62 to 112 clarify what is meant by a faithful person. In verse 62 we read: *Indeed, the faithful, the Jews, the Christians, and the Sabaeans —those of them who have faith in God and the Last Day and act righteously they shall have their reward near their Lord, and they will have no fear, nor will they grieve.*

Then verses 81 and 82: state the characteristics that would qualify a person for either punishment or reward.

> Indeed, whoever commits misdeeds and is besieged by his iniquity —such shall be the inmates of the Fire, and they shall remain in it [forever]. Moreover, those who have faith and do righteous deeds, —they shall be the inhabitants of Paradise; they shall remain in it [forever]. Q. 2:82

Simple confessions such as "I am Muslim, I am Christian, I am a Jew, I am Sunni, I am Shi'i" would not be sufficient to save a person. Rather, if evil occupies a person's heart, they will become inmates of Hell, regardless of their confessions. Those who believe in God and commit good deeds will end up in Paradise. Tabatabai notes that if we place these sets of verses together, God's requirements from us become clear: first to believe in him submissively, and second to commit righteous deeds. It can be difficult to come to terms with this understanding of religion, as many have been brought up with the idea that the names or titles are important. However, Tabatabai argues otherwise; those names and titles are not important, rather the way people turn to God and their actions are of far more importance. In the case of Muslims, we also know and confess that the Prophet Muhammad is the Messenger of God. Thus, we can never turn to Christianity or any other religion with the knowledge about Prophet Muhammad. If we do so, it means that we do not submit the God. However, if someone does not know it, or is not convinced about it but they still do their best, of course, God would reward them.

This understanding of faith is undoubtedly different from the manufactured theologies and religious delimitations that people have created. Further, it provides a more peaceful and harmonious understanding of religion. However, one might question the need to call people to Islam or to any faith. If all monotheistic faiths are the same, what is the difference between various beliefs? The equivalent would be to ask if someone has GCSE qualifications what is the point of them going to university? What is the point of continuing to learn since they have GCSEs, and they can find a job? Hence, it is all about perfecting our religious understanding. If we strive to acquire the best understanding of religion, then we must follow the right guide(s), therefore following the teachings of Prophet Muhammad becomes crucial to perfect our understanding of religion. Consequently, if we believe that Prophet Muhammad is the Messenger of God, and he has brought a message which negates certain tenets of other faith groups then we have the responsibility to share this understanding of faith with other people, because we believe that this is the best understanding of worshipping God Almighty.

Therefore, salvation should not be confused with correctness of faith. Indeed, certain tenets of the monotheistic religions are drastically different; for example, Muslims categorically deny the concepts of the Trinity and Jesus being the son of God. However, if some people believe in this faith, and they try to do their best to submit themselves to God and do good deeds, they will absolutely attain salvation. However, they may be placed in lower levels of Paradise compared to people who have correct faith and commit the right deeds. Human beings are not monolithic in the sense that they will all be placed in the same level in Paradise. There is a spectrum of positions in Hell and Paradise and perfectionism in faith gives us the opportunity to elevate our status in Paradise. However, if people are convinced that Prophet Muhammad is the Messenger of God, but they deny it because of some personal gains (whether material gains or non-material gains), their faith would not be included in this category.

'Alī Akbar Qurashī (b. 1928), a prominent contemporary Shi'i exegete, contends that there are two prerequisites for salvation: one is to submit, and the other is to do good. Labels such as Muslim, Christian, Jew, Sunni or Shi'i, are not sufficient to save people.[249] This understanding of faith is mentioned in various verses of the Quran:

> Say, 'O People of the Book! You do not stand on anything until you observe the Torah and the Evangel and what was sent down to you from your Lord.' Surely many of them will be increased by what has been sent down to you from your Lord in rebellion and unfaith. So do not grieve for the faithless lot. (Q. 5:68)

The verse suggests that receiving the Book of God is not useful unless the instructions of the Book are followed.

وَقَالَتِ الْيَهُودُ لَيْسَتِ النَّصَارَىٰ عَلَىٰ شَيْءٍ وَقَالَتِ النَّصَارَىٰ لَيْسَتِ الْيَهُودُ
عَلَىٰ شَيْءٍ وَهُمْ يَتْلُونَ الْكِتَابَ كَذَٰلِكَ قَالَ الَّذِينَ لَا يَعْلَمُونَ مِثْلَ قَوْلِهِمْ
فَاللَّهُ يَحْكُمُ بَيْنَهُمْ يَوْمَ الْقِيَامَةِ فِيمَا كَانُوا فِيهِ يَخْتَلِفُونَ ﴿113﴾

The Jews say, 'The Christians stand on nothing,' and the Christians say, 'The Jews stand on nothing,' though they follow the [same] Book. So said those who had no knowledge, similar to what they say. God will judge between them on the Day of Resurrection concerning that about which they used to differ.

Razi makes an insightful observation about this verse. He states that "what happened to Jews and Christians exactly happened to the *umma* of the Prophet; every group declared the other to be disbelievers, and claimed they would not attain salvation."[250] Without certain knowledge, different groups, such as Jews, Christians, Muslims and among the Muslim groups Mutazilites, Asharites, Sunnis, and Shiʿis, all alleged that their group could exclusively attain salvation and the rest will end up in Hell. On the other hand, God Almighty is clear about the matter as mentioned in the verse, *though they follow the [same] Book*; the Books of God mention the prerequisite for salvation and disbelief. In relation to theological conflicts between various Muslim groups Razi observes that despite reciting the same Quran, these Muslim groups declare each other to be disbelievers.

Tusi in *Tibyān* notes that there is a disagreement about the time and the circumstance of revelation of this verse among Muslim exegetes. Ibn Abbas has reportedly said that when the Christians of Najran came to Medina and the incident of *Mubāhala* took place, the Christians did not only argue with the Prophet but they also argued with the Jews. Rāfiʿ b. Khuwaylid (d. unknown) who was a Jewish scholar of Medina said to the Christians "you have no share of faith and Jesus was not a Prophet of God." In response one of the Christians of Najran said, "you have no share of faith and Moses was not the Prophet of God."[251] They then took this argument to the Prophet and as a result this verse was revealed. If this tradition about the circumstance of revelation is correct, it indicates the degree of hostility between the Jews and Christians at the time. The Bible clearly states that Moses is a prophet but some Christians out of anger and hostility may have denied their own Book to insult the Jews.

Another tradition, attributed to Imam Hasan may refer to the same episode mentioned in the tradition attributed to Ibn Abbas, but focusing on a different perspective. The tradition states that this verse is revealed about the Jews and Christians who came to the Prophet and said:

> 'O Muhammad, judge between us!' The Prophet told: 'What is the matter?' The Jews said: 'We believe in God, and we are his friends. Christians have no share of the faith and they

> are on the wrong.' The Christians then replied by saying: 'No, this is not right we are the true believers in God, and we are His Friends. The Jews have no share of faith, they are on the wrong.' The Prophet then told them, 'All of you are in error, you are making false statements, and you have gone out of faith and following God's commands.' The Jews, protested by saying, 'how do you say that we have gone out of faith and following God's commands? We read the Book of God?' The Prophet responded, 'you have disagreed among each other about the Book of God, and you are not acting upon your Book, and if you do not act upon your Book, then of course you are not believers in your Book, and the Book will become a liability upon you; not an advantage for you.'[252]

The remarks of Imam Hasan are relevant and support the conclusion of the discussion in the previous verses. Those who receive a sacred book and claim to believe in it must also submissively follow the instructions mentioned in that Book. If they do not, the book becomes a liability for them instead of an advantage. In other words, it becomes an evidence to be used against them on the Day of Judgment. This view is in line with traditions that state that Muslims who are oppressors and wrongdoers will be taken to Hell before the disbelievers. They would protest, asking why God placed them into Hell before the disbelievers while they believed in his Book. God would reply that they had knowledge whilst the disbelievers did not know.

So said those who had no knowledge; There has been much debate among Muslim exegetes about the identity of the group. Some argue that "those" in the verse refers to the disbelievers (*mushrikūn*) and the "knowledge" that the Quran mentions is the knowledge of the Book. The evidence for this is from the verses of the Quran that state that the people to whom we gave the Book disagreed about it after knowledge came to them;[253] here, knowledge refers to the knowledge provided in the Book of God. Without the Book and knowledge it provides, we would have some idea about God and his creation through contemplation, experience and study. However, it would have been impossible for us to know about the Day of Judgment, Heaven and Hell and the human journey towards God. Human beings cannot attain this type of knowledge without accessing the Book of God. Therefore, "those who had no knowledge" is understood as referring to the disbelievers who do not have knowledge of the Book of God.

Additionally, "those who do not know" may refer to Muslims who may make the same wrongful claim; saying that it is the Jews or Christians who have no share of faith. Therefore, we may conclude that anyone who speaks with an exclusivist (or sectarian) attitude about religion is an ignorant person who rejects some of the core tenets of the faith as mentioned in the Book of God.

God will judge between them on the Day of Resurrection concerning that about which they used to differ. The Quran states that there will be no argument in Hereafter. God will not inform the Christians that "they are right over the Jews" or that "Shi'is are right over the Sunni's" or vice versa. Rather, on the Day of Resurrection the truth will be revealed and that would be the judgment between people. Once the truth is revealed, everyone will know what share of the truth they have. They will also come to understand the parts of their faith that are correct and distinguish them from the part of their faith that was false.

وَمَنْ أَظْلَمُ مِمَّن مَّنَعَ مَسَاجِدَ اللَّهِ أَن يُذْكَرَ فِيهَا اسْمُهُ وَسَعَىٰ فِي خَرَابِهَا ۚ
أُولَٰئِكَ مَا كَانَ لَهُمْ أَن يَدْخُلُوهَا إِلَّا خَائِفِينَ ۚ لَهُمْ فِي الدُّنْيَا خِزْيٌ وَلَهُمْ فِي
الْآخِرَةِ عَذَابٌ عَظِيمٌ ﴿114﴾

Who is a greater wrongdoer than him who denies access to the mosques of God lest His Name be celebrated therein, and tries to ruin them? Such ones may not enter them, except in fear. There is disgrace for them in this world, and there is for them a great punishment in the Hereafter.

There is an apparent shift away from the discussion in the previous verses. The previous verses were about the disputes between the Jews and Christians, but this verse discusses the safety of mosques. Some exegetes have attempted to connect this verse to the previous set of verses. The first opinion[254] suggests that the word *masājid* does not to signify "mosques"; rather it refers to anywhere God is being worshipped. This is based on the idea that any place in which people humble themselves before God is called *masjid* (pl. *masājid*). Therefore, in addition to the arguments that the "Jews stand on nothing" or "Christians stand on nothing" there has been a history of destruction of sites of worship that belong to opposing religious groups. Some followers of these faiths have destroyed each other's temples especially when they conquered new lands. By mentioning this verse, in this context, God condemns these actions. Each group should be free to worship God in their own way.

According to the second opinion,[255] the verse is connected to the previous set of verses because it calls upon the Jews and Christians to protect places of worship, stating that they worship God, and they know that Muslims worship the same God. There might be theological differences, but overall Jews, Christians and Muslims are of the same faith. The pagans who did not believe in worshipping God at all, destroyed mosques. When the Prophet was in Mecca, the pagans destroyed any attempt by Muslims to build a mosque. Therefore, the verse urges the Jews and Christians that if they wish to criticise anyone, they should direct their criticism to those pagans who destroyed the place of worship for Muslims.

According to the third view,[256] held by Ibn Abbas and his student Mujahid, the verse refers to the Romans. When they entered Jerusalem, the Romans destroyed the temple. Muslims then restored the temple when they conquered Jerusalem. Ibn Abbas and Mujahid connect this verse to the previous set of verses by arguing that although the Jews and Christians attacked each other, the pagan Romans attacked places of their worship, with no regard for whether they belonged to Jews or Christians.

such ones may not enter them, except in fear. It is very challenging to combine this phrase with the previous sentence that would read, "those who destroy the mosques may not enter them, except in fear." Ayyashi states[257] that those who destroy the mosques would never believe in God, except under the threat of sword. If Muslims have power, they become fake believers out of fear. They would then enter mosques and pray with Muslims, but they would do it out of fear of the Muslims as opposed to any true belief. Ayyashi elaborates on his position by referring to the hypocrites of Medina, who feigned faith out of fear of the Muslims. This may be applicable to hypocrites within every faith. When they were in power, they fought viciously to destroy the faith and its places of worship, but when they were overpowered by the believers, they pretended to join them in faith out of fear. The verse alludes to the fact that they entered places of worship under the influence of this fear.

On the other hand, Kashani,[258] argues that this sentence is the Quran's foretelling of the Muslim victory over the Arab pagans. Consequently, these pagans would embrace Islam and then enter the mosques, out of fear.

There is another interpretation of this sentence of the verse that disbelievers should never enter mosques except if they enter undercover and fearfully. Therefore, some Muslim scholars infer from this sentence that disbelievers should not enter any mosque or the Great Mosque of Mecca. However, there is no evidence that this verse refers to the exclusion of disbelievers from entering the Great Mosque of Mecca. There is also no indication that this verse tells us anything about the exclusion of disbelievers from entering mosques. The context of the verse is completely different and does not relate to banning disbelievers from entering mosques. Rather, the context is about those who try to destroy mosques or true faith and those who may enter mosques with fear. In conclusion, such inferences based on this verse are baseless.

Tabrisi in *Majmaʿ al-bayān*, argues that when this verse was revealed, the Prophet announced, "no disbeliever is allowed to come the Great Mosque of Mecca after this year and no naked person is allowed to circumambulate the Kabah."[259] The veracity of this tradition is questionable, but even if it is true, it refers to prohibition of certain *acts* of disbelievers. Some of the disbelievers held the view that they must not circumambulate the Kabah wearing the clothes in which they had committed sins; therefore, they removed all their clothes and circumambulated the Kabah naked. This was an obscene and disturbing practice for the Prophet; thus, he prohibited the practice at the time. This incident is not related to the banning of disbelievers from entering mosques. Rather, it concerns ending an obscene tradition of the disbelievers around the Kabah. It is important to remember that while the verse refers to the prohibition of certain acts, we should not generalise these interpretations to include blanket rulings.

وَلِلَّهِ الْمَشْرِقُ وَالْمَغْرِبُ ۚ فَأَيْنَمَا تُوَلُّوا فَثَمَّ وَجْهُ اللَّهِ ۚ إِنَّ اللَّهَ وَاسِعٌ عَلِيمٌ ﴿115﴾

To God belong the east and the west: so whichever way you turn, there is the face of God! God is indeed All-bounteous, All-knowing.

This verse is an introduction to the discussion on the change of the qibla (direction of prayer), however, it is also connected to the previous verses concerning the dispute of the People of the Book. It implies that the *direction* people turn towards God to worship him is not as significant as the *quality* of their worship to God. Hence, they should not accuse each other of not believing in God or criticise the different directions they stand to worship him. God Almighty is everywhere, and people may worship him in any direction he commands.

Some exegetes have disputed whether the verse is related to the change of the direction of prayer on the grounds that the issue is discussed in later verses. There are three main opinions deduced from the verse. Some argue that this verse is about the change of the direction of prayer. Others say that the verse refers to the recommended prayers. For example, if a Muslim is travelling and unable to stand in the direction of prayer, they can stand facing any direction they wish. Finally, some argue that this verse refers to those who may miscalculate the direction of prayer by more than 90 degrees.[260] However, these three views are based on traditions and none of them can be inferred from the verse itself.

To God belong the east and the west; Tusi highlights that east and west are preceded by the definite article. In other parts of the Quran, east and west are referred to in their plural forms (for example, Q. 7:137, 37:5, 70:40). This is because the sun rises from different places and sets in different places. Those verses refer to every east and every west. However, this verse distinctively refers to the singular because the east and the west are referred to as concepts (rather than specific places) in order to indicate that anywhere which is east or west belongs to God.[261]

the face of God; Some Shi'i traditions[262] state that "the face of God" refers to the Prophet and the Imams. These traditions need to be reconciled with the meaning of the verse that states, whichever way you turn, there is the face of God." Firstly, it is important to note that these traditions are based on *ta'wīl* (esoteric interpretation of the Quran) which is different from *tafsir* (exegesis) of the Quran. The *tafsir* seeks to understand the meaning of the expressions in the Quran, whereas *ta'wīl* seeks to reveal the applications of the verses which are not apparent from their litteral meanings. These traditions imply that whilst the face of God is apparent everywhere we turn, there is another aspect of the face of God which is hidden from people. When the term "face of God" is used to refer to the Prophet and Imams it means that these personalities are the representatives of God and people shoud turn to them if they want guidance. In the same way that the face is the outward representation of a thing, these honourable people represent God in guiding people. In other words, when people need to ask questions and seek guidance from someone, they need to face them. We cannot face God directly and ask him questions and seek guidance from him. But we can do it through the medium of the Prophet and Imams. Hence, in this sense they are the face of God.

This is a deeper application of the verse or *ta'wil* of the expression, but the *tafsir* of the verse may be best explained in a tradition from *al-Tawhīd*[263] by Ibn Babawayh attributed to Imam Ali and reported by Salmān al-Fārisī (d. 36/656-57). An archbishop came to Imam Ali and asked him certain questions, one of which concerned "the face of God". Before answering the archbishop, Imam Ali asked for some firewood, and he set up a fire. Imam Ali then asked: "where is the face of this fire?" The archbishop replied, "everywhere is its face". Imam Ali then said, "This is something created by me and you cannot distinguish where the face is. Of course, the example is not similar to God, but when we talk about "the face of God," we talk about something that has no direction." What Imam Ali means is that you cannot attribute direction to God, but you can say that "the face of God" is everywhere. The face is the way that you recognise him. We recognise God through his creation and signs which are present everywhere, so wherever we turn it is the face of God.

وَقَالُوا اتَّخَذَ اللَّهُ وَلَدًا ۗ سُبْحَانَهُ ۖ بَل لَّهُ مَا فِي السَّمَاوَاتِ وَالْأَرْضِ ۖ كُلٌّ لَّهُ قَانِتُونَ ﴿116﴾

And they say, 'God has taken a son.' Immaculate is He! Rather to Him belongs whatever is in the heavens and the earth. All are obedient to Him,

بَدِيعُ السَّمَاوَاتِ وَالْأَرْضِ ۖ وَإِذَا قَضَىٰ أَمْرًا فَإِنَّمَا يَقُولُ لَهُ كُن فَيَكُونُ ﴿117﴾

the Originator of the heavens and the earth; and when He decides on a matter, He just says to it, 'Be!' and it is.

And they say, 'God has taken a son.' As previously discussed, the verses remain relevant to the debate between the Muslims, Christians and Jews of Medina. While some Christian groups believed that God had begotten a son, others maintained that God had adopted a son. However, the exegetes have not limited this verse to Christian theology. The idea that God had some offspring is an ancient concept present in early human history. People of the past needed sons for both practical and selfish reasons: practically they needed the support and strength of male offspring to grow in influence, power and fame in the society. The inevitability of death meant that people developed the idea that their existence and legacy would continue through their male offspring. This would grant them a false perception of immortality. In the Greco-Roman world, people foolishly projected the same ideas to their creator whom they had imagined in human form. Within the context of a patriarchal society, people assumed that like human beings, God needed a son to take care of his affairs and continue his existence through his sons.

Furthermore, some factions amongst the Jews, Christians and the disbelievers thought that God had adopted a son: *The Jews say, 'Ezra is the son of God,' and the Christians say, 'Christ is the son of God.' That is an opinion that they mouth, imitating the opinions of the faithless of former times. May God assail them, where do they stray?* (Q. 9:30)

The idea of adopting son was common practice among the Roman nobles, who often favoured their adopted sons over their biological sons. The adoption is based on merit. In other words, Roman nobles adopted the brightest and the most valiant young males to increase the prestige of their family and to continue their existence through them. In fact, some Roman emperors granted their legacy to the adopted sons, whose merit would often surpass their own biological sons.[264]

Immaculate is He! The Islamic arguments against the idea that God would have a child stem from an understanding that God is unique and absolute and that there is none like him. Therefore, the verse categorically rejects these beliefs using the phrase "Immaculate is He!" The expression carries a sense of disassociation, implying that God is above everything that human mind may imagine about him, hence people must not attribute their own qualities and needs to a supreme being.

Rather to Him belongs whatever is in the heavens and the earth. All are obedient to Him, the Originator of the heavens and the earth; This is an emphatic reminder that God is the originator of everything and has absolutely no need to adopt a son to undertake his tasks or help him in any way. This is further clarified in the next part of the verse.

He just says to it, 'Be!' and it is. There are two ways in which God creates: one is *amr* (outside of the time or instant creation) and the other is *khalq* (inside the time or gradual creation). The subject is a complex one and needs further clarification. Creation started at a point, which is to be distinguished from a "point in time" because time was created by the creation. According to current scientific understanding, the universe was a small mass and then there was the big bang and explosion which led to the development of the universe. If we assume that this theory is the correct version of the event that led to the formation of the universe, it would be categorised as *khalq*.

Khalq implies that the creation has a process. God has set a time for the creation and expansion of the universe. While everything related to the creation and expansion of the universe occurs within time, God manages it outside of time. In this way he is outside of the creation process. He remains outside of it, from the beginning until the end.

However, there are times when God wills things to happen instantly - for example in the creation of the universe, everything began with the explosion of the small mass. God created this mass instantly, it appeared out of nothing without going through any process, which is called *amr*. Therefore, the main difference between the two ways of the creation is that one occurs instantly and the other occurs gradually, but for God both are encapsulated in the phrase *He just says to it, 'Be!' and it is*, because he is outside of the time.

The two instances of creation are explained in the Surah Qamar (The Moon): *Indeed, We have created everything in a measure (khalq), and Our command (amr) is but a single [word], like the twinkling of an eye.* (Q. 54:49-50) The verse states that God has created everything with a measure, especially in time; however to God, it is one command. The beginning of the creation and the Day of Judgment are both in the present time for God - he said "be" and everything happens.

وَقَالَ الَّذِينَ لَا يَعْلَمُونَ لَوْلَا يُكَلِّمُنَا اللَّهُ أَوْ تَأْتِينَا آيَةٌ كَذَٰلِكَ قَالَ الَّذِينَ مِن
قَبْلِهِم مِّثْلَ قَوْلِهِمْ تَشَابَهَتْ قُلُوبُهُمْ قَدْ بَيَّنَّا الْآيَاتِ لِقَوْمٍ يُوقِنُونَ ﴿118﴾

Those who have no knowledge say, 'Why does not God speak to us, or come to us a sign?' So said those who were before them, [words] similar to what they say. Alike are their hearts. We have certainly made the signs clear for a people who have certainty.

إِنَّا أَرْسَلْنَاكَ بِالْحَقِّ بَشِيرًا وَنَذِيرًا ۖ وَلَا تُسْأَلُ عَنْ أَصْحَابِ الْجَحِيمِ ﴿119﴾

Indeed, We have sent you with the truth, as a bearer of good news and as a warner, and you will not be questioned concerning the inmates of hell.

Those who have no knowledge; These people who have no knowledge may be the disbelievers who have not received any guidance and knowledge from God. Or it may refer to the People of Book, Christians, Jews and Muslims, who have already received knowledge from God, but they are ignorant of what they have received. Kashani in *Tafsīr al-ṣāfī* contends that the verse refers to both groups.

'Why does not God speak to us, or come to us a sign?' Some had asked why a miracle had not come to them as a sign. They wanted to see something extraordinary about God with their own eyes. The verse informs us that these expectations are not new. Throughout history, people have made similar demands; that they wanted to have direct communication with God, so that they may believe in him. Or they demanded a miracle to see God or his signs with their own eyes, so that they may believe in him.

The souls of people are similar in their ambitions and desires. However, God has made his signs clear for those who want to believe, if they do not want to believe - they would ignore those signs about God. There is a similar verse in Surah al-Furqān (The Criterion): *Those who do not expect to encounter Us say, 'Why have angels not been sent down to us, or why do we not see our Lord?' Certainly, they are full of arrogance within their souls and have become terribly defiant.* (Q. 25:21)

In this verse, those who do not wish to believe bring forth similar arguments that they wish to communicate with by God directly, and God's answer to these arguments answers the heart of the matter: *Certainly, they are full of arrogance within their souls and have become terribly defiant.* The reply exposes that this was not a sincere request, rather it stemmed from human arrogance. To clarify the matter further, consider the possibility of worshipping a visible god. In order to see God, he would need to have a physical existence, and this implies limitations, in the same way that human beings are limited. This is not a being that could be worshipped.

Therefore, the idea of being able to see God, or believing in a visible God, is due to the short-sightedness of human beings. Further, it is also arrogant to assume that human beings are all equally capable of communicating and grasping God. This requires the development of certain qualities which begin with humility towards God. If people want to believe in God, they do not need to physically see him or communicate with him directly. His signs are clear, such as God's signs in nature and the signs that are sent through his messengers.

Indeed, We have sent you with the truth, as a bearer of good news and as a warner; The verse refers to the Prophet as the "bearer of good news." His "good news" is the news about the immortality of the human soul and eternal life that awaits everyone after the death. Human beings will not perish upon death - instead they will continue a different stage of their eternal journey towards God. The "good news" is that people will be showered with the mercy of God and will live in joy and happiness in the proximity of God Almighty. The "good news" is that people live near him like his friend, they will love their Maker and he will love people. The "good news" is that people will receive satisfaction from God. This is great news for all of humanity and we would not able to know this news if the Prophet had not come to us.

As mentioned in the Surah al-Nabā' (Tidings): *What is it about which they question each other? [Is it] about the great news...* (Q. 78:1-2) There is no greater news in the world than the news that human life continues after death. We could have never obtained this news without the divine message. However, this is also a great warning that we will meet God Almighty one day and be held accountable for our deeds. This is why the Prophet is also referred to as a "warner." Here "bearer of glad tidings" and "warner" are two complementary epithets of the Holy Prophet.

and you will not be questioned concerning the inmates of hell. Finally, verse 119 tells the Prophet that he will not be held responsible for those who reject the message. The only thing the Prophet is charged to do is to offer guidance - it is then up to the hearts of people to accept and follow the message with the support of God. He is aware of who should be directed towards the message and who should be barred from it.

وَلَن تَرْضَىٰ عَنكَ الْيَهُودُ وَلَا النَّصَارَىٰ حَتَّىٰ تَتَّبِعَ مِلَّتَهُمْ ۗ قُلْ إِنَّ هُدَى اللَّهِ
هُوَ الْهُدَىٰ ۗ وَلَئِنِ اتَّبَعْتَ أَهْوَاءَهُم بَعْدَ الَّذِي جَاءَكَ مِنَ الْعِلْمِ ۙ مَا لَكَ مِنَ اللَّهِ
مِن وَلِيٍّ وَلَا نَصِيرٍ ﴿120﴾

Never will the Jews be pleased with you, nor the Christians, unless you followed their creed. Say, 'Indeed, it is the guidance of God which is the [true] guidance.' And should you follow their desires after the knowledge that has come to you, you will not have against God any guardian nor any helper.

Never will the Jews be pleased with you, nor the Christians, unless you followed their creed; The Prophet would always speak kindly to the Jews of Medina, and to try to please them, so that they would stop their animosity against the Prophet and Muslims. He tried to defuse the tension through his kindness and avoiding the things that would displease them. Therefore, in this verse, God tells the Prophet that they would never become satisfied with him unless he leaves this faith, by denouncing the prophethood and following them.

Certainly, the context of the verse is about the Jews of Medina and the Christians who interacted with the Prophet while he was in Medina. However, in general, whilst dialogue and open discussion with those of other faiths is important, this does not mean that those with different beliefs will ever be fully happy with Muslims, as there will always be differences in of opinion. Similarly, this statement is also applicable to Muslims who would also never be fully satisfied with the Jews and Christians because Muslims follow a different faith. Consequently, if we interpret the verse in general terms, Muslims' interactions with other faiths should be based on certain principles, not on an emotional expectation to win their hearts or vice versa. It is not possible to achieve this. Instead, we should try to establish certain principles and work towards achieving wholesome coexistence and harmony. This achievement would be the best outcome of establishing relationships with the members of other faith communities.

Say, 'Indeed, it is the guidance of God which is the [true] guidance.' The verse is responding to demands on the Prophet made by the Jews and Christians. However, the Prophet cannot forsake true guidance in order to simply please the Jews and Christians - he needs to act upon the guidance that he has received from God. From this we understand that human beings cannot attain total guidance in their lives unless they are guided by God. Even though it is important to study, analyse and contemplate, and make ethical judgments on the subjects, we still need divine guidance to supplement it.

and should you follow their desires after the knowledge that has come to you; Here, God speaks in the context of a religious dialogue between Muslims, Jews and Christians. The Jews and Christians brought arguments against the Prophet referring back to their books by quoting Moses and Jesus. However, the verse suggests that these were not the exact statements of the previous prophets, rather they were a reflection of the desires of the Jews and Christians in the Book. The Books of the Jews and Christians are polluted with the desires of the Jewish of the Christian scholars. Hence, the Prophet is told not to exchange the knowledge of the Quran with the claims of the Jews and Christians. This a general principle of God that if people leave the faith for their desires, God will leave them to themselves. He would not be their guardian anymore and he would not look after their affairs.

الَّذِينَ آتَيْنَاهُمُ الْكِتَابَ يَتْلُونَهُ حَقَّ تِلَاوَتِهِ أُولَٰئِكَ يُؤْمِنُونَ بِهِ ۗ وَمَن يَكْفُرْ بِهِ فَأُولَٰئِكَ هُمُ الْخَاسِرُونَ ﴿121﴾

Those to whom We have given the Book follow it as it ought to be followed: they have faith in it. As for those who defy it - it is they who are the losers.

Those to whom We have given the Book follow it; The verse alludes to one of the main principles in the Quran. Whenever a nation, especially the Jews and Christians, are mentioned, exceptions within these nations always follow to make it clear that those statements do *not* include all the Jews and Christians. The verse, therefore, states that despite the existence of Jews and Christians who diverted from the right path by interpreting their Books according to their desires, there are some Jews and Christians who follow their Books correctly and remain obedient to God.

Some of the exegetes contend that "it" mentioned in the sentence, "they have faith in it" refers to the Quran. Thus, the meaning of the sentence reads, "they initially followed their own Books (the Torah or the Bible) correctly and when the Quran was revealed, they then received the guidance by believing in the Quran." On the other hand, some argued that "it" does not refer to the Quran, but it means "they really believed in their own Books."

follow it as it ought to be followed; This is a powerful statement. Although the verse addresses the Jews and Christians it is also relevant to Muslims and their relationship with their Book. It urges them follow the Quran "as it ought to be followed." Regarding this verse, Imam Jafar al-Sadiq is reported to have said:

> They recite the verses of the Quran with measured pace, they ponder upon its verses and understand it and they act upon its rulings. They

> place hope in the promises, and they are cautious about their warnings. They take lessons from its stories and comply with its commands and avoid its prohibitions. I swear by God, it is not just memorising its verses and mastering its pronunciation ...[265]

This tradition explains that when reading the Quran, the focus should be on its meaning with the aim of adopting and implementing its teachings. The reading should not be a means to an end. When a person picks up the Quran to read it and sincerely search for guidance from God, they must leave their presupposed ideas and theologies to one side. In fact, one of the hindrances to understanding the Quran is the theology that we are subscribed to already. This is because we often try to justify and explain verses in the light of our own theology and understanding rather than adapting our understanding to what the Quran tells us.

يَا بَنِي إِسْرَائِيلَ اذْكُرُوا نِعْمَتِيَ الَّتِي أَنْعَمْتُ عَلَيْكُمْ وَأَنِّي
فَضَّلْتُكُمْ عَلَى الْعَالَمِينَ ﴿122﴾

O Children of Israel, remember My blessing which I bestowed upon you, and that I gave you an advantage over all the nations.

وَاتَّقُوا يَوْمًا لَا تَجْزِي نَفْسٌ عَنْ نَفْسٍ شَيْئًا وَلَا يُقْبَلُ مِنْهَا عَدْلٌ وَلَا
تَنْفَعُهَا شَفَاعَةٌ وَلَا هُمْ يُنْصَرُونَ ﴿123﴾

And beware of the Day when no soul shall compensate for another, neither shall any ransom be accepted from it, nor shall any intercession benefit it, nor will they be helped.

These verses are a repetition of verses 47 and 48 which signified the beginning of the discussion about the Israelites. The repetition of the verses here suggests that the discussion about the Israelites has come to the end and a new related topic will be discussed, which is the change in the direction of the prayer.

As previously noted, the most important blessing that God granted to the Israelites was his guidance. At the time, God gave guidance to the Israelites, whilst other nations in the world were worshipping idols as the guidance of Abraham had been lost. Under these circumstances, the guidance that the Israelites received was a great blessing. Of course, this does not mean that the Israelites were blessed over all other nations in every time. Rather, this reference is time specific to when they received the guidance while the other nations were still worshipping idols. The guidance is a great advantage which comes with great responsibility. Therefore, the Israelites were warned about the Day of Judgment, when only their righteous deeds would be of help to save them from the punishment.

وَإِذِ ابْتَلَىٰ إِبْرَاهِيمَ رَبُّهُ بِكَلِمَاتٍ فَأَتَمَّهُنَّ ۖ قَالَ إِنِّي جَاعِلُكَ لِلنَّاسِ إِمَامًا ۖ قَالَ
وَمِن ذُرِّيَّتِي ۖ قَالَ لَا يَنَالُ عَهْدِي الظَّالِمِينَ ﴿124﴾

And when his Lord tested Abraham with certain words, and he fulfilled them, He said, 'I am making you the Imam/Leader of mankind.' Said he, 'And from among my descendants?' He said, 'My pledge does not extend to the unjust.'

Verses 122 and 123 marked the end of a section in the Surah al-Baqarah. From verse 124, the focus moves to the change of the direction of prayer (*qibla*) from Jerusalem to the Kabah in Mecca. It is of great significance that the discussion about the importance of the Kabah begins with the story of Prophet Abraham. The verse details how he was made a Leader (Imam) for mankind and how he built the Kabah to prepare the way for the injunction of the change of the direction of prayer. The verse is a reminder to Muslims that the Kabah was built by their forefather Prophet Abraham, and it was blessed because of Abraham's impeccable faith in God.

And when his Lord tested Abraham with certain words, and he fulfilled them; The significance of the House of God in Mecca was given new spirit by Abraham's contribution. There are many narrations concerning the "words" God Almighty tested Abraham with. However, these narrations do not usually correspond with the context of the verse. It is likely that these tests surpassed the tests that ordinary people endured. He was tested by the commands of God. For example, God commanded him to slaughter his son Ishmael. This is not an ordinary test and God did not intend Abraham to do it; God just mentioned the word of it. God's intention was to test Abraham and he fulfilled the test. As mentioned in the Surah al-Ṣāffāt (Those who set the Ranks) after Abraham fulfilled the test God said, *it was a manifest test* (Q. 37:106) and you passed it. This is one of the examples mentioned in the Quran, and it is probable that he went through many tests like this. By strengthening his faith through tests from God, Prophet Abraham was able to fulfil his potential.

He said, 'I am making you the Imam/Leader of mankind.' Prophet Abraham was steadfast and, due to his great resolution, God made him an "Imam of mankind." He received leadership after he was strenuously tested, and he became a role model for all who wish to get close to God. The story of the command to slaughter Prophet Ishmael, begins with Prophet Abraham informing his son ... *I see in a dream that I am sacrificing you, what do you think [I should do]?'* In submission Prophet Ishmael replies *Father! Do whatever you have been commanded. If God wishes, you will find me to be patient.* (Q. 37:102) Prophet Ishmael submitted to death but Prophet Abraham had to slaughter his own son, which was significantly harder. They both submitted to the command of God Almighty. In a later verse, God tells Prophet Abraham that *You have indeed fulfilled the dream! Thus, indeed do We reward the virtuous!* (Q. 37:105) In other words, this process was the "word" by which God tested Abraham.

These verses indicate that the Imama or Divine leadership was bestowed on Prophet Abraham when he was very old. He says *All praise belongs to God, who, despite [my] old age, gave me Ishmael and Isaac. Indeed, my Lord hears all supplications.* (Q. 13:39) He attained the status of the leadership after Ishmael was grown up. Similarly, when Prophet Abraham was given the good tidings of a son, *He said, 'Do you give me good news though old age has befallen me?'* (Q. 15:54) Based on these verses, and some other verses of the Quran, it is certain that Abraham received the leadership in a very old age after he was already a prophet.

There is tradition mentioned in *al-Kāfī,*[266] attributed to Imam Jafar al-Sadiq regarding the status of Prophet Abraham's leadership and his request for his progeny. The traditions fits with the context of this verse. Usually, God appoints his prophets from among the *truthful*, the *witnesses* and the *righteous*. They are people who have wisdom, knowledge and other qualities. Due to their great qualities, Joseph and Moses were granted knowledge when they reached the age of maturity: *When he (Joseph) reached maturity, We gave him judgment and [sacred] knowledge, and thus do We reward the virtuous.* (Q. 12:22)

Similarly, God granted Abraham knowledge even before appointing to be a Prophet. He was then made a *Nabī* (a prophet of God who does not have a particular mission and was not given a sacred Book), and after this stage, he became a *Rasul* or Messenger (a prophet of God who has a particulate mission and was given a sacred Book). After becoming a Messenger of God, Abraham then became a friend of God. Not many Messengers of God have attained this status of becoming a friend of God. Finally, God appointed Abraham as the Leader or Imam over the faithful. A culmination of all these qualities resulted in God telling Abraham that he would appoint him as an Imam for people.

And from among my descendants? At this point Prophet Abraham was overwhelmed with the magnanimity of this blessing. Notice that Prophet Abraham did not ask for prophethood, friendship or any similar position for his progeny, but he asked for leadership, because he grasped the greatness of this position.

He said 'My pledge does not extend to the unjust.' Imam Jafar al-Sadiq explained God's response by saying that "reckless people cannot guide righteous people,"[267] hence God's response to Abraham indicated that the status of leadership cannot be given to foolish people and anyone who commits sin is a foolish person.

Exegetes have debated over the meaning and extent of leadership as mentioned in the Quran. Some contend that leadership means prophethood, because a prophet should be obeyed by the people. This explanation does not make sense, as Prophet Abraham had already been appointed as a prophet long before becoming an Imam. Other exegetes have argued that the leadership means caliphate or guardianship over people in their worldly and religious affairs. This explanation also does consider that every prophet has had this type of leadership over their people, especially the ones who are Rasul, or who were sent with a mission. Consequently, neither explanation give an appropriate meaning of the leadership mentioned in the verse.[268]

Here it is important to highlight the universality of the expression of "the Imam or Leader of mankind". This implies that the appointment of leadership (*imamate*) is not restricted to time and place. Upon testing Prophet Abraham with extraordinary tests, God granted him the position of being a universal role model for humanity. Therefore, in the Quran, God often refers to Prophet Abraham as a role model to human beings. This great status cannot be blocked or taken away, whereas a political or religious position could be usurped by people. When Prophet Abraham realised the dignity of the status of the leadership, he asked it to be continued through his progeny.

Here, the unjust can be described as those who are polytheists and disobey God. This is understood from the verse, *Luqman said to his son, as he advised him: 'O my son! Do not ascribe any partners to God. Polytheism is indeed a great injustice.* (Q. 31:13)

Another meaning of "unjust" includes those who are oppressors and are unjust towards others. However, "unjust" in this verse refers to those who commit idolatry or sin. There are three categories of unjust people. The first category includes those who commit sins for their entire lives; the second category includes those who commit sin at the early stages of their lives, but then repent and reform, and the third category includes those who are good initially, but later become sinners, hence they become unjust. Aside from these groups of unjust people, there are the people who have never committed a sin in their lives.

It is implausible that Prophet Abraham would have asked God to give the status of leadership to those of his progeny who were unjust during their entire lives or those who were initially good but then became unjust people. It is more likely that Prophet Abraham asked God to give the status of leadership to those who were initially unjust, but then repented and reformed. However, God declined this request on the grounds that the position of leadership requires immaculate obedience and perseverance. The verse also indicates that God granted Abraham's request to those of his progeny who had never been unjust.

Further, the verse mentions that Prophet Abraham was the leader of all humanity, including the Jews, Christians, and Muslims. He was the leader of all the prophets who came after him, including the Prophet Muhammad. As the Quran says: *We revealed to you [Muhammad] to follow the religion of Abraham...* (Q. 16:123) In this way, the just progeny of Prophet Abraham who followed the teachings of Abraham were made the leaders for humanity.

Remarkably, it does not seem that the progeny of Prophet Abraham who attained the status of the leadership also went through the same tests before reaching this status. This is because his progeny was rewarded with leadership because of the tests that Abraham endured. For example, the ninth Imam Muhammad al-Jawad (d. 220/835) and the tenth Imam Ali al-Hadi (d. 254/868) became leaders at very young ages, yet they did not go through those tests before attaining those leadership positions. Therefore, we may argue that Abraham's tests were enough to benefit his progeny. This is a demonstration of God's overflowing mercy, that he grants the reward of a father's righteous action to his descents.

There are criteria mentioned in the Quran for people to become the Imam (leader) without going through those tests that Abraham had to endure. One of the verses mentions Isaac and Jacob. Both prophets were tested severely, especially Prophet Jacob through the separation of his beloved son Prophet Joseph. However, these tests were not as severe as the tests that Abraham had to bear: *And amongst them (the Israelites) We appointed imams to guide [the people] by Our command, when they had been patient and had conviction in Our signs.* (Q. 32:24)

There are two criteria mentioned in the verse for being the Imam. The first is patience, which refers to total submission to God. Total submission is to have patience in everything. Knowing that there is wisdom behind their affairs, and if we believe in this wisdom, it means we have patience. The second is to have absolute conviction in the signs of God. Absolute conviction is more than having strong faith. It is when the heart is lit with a light which enables a person to see everything as the work of God. At this stage, a person can *see* the signs of God; not only have knowledge of them. Faithful people generally know that everything is at the hand of God Almighty, but when they *see* these signs, they gain absolute conviction.

Further, the Quran provides additional criteria for leadership:

> And We gave him (Abraham) Isaac, and Jacob as well, and each of them We made righteous. We made all of them imams, guiding by Our command, and We inspired them with the performance of good deeds, the maintenance of prayers, and the giving of *zakat,* and they used to worship Us. (Q. 21:72-73)

The third and fourth criteria that Imams or leaders need to possess are: inspired knowledge and determination to act upon that knowledge. The word "*awaḥaynā*" means that God did not merely reveal to them knowledge of what is good or bad, rather he inspired them with the instances of good deeds. They are required to act upon this knowledge to attain and preserve the leadership. Therefore, leadership or *imama* is not something that people can choose or nominate; it can only occur with the guidance of God.

It is clear from the Quranic introduction to the subject that God first clarifies the position of Abraham and then discusses the relation between Prophet Abraham and the Kabah.

وَإِذْ جَعَلْنَا الْبَيْتَ مَثَابَةً لِّلنَّاسِ وَأَمْنًا وَاتَّخِذُوا مِن مَّقَامِ إِبْرَاهِيمَ مُصَلًّى وَعَهِدْنَا إِلَىٰ إِبْرَاهِيمَ وَإِسْمَاعِيلَ أَن طَهِّرَا بَيْتِيَ لِلطَّائِفِينَ وَالْعَاكِفِينَ وَالرُّكَّعِ السُّجُودِ ﴿125﴾

And [remember] when We made the House a place of return for mankind and a sanctuary [declaring], 'Take the venue of prayer from Abraham's Station.' We charged Abraham and Ishmael [with its upkeep, saying], 'Purify My House for those who go around it, [for] those who make it a retreat and [for] those who bow and prostrate.'

And [remember] when We made the House a place of return for mankind and a sanctuary; The word "*mathāba*" is sometimes translated as "to reward", however most exegetes have interpreted the word to mean "to return". Hence, the Kabah is a place where people return and perform pilgrimage. Furthermore, in the first sentence, God refers to the House as a place of return for all mankind on the condition that people wish to return to God. Since the time of Prophet Abraham this House has become so prominent that all the messengers of God and numerous nations knew of this sanctuary. Both Sunni and Shi'i hadith collections include sections about the traditions regarding the sanctity of the Kabah. These reports indicate that Prophet Abraham was an extremely respectable figure internationally, and therefore, God chose him to build the House and he made it a source of sanctity for everyone.

'Take the venue of prayer from Abraham's Station.' There are differing views about "Abraham's Station" (*Maqām Ibrāhīm*) mentioned in the verse. It is known to be a stone near the Kabah where Prophet Abraham stood, and his footprint is marked on it. However, some exegetes have suggested that "Abraham's Station" does not refer to this stone, but to the place where he resided, which is the whole of Mecca. This is because the sanctity of the whole city comes from Abraham, thus wherever he resided and worshipped ought to be sacred. Having said this, there are numerous traditions that explicitly state that the place of prayer should be beside or behind the stone where Abraham stood.[269]

We charged Abraham and Ishmael [with its upkeep, saying], 'Purify My House... When Abraham and Ishmael built the Kabah in the desert, pure water was not readily available. Therefore, we may conclude that the command of "Purify My House" mentioned in the verse refers to a spiritual, rather than physical purification. In other words, God commands Prophet Abraham to prepare the House in a pure way for the pure visitors to claim its benefits.

"My House" refers to the fact that the House being built by Abraham and Ishmael did not belong to any person; rather through claiming its ownership, God franchised his house to be the property of anyone who wishes to return to God. Abraham and Ishmael built and purified the Kabah but neither Abraham nor Ishmael had any authority over the it.

...for those who go around it, [for] those who make it a retreat and [for] those who bow and prostrate. The meaning of these three groups of people are very interesting. The literal meaning of *al-ṭā'ifin* is "those who go around it," refers to the "traveller." Similarly, the meaning of the word *al-'ākifin* is literally "those who make it a retreat," however in this context it would mean "those who reside [in Kabah]". Thus, these qualities, are applicable to anyone who visits the House of God regardless of their religious affiliation.

وَإِذْ قَالَ إِبْرَاهِيمُ رَبِّ اجْعَلْ هَٰذَا بَلَدًا آمِنًا وَارْزُقْ أَهْلَهُ مِنَ الثَّمَرَاتِ مَنْ
آمَنَ مِنْهُمْ بِاللَّهِ وَالْيَوْمِ الْآخِرِ ۖ قَالَ وَمَنْ كَفَرَ فَأُمَتِّعُهُ قَلِيلًا ثُمَّ أَضْطَرُّهُ إِلَىٰ
عَذَابِ النَّارِ ۖ وَبِئْسَ الْمَصِيرُ ﴿126﴾

And when Abraham said, 'My Lord, make this [place] a secure town, and provide its people with fruits —such of them as have faith in God and the Last Day,' He said, 'As for him who is faithless, I will provide for him [too] for a short time, then I will shove him toward the punishment of the Fire, and it is an evil destination.'

Up to verse 125, God talks about his command to Abraham and Ishmael to build the House. However, from the verse 126 onwards, there is a change in the tone of the verses as Prophet Abraham and Prophet Ishmael begin to make requests to God whilst building the House. They were aware of the greatness of the task and the honour they were given, therefore while they were raising the walls of the House, they were constantly praying. Of course, God accepted these prayers and made the city a secure place for its inhabitants and travellers who come to visit the House of God. There are two versions of Abraham's prayer in the Quran, the second prayer is mentioned in the Surah Ibrāhīm, *When Abraham said, 'My Lord! Make this city a sanctuary.* (Q. 14:35) Although these two prayers seem similar, they were made during different stages of the formation of the city of Mecca. The first instance (Q. 2:126), was before there was a city. The second instance (Q. 14:35) took place at a later stage when Mecca emerged like a city around the House.

God also accepted the request of Prophet Abraham to make Mecca a thriving city. Mecca turned into a centre of trade and business. However, not only did God favour the believers, but he also blessed Mecca by making it clear that when God provides for believers, others would the provision useful for other as well. This is clearly expressed in the verse,

> Say, 'Who has forbidden the adornment of God which He has brought forth for His servants, and the good things of [His] provision?' Say, 'These are for the faithful in the life of this world, and exclusively for them on the Day of Resurrection.' Thus, do We elaborate the signs for a people who have knowledge. (Q. 7:32)

God bestows his blessings to everyone, of course; believers benefit from both physical and spiritual blessings of God, and the disbelievers only benefit from the worldly blessings. But when God bestows his blessings upon his servants, he does not discriminate. People can choose how much they take from it. In fact, this world is the world of mixing; people and their deeds are mixed. However, on the Day of Judgment which is the also the Day of Separation (*Yawm al-faṣl*) (Q. 37:21, 44:40-42, 72:12-14), the worldly blessings would not be of use - only the spiritual blessings would matter for the believers.

In summary, Prophet Abraham asked for two great blessings from God which are also the two main components of a good life: security and provision.

وَإِذْ يَرْفَعُ إِبْرَاهِيمُ الْقَوَاعِدَ مِنَ الْبَيْتِ وَإِسْمَاعِيلُ رَبَّنَا تَقَبَّلْ مِنَّا ۖ إِنَّكَ أَنْتَ
السَّمِيعُ الْعَلِيمُ ﴿127﴾

As Abraham raised the foundations of the House with Ishmael, [they prayed]: 'Our Lord, accept it from us! Indeed, You are the All-hearing, the All-knowing.'

As Abraham raised the foundations of the House with Ishmael; At the time of raising walls of the Kabah, Prophet Abraham and Prophet Ishmael's achievement may have been ostensibly humble. But over the course of time, Prophet Abraham's legacy and the central of role of the Kabah for the various religious traditions, especially for

Islam, has demonstrated that both Abraham and Ishmael knew the implications of their actions. They were pioneers of a new era in human history through their role in firmly establishing the foundation of the monotheistic religion. Their exact feelings and their circumstances are not known, but it is obvious that both Abraham and Ishmael understood the significance of their actions.

'Our Lord, accept it from us!' This prayer does not imply that Abraham and Ishmael were asking for a reward from God. Rather, they were simply asking for God to grant the required effect to such an important achievement. This is the case for every worship we perform - if God accepts it, the required effect will follow, otherwise it would not be brought forth. Take the example of prayer - if God accepts it from a person, their heart will become humble. As the Quran suggests *... prayer prevents people from [committing] indecency and evil deeds...* (Q. 29:45) Consequently, the indication of God's acceptance of our prayer is that it prevents a person from committing indecency and evil deeds. In other words, if God accepts a person's prayer, they would not commit indecency and evil deeds and if he does not accept the prayers, they would continue to commit indecency and evil deeds.

Of course, God only accepts from the righteous: ... *God only accepts from the righteous.* (Q. 5:27) It is evident that the prayer of Prophet Abraham and Prophet Ishmael was accepted. Every year millions of people wait and yearn to visit the House of God which was built and purified by these two personalities.

رَبَّنَا وَاجْعَلْنَا مُسْلِمَيْنِ لَكَ وَمِن ذُرِّيَّتِنَا أُمَّةً مُّسْلِمَةً لَّكَ وَأَرِنَا مَنَاسِكَنَا
وَتُبْ عَلَيْنَا إِنَّكَ أَنتَ التَّوَّابُ الرَّحِيمُ ﴿128﴾

'Our Lord, make us submissive to You, and [raise] from our progeny a nation submissive to You, and show us our rites [of worship], and turn to us clemently. Indeed, You are the All-clement, the All-merciful.'

This verse details Prophet Abraham and Prophet Ishmael's four requests from God in addition to the security, provision and acceptance of their pure deeds. Up to verse 128, they had made seven requests from God, and in the following verse they make one final request. This does not mean that their requests were limited to these eight instances, rather, God only chooses the best of everything and most relevant circumstances to include in the Quran.

'make us submissive to You,' This request came after Prophet Abraham became the Imam, though some have argued that there is a slight possibility that he might not have been appointed as the Imam yet, but it is certain that he was a Rasul.

This is a beautiful and insightful request because faith begins with submission, and it ends with submission. In the case of Islam, the first step of faith is to submit to the Prophet as the Messenger of God. When a student enters a university, they do not automatically become scientists or philosophers; they still need to continue their studies to reach those levels. However, they achieve the first and most important step which is to be admitted into the university. In the same way, people are admitted into a type of university by becoming Muslims. Here, their journey begins. By accepting Islam, Muslims do not necessarily attain faith fully; however, they may attain it partially. This is the meaning of the verse, *The Bedouins say, 'We have faith.' Say, 'You do not have faith yet; rather say, "We have embraced Islam," for faith has not yet entered into your hearts...'* (Q. 49:14)

The deeper we go into practicing the religion the more submissive our hearts become to God. The highest level of submission is felt when we submit to God alone from the deepest levels of our hearts and souls. We are all at different levels of faith, but if we test ourselves, we may realise that our lower-self (*nafs*) is defiant towards God. Even if we do not openly manifest our defiance, it may lurk inside our hearts, though we try to suppress it. This means that our soul has not submitted to God fully. Total submission to God comes after the feeling of absolute tranquillity; when faith is added upon faith: *It is He who sent down composure into the hearts of the faithful that they might enhance their faith...* (Q. 48:4)

There is a direct correlation between an increase in faith and a feeling of tranquillity. When faith is strong, the person does not complain about their circumstances, instead they are absolutely calm, no matter how many calamities befall them. It is not that these people do not suffer; rather, the suffering does not change anything in their attitude. Instead, they see the situation as a blessing and a pleasant experience, as they have attained the special attention of God through being tried by him. They know that they are being treated through a hidden wisdom of God in order to take them to higher levels of faith. The submission that Abraham and Ishmael asked for from God in this verse refers to their wish to achieve the highest stage of faith.

'[raise] from our progeny a nation submissive (*ummatan muslimatan*) to You,' Prophet Abraham and Prophet Ishmael asked God to raise a group of people from their progeny who are submissive to God like they were. This request is not for all of their progeny, only for a deserving group among them who would be submissive to God to the level and calibre of Abraham and Ishmael. It is this elite group who are meant to be the role models for all humanity as mentioned in, *Thus We have made you a middle nation (umma) that you may be witnesses (role model) to the people, and that the Apostle may be a witness (role model) to you.* (Q. 2:143) Otherwise, it would not be possible to say that all Muslim nations have been role models for all other nations. We know that in the past, Muslims such as Umayyads and Abbasids have committed heinous crimes against humanity, and in the present-day Muslims continue to commit crimes such as allying themselves with international criminals. They cannot be considered as role models for other nations. Therefore, we can conclude that *umma* has a specific meaning in this verse and refers to a specific group of people who are given the status of leadership.

There is a clear indication in the Quran that the believers should not automatically assume that they have the quality of being included in such an *umma*. Rather, they have to follow this special group (*umma*) as their spiritual and social leaders. *There has to be a nation (umma) [appointed by God] among you summoning to the good, bidding what is right, and forbidding what is wrong. It is they who are the felicitous.* (Q. 3:104)

There has been great confusion about the translations and interpretations of these verses, and based on incorrect interpretations, the current terrorist groups such as ISIS and al-Qaida have killed innocent people in the name God, claiming that they are the *umma* mentioned in the verse. The correct interpretation of the verse in the light of the other Quranic verses which refer to the *umma* is that believers should not envy a group among them who have been given the divine leadership. These qualities cannot be gained by collusion or nomination. Shi'i commentaries refer to this group of people as the Prophets and Imams from his progeny.

Tabatabai has also adopted the same interpretation. He says that it is clear that the use of *umma* in this verse is not a reference to the whole Muslim nation that follows the Prophet but a particular nation of submissive servants of God like Abraham and Ishmael. They are from their offspring and in fact the next verse, *'Our Lord, raise among them an apostle from among them...'* (2:129) also refers to the same submissive nation from whom came Prophet Muhammad. Moreover, Abraham's prayer to protect him and his sons from idol worship, to keep them away from polytheism and error, is the divine protection that gave them infallibility (*'iṣma*). Amongst the Arabs, many of the idol worshippers were descendants of Abraham. This again proves that Abraham's prayer for his 'children' or 'sons' to be protected was for a particular group amongst them.[270]

Tabatabai has argued that this restricted meaning of *umma* refers to a small elite group who are the infallible Imams descended from the Prophet. In the case of other verses (such as Q. 2:143, 3:104 and 3:110), he has argued that the use of the word *umma* refers to all Muslims who follow the Prophet as these verses came to be assumed much later, for various reasons.[271]

'show us our rites (*manāsika*) [of worship],' The Arabic word *nusuk* (pl. *manāsika*) was initially used to refer to a way of offering a sacrificing to God. Later, the meaning expanded to include any kind of worship for God. There are two ways to understand this part of the verse; one is that it means "show us how we have to worship you in pilgrimage." When this verse was revealed, Muslims understood the other forms of worship, but they were yet to understand how to perform the pilgrimage as it had not been legislated at this time. The second way to understand this is that Muslims already understood how to perform the act of pilgrimage, but they wanted to know about the meaning or reality of the worship. The pilgrimage rituals include throwing pebbles, circumambulating the Kabah, and visiting many locations, and so it is possible that the early Muslims asked to know about the purpose and meaning of these worships performed in the pilgrimage. Thirdly, they may have been asking about the outcome or the reward of the worship.

'and turn to us clemently. Indeed, You are the All-clement, the All-merciful.' Most Muslims believe that the prophets are infallible, and repentance is only required when someone sins. Therefore, there are several explanations for Prophet Abraham's request for God to *turn to us clemently* or *accept our repentance.* The previous verses concern the debate about the direction of prayer in Medina, where most Muslims lived at that time. In this verse however, the meaning is more general, stating that wherever set out to travel, turn your face towards the Kabah in prayer. In this verse, God addressed the Prophet individually to show the importance of this ruling, which is reiterated by *Indeed, it is the truth from your Lord.* The next verse repeats this command and then generalises it to all Muslims.

رَبَّنَا وَابْعَثْ فِيهِمْ رَسُولًا مِّنْهُمْ يَتْلُو عَلَيْهِمْ آيَاتِكَ وَيُعَلِّمُهُمُ الْكِتَابَ
وَالْحِكْمَةَ وَيُزَكِّيهِمْ إِنَّكَ أَنتَ الْعَزِيزُ الْحَكِيمُ ﴿129﴾

'Our Lord raise amongst them an apostle from among them, who should recite to them Your verses, and teach them the Book and wisdom, and purify them. Indeed, You are the All-mighty, the All-wise.'

This is the climax of Prophet Abraham and Prophet Ishmael's request from God. They ask that he should raise an apostle (or *rasūlan*) from among their selected and submissive progeny (*umma*). It is certain that this verse refers to Prophet Muhammad and his pure progeny, the Twelve Imams and Lady Fatima. While there were many prophets from the progeny of Prophet Abraham through Prophet Isaac, from the line of Prophet Ishmael who made this request with Prophet Abraham, there is only one prophet, Prophet Muhammad and his line continued with the Imams and his daughter Lady Fatima.

The way in which the prayer of Prophet Abraham is answered through the Prophethood of Muhammad and the Imama of the Ahulbayt is a clear indication of the lack of significance of time in the eyes of God Almighty. In response to a request from one of the greatest human beings, God sends the greatest person and perfect human being around 2500 years later. Time is irrelevant to God - as discussed previously, he is outside of the time, thus he does not need to rush to fulfil his favours and promises. It is astonishing that Prophet Muhammad came as a result of the request of his forefather Prophet Abraham.

'who should recite to them Your verses;' This refers to how the Prophet recited the revelations of God to the people. Some of the revelation is knowledge of "the Book" and some is "wisdom" - all of them together are sufficient for purification. The "Book," refers to that which is written or prescribed for worshippers such as *fasting is prescribed (kutiba) upon you...* (Q. 2:183) *Fighting is prescribed (kutiba) upon you...* (Q. 2:216) or *...Indeed, prayer (ṣalāt) has been prescribed (kitāban) upon the believers for specified times.* (Q. 4:103) Therefore, when these verses mention the Book, they refer to the prescriptions that are mentioned in divine revelations.

'wisdom;' refers to the knowledge which is given to people from the Book. This knowledge may be about God, the meaning of life, or the Hereafter. Some only practice the Book, or the rituals mentioned in the Book, but they may not have any wisdom or knowledge about God, and so they do not know the real meaning and purpose of the rituals that they practice. It is important to have both qualities; the Book and wisdom are two qualities which form a teaching which then purifies a person.

'You are the All-mighty, the All-wise.' At the end of the verse, God is described as, al-'Azīz, which means Invincible or All-Mighty who can never be overcome by any other being. Another meaning of al-'Azīz is the one who can do anything he wants; some things may be powerful (*qādir*), but they cannot do anything. In this way al-'Azīz is one who has power and ability.

وَمَن يَرْغَبُ عَن مِّلَّةِ إِبْرَاهِيمَ إِلَّا مَن سَفِهَ نَفْسَهُ ۚ وَلَقَدِ اصْطَفَيْنَاهُ فِي الدُّنْيَا ۖ
وَإِنَّهُ فِي الْآخِرَةِ لَمِنَ الصَّالِحِينَ ﴿130﴾

And who will [ever] renounce Abraham's creed (millat) except one who fools himself? We certainly chose him in the [present] world, and in the Hereafter, he will indeed be among the Righteous.

And who will [ever] renounce Abraham's creed (*millat*) except one who fools himself? The word *millat* mentioned in the verse is often translated as "faith", "creed" and "religion", but these words are not used in the way we usually understand them. Instead of referring to a specific religion or creed, the word *millat* refers to the way by which a faithful person should face God or the way in which faith is acceptable to God. This meaning indicates that people may believe in God in different ways. However, one of these faiths is the most correct to follow even though the other faiths may eventually lead their followers to salvation. In this verse, the expression the creed (*millat*) of Prophet Abraham is the correct faith, which would lead its followers directly to salvation. On the other hand, Judaism and Christianity, whose followers are addressed in these verses, are regarded in some ways as deviations from the most correct path towards salvation. Thus, they are called back to the most correct path for the salvation; the faith of Prophet Abraham.

Therefore, some exegesis argued that in this verse, the creed of Abraham may refer to the religion of Islam, as he himself refers to his creed as "submission." Many rituals of the creed of Abraham may have been different to the rituals of Islam, but at their core the creed of Abraham and Islam are the same.

except one who fools (*safiha)* himself? The word *safiha* mentioned in the verses describes a person who cannot distinguish between what is good and what is bad. Thus, in reference to the Jews and Christians who lived at the time of the Prophet, the verses states that if they turn away from the creed of Prophet Abraham or Islam, they are not able to distinguish between benefit and harm.

"We certainly chose (*iṣṭafā*) him in the [present] world, and in the Hereafter, he will indeed be among the Righteous." The justification for following the creed of Prophet Abraham is reemphasised at the end of the verse. The meaning of word "chose" (*iṣṭafā)* is important; it specifically refers to choosing the purest part of a thing. This means that God chose Abraham from the entire human race and he was the purest of all by virtue of his relation to God.

إِذْ قَالَ لَهُ رَبُّهُ أَسْلِمْ قَالَ أَسْلَمْتُ لِرَبِّ الْعَالَمِينَ ﴿131﴾

When his Lord said to him, 'Submit,' he said, 'I submit to the Lord of all the worlds.'

God asked Prophet Abraham to submit to him, and when Prophet Abraham responded with complete submission, God chose him above all other human beings. Many exegetes have argued that this submission was a special type of submission not like what ordinary believers go through. Certainly, as the verse testifies, this type of submission took place after Abraham was granted prophethood and naturally was a state after all those monumental states that Abraham had achieved. Therefore, in *Majma' al-bayan*,[272] the "submission" was interpreted as submission in perseverance of monotheism (*tawhīd*). In other words, he went deeper and deeper in by absorbing monotheism as mentioned in the verse of the Quran, *Know [O Muhammad], that there is no deity except God!* (Q. 47:19)

Prophet Muhammad was preaching the existence of one true God from the beginning of his ministry. He was chosen as a prophet because he believed in one God. However, in the verse quoted above (Q. 47:19), when God says *Know*, he refers to a deeper understanding and deeper practice of monotheism than what the Prophet previously held. In the same manner, in the verse 131 of Surah Baqarah, God called Abraham to a deeper understanding and practice of monotheism and when he achieved it, he was elevated to the status of ultimate human being. Tabatabai also accepts this interpretation of the verse.[273]

In summary, submission to God has different levels and our souls have varying capacities and depths. Consequently, when we delve deeper, we may realise that there are many deeper levels of our soul that are not submitted to God entirely. This may be through committing sins as a result of our negligence of God. Our negligence of God results in a lack of concentration during prayer, and constant worry about our past and our future. This is a sign of thinking that we are independent from God. We need to follow the examples of Prophet Abraham, Prophet Muhammad, the other great prophets and Imams. They have submitted their whole existence to God in the deepest levels of their souls and for this very reason they were chosen to lead people and were given the greatest status that human beings may ever attain.

وَوَصَّىٰ بِهَا إِبْرَاهِيمُ بَنِيهِ وَيَعْقُوبُ يَا بَنِيَّ إِنَّ اللَّهَ اصْطَفَىٰ لَكُمُ الدِّينَ
فَلَا تَمُوتُنَّ إِلَّا وَأَنتُم مُّسْلِمُونَ ﴿132﴾

Abraham enjoined this [creed] upon his children, and [so did] Jacob, [saying], 'My children! God has indeed chosen this religion for you; so never die except as muslims.'

Abraham enjoined this [creed] upon his children, and [so did] Jacob; After Prophet Ishmael and Prophet Isaac were born, their father Prophet Abraham married other wives at a very old age and had four other sons. This in indicated in this verse as the plural version of children is used, as opposed to the dual form. Prophet Abraham advised all his sons, but naturally not all of them were as pure as Ishmael and Isaac who became the founding fathers of the two branches of the Abrahamic faith. Prophet Jacob also did the same by warning his children about their religious commitment.

The warning highlights some very interesting and important aspects of faith. Firstly, when Prophet Abraham and Prophet Jacob issued these warnings to their children, the faith had already been established. Prophet Abraham had purified and ushered the faith into maturity and presented it to his progeny. This process demonstrates that faith in God is not a mechanical process in the sense that it was defined in the heavens by God and dictated upon people. Rather it takes form in the soul of people, and faith was made in the soul of Abraham. Once Prophet Abraham perfected the faith in his soul, God Almighty offered it to humanity. The process also highlights the position Prophet Abraham to the concept of monotheism.

True faith was engraved in Abraham's soul and his followers were asked to adopt this perfected version of faith; thus, they were called *the nation of Abraham*. Furthermore, the Quran refers to Abraham as a nation, *Abraham was a nation...* (Q. 16:120) This is also why Prophet Muhammad was asked to follow this perfected version of faith, and he was referred as from *the nation of Abraham.*

Faith in God is a lifelong process, not a single action of embracing faith; rather, it is a continual practice by which faith gradually establishes itself in the soul fully.

أَمْ كُنتُمْ شُهَدَاءَ إِذْ حَضَرَ يَعْقُوبَ الْمَوْتُ إِذْ قَالَ لِبَنِيهِ مَا تَعْبُدُونَ مِن بَعْدِي
قَالُوا نَعْبُدُ إِلَٰهَكَ وَإِلَٰهَ آبَائِكَ إِبْرَاهِيمَ وَإِسْمَاعِيلَ وَإِسْحَاقَ إِلَٰهًا وَاحِدًا
وَنَحْنُ لَهُ مُسْلِمُونَ ﴿133﴾

Were you witnesses when death approached Jacob, when he said to his children, 'What will you worship after me?' They said, 'We will worship your God, and the God of your fathers, Abraham, Ishmael, and Isaac, the One God, and to Him do we submit.'

The Jews of Medina claimed that they were Israelites as they follow the teachings of Jacob (Israel), and they used this claim to argue against the Prophet. However, the verse suggests that Jacob followed the teachings of Abraham and advised his sons accordingly; Judaism had not been established at the time of Jacob. The Prophet told the Jews of Medina that he was following the faith of Abraham and invited them to the same faith if they were truthful in claiming that they are followers of the heritage of Jacob.

'What will you worship after me?' They said, 'We will worship your God, and the God of your fathers, Abraham, Ishmael, and Isaac;' This is a curious reply as Prophet Jacob's sons make reference to "*your* God". This is because when we define God, he becomes "our God". By saying that *We will worship your God...* Prophet Jacob's sons reaffirm that they will worship God, the way their father and forefathers defined God. When the magicians of Pharaoh believed in Moses, they said *We believe in the Lord of the worlds, the Lord of Moses and Aaron.* (Q. 7:121-122) The magicians believed in the way Prophet Moses and Prophet Aaron defined God. Correspondingly, Muslims believe in the God of Muhammad; the way *he* described God Almighty.

'and the God of your fathers, Abraham, Ishmael, and Isaac;' Prophet Ishmael was the uncle of Prophet Jacob however in many instances in the Arabic language, the word father (*āb*) is also used to refer uncle. This is also the case in the story of Prophet Abraham mentioned in the Quran. Āzar, the person Prophet Abraham refers to as his father, the idol maker, is in fact his uncle: *When Abraham said to his uncle Āzar, "Do you take idols as deities? I see you and your people to be in manifest error."* (Q. 6:74) It is important to note that God does not usually mention names in the Quran except the names of the prophets. However, in this verse Āzar's name was mentioned to distinguish his uncle from Prophet Abraham's biological father who had passed away.

تِلْكَ أُمَّةٌ قَدْ خَلَتْ لَهَا مَا كَسَبَتْ وَلَكُم مَّا كَسَبْتُمْ وَلَا تُسْأَلُونَ عَمَّا كَانُوا يَعْمَلُونَ ﴿134﴾

That was a nation that has passed: for it there will be what it has earned, and for you there will be what you have earned, and you will not be questioned about what they used to do.

This verse concludes the dialogue between the Jews of Medina and the early Muslims. It is a warning to the Jews and to people in general that they should stop taking pride in the heritage of their forefathers, and instead focus on their faith and deeds.

وَقَالُوا كُونُوا هُودًا أَوْ نَصَارَىٰ تَهْتَدُوا قُلْ بَلْ مِلَّةَ إِبْرَاهِيمَ حَنِيفًا وَمَا كَانَ مِنَ الْمُشْرِكِينَ ﴿135﴾

And they say, 'Be either Jews or Christians, that you may be [rightly] guided.' Say, 'Rather [we will follow] the creed of Abraham, a *ḥanīf* and he was not one of the polytheists.'

And they say, 'Be either Jews or Christians...' It is evident from the verse that the Jews invited people to Judaism and the Christians invited people to Christianity. However, the verse ostensibly questions the benefit of following the two religions because the followers of these religions did not have the pure guidance that Prophet Abraham had cultivated.

Say, 'Rather [we will follow] the creed of Abraham,' Prophet Abraham was the archetype of human perfection and submission to God. The definition of pure divine religion was embodied in the soul of Prophet Abraham. Before this point, faith had been an abstract concept, but through Prophet Abraham, God showed humanity the most perfect form of faith. Through overcoming many hurdles, Prophet Abraham demonstrated that human beings have the capacity to follow a pure form of faith. The verse shows that those who came after Prophet Abraham were asked to follow his legacy, including Prophet Muhammad. By inviting people to follow the faith of Prophet Abraham, the verse shows that there is only one religion that all prophets came to teach and that God appointed Abraham as its Leader (Imam).

'a *ḥanīf,*' The word *ḥanīf* is used to describe Prophet Abraham and those who follow him. Exegetes often cite two meanings for *ḥanīf*: first, *ḥanīf* is a person who is upright and has not diverted from the true path in any way; second, it describes something which is inclined towards the centre or the truth. Here, *hanīf* describes the faith of Prophet Abraham.

'and he was not one of the polytheists.' The last section of the verse refers to the allegations of the Jews who argued that as the faith of *ḥanīf* emerged from Mecca, it is under the influence of polytheism. However, the Prophet categorically refutes this allegation by arguing that they follow the legacy of Prophet Abraham, and he was surely not a polytheist.

قُولُوا آمَنَّا بِاللَّهِ وَمَا أُنزِلَ إِلَيْنَا وَمَا أُنزِلَ إِلَىٰ إِبْرَاهِيمَ وَإِسْمَاعِيلَ
وَإِسْحَاقَ وَيَعْقُوبَ وَالْأَسْبَاطِ وَمَا أُوتِيَ مُوسَىٰ وَعِيسَىٰ وَمَا أُوتِيَ
النَّبِيُّونَ مِن رَّبِّهِمْ لَا نُفَرِّقُ بَيْنَ أَحَدٍ مِّنْهُمْ وَنَحْنُ لَهُ مُسْلِمُونَ ﴿136﴾

Say, 'We have faith in God, and that which has been revealed to us, and that which was revealed to Abraham, Ishmael, Isaac, Jacob and the Tribes, and that which Moses and Jesus were given, and that which the prophets were given from their Lord; we make no distinction between any of them, and to Him do we submit.'

Say, 'We have faith in God,' Here, Islam is described to the Jews and Christians through the prophets. Faith in one God is the shared tenet in Judaism, Christianity and Islam: albeit with differing understandings of God. However, belief in one God is not sufficient to make a religion. Revelation provides details about the purpose of life, the duties and responsibilities of human beings, and the attributes of God and the Hereafter. Believing in one God may make a person spiritual, but it does not make them religious people and it will not be sufficient on the Day of Judgment. When God guides, we need to follow that guidance; purely believing in him but not following his guidance is not enough.

'and that which has been revealed to us, and that which was revealed to Abraham, Ishmael, Isaac, Jacob,' The second stage of the faith is mentioned in the verse: to accept the revelation of God. This is what distinguishes Muslims from the Jews and Christians. In addition to what was revealed to the Prophet of Islam, Muslims also believe in the previous revelations. Moreover, believing in Prophet Ishmael distinguishes Muslims from the Jews as they do not accept Ishmael as a prophet. In addition, believing in Prophet Abraham distinguishes Muslims from Christians as they do not believe Abraham was a prophet. The Christians believed that Abraham was the father of the nation. Thus, we can conclude that there are differences how the Muslim accept the prophets; unlike the Jews and Christians, Muslims accept all the prophets and revelations that they have received.

'and the Tribes,' *Al-asbāṭ* or Tribes, it is the plural of Arabic word *sabṭ* which means grandson. Originally, it refers to the grandchildren of Prophet Abraham through Jacob and his twelve children, including Prophet Joseph. However, *al-asbāṭ* does not refer to the twelve children of Jacob, but the tribes that came from the twelve children of Jacob. Most of the Sunni exegetes have interpreted the verse to mean that all the twelve sons of Prophet Jacob were prophets and received revelation.

On the other hand, all the Shi'i exegetes and a minority of Sunni exegetes have rejected this interpretation on the grounds that the brothers of Prophet Joseph committed a grave sin by attempting to murder Prophet Joseph and then lying to their father about what had happened. Of course, the story ended well for everyone, as God saved Prophet Joseph and softened the hearts of his brothers who were remorseful in the end. Yet, it was not possible for them to become prophets after they had committed a grave sin. There is a conflict between the apparent meaning of the verse and the theological doctrine that a majority Shi'i scholars and a minority Sunni scholars have maintained that prophets cannot commit grave sin. This group of exegetes developed an alternative interpretation by saying the verse refers to *some* of the sons of Prophet Jacob such as Prophet Joseph and it does not include all the sons of Prophet Jacob.

However, this interpretation is not tenable as it stretches the meaning away from the apparent meaning of the text. A better interpretation may be that the Twelve Tribes do refer to Jacob's descendants who came from these tribes. We know from the religious texts that each tribe of the Twelve Tribes had their own prophets. At some point, tribalism become so strong among the Israelites that the members of the tribes refused to listen and follow the prophets of other tribes, hence each tribe were sent their own prophets. Previous verses of this surah have detailed how Prophet Moses dealt with a strong sense of tribalism among the Jews. When they needed water in the desert, he struck the rock with his staff and twelve rivulets emerged from rock to go to each tribe to quench their thirst. They were simply not able to share the water from a common source and would have fought with each other if they had received it altogether.

'which Moses and Jesus were given;' The choice of words in this sentence is interesting. In the cases of Abraham, Ishmael, Isaac, Jacob and the Tribes the verse uses the phrase *which was revealed* to describe the guidance sent to them. However, for Moses and Jesus, the phrase *were given* is used. Seemingly, *were given* refers to the Books which were given to Moses and Jesus. God revealed these Books to the Jews and Christians, and they followed these Books, thus Muslims also believe in them, with some reservations that some parts of the Books have been distorted.

'we make no distinction between any of them, and to Him do we submit.' Finally, if it is established that God sent down divine revelation, Muslims need to follow it in the same way they follow the revelation that came down to the Prophet Muhammad. This does not mean that Muslims need to follow the laws of these creeds, but they need to follow the core teachings of these creeds, which are the same as Islam. There is another mention of submission at the end of the verse, again, highlighting its centrality in faith and worship.

فَإِنْ آمَنُوا بِمِثْلِ مَا آمَنتُم بِهِ فَقَدِ اهْتَدَوا ۖ وَّإِن تَوَلَّوْا فَإِنَّمَا هُمْ فِي شِقَاقٍ ۖ
فَسَيَكْفِيكَهُمُ اللَّهُ ۚ وَهُوَ السَّمِيعُ الْعَلِيمُ ﴿137﴾

So if they believe in the like of what you believe in, then they are certainly guided; and if they turn away, then they are only [steeped] in defiance. God shall suffice you against them, and He is the All-hearing, the All-knowing.

---

and if they turn away, then they are only [steeped] in defiance; When the previous verses were revealed to the Prophet, the Jews refused to accept that the Christians were following the right prophet, thus they were "in defiance". Of course, the Christians were also "in defiance". There were not many Christians in Arabia, but historical sources cite that the Christians of Najran would visit the Prophet for religious discussions and rejected the message of Prophet Muhammad. Therefore, the verse alludes to the mindset of those who hear about the divine revelation but reject it. This was not because the Prophet was wrong, but because they were in defiance due to their prejudice. This "defiance" (*shiqāq*) mentioned in the verse is interpreted as disbelief because rejecting the truth in any way is a type of disbelief. It is classed as a disbelief if people knowingly reject something which comes from God.

The polytheists of Medina held the Jews of Medina in high regard. They were learned people who were deemed to have high moral values and a systematic belief system, as well as a Scripture. Therefore, their rejection of the Prophet had a significant negative impact on the mindset of the polytheists of Medina. The Jews also held military and political leverage in Medina. Therefore, the Prophet had to reconcile his mission with the position of the Jews and try to build a peaceful co-existence with them in Medina. In this vein, the last part of the verse refers to the Jews' defiant attitude towards the Prophet. God tells his Prophet that *if they turn away, then they are only [steeped] in defiance. God shall suffice you against them...* In hindsight, the early history of Islam shows that the promise of God was realised - despite all their power and influence, the Jews of Medina could not pose significant danger to Muslims. The Prophet dissipated their defiance and betrayal on several occasions.

صِبۡغَةَ ٱللَّهِۖ وَمَنۡ أَحۡسَنُ مِنَ ٱللَّهِ صِبۡغَةٗۖ وَنَحۡنُ لَهُۥ عَٰبِدُونَ ﴿138﴾

The *ṣibqa* of God, and who has *ṣibqa* better than God? And Him do we worship.'

The *ṣibqa* of God; The previous verses discussed pure faith and pure religion as submission to God and belief in all the prophets and messengers without making any distinction. This verse is mentioned to refer to such a pure faith as *ṣibqa* of God. Literally *ṣibqa* means colour, therefore most of the translators have rendered it as "the colouring of God." Figuratively, "the colouring of God" refers to the faith of people which has been shaped in their hearts with the guidance of God.

Therefore, many early exegetes have interpreted "*ṣibqa*" as religion. Tusi and some other early exegetes argue that "the colouring of God" means "configuration (*fiṭra*) of God" like what is mentioned in the verse: *Direct your face toward the pure faith, stand firm and [adhere to] the configuration (fiṭra) of God upon which He has created people...* (Q. 30:30) God has created and configured people to worship him, thus worshipping God is the best of actions.[274]

However, many later exegetes such as Tabrisi have related the word *ṣibqa* to the Christian and sometimes Jewish practice of baptising children with yellow water.[275] These exegetes believe that the colour mentioned in the verse alludes to the yellow water which gave a yellow colour to the children during the baptism. The purpose of baptism is to purify children and make them Christians. Therefore, according to this interpretation, the verse suggests that rather than becoming pure through baptism with yellow water, true purity comes from the acceptance of the correct form of faith which is the religion of Islam. Either of these interpretations may be correct.

قُلْ أَتُحَاجُّونَنَا فِي اللَّهِ وَهُوَ رَبُّنَا وَرَبُّكُمْ وَلَنَا أَعْمَالُنَا وَلَكُمْ
أَعْمَالُكُمْ وَنَحْنُ لَهُ مُخْلِصُونَ ﴿139﴾

Say, 'Will you argue with us concerning God, while He is our Lord and your Lord, and our deeds belong to us, and your deeds belong to you, and we worship Him dedicatedly?'

'Will you argue with us concerning God, while He is our Lord and your Lord, This verse refers to the people who would argue about God. The nature of the argument was not about the existence of God or his attributes, rather the argument was focused on whether he sent down revelation to Prophet Muhammad. The Jews and Christians of the region commonly held the view that God only sent down revelation to the Jews and Christians. Moreover, the Jews believed that the revelation should only come to the Children of Jacob. Within this context the argument of the verse is based on God being everyone's

Lord. Therefore, it is not possible that he gives revelation to a certain group but withdraws such a privilege from other groups. Furthermore, if he is everyone's Lord, it is possible that he gives revelation to Muslims and others as well. The undertone of the verse goes back to our previous discussions regarding the severe criticism of sectarianism and racism in the Quran.

and we worship Him dedicatedly; The word "dedicatedly" (*mukhliṣūn*) comes from the Arabic word *ikhlāṣ* which means dedicated, pure, sincere worship of God. Sincere worship of God, which is done with *ikhlāṣ*, is not mixed with any other type of worship. Our aim is to be purely dedicated to God Almighty.

أَمْ تَقُولُونَ إِنَّ إِبْرَاهِيمَ وَإِسْمَاعِيلَ وَإِسْحَاقَ وَيَعْقُوبَ وَالْأَسْبَاطَ كَانُوا هُودًا أَوْ نَصَارَىٰ ۗ قُلْ أَأَنتُمْ أَعْلَمُ أَمِ اللَّهُ ۗ وَمَنْ أَظْلَمُ مِمَّن كَتَمَ شَهَادَةً عِندَهُ مِنَ اللَّهِ ۗ وَمَا اللَّهُ بِغَافِلٍ عَمَّا تَعْمَلُونَ ﴿140﴾

Do you say that Abraham, Ishmael, Isaac, Jacob, and the Tribes were Jews or Christians? Say, 'Is it you who know better, or God?' And who is a greater wrongdoer than him who conceals a testimony that is with him from God? And God is not oblivious of what you do.

Do you say that Abraham, Ishmael, Isaac, Jacob, and the Tribes were Jews or Christians? The verse continues to confront the sectarian argument raised by the Jews and Christians who interacted with the Prophet; do they dare challenge the great prophets, who were neither Jews nor Christians? The foundation of Judaism was laid by Prophet Moses through his emancipation of the Jews and receiving the Ten Commandments. The great prophets Abraham, Ishmael, Isaac, Jacob and their progeny who had lived before Moses could therefore not be formally classified as Jews in this sense.

Say, 'Is it you who know better, or God?' This question is asked in order to counter the next argument that these prophets were also Jews and Christians, but they lived before Moses and Jesus. Here, the verse is challenging the idea of giving names to the religion of God and then restricting guidance to an elite group. Rather, there is one religion of God and various prophets have come to teach and rectify this religion. Whoever follows the pure religion of God, regardless of their affiliation to a certain group, would be saved.

And who is a greater wrongdoer than him who conceals a testimony that is with him from God? The "testimony" (*shāhadatan*) mentioned in the verse is the acknowledgment that at the end of time, revelation will come to a descendant of Prophet Ishmael. This testimony was mentioned in their Books, but they chose to conceal it. God is aware of what people do.

تِلْكَ أُمَّةٌ قَدْ خَلَتْ لَهَا مَا كَسَبَتْ وَلَكُم مَّا كَسَبْتُمْ وَلَا تُسْأَلُونَ عَمَّا كَانُوا يَعْمَلُونَ ﴿141﴾

That was a nation that has passed: for it there will be what it has earned, and for you there will be what you have earned, and you will not be questioned about what they used to do.

This verse focuses the reader's attention to the present. What we do for ourselves is important and the achievements of the previous prophets and their specific faith would not benefit us. Therefore, there is no need to try to take credit for what they did. We need to act for ourselves and achieve salvation through good deeds and pure intention.

سَيَقُولُ السُّفَهَاءُ مِنَ النَّاسِ مَا وَلَّاهُمْ عَن قِبْلَتِهِمُ الَّتِي كَانُوا عَلَيْهَا ۚ قُل لِّلَّهِ الْمَشْرِقُ وَالْمَغْرِبُ ۚ يَهْدِي مَن يَشَاءُ إِلَىٰ صِرَاطٍ مُّسْتَقِيمٍ ﴿142﴾

The foolish among the people will say, 'What has turned them away from the qibla (the direction of prayer) they were following?' Say, 'To God belong the east and the west. He guides whomever He wishes to a straight path.'

From verse 142 onwards, ten verses are related to the change in the direction of prayer. The previous verses provided a brief history of the Kabah, emphasising its significance as a House of worship, ushering readers to the climax which was the change of the *qibla* (the direction of the prayer) from Jerusalem to the Kabah.

The foolish among the people; These are people who questioned and speculated about the change of the *qibla* without having any insight into the divine wisdom. At the time when the *qibla* was changed, there were many social, theological, and political debates taking place in Medina. There were several groups in Medina who may be included in this group of "foolish people," but the verse does not explicitly identify these people. Some exegetes have suggested that there may be three groups included in "foolish people" mentioned in the verse. Reports[276] attributed to Ibn Abbas and al-Barā b. 'Azib (d. 71/690) state that "foolish people" refers to the Jews of Medina. Bayt al-Maqdis, which is in Jerusalem, was the initial *qibla* of Muslims as well as the prayer of direction of the Jews. Changing the direction of *qibla* from Bayt al-Maqdis to the Kabah was significant to Muslims as a way of distinguishing themselves from the Jews in this respect. At the same time, for the Jews of Medina, changing the direction of prayer was a matter of anxiety and concern as it was an overt demonstration that Muslims were departing from the tradition of the Jews. It is understandable that at a time of great changes, people may express opposition and resistance. This was the position of the Jews of Medina who may have questioned the sudden change in the direction of prayer.

On the other hand, Hasan al-Basri and some others have argued that "foolish people" refers to the polytheists of Mecca who began mocking the Prophet when they heard about the change in the direction of prayer. A third group of scholars argued that "foolish people" refers to the hypocrites. The hypocrites did not have faith in God or the Prophet, but they pretended to be Muslims in order to protect their privileges in society. Through the change of *qibla*, they had the opportunity to criticise the Prophet and express their hostility to Islam in a subtle manner. They reportedly questioned God's ability to decide the direction of prayer.

In the absence of convincing evidence as to whom the word "foolish people" specifically refers to, it may be that all these groups referred as "foolish people". It is possible that the members of these three groups wanted to seize the opportunity to attack the Prophet and Islam.

The argument over the change on the direction of prayer provided a great opportunity to the Prophet's enemies. From their perspective, there has been in sudden change in God's plan which suggested that God was not omniscient. This argument also weakened the faith of some Muslims and even led some of them to disbelief. Therefore, Muslim scholars have made a great effort to explain the change of the direction of *qibla* theologically by developing the concepts of "abrogation" (*naskh*) and "revision" in Divine Destiny (*bad'a).*

In this vein, Tusi, in his *tafsīr* discusses the topic at length, responding to the criticisms of Sunni scholars regarding *bad'a* and justifying the position of the Shi'i scholars. Tusi's main argument[277] in support of the concept is that *bad'a* (revision) is related to the change of circumstances related to time and place. In certain situations, these variables change, then the relevant ruling may also change. The change of the direction of the *qibla* took place after the Prophet and Muslims emigrated from Mecca to Medina. The conditions and priority of Muslims changed as the time and place had also changed. Mecca became more important than Jerusalem, thus God changed the direction of *qibla*. This explanation shows that *bad'a* does not entail a change in Divine Will.

وَكَذَٰلِكَ جَعَلْنَاكُمْ أُمَّةً وَسَطًا لِّتَكُونُوا شُهَدَاءَ عَلَى النَّاسِ وَيَكُونَ
الرَّسُولُ عَلَيْكُمْ شَهِيدًا ۗ وَمَا جَعَلْنَا الْقِبْلَةَ الَّتِي كُنتَ عَلَيْهَا إِلَّا لِنَعْلَمَ
مَن يَتَّبِعُ الرَّسُولَ مِمَّن يَنقَلِبُ عَلَىٰ عَقِبَيْهِ ۚ وَإِن كَانَتْ لَكَبِيرَةً إِلَّا عَلَى
الَّذِينَ هَدَى اللَّهُ ۗ وَمَا كَانَ اللَّهُ لِيُضِيعَ إِيمَانَكُمْ ۚ إِنَّ اللَّهَ بِالنَّاسِ لَرَءُوفٌ
رَّحِيمٌ ﴿143﴾

Thus, We have made you a middle nation that you may be witnesses to the people, and that the Apostle may be a witness to you. And We did not appoint the qibla you were following but that We may ascertain those who follow the Apostle from those who turn back on their heels. It was indeed a hard thing except for those whom God has guided. And God would not let your prayers go to waste. Indeed, God is most kind and merciful to mankind.

Thus, We have made you a middle nation; This is an oft-repeated sentence in the Quran. Muslims claim that they are the "middle nation". Regarding the meaning of middle (*wasaṭ*), it may mean *wāsiṭ*, something in the middle or the medium between two things. Or it may allude to *'adl*, justice or the middle between two extremes. Thus, the verse would read, "we have made you a just *umma*" an *umma* that is away from extremism from both sides; neither lacking vigour nor having too much vigour. There is one more meaning to *wasaṭ* which means to have the best of everything *(afḍal)*.

Umma often refers to a group of people; usually up to ten people or more. For example, *when Moses arrived at the well of Madyan, he found a crowd of people (ummatan)...* (Q. 28:23) Usually exegetes use the word *umma* to mean "nation," and Sunni commentators used this meaning here. However, Shi'i scholars have interpreted it as a "group among the nation".

It is problematic to render *umma* as the whole nation since the nation of Islam cannot be considered collectively as a role model for humanity. There have always been tyrants, oppressors and criminals among those who call themselves Muslim. Their character could not be considered as exemplary. Therefore, some Muslim scholars have interpreted the word *umma* in this verse as the faith of Islam rather than the collective followers of Islam. They considered Islam as a moderate religion, meaning that it takes the middle path between two extreme views. However, it is clear that the verse refers to actual people; it does not refer to the creed for it says, "*you may be witnesses to the people, and that the Apostle may be a witness to you.*"

Clearly, the word *umma* does not refer to all Muslims; in fact, according to Shi'i commentators the word *umma* in this verse refers to our role models, who are the Imams. They have the character traits alluded to in the verse. They were just and morally upright, thus capable of being role models. They were exemplary in performing their religious duties and so they were mediums between the Prophet and the people, and the proofs of God over people. Similar verses in the Quran support this view. For example, the last two verses of Surah al-Hajj clearly nominate the chosen elite among the believers to be the witnesses of the *umma*:

> O you who have faith! Bow down and prostrate yourselves, and worship your Lord, and do good, so that you may be felicitous. And strive hard in [the path] of God, a striving which is worthy of Him. He has chosen you and has not placed before you any obstacle in the religion, the faith of your father Abraham. He named you 'Muslims' before, and in this, so that the Apostle may be a witness to you, and that you may be witnesses to mankind. So, maintain the prayer, give the zakat, and hold fast to God. He is your master an excellent master and an excellent helper. (Q. 22:77-78)

Therefore, the whole Muslim nation can be described as "a middle nation" for the sake of these people.

This is a stylistic feature of the Quran. It uses general terms to allude to particular groups or people. For example, it says *your Lord's best word [of promise] was fulfilled for the Children of Israel because of their patience.* (7:137) Obviously, not all the Israelites were patient, since in the Quran God criticises the Israelites for their impatience, greed and disobedience. But there were certain people among the Israelites who were special in the eyes of God due to their spiritual qualities, and thus God saved their nation for their sake.

that you may be witnesses to the people, and that the Apostle may be a witness to you; *Shahīd* (plural *shuhadā'*) may mean someone who witnesses something, or it may mean a proof (*hujja*). *Shahīd* refers to a person whom others are measured against in comparison. In this sense the *shahīd* is a role model because a role model is someone according to whom we judge our belief and actions. Therefore, the verse would mean, "we have made you a role model for the people."

And We did not appoint the qibla you were following but that We may ascertain those who follow the Apostle from those who turn back on their heels; God acknowledges the difficulty of accepting the change of the direction of the *qibla*. The people of Medina were often inclined towards Bayt al-Maqdis in Jerusalem due to the influence of the Jews of Medina who prayed towards Bayt al-Maqdis and greatly revered it. The Emigrants (*Muhājirūn*) who had come from Mecca, on the other hand, inclined towards the Kabah due to their past. One may imagine that when the *qibla* was towards Jerusalem, the people of Medina were pleased. When the direction was changed, the people of Mecca became pleased. God says in the verse that this is a test for all people to uncover their real reasons behind following the Prophet. Did they pray towards *qibla* because of their own inclinations or because of God's decree? It is important to clarify that the primary aim of the change of *qibla* was not to test people; rather, the main aim was to respond to the change in circumstances in the mission of the Prophet. In general, all the events that take place in our lives are tests of faith and commitment to the Divine Decrees. However, they are also related to the time and place people live in.

According to Muslim sources, after the *change* of qibla, some Muslims turned away from Islam, questioning the wisdom of the decision of God and his Prophet. This is why God said, *We made it a test to separate who are weak and strong in their faith.* This issue highlighted an underlying problem within the Muslim community that some people followed the Prophet because they really believed in him, and others followed him because some aspects of the religion "made sense" to them. The second group of people then departed from the faith,when some aspects of the faith "did not make sense" to them.

The example of people who subscribe to the view of the second group of people are abundant in modern societies. Due to their predetermined convictions, worldviews and cultural background, some people may claim that certain aspects of the religion do not make sense to them. When we do not understand something within our religion, it is important to reflect on our social and cultural biases and to try to acquire more knowledge in order to understand God's perspective.

قَدْ نَرَىٰ تَقَلُّبَ وَجْهِكَ فِي السَّمَاءِ ۖ فَلَنُوَلِّيَنَّكَ قِبْلَةً تَرْضَاهَا ۚ فَوَلِّ وَجْهَكَ
شَطْرَ الْمَسْجِدِ الْحَرَامِ ۚ وَحَيْثُ مَا كُنتُمْ فَوَلُّوا وُجُوهَكُمْ شَطْرَهُ ۗ وَإِنَّ
الَّذِينَ أُوتُوا الْكِتَابَ لَيَعْلَمُونَ أَنَّهُ الْحَقُّ مِن رَّبِّهِمْ ۗ وَمَا اللَّهُ بِغَافِلٍ عَمَّا
يَعْمَلُونَ ﴿144﴾

We see you turning your face about in the sky. We will surely turn you to a qibla of your liking: so turn your face towards the Holy Mosque, and wherever you may be, turn your faces towards it! Indeed, those who were given the Book surely know that it is the truth from their Lord. And God is not oblivious of what they do.

We see you turning your face about in the sky; This is the central verse about the change of the direction of prayer. In the Arabic language, the term "We see" (*qad narā*) implies repetition. Therefore, the accurate meaning of the verse, is that "We repeatedly see you turning your face about in the sky" and it seems to be referring to the Prophet's anticipation for revelation or his request to God for revelation and further instructions about the change of the *qibla*. What we understand from the verse and some traditions is that the Prophet was concerned about the *qibla* due to his encounters with the Jews of Medina.

The Prophet was previously in Mecca for 13 years where he prayed towards Jerusalem without any problem. According to Muslim traditions, the change of the *qibla* took place two months before the Battle of Badr, which places the event 17 months after the emigration from Mecca to Medina. Both the Quran and Muslim traditions report that this period saw major debates between the Jews of Medina and Muslims. It seems that the undertone of these debates was that the Jews taunted Muslims by saying that Islam was an offshoot of Judaism. After all, Muslims followed the same *qibla* as the Jews, the same prophets, and the same God. This is very same premise that some Western scholars have argued - that Islam is an unorthodox offshoot of Judaism. Understandably, this attitude of the Jews of Medina made the Prophet unhappy; therefore, he sought an independent identity for Muslims for which the change of *qibla* played a crucial role.

We will surely turn you to a qibla of your liking; God granted the Prophet's prayer by changing the qibla to the Kabah where the foundation of the monotheistic religion was laid by Prophet Abraham. The verse also indicates Prophet Muhammad's great affinity with Prophet Abraham and the great example that he set for his progeny and the faithful. This is a remarkable situation; God Almighty follows the liking of his Prophet by turning the *qibla* from Jerusalem to Mecca.

"so turn your face towards the Holy Mosque, and wherever you may be, turn your faces towards it!" This verse gave rise to some discussion regarding whether the *qibla* referred to the Holy Mosque

(*Masjid al-Ḥarām*) or the Kabah. *Masjid al-Ḥarām* is not a fixed area and it has been expanded significantly since the time of the Prophet. Here, *Masjid al-Ḥarām* is mentioned in the verse rather than the Kabah. There is consensus among the commentators that the reason for this is because it is impossible and impractical to turn towards the Kabah accurately from a distance due to its size. Therefore, according to the Islamic law, the *qibla* of people who live in and around *Masjid al-Ḥarām* is Kabah and for those who live elsewhere, the *qibla* is *Masjid al-Ḥarām* which is a much larger area. This ruling is purely based on practicality, and it indicates that the direction is important not the accuracy of it.

Indeed, those who were given the Book surely know that it is the truth from their Lord. And God is not oblivious of what they do. The context here suggests that the last section of the verse addresses the Jews of Medina. According to reliable traditions, they had the knowledge that the last Prophet would pray towards two directions. Therefore, the verse shifts the debate between the Jews of Medina and Muslims by using the change of the direction of the prayer as a proof of the prophethood of Muhammad.

وَلَئِنْ أَتَيْتَ الَّذِينَ أُوتُوا الْكِتَابَ بِكُلِّ آيَةٍ مَّا تَبِعُوا قِبْلَتَكَ ۚ وَمَا أَنتَ بِتَابِعٍ قِبْلَتَهُمْ ۚ وَمَا بَعْضُهُم بِتَابِعٍ قِبْلَةَ بَعْضٍ ۚ وَلَئِنِ اتَّبَعْتَ أَهْوَاءَهُم مِّن بَعْدِ مَا جَاءَكَ مِنَ الْعِلْمِ ۙ إِنَّكَ إِذًا لَّمِنَ الظَّالِمِينَ ﴿145﴾

Even if you bring those who were given the Book every [kind of] sign, they will not follow your qibla. Nor shall you follow their qibla, nor will any of them follow the qibla of the other. And if you follow their desires, after the knowledge that has come to you, you will indeed be one of the wrongdoers.

Every [kind of] sign; This alludes to every kind of argument. Even though the Jews already knew that the last Prophet would have two directions of prayer, they would not follow the Prophet and his *qibla*. The verse informs us that the debate around the change of *qibla* continued long after it was changed. Muslims continued to try to convince the Jews of Medina about the righteousness of the Prophet and the justification of the change of the *qibla*.

nor shall you follow their qibla; Debating with people who are not ready to engage in understanding the other side of an argument is a futile exercise. These debates are not truth-seeking, and the Quran advises not to argue with close-minded individuals.

nor will any of them follow the qibla of the other; There was also a dispute about the direction of prayer among the Jews and Christians. Although this is the most likely interpretation of the verses, there is a lack of evidence about the precise contents of the Holy Books of the Jews and Christians of the time. This information is crucial since some of the statements of the Quran about the belief system of the Jews and Christians at the time of revelation may be different to the belief system of contemporary Jews and Christians. For example, there is evidence that some of the Christians in the Northern Arabian Peninsula followed the *Maryamiyya* sect of Christianity, possibly referring to Greek Orthodox Patriarchate, who at the time considered Saint Mary as a goddess. They possessed holy books that are different to the Gospels available today. Drawing on the possibility that the Jews and Christians followed different directions of prayer to each other, the verse may be focusing on this in order to de-emphasise the issue of Muslims having their own direction of prayer.

And if you follow their desires, after the knowledge that has come to you, you will indeed be one of the wrongdoers. The last section of the verse addresses Muslims through the Prophet. There was an ongoing debate among the Jews and Muslims in Medina about the teachings and legitimacy of the Prophet Muhammad. Some of the arguments that the Jews put forward caused some Muslims to become confused and to begin to question the need to change their *qibla* and this led them to doubt their faith. In return, the verse warns these Muslims that if they follow their desires, they are from wrongdoers.

الَّذِينَ آتَيْنَاهُمُ الْكِتَابَ يَعْرِفُونَهُ كَمَا يَعْرِفُونَ أَبْنَاءَهُمْ ۖ وَإِنَّ فَرِيقًا مِّنْهُمْ لَيَكْتُمُونَ الْحَقَّ وَهُمْ يَعْلَمُونَ ﴿146﴾

Those whom We have given the Book recognise him just as they recognise their sons, but a part of them indeed conceal the truth while they know.

The Jews of Medina knew from their books that the last Prophet would pray towards two directions. Therefore, when the change of the *qibla* took place, it was a clear sign that Muhammad was the last Prophet. The second possible interpretation of the verse suggest that the pronoun "*ha*" refers to the change of *qibla*, instead of the Prophet, so it reads "Those whom We have given the Book recognise it"; meaning that they knew that the change of the *qibla* was justified.

but a part of them indeed conceal the truth while they know, The structure of this phrase is often used in the Quran to distinguish those who are sincere in their faith. God is critical of those who conceal the truth "while they know" thereby highlighting their intention and acknowledging that there was a group of Jews who did not conceal the truth and remained sincere in their faith.

الْحَقُّ مِن رَّبِّكَ ۖ فَلَا تَكُونَنَّ مِنَ الْمُمْتَرِينَ ﴿147﴾

This is the truth from your Lord; so do not be among the sceptics.

Here, Muslims are asked to remove their doubts and refrain from futile debates about the change of *qibla* and continue with their other affairs.

The address of the verse is to the Prophet; however, Muslims are meant to take notice. Certainly, the Prophet never would be sceptical about what was revealed to him; thus, it is a command for others.

This is the truth from your Lord; Two views have been stated regarding the sentence structure of this verse. "The truth is from your Lord," (*al-haghghu min rabbika*) may form the subject and predicate of a nominal sentence. Hence it means that "the truth only comes from your Lord, and you should not listen to anyone else after the truth has come to you." The other structural possibility is that "the truth" is the predicate of an elided subject *huwa,* here it would mean, "this is the truth" from your Lord, meaning that the change of the direction of the prayer is the truth from your Lord.

وَلِكُلٍّ وِجْهَةٌ هُوَ مُوَلِّيهَا فَاسْتَبِقُوا الْخَيْرَاتِ أَيْنَ مَا تَكُونُوا يَأْتِ
بِكُمُ اللَّهُ جَمِيعًا إِنَّ اللَّهَ عَلَىٰ كُلِّ شَيْءٍ قَدِيرٌ ﴿148﴾

Everyone has a cynosure [center of attention] to which he turns; so, take the lead in all good works. Wherever you may be, God will bring you all together. Indeed, God has power over all things.

Everyone has a cynosure to which he turns; The specific direction is not of importance; after all, every individual has been given a cynosure to which they turn. The importance lies in obeying God. This is true for all aspects of our lives. There is no point of debating over the precise day of Eid or other holy occasions. What matters the most is that once people have been given clear instructions, they need to rush to deliver God's command. This ethos is echoed in other verses of the Quran, for example in the verse: *Virtue is not to turn your faces to the east or the west; rather, virtue is [personified by] those who have faith in God and the Last Day...* (Q. 2:177) The verse clearly notes that virtue is not nit-picking minute details of God's commands but to implement them with utmost commitment.

Wherever you may be, God will bring you all together. Indeed, God has power over all things. The last section of the verse marks God's final remarks on the change in the direction of prayer and the futility of needless debate. There are two additional verses (Q. 2:149-150) which serve to reaffirm the change of *qibla*. These verses show that the aim of the change of the direction of the *qibla* was to provide Muslims with an identity independent from the Jews of Medina. However, the undertone of this set of verses suggests that *qibla* in itself has no value to God Almighty. For God, it is important that people should obey divine commands and exert utmost effort to commit virtuous acts. In the end, God will gather everyone on the Day of Judgment, regardless of their location, direction, and affiliation.

وَمِنْ حَيْثُ خَرَجْتَ فَوَلِّ وَجْهَكَ شَطْرَ الْمَسْجِدِ الْحَرَامِ وَإِنَّهُ لَلْحَقُّ مِن رَّبِّكَ وَمَا اللَّهُ بِغَافِلٍ عَمَّا تَعْمَلُونَ ﴿149﴾

Whencesoever you may go out, turn your face towards the Holy Mosque. Indeed, it is the truth from your Lord, and God is not oblivious of what you do.

The previous verses concern the debate about the direction of prayer in Medina, where most Muslims lived at that time. In this verse however, the meaning is more general, stating that whenever setting out to travel, turn your face towards the Kabah in prayer. In this verse, God addressed the Prophet individually to show the importance of this ruling, which is reiterated by *Indeed, it is the truth from your Lord.* The next verse repeats this command and then generalises it to all Muslims.

وَمِنْ حَيْثُ خَرَجْتَ فَوَلِّ وَجْهَكَ شَطْرَ الْمَسْجِدِ الْحَرَامِ ۚ وَحَيْثُ مَا
كُنتُمْ فَوَلُّوا وُجُوهَكُمْ شَطْرَهُ لِئَلَّا يَكُونَ لِلنَّاسِ عَلَيْكُمْ حُجَّةٌ إِلَّا
الَّذِينَ ظَلَمُوا مِنْهُمْ فَلَا تَخْشَوْهُمْ وَاخْشَوْنِي وَلِأُتِمَّ نِعْمَتِي عَلَيْكُمْ
وَلَعَلَّكُمْ تَهْتَدُونَ ﴿150﴾

And whencesoever you may go out, turn your face towards the Holy Mosque, and wherever you may be, turn your faces towards it, so that the people may have no argument against you, neither those of them who are wrongdoers. So do not fear them, but fear Me, that I may complete My blessing on you and so that you may be guided.

And whencesoever you may go out, turn your face towards the Holy Mosque, and wherever you may be, turn your faces towards it; The verse reiterates the previous verses about the change of the direction of the *qibla* to make a new statement. In fact, there are three repetitions in the set of verses that discusses the change of *qibla*. Some Western scholars considered the repetitious style of the Quran as an "inconsistency". However, the supposed repetitions are a stylistic feature of the Quran. When God addresses an important matter, he repeats his instructions while drawing attention to different aspects of the issue being addressed. By doing so, he keeps the focus on the subject while setting out the relevant issues. Therefore, each of the three instances about change of *qibla* draws attention to a different aspect of the change of the *qibla*.

In the first instance, the verses described the Prophet's wish to change the direction of the *qibla* due to the constant attacks from the Jews of Medina who accused Islam of being a heretic offshoot of Judaism. The second verse refers to the existence of the information about the change of the *qibla* in the religious texts of the Jews, and their knowledge that the last Prophet would have two directions of prayer. Finally, in this verse, there is an emphasis that the changing of the *qibla* would end the arguments against Muslims.

so that the people may have no argument against you; The arguments against Muslims included the accusation that, if Islam was an independent religion, in the sense it had a different prophet and holy book, it would also have an independent direction of prayer that was different to the Jews. Secondly, it is possible that if the Jews of Medina had information in their scriptures about the last Prophet having two directions of prayer, then they may have questioned the Prophet about this prior to the change. It is important to note that this postulation is highly speculative and rests on a number of assumptions about the contents of the Jewish scripture.

So do not fear them, but fear Me; These verses illustrate the importance and influence the Jews of Medina had over Muslims. Muslims of Medina cared about what the Jews thought about their religion, the way on which they reacted to new revelations and their opinion of the Prophet. The Jews were influential in Medina as Muslims regarded them highly due to the monotheistic connection. However, God instructed Muslims to change this mindset as they needed to come out of the influence of the Jews, and these types of verses have a purpose of withdrawing the Jewish influence on Muslims.

I may complete My blessing on you and so that you may be guided. The blessing mentioned in the verse may have two meanings: first, the blessing of an independent identity granted to Muslims; and second, the blessing granted as a reward for following God's instructions.

كَمَا أَرْسَلْنَا فِيكُمْ رَسُولًا مِّنكُمْ يَتْلُو عَلَيْكُمْ آيَاتِنَا
وَيُزَكِّيكُمْ وَيُعَلِّمُكُمُ الْكِتَابَ وَالْحِكْمَةَ وَيُعَلِّمُكُم مَّا لَمْ
تَكُونُوا تَعْلَمُونَ ﴿151﴾

As We sent to you an Apostle from among yourselves, who recites to you Our signs, and purifies you, and teaches you the book and wisdom, and teaches you what you did not know.

When Abraham was building the House of God, he supplicated saying: *Our Lord, raise amongst them an apostle from among them, who should recite to them Your signs, and teach them the Book and wisdom, and purify them. Indeed, You are the All-mighty, the All-wise.* (Q. 2:129)

As We sent to you an Apostle from among yourselves; The Arabs were *ummiyyūn*, those who had not been given any scripture. In other words, they were gentiles; Jews referred them *ummiyyūn* on the grounds that the Jews were given scripture, but the gentiles were not given scripture. By sending them a messenger with revelation, scripture and guidance, God then completed his blessing over the people.

who recites to you Our signs, and purifies you, and teaches you; Three beautiful qualities of the Prophet are mentioned in the verse. Interestingly, these are the three requests that Abraham made in his supplication. "Recites to you Our signs" refers to how Prophet Muhammad conveyed the revelation to Muslims and informed them about this world and the Hereafter.

The Prophet purifies Muslims from inward and outward evils as mentioned in Q. 6:120: *Renounce outward sins and the inward ones...* The inward evils include polytheism, disobedience to God, holding grudges, greed, jealousy and the like. The outward evils include fornication, adultery, openly committing various sins and on the like. This verse asserts that the Prophet would purify his followers from these evils.

and teaches you the book and wisdom; The book (*kitāb*) mentioned in the verse is not the scripture; rather it refers to the obligatory rituals mentioned in the Quran such as praying, fasting and giving alms. Every believer should know their responsibility towards God. These responsibilities have been conveyed and taught to Muslims by the Prophet and this is what is referred to as the book. "Wisdom" (*hikma*) is the theology, belief and teachings which Muslims believe in. Therefore, the difference between the book and wisdom is that the book is the practical instructions Muslims need to follow, and the wisdom is the theology of the religion.

And teaches you what you did not know. Refers to the unknown aspects of this world which are impossible to know without divine help and guidance. There are many aspects of the world that human beings can acquire knowledge of independently, including knowledge of science and technology. However, there are some aspects of the world that no person can acquire knowledge of independently including the knowledge of life after death, the connection between human beings and angels, and the human spirit.

فَاذْكُرُونِي أَذْكُرْكُمْ وَاشْكُرُوا لِي وَلَا تَكْفُرُونِ ﴿152﴾

Remember Me, and I will remember you, and thank Me, and do not be ungrateful to Me.

This verse, coupled with another verse in Surah Tawba, make an interesting conversation in the Quran. Here, the verse says, *Remember Me, and I will remember you,* and in Surah Tawba, *... they forget God, so He forgets them...* (Q. 9:67)

God bestows some blessings on everyone unconditionally. However, if people wish to move towards him, the move should be initiated by people, and this is followed by blessings from God Almighty. God sends down his special blessings on those who remember him. If they forget him, he withdrawn his blessings. In other words, if people expose themselves to God's blessing, they will receive his blessings and if they block the blessings by turning away, they will not receive it.

In this sense, these two verses are a clear manifestation of absolute human free will. Of course, this verse is not referring to material blessings, rather, it speaks of the spiritual blessing that leads to closeness to God. There is a clear distinction between spiritual blessings and material blessings. Many non-believing nations in the past and present have excelled in material blessings both individually and collectively. Some Muslims wonder why material blessings such as good health, wealth, safety and security are given to non-believing nations. But it is important to remember that these blessings are material and have been given to them due to their other actions. Spiritual blessings are related to becoming close to God and this is only achievable through remembrance of God. Furthermore, according to many traditions God will remember us in the same way as we remember him.

There are of three types of remembrance of God: first is uttering the names of God with the tongue. This is what Muslims practise in ritual prayers and other occasions. Second, is remembrance by action; any good deed done for the sake of God falls under this category. Third, is rembrance through contemplating the greatness of God, his blessings and creation. The benefit of remembering God also manifests in this world but it would be amplified in the Hereafter: *...Remember God abundantly...* because the benefits of it would come in the Hereafter. (Q.8:40, 62:10)

One might wonder why remembrance of God is integral to attaining spiritual elevation. Thankfulness does not reach him, in the sense he does not benefit from it, nor does he feel better when people thank him. We feel gratified when someone thanks us, but the same feelings are not applicable to God. We are the ones who benefit from our interactions with God. God does not gain or lose anything as a result of our deeds. Thanking God is an acknowledgment that we understand that what we have is solely from him. It is also humbling and softens the hearts. In return, this process makes us obedient and patient towards God. In this way, we are the principal recipients of our thankfulness towards God. He encourages us to be thankful and to remember and worship him, because these actions bring us close to him and this is his Divine Will.

يَا أَيُّهَا الَّذِينَ آمَنُوا اسْتَعِينُوا بِالصَّبْرِ وَالصَّلَاةِ ۚ إِنَّ اللَّهَ مَعَ الصَّابِرِينَ ﴿153﴾

O you who have faith! Take recourse in patience and prayer; indeed, God is with the patient.

وَلَا تَقُولُوا لِمَنْ يُقْتَلُ فِي سَبِيلِ اللَّهِ أَمْوَاتٌ ۚ بَلْ أَحْيَاءٌ وَلَٰكِنْ لَا تَشْعُرُونَ ﴿154﴾

And do not call those who were slain in God's way 'dead.' Rather they are living, but you are not aware.

These two verses introduce a new subject; God is preparing Muslims for sacrifice. The verse is also related to the previous verses in the sense that the change of *qibla* created a new and independent identity for Muslims that the polytheists of Mecca and Jews of Medina could not tolerate. Therefore, a war became inevitable.

O you who have faith! As discussed above, this advice was given to the Jews of Medina in verse 45 of this surah, when the conversation with the Jews began *Take recourse in patience and prayer and it is indeed hard except for the humble.* In the verse at hand (Q. 2:153), it is assumed that the believers should already be humble as they are addressed as those who have faith. Therefore, this verse puts forward another aspect to *patience and prayer* that *God is with the patient.*

Take recourse in patience and prayer; In Q. 2:45, most of commentators interpreted "patience" (*ṣabr*) as fasting, however, in this verse "the patient are those who control themselves in the face of difficulties." In this regard, Tusi defines a patient person as "someone who resists, in the face of what his desires call him towards."[278] Desires may call towards what is forbidden or they may not tolerate whatever calamities fall upon a person individually or collectively. A patient person resists these desires in the face of difficulty.

Indeed, God is with the patient. This is a beautiful, reassuring and oft-repeated phrase in the Quran. When God is *with* a person, it means that they have the support, guidance and blessings of God and that he will take the person out of the calamity with his interventions. One of the severest calamities is the loss of loved ones, for example through war. This is the connection to verse 154: *And do not call those who were slain in God's way 'dead.' Rather they are living, but you are not aware.* To start with the end of verse, "are not aware" draws attention to the fact that, when somebody dies, people often assume that the deceased has been cut off from this world. God tells us that we do not have the awareness to realise that those who are killed in the way of God are alive. Of course, it is not limited to those who are killed in the way of God - everyone who has moved from this world to the next is alive. They continue the next stage of their journey in *barzakh*, while waiting for the Day of Judgment.

And do not call those who were slain in God's way 'dead.' When there is a war or fighting, it may be assumed that even the ones who are killed whilst fighting the right cause have died in vain. In fact, they may be considered to have died for no reason and their death may even be considered as a waste, especially if they are young. However, God tells us that this is not the case, they are alive, but people do not grasp it.

Rather they are living, but you are not aware. In addition, we understand from the other verses of the Quran (Q. 3:169) that they are granted a high position and privileges. In conclusion, the verse prepares Muslims mentally and spiritually for a sudden and brutal death in the imminent fight with their enemies.

وَلَنَبْلُوَنَّكُم بِشَيْءٍ مِّنَ الْخَوْفِ وَالْجُوعِ وَنَقْصٍ مِّنَ الْأَمْوَالِ
وَالْأَنفُسِ وَالثَّمَرَاتِ وَبَشِّرِ الصَّابِرِينَ ﴿155﴾

We will surely test you with a measure of fear and hunger and a loss of wealth, lives, and fruits; and give good news to the patient.

We will surely test you; Divine tests and trials are not done in order for God to know something that he would not know otherwise. They are to evoke and train the capacities and abilities of humankind. The means of such trials may be bitter or pleasant as Q. 7:168 states about the Israelites, *We tested them with good and bad [times] so that they may come back.*

and give good news to the patient, Those who are patient have been referred to in the previous verses, "*indeed God is with the patient.*" (Q. 2:153) These two occasions refer two different levels of patience for two different categories of people of faith: the first type of patience is that believers cope with the calamities that befall them, and they do not complain and endure the calamities. Yet they may not know how the wisdom of God operates through calamities. This is the type of patience mentioned in this verse, (Q. 2:155) *give good news to the patient* that they would be rewarded with Paradise even if they do not understand the wisdom behind the calamities.

The second type of patience is that believers are aware of the inner workings of the system that God has established in this world and the role that calamities play in this system. They do not simply cope with the calamities but embrace them with the knowledge that the calamities are a means to elevate their spiritual station. This is the type of patience mentioned in 2:153 *indeed God is with the patient.*

الَّذِينَ إِذَا أَصَابَتْهُم مُّصِيبَةٌ قَالُوا إِنَّا لِلَّهِ وَإِنَّا إِلَيْهِ رَاجِعُونَ ﴿156﴾

—those who, when an affliction visits them, say, 'Indeed we belong to God, and to Him do we indeed return.'

When people are afflicted with calamities, many become angry with God and complain or make accusations against him. This verse, on the other hand, states that those who have the second type of patience mentioned in the previous verse do not complain to God, or accuse him of not knowing how to manage the affairs of his creation, rather, they say *"Indeed we belong to God, and to Him do we indeed return."*

Indeed, we belong to God, and to Him do we indeed return. In its simplest form, *Indeed, we belong to God* expresses faith in God and *to Him do we indeed return* expresses faith in the Day of Judgment as if to reveal that the root of patience (*ṣabr*) is faith in God and the Last Day.

There is a fascinating explanation of this verse in *Nahj al-balāgha*; Imam Ali said: "When we say 'Indeed we belong to God', in a way we confess, we are owned by God Almighty. Then when we say 'to Him do we indeed return' we confess to our distraction in this world when we are to move to the next world."[279] The verse does not refer to just expressing this phrase, or an utterance that Muslim should use, as is very common, especially in when someone had lost a loved one. Rather, the verse reveals the attitude of the heart and mind that embraces the calamity which in return leads to a God-centric outlook on the world. If such realizations take deep root in a person's heart, it can bring out utmost patience and eradicate all forms of sorrow, fear and anguish and remove all forms of heedlessness from the heart.

أُولَٰئِكَ عَلَيْهِمْ صَلَوَاتٌ مِّن رَّبِّهِمْ وَرَحْمَةٌ ۖ وَأُولَٰئِكَ هُمُ الْمُهْتَدُونَ ﴿157﴾

It is they who receive the blessings of their Lord and [His] mercy, and it is they who are the [rightly] guided.

It is they who receive the blessings of their Lord; The commentators explain that "*the blessings of their Lord*" refers to purification of the soul, benevolence, subtle blessing, forgiveness and mercy from God. There are three rewards mentioned in this verse as the reward of the patient: blessing of their Lord, a type of mercy and guidance.

Here, *ṣalawāt* is the word used for "blessing". Muslims send *ṣalawāt* on the Prophet, a prayer where Muslims ask God to bless the Prophet. This is not the type of *ṣalawāt* mentioned in this verse. This *ṣalawāt* comes from God and is an indication of a blessing or reward. There are other occasions in the Quran that God and his angels send blessings to the people: *It is He who blesses you, and so do His angels, that He may bring you out from darkness into light, and He is most merciful to the faithful.* (Q. 33:43)

From these verses we understand that *ṣalawāt* from God is a reward for the pious; it is not a prayer as we say for the Prophet. The intent of this reward can be understood from the verse, "*so that He may bring you out from darkness into light.*" Therefore, the blessing or *ṣalawāt* from God brings about openness of the heart, and the guidance that comes to the heart.

and [His] mercy, and it is they who are the [rightly] guided. When someone has the attitude and mindset of patience mentioned in verses 2:153 and 156, then the heart is opened; guidance, and the blessings of God pour into the recipient's heart. This is why the verse states that upon receiving blessings of their Lord, they receive "mercy" (*raḥma*). God rewards them with extra blessings because they are enduring an affliction. Finally, this blessing takes people into "light" as mentioned in Q. 33:43, and this light is the guidance.

The overall message of this set of verses demonstrates that afflictions that fall upon believers are not to be detested. After all, if believers have the right attitude, afflictions will lead to the mercy and guidance of God. From the relevant verses of the Quran and the teachings of the Prophet and Imams we gather that this world is a place of affliction. If a person believes in God and stands firm in the face of these afflictions, without wavering, there will be a great reward in the end.

إِنَّ الصَّفَا وَالْمَرْوَةَ مِن شَعَائِرِ اللَّهِ ۖ فَمَنْ حَجَّ الْبَيْتَ أَوِ اعْتَمَرَ فَلَا جُنَاحَ
عَلَيْهِ أَن يَطَّوَّفَ بِهِمَا ۚ وَمَن تَطَوَّعَ خَيْرًا فَإِنَّ اللَّهَ شَاكِرٌ عَلِيمٌ ﴿158﴾

Indeed, Ṣafā and Marwa are among God's sacraments. So, whoever makes hajj to the House, or performs the ʿumra, there is no sin upon him to circuit between them. Should anyone do good of his own accord, then God is indeed appreciative, All-knowing.

This verse is connected to the earlier verses about the Hajj (Pilgrimage) but there are other verses included in between.

Indeed, *Ṣafā* and *Marwa* are among God's sacraments; *Ṣafā* literally means solid stone which is pure in the sense that no other material has penetrated inside it to make it a hybrid stone. It seems there was a small mountain which was made of a pure, solid stone at the current location of Mount *Ṣafā*. *Marwa,* on the other hand, means soft stone which may have mixed with other substances and is no longer pure. Therefore, these two locations in Mecca where Muslims visit for the Hajj are named after two different types of rock which were initially there but have now been lost. The word *sha'ā'ir* ("Sacraments", singular *sha'īra),* is used in the verse to mean a sign. Any place where Muslims worship God is a sign. In fact, any worship such as prayer, fasting and the place where worship is performed, such as the Kabah, *Ṣafā* and *Marwa*, in itself could be called a sign. Furthermore, the word *sha'īr* originates from *shu'ūr* which means "awareness". Therefore, the sign makes us aware of the connection between a certain prayer or place of worship and God.

So, whoever makes *hajj* to the House; The Arabic word *hajj* means "to intend", and, in the verse, it is used literally to mean, "whoever intends to visit the House". Figuratively it has been used as the name of the ritual of Muslim Pilgrimage. The other ritual which also involves visiting the Kabah, but it is not considered the Pilgrimage, is the *'umra,* derived from the word *i'tamara.* The word *'umra* literally means "to visit", and it is figuratively used to refer to visiting the Kabah without the intention of performing the Pilgrimage. In contrast to Hajj, *'umra* can be performed any time of the year, but Hajj must be performed in a specific time period.

there is no sin upon him to circuit between them. There has been a lengthy discussion among the Muslim jurists, but in general they state that it is not obligatory to circuit between *Ṣafā* and *Marwa*. However, the context of the revelation, and a number of hadith indicate that it had been obligatory to circuit between *Ṣafā* and *Marwa* but this was made a voluntary ritual at the time of the Prophet. In this way, there is no contradiction between the verse, the *ahadith* and the context. Prophet Abraham's followers have circuited between the two places, but God made it a voluntary act for Muslims. The reasons behind the circuit between *Ṣafā* and *Marwa*, are in numerous traditions but the overall theme of these traditions is that the purpose of the ritual is to humble oneself before God.

"Should anyone do good of his own accord, then God is indeed appreciative, All-knowing." This sentence highlights that God is not in need of our appreciation. We show appreciation to God because he has given us blessings. We cannot give any blessing to God, but he thanks us because we have shown him gratitude.

إِنَّ الَّذِينَ يَكْتُمُونَ مَا أَنزَلْنَا مِنَ الْبَيِّنَاتِ وَالْهُدَىٰ مِن بَعْدِ مَا بَيَّنَّاهُ لِلنَّاسِ
فِي الْكِتَابِ أُولَٰئِكَ يَلْعَنُهُمُ اللَّهُ وَيَلْعَنُهُمُ اللَّاعِنُونَ ﴿159﴾

Indeed, those who conceal what We have sent down of manifest proofs and guidance, after We have clarified it in the Book for mankind, —they shall be cursed by God and cursed by the cursers,

---

Indeed, those who conceal what We have sent down of manifest proofs and guidance; According to Tabrisi the verse refers to the Jewish Rabbis who concealed the prophethood of Muhammad or the signs that indicated his prophethood from the Jews and non-Jews of Medina.[280] There are two intriguing points in this verse, first, there is a difference between "manifest proofs" (*al-bayyināt*) and "guidance" (*al-hudā*)". In the Quran the word *bayyina* (sing. of *bayyināt*) is used to refer to a miracle or a clear argument which cannot be refuted. Both meanings are possible in this verse. Some commentators have suggested that when *bayyina* is used together with *hudā,* it refers to the creed (*'aqīda)* or principles of the religion (*uṣūl al-dīn*) and *hudā* refers to the Islamic law (*sharia*) or ancillaries of the religion (*furū' al-dīn*).

Of course, *sharia* is a type of guidance - Muslims have been guided about how to pray and regulate their daily affairs. *Bayyināt* refers to the things that are higher than *sharia*. A more plausible explanation for the word *bayyināt* may be that in the Torah, there were clear signs (*bayyināt*) and guidance (*hudā*) by which people were guided towards Prophet Muhammad. The very reason that the Jews settled in Medina was to await the promised Prophet; therefore, they had this guidance with them.

after We have clarified it in the Book for mankind; This caveat points out the fact that the curse came into effect only after the clear warning was given to people. The consequence of the concealment and deviation from the truth was so dramatic that God sent a clear warning before the punishment took effect.

they shall be cursed by God; The verse ends with a curse (*laʿna*) on those who conceal the clear signs and guidance. The literal meaning of *laʿna* is to distance someone from one's grace and blessing. Cursing someone means you do not wish to include them in your blessing. Thus, when God curses Satan, it means that he distanced him from his mercy. This is the true meaning of the curse mentioned in the Quran. When people curse the wrongdoers, it means that they pray to God to distance the wrongdoers from his mercy. In this sense, *laʿna* is the opposite of *salawāt* (salutations) where people ask God to include someone in his mercy. This, when Muslims send *salawāt* (salutations) to the Prophet, they ask God to include him in his mercy.

The Quran refers to both salutation and curse. Certain people are included in God's mercy (for example, Q. 9:99, 23:9, 33:56) and some are distanced from his mercy (including Q. 3:61, 3:87, 24:23, 28:42. The cursed people mentioned in this verse were the ones who deterred others from the message of God and tried to obstruct God's message.

they shall be cursed by God and cursed by the cursers. The curious part of the process of cursing is that it is not only God who curses them. The verse indicates that the others ("the cursers") do the same. The cursers refer to those who are able to influence this world, such as the angels, prophets and saints. The commentators have provided lengthy and detailed discussions regarding "the cursers". Although they have mostly agreed that the cursers include the beings who have an influence in this world, some went so far as to claim that any creature who lives on the earth, including animals, can curse. Mujahid is one of the proponents of this interpretation and notes that due to certain kinds of wrongdoing of some communities, God withdraws his blessings such as rain, and communities are stricken with drought and famine. This affects the lives of the animals who live in the vicinity, so consequently they curse the wrongdoers of the community from their hearts.[281] It is important to note that this is a marginal view among the commentators.

إِلَّا الَّذِينَ تَابُوا وَأَصْلَحُوا وَبَيَّنُوا فَأُولَـٰئِكَ أَتُوبُ عَلَيْهِمْ ۚ وَأَنَا التَّوَّابُ الرَّحِيمُ ﴿160﴾

except such as repent, make amends, and clarify, —those I shall pardon, and I am the All-clement, the All-merciful.

The verse lays out conditions for the exemption from this curse. The condition is that the atonement should be accompanied with amendments and clarifications. It means that those who conceal the truth should repent and then publicly admit that they had been concealing the truth and clarify what the truth is. If someone repents and does not declare the truth, their situation would be incomplete. The verse is clear that the curse would be removed only after they repent and make a public declaration to rectify their position. Their judgment is with God Almighty.

إِنَّ الَّذِينَ كَفَرُوا وَمَاتُوا وَهُمْ كُفَّارٌ أُولَـٰئِكَ عَلَيْهِمْ لَعْنَةُ اللَّهِ وَالْمَلَائِكَةِ وَالنَّاسِ أَجْمَعِينَ ﴿161﴾

Indeed, those who turn faithless and die while they are faithless, —it is they on whom shall be the curse of God, the angels and all mankind.

The verse addresses those who turn away from the faith after they initially accepted faith, and then commit to misguide people. This is different to not believing in God, rather it is committing to the act of concealing the truth. In this way, it is connected to the previous verse about those who do not rectify the mischief that they have caused.

خَالِدِينَ فِيهَا ۖ لَا يُخَفَّفُ عَنْهُمُ الْعَذَابُ وَلَا هُمْ يُنظَرُونَ ﴿162﴾

They will remain in the curse [forever], and their punishment shall not be lightened, nor will they be granted any respite.

Whilst those who misguide people do not change and reform their evil characteristics, God's curse will remain on them, thus they will remain in Hell. There is a possibility of exiting Hell if people rectify their evil attributes. However, those who are not able to rectify their evil, would remain in Hell forever.

وَإِلَٰهُكُمْ إِلَٰهٌ وَاحِدٌ ۖ لَّا إِلَٰهَ إِلَّا هُوَ الرَّحْمَٰنُ الرَّحِيمُ ﴿163﴾

Your god is the One God, there is no god except Him, the All-beneficent, the All-merciful.

This statement emphasises that nothing can be concealed and all the prophets have come to give the same message.

Your god is the One God; This statement declares the most basic tenet in monotheism, that it is God who deserves to be worshipped. There is no being in this world who deserves to be worshipped except the one who is God Almighty. All human beings have only this one God. The word *wāḥid* can refer to mean numerical one or it may mean all the qualities that make him deserve to be worshipped.

there is no god except Him; This draws attention to another important point that there is no other deity in this world deserving of worship. Thus, the verse strongly emphasises the doctrine of monotheism.

the All-beneficent, the All-merciful. These qualities are used to explain *why* God Almighty deserves to be worshipped. The All-beneficent (*Raḥmān*) refers to the general mercy for the creation and the All-merciful (*Raḥīm*) means someone who listens to the believers, forgives, and provides for them.

Here, the content of revelation is also important. Tabrisi notes that when the verse was revealed in Mecca, there were 360 idols being worshipped.[282] Denouncing all the other deities and reaffirming oneness of God sent shockwaves through the Meccan community. In anticipation of their request for proof for the one God, the verse emphasises the attributes of God: "the All-beneficent, the All-merciful". The following verse, which gives a detailed description of God and proof regarding his creation, gives further credence to this view.

إِنَّ فِي خَلْقِ السَّمَاوَاتِ وَالْأَرْضِ وَاخْتِلَافِ اللَّيْلِ وَالنَّهَارِ وَالْفُلْكِ الَّتِي تَجْرِي فِي الْبَحْرِ بِمَا يَنفَعُ النَّاسَ وَمَا أَنزَلَ اللَّهُ مِنَ السَّمَاءِ مِن مَّاءٍ فَأَحْيَا بِهِ الْأَرْضَ بَعْدَ مَوْتِهَا وَبَثَّ فِيهَا مِن كُلِّ دَابَّةٍ وَتَصْرِيفِ الرِّيَاحِ وَالسَّحَابِ الْمُسَخَّرِ بَيْنَ السَّمَاءِ وَالْأَرْضِ لَآيَاتٍ لِّقَوْمٍ يَعْقِلُونَ ﴿164﴾

Indeed in the creation of the heavens and the earth, and the alternation of night and day, and the ships that sail at sea with profit to men, and the water that God sends down from the sky — with which He revives the earth after its death, and scatters therein every kind of animal— and the changing of the winds, and the clouds disposed between the sky and the earth, are surely signs for a people who apply reason.

Continuing from the previous verse which addressed the polytheists of Mecca, this verse, makes a case for monotheism. It is important to remember that the polytheists of Mecca believed in one creator god, however, they also believed that he delegated his powers to lower deities who were symbolised by the idols.

The way that God creates can sometimes be taken for granted - some may even assume that creation always existed or came into existence by "coincidence." However, even the smallest creation of God, the atoms, are designed with sophistication such that even these atoms are synchronised with each other and the world around them. Taking time to contemplate over this shows that the design is astonishing and deserves great admiration, which makes it impossible to think that these matters came into existence coincidentally.

The way God created the heavens and the earth is called "*khalq*" which is different to "*ibdā*ʿ and *inshā*". "*Ibdā*ʿ and *inshā*" mean bring about something out of nothing, however, "*khalq*" means to make something out of something else or creation through transformation. God has created this world through the atoms. At this stage of human advancement, scientists understand that the atoms miraculously work in a harmonious and constant manner to give shape to the world around us.

the alternation of night and day; This refers to the orderly manner in which time is running; without any interruption and convolution.

the ships that sail at sea with profit to men; This refers to the human misconception that because ships are made by the hands of human beings, credit for their creation should lie with human ingenuity. On the contrary, it is due to the grace of God that ships sail on the waters. Buoyancy is a great blessing from God that can easily be overlooked. People may invent aeroplanes, space shuttles, rockets, computers and other technologies and may wrongfully think this is all due to their own intellect and success. On the contrary, it is God who created the space, sky and seas and made them suitable for human beings to take advantage of them to travel and exploit them for other activities. All these creations run smoothly and in harmony with other elements operating in the world.

the water that God sends down from the sky —with which He revives the earth after its death, and scatters therein every kind of animal; This part of the verse speaks of the miracle of water which works in a systematic and organised way. Water evaporates in the oceans, water clouds are driven through the winds to the places where people and the natural habitat require it, and then it is poured down. This process has endured since the beginning of creation. A little increase in this process may cause floods and a little decrease may cause famine - everything is done in a just and measured way.

Of course, God states in the Quran that sometimes he makes amendments to this organised system by withdrawing it from some and pouring it down on others so that people are reminded that there is a creator who organises the natural events and he is also able to make changes so that people do not take it for granted. *Certainly, We have alternated it among them.* (Q. 25:50) This may only be grasped by "people who apply reason."

وَمِنَ النَّاسِ مَن يَتَّخِذُ مِن دُونِ اللَّهِ أَندَادًا يُحِبُّونَهُمْ كَحُبِّ اللَّهِ ۖ وَالَّذِينَ
آمَنُوا أَشَدُّ حُبًّا لِّلَّهِ ۗ وَلَوْ يَرَى الَّذِينَ ظَلَمُوا إِذْ يَرَوْنَ الْعَذَابَ أَنَّ الْقُوَّةَ لِلَّهِ
جَمِيعًا وَأَنَّ اللَّهَ شَدِيدُ الْعَذَابِ ﴿165﴾

Among the people are those who set up compeers besides God, loving them as if loving God —but the faithful have a more ardent love for God— though the wrongdoers will see, when they sight the punishment, that power, altogether, belongs to God, and that God is severe in punishment.

Among the people are those who set up compeers besides God; The previous verse discussed God's "signs" to emphasise that the management of this world belongs to God alone. Within this context, verse 165 states that despite all those signs and proofs about God's presence and his management of the world, there are some people who take compeers (*andād*) beside God. In other words, they equate some divinities with God. Equating a divinity with God entails giving the attributes or qualities of God to these divinities. This is also mentioned in Q. 7:180, *leave those who deviate in his names (asmā').* "Deviating in his names," means attributing God's qualities to other divinities or attributing the evils of others to God. This is a common phenomenon and even believers may become confused and commit this sin. For example, due to their actions and intentions, believers may distance themselves from God, but they can blame God by saying it is God who created this distance. However, God does not change he is always there for us, constantly pouring down his mercy on the believers. It is our hearts that have the problem; something in our hearts change and we blame God for it. This is a subtle type of deviation (*ilhād*) in the attributes of God, by way of attributing the shortcomings of others to God. Further, people may also attribute the qualities of God to others, such as holding power, giving provisions, and the general management of this world. This is the very act of equating God with others.

loving them as if loving God; This confusion can lead some to polytheism. Others have falsely attributing divine qualities to the prophets, Imams, saints and angels. This confusion creates false love; when people think that something has power or influence, they begin to form an attachment to them.

This was the case with the polytheists of Mecca who are described in this verse. In some other cases, we might form an attachment to our own "self" especially if we have power or influence. However, believers are supposed to love God more than themselves by acknowledging their shortcomings and accepting responsibility for them, rather than attributing them to God.

Commentators have often struggled to find the most correct explanations for this verse. From the text it seems the addressees of the verse are the polytheists, but this understanding can also be problematic.

those who set up compeers besides God, loving them as if loving God; This refers to an understanding of what it means to love God, which cannot apply to the polytheists. The commentators have brought forward three explanations: first, "they like those divinities in the same way that Muslims love God". This view accepts that polytheists cannot love God, so they argue that the verse refers to how Muslims love God. Love is a feeling that we hold for many things including our family, children, friends. This love should not be equal to our love for God.

There are different types of love, for example, love for a spouse is different to love for children, or friends and relatives. In the same way, love for God is different to all other types of love. God never tells us that we should not love anybody or anything else but God; however, it is important to be careful not to love people and things in the way that we love God.

The second view suggested that the polytheists did believe in God, so they loved him but took other divinities alongside their gods and loved them too. So "loving them" refers to their love for the idols. The third view argued that "loving them" refers to loving the worship of idols as they worship God.

Furthermore, there has been a disagreement about the nature of compeers (*andād*), mentioned in the verse. The compeers may refer to the idols or other things that people equate with God or it may refer to leaders of the community. In the latter case, some people are infatuated with their leaders and follow them without question, in the way that they are meant to follow the commands of God. This could even refer to spiritual leaders, such as the prophets, angels and Imams. This love takes the form of attributing the qualities of God to these creations.

The starkest example of it may be the attribution of divine qualities to the Imams by the extremist Shi'is (*qulāt*) who wrongly thinking that they can give sustenance to people or answer to prayers directly. Unfortunately, some of the major Shi'i hadith collections have been infiltrated with some of these extremist ideas. Thus, the veracity of reports must always be scrutinised against these Quranic principles to avoid promoting wrong ideas.

though the wrongdoers will see, when they sight the punishment; The Arabic word "*law*" (though) has two meanings; one is "to wish" and the other is "condition". Both meanings could be used in this verse without contradicting the overall meaning of the verse.

that power, altogether, belongs to God; This shows why these wrongdoers will become regretful in the Hereafter. On the Day of Judgment when the truth is disclosed, they will see that nothing has power except God.

This world is called the world of *mulk* where everything operates according to the causality that God has set in order and he is the one who empowers and influences it. People cannot see the power behind the causality unless they look for the signs of God in creation. They can only discover how this causality operates, and this is what modern science and technology achieves. However, in the Hereafter, a veil will be lifted, and everyone will see that it is God who manages everything. This is why the Quran refers to the Day of Judgment as "the Day of Truth".

God is severe in punishment; Tabatabai has an insightful theological discussion regarding this phrase.[283] He puts forward the apparent contradiction between God's unlimited mercy and his attribute of being severe in punishment. He also contemplates the nature of the punishment. In his response, he makes a distinction between our qualities and God's qualities. For example, we can be merciful and God is merciful. Our mercy is driven by the softness of our heart or by pity. In other words, human mercy is driven by external influences on human emotions. On the other hand, nothing can influence God, thus, he has no emotions. His mercy is constant and available for those who work towards attaining it. It is the same for punishment; God does not become angry or vengeful in the way that human beings can. Instead, people receive the consequences of their actions from God. The negative qualities that humans have embodied in this world will bring about punishment in the Hereafter. Those punishments are severer and harder, and this is why God is referred to as being "severe in punishment."

Further, Tabatabai notes that being precluded from the blessing of God is the harshest punishment for people. People who are self-centred and egoistic are always being punished, even in this world. They cannot attain whatever they desire, and selfish people are always chasing their own desires, thus they have to live in constant disappointment and the heart is imbued with vices such as jealousy and greed. In the Hereafter, these feelings are amplified. The power of God becomes manifest, and people will see the blessings that others receive which they might not have achieved. The intensity of these feelings become so great that it would overtake the intensity of Hellfire.

On the Day of Judgment, when people see that all power belongs to God, there can be no more polytheism (*shirk*) anymore. Even though there is no polytheism, some people end up in Hell due to the vicious attributes of their souls - these people have become the embodiment of polytheism. People witness the power of God, nobody can have any influence over that power, but those vicious people cannot accept it. They tell lies to God Almighty: *The day when God will raise them all together, they will swear to Him, just like they swear to you [now], supposing that they stand on something. Look! They are indeed liars!* (Q. 58:18) Although in the Hereafter people witness the power of God, they try to cheat God as cheating has become part of their nature which they cannot change, and their vicious state brings about their punishment.

Through an understanding of all the signs, the verse concludes that there is one manager in the world. People in different parts of the world may worship different gods, especially in the past, but everywhere in this planet the water cycle works in the same way, regardless which deity people worship. Therefore, the idea of different gods is nothing but created illusion. Yet, despite the obvious signs, some people may still take equals to God. On the Day of Judgment, they will see that all those equals amount to nothing, but illusions. They will be subjected to a severe punishment. It is also important to remember that these equals may not always be idols; they may be people, angels, or even oppressors who forced people to follow them through manipulation. The following verse corroborates this view.

إِذْ تَبَرَّأَ الَّذِينَ اتُّبِعُوا مِنَ الَّذِينَ اتَّبَعُوا وَرَأَوُا الْعَذَابَ وَتَقَطَّعَتْ بِهِمُ الْأَسْبَابُ ﴿166﴾

When those who were followed will disown the followers, and they will sight the punishment while all their means of recourse will be cut off,

When those who were followed will disown the followers; This verse is directly linked to the previous verse and mentions the state of those who take equals to God. On the Day of Judgment, those who were followed in this world will disown their followers by admitting that they never had any power over anything in the world or the Hereafter. Thus, they admit that should not have been followed. Most prominent among them is Satan who will say:

> God gave you the right promise and I gave you the wrong promise. I had no authority over you, except that I called you and you responded to me. So do not blame me but blame yourselves. I cannot respond to your distress calls, neither can you respond to my distress calls. Indeed, I disavow your taking me for [God's] partner aforetime. There is indeed a painful punishment for the wrongdoers. (Q. 14:22)

Here, "following" referred to in the verse is done by consent and choice, not by force. God is just, and he does not punish anyone for committing acts under duress. In unauthorised following, the followed ones would disavow their followers on the Day of Judgment. In the previous verse, the "punishment" they will have to endure on the Day is discussed.

while all their means of recourse will be cut off; This may either refer to the connections between the followed and follower or that every means of recourse for that person is cut off.

وَقَالَ الَّذِينَ اتَّبَعُوا لَوْ أَنَّ لَنَا كَرَّةً فَنَتَبَرَّأَ مِنْهُمْ كَمَا تَبَرَّءُوا مِنَّا ۗ كَذَٰلِكَ
يُرِيهِمُ اللَّهُ أَعْمَالَهُمْ حَسَرَاتٍ عَلَيْهِمْ ۖ وَمَا هُمْ بِخَارِجِينَ مِنَ النَّارِ ﴿167﴾

and when the followers will say, 'Had there been another turn for us, we would disown them as they disown us [now]!' Thus, shall God show them their deeds as regrets for themselves, and they shall not leave the Fire.

---

and when the followers will say, 'Had there been another turn for us, we would disown them as they disown us [now]!' Those who followed false equals to God would ask for another chance to come back to the world and disown their false gods. "Disowning" refers to their false illusions about the benefits of things that would be useless in the Hereafter when everything will show itself in the light of God. On the Day of Judgment everyone will see the consequences of their actions as a result of the wisdom of God. It is by the mercy of God that he keeps the records of people's deeds and returns the benefits of their deeds to them in the Hereafter, if they are good people. However, the same mercy of God would work against vicious people whose evil deeds will be returned to them as punishment. These evil people will regret that they followed false deities or relied on anyone apart from God.

they shall not leave the Fire; This is an indication of their eternal stay in Hell. It may seem harsh to remain in Hell forever, for actions that have been committed in the short span of time that a person lives in the world. To explain this further, there are different types of people in Hell: the first type are *the fuel of Hell.* (Q. 3:10, 66:6) This group of people will cause Hell to blaze because of their internal vices. The second type is not the fuel of Hell, but they are burnt in the fire of the first group of people. The fire in Hell is not the fire that we have in this world; it comes from within people as clearly stated in Q. 66:6, *O you who believe! Protect yourselves and your families against a Fire (Hell) whose fuel is men and stones, over which are (appointed) angels stern (and) severe, who disobey not the commands they receive from Allah, but do that which they are commanded.*

The first group of people can never leave because they are the source of fire, unless they reform their evil attributes. This is the best way of understanding the "eternity" of Hellfire mentioned in the Quran. It may be easier for the second type to exit Hell as they are not the fuel of Hell but are there because they followed the people who are the fuel of Hell. Evil is not part of their nature, and they have blindly followed vicious beings whose evil has become part of their nature. There are some verses of the Quran, and many narrations which indicate that there would be a way to exit from Hellfire for those who can reform themselves.

Thus, shall God show them their deeds as regrets for themselves; Tabrisi in *Majmaʿ al-bayān* contends that there is an implication in this verse that people have free will; the power of choice between the right and wrong.[284] Regret is only possible for the actions that a person has the power to do but chose not did not do. For example, people never regret not being able to fly without a medium, because they could never have done it. In this way, the verse says *God shows them their deeds* as a matter of regret for them, it means that they had the power of choose between the right and wrong, and they choose their deeds. Therefore, they have the regret mentioned in the verse.

يَا أَيُّهَا النَّاسُ كُلُوا مِمَّا فِي الْأَرْضِ حَلَالًا طَيِّبًا وَلَا تَتَّبِعُوا خُطُوَاتِ الشَّيْطَانِ إِنَّهُ لَكُمْ عَدُوٌّ مُبِينٌ ﴿168﴾

O mankind! Eat of what is lawful and pure in the earth, and do not follow in Satan's steps. Indeed, he is your manifest enemy.

At the time of the advent of Islam, the polytheists of Mecca had a very complicated system of defining the types of meat that were lawful and unlawful to eat. Some of these laws are mentioned in the Quran: *God has not prescribed any such thing as Baḥīra, Sā'iba, Wāṣila, or Ḥam; but those who are faithless fabricate lies against God, and most of them do not apply reason.* (Q. 5:103) These four categories made up some part of their complex system of lawful and unlawful meat.

Eat of what is lawful and pure in the earth; In this verse God commands people not to follow such arbitrary and superstitious ways of categorising the edibility of meat; rather they are to eat whatever God has created and made permissible for his creation. The verse indicates that the primary principle in eating food is that everything is lawful or halal unless God has specifically mentioned that something is unlawful or haram. It is not the other way around as some groups such as the Akhbārīs[285] claim that everything is unlawful unless God verifies that it is lawful.

do not follow in Satan's steps; This refers to how Satan often whispers doubts into our minds in the form of a preacher justifying certain values. For example, there are many people who are vegan in the society and, of course, there is nothing wrong with being a vegan. However, it becomes problematic if vegans started preaching that eating meat is wrong in the eyes of God. According to the verse at hand this attitude is considered as "Satan's steps." This is because there are many arguments that non-meat eaters use to convert people to vegetarianism or veganism including "it is unethical to eat kill and eat animals, it is animal cruelty, animal farms are polluting to the environment, it is not sustainable" and so on. Some of these arguments are justified, but we also know that everything is the creation of God and the cycle of life works in this way. Everything works in harmony and balance, so there is no need to disrupt this balance. The Quran already discourages people from excessive consumption of any kind of food, so we can apply this to eating meat as well. Everything should be consumed moderately and responsibly, but a complete ban on consumption of meat is not Islamic. If Satan whispers to people about something which is not mentioned in Islamic law, they should avoid listening to him.

According to traditions attributed to Ibn Abbas, at the time of the Prophet, many Arab tribes made certain types of farm products unlawful for themselves as was mentioned in Q. 5:103. *Baḥīra,* mentioned in the verse, is a camel who was born as the fifth child of the mother and Arabs made it unlawful to slaughter the fifth child of a camel. *Sā'iba* was a she-camel which had given birth to 10 camels and, based on the productivity of the camel, Arabs decided to free the camel who gave birth to 10 camels, and it was forbidden to harm them or eat their meat. *Wāṣila* was a lamb who was born with another lamb. If a lamb was born together with another lamb, they spared one of these lambs by making it unlawful to harm it or eating the meat out of their benevolence. *Ḥam* refers to a male camel, who had produced 10 camels, and the Arabs made it unlawful to harm them. These are only some of the animals that the Arabs of Mecca made unlawful. Some other examples include those animals who were then freed because they had taken their owners to the Kabah. In this intricate but arbitrary system of rules, there were many other categories of animals which were forbidden to eat therefore, many people were confused as to what to eat or not eat.

God conveys his message clearly in this verse that these artificial categorisations are the work of Satan and people must avoid falling into Satan's trap. It was a kind of anthropomorphism to attribute human feelings to the farm animals or take on animal feelings upon ourselves. According to God, these are the result of human imagination. Therefore, humans are commanded to eat from what God has made permissible for people, with the limitation that this is done with moderation. These clear instructions may seem to be unsympathetic. The Arabs at the time thought their rules were kind gestures to their animals, stemming from their benevolence and gratitude to the farm animals who had generously provided for them. Contemporary debates in animal rights have often been polluted with these types of arguments. According to the verse, the source of such ideas is the whispering of Satan. It does not matter how nice and kind these ideas might seem.

إِنَّمَا يَأْمُرُكُم بِالسُّوءِ وَالْفَحْشَاءِ وَأَن تَقُولُوا عَلَى اللَّهِ مَا لَا تَعْلَمُونَ ﴿169﴾

He only prompts you to [commit] evil and indecent acts, and that you attribute to God what you do not know.

He only prompts you to [commit] evil and indecent acts; Satan tricks people into doing evil. The verse draws attention to the fact that this may begin with some innocent and seemingly virtuous idea. However, because the idea does not stem from the religious justification, in the later stages it may lead to evil and indecent acts. Therefore, the verse warns people not to be deceived by false ideas and perceptions. Although they may seem nice, they are ploys to trick people into evil and indecency. Therefore, it is always important to recognise the source of an argument, and whether it has any basis in God's framework of right and wrong.

you attribute to God what you do not know; This phrase has been a matter of lengthy discussion and debate among the scholars of jurisprudence. Human nature is inclined to make assumptions on God's behalf due to our preconceived ideas of what we expect of God. People develop their own values and consciences, and they expect others to be in conformity with them. We can easily extend these expectations to God. However, this is certainly a wrong and deceitful path as we cannot assume to know better than God. To avoid falling into the trap of Satan, we must carefully follow what is said in the scriptures. This does not mean that people cannot behave according to their worldviews, as long as they attribute these views to themselves and not God. Attributing personal views to God leads to making value judgments based on these views. This is why Muslim scholars are not allowed to follow conjecture in the matters of religion.

وَإِذَا قِيلَ لَهُمُ اتَّبِعُوا مَا أَنْزَلَ اللَّهُ قَالُوا بَلْ نَتَّبِعُ مَا أَلْفَيْنَا عَلَيْهِ آبَاءَنَا ۗ أَوَلَوْ
كَانَ آبَاؤُهُمْ لَا يَعْقِلُونَ شَيْئًا وَلَا يَهْتَدُونَ ﴿170﴾

When they are told, 'Follow what God has sent down,' they say, 'We will rather follow what we have found our fathers following.' What, even if their fathers neither applied any reason nor were guided?!

We will rather follow what we have found our fathers following; This is the response from people after the command in the previous verse warning them to follow God's instructions alone and not simple conjecture. However, people disregarded God's instructions about what is lawful and unlawful and preferred to remain on their forefather's traditions. In response to this, God states "What, even if their fathers neither applied any reason nor were guided?!"

Kashani makes a remarkable consideration in commenting on this verse.[286] He states that Muslims are not permitted to follow anyone without having sound justification and good reasoning. Muslims should look for the criteria of justification and good reasoning even from those they follow in religious matters, such as *fatwas* of the religious scholars. Kashani's point is relevant to contemporary Muslims. For example, some people follow certain *marja'* (pl. *marāji'*) or source of emulation in the Twelver Shi'i tradition, simply because their fathers followed the same *marja'* or because that *marja'* has the largest following. This way of thinking is not justified. We need to find the most capable and learned *marja'* to follow in religious matters. The criteria for following a particular *marja'* should be based on their ability to act based on clear evidence and reasoning. We do not just follow a person; we follow their evidence which is rooted in the teachings of the Prophet and Imams.

The traditions of our forefathers are not necessarily bad or evil, however the real issue here comes from acting without evidence or understanding. If their practice is based on reasoning and evidence, of course there is no harm in following their practice. Otherwise, following forefathers is nothing but close-mindedness and people will be held accountable for it on the Day of Judgment. Muslims have many practices in contemporary communities which are often contrary to Islamic law and reason. Yet we continue to practice these because it is the tradition of our forefathers. We need to review our practices and traditions according to Islamic law and reasoning and root out the practices which are not compatible with Islamic law and reasoning. Otherwise, we may be in the same category that the verse at hand rebukes.

وَمَثَلُ الَّذِينَ كَفَرُوا كَمَثَلِ الَّذِي يَنْعِقُ بِمَا لَا يَسْمَعُ إِلَّا دُعَاءً وَنِدَاءً ۚ صُمٌّ بُكْمٌ عُمْيٌ فَهُمْ لَا يَعْقِلُونَ ﴿171﴾

The parable of the faithless is that of someone who shouts after that which does not hear [anything] except a call and cry: deaf, dumb, and blind, they do not apply reason.

This verse comes in the middle of the discussion about the ruling of God concerning the polytheists and the Jews. It gives a sudden pause to the ongoing debate to make an important point that despite calling people to the truth, the Prophet should not expect that all of them would understand him.

The parable of the faithless is that of someone who shouts after; In this parable, "someone who shouts after" refers to the Prophet who calls the faithless to the religion of God, yet those who are being called upon it are like cattle, they do not understand what the Prophet is telling them. They do not hear, see and most importantly do not process his call.

Similar points have been made in many other places of the Quran indicating that there are some who are irresponsive to the message of God. This is not because they do not have human feelings and reasoning, rather it is because they do not grasp the gravity of the teachings of the

Prophet. In this way the means of communication between the Prophet and the faithless is cut. People experience life on different levels. First is the vegetative life; the aspect of life that is related to human growth. Like vegetables and all living things, people need nutrition to grow and prosper. Second is the animal life, which includes movement, feelings, reproduction and raising children. The third is human life which is the highest form of life. Humans have higher values that animals may lack. Of course, we do not possess much knowledge about animals, but based on our existing knowledge, we assume that they lack certain qualities that humans have. Some of these values include a sense of justice, honesty, and gratitude. These values are found in humans universally. The Quran states that there is another level of life that people should have: connection to God Almighty. This entails knowing him better through certain tools that God has placed in our innate nature (*fiṭra*). If we do not have this connection, we cannot fulfil our true potential, therefore, we remain stagnant around the three levels, vegetative life, animal life and human life.

If people have not established this connection with God, or have not made any attempt to establish it, then they do not hear the message of God in the real sense. They hear it with their ears but they do comprehend it. They are blind because they see it with their eyes, but they do not process the guidance correctly. They are dumb because they cannot repeat the statements of faith, in the sense that it does not go through their heart.

يَا أَيُّهَا الَّذِينَ آمَنُوا كُلُوا مِن طَيِّبَاتِ مَا رَزَقْنَاكُمْ وَاشْكُرُوا لِلَّهِ إِن كُنتُمْ إِيَّاهُ تَعْبُدُونَ ﴿172﴾

O you who have faith! Eat of the good things We have provided you, and thank God, if it is Him that you worship.

Eat of the good things We have provided you; After taking a short break from the discussion, verse 172 returns to the subject of eating what is lawful, this time in a milder tone. The verse mentions thanking and worshipping God and urges believers to eat from the animals that he has made lawful, therefore abolishing the previous polytheistic customs.

if it is Him that you worship; One of the major pillars of worship is to thank God (*shukr*). If there is no thanksgiving, there is no worship. In fact, the performance of worship is about thanksgiving to God. There is a striking definition of thanksgiving (*sukhr*) to God in Tabrisi's *Majma' al-bayān*.[287] He states that *shukr* is acknowledging the blessings of God; and acknowledging that these blessings originate from him alone. This is the root of the *shukr* and this creates reverence for God in the heart. However, most of the time, we are negligent of this, and assume that we are earning everything ourselves. If we remove this false perception and acknowledge that everything comes from God alone, out of nothing, then the sense of *shukr* and reverence of God would develop to our hearts.

Tabrisi continues to define *shukr* by dividing it to two types: First is whenever people remember a blessing, they acknowledge that it comes from God. Second is that people obey what the source of the blessing asks. The second type can be regarding God Almighty or other people. When someone gives us something, they may ask from us in return and in the spirit of gratitude, we would feel obliged to comply with the request. However, there is one kind of *shukr* which is only due to God Almighty and that is worship. In this sense worship is all about thanksgiving. The highest level of thanksgiving is absolute obedience to God alone. Therefore, our worship should be accompanied with humility and gratitude.

In summary, *shukr* or thanksgiving is part of human nature. People universally understand that they must be grateful for the blessings that they receive. *Shukr* has two pillars; one is the acknowledgment of a blessing and second to the fulfilment of the request of the one who has given us the blessing. When it comes to God this translates into worship. Worship means to obey God no matter what he commands. There is also one other aspect of *shukr*, which is to use the blessing in a way which would not displease the bestower of the blessing. For example, if a person lends some money to his neighbour and the neighbour then buys a pistol with the money and kills the lender's children. This would be the most blatant form of disgracefulness to show how committing evil against God's creatures with the blessings which are provided by God. Thus, a very important aspect of *shukr* is to use the blessings in a way that does not displease the Provider.

إِنَّمَا حَرَّمَ عَلَيْكُمُ الْمَيْتَةَ وَالدَّمَ وَلَحْمَ الْخِنْزِيرِ وَمَا أُهِلَّ بِهِ لِغَيْرِ اللَّهِ ۖ
فَمَنِ اضْطُرَّ غَيْرَ بَاغٍ وَلَا عَادٍ فَلَا إِثْمَ عَلَيْهِ ۚ إِنَّ اللَّهَ غَفُورٌ رَحِيمٌ ﴿173﴾

He has forbidden you only carrion, blood, the flesh of the swine, and that which has been offered to other than God. But should someone be compelled, without being rebellious or aggressive, there shall be no sin upon him. Indeed, God is All-forgiving, All-merciful.

He has forbidden you only carrion, blood, the flesh of the swine, and that which has been offered to other than God; The use of the word "only" is interesting as it does not include other things which are unlawful for Muslims to eat such as predator animals, as well as certain types of birds and fish.

A verse in Surah An'ām shows that aside from these four unlawful types of meat, there are more unlawful things to eat:

> Say, 'I do not find in what has been revealed to me that anyone be forbidden to eat anything except carrion or spilt blood, or the flesh of swine —for that is indeed unclean— or an impiety offered to other than God.' But should someone be compelled, without being rebellious or aggressive, indeed your Lord is All-forgiving, All-merciful. (Q. 6:145)

Based on Q. 6:145, some jurists in the past have argued that only these four types of meat are unlawful, and everything else is lawful for Muslims to eat. However, this position has now evolved. The Imams were questioned about why the Quran only mentions these four types of meat as unlawful. They replied that the four types of meat mentioned in the verses represent the most serious violations.[288]

To support this view, it is important to look at the context in which the verses were revealed. At the time of revelation, the Arabs used to eat cattle and designated lawful and unlawful different parts of cattle meat. The verses, therefore, specifically refer to the certain parts of cattle meat and reassert the unlawful parts of cattle meat. Arabs did not eat predatory animals or birds; therefore, it is likely that this is the reason why these verses did not discuss the other types of unlawful meat. The context of Q. 6:145 reinforces this view, as Q. 6:144 makes clear that the verse only refers to cattle meat which is the main focus of the verses:

> And two of camels and two of oxen. Say, 'Is it the two males that He has forbidden or the two females, or what is contained in the wombs of the two females? Were you witnesses when God enjoined this upon you?' So, who is a greater wrongdoer than him who fabricates a lie against God to mislead the people without any knowledge? Indeed, God does not guide the wrongdoing lot.

To conclude, these verses explain the exclusive set of rulings regarding cattle. Thus, the instruction "He has forbidden you only" refers to the meat which is among the cattle meat only, "carrion, blood, the flesh of the swine, and that which has been offered to other than God." This does not preclude other animals from being unlawful to eat. Furthermore, when the Prophet was asked later about the other animals, he also included these animals in the category of what is unlawful to consume.

But should someone be compelled, without being rebellious or aggressive; If a person is compelled to eat unlawful food in life threatening circumstances the ruling changes and the unlawful becomes lawful. Regarding this issue, there is a tradition in Ibn Babawayh's *Kitāb man lā yaḥḍuruh al-faqīh* attributed to Imam Jafar al-Sadiq, which reads: "Whoever is in dire need of carrion, blood, the flesh of the swine but does not eat until he dies, he dies as a disbeliever."[289] Here, the person would be classed as a disbeliever because they would be rejecting the ruling of God, perhaps thinking that their values are more esteemed than what God has set out.

إِنَّ الَّذِينَ يَكْتُمُونَ مَا أَنزَلَ اللَّهُ مِنَ الْكِتَابِ وَيَشْتَرُونَ بِهِ ثَمَنًا قَلِيلًا ۙ
أُولَٰئِكَ مَا يَأْكُلُونَ فِي بُطُونِهِمْ إِلَّا النَّارَ وَلَا يُكَلِّمُهُمُ اللَّهُ يَوْمَ الْقِيَامَةِ وَلَا
يُزَكِّيهِمْ وَلَهُمْ عَذَابٌ أَلِيمٌ ﴿174﴾

Indeed those who conceal what God has sent down of the Book and sell it for a paltry gain —they do not take in, into their bellies, [anything] except fire, and God shall not speak to them on the Day of Resurrection, nor shall He purify them, and there is a painful punishment for them.

God's conversation with the Jews of Medina serves as a prelude to the discussion on the types of unlawful meat. The discussion concerning the polytheists and their consumption of eating unlawful meats acted as a break from this discussion which may have been as a result of a pressing need in the context of the lives of the Muslim in Medina. With verse 174, the chapter goes back to discuss the Jews. Almost all the commentators agree that the subject matter of this verse are the Jewish scholars. Tusi contends that the verses refer to the minority of Jewish scholars who concealed what had been revealed in their books. It is important to remember that not all the Jews of Medina were scholars and among the Jewish scholars not all were concealing the revelation. Thus, the Quran neither criticises all the Jews nor condemns them all to Hellfire. Rather, the verses single out this minority within the scholarly Jewish community.

Indeed those who conceal what God has sent down of the Book and sell it for a paltry gain; Here, the Book refers to the Torah and what they concealed refers to the signs of the Prophet Muhammad.

and sell it for a paltry gain; By concealing true guidance from their people, the Jewish scholars sold it for a very cheap price. The cheap price referred to here was most probably leadership, power and position within the community. Had they confessed that they concealed the guidance and converted to Islam, they would have lost the leadership of the Jews.

—they do not take in, into their bellies, [anything] except fire; The metaphor used for their concealment refers to something that they had consumed. The leadership and power that the Jewish scholars enjoyed came with valuable income streams and religious taxes. They continued to possess these material gains in exchange of their concealment of the guidance - by doing so they were like people who eat fire. Some commentators suggest that the verse reads: "they fill their bellies."

The idea that their actions in this world manifest as fire on the Day of Judgment draws attention to the notion of *tajassum al-ʿamāl* or the embodiment of our actions on the Day of Judgment. For example, those who devour the property of orphans will manifest as them as eating fire in Hell. Similarly, those Jewish leaders who concealed the revelation for personal gains would be eating fire in Hell.

God shall not speak to them on the Day of Resurrection; The apparent implication of this statement is that God does speak to people when they meet him on the Day of Judgment with some exceptions. Meeting God is mentioned in the Quran in the verse, *O mankind, you are labouring towards your Lord and you will meet him.* (Q. 84:6) We do not have knowledge of what the meeting entails, but it would not be a mystical experience that is believed to take place in this world. Every individual will meet God and this meeting may include grasping an understanding of God. In this meeting, God will speak to some people in the way that he speaks to his prophets in this world. Speaking with God is the greatest honour a person can have in the Hereafter, and this honour is even greater than speaking with God in this world. This is because this conversation will take place without the medium of angels. The direct conversation with God provides evidence for the growth of the human soul. The conversations with God will not be restricted to the Day of Judgment, but will continue in Paradise. One of the most pleasurable and honoured rewards of Paradise is conversing with God Almighty.

However, as the verse mentions, God will not speak with people who had concealed his revelation. Having said that, there are other occasions in the Quran where God speaks to some depraved souls. For example, *We will question those to whom messengers were sent...* (Q. 7:6) or when people of Hell ask God to release them from the fire, *He will say, 'remain despised therein and do not speak to Me.'* (Q. 23:108). However, it is possible that these interrogations may be part of a collective address and not individual conversations. Furthermore, some commentators have argued that these are not conversations with the wrongdoers[290] - rather they are angry rebukes.

nor shall He purify them; The Arabic word *yuzakkīhim* may have two meanings, one is to "purify" and the other is "praise." Both meanings are plausible here and it is possible that both would happen on the Day of Judgment: God neither shall purify nor praise those who conceal the guidance. Those who are to enter Paradise need to be purified, regardless of how good they had been in this world. The level of purity required to be admitted into Paradise cannot be acquired by anyone except by the grace of God. Therefore, God will purify many people before admitting them into Paradise. However, he will not purify some people, including these Jewish leaders who believed in God and were religious, but concealed his guidance, therefore, they would not be able to enter Paradise at all.

It is astonishing to imagine that people will meet God and converse with him and in this conversation, he will praise them for their achievements in the world. Of course, the concealers of guidance would be excluded from this praise. We read in the Quran that God praises some of his servants in this world. For example, God praises

Prophet Job (Ayyub) in this world: ... *We found him (Job) patient, an excellent servant...* (Q. 38:44) Imagine if we meet with our Lord on the Day of Judgment and he praises us by saying "an excellent servant!" This would be the indication of our full accomplishment and would be more satisfying than Paradise.

In summary, many verses of the Quran often discuss exclusions and exceptions to general rules and statements. In this specific case, we are told that people who conceal the guidance would be deprived of certain privileges. Therefore, these verses imply that God would converse with most people and praise them during this conversation. The verse also indicates that God is taking people to a level where they would be able to speak to him and he would praise them directly. He will send us to Paradise which is his neighbourhood and many other things that he has destined for human beings.

Hell is not the destiny for the human species, as the purpose of the human creation is to be honoured and to be made the inhabitants of Paradise. Those who go to Hell are the exceptions to the general rule as it is not God's purpose to send them to Hell. But regardless of the warnings and evidences they chose to be evil and go to Hell.

there is a painful punishment for them. The very fact that God will not converse with them and will not praise them, is a great punishment. This would then be followed by other punishments that would be materialised in Hell. The great majority of these punishments would be carried in the soul of the offenders.

أُولَٰئِكَ الَّذِينَ اشْتَرَوُا الضَّلَالَةَ بِالْهُدَىٰ وَالْعَذَابَ بِالْمَغْفِرَةِ ۚ فَمَا أَصْبَرَهُمْ عَلَى النَّارِ ﴿175﴾

They are the ones who bought error for guidance, and punishment for pardon: how patient of them to face the Fire!

The verse refers again the minority group of Jewish scholars of

Medina, who exchanged the true teachings of the Torah for their personal, familial and tribal interests. In return, they will receive punishment in the Hereafter.

how patient of them to face the Fire! This is a curious expression. Superficially, it can be interpreted as God's amazement of how these wrongdoers are created to endure Hellfire. As Hellfire is so severely painful, it is not designed to be endured by any creation. However, the way a human being is created means that they are able to endure it.

In a tradition attributed to Imam Jafar al-Sadiq, there is an alternative interpretation of the verse which suggests that God is appalled to see how the wrongdoers persevere in their mischief whilst knowing that these actions would lead them to Hellfire.[291] Some people are not aware that their actions will lead them to Hellfire, but they persist in the evil deeds because they have lost hope in the mercy of God or because they become overwhelmed with their desires and emotions, and senselessly continue their wrongful ways.

ذَٰلِكَ بِأَنَّ ٱللَّهَ نَزَّلَ ٱلْكِتَابَ بِٱلْحَقِّ ۗ وَإِنَّ ٱلَّذِينَ ٱخْتَلَفُوا۟ فِى ٱلْكِتَابِ
لَفِى شِقَاقٍۭ بَعِيدٍ ﴿176﴾

That is so because God has sent down the Book with the truth, and those who differ about the Book are surely in extreme defiance.

That is so because God has sent down the Book with the truth; This expression explains why the punishments mentioned in the previous verses are so severe. It is because God has revealed *the Book with the truth*. The Arabic word used for truth in the verse is *haqq*. *Haqq* can have several meanings. One meaning of *haqq* is a statement which corresponds with reality. This is the meaning used in *O People of the Book! Do not exceed the bounds in your religion, and do not attribute anything to God except the truth (haqq).* (Q. 4:171)

The other meaning is anything real and not fantastical, like *On that day God will pay them in full their due recompense, and they shall know that God is the Manifest Reality (haqq).* (Q. 24:25) A third meaning of *haqq* is anything which is logical and based on wisdom. *He created the heavens and the earth with reason (haqq).* (Q. 64:3) In this verse, *God has sent down the Book with the truth,* the '*truth*' may have been used in the first sense, which means a true statement. It also may mean that God has sent the Book with and based on wisdom.

and those who differ about the Book are surely in extreme defiance. *Shiqāq* (defiance) is used here to denote the fact that their rejection is not because they do not know the truth; rather, it is because they defy the truth (*haqq*), and that is why they deserve the dire consequences mentioned in the previous verses.

لَيْسَ الْبِرَّ أَنْ تُوَلُّوا وُجُوهَكُمْ قِبَلَ الْمَشْرِقِ وَالْمَغْرِبِ وَلَٰكِنَّ الْبِرَّ مَنْ
آمَنَ بِاللَّهِ وَالْيَوْمِ الْآخِرِ وَالْمَلَائِكَةِ وَالْكِتَابِ وَالنَّبِيِّينَ وَآتَى الْمَالَ
عَلَىٰ حُبِّهِ ذَوِي الْقُرْبَىٰ وَالْيَتَامَىٰ وَالْمَسَاكِينَ وَابْنَ السَّبِيلِ وَالسَّائِلِينَ
وَفِي الرِّقَابِ وَأَقَامَ الصَّلَاةَ وَآتَى الزَّكَاةَ وَالْمُوفُونَ بِعَهْدِهِمْ إِذَا عَاهَدُوا
وَالصَّابِرِينَ فِي الْبَأْسَاءِ وَالضَّرَّاءِ وَحِينَ الْبَأْسِ أُولَٰئِكَ الَّذِينَ صَدَقُوا
وَأُولَٰئِكَ هُمُ الْمُتَّقُونَ ﴿177﴾

Righteousness is not to turn your faces to the east or the west; rather, righteousness is [personified by] those who have faith in God and the Last Day, the angels, the Book, and the prophets, and who give their wealth, for the love of Him, to relatives, orphans, the needy, the traveller and the beggar, and for [the freeing of] the slaves, and maintain the prayer and give the zakat, and those who fulfil their covenants, when they pledge themselves, and those who are patient in stress and distress, and in the heat of battle. They are the ones who are true [to their covenant], and it is they who are the Godwary.

Verse 177 is crucial in defining who the righteous people are in the eyes of God. Righteousness has been misunderstood and often used to describe good people who do not believe in God. Conversely, there are people who observe all the obligatory and recommended rituals of the religion, yet they may behave badly with their relations, neighbours, and co-workers. These conflicting behaviours of people have led to some confusion about the definition of righteous people. In this way, the verse at hand is of seminal importance in providing the definition of righteous people.

Righteousness is not to turn your faces to the east or the west; The beginning of the verse alludes to the change of the direction of the *qibla.* This draws attention to the futility of debating the conventional matters of religious law which may be changed by the prophets. It warns the audience that it is not accurate to limit the definition of righteousness to the direction of prayer.

righteousness is [personified by] those who have faith in God and the Last Day; The verse goes on to provide a broad definition of righteousness. Having faith in God and the Last Day are the pillars of sound human comprehension of this world. Some people may be very kind and charitable, but if they are mistaken about the reality of this creation, they may be considered to possess one aspect of righteousness, but they are not fully righteous. Having faith in God is the reality of this world and faith in the Day of Judgment is the reality of the human destination.

the angels, the Book, and the prophets; Faith in the existence of "the angels" is also of significance importance here. This is because believing in angels broadens our understanding of the way the world operates. Science often leads us to think that everything in this world operates through a chain of cause and effect. However, believing in angels affirms that there is a hidden aspect to this beyond the system of cause and effect, which manages the affairs of this world and enables the system of cause and effect to work. It is important to know that this world is not simply left to itself.

Faith in "the Book, and the prophets" represents faith in the guidance of God. He has not left us alone in this world and he supports us with his books and prophets. The reason why having faith in the prophets is distinguished from having faith in the books is because of the importance of following the prophets in their good character. These selected people have conveyed the message of God; therefore, they are the ones who should be followed and obeyed.

The five pillars mentioned in the verse are the basic requirements of righteousness. The absence of any of these five pillars may make it difficult to classify a person as righteous. For example, atheists and agnostics do not believe in some or all of these pillars, therefore, regardless of their charitable or spiritual achievements, we cannot define them as righteous persons. A righteous person should have these five internalised characteristics as a minimum. These characteristics are related to a person's internal realm. The verse then continues to convey the remaining characteristics of a righteous person which are related to the outward expressions of righteousness which are related to their relationships with other people.

who give their wealth, for the love of Him; The charity mentioned in this verse is not *zakat* (almsgiving) or *khums,*[292] rather, it refers to an overall generosity and a humanitarian duty which would prove their righteousness. Turning our face to the east or west or trying to implement the conventional rulings of the religious laws does not prove our righteousness. Instead, giving away our wealth for the love of God, is the foremost criteria for our commitment to the faith.

There is a technical discussion about the nature of the pronoun *ha* that is attached to the word "love" (*ḥubb*). Some commentators interpret the sentence to mean "despite their love of it" or "give away their wealth despite the love of it." The second meaning is more generally accepted by the commentators. Love for wealth should not be confused with someone who is immersed in the material life or someone who has extensive love for the material world. Rather, it refers to someone who *needs* that wealth and despite their own need for it, they still give it to others in need; preferring them over themselves. If we love the wealth without need, it means our hearts are afflicted with the disease of greed.

Some commentators such as Ibn Masud explain that those "who give their wealth for the love of Him" refers to those who give when they are still healthy and have the expectation of a long life, as opposed to a person who may be nearing the end of their life and looking to distribute their wealth.[293] It must be given before losing the expectation of having a long life. Furthermore, the person should also fear that they may not be able to replace the wealth at any point. These two conditions must be met in order to consider that they are giving for the love of God.

Some other commentators provided alternative interpretations suggesting that it refers to people who are of a generous nature and love to give charity. However, this is an improbable explanation as if somebody already has a generous character it would be easy for them to part from their wealth. They are not equal to those who are in need of wealth and do not have the natural disposition to give charity. Due to their faith and love of God, they give what they have to charity.

to relatives orphans, the needy, the traveller and the beggar, and for [the freeing of] the slaves; There is a tradition attributed to the Prophet which explains that Muslims prioritise giving their wealth to their relatives. The traditions states that the best relative to whom we should give charity to is the one whom we know has a hidden or open animosity for us.[294] This is because the Prophet anticipated that generosity would ease the existing animosity between relatives. It takes a lot of spiritual strength to give charity to someone whom we know has animosity against us, but this is the most rewarding.

After the relatives, we should give our wealth to the orphans and the needy as they represent the weakest layer of the society and there is a general duty upon everyone to look after them. The traveller may not be poor, but they are cut off from their resources due to being away from their hometown, which includes their assets and their support network. Of course, in the modern world, we have international credit cards, debit cards and mobile phone apps which allow travellers to remain connected to their resources. Previously, it was common for people to be robbed by criminals or to consume their own provisions before reaching their destination. In such cases it was not possible for them to replenish their supplies and they had to rely on the help of the strangers. Therefore, Muslims were asked to help the travellers who were in need of provisions.

The next category are the *sā'ilīn* which is often translated as the beggars. However, *sā'ilīn* carries the meaning of "those who ask"; some people may not be poor but may still ask for a favour.

Freeing of slaves was one of the most important ethical teachings of Islam, and believers were expected to free their slaves for the love of God. At this point, we may want to touch upon an important dilemma; why the Divine Books, the Torah, Bible and Quran did not abolish the practice of slavery outright, and instead encouraged their followers to treat slaves with kindness by setting them free.

The reason lies within the structure of old societies in which slavery was a functional institution. In those days, there were widespread wars and conflicts which meant that that if people did not want to take captives in war, they would have had to kill all their enemies. The winning side had only two options, either to capture the opposing side or to kill them all. There were no other alternatives. Therefore, slavery was the lesser evil compared to massacring the losing side and there was a consensus among the previous generations about the benefits of this system.

This is very different to the slave trade that operated in the 18th and 19th centuries, where people of African ancestry were hunted down like wild animals, kidnapped and shipped back to Europe and America. They underwent a great deal of torture, suffering and other forms of inhuman treatments, especially at the hands of the notorious cotton industry in America. This slavery came about as a result of human greed and arrogance and no monotheistic religion may justify these actions.

Like the verse at hand, Islam right from the beginning aimed to remove slavery gradually from the society by strongly encouraging Muslims to free slaves and set out strict terms to protect the dignity and well-being of slaves. Freeing slaves was one of the preconditions of achieving human salvation and it was often considered a proof of a person's faith.

Modern societies no longer meet the conditions that provided a limited justification to the institution of slavery. Therefore, there is no religious legitimacy for it now and it is against Islam to have slaves. Certain terrorist groups like ISIS, in the pretext of Islamic law, have tried to reinstate slavery but like many other atrocities and crimes they have committed in the name of religion, it has no religious justification. What they have done was a clear perversion of the faith.

and maintain the prayer and give the *zakat*; After discussing the faithful ways to distribute wealth, some further obligations are mentioned. First, the mention of *zakat* here shows that the previous instances of financial commitments stated in the verse are differentiated from *zakat* or considered outside the obligatory duties of the Muslims. Therefore, based on this verse, the obligatory parts of the faith such as maintaining the prayer and giving the *zakat* follow from the financial commitments mentioned previously in the verse. First, the ideological commitments such as having faith in God and the Last Day, the angels, the Book, and the prophets. Second, the social and financial commitments such as giving out wealth to relatives, orphans, the needy, the traveller and the beggar. Third, the religious obligations such as maintaining prayer and *zakat.* Fourth, the ethical commitments including fulfilling covenant as pledges as in the phrase, *those who fulfil their covenants, when they pledge themselves.*

and those who fulfil their covenants, when they pledge themselves; This refers to a general covenant which includes Muslim commitments between themselves and with non-Muslims (Christians, Jews, Hindus and atheists). Any commitment made by a Muslim must be honoured. This obligation is explicitly stated in Surah Tawba. The first three verses of the surah declare universally the annulment of the peace agreements made with the polytheists, but the fourth verse exempts those polytheists who complied with their agreements. The verse consequently enforces the covenant made by this group of polytheists:

> barring the polytheists with whom you have made a covenant, and who did not violate any [of its terms] with you, nor backed anyone against you. So, fulfil the covenant with them until [the end of] its term. Indeed, God loves the Godwary. (Q. 9:4)

Honouring covenants is not only a religious concept, but it is one of the fundamental principles of human ethics that allows people to co-exist. Families, communities, nations and states need to honour their covenants and agreements to live in peace together. However, some powerful countries can easily break their covenants based on a change in their national interests which makes the world a dangerous and unpredictable place to live.

those who are patient in stress and distress, and in the heat of battle; Finally, the fifth criteria for righteousness is the preservation of patience at all times. Patience is one of the most important components of faith and there are many different instances of it. This verse draws attention to these different instances of patience including patience in the face of poverty (*al-ba'sā*). There is a relevant hadith mentioned in *Nahj al-balāgha* stating that,

> the world and faith are based on four things... one of them is that wealthy people who do not refrain from giving out from their wealth, and poor people who are patient and do not sell their religious values for the worldly gains... If the wealthy people refrain from giving, poor people lose patience and they sell their religious values for the worldly gains...[295]

The second instance of patience mentioned is patience in the face of disease, pain and other health problems (*al-ḍarrā*). The third instance of patience mentioned is the patience in the heat of battle (*ḥīna al-ba'si*). These are the three most difficult situations to be patient in life.

they are the ones who are true [to their covenant], and it is they who are the Godwary. The final section of the verse reinforces the notion that the verse gives the description and characteristics of true believers. People have different degrees of faithfulness, so one person may not have all these characteristics in them, but this does not mean that they do not have faith. These qualities are very difficult to attain but attainment of these qualities results in perfect faith. This is the purpose of mankind in this world. Some special people like the prophets, imams, and saints are able to attain these qualities in this world. However, most people will attain some of these qualities in this world and God will compensate the rest through his mercy in the Hereafter.

Another rationale for mentioning these qualities in the verse is to articulate the holistic nature of faith. Faith should not be judged on the basis of some rituals we perform. Rather they are part of the layered framework mentioned in the verse. This point relates back to the Jews of Medina who harshly and superfluously criticised Muslims for changing the direction of the *qibla*. Their focus was on the outward aspect when there were more fundamental aspects of faith to consider. Praying towards a certain direction is not related to the quality of faith - the real measurement of faith are the qualities mentioned in the verse.

In this vein, Tusi and Tabrisi state in their commentaries that Shi'i scholars have postulated that this verse is about Imam Ali.[296] This is because all Muslims who lived at the time knew that Imam Ali possessed all these qualities mentioned in this verse. These qualities could not be found all together in any other person of his time, except for Prophet Muhammad who is the best of God's creation. There was no disagreement among the *umma* in this regard. There is no unanimous agreement on any other person in the early history of Islam; Sunnis revered their own leaders but rejected Shi'i leaders. On the other hand, Shi'is revered their own leaders, but rejected Sunni leaders. Nevertheless, they both agree on the outstanding merits of Imam Ali.

يَا أَيُّهَا الَّذِينَ آمَنُوا كُتِبَ عَلَيْكُمُ الْقِصَاصُ فِي الْقَتْلَى الْحُرُّ بِالْحُرِّ
وَالْعَبْدُ بِالْعَبْدِ وَالْأُنْثَىٰ بِالْأُنْثَىٰ فَمَنْ عُفِيَ لَهُ مِنْ أَخِيهِ شَيْءٌ فَاتِّبَاعٌ
بِالْمَعْرُوفِ وَأَدَاءٌ إِلَيْهِ بِإِحْسَانٍ ذَٰلِكَ تَخْفِيفٌ مِنْ رَبِّكُمْ وَرَحْمَةٌ فَمَنِ
اعْتَدَىٰ بَعْدَ ذَٰلِكَ فَلَهُ عَذَابٌ أَلِيمٌ ﴿178﴾

O you who have faith! Retribution is prescribed for you regarding the slain: freeman for freeman, slave for slave, and female for female. But if one is granted any extenuation by his brother, let the follow up [for the blood-money] be honourable, and let the payment to him be with kindness. That is a remission from your Lord and a mercy; and should anyone transgress after that, there shall be a painful punishment for him.

Retribution is prescribed for you; From this point on in the surah, some laws and legislations are mentioned. The first is about *qiṣāṣ* (retribution in intentional crimes). Whenever the phrase "prescribed for you" (*kutiba*) is mentioned in the Quran, it refers to the prescription of God's law. Verse 151 also included this phrase, and the discussion of its meaning can be found there. The verse at hand states that it is the law of God that the believers must implement retribution regarding the slain. This retribution must be implemented in commensuration with the legal and social status of the offenders and victims. Their status is not related to the power or wealth of the people in question, rather it is related to the type of financial damage that the offence may have brought upon the relatives of the victim. Therefore, it is more related to levy the accurate compensation or punishment that would redeem the financial loss.

freeman for freeman, slave for slave, and female for female; If the offender is a freeman who killed another freeman, then he could be killed. If a slave is killed by a slave, then the offender slave could be killed. The same is applicable to the female offender killing a female victim. However, if a freeman kills a slave, it would be more than just a loss of life; the slave has a financial value as well, therefore, the offender would be punished severely and pay for the financial loss. In the case of killing of a female by a male, the family of the victim could have two options: one is to pay the financial difference of the male and female and have the *qiṣāṣ* implemented; the second option is to take a financial compensation from the offender.

The ruling may seem discriminatory against women. However, it should noted that if a female is killed, the blood money would go to the men of the family; this may be her husband or her sons. On the other hand, if a male is killed, the blood money would usually go to the wife and children of the victim. Because men were the sole bread-winners, at the time; so if a man was killed it meant the sole income of the family was cut off. Therefore, the compensation would have been double in order to balance the loss of the victim's family and the financial loss that could occur due to the execution of the offender whose wife and children would also be punished for the actions of the husband.

If the offender husband had been executed right away, his wife would have needed to seek re-marriage to support herself and would not have been able to provide for her children.

But if one is granted any extenuation by his brother, let the follow up [for the blood-money] be honourable, and let the payment to him be with kindness. It is also important to note that *qiṣāṣ* is not obligatory in Islam. The following sections of the verse suggest that taking the blood-money or forgiving the offender, without taking any kind of compensation are the most encouraged forms of behaviours.

Historically, in most cases, taking blood-money has dissipated quarrels between warring parties and in the rarest instances *qiṣāṣ* has been implemented. The language of the verse is interesting and addresses the warring parties as "brother(s)", because these kinds of events are inevitable in society, but the emphasis here is on not to break the bondage of the society. This is a great lesson for us; if God does not want us to break the bondage of society for a crime as evil as murder, what about pettier crimes? Sometimes we harbour hatred against each other for trivial things such as financial matters or family issues for which we think there cannot be any hope of reconciliation between warring parties. Yet, this verse indicates that such events should not break the bondage of the society.

Furthermore, the verse also lays out the ethics of settling the dispute with blood-money; the sum should not be too much so that the offender or the family cannot afford it. Also, the family of the offender needs to pay the agreed blood-money in a timely manner, with kindness and gratitude, so that victim's family does not suffer further. Both sides should behave honourably and work towards mending the scars of such a tragic event.

That is a remission from your Lord and a mercy; This refers to the arrangement of the blood-money and the encouragement to forgive the offender and to settle disputes in the society and create an environment for a peaceful coexistence and harmony. Some commentators have claimed the "remission" mentioned in the verse includes *qiṣāṣ* as well, but this explanation does not seem to be plausible as *qiṣāṣ* is a retribution not a remission.

and should anyone transgress after that, there shall be a painful punishment for him. In Islamic law, the right to forgive belongs to the heirs. If one of the heirs forgives and all the rest do not forgive, the offender would be spared based on the forgiveness of only one heir. For example, if a murder victim left behind five daughters and five sons, and if one child out of the ten consents and forgives, then the offender would be pardoned. Consequently, all the siblings must split the blood-money among themselves. After this point, *qiṣāṣ* can no longer be implemented. It is sometimes possible that upon reaching a settlement on the payment of a blood-money, some of the siblings may try to refuse the blood-money and seek revenge instead. Or they may take the compensation, but then change their mind afterwards and decide to kill the offender. In Islamic law, the right to choose the appropriate punishment for the offender from the available options belongs to the heirs of the victim, however the right to execute the appropriate punishment belongs to the government.

Individuals may ask for *qiṣāṣ* but they cannot execute it - they need to go to the courts of law and make their claims. It is up to court to decide the outcome and relevant authorities to execute the verdict of the court. Therefore, the verse refers to the individual's infringement of the legal process. Other verses of the Quran also point out the right of the heir of the victim to choose between *qiṣāṣ* or compensation:

> Do not kill a soul [whose life] God has made inviolable, except with due cause, and whoever is killed wrongfully, We have certainly given his heir an authority [to choose between *qiṣāṣ* or compensation]. But let him not commit any excess in killing, for he enjoys the support [of law]. (Q. 17:33)

The right of execution of the appropriate option is with the government and its courts. *Let him not commit any excess* mentioned in Q. 17:33 also draws attention to the fact that *qiṣāṣ* should only be implemented on the offender who committed the actual killing. This legal framework was aimed at curbing the ancient Arab custom of avenging all the family members of a murderer.

وَلَكُمْ فِي الْقِصَاصِ حَيَاةٌ يَا أُولِي الْأَلْبَابِ لَعَلَّكُمْ تَتَّقُونَ ﴿179﴾

There is life for you in retribution, O you who possess intellects! Maybe you will be Godwary!

There is life for you in retribution; The verse discusses the philosophy of implementing *qiṣāṣ* or compensation in the case murder. There was a saying among the Arabs, before this verse was revealed: "killing would drive away further killing," (*al-qatlu yanfi al-qatl*). It meant that if somebody had been murdered and the offender was then executed, fighting between families and tribes would have stopped. However, there was neither such a law in Arabia, nor a central government to implement this law. Therefore, there had been unending vendettas between families and tribes that took many lives and created instability in the society. This verse filled that vacuum, and its meaning is similar to the Arab saying mentioned, but of course, it is more eloquent.

At first glance, there seems to be a paradox in the verse, that life can be found through killing and the verse seems to endorse killing with this sentence. People often think that if a person is killed, the harm is already done, so executing the offender will only bring further harm. Instead, the life of the offender should be preserved by saving the offender from death. In this context, "There is life for you in retribution" may have meant that by taking the life of the offender, the state stops the blood feud and any further killings between families and clans. Until recent times, there has been a custom of blood feud in many communities that if a person is killed for whatever reason, their surviving relatives had the right to kill all the male members of the offender.

This blood feud still exists in some communities but has almost disappeared in modern societies. Given the strong presence of such a custom in pre-modern Arabia, the verse put an end to further bloodshed by the execution of the offender by the courts of law. Furthermore, the execution of the offender was a strong deterrent for people who often thought imprisonment brought honour instead of shame to the family. However, the execution penalty in retribution to murder was a deterrent for them. In summary, to acknowledge its efficacy in the reduction of the blood-feud related killings, the verse states that there is life in killing or retribution under the supervision of the courts of law.

However, there is an opposing argument to this interpretation of the verse from those who argue that capital punishment for murder is not effective. According to some statistics, societies where capital punishment is implemented on murderers, murder rates remain almost the same as the societies where capital punishment is not implemented. However, this view does not consider the social and cultural differences in the countries that they compare, therefore; it lacks accuracy. It is not possible to compare a third world agricultural society with a prosperous European society. Some values and structures including familial and tribal honour, blood feuds and the like, have lost much of their relevance due to the effect of mass industrialisation. Therefore, it may be possible for Muslim jurists to revisit the relevant rulings of Islamic law to find an alternative punishment for these crimes which better responds to the changing needs of the society. However, this is a matter of discussion for Muslim jurists.

O you who possess intellects! Maybe you will be Godwary! This is a powerful phrase that draws attention to the issues mentioned above. In the context of the Arabian society, where the verses of retribution were revealed, this verse helped to reduce blood-feuds and further killings of innocent people. Therefore, upholding these laws led to justice and peace in the society and consequently achieved the nearness to God.

كُتِبَ عَلَيْكُمْ إِذَا حَضَرَ أَحَدَكُمُ الْمَوْتُ إِنْ تَرَكَ خَيْرًا الْوَصِيَّةُ
لِلْوَالِدَيْنِ وَالْأَقْرَبِينَ بِالْمَعْرُوفِ حَقًّا عَلَى الْمُتَّقِينَ

Prescribed for you, when death approaches any of you and he leaves behind any property, is that he makes a bequest for his parents and relatives, in an honourable manner, —an obligation on the Godwary.

فَمَنْ بَدَّلَهُ بَعْدَمَا سَمِعَهُ فَإِنَّمَا إِثْمُهُ عَلَى الَّذِينَ يُبَدِّلُونَهُ ۚ إِنَّ اللَّهَ سَمِيعٌ
عَلِيمٌ ﴿181﴾

And should anyone alter it after hearing it, its sin shall indeed lie on those who alter it. Indeed, God is All-hearing, All-knowing

---

Verse 180 relates to inheritance left behind by a deceased person. There is some and is controversy between Shi'i and Sunni Muslims about the interpretation of this verse. Sunnis believe that this verse was abrogated as there is another verse about the inheritance share:

> God enjoins you concerning your children: for the male shall be the like of the share of two females, and if there be [two or] more than two females, then for them shall be two-thirds of what he leaves; but if she be alone, then for her shall be a half; and for each of his parents a sixth of what he leaves, if he has children; but if he has no children, and his parents are his [sole] heirs, then it shall be a third for his mother; but if he has brothers, then a sixth for his mother, after [paying off] any bequest he may have made or any debt [he may have incurred]. Your parents and your children —you do not know which of them is likelier to be beneficial for you. This is an ordinance from God. Indeed, God is All-knowing, All-wise. (Q. 4:11)

Sunni scholars have mostly argued that Q. 4:11 provides a detailed description of the right of inheritance in this verse and therefore it has abrogated Q. 2:180. On the other hand, Shi'i scholars have argued that this verse was not abrogated - rather, it is an addition to Q. 4:11. Aside from these two main views, it is important to note that there are some marginal views on the interpretation of the verse.

The Shi'i view on the verse and explanation means that there are relatives who do not have a share of inheritance.[297] For example, if a man dies and leaves behind a wife and children, his siblings would not have a share in the inheritance. However, it is recommended that a wealthy person should make a will for those who would not receive a share from the inheritance otherwise and distribute a third of this wealth to them. The remaining two-thirds of inheritance goes to actual beneficiaries such as the deceased person's wife and children. There are numerous traditions attributed to Shi'i Imams in this respect, and this is the established Shi'i view regarding the interpretation of this verse. If after a person has died, the beneficiaries challenge this will, then the deceased person has no blame, and the sin is with those who alter the will.

فَمَنْ خَافَ مِن مُّوصٍ جَنَفًا أَوْ إِثْمًا فَأَصْلَحَ بَيْنَهُمْ فَلَا إِثْمَ عَلَيْهِ إِنَّ اللَّهَ غَفُورٌ رَّحِيمٌ ﴿182﴾

But should someone, fearing deviance or sin on the testator's behalf, set things right between them, there is no sin upon him. Indeed, God is All-forgiving, All-merciful."

The verse further elaborates the inheritance law. If a wealthy person makes a will, they can leave a portion of their wealth to their relatives who would not have received it otherwise. There are two ways to interpret the verse at hand: first, if the testator or deceased person breaches the law by giving one of the children more than the others by denying them the share stipulated in Islamic law, then the inheritors have the right to amend the will. The inheritors also have the right to amend the will if the testator donates a portion of his inheritance to an unlawful cause. This interpretation, therefore, clarifies the previous verse where it stipulates that inheritors have no right to amend a will. The exception here is in the case of a breach in Islamic law, where the inheritors must amend the will to follow Islamic law.

The second interpretation of the verse is that when a will is made in the presence of the inheritors and the testator informs the inheritors about the will, some of them may object to the contents of the will. It is a very unpleasant situation, but the testator should then amend the will to make peace between the inheritors. However, the first meaning makes more sense.

يَا أَيُّهَا الَّذِينَ آمَنُوا كُتِبَ عَلَيْكُمُ الصِّيَامُ كَمَا كُتِبَ عَلَى الَّذِينَ مِن قَبْلِكُمْ لَعَلَّكُمْ تَتَّقُونَ ﴿183﴾

O you who have faith! Prescribed for you is fasting as it was prescribed for those who were before you, so that you may be Godwary.

O you who have faith! This is a very well-known verse in the surah. There is a very beautiful tradition about the opening of this verse attributed to Imam Jafar al-Sadiq: "The enjoyment of "O" (*yā*) by which God addresses the faithful removes all the difficulties of worship when he is directly addressing the people."[298] In this tradition, Imam Jafar al-Sadiq expresses the joy of a believer who is directly addressed by the Creator. It is recommended that whenever we read a verse of the Quran that addresses believers, we should utter the word "*Labbayk*" (an affirmative response to the call of God) to confirm that we are responding to the call of God when he says "O you who have faith."

Prescribed for you is fasting; The original meaning of the word *ṣiyām* is to refrain from something; it may mean refraining from eating, drinking, speaking or the like. The word is used to refer to refraining from speaking in Surah Maryam *Eat, drink, and be comforted. Then if you see any human, say, 'Indeed I have vowed a fast (ṣawman) to the All-beneficent, so I will not speak to any human today.'* Therefore, the word *ṣiyām* may have different meanings in different contexts.

as it was prescribed for those who were before you; Here, the verse explicitly states that fasting was also prescribed for the previous nations but does not state the specific time they were prescribed to fast. The verse is clear that fasting has been practiced to the previous nations and may be traced back as far as Prophet Adam. It can be understood that God wanted to the reassurance Muslims that fasting was not something new.

We do not know if the previous generations fasted in the month of Ramadan or about the nature of their fasts. Some Muslims believe that previous nations initially fasted in the month of Ramadan, and they then changed the timing according to their convenience. On the other hand, Shi'i Imams have been explicit that fasting in the month of Ramadan has only been prescribed for Muslims.

so that you may be Godwary. Fasting is instrumental in attaining a higher spiritual status. Therefore, it is understandable that God commanded believers to practice fasting from the earliest times. Fasting has been implemented as part of spiritual development. Based on experience, many non-Abrahamic faiths have adopted the practice of fasting in order to boost their spirituality.

أَيَّامًا مَّعْدُودَاتٍ ۚ فَمَن كَانَ مِنكُم مَّرِيضًا أَوْ عَلَىٰ سَفَرٍ فَعِدَّةٌ مِّنْ أَيَّامٍ
أُخَرَ ۚ وَعَلَى الَّذِينَ يُطِيقُونَهُ فِدْيَةٌ طَعَامُ مِسْكِينٍ ۖ فَمَن تَطَوَّعَ خَيْرًا فَهُوَ
خَيْرٌ لَّهُ ۚ وَأَن تَصُومُوا خَيْرٌ لَّكُمْ ۖ إِن كُنتُمْ تَعْلَمُونَ ﴿184﴾

That for known days. But should any of you be sick or on a journey, let it be a [similar] number of other days. Those who find it straining shall be liable to atonement by feeding a needy person. Should anyone do good of his own accord, that is better for him, and to fast is better for you, should you know.

Verse 184 then states those who are exempted from fasting due to their conditions. These include sick people and travellers who do not need to fast. If they are able, they then can make up for the missing days by fasting on other days. Otherwise, they can make up their fasts by feeding a certain number of poor people. A debate regarding the exemption of fasting for travellers in modern times stems from the relative speed and ease of travelling long distances by car, train or plane. Some have argued that due to the lack of hardship, there is no need for travellers to abstain from fasting. However, the verse is clear that sick people and travellers should not fast, therefore, it is unlawful for travellers to fast. Although travelling may seem to have been previously more difficult but, it was a more pleasant experience. People travelled in open air, with their friends and relatives without being constrained into tiny spaces and rushed through one place to another like a sheep in a herd. They had their own horses, camels and could move on at their own convenience. There is an argument to say that it was a more pleasurable and relaxed experience than it is today.

Unfortunately, modern mass transportation is driven with profit making and has little regard for human dignity. Furthermore, travellers are not only exempted from fasting during the days of travel; if they are staying in their destinations less than ten days, they are also not allowed fast during those days, so the exemption is not just related to the difficulties of travelling. It is related to the physiological state of a traveller. When people travel, they enter a different state of mind which may include stress about the travel itself, or the business they may attend to at their destination and other issues related to travelling. Therefore, they may not be able to benefit from fasting as they would have, if they had not travelled. Therefore, many scholars have felt the need to make a case for travellers to not fast. Yūsuf b. al-Hakam (d. unknown) narrates a brilliant point:

> I asked ʿAbdullāh b. ʿUmar (d. 74/693) that could we fast while we are travelling as it is not difficult for me to fast and I do not like to miss Ramadan fasting? ʿAbdullāh b. ʿUmar replied: 'If you give a gift to someone, and that person throws it back to you, wouldn't you become angry? God has given this exemption to you as a gift while you are travelling...'[299]

This is indeed a beautiful way of explaining the matter; God has given Muslims a gift and they should take it without questioning it. There are also many narrations attributed to the Shiʿi Imams that breaking fast while travelling is obligatory and it is not matter of choice.

Those who find it straining shall be liable to atonement by feeding a needy person; The group of people refers to those who can fast, but they do it with hardship. This is a distinct category to those who are sick or need to travel. In Islamic law, there is a disagreement about the exact definition of this group of people. There is also a difference between Shi'i and Sunni scholars regarding the definition of this group. While some have suggested that it refers to elderly people who can fast with difficulty and hardship, some others have suggested that it refers to pregnant or breast-feeding women. According to Shi'i scholars, this category only includes the elderly. Pregnant and breastfeeding women should make up for their missed fasting after they have completed breastfeeding. However, the elderly who are able to compensate the fast can do so by feeding a poor person.

Should anyone do good of his own accord, that is better for him; Though the obligation is to feed a single needy person, it is better to feed more than one person if the person has means to do so.

and to fast is better for you, should you know. This is often understood to be the beginning of a separate sentence. Therefore, it is not related to the previous sentence which warrants elderly people to feed a needy person. This sentence is related to the whole idea of fasting and encourages people to fast. However, Kashani and Tabrisi make a strong case against this interpretation and suggests that this is not a new sentence and refers to those for whom fasting is difficult, saying that it is better for them to fast. This interpretation fits well within the context where although they have the option of feeding a poor person, fasting is better for them due to its boundless spiritual blessing.

شَهْرُ رَمَضَانَ الَّذِي أُنزِلَ فِيهِ الْقُرْآنُ هُدًى لِّلنَّاسِ وَبَيِّنَاتٍ مِّنَ الْهُدَىٰ
وَالْفُرْقَانِ فَمَن شَهِدَ مِنكُمُ الشَّهْرَ فَلْيَصُمْهُ وَمَن كَانَ مَرِيضًا أَوْ
عَلَىٰ سَفَرٍ فَعِدَّةٌ مِّنْ أَيَّامٍ أُخَرَ يُرِيدُ اللَّهُ بِكُمُ الْيُسْرَ وَلَا يُرِيدُ بِكُمُ
الْعُسْرَ وَلِتُكْمِلُوا الْعِدَّةَ وَلِتُكَبِّرُوا اللَّهَ عَلَىٰ مَا هَدَاكُمْ وَلَعَلَّكُمْ
تَشْكُرُونَ ﴿185﴾

The month of Ramadan is one in which the Quran was sent down as guidance to mankind, with manifest proofs of guidance and the Criterion. So let those of you who witness it fast [in] it, and as for someone who is sick or on a journey, let it be a [similar] number of other days. God desires ease for you, and He does not desire hardship for you, and so that you may complete the number, and magnify God for guiding you, and that you may give thanks.

The verse begins with the specification of the time when fasting must be observed which is in the holy month of Ramadan. The previous verse mentions "the number of days" which makes the period of fasting a very precise practice, which can sometimes lead to heated debates among scholars as they are scrupulous in observing the command of God and they do their best to accurately find out when the fasting should begin.

in which the Quran was sent down; Tusi mentions two possible opinions to explain this phrase.[300] The first opinion is held by mostly Shiʿi scholars, which is that God sent down the whole Quran on the Night of Power (*Laylat al-Gadr*), which is in the month of Ramadan (according to Shiʿis, most likely to be on the 23 night of Ramadan), from Higher Heaven to the Lower Heaven from where God revealed it to the Prophet gradually. Tusi attributes this opinion to Ibn Abbas, Saʿīd b. Jubayr, Hasan al-Basri and Imam Jafar al-Sadiq. Another verse which explains what is meant by the Quran coming down to the Lower Heaven is in Surah al-Ṭalāq:

> It is God who has created seven heavens, and of the earth [a number] similar to them. The command gradually descends through them, that you may know that God has power over all things, and that God comprehends all things in knowledge. (Q. 65:12)

This verse refers to seven levels or dimensions of creation and whenever the Quran refers to the seven heavens it is referring to the seven levels or dimensions of creation. Each level is the habitat of a different group of angels. We know that angels do not live in this physical world, therefore, heavens are dimensions beyond the physical world. God sends down his commands through these heavens which are revealed step by step from the seventh dimension to the lowest dimension. In other words, the angels translate the command of God to the lower stages of creation. In this way, when the Quran was sent down to the Lower Heaven it arrived to where the angel Gabriel could read and convey it to the Prophet.

Among those who hold the first opinion, some suggested that the Quran was revealed to the heart of the Prophet as a whole on the Night of Power, as a concept which was later translated into words through angel Gabriel.

The second opinion is that revelation began on the Night of Power and continued gradually after that. This view is held mostly by Sunni scholars, however, there are a limited number of Shi'i scholars who also have adhered to this view. One of the criticisms of the second view is that it is well-known that the first revelation came to the Prophet on the 27th of Rajab; not in the month of Ramadan. The implication of this is that either the Quran was wholly revealed in the month of Ramadan or that revelation began in the month of Ramadan. Either way the verse gives the honour and status of this special occasion to the month of Ramadan. In this month, the blessings of God descend to the earth, especially through the blessing of guidance, the Quran.

as guidance to mankind, with manifest proofs of guidance and the Criterion. The Quran is the general guidance for people which sets out the purpose and destiny of creation and the duties of people towards God. It also explains the "manifest proofs of guidance" which are the details of how to fast, pray and give charity as well as the rules of inheritance, and ritual cleaning and many more.

The difference between "the Criterion" and "manifest proofs of guidance" is best explained by a tradition attributed Imam Jafar al-Sadiq: "The Quran is the whole book, 'the Criterion' are those verses which include unequivocal (*muhkam*) verses or clear injunctions which are clear and obligatory to follow."[301]

Kashani has an interesting view on the Quran being revealed every year on the Night of Power to the Twelfth Imam al-Mahdi. He explains that the *interpretation* of the Quran is revealed to Imam al-Mahdi every year. This is simply an anecdote based on some Shi'i narrations.

The verse then repeats the previous rulings which grant exemptions to the sick, and the traveller who would then be able to make up for the missed days in equal numbers after the end of Ramadan. However, they are not allowed to fast while they are sick or travelling.

God desires ease for you, and He does not desire hardship for you; This is the reason why those who are sick or travelling should not fast. Some people may still fast while they are sick or travelling, but God does not burden people with this hardship. Rather, his intention is to ease our difficulties. Yet the benefits of fasting are so great that if people are not able to fast in Ramadan, they should compensate in equal numbers after Ramadan so that they are not deprived of those benefits. The number of days is therefore important and missing days must be made up in strictly equal numbers. In general, the obligatory worships, daily prayers, fasting, giving alms and going to Hajj have such significant spiritual benefits that God encourages believers to adhere to them. Otherwise, there are many other worships which are not obligatory despite having many benefits in them. This is because they are not required in order to enter Heaven. However, the obligatory worships are deeply necessary and required for entry to Heaven; without the obligatory prayers, a person would have to wait for a long time before qualifying to go into Heaven.

This period of waiting would take place in *al-ṣir'āṭ* (lit. obvious path or main way) which is the lifeline that God has given us. God can keep people there for as long as several thousand years, so that they would be able to attain the necessary pre-requisites that they had not attained during their lifetime. However, this attainment would be in the form of compensation for what they had missed in the world, and therefore it would take a very long time. It is much quicker for people to attain the necessary pre-requisites in this world and the key to attain the necessary pre-requisites is to duly perform the obligatory worships which includes fasting.

so that you may complete the number, and magnify God for guiding you, and that you may give thanks. Through performing the obligatory worships, believers also acquire awareness about the magnitude of God and the knowledge of God shines in their hearts. People are not able to see or experience God in anyway except through the enlightenment of the heart which is only possible with worship. When this process is completed, believers would then be able to thank God Almighty for the guidance that he has given to the believers.

وَإِذَا سَأَلَكَ عِبَادِي عَنِّي فَإِنِّي قَرِيبٌ ۖ أُجِيبُ دَعْوَةَ الدَّاعِ إِذَا دَعَانِ ۖ
فَلْيَسْتَجِيبُوا لِي وَلْيُؤْمِنُوا بِي لَعَلَّهُمْ يَرْشُدُونَ ﴿186﴾

When My servants ask you about Me, [tell them that] I am indeed nearmost. I answer the supplicant's call when he calls Me. So, let them respond to Me, and let them have faith in Me, so that they may fare rightly.

When My servants ask you about Me; The verse does not specify the type of question the enquirer asks about God. It is reported that someone had asked the Prophet about God, prior to the revelation of this verse. Quranic exegetes refer to traditions reported by Hasan al-Basri and Qatada in this regard, that a person or a group of people asked the Prophet about God, and although it is difficult to establish the veracity of these traditions, it is probable that the verse was revealed in response to their question. However, this verse addresses mankind's general question about our relationship with God and his attitude towards creation.

[tell them that] I am indeed nearmost. The word "nearmost" (*qarībun*) used in the verse, has led to many discussions among the commentators as God does not have proximity in terms of physical distance. God is the creator of space so he cannot be in a space. Therefore, we cannot say that he is physically close to us. Tabrisi comments that the verse implies that God has no physical place, because, if he had a space, he could not be close to all of his creation at the same time.[302]

The relation between God and his creation is complicated and paradoxical. He is with everything but in everything. He is outside everything but not remote from anything. In a sense our mind cannot comprehend the nature of the relationship God has with his creations. Our minds are set to understand things within the context of space and time, and it is difficult, if not impossible to imagine something outside of time and space. Therefore, our eyes cannot see him, and even our imagination is not able to grasp him fully. As one verse of the Quran explains, *The sights do not apprehend Him, yet He apprehends the sights, and He is the All-attentive, the All-aware.* (Q. 6:103)

Although we neither know the extent of the closeness of God to us nor the nature of this closeness, we know that God is intimate with his creation. Tusi notes that God's statement "*I am indeed nearmost*" may have two meanings.[303] Firstly, that he responds quickly, especially when a faithful person asks something from God. Secondly, that he hears us from close proximity.

I answer the supplicant's call when he calls Me. This is a call from the heart of a believer to God. God responds to this heart connection. Shaykh Tusi articulates this well, that God's response would not be exclusive to Muslims.[304] Anyone (Muslim or non-Muslim) who calls upon God from the bottom of their hearts, will receive the attention and response of God. Anyone who acknowledges God and then desperately calls upon him, would receive his attention as it is mentioned in the Quran: *"Or who answers the call of the distressed [person] when he invokes Him and removes his distress, and makes you the earth's successors? What! Is there a god besides God [Almighty]? Little is the admonition that you take."* (Q. 27:62) This verse is addressing the polytheists of Mecca, not Muslims. God reasserts that if people call upon him, he will respond, but this call must come from the bottom of heart instead of tip of the tongue.

So, let them respond to Me and let them have faith in Me; Calling upon God at the time of desperation and getting his attention is a reciprocal process. Upon receiving God's positive response to a call, the caller then needs to respond to God's call to having faith in him. This faith includes believing in the existence of God and his message and messengers. However, some exegetes have suggested that "let them have faith in Me" does not refer to having faith in God per se, rather it refers to having faith in his power and magnanimity to respond to those who call upon him from bottom of their hearts. This opinion is more plausible.

so that they may fare rightly. Calling upon God (*du'ā*) in a time of need, leads to spiritual growth and elevation. Even though God is able to give without the need for asking, it is still important for people to ask him. This is because of the spiritual effect of making *du'ā*; it grants spiritual elevations to people, and this is exactly what God wants people to do.

Kashani asks why many of us make requests from God, but he does not answer them and how does this relate to "I answer the supplicant's call when he calls Me"?[305] To answer to this question, the first requirement is that *du'ā* needs to come from the bottom of our hearts. It is reported that: "Do not command God, ask from him humbly!"

We may often command God to give us what we want, but this is not a *du'ā*. Rather, to make *du'ā* is to beseech God with utmost humility. The second requirement for a *du'ā* to be answered is that it should be in accordance with the wisdom or equilibrium of the management of creation. If these two requirements are met, the response would certainly come. If the *du'ā* meets the first requirement but fails the second, then God would grant us something different that would not upset the equilibrium of the management of the creation and would satisfy our needs.

أُحِلَّ لَكُمْ لَيْلَةَ الصِّيَامِ الرَّفَثُ إِلَىٰ نِسَائِكُمْ ۚ هُنَّ لِبَاسٌ لَّكُمْ وَأَنتُمْ
لِبَاسٌ لَّهُنَّ ۗ عَلِمَ اللَّهُ أَنَّكُمْ كُنتُمْ تَخْتَانُونَ أَنفُسَكُمْ فَتَابَ عَلَيْكُمْ
وَعَفَا عَنكُمْ ۖ فَالْآنَ بَاشِرُوهُنَّ وَابْتَغُوا مَا كَتَبَ اللَّهُ لَكُمْ ۚ وَكُلُوا
وَاشْرَبُوا حَتَّىٰ يَتَبَيَّنَ لَكُمُ الْخَيْطُ الْأَبْيَضُ مِنَ الْخَيْطِ الْأَسْوَدِ مِنَ
الْفَجْرِ ۖ ثُمَّ أَتِمُّوا الصِّيَامَ إِلَى اللَّيْلِ ۚ وَلَا تُبَاشِرُوهُنَّ وَأَنتُمْ عَاكِفُونَ فِي
الْمَسَاجِدِ ۗ تِلْكَ حُدُودُ اللَّهِ فَلَا تَقْرَبُوهَا ۗ كَذَٰلِكَ يُبَيِّنُ اللَّهُ آيَاتِهِ لِلنَّاسِ لَعَلَّهُمْ
يَتَّقُونَ ﴿187﴾

You are permitted, on the night of the fast, to go into your wives: they are a garment for you, and you are a garment for them. God knew that you used to betray yourselves, so He pardoned you and excused you. So now consort with them, and seek what God has ordained for you, and eat and drink until the white streak becomes manifest to you from the dark streak at the crack of dawn. Then complete the fast until nightfall, and do not consort with them while you dwell in confinement in the mosques. These are God's bounds, so do not approach them. Thus, does God clarify His signs for mankind so that they may be Godwary.

Upon providing some general information about the significance of fasting during the month of Ramadan in the previous verses, this verse provides some detailed rulings about fasting. The rulings are mostly about the relation between husband and wife.

You are permitted, on the night of the fast, to go into (*al-rafath*) your wives; Here, the verse is explicit in providing the boundaries of fasting regulating the physical relationship between husband and wife. Partners need to abstain from sexual contact while in the state of fasting, however, when the fasting is over, they may approach each other.

The Arabic word *al-rafath* is used figuratively to refer to intercourse. It literally means "intimate words which are mentioned explicitly". The same word is also used in Q. 2:197 to forbid sexual intercourse while performing Hajj: ... *whoever decides on Hajj [pilgrimage] therein, [should know that] there is to be no sexual contact (rafatha)...*

God never uses explicit words to describe issues which are related to human modesty such as sexual relationships between husband and wife. According to the verse, believers are permitted to approach their lawful partners after sunset, upon breaking their fasting.

they are a garment for you, and you are a garment for them; Here the reason for this permission is mentioned. This is one of the most beautiful expressions mentioned in the Quran. It means partners are so close to each other that it is impossible to avoid intimacy for a long time. Furthermore, garments protect us from heat and cold and cover our private parts. Garments are also an adornment for people. In the same way, a husband and wife protect each other from deviation and shortcomings and become a means of comfort for each other. Therefore, the choice of the metaphor of garment to describe the connection between husband and wife is meaningful.

God knew that you used to betray yourselves, so He pardoned you and excused you. The initial ruling for husbands and wives was different and stricter than the rule laid out in the verse above. Previously, intercourse was forbidden during the period of the fasting day as well as the night for the complete month. However, many found this to be difficult, and therefore this verse abolished the old ruling.

If this was the case, one might wonder why God ordained such as difficult ruling at first. If he had already known that it was difficult for some couples to abstain from intercourse during the month of Ramadan, there must be some wisdom in forbidding it and then relaxing the ruling. The answer may be that sometimes God wants to emphasise the significance of some acts. After this, God removed the negative effects of having intercourse during Ramadan.

It was a similar case with the night prayers. God initially ordained them to be obligatory for believers: *O you wrapped up in your mantle! Stand vigil through the night, except a little, a half, or reduce a little from that or add to it and recite the Quran in a measured tone.* (Q. 73:1-4) The verse urged the Prophet during the early periods of the revelation to keep up the night prayers and his companions also prayed night prayers as an obligatory worship. It was very difficult for some of the early believers, thus, after some time, God withdrew the commandment with Q. 73:20, and made the status of night prayer a recommended, but not obligatory act.

So now consort with them and seek what God has ordained for you; Exegetes have varying opinions about the meaning of this sentence. One group has argued that the verse commands to consort with your partners to seek virtuous children that God has for you in your destiny. Therefore, some say that on the nights of Ramadan it is not recommended to have intercourse except for with the intention of having good children. However, this view is puritanical and does not comply with the other phrases in the verse. The second group suggests that the verse commands us to seek whatever God has written for you in terms of this permission; seek that permission and go to your spouses.

and eat and drink until the white streak becomes manifest to you from the dark streak at the crack of dawn. The next part of the verse provides specific instructions regarding the beginning of the fast in Ramadan. When the distinguishing time of the morning arrives in the horizon, the time of fasting begins.

There has been disagreement among the Shi'i scholars about the beginning of the night: whether night falls at sunset, when the sun levels with horizon, or whether the sun needs to set until the redness in the eastern sky appears. Tabrisi makes an interesting intervention by combining the two views: he states that the night starts when the sun levels with the horizon but in the urban and mountainous areas it is difficult to observe this, therefore, in such places the sign of sunset is the appearance of the redness in the eastern sky which happens approximately 10 minutes after. However, in flat landscapes where the sunset can be seen, night begins when the sun levels with horizon.[306] This is the view of the Sunni school of thought. Among the contemporary Shi'i scholars Muhammad Taqi Bahjat (d. 2009) and Naser Makarem Shirazi (b. 1927) have held this view as well. Most of the other contemporary Shi'i scholars hold the later view that the sun must set until the redness in the eastern sky appears.

These are God's bounds, so do not approach them. Thus, does God clarify His signs for mankind so that they may be Godwary. This is extremely powerful. In the Quran, whenever the boundaries of God are mentioned, they are coupled with powerful statements. Instead of warning against trespassing God's boundaries, it says "do not approach them." There are certain things which are defined for us, in terms of worship and our social relations and there are some issues which cause much debate between people such as the benefits and harms of drinking alcohol, or the boundaries of the relationship between men women. God regulates these important affairs in the Scriptures so that human beings stop arguing about them and focus on social and spiritual affairs. God calls these affairs "God's bounds"; naturally, human nature can trespass these bounds easily, but he asks people to not to approach them for their own good. In summary the verses on the fasting began with the understanding that the end goal is to achieve piety (*taqwā*) and the discussion ends a reminder about piety again.

وَلَا تَأْكُلُوا أَمْوَالَكُم بَيْنَكُم بِالْبَاطِلِ وَتُدْلُوا بِهَا إِلَى الْحُكَّامِ
لِتَأْكُلُوا فَرِيقًا مِّنْ أَمْوَالِ النَّاسِ بِالْإِثْمِ وَأَنتُمْ تَعْلَمُونَ ﴿188﴾

Do not eat up your wealth among yourselves wrongfully, nor proffer it to the judges in order to eat up a part of the people's wealth sinfully, while you know [that it is immoral to do so].

This verse further elaborates on God's limits, which include respecting personal property. There are definitive regulations about the specific ways of exchanging personal property. There are also certain ways in which personal property is exchanged, which include some strictly forbidden practices such as *rib'a* (usury).

Do not eat up your wealth among yourselves wrongfully; (*bi al-bāṭil*). "Wrongfully" here refers to ways which are unacceptable according to Islamic law. There are a number of *bāṭil* ways in which property can be exchanged, such as through oppression, betrayal, stealing, usurpation, gambling and the like. It is unfortunate to see that some of these wrongful ways to exchange property have become part of the fabric of non-Muslim communities despite their destructive effects on the individuals and communities. Many desperate people suffer from high interest loans and gambling addictions, yet corporates are encouraged to carry out their business. Islam forbids this unlawful way of exchanging property.

nor proffer it to the judges; This phrase draws attention to prohibition of wrongful ways of being litigious against others. If people have ill-intentions, they may always find loopholes in the laws and take advantage of these loopholes by producing false evidence to wrongfully seize another person's property. Another meaning of it may refer to paying bribes to judges so that they may rule in favour of the dishonest party to take over another's property.

in order to eat up a part of the people's wealth sinfully, while you know [that it is immoral to do so]. People often know the truth in their heart that although they may have the means to take over another's properties, it is the wrong thing to do. If they go against it to deceitfully seize another person's property this is a great sin against God.

يَسْأَلُونَكَ عَنِ الْأَهِلَّةِ ۖ قُلْ هِيَ مَوَاقِيتُ لِلنَّاسِ وَالْحَجِّ ۗ وَلَيْسَ الْبِرُّ بِأَنْ تَأْتُوا
الْبُيُوتَ مِنْ ظُهُورِهَا وَلَٰكِنَّ الْبِرَّ مَنِ اتَّقَىٰ ۗ وَأْتُوا الْبُيُوتَ مِنْ أَبْوَابِهَا ۚ
وَاتَّقُوا اللَّهَ لَعَلَّكُمْ تُفْلِحُونَ ﴿189﴾

They question you concerning the new moons. Say, 'They are timekeeping signs for the people and [for the sake of] Hajj.' It is not piety that you come into houses from their rear; rather piety is [personified by] one who is Godwary, and come into houses from their doors, and be wary of God, so that you may be felicitous.

They question you concerning the new moons; This verse marks the beginning of a new discussion in Surah al-Baqarah by quoting a question asked to the Prophet. There are around 15 cases where the Quran quotes questions which were asked from the Prophet. Several of these questions are mentioned in Surah al-Baqarah and one example is mentioned in this verse. There is a view among the commentators that these questions indicate that the early followers were mostly obedient to the instructions of the Prophet and questioned him little when he brought new rulings. This is different to the experience of Prophet Moses found earlier in the surah.

Although Prophet Muhammad did not receive resistance from his companions to the extent that Prophet Moses received resistance from his followers, not every question that the followers of the Prophet put to him are included in the Quran. Some of the questions are included in the hadith literature. It is impossible to imagine that his followers asked only fifteen questions to the Prophet. Also, asking a question to the Prophet should not be considered a negative trait, so long as the questions were genuine. In fact, it can be taken as a sign of the sincerity of the believers made a life changing commitment by submitting to the religion of God and who wish to further understand the religious teachings. These questions may have been included in the Quran as they required revelation to answer them or because they asked just as revelation was about to come, and the answer was also included in the revelation.

This question was asked about the crescents of the moon. The translation is often rendered as "the new moons" but the real meaning is more complex. It is not clear from the verse whether the exact question was related to the crescents of the moon. However, the answer mentioned in the verse tells us that the question was not about the crescents themselves rather it was about the *benefit* of the crescents of the moon for religious matters. Muslims rely on both the Moon and Sun to determine the time and dates that enable them to perform their religious obligations. The solar calendar is complex and requires complicated calculations. Hence ordinary people were not able to use it easily, especially without the use of calculators and other technology. However, the lunar calendar was easier to use and could be determined through observation rather than calculation. For this reason, God chose the lunar calendar for people to use to determine religious matters as indicated in the verse. Furthermore, the verse also points out the relevance of lunar calendar "[for the sake of] Hajj". It seems Hajj is included as a prelude to the following verse which discusses fighting and *jihad* in the way of God. It is known that in Dhul Hijja, fighting was not permitted.

It is not piety that you come into houses from their rear; rather piety is [personified by] one who is Godwary, and come into houses from their doors, and be wary of God, so that you may be felicitous. This part of the verse does not seem to be directly related to Hajj, but it draws attention to a practice of some of the tribes of Quraysh at the time of pagan faith. These tribes were called *ḥums* or zealots and included those who were fervent in pursuing their faith. When they wanted to go for pilgrimage, they included additional rituals to show off their dedication to their faith. They would say, we do not enter our house from the same door that we had left for pilgrimage. So, they would make a hole at the furthest back of their house and entered their house from that hole when they returned from their pilgrimage.

One may imagine many other arbitrary rituals that may have been developed around this practice. What makes this ritual important is that it was believed to be a sign of piety for the pagan Arabs, and the Quran objects to this false perception. In fact, the Quran outwardly declares that this practice is not an indication of piety; rather piety comes from fear of God and refraining from things that he has prohibited. Also, piety is doing what he has ordained upon us for his sake. Some Muslims attempt to add extra embellishments to the rituals with the intention that these additions are a sign of their dedication to God more than the others. So, this verse is not only referring to the pagan Arabs of Mecca who lived at the time of the Prophet, but it also refers to Muslim zealots who similarly attach innovations to the rituals.

come into houses from their doors, and be wary of God, so that you may be felicitous. Here the verse reemphasises not to add embellishments to God's commands, rather, we must carry out God's commands in the way he has ordained upon us; nothing more or nothing less.

وَقَاتِلُوا فِي سَبِيلِ اللَّهِ الَّذِينَ يُقَاتِلُونَكُمْ وَلَا تَعْتَدُوا ۚ إِنَّ اللَّهَ لَا يُحِبُّ الْمُعْتَدِينَ ﴿190﴾

Fight in the way of God those who fight you, but do not transgress. Indeed, God does not like transgressors.

This is one of the first verses to be revealed permitting Muslims to wage defensive war or *jihad* against the polytheists of Mecca. As it is clear from the verse, permission to fight is only granted against those who wage war against Muslims. That is why some exegetes contend that this verse was abrogated (*mansukh*) by the verses which seemingly permit war unconditionally, for example, *O you who have faith! Fight the faithless who are in your vicinity, and let them find severity in you, and know that God is with the Godwary.* (Q. 9:123)

It is important to note the context of this verse in Surah al-Tawba refers to those polytheists who were in breach of a peace treaty with the Prophet, or those who were creating constant mischief. Even so, Muslims may not have adhered to this condition either because they believed that the verse was abrogated or held that it was not practical. After the death of the Prophet, Muslims undertook a massive expansion campaign and conquered many lands in the name of Islam and *jihad*, however, many conditions of *jihad* were not observed.

Therefore, there is an apparent contradiction between the instructions of the Quran that *jihad* is only allowed defensively and the practices of early Muslims waging offensive *jihad*. This contradiction is problematic for the commentators and contemporary Muslims alike. Kashani suggests that the verse itself may offer an answer by the addition, *but do not transgress*. He interprets this addition as God's command thereby banning the initiation of war by Muslims, since initiation of war is considered in his view as transgression.[307] An exception to this may be for a war that is waged after calling a people to Islam and they reject. This has been the stance that the Sunni world and some Shi'i scholars have taken, who are of the view that if a non-Muslim people fail to accept the invitation to Islam, they are entitled to wage *jihad* against them.

This understanding does not make sense. Wars often occur between rulers, so when Muslim rulers invite non-Muslim rulers to Islam; the invitation only reaches the rulers or politicians. It does not genuinely reach the ordinary people. Consequently, it cannot be claimed that the process of inviting a country to Islam involves calling its people to Islam. In any case, existing rulers of a country often have well-established security and propaganda mechanisms to suppress any call to another faith. Consequently, it would not be realistically possible to invite nations to Islam in the true sense, which means calling for *jihad* in these circumstances is unjustifiable.

Razi, along with many other exegetes, have contended that this verse was abrogated by the following verse:[308] *And kill them wherever you confront them, and expel them from where they expelled you, for faithlessness is graver than killing*. (Q. 2:191) This verse will be discussed in depth later, however although this is a strange viewpoint, the majority of Muslims support it. It is evident that the command of Q. 2:191 *And kill them wherever you confront them* is in relation to engagement on the battlefield in a war which was warranted defensively in Q. 2:190. The verses are neither separate from each other nor a replacement to each other. The former verse sanctions waging defensive war whilst the later verse sanctions killing enemies who participate in the war. Killing is the natural consequence of any war. When a war starts, armies gather to fight and kill, to retreat, regroup, and fight back, therefore the verses states *And kill them wherever you confront them.*

The scholars who believed in the abrogation of verse 190 attempt to justify the early history of Islam in light of the verses of the Quran. The early Muslims waged offensive wars after the death of the Prophet in which they conquered lands and accrued an unimaginable amount of wealth. However, many of those wars were primarily motivated by materialistic and expansionist ambitions. This was the case especially during the Umayyad reign, when wars were often waged to increase political power, exploit wealth and increase tax revenues. People of newly occupied lands were often discouraged from converting to Islam as the conversion would reduce the amount of tax that would be payable to the state. Therefore, Shiʿi Imams did not participate in these battles after the Prophet's demise. Although Imam Ali was the most decorated warrior of Islam during the Prophet's life and had decisive roles in many battles, he never joined any war expeditions after the Prophet died. Also, Imam Hasan and Imam Husayn only participated in fighting during the caliphate of Imam Ali. After his death, they both abstained from participating in battles. This may be because they were aware of the motivations behind these wars, and how offensive wars were prohibited in Islam.

Nevertheless, given the verse at hand, it is clear that the Quran only sanctions defensive *jihad*. The idea of abrogation may have been improvised to justify the offensive wars waged in the early history of Islam. The selective use of the concept of abrogation to justify particular religious views is documented in John Burton's well-known work *The Collection of the Quran.*[309] The discourse of abrogation built around this verse may be another stark example of the use of the concept of abrogation to support certain acts. The obvious motivation is to justify the misdeeds or incorrect views of early Muslims.

The views of Shi'i scholars on this topic are fundamental in the correct understanding to the Islamic perspective of *jihad*. The Shi'i scholars maintain that offensive *jihad* was only permissible during the times of the Holy Prophet and the infallible Imams. It is important to note that there is a minority of Shi'i scholars who maintain that a legal jurist in charge of an Islamic government who has embodied all the necessary qualities such as piety, justice, knowledge, political acumen and the like *(faqīh al-jāmi' li-shārā'iṭ)* can wage offensive *jihad*. However, this is the marginal view held by a minority of Shi'i scholars including two prominent Shi'i jurists, Mufid (d. 413/1022) and Sallār al-Daylamī (d. 463/1071). It may be interesting to note that amongst the contemporary Shi'i scholars, Khomeini (d. 1989) is against the idea of waging offensive *jihad* by a qualified jurist, whilst Khoei (d. 1992) argued that a qualified jurist could indeed wage offensive *jihad*.

Looking back at the available historical data from the time of the Prophet, it seems that the Prophet did not wage any offensive wars during his lifetime, although he did launch pre-emptive attacks against the enemy. For example, during the Expedition of Tabuk at 9/630, Prophet Muhammad received the news of an imminent Byzantine invasion of Muslim lands. In response, the Prophet assembled an unprecedentedly large army to meet the Byzantine army at their borders, however the Byzantine army did not arrive. Thus, the Prophet returned without engaging in any battle, although he passed many non-Muslim areas on the expedition.

On the other hand, the story of Solomon and Queen Sheba demonstrates the other side of the spectrum. There was no provocation from Yemen, Queen Sheba's country, on Prophet Solomon. Prophet Solomon was informed that the people of Yemen worshipped the Sun (Q. 27:23-24). Prophet Solomon then sent Queen Sheba an ultimatum (Q. 27:28) which could be regarded as an initiation of war. However, a further investigation into these events can offer a different perspective. Firstly why did Prophet Solomon have such a great interest in Yemen in particular? There were many idolaters situated around the Kingdom of Solomon that he did not approach. It is possible that the significance of an idolater nation in Yemen may have been greater for the Arabian

Peninsula and the potential military and strategic threat that it posed to the believers' community. Instead, it may be that Prophet Solomon had sensed that Queen Sheba was a wise woman (Q. 27: 34-36) and her heart was inclined towards faith and that Queen Sheba would embrace the true religion and encourage her people to embrace *tawhid*. The idea that Prophet Solomon singles out Queen Sheba from other disbelieving people strengthens the second view that Prophet Solomon was interested in helping Queen Sheba who was already inclined towards faith. The relevant verses of Chapter 27 of the Quran provide further information about the spiritual qualities and acumen of Queen Sheba.

وَاقْتُلُوهُمْ حَيْثُ ثَقِفْتُمُوهُمْ وَأَخْرِجُوهُم مِّنْ حَيْثُ أَخْرَجُوكُمْ وَالْفِتْنَةُ
أَشَدُّ مِنَ الْقَتْلِ وَلَا تُقَاتِلُوهُمْ عِندَ الْمَسْجِدِ الْحَرَامِ حَتَّىٰ يُقَاتِلُوكُمْ فِيهِ
فَإِن قَاتَلُوكُمْ فَاقْتُلُوهُمْ كَذَٰلِكَ جَزَاءُ الْكَافِرِينَ ﴿191﴾

And kill them wherever you confront them, and expel them from where they expelled you, for corruption (fitna) is graver than killing. But do not fight them near the Holy Mosque unless they fight you therein; but if they fight you, kill them; such is the requital of the faithless.

As noted above, some commentators contend that this verse abrogates the previous verse (190) as it can be interpreted as a general verse which advocates the killing of all disbelievers. These commentators often understand the word *fitna* in the verse as "faithlessness" which they regard as the source of corruption on the earth. The discussion of abrogation above concluded that aside from a few select of cases, there is no indication of verses abrogating each other. Rather, in most cases what is regarded to be the "abrogating" or "abrogated" verses often address the exigencies of different contexts and situations. In some other cases, a set of verses elaborate the same theme from different perspectives. The verses above have been revealed simultaneously, thus, it is highly unrealistic that the previous verse (190) would have been abrogated with the next verse (191). As these are sequential verses, there is no reason to think that God immediately has changed his view on the issue of fighting with disbelievers.

That is why Tabatabai's opinion seems quite plausible here. He says the verse does not warrant Muslims to fight every faithless person; rather the verse is revealed explicitly about the disbelievers of Mecca who were plotting to fight and eradicate Muslims.[310] There was already a de facto state of war between Muslims and the Meccan disbelievers, and with this verse, Muslims were authorised to fight and kill them when necessary. Therefore, there is no ground for some contemporary Muslims to claim that waging unprovoked and offensive war against disbelievers is justified. This ideology stems from a fundamental misunderstanding of the basic tenets of Islam and the Quran. In accordance with the example of the Prophet and Imams, Muslims must abstain from waging offensive wars and causing bloodshed and unnecessary pain on the earth. As a rule, Muslims are *only* allowed to resort to violence to defend themselves and defend the oppressed from immediate danger.

And kill them wherever you confront them and expel them from where they expelled you; Muslims are permitted to kill their enemies or expel them wherever they confront them in defensive *jihad*. Again, such rulings by no means warrant the terrorist activities of some who claim to have the authority to wage *jihad* in the name of Islam and kill or wound mostly innocent civilians. Islam despises such behaviours which are often motivated by individual ambitions of attaining power. Waging jihad is strictly regulated in both Shi'i and Sunni legal systems, and only legitimate leaders of the Muslim community may take decisions about waging war. When a defensive *jihad* is waged, the rights and wellbeing of civilians, animals and plants must be preserved. Killing is only warranted in the actual battlefield, not elsewhere. In this regard, the actions of some so-called "jihadist" groups is no different than the immoral and opportunist actions of some of the modern nation-states that have no regard for civilian, animal and environmental rights.

for corruption (*fitna*) is graver than killing. Due to the practices of early Muslims, the commentators have often inclined to interpret the word *fitna* as "disbelief." They wanted to associate disbelief with *fitna* to justify the offensive *jihad* campaign of the early Muslims against non-Muslim states. However, this interpretation is a theological and ideological reading of the Quran. The corruption (*fitna*) refers to the hostile actions of Meccan disbelievers who killed, tortured and expelled Muslims and dispensed every effort to suppress the message of the Prophet. Of course, this transgression is worse than shedding blood because it causes constant distress and affliction for people and interrupts the development of faith in a brutal way. Therefore, the verse warrants fighting and killing for self-defence. It may also be interpreted to mean that for a decent human being living in situations of constant humiliation is worse than fighting and dying on the battlefield.

But do not fight them near the Holy Mosque unless they fight you therein; but if they fight you, kill them; This statement further strengthens the view that the verse addresses a specific conflict situation with Meccan disbelievers who had openly declared war against Muslims. The verse first discourages Muslims from shedding blood in the Sacred Mosque of Mecca that surrounds the Holy Kabah. However, if the disbelievers continue their hostilities around the Holy Kabah, the verse permits Muslims to fight them there as a retaliatory action.

such is the requital of the faithless. This refers to fighting the polytheists near the Holy Mosque. If the disbelievers initiate a fight against Muslims and continue their fight in the Holy Mosque of Mecca, they deserve to be fought and killed even inside the Holy Mosque; that is their requital. Everyone and everything must be respected in the Holy Mosque. Yet, because of the gravity of their hatred and aggression, if they disrespect the Holy Mosque by fighting in it, then they would have to be disrespected too.

فَإِنِ انتَهَوْا فَإِنَّ اللَّهَ غَفُورٌ رَّحِيمٌ ﴿192﴾

But if they relinquish, then God is indeed All-forgiving, All-merciful.

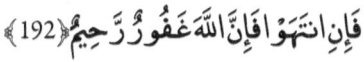

This verse goes on to mention that if the disbelievers of Mecca end their aggression against Muslims, then Muslims should cease any hostilities towards them in turn. This is despite the aggressors being disbelievers and Muslims acting in self-defence. God does not like fighting and bloodshed, thus he encourages Muslims to take a peaceful stance. Muslims are allowed to resort to violence to protect themselves only. As soon as the hostilities cease, Muslims should also stop fighting so that peace and harmony may be reinstated and there would be an opportunity for the religion of God to continue to flourish. This is reinforced by Q. 8:61: *And if they incline toward peace, then you too incline toward it, and put your trust in God. Indeed, He is the All-hearing, the All-knowing.*

Therefore, the ethics of war is distinct in Islam: in a conflict situation, if a warring side decides to cease hostilities, it is often understood to be a sign of weakness and inability to continue to fight. Thus, the opposing side would usually take full advantage of the situation by either attempting to wipe out the enemy or demand a complete surrender and submission from them. However, the verse stipulates that Muslims should just stop fighting and immediately reinstate peace once the threat is eliminated, without any further escalations.

Islam does not aim to proselytise non-Muslims forcefully; otherwise, it would have been easy for God to coerce everyone into embracing Islam. This is entirely against the Quranic teachings of free will and the human objective to self-purify the soul. One of Islam's basic tenets is that there is no compulsion in religion; and Islam does not allow forceful conversion of people to Islam.

وَقَاتِلُوهُمْ حَتَّىٰ لَا تَكُونَ فِتْنَةٌ وَيَكُونَ الدِّينُ لِلَّهِ ۖ فَإِنِ انتَهَوْا فَلَا عُدْوَانَ إِلَّا
عَلَى الظَّالِمِينَ ﴿193﴾

Fight them until corruption (fitna) is no more, and religion becomes [exclusively] for God. Then if they relinquish, there shall be no reprisal except against the wrongdoers.

The verse clearly stipulates that the limits of violence in Islam are until the cessation of hostilities. When the threat is gone, Muslims must stop fighting and go on peacefully with their lives.

Religion becomes [exclusively] for God. This phrase could be interpreted as "until everyone submits to Islam." However, this interpretation is incorrect and the result of the false attribution to Quran and Islam which again stems from the scholarly effort to reconcile the verses of the Quran with the early misconducts of Muslims such as waging war against non-Muslim states in order to acquire wealth. A more accurate interpretation would be "until Muslims can follow their faith in God freely," not to be coerced into anything else.

Then if they relinquish, there shall be no reprisal except against the wrongdoers. This ending of the verse reasserts the stipulation that when hostilities cease, fighting should also cease.

الشَّهْرُ الْحَرَامُ بِالشَّهْرِ الْحَرَامِ وَالْحُرُمَاتُ قِصَاصٌ فَمَنِ اعْتَدَىٰ عَلَيْكُمْ فَاعْتَدُوا عَلَيْهِ بِمِثْلِ مَا اعْتَدَىٰ عَلَيْكُمْ وَاتَّقُوا اللَّهَ وَاعْلَمُوا أَنَّ اللَّهَ مَعَ الْمُتَّقِينَ ﴿194﴾

A sacred month for a sacred month and all sanctities require retribution. So, should anyone aggress against you, assail him in the manner he assailed you, and be wary of God, and know that God is with the Godwary.

A sacred month for a sacred month and all sanctities require retribution; The lunar months of Dhu al-Qa'da, Dhu al-Hijja, Muharram and Rajab have been known as the sacred months, most likely since the time of Prophet Abraham. All hostilities were strictly prohibited during these months. According to the verse, if the sanctity of sacred months is violated by the enemy, then it is justifiable for Muslims to fight back during these sacred months. It means that at any point Muslims are allowed to launch a counterattack against the enemy and a series of follow up attacks if necessary.

So, should anyone aggress against you, assail him in the manner he assailed you. This sentence refers to an extremely important aspect of the ethics of hostility, which is the proportionality of reactions. It highlights the fact that hostility should not lead to extravagance in retaliation. That is why God warns Muslims to fear God when they defeat the enemy and have full power over them. They should not transgress the limits during retaliation. Their response must be proportionate to the nature of the threat or hostility that they received from their enemies, and they need to avoid any disproportionate retribution. Even though the defeated enemy may have no power to enforce justice from Muslims, they should know that God is watching and have to be fearful of him, and they should "*know that God is with the Godwary*".

وَأَنفِقُوا فِي سَبِيلِ اللَّهِ وَلَا تُلْقُوا بِأَيْدِيكُمْ إِلَى التَّهْلُكَةِ وَأَحْسِنُوا
إِنَّ اللَّهَ يُحِبُّ الْمُحْسِنِينَ ﴿195﴾

Spend in the way of God, and do not cast yourselves with your own hands into destruction; and be virtuous. Indeed, God loves the virtuous.

This verse continues the overarching theme of the ethics and rules of war in Islam.

Spend in the way of God; This refers to spending wealth on war capabilities when a war is being fought. This may include providing logistical or financial support to the army during these times. Depending on the context, spending may even have a more general meaning, such as any effort spent for the fulfilment of Islamic teachings or improving social and individual life. There is a condition on fighting which is that it must be "in the way of God" which means that fighting must always be for a good cause, for example, to defend the lives and properties of the faithful or the oppressed.

and do not cast yourselves with your own hands into destruction; This is an oft-quoted verse of the Quran and has been interpreted in two different ways depending on the interpretation of the Arabic preposition *bā* (with) before the phrase "your hands." Some say that *bā* in this verse is redundant and in Arabic grammar, a redundant *bā* is used to emphasise the purport of a sentence. Using this meaning, the translation of the verse becomes, "do not cast your own hands into destruction" and hands often signifies one's own self since hands are a medium by which people act. Therefore, the meaning becomes "do not cast yourself into destruction." However, others have said that this *bā* is used in the sense of causation (*sababiyya*). Thus, it gives the meaning; "do not cast yourselves with (*bā*) your *own* hands into destruction." In the context of this verse, it is quite clear that the first meaning is not intended. The verse is trying to warn that if you do not spend in the way of *jihad*, when a war or imminent threat approaches, then you will expose yourself to destruction by allowing the enemy to attack and catch you off guard.

There may be a way to justify the first meaning too. Spending, whether for battle preparations or any other rewarding cause, should not exceed the limits in a way that would cause people to fall into a state of destitution and destruction. As it is mentioned in the Surah Isrā': *Do not keep your hand chained to your neck, nor open it altogether, or you will sit blameworthy, regretful.* (Q. 17:29) In this sense, the verse advises the charitable people that they should be prudent; while they discharge their material duties in the best possible way towards God, they should also consider their own welfare and their families. If they do not, they would be to blame for their own need and destitution.

وَأَتِمُّوا الْحَجَّ وَالْعُمْرَةَ لِلَّهِ ۚ فَإِنْ أُحْصِرْتُمْ فَمَا اسْتَيْسَرَ مِنَ الْهَدْيِ ۖ وَلَا
تَحْلِقُوا رُءُوسَكُمْ حَتَّىٰ يَبْلُغَ الْهَدْيُ مَحِلَّهُ ۚ فَمَنْ كَانَ مِنْكُمْ مَرِيضًا
أَوْ بِهِ أَذًى مِنْ رَأْسِهِ فَفِدْيَةٌ مِنْ صِيَامٍ أَوْ صَدَقَةٍ أَوْ نُسُكٍ ۚ فَإِذَا أَمِنْتُمْ فَمَنْ
تَمَتَّعَ بِالْعُمْرَةِ إِلَى الْحَجِّ فَمَا اسْتَيْسَرَ مِنَ الْهَدْيِ ۚ فَمَنْ لَمْ يَجِدْ فَصِيَامُ
ثَلَاثَةِ أَيَّامٍ فِي الْحَجِّ وَسَبْعَةٍ إِذَا رَجَعْتُمْ ۗ تِلْكَ عَشَرَةٌ كَامِلَةٌ ۗ ذَٰلِكَ لِمَنْ لَمْ
يَكُنْ أَهْلُهُ حَاضِرِي الْمَسْجِدِ الْحَرَامِ ۚ وَاتَّقُوا اللَّهَ وَاعْلَمُوا أَنَّ اللَّهَ شَدِيدُ
الْعِقَابِ ﴿196﴾

Complete the Hajj and the ʿumra for God's sake, and if you are prevented, then [make] such [sacrificial] offering as is feasible. And do not shave your heads until the offering reaches its [assigned] place. But should any of you be sick, or have hurt in his head, let the atonement be by fasting or charity, or sacrifice. And when you have security —for those who enjoy [release from the restrictions] by virtue of the ʿumra until the Hajj— let the offering be such as is feasible. As for someone who cannot afford [the offering], let him fast three days during the Hajj and seven when you return; that is [a period of] ten complete [days]. That is for someone whose family does not dwell by the Holy Mosque. And be wary of God, and know that God is severe in retribution.

This verse details many aspects of the ritual of Hajj and ʿumra, both of which are obligatory on Muslims.

Complete the hajj and the ʿumra for God's sake; The word "complete" here may refer to two aspects of Hajj: firstly, fulfilling the rituals of Hajj in keeping with following the instructions in meticulous detail and having the correct intention. Secondly, the phrase emphasises that once a pilgrim embarks on the ritual of Hajj by wearing the *iḥrām* (prescribed attire that pilgrims should wear at the start of Hajj), it must be completed without interruption at any point. Given the meaning of the second phrase, *for God's sake*, that will be discussed into below, the second meaning is more plausible.

The specific mention of the phrase "for *God's sake* (*lillāh*)" may be related in order to highlight that the sole purpose for going for Hajj should be for "*God's sake*". Before the advent of Islam and shortly after, people performed pilgrimage to the Kabah for different reasons. This was mostly to worship the idols which resided there. Aside from this, they also had other motives to visit the Holy Kabah as the pilgrimage was a great opportunity to negotiate business and political deals.

In fact, before the advent of Islam, very few people went to the Kabah to worship God Almighty. This is mentioned several times in the Quran (Q. 29:61 and 31:25), although the idolaters of Mecca believed in an Almighty God, they also believed that he had delegated his powers and the management of this world to the idols. This is why people mostly worshipped the idols for their worldly needs.

After the advent of Islam, Muslims did not go to Hajj to worship the idols. Nevertheless, for some, it was merely the continuation of the cultural activity, and they also used the pilgrimage as an opportunity to attend to some other businesses whilst they went for Hajj. For *"God's sake"* mentioned in the verse, denies the different motivations for going for Hajj and emphasises that it be performed exclusively for the sake of God.

If you are prevented, then [make] such [sacrificial] offering as is feasible. The previous sentence instructed that Hajj must be completed, however, in case a person is prevented from completing the ritual of Hajj due to either internal or external reasons (such as getting sick, having no physical strength or being blocked by an enemy), they should then make a sacrificial offering as a recompense. This was what the Prophet did after the Treaty of Hudaybiyya (6/629) when the idolaters prevented him and other Muslims from completing their Hajj. Upon signing the treaty, the Prophet and Muslims offered sacrificial animals and then removed their *iḥrām*.

And do not shave your heads until the offering reaches its [assigned] place. This sentence stipulates that if the pilgrims need to break the ritual of Hajj, they should not abandon the state of *iḥrām* immediately. They must wait until the animals are sacrificed. After that, they may go out of the state of *iḥrām*, at which point they also shave their heads.

But should any of you be sick, or have hurt in his head, let the atonement be by fasting, or charity, or sacrifice. The ritual of Hajj begins when the pilgrims enter the state of *iḥrām*. Whilst in this state, certain acts become impermissible or haram for them. One of those acts is cutting or shaving their hair. After completing the pilgrimage, the male pilgrims need to shave the hair on their heads to mark of the end of the ritual. However, if they have a disease which affects their scalp or have sustained an injury to their heads, they may then defer shaving their head hair and instead offer "*fasting, or charity, or sacrifice*". Going into such great detail about the specific rituals of Hajj in the Quran indicates the significance of these ritual in Islam.

And when you have security —for those who enjoy [release from the restrictions] by virtue of the 'umra until the Hajj— let the offering be such as is feasible. There are two different types of pilgrimage to the Kabah: 'umra and Hajj. The former can be done any time of the year, whilst the latter may only begin on the 8th of Dhu al-Hijja. However, those who travel from afar must combine Hajj and *'umra* during the months of Hajj which are Shawwal, Dhu al-Qada, and Dhu al-Hijja. This type of pilgrimage is called *hajj al-tamattu'*. As the pilgrims must put on *iḥrām* for *'umra* when they begin this type of pilgrimage, there may be an assumption that they need to be in the state of *iḥrām* after they complete 'umra until the time when Hajj begins on the 8th of Dhu al-Hijja. This could take several weeks. The verse clarifies that after performing the *'umra,* pilgrims can put aside their *iḥrām* until the 8th of Dhu al-Hijja when they must put back the *iḥrām* again. During this time, they are allowed to partake in what was forbidden for them whilst in the state of *iḥrām*. These pilgrims need to offer a sacrifice as a necessary part of the pilgrimage.

As for someone who cannot afford [the offering], let him fast three days during the Hajj and seven when you return; that is [a period of] ten complete [days]. Those who perform *hajj al-tamattu'*, but cannot afford a sacrifice, must fast for ten days: three days while in Hajj and seven days when they return home.

That is for someone whose family does not dwell by the Holy Mosque. This type of pilgrimage is for those who live a distance from the Holy Mosque, which is farther than 96 km radius around the Kabah. For those who live inside that radius, they must perform either *hajj al-qirān*, or *hajj al-ifrād*. In these two types, *'umra* and Hajj cannot be combined together the way it was in *hajj al-tamattu'*.

الْحَجُّ أَشْهُرٌ مَعْلُومَاتٌ ۚ فَمَنْ فَرَضَ فِيهِنَّ الْحَجَّ فَلَا رَفَثَ وَلَا فُسُوقَ وَلَا جِدَالَ فِي الْحَجِّ ۗ وَمَا تَفْعَلُوا مِنْ خَيْرٍ يَعْلَمْهُ اللَّهُ ۗ وَتَزَوَّدُوا فَإِنَّ خَيْرَ الزَّادِ التَّقْوَىٰ ۚ وَاتَّقُونِ يَا أُولِي الْأَلْبَابِ ﴿197﴾

The Hajj [season] is in months well-known; so whoever decides on Hajj [pilgrimage] therein, [should know that] there is to be no sexual contact, vicious talk, or disputing during the Hajj. And whatever good you do, God knows it. And take provision, for indeed the best provision is Godwaryness. So be wary of Me, O you who possess intellects!

Continuing the rulings of Hajj, this verse defines the specific times in which Hajj must be performed which are in the lunar months of Shawwal, Dhu al-Qada, and the first ten days of Dhu al-Hijja. Pilgrims are not allowed to perform Hajj outside these months.

so whoever decides on Hajj [pilgrimage] therein, [should know that] there is to be no sexual contact, vicious talk, or disputing during the Hajj. During Hajj, three main things are forbidden for Muslims: sexual contact (*rafath*), vicious talk (*fusūq*) and quarrel (*jidāl*). Couples are forbidden from any form of sexual relation or contact while they are in Hajj attire (*iḥrām*). Malicious talk, according to the commentators, refers to three misdeeds: lying, swearing and boasting to humiliate others. Of course, these transgressions are always sinful, and Muslims are forbidden from committing them anywhere. However, due to the sanctity of Hajj and the importance of the occasion, God warns the pilgrims to be extra careful and abstain from committing such misdeeds during their pilgrimage.

Finally, a pilgrim should not insist on their opinions to the extent that it may lead to a quarrel. The pilgrimage is an occasion for soul-searching and contemplation. It is where the lower self must be restrained, and the spirit must gain strength and find its way into the world of super material. This cannot be achieved except in an environment of brotherhood, harmony, and alliance.

And whatever good you do, God knows it. This sentence implicitly encourages the pilgrims to do all types of good in Hajj. The phrase "God knows it" is another expression for God rewarding what they do. However, it is a more powerful and intimate way of saying it, since any pilgrim would like to be seen as obedient and well-disposed by the Lord. This statement in itself is like a reward for the pilgrim, because the utmost joy and happiness of a true believer is to know that his Lord is aware of the good that they do for his sake.

And take provision, for indeed the best provision is Godwaryness. *Zād* is the provision of the traveller. The recommendation for *tazawwud* (taking provision) implies that Hajj is a spiritual occasion from which provision could be taken for a future journey, the journey to God. This phrase gives a beautiful hint that in Hajj there are many opportunities to attain spiritual provision which should not be neglected. Those whose spirit is aware can gain spiritual provisions from this unique journey for their transient life in this world as well as for their coming eternal life.

So be wary of Me, O you who possess intellects. There is a beautiful and delicate shift in the pronoun and address (*iltifāt*) in this last sentence. Previously in the verse, God was referred to in the third person, "he," and now there is a shift to the first person (*be wary of me*). The direct address is to give great importance to God-wariness (*al-taqwā*) and to remove any sense of distance between God and the Godwary. However, this address is to those *who possess intellect* (*ūlū al-albāb*) because they are the ones who enjoy the utmost merits of this spiritual journey whilst others only take smaller advantages and benefits of it. *Albāb* is the plural of *lubb* which is the core and kernel of intellect. It is that aspect of intellect which seeks deeper meanings of life, creation and existence, and is not satisfied with the exterior basic understanding of things.

لَيْسَ عَلَيْكُمْ جُنَاحٌ أَن تَبْتَغُوا فَضْلًا مِّن رَّبِّكُمْ ۚ فَإِذَا أَفَضْتُم مِّنْ
عَرَفَاتٍ فَاذْكُرُوا اللَّهَ عِندَ الْمَشْعَرِ الْحَرَامِ ۖ وَاذْكُرُوهُ كَمَا هَدَاكُمْ وَإِن
كُنتُم مِّن قَبْلِهِ لَمِنَ الضَّالِّينَ ﴿198﴾

There is no sin upon you in seeking your Lord's grace [during the Hajj season]. Then when you stream out of ʿArafāt, remember God at the Holy Mashʿar, and remember Him as He has guided you, and earlier you were indeed among the astray.

The rituals of Hajj were ordained by God at the time of Prophet Abraham after he constructed the Kabah. Over time, the same rituals were practiced by the pilgrims even after the introduction of idolatry in Arabia about four centuries before Islam. So, although at the time of revelation the main body of the rituals were the same as what Prophet Abraham had ordained, certain innovations had been added by idolaters. That is why although the rulings of Hajj mentioned in the Quran approve of the rituals of the time in general, they also abrogate some aspects of Hajj which were introduced by the idolaters.

There is no sin upon you in seeking your Lord's grace [during the Hajj season]. This verse shifts the focus from spiritual earning and piety as the main purpose of Hajj in the previous verse to the daily physical needs of pilgrims. Over centuries, some idolaters had developed stringent rulings about Hajj, as they regarded pilgrimage to Kabah amongst the holiest of all rituals.

As previously mentioned there was a group from the idolaters who called themselves "The Zealots" and believed in the performance of pilgrimage in the strictest sense possible. The Zealots considered any type of business conducted during the pilgrimage to be unlawful. This also included the money paid to workers for their services during the pilgrimage. For this reason, they barred servicemen from performing pilgrimage, claiming that they were only there to do business and not to perform the pilgrimage. In this verse, God corrects this misunderstanding by striking a balance between this world and the Hereafter.

Then when you stream out of ʿArafāt, remember God at the Holy Mashʿar; The first act of Hajj, after wearing the *iḥrām* is to go to ʿArafāt. The verse mentions that from this stage onwards the believers should always remember God and be grateful for his blessings upon them. Furthermore, the command to remember God in Mashʿar al-Ḥarām, which is close to Minā, alludes to the ritual of staying in Mashʿar overnight, praying and supplicating in that area until morning, before proceeding to Eid rituals in Minā.

Mashʿar is derived from *shuʿūr* meaning consciousness and awareness. Remembering God in Mashʿar should create a new awareness (*shuʿūr*) of God in the pilgrim that was not there before. The astonishing scene of multitudes of people of different races, ethnicities and cultures all in the same unifying attire lying side by side under the starry sky over the stretch of Mashʿar, is a reminder to every one of the insignificance of man and the glory of God. The scene is like a small blueprint of the Great Resurrection in the Hereafter. So, "*remember God at the Holy Mashʿar.*"

and remember Him as He has guided you, and earlier you were indeed among the astray. Guidance is the greatest blessing God has favoured upon humanity. "Remember Him as He has guided you" may be understood in two ways. The first meaning is to remember God as a token of gratitude because he has guided you while before you were among the astray. The second meaning is to remember him the way he has taught you to remember him in your prayers and rituals.

ثُمَّ أَفِيضُوا مِنْ حَيْثُ أَفَاضَ النَّاسُ وَاسْتَغْفِرُوا اللَّهَ ۚ إِنَّ اللَّهَ غَفُورٌ رَحِيمٌ ﴿199﴾

Then stream out from where the people stream out, and plead to God for forgiveness; indeed, God is All-forgiving, All-merciful.

Then stream out from where the people stream out; The Arabic word *thumma* used in the verse is usually to indicate the order of events. However, this verse is intended to reiterate the previous statement to move out of Arafāt and is used here for emphasis. Therefore, the meaning of the two verses would be "when you stream out of Arafāt, remember God at the Holy Mash'ar, and I emphasise that you move out from where the people move out from Arafāt."

This emphasis is to address the false privileges that the Quraysh had considered for themselves. The Quraysh used to call themselves *"ḥums"* (firm in religion) and, as they considered themselves the offspring of Prophet Abraham and custodians of the Kabah, giving them superiority over people of other Arab tribes. They thought going out of the Ḥaram area was not appropriate for them during the Hajj season. And since Arafāt was just outside Ḥaram area, they stayed in Mecca and avoided joining the other pilgrims in proceeding to the plain of 'Arafāt even though they knew that it was among the rites of Hajj and a part of the Abrahamic creed. Quashing these imagined privileges, the Quran commands that they all must move out to 'Arafāt and from there go towards Mash'ar and remember God there.

and plead to God for forgiveness; indeed, God is All-forgiving, All-merciful. Those who have prejudiced views and discriminatory ideas and see themselves as superior to other people should ask for forgiveness when unity is the substance of the occasion and humbleness is its essence.

There are two types of forgiveness mentioned in the Quran: the first is 'afw and the second is *maghfira*. The verse here asks the pilgrims to ask *maghfira* from God rather than *'afw*. 'Afw is the standard quality of forgiveness which passes between God and his creatures; both God and people can forgive ('afw) other people. However, *maghfira* is a specific quality that is only attributed to God as he alone has the ability to grant it.

The following example can help to illustrate the subtle difference between *'afw* and *maghfira*. If some people have wronged others, the wronged people have the power of forgiving ('afw) the wrongdoers; consequently, the wrongdoers would be saved from the punishment as a result of the forgiveness. However, the wrongdoers will still suffer as their action will leave a scar upon their souls, which they have no power to erase. God alone can erase the effects of wrongdoing through his forgiveness (*maghfira*). God's forgiveness means that the soul of the wrongdoer would not lose its ability to receive blessings from the Almighty. Therefore, in the Quran, God states that before entering Paradise, he would give them the good news of *maghfira*: Q. 3:133-136, 47:15 and 57:20-21. In this way *maghfira* is the precondition of entering Paradise.

فَإِذَا قَضَيْتُم مَّنَاسِكَكُمْ فَاذْكُرُوا اللَّهَ كَذِكْرِكُمْ آبَاءَكُمْ أَوْ أَشَدَّ ذِكْرًا ۗ
فَمِنَ النَّاسِ مَن يَقُولُ رَبَّنَا آتِنَا فِي الدُّنْيَا وَمَا لَهُ فِي الْآخِرَةِ مِنْ خَلَاقٍ ﴿200﴾

And when you finish your rites, then remember God as you would remember your fathers, or with a more ardent remembrance. Among the people some say, 'Our Lord, give us in this world,' but for such, there is no share in the Hereafter.

The verse discusses the end of the ritual of Hajj and urges Muslims to remember God upon its completion. Some commentators purport that "remembrance" here refers to the *takbīrāt*[311] which must be uttered after daily prayers in Minā. In contrast, others have suggested that the remembrance here does not refer to the utterance of the *takbīrāt,* but instead refers to a deep contemplation of God when pilgrims reside in Minā.

Then remember God as you would remember your fathers; This phrase may also refer to the pre-Islamic pilgrimage ritual of reciting poetry and gathering with friends and relatives to talk about their tribal merits in order to pass the time in Minā. God Almighty does not condemn this practice. It is always good to honour forefathers and be grateful for their achievements that led believers towards the path of God, as long as it is not done in a boastful way. The verse advises Muslims that in the same way that they used to remember their forefathers or with more emphasis (or as a result of deep contemplation), they should remember God too. Whatever achievements their forefathers had made was due to the grace of God.

And among the people, there are those who say, 'Our Lord, give us in this world,' but for such, there is no share in the Hereafter. Hajj is a ritual in which God has insisted that the pilgrims should ask him of his grace and bounties. It is a difficult form of worship, which involves travelling long distances and significant financial and physical commitments. Therefore, upon the completion of such a difficult task, some may ask for worldly and other-worldly blessings. God acknowledges this expectation in the verse. However, he encourages the believers to ask for something more comprehensive; bounties that would benefit them both in this world and the Hereafter. In general, believers should not only have materialistic expectations from God. Instead, they should ask for long-lasting rewards, which may help them in this world and allow them to achieve their ultimate ambition of securing higher stations in the Hereafter. Otherwise, they risk ending up with nothing in the Hereafter. This section of the verse refers to idolaters whose main aim for performing the pilgrimage was merely worldly and seeking material gains from the Hajj. They did not believe in the existence of the Hereafter, so their attitude towards pilgrimage was ultimately wrong.

وَمِنْهُم مَّن يَقُولُ رَبَّنَا آتِنَا فِي الدُّنْيَا حَسَنَةً وَفِي الْآخِرَةِ حَسَنَةً وَقِنَا
عَذَابَ النَّارِ ﴿201﴾

And among them, there are those who say, 'Our Lord, give us good in this world and good in the Hereafter, and save us from the punishment of the Fire.'

Having criticised the worldly or materialistic expectations of the first group, God advises believers about how to ask him of his grace. They should ask for goodness in this world and the Hereafter and request to be saved from the Hellfire. This is, indeed, fascinating; the pilgrims perform Hajj for the sake of God, and then when they want to ask for a reward for it, God stops to teach them what to ask for and how to ask for it. This is because we are unaware of our own benefits, and the extent of the bounties of God who is intent to give to the rightful people as much as they have the capacity to take.

In this regard, Qushayri explains that some people are extremely self-centred. Hence, they cannot see anything but themselves and when they do something, it is for material gain alone, so their heart never turns towards God.[312] Consequently, their heart cannot achieve anything in relation to God, neither his remembrance, mercy or rewards.

Having said that, the verses imply that just through performing Pilgrimage even these self-centred people, who usually lose out on the rewards of the Hereafter, would gain something. This is because those who perform the Pilgrimage achieve some reward in this world even if they are disbelievers. However, they may be deprived of the rewards of the Hereafter if they do not care about the Pilgrimage or are not conscious of it. Even if the believers follow the instructions of God sincerely, they would still be concerned that even if they perform their duties, it is not certain that they would be spared from the Hellfire. The attitude of the true believers is mentioned in the Quran: *and who give whatever they give while their hearts tremble with awe that they are going to return to their Lord.* (Q. 23:60)

أُولَٰئِكَ لَهُمْ نَصِيبٌ مِّمَّا كَسَبُوا ۚ وَاللَّهُ سَرِيعُ الْحِسَابِ ﴿202﴾

Such shall partake of what they have earned, and God is swift at reckoning.

The verse refers to the second group of people mentioned in the previous verse (201), who are encouraged to ask for goodness both in this world and the Hereafter upon completion of Hajj. *What they have earned* appears to refer to the reward that they have earned as a result of performing Hajj. Depending on their intention, sincerity and the quality of their worship during Hajj, believers gain rewards, and God compensates them swiftly. God grants the reward of good deeds immediately in the heart of the believers so that they have the capacity to do better with the rewards that they have been granted and receive more reward from God in return.

وَاذْكُرُوا اللَّهَ فِي أَيَّامٍ مَّعْدُودَاتٍ ۚ فَمَن تَعَجَّلَ فِي يَوْمَيْنِ فَلَا إِثْمَ عَلَيْهِ
وَمَن تَأَخَّرَ فَلَا إِثْمَ عَلَيْهِ ۚ لِمَنِ اتَّقَىٰ ۗ وَاتَّقُوا اللَّهَ وَاعْلَمُوا أَنَّكُمْ إِلَيْهِ
تُحْشَرُونَ ﴿203﴾

Remember God in the appointed days. Then whoever hastens off in a couple of days, there is no sin upon him, and whoever delays, there is no sin upon him —that for one who has been Godwary— and be wary of God, and know that toward Him you will be mustered.

Remember God in the appointed days; This is the last verse in the series of verses discussing the ritual of Hajj. *The appointed days* refers to the three days (11th, 12th and 13th) of Dhu al-Hijja which are called *Ayyām al-tashrīq* (Days of Sunshine). The name *Ayyām al-tashrīq* was used before the advent of Islam. When people performed the pilgrimage to the Kabah, they sacrificed animals at the final stage. On these three days, they sliced the meat of the sacrificed animals and left them under sunlight to dry so that they could be preserved and consumed on their return journey and thereafter. However, God instructs people to remember him in between their activities during these three days. The verse is a reminder that the purpose of staying in Minā in these days is not to spread and store meat but to take the provision of reflection, remembrance, and God-consciousness.

Then whoever hastens off in a couple of days, there is no sin upon him, and whoever delays, there is no sin upon him; The second part of the verse goes on to give good news to the pilgrims that whoever performs the Hajj, with a pure intention and attention, their sins will be forgiven whether they stay two or three days in Minā.

وَمِنَ النَّاسِ مَن يُعْجِبُكَ قَوْلُهُ فِي الْحَيَاةِ الدُّنْيَا وَيُشْهِدُ اللَّهَ عَلَىٰ مَا فِي قَلْبِهِ
وَهُوَ أَلَدُّ الْخِصَامِ ﴿204﴾

Among the people is he whose talk about worldly life impresses you, and he holds God to witness to what is in his heart, though he is the staunchest of enemies.

Although the discussion on the ritual of Hajj completed in the previous verse, it appears that this verse continues with the description of the materialistic thinking of people mentioned above in the verse *Among the people there are those who say, 'Our Lord, give us in this world,' but for such, there is no share in the Hereafter.* (Q. 2:200) Narrations state that the verse was sent down in response to a wealthy Meccan, Akhnas b. Shurayq, who lived at the time of the Prophet and was his staunch enemy. He was a Meccan chief and was known to be an eloquent speaker; he used his oratory skills to try to trick the Prophet. It may be possible that the verse was revealed in response to his behaviour during one of these occasions.

However, the advice is this verse applies to all people. It is the style of the Quran to pick an example of an incident or individual and to give a general statement about the qualities and attitudes of people. Therefore, there is no reason to delve into whether the verses address this specific individual or not; our focus should be on comprehending the overall message of the verse.

As the verse addresses the Prophet, we can assume that the Prophet would not have been impressed with this man's talk of material gains such as money, wealth, and glory, since these things never impressed the Prophet. But the verse suggests that something in his speech impressed the Prophet; it seems he also spoke on the importance of the wellbeing of people, the importance of looking after the needy and the weak, and the destructive nature of wars and bloodshed. People may hear the same kind of insincere rhetoric and propaganda from some contemporary politicians who would say whatever it takes for them to gain the support of the masses.

وَإِذَا تَوَلَّىٰ سَعَىٰ فِي الْأَرْضِ لِيُفْسِدَ فِيهَا وَيُهْلِكَ الْحَرْثَ وَالنَّسْلَ ۗ وَاللَّهُ لَا يُحِبُّ الْفَسَادَ ﴿205﴾

And if he were to wield authority, he would try to cause corruption in the land, and to ruin the crop and the stock, and God does not like corruption.

The verse then details the attributes of worldly manipulative orators, who deceive people with their rhetoric and take advantage of their trust to gain power and influence. If such people succeed in their effort to gain control (*tawallā*), they will then cause corruption on the earth.

Tawallā may have two meanings here: the first is to take rulership or authority; the second is to turn away. The first meaning is more applicable in this verse. The core of this type of selfish motivation is usually due to worldly ambitions. When they get an opportunity to fulfil their aspirations, they will inevitably cause corruption. As their sole aim is to quench their insatiable ambitions, these people will claim and take anything they like by force. In such cases, God withdraws his blessings, and they are left to themselves. This is the meaning of the phrase, "*God does not like corruption*" in the verse.

وَإِذَا قِيلَ لَهُ اتَّقِ اللَّهَ أَخَذَتْهُ الْعِزَّةُ بِالْإِثْمِ فَحَسْبُهُ جَهَنَّمُ وَلَبِئْسَ الْمِهَادُ ﴿206﴾

And when he is told, 'Be wary of God,' conceit seizes him sinfully; so let Hell suffice him, and it is undoubtedly an evil resting place!

And when he is told, 'Be wary of God,' conceit seizes him sinfully; When people like this are warned about their misdeeds and advised to be Godwary, *conceit seizes him sinfully* and pride takes over them. Some commentators have explained this phrase to mean that the pride of these individuals leads them to sin. On the other hand, others have contended that by perpetually committing sins, they are drawn to a life of pride and arrogance. For Tabatabai, the great evils in people's hearts are produced as a result of the accumulation of smaller sins that they may commit. These sins eventually grow into arrogance, pride and many vices.

so let Hell suffice him, and it is undoubtedly an evil resting place! One might wonder how God will treat these arrogant people who are not wary of God and continue their misdeeds? The first punishment from God is to allow them to have the sense of false pride and dignity, which is, in fact, nothing but arrogance. They would not be able to see their mistakes, and this would deprive them of the opportunity to listen to any admonition and repent. Aside from this, God often does not stop people from committing misdeeds in this world. It is the nature of this life that God allows people to do good or evil so that they can be held accountable or rewarded on the Day of Judgment. Arrogant people as described in these verses would be brought to Hell, and this is an appropriate punishment for them.

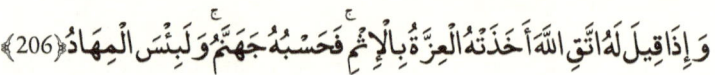

وَمِنَ النَّاسِ مَن يَشْرِي نَفْسَهُ ابْتِغَاءَ مَرْضَاتِ اللَّهِ وَاللَّهُ رَءُوفٌ
بِالْعِبَادِ ﴿207﴾

And among the people is he who sells [or dedicates] his soul seeking the pleasure of God, and God is most kind to [His] servants.

And among the people is he who sells [or dedicates] his soul seeking the pleasure of God; On the opposite side of the spectrum, there are people who completely dedicate their lives to God even though they are not gifted with oratory skills, wealth or influence. The characteristics of these people are that they do things for the sake of God alone. They bargain with God, giving everything they have, including their lives, in return for God's pleasure. As a result of their complete dedication, these people would be rewarded with a sense of tranquillity in this world and with the endless bounties and blessings in the Hereafter. The category of this kind of devoted believer includes a vast range of people. However, the consensus among the commentators is that those who die and suffer in the way of enjoining good and forbidding evil are included in this category.

There has been an eternal struggle between the two types of people described in these verses. The first are arrogant people who aspire to take advantage of weak and ignorant people and the second type of people described, have devoted their souls to God and continuously try to enjoin good and forbid evil.

and God is most kind to [His] servants. Although God does not directly stop the arrogant people, he supports and encourages his faithful servants to struggle against them to defend the rights of the masses who are the third group of people. In this way, God does not leave the arrogant and oppressors without reproach. He fights their corruption through his devoted servants. This is the how God shows his kindness to his servants and does not leave them alone in the face of oppression and corruption. This explanation has been mentioned elsewhere in the Quran:

> Why should you not fight in the way of God and the abased men, women, and children, who say, "Our Lord, bring us out of this town whose people are wrongdoers, and appoint for us a guardian from You, and appoint for us a helper from You?" (Q. 4:75)

There will always be some corrupt people, whilst there will be others striving to serve God and fight against corruption. God also supports his servants to stop the domination of corruption on the earth so that the people may have a decent life and the opportunity to receive God's message.

يَا أَيُّهَا الَّذِينَ آمَنُوا ادْخُلُوا فِي السِّلْمِ كَافَّةً وَلَا تَتَّبِعُوا خُطُوَاتِ الشَّيْطَانِ ۚ إِنَّهُ لَكُمْ عَدُوٌّ مُبِينٌ ﴿208﴾

O you who have faith! Enter into submission, all together, and do not follow in Satan's steps; he is indeed your manifest enemy.

The mystics have placed great significance on the implementation of this particular verse as it is one of the most spectacular verses of Surah Baqarah.

O you who have faith! Enter into submission, all together; Mahdī Baḥr al-'Ulūm (d. 1212/1797) in *Risāla* al-*sayr wa-al-sulūk*[313] delves into the contents of this verse in detail. The word "*kāffatan*" (wholeheartedly / all together) is either an adverb for "submission" or adverb for "enter." If it is the adverb for the latter, the meaning becomes "enter into submission (Islam) altogether." However, if it is an adverb for the former, the meaning becomes "enter into Islam wholeheartedly." This meaning makes more sense; it urges Muslims to embrace the faith in its entirety, not selectively. Consequently, it asks Muslims to upgrade their faith to a higher grade of faith. Most of those who have embraced Islam have not submitted in all aspects or every detail of the faith, either in terms of observing the rituals or surrendering their hearts to God.

Elsewhere in the Quran the believers are expected to elevate their faith in God and his Messenger: *O you who believe, believe in God and His messenger!* (Q. 4:136) or *For your god is one God, so submit to Him.* (Q. 22:34) Both verses address the believers and teach them a fundamental piece of advice: submit to your Lord wholeheartedly.

Baḥr al-'Ulūm, explains that the verse is an instruction for the sincerity of the heart (*ikhlāṣ*). The starting point for his discussion is the well-known tradition attributed to the Prophet that "whoever purifies their heart for 40 days for the sake of God, the springs of wisdom would flow from their heart to the tongue." This purification is a process that needs training through various stages to reach this status. The first stage is called the *primary submission* to the faith. People confess their faith and then observe the rituals. Most Muslims find themselves at this stage. The second stage is full submission to the faith. Here, believers embrace the faith wholeheartedly. They not only submit that there is no god but God, they also see everything from God as being correct and fair.

A tradition from Imam Jafar al-Sadiq details these stages and Baḥr al-'Ulūm uses this tradition to explain that at the first stage, although believers practice the rituals and believe in God, when a calamity befalls them, they begin to question the wisdom of God, either openly or in their heart. When believers reach the second stage (through practice and contemplation), they realise everything comes from God alone, and no one possesses anything. All possessions belong to God, and everyone and everything is absolutely dependent on him; many find it difficult to accept in this fact. Both those who have the first type of faith and those who have the second type of faith will go to Paradise, but of course, those who have the second type of absolute faith will attain higher stations there.

And do not follow in Satan's steps; he is indeed your manifest enemy. This verse reveals that due to the influence of Satan on the believer's heart and mind, it can be hard to move from the first stage of faith to the second. Satan has access to the most profound and darkest parts of our hearts, and he is well acquainted with our weaknesses and doubts. So, he whispers to people and moves them away from total submission. The foremost example of this is the whispering of Satan to Prophet Abraham over slaughtering his child Ishmael. Ordinary people are not tested like Abraham, and of course, they are not given a status like Prophet Abraham. Nevertheless, we experience the whisperings of Satan every day in our heart. By instigating doubt and disobedience, he prevents us from submitting completely to the wish and wisdom of God. He hates humanity, and because of his animosity, he does not want people to enter Paradise or achieve a higher status within Paradise.

فَإِن زَلَلْتُم مِّن بَعْدِ مَا جَاءَتْكُمُ الْبَيِّنَاتُ فَاعْلَمُوا أَنَّ اللَّهَ عَزِيزٌ
حَكِيمٌ ﴿209﴾

And should you stumble after the manifest proofs that have come to you, know that God is All-mighty, All-wise.

People are always tested with difficult situations, and it is possible that some may stumble in the face of adversity. In these situations, a person is faced with two basic options: the first option is to recollect themselves and do the right thing when it becomes clear that they are in the wrong. The second option is that even after they have obtained clear evidence that they are in the wrong, they insist on their misdeed due to their stubbornness and arrogance. In either case, they would be subject to the system that God has created. They would be either rewarded for acknowledging that they were in the wrong and repenting for their mistakes and receive the blessings of God in return. Alternatively, if they insist on their misdeed, they would be punished because of their actions.

Both the punishment and reward are consequential, not conventional. That is to say that they receive the consequences of their actions because of the system that is set to govern this world and the Hereafter, based on justice and wisdom. God is not affected by people's actions: he does not need to punish wrongdoers, because their actions have no influence over him. If people do good deeds, they do good to themselves, and if they do evil deeds, they harm themselves. Both rewards and punishments are intense in the Hereafter because the human soul is so powerful that it may only be appeased with great rewards or tamed with harsh punishments. As it is mentioned elsewhere: *[O Muhammad], inform My servants that I am the Forgiving and Merciful. But my punishment is a very severe punishment.* (Q. 15:49-50)

هَلْ يَنظُرُونَ إِلَّا أَن يَأْتِيَهُمُ اللَّهُ فِي ظُلَلٍ مِّنَ الْغَمَامِ وَالْمَلَائِكَةُ وَقُضِيَ الْأَمْرُ وَإِلَى اللَّهِ تُرْجَعُ الْأُمُورُ ﴿210﴾

Do they await anything but that God should come to them in the shades of the clouds, with the angels, and the matter be decided [once and for all]? And to God, all matters are returned.

Do they await anything but that God should come to them in the shades of the clouds, with the angels, and the matter be decided [once and for all]? There are a some of essential aspects in this particular verse: at first sight, the verse is not specific about who it addresses yet there is a threat of collective punishment. Second, the phrase, "God should come to them in the shades of the clouds?" seems baffling. Some commentators, based on various traditions, have argued that the verse addresses the Meccan disbelievers. However, the verse follows the end of the series of verses dealing with the rituals of Hajj, and the attention of the verses shifted to the believers. Thus, it is improbable that this verse refers to the disbelievers. Therefore, it is obvious from the context of the verses that it is addressing Muslims. In this regard, it is one of the most surprising verses of the Quran which threatens Muslims with a great punishment.

As mentioned, all the verses of Surah al-Baqarah were revealed in Medina, so what was the situation at the time in Medina which evoked such a harsh warning from God? In order to answer this question, we must first delve into an aspect of faith which is usually ignored in Muslim communities. When the Quran talks about believers being protected and supported by God or believers ending up in Paradise, the Quran is referring to the *true* believers. These are believers who have attained the faith in the depths of their hearts and not only by their tongues.

It seems that the verse above addresses the type of believers whose faith remained on their tongues and had not penetrated their hearts, though they were regarded as Muslims because they had professed faith. However, they had not fully committed themselves to the basic principles of the faith. Thus, their souls remained rebellious. In this way, the verse acts as a continuation of the previous verse which draws attention to those believers who *stumble after the manifest proofs that have come* and decide to follow the footsteps of Satan. The first aspect of the verse therefore clarifies who is being addressed in the verse.

God should come to them in the shades of the clouds; As mentioned previously, God does not have physical attributes, hence would not "come" or "go" in the literal sense. These qualities are for limited beings, and he is above physical limitations. Therefore, the expressions in the Holy Quran which refer to God's physical actions and traits should be interpreted as God's command.

The metaphor in this verse is of a cloud and it refers to the cloud's ability to bring heavy rain and storm that may cause flooding and devastation. God's command may come in that form, and the angels also carry God's command. However, Tabatabai contends that the mediums of angels and the chain of causation at work in nature does not imply that God is not working in creation directly.[314] All the mediums and causes only work because God directly gives them life and effect, and without his presence nothing would work. So, it is true to say that the winds move the clouds and at the same time it is accurate to say that God moves them. He has set a system in which the angles play a role as well as the chain of causes and effects. He allows them to carry out the commands to bless them as well. But overall, he is the one who manages everything as it is mentioned in the Quran: *Indeed, God is the splitter of the grain and the pit. He brings forth the living from the dead, and He brings forth the dead from the living. That is God! Then where do you stray?* (Q. 6:95) People too often only see the chain of causes and effects that God has set in motion. Yet he is the one who set the system, and he exists in every atom of this world, but people are mostly unaware of it.

The commentators have interpreted *God should come to them in the shades of the clouds,* as God's command coming for punishment to be brought down on them from the clouds. However, based on Tabatabai's interpretation, God himself brings that punishment since he is present everywhere and in everything.

and the matter be decided [once and for all]. This phrase explains that the punishment of God would come when the false believers have been separated from the true believers. At this point, it is plausible that since the verse is addressing the believers, it is probable that it also warns some the companions of the Prophet as well. It is inherently wrong to assume that everybody who was around the Prophet had a firm belief in him.

سَلْ بَنِي إِسْرَائِيلَ كَمْ آتَيْنَاهُم مِّنْ آيَةٍ بَيِّنَةٍ ۗ وَمَن يُبَدِّلْ نِعْمَةَ اللَّهِ مِن بَعْدِ مَا
جَاءَتْهُ فَإِنَّ اللَّهَ شَدِيدُ الْعِقَابِ ﴿211﴾

Ask the Children of Israel how many a manifest sign We had given them. And whoever changes God's blessing after it has come to him, indeed God is severe in retribution.

The previous verse addressed the believers and warned them about the quality of their faith in order to urge them to have sincere faith in God and his Prophet. This verse provides an example of a past religious community who were given undeniable proofs and signs, yet sold God's bounties for a paltry gain and changed his blessing into curse. The verse acts as a reminder to Muslims that they are not an exception, and if they follow the path of previous communities they will meet the same end.

The verse also reprimands the Jews of Medina, reminding them that despite all the signs and miracles they were shown, including the defeat of the magicians by Moses's staff, splitting the sea, sending them *Manna* and *Salwa*, and many other examples, they did not wholeheartedly follow the Torah. Furthermore, they concealed the qualities of the awaited prophet to deny that Mohammad is that awaited one. In short, the Israelites had all the worldly and heavenly blessings from God, yet these blessings made them arrogant and instead moved them away from the faith. They rejected their prophets and fought against the instructions of God; in the end they will pay for their disobedience.

زُيِّنَ لِلَّذِينَ كَفَرُوا الْحَيَاةُ الدُّنْيَا وَيَسْخَرُونَ مِنَ الَّذِينَ آمَنُوا وَالَّذِينَ
اتَّقَوْا فَوْقَهُمْ يَوْمَ الْقِيَامَةِ وَاللَّهُ يَرْزُقُ مَنْ يَشَاءُ بِغَيْرِ حِسَابٍ﴿212﴾

Worldly life has been glamorised for the faithless, and they ridicule the faithful. But those who are Godwary shall be above them on the Day of Resurrection, and God provides for whomever He wishes without any reckoning.

Worldly life has been glamorised for the faithless; Although some commentators have held that "the faithless" in the verse refers to the chieftains of Mecca who fought against Muslims, it is almost certain that this entire chapter was revealed in Medina. Hence, this set of verses may address the hypocrites in Medina who pretended to be believers. The verse makes a clear distinction between those who only declared their faith but did not fully embrace the faith and those who surrendered to the faith and attained piety. The hypocrites, and even some Muslims of weak faith, despite professing belief, only focused on this world because the worldly life has been glamorised for them. On the other hand, pious believers are not deceived by the glamours of this life, and they do not forget about the Hereafter.

Muslims can sometimes fall into these traps, especially if they are solely focused on gaining wealth, even if it means infringing upon the boundaries of faith and imitating the unethical ways through deceit and cheating. The world becomes the end for such people, and despite their simple confession of Islam, they forget the most basic tenet of faith is that this world is simply a means to attain a higher station in the Hereafter.

and God provides for whomever He wishes without any reckoning. Commentators have mentioned a breadth of interesting opinions on the concept of providing without reckoning. One suggested meaning is that it refers to the number of blessings that God has provided for people in this world without measure. One can just imagine the range of blessings which cannot be counted. From the faculties that God has blessed man within his soul and body, to the sun without which life would not have been possible on the earth. The firm shield of atmosphere which surrounds the earth and protects it from meteorites and harmful rays. And the provisions that have been endowed for him in the earth from different types of fruits, crops and meat to the mines and minerals, to different wave frequencies scattered in the air and the list could go on to fill all the pages of all the books and would still not be exhausted. "*And if you enumerate God's blessings, you will not be able to count them. Indeed, God is All-forgiving, All-merciful*". (Q. 16:18) This generalised meaning of God's provision does not accurately correspond with the contents of the verse, as the verse explicitly states that the provision without reckoning is not for all but "*for whomever He wishes*".

The second understanding is that there is no correlation between the faith of people and the worldly blessings they receive. Some people may be intelligent, articulate, talented, and rich yet they may be disbelievers. On the other hand, some people may be poor and oppressed yet they may have solid faith in God and his messenger. A person's faith should never be judged based on their worldly position.

According to a third view, the verse alludes to the blessings that the believers receive in the Hereafter. God's reward to the believers in the Hereafter are not necessarily proportionate to their worldly deeds. He would give them much more than what they deserve in the Hereafter. "*There they will have whatever they wish, and with Us there is yet more*". (Q. 50:35)

A fourth interpretation suggests that God can give to whomsoever he wishes, and nobody can hold him accountable for it. Nobody can challenge or question his wisdom of how or why he provides for people. Our minds, thoughts and information are too insignificant to able to comprehend the wisdom behind God's acts.

The fifth suggestion is that God does not supply from a reserved or set amount in a way that he is in need of recounting and rationing what he provides. His treasures are infinite and no matter how much he spends they remain the same. *That which is with you will be spent but what is with God shall last.* (Q. 16:96) Since his source of bounty is infinite, it does not matter how much he provides for people. In other words, no matter how much of his treasures God gives away, the total amount will always remain the same.

كَانَ النَّاسُ أُمَّةً وَاحِدَةً فَبَعَثَ اللَّهُ النَّبِيِّينَ مُبَشِّرِينَ وَمُنذِرِينَ وَأَنزَلَ
مَعَهُمُ الْكِتَابَ بِالْحَقِّ لِيَحْكُمَ بَيْنَ النَّاسِ فِيمَا اخْتَلَفُوا فِيهِ وَمَا
اخْتَلَفَ فِيهِ إِلَّا الَّذِينَ أُوتُوهُ مِن بَعْدِ مَا جَاءَتْهُمُ الْبَيِّنَاتُ بَغْيًا بَيْنَهُمْ فَهَدَى
اللَّهُ الَّذِينَ آمَنُوا لِمَا اخْتَلَفُوا فِيهِ مِنَ الْحَقِّ بِإِذْنِهِ وَاللَّهُ يَهْدِي مَن يَشَاءُ إِلَىٰ
صِرَاطٍ مُّسْتَقِيمٍ ﴿213﴾

Mankind were a single community; then God sent the prophets as bearers of good news and as warners, and He sent down with them the Book with the truth, that it may judge between the people concerning that about which they differed, and none differed in it except those who had been given it, after the manifest proofs had come to them, out of envy among themselves. Then God guided those who had faith to the truth of what they differed in, by His will, and God guides whomever He wishes to a straight path.'

This is one of the most important verses of the Quran. It is connected to the previous set of verses on the categories of faith. The verse reminds us that the state of faith in the heart of people remained the same. Whenever God sent down a Book for people as guidance, people started to disagree about its content because of their internal weaknesses such as jealousy and envy. Even though God's guidance is clear, people tend to distort the guidance due to their internal weaknesses. Thus, only sincere people have followed the guidance and the others, whose faith was superficial, followed the path of misguidance. They had a distorted form of religion, and God will not accept this on the Day of Judgment.

Mankind were a single community; According to commentators, there are two main views on the interpretation of the phase "single community." According to the first view, it refers to the fact that from the beginning of human history, people have always been inclined to a primitive understanding of faith and worshipped animations of certain objects. They did not have any notion of monotheism, so they were a single community of disbelievers. It appears that this view has been under the influence of the science of anthropology which holds a similar understanding of the development of religions.

The second group of commentators contend that the "single community" refers to a single community of believers. They disputed about the faith and most of them then disbelieved. These commentators maintain that God revealed this verse as a consolation to the Prophet, showing that it is not the fault of the prophets if people falter and abandon the faith as this has happened many times since the time of Prophet Adam.

A third view is presented by Shi'i commentators from explanations found in traditions from Shi'i Imams. According to this view given in *Tafsīr al-'ayyāshī* the "single community" refers to neither believers nor disbelievers completely.[315] Rather, the "single community" refers to a single human nature (*fiṭra*) which has qualities innate to human beings such as respecting the rights of others, honesty, justice, integrity and generosity. People had lived with these inbuilt values since the start of time. However, human nature does not only consist of good values;

it also consists of certain vices such as jealousy, greed and arrogance. Eventually human vices prevailed, and strong, intelligent people began to take advantage of the weaker ones. This is how slavery and exploitation of the weak, including women, emerged.

As a response to the abuse and misuse of the *fiṭra*, God sent the prophets and prescribed laws to clarify the boundaries of right and wrong. If people had lived on the good side of their *fiṭra*, there would not have been the need for the prophets and laws coming from God. Tabatabai considers this to be the origins of human laws.[316] Every nation thereafter, whether secular or religious, based their laws upon the laws sent down by God. There are many traditions from Shiʿi Imams that support this view.

As previously discussed, the *fiṭra* is also the covenant between God and his creation. People are expected to act upon this covenant even if they do not have access to the direct guidance of God. The prophets, Imams and saints are people of *fiṭra*; they always act upon the good side of their *fiṭra*, and this is why they are so special. However, ordinary people often falter and go between their good *fiṭra* and vices. Therefore, there is a need to guide people through prophets and revelation as they act as a reminder for the people. This guidance also serves the purpose of perfecting one's faith and elevating their status. However, if people live in remote places and do not have access to this guidance, they would still be held accountable for not following their *fiṭra*. If they were on the right side of their *fiṭra*, then regardless of the religion, they may be rewarded in Paradise.

then God sent the prophets as bearers of good news and as warners, and He sent down with them the Book with the truth, that it may judge between the people concerning that about which they differed; It is probable that the digression in human nature began before the ministry of Prophet Noah. Between Prophet Adam and this time people were mostly true to their *fiṭra* and acted on the good side of human nature. Therefore, during this period, these people did not need to have divine laws; because, in its pure form, human nature is concurrent with divine laws. However, before Prophet Noah, human nature gave in to greed and desires and people deviated from their true nature. There may be a direct correlation between this deviation from human nature and the advancement of human civilisation, as this deviation enabled some people to accumulate more wealth than others, and they realised that it is easy for them to exploit the weak in order to increase their own wealth and power. This perverted attitude then gave rise to the invention of deviant faiths such as idol worshipping which could easily be manipulated and controlled by the elites. Furthermore, religion was used as a tool to legitimise and further reinforce authority and dominance over the weak.

At this point, God sent Prophet Noah with divine laws to correct the deviant human course by setting down the boundaries of justice and good behaviour between people. The Book refers to the divine Books that God sent down to people through his messengers. It is referred to as a single Book because, in essence, these books were all the same. God mentions this in several verses of the Quran such as:

> He has prescribed for you the religion which He had enjoined upon Noah and which We have [also] revealed to you, and which We had enjoined upon Abraham, Moses and Jesus, declaring, 'Maintain the religion, and do not be divided in it.' (Q. 42:13)

To be clear, God did not send down different religions to these prophets, rather, it was the *same* religion. God sent the same Book to Prophet Noah that he also sent to Abraham, Moses, Jesus and Muhammad. But people have interpreted the Book based upon their own vested interests, thus giving a false impression that there are different books which preach different monotheistic religions.

that about which they differed; This refers to the different interpretations of the faith which began early on; most probably from the period of revelation onwards. In the case of Islam, we may consider this to include those people who were with the Prophet until right after his death when they began to disagree on the meaning of the Book and the advice of the Prophet. A stark example of such corrupt human tendencies can be seen in the behaviour of some early Muslims who fought against the rightful Imam and killed each other soon after the death of the Prophet due to their envy and personal interests.

There is a crucial question to mention at this point: is it not natural for the faithful to disagree on the interpretation of the Book? When people read even a simple text, they disagree on its interpretation and have their own opinions, therefore reason dictates that it should be natural to disagree on the interpretation of the Book of God, as people may have a difference of opinion on its meaning. If this is the case, God should not consider these disagreements as being evil. However, this verse does not talk about having a difference of opinions; it talks about the clear instruction provided by the Messenger of God and people's breach of these clear instructions as a result of their envy and ambitions. Otherwise, there is no harm if people have a difference of opinion about abstract matters of religion.

These disagreements have occurred after every prophet, and this provides a good justification for the argument that prophets should be succeeded by appointed people in order to prevent such disagreements or at least to minimise their effects on the religion. The Book of God is not enough to eliminate all these disagreements. Ultimately, people have the will and ability to manipulate the meaning of the Holy Text:

> And when there came to them an apostle from God, confirming that which is with them, a part of those who were given the Book cast the Book of God behind their back, as if they did not know [that it is God's Book]. (Q. 2:101)

Therefore, there needs to be trusted successors to the prophets to ensure that the actual and true meaning of the text is preserved. Shi'is believe that the Imams were tasked with the preservation of the true meaning of the text of the Quran and the interpretation of the faith.

then God guided those who had faith to the truth of what they differed in, by His will, and God guides whomever He wishes to a straight path. The overall test for people is to follow the appointed trustees of the Book and faith. Despite the efforts of envious people, with the help of God, true believers are not affected by these disagreements and confusion over the interpretation of the faith, and they will continue to follow the appointed trustees of the Book and the faith.

أَمْ حَسِبْتُمْ أَنْ تَدْخُلُوا الْجَنَّةَ وَلَمَّا يَأْتِكُمْ مَثَلُ الَّذِينَ خَلَوْا مِنْ
قَبْلِكُمْ مَسَّتْهُمُ الْبَأْسَاءُ وَالضَّرَّاءُ وَزُلْزِلُوا حَتَّىٰ يَقُولَ الرَّسُولُ
وَالَّذِينَ آمَنُوا مَعَهُ مَتَىٰ نَصْرُ اللَّهِ ۗ أَلَا إِنَّ نَصْرَ اللَّهِ قَرِيبٌ ﴿214﴾

Do you suppose that you shall enter Paradise though there has not yet come to you the like of [what befell] those who went before you? Stress and distress befell them, and they were shaken until the apostle, and the faithful who were with him said, 'when will God's help [come]?' Look! God's help is indeed near!

Those *who had faith to the truth of what they differed in* (who are mentioned in the previous verse), are urged to remain steadfast on the path of God and not waver in the face of hardship and difficulties. Remaining steadfast in faith with the goal of achieving Paradise requires the faithful to face difficulties. When previous nations wanted to be firm in their faith, stress and distress befell upon them until God's help arrived.

Do you suppose that you shall enter Paradise though there has not yet come to you the like of [what befell] those who went before you? According to Tabrisi, there are two reasons that this verse is mentioned here: one is to inform the Prophet and believers that they would certainly face difficulties. Secondly, to console them by informing them that facing difficulties is not exclusive to them; previous prophets and believers have also faced similar difficulties.[317]

There are many other verses of the Quran, which are also supported by historical information, which show that monotheistic faiths have received extremely hostile reactions throughout history. Prophets and followers of these faiths were persecuted viciously; tortured, enslaved and killed by the rulers and elites. The pagan Romans, for example, were particularly brutal against the Christians. As well as the followers of Prophet Noah, Prophet Shu'ayb, and of course, the Jews who suffered under the Pharaoh.

Stress and distress befell them, and they were shaken; These calamities had such profound impacts and even led those believers to question the veracity of their faith. Believers by nature expect God to help them in their hour of need. If the help of God does not come when they expect it, and the difficulties continue, the faithful might lose their patience and their faith could be shaken. This is the exact moment the verse refers to "they were shaken," this is the point when somebody's faith can be verified and be categorised as a true believer. This is the status that God wants people to achieve, thus he withholds his support until the verification process is complete.

As it is mentioned in the Quran, for true believers, the victory of God is guaranteed: *God has decreed: 'I and My messengers will prevail.' God is most powerful and mighty.* (Q. 58:21) or *O you who believe! If you help God, He will help you and make you stand firm.* (Q. 47:7) If believers help the cause of God, in return, God will help the believers, so the help is guaranteed. However, God's help does not come right away; it comes at a later stage to test the faith of the believers.

There is an important issue which has also puzzled the commentators here. How is it possible that the messengers of God were shaken as well as the believers? God's messengers, prior to their appointment, received extensive spiritual training and already knew that God's help comes at an appointed stage. It appears that messengers' questioning about God's help is not related to their weakness in their faith but instead to ask God to speed up his help so that their followers may have a lighter test.

يَسْأَلُونَكَ مَاذَا يُنفِقُونَ ۖ قُلْ مَا أَنفَقْتُم مِّنْ خَيْرٍ فَلِلْوَالِدَيْنِ وَالْأَقْرَبِينَ
وَالْيَتَامَىٰ وَالْمَسَاكِينِ وَابْنِ السَّبِيلِ ۗ وَمَا تَفْعَلُوا مِنْ خَيْرٍ فَإِنَّ اللَّهَ بِهِ
عَلِيمٌ ﴿215﴾

They ask you as to what they should spend. Say, 'Whatever wealth you spend, let it be for parents, relatives, orphans, the needy, and the traveller.' And whatever good that you may do, God indeed knows it.

There seems to be a discrepancy between the question and the answer mentioned in the verse. The believers ask what they should spend as charity. However, in the answer, God does not tell them *what* they should spend. Instead, he states to *whom* they should give charity. The reason for the answer is clear; God is telling the believers it does not matter how much and to what extent they wish to spend; certainly, the more the better. The issue is not how much they should spend, but to whom they should give charity. In addition to that, the verse is reluctant to give a direct answer which may lead to an inconvenient obligation. In fact, three verses later (Q. 2:218) the question is repeated, and the questioners insist on a direct answer. The direct answer is that you should give whatever is extra to your expenses. Something that a very small minority of the believers could do.

Whatever wealth you spend; The term used for wealth here is *khayr*. *Khayr* literally means "good and beneficial". In other places in the Quran, *khayr* is used also to mean wealth (Q. 100:8). Using the term *khayr* for wealth means that firstly, the source of what is given as charity must be good and lawful (*halal*). Secondly, what is given must be of good quality and not something that the giver themselves would not like to receive. Finally, it must be beneficial; something that could be of considerable use.

let it be for parents, relatives, orphans, the needy, and the traveller; The verse then mentions the categories of people to whom charity should be given in order of their priority: parents, relatives, orphans, the needy, and the traveller. Here, relatives, especially parents, have priority over other people who may be in need. Some may think that the those who are related to them are not qualified to receive sincere charity, while the Quran instructs Muslims otherwise.

Travellers are considered to be those who used up their money and provision in the middle of their journey. This may rarely happen in our time, but in in previous generations, due to the length and unpredictability of journeys as well as attacks from bandits on the way, it was common for travellers to run out of money. Therefore, it was considered as charity to help these stranded travellers by giving them enough money to complete their journey.

كُتِبَ عَلَيْكُمُ الْقِتَالُ وَهُوَ كُرْهٌ لَّكُمْ وَعَسَىٰ أَن تَكْرَهُوا شَيْئًا
وَهُوَ خَيْرٌ لَّكُمْ وَعَسَىٰ أَن تُحِبُّوا شَيْئًا وَهُوَ شَرٌّ لَّكُمْ وَاللَّهُ يَعْلَمُ
وَأَنتُمْ لَا تَعْلَمُونَ ﴿216﴾

Warfare has been prescribed for you, though it is repulsive to you. Yet it may be that you dislike something while it is good for you, and it may be that you love something while it is bad for you, and God knows, and you do not know.

The focus of the chapter now shifts to the subject of warfare. The meaning of warfare (*qitāl*) is very important for the study of this verse. The meaning of the Arabic word *qitāl* implies mutual killing in a fight. The Quran is clear that there are certain situations in which war is unavoidable. Muslims are expected to fight and kill their enemies in these situations. Therefore, it is safe to argue that here *qitāl* refers to one of the instances of *jihad*.

The reason for this distinction is that there has been a trend, amongst some Muslim scholars, who try to eliminate the idea of "violence" in

Islam altogether. They often argue that violence has no place in Islam, and instead *jihad* is simply a personal and collective endeavour to attain higher spiritual or social qualities. However, this a view clearly contradicts the Quran, as verses such as these explicitly encourage Muslims to fight and kill when it is necessary. Of course, Islam ideally promotes peace and harmony between people, but it is also a realistic faith; when people's life or wealth are in danger, they have a legitimate right to defend themselves, and under such circumstances, violence is not only warranted, but also prescribed until the imminent danger has dissipated.

though it is repulsive to you; Commentators have provided lengthy discussions on why warfare may be repulsive to believers, while it is a command of God. Of course, fighting is not something people naturally enjoy. It brings about harm to both sides, leads to death, destruction and many other atrocities. Also, as Tabatabai demonstrates very well, in its core, Islam advocates peace and harmony.[318]

As a matter of fact, one of the reasons that early Muslims were attracted to Islam, especially the people of Medina, was because they saw Islam as a means to put an end to the ongoing feuds and conflicts, thus bringing peace to their society. Islam propagates kindness and respect for other human beings and despises unjust killing and unwarranted harm to others. These beliefs had been carved into the hearts of the early believers. Therefore, it was normal for them to be repulsed by the command to fight. However, God states in the verse that despite the many downsides to fighting and violence, when the time comes in which believers have no other choice but to defend themselves, then fighting becomes an obligation on them.

Yet it may be that you dislike something while it is good for you, and it may be that you love something while it is bad for you, and God knows, and you do not know. Many commentators have related this section of the verse to either gaining war booties or attaining martyrdom as a result of participating in a war. However, this interpretation stems from the idea of the permissibility of offensive *jihad* which emerged as a result of efforts to justify the actions of the early Muslim generations. In Islam, war is never justified by gaining booties or land. As a matter of fact, if the intention of believers who are participating in a war is related to gaining booties, and if they are killed during the war, they will not attain martyrdom. It is true that booties may be a by-product of a victorious war. But gaining booty cannot be a motivation for Muslims in *jihad*, and certainly God would never make such a connection between war and gaining booties as *khayr*.

Rather, this section of the verse leads to an understanding that Muslims may want to coexist in peace with those who pose a danger to them, but their enemies may plot to destroy them or drive them out of their lands. In order to avoid these gruesome situations happening, God tells believers to defend themselves so that they may avoid a dreadful destiny. It is obvious that a nation who cannot defend itself against arrogant warmongers and trespassers of human values would be vunerable and weak and doomed to annihilation and oppression.

يَسْأَلُونَكَ عَنِ الشَّهْرِ الْحَرَامِ قِتَالٍ فِيهِ قُلْ قِتَالٌ فِيهِ كَبِيرٌ وَصَدٌّ عَن
سَبِيلِ اللَّهِ وَكُفْرٌ بِهِ وَالْمَسْجِدِ الْحَرَامِ وَإِخْرَاجُ أَهْلِهِ مِنْهُ أَكْبَرُ عِندَ اللَّهِ
وَالْفِتْنَةُ أَكْبَرُ مِنَ الْقَتْلِ وَلَا يَزَالُونَ يُقَاتِلُونَكُمْ حَتَّىٰ يَرُدُّوكُمْ عَن
دِينِكُمْ إِنِ اسْتَطَاعُوا وَمَن يَرْتَدِدْ مِنكُمْ عَن دِينِهِ فَيَمُتْ وَهُوَ
كَافِرٌ فَأُولَٰئِكَ حَبِطَتْ أَعْمَالُهُمْ فِي الدُّنْيَا وَالْآخِرَةِ وَأُولَٰئِكَ أَصْحَابُ
النَّارِ هُمْ فِيهَا خَالِدُونَ ﴿217﴾

They ask you concerning warfare in the holy month. Say, 'It is an outrageous thing to fight in it, but keep [people] from God's way, and to be unfaithful to Him, and [to keep people from] the Holy Mosque, and to expel its people from it are more outrageous with God. And corruption is graver than killing. And they will not cease fighting you until they turn you away from your religion, if they can. And whoever of you turns away from his religion and dies faithless —they are the ones whose works have failed in this world and the Hereafter. They shall be the inmates of the Fire, and they shall remain in it [forever].'

The verse is extremely relevant to Muslims today. It was revealed in relation to the propaganda of the Meccan polytheists about Prophet Muhammad's apparent disregard for the holy months. It was an established custom since the time of Abraham to cease all fighting in the holy months. It seems that the verse is related to the raid on Nakhla (2/623); a small expedition force led by 'Abdullāh b. Jaḥsh (d. 3/625) who was the brother-in-law of Prophet Muhammad. The Prophet tasked him to spy on the Meccans and capture one of their caravans. The expedition was a response to the Meccans having confiscated homes and properties of Muslims which were left in Mecca after the Emigration. The force achieved its objective, but mistakenly carried out the fighting on the first day of Rajab, one of the forbidden months for fighting. Subsequently the Muslims came under an organised propaganda attack for their disregard for the cessation of hostilities during the forbidden months. In response to this incident, God revealed the verse in which he first clarified that fighting in the holy months is outrageous, yet there are other acts which are more outrageous than fighting in the holy months.

Similarly, in the present day, Muslims do things which go against the established norms and consequently they come under heavy criticism by those who are hostile against Islam and Muslims. However, when the rights of Muslims are being flagrantly breached, they either ignore it or find justification for it. This was also the case at the time of the Prophet - when Muslims' property was plundered and they were tortured, the Meccan polytheists tried to justify their actions, yet when Muslims implemented retaliatory measures to defend themselves and take back what was rightfully theirs, they came under heavy propaganda attack.

but to keep [people] from God's way, and to be unfaithful to Him, and [to keep people from] the Holy Mosque, and to expel its people from it are more outrageous with God. This part of the verse highlights the appalling behaviour of the polytheists against Muslims in order to demonstrate the hypocrisy of the polytheist's mentality. Their hatred towards Islam made life miserable for the early Muslims. They tortured and killed Muslims and enforced an economic boycott on them. This led to unbearable suffering and starvation which finally drove Muslims out of their lands. When they had fled, the polytheists confiscated all the property that belonged to Muslims. These assaults against Muslims created *fitna* or corruption which is much worse than fighting in the holy months.

And they will not cease fighting you until they turn you away from your religion, if they can. And whoever of you turns away from his religion and dies faithless —they are the ones whose works have failed in this world and the Hereafter. They shall be the inmates of the Fire, and they shall remain in it [forever]. The verse then discusses the issue of apostasy (*irtidād*). There are some legal rulings concerning apostasy and its implementation, which will not be discussed here as this is something that Muslim majority countries should navigate themselves based on their interpretation of the Islamic legal sources. However, there are some religious implications of apostasy and apostates' situation in the Hereafter. One of the most important religious matters regarding the apostates concerns the good deeds that they have done in this world before turning away from faith. Do they not deserve to be rewarded for the good deeds they have done, despite their later denial of faith? The verse is clear regarding this question: "they are the ones whose works have failed in this world and the Hereafter." Their good deeds would be void not only in Hereafter but in this world as well.

Muslim theologians, both Shi'i and Sunni, from the early periods have discussed the meaning of the invalidation of good deeds as a result of apostasy. This topic is often discussed under the section of "fulfilment" (*muwafāt*). They have often suggested that apostasy invalidates the effects of good deeds. In this way, good deeds do not provide the required effect. For example, giving charity should attract certain benefits in this world and the next, but in the case of apostates, these benefits are not attracted and the charity does not have the desired effect. This is also mentioned elsewhere in the Quran: *And we will turn to the deeds that they have done and disperse them like dust.* (Q. 25:23)

One might wonder why faith is such an important ingredient in making good deeds effective, and why a person's good deeds are void when they are not accompanied by faith. If a person has faith, even their seemingly insignificant good deeds are taken into consideration. It seems that good deeds only have a positive effect on a person's soul if there is faith to accommodate them. For example, if a person wishes to light a candle, they can only do so in an environment where oxygen is present. With oxygen present, a person can light as many or as few candles as they wished, and they would all glow with light. However, if the oxygen in the room is removed, it would not matter if there was one or one hundred candles, none would glow with the light the person desired. Oxygen here is the precondition to light candles, and similarly, faith is the prerequisite for good deeds having an effect. Without faith in God, good deeds would be like candles without oxygen - regardless of their number, they would not glow.

Of course, this does not mean that faithless charitable people would not receive any benefits of their good deeds. They do get benefits for their deeds in this world; they may be honoured by people or blessed with further wealth for their charitable works. This verse mainly refers to the benefits seen in the Hereafter. The Hereafter operates differently from this world. There, faith is the ultimate prerequisite for people to receive blessings and benefits. According to Mutazilite scholars, if people go back and forth into faith but they are faithful at the moment of death, then all their previous good deeds would return with benefit in the Hereafter, regardless of how many times they went outside of the faith and came back.

Mufid in his book on theology *Awā'il al-maqālāt fi al-madhāhib wa-al-mukhtārāt* makes a distinction between Mutazilite and Shi'i schools of thought.[319] He puts forward a different view from the Mutazilite scholars who argue that if a person loses faith before death, none of their good deeds would be accepted. Mufid disagrees with this view which had also been accepted by Shi'i theologians up to his time, including the theologians of the influential Nawbakhtī family. Based on his interpretation of the Shi'i narrations, Mufid contends that if people have attained real faith in some parts of their lives, that faith would never go away and eventually they would die as a faithful person.[320] So even though a person may denounce faith by their tongue, faith is deeply rooted in their hearts and they may not even be aware of it. However, if these people had not attained true faith, instead only having attained a superficial level of faith, and then professed disbelief, they would die in the state of disbelief. In one of the relevant Shi'i narrations attributed to Imam Jafar al-Sadiq, it is reported that "whoever does only one true and sincere prostration for God, God would never punish him."[321] This tradition indicates that sincere faith continues until the time of death, even if people may not be aware of its existence in their heart as they may denounce their faith by their tongue.

إِنَّ الَّذِينَ آمَنُوا وَالَّذِينَ هَاجَرُوا وَجَاهَدُوا فِي سَبِيلِ اللَّهِ أُولَٰئِكَ يَرْجُونَ
رَحْمَتَ اللَّهِ وَاللَّهُ غَفُورٌ رَحِيمٌ ﴿218﴾

Indeed, those who have become faithful and those who have migrated and waged jihad in the way of God —it is they who expect God's mercy, and God is All-forgiving, All-merciful.

This verse specifically refers to the expedition group who infiltrated into Mecca and raided the caravan by mistake, although the purport of the verse is not restricted to them. 'Abdullāh b. Jaḥsh and his companions infiltrated enemy lines and endangered their lives in the service of God and his Messenger, yet when they returned to Medina, they came under severe criticism even by some fellow Muslims because they had mistakenly made the attack in the holy month. However, God supports them and reassures them that their mistake was forgiven, but he will not forgive the mischief of the people of Mecca and their oppression towards Muslims.

يَسْأَلُونَكَ عَنِ الْخَمْرِ وَالْمَيْسِرِ ۖ قُلْ فِيهِمَا إِثْمٌ كَبِيرٌ وَمَنَافِعُ لِلنَّاسِ
وَإِثْمُهُمَا أَكْبَرُ مِنْ نَفْعِهِمَا ۗ وَيَسْأَلُونَكَ مَاذَا يُنْفِقُونَ قُلِ الْعَفْوَ ۗ كَذَٰلِكَ
يُبَيِّنُ اللَّهُ لَكُمُ الْآيَاتِ لَعَلَّكُمْ تَتَفَكَّرُونَ ﴿219﴾

> They ask you concerning wine and gambling. Say, 'There is a great sin in both of them, and some profits for the people, but their sinfulness outweighs their profit.' And they ask you as to what they should spend. Say, 'All that is surplus.' Thus, does God clarify His communications for you so that you may reflect.

They ask you concerning wine and gambling. Say, 'There is a great sin in both of them' As noted earlier, the whole surah including this verse was revealed in Medina. Therefore, it is a wonder that Muslims were still not clear about the prohibition of alcohol and gambling so long after the first revelation. This is despite the fact that the verse had already been revealed in Mecca and forbidding "*sin*" (*ithm*) by which drinking wine and gambling are described in this verse.

> Say, 'My Lord has only forbidden indecencies, the outward among them and the inward ones, and sin (*ithm*) and undue aggression, and that you should ascribe to God partners for which He has not sent down any authority, and that you should attribute to God what you do not know.' (Q. 7:33)

Muslims then emigrated to Medina, but some believers still drank alcohol and gambled. From the perspective of the Prophet and Islam, it was clear that both these acts were forbidden from the very beginning. The Prophet never drank alcohol nor gambled during his lifetime. However, up to this point, certain people took this prohibition lightly and used to justify their actions by interpreting the prohibition as a voluntary choice. For this reason, the matter is clarified again at this point in time and the believers are told that there is great sin (*ithm*) in them although there may be some benefits too.

Islam prohibits alcohol due to its intoxicating effect which impairs a person's ability to comprehend, make sound decisions, or progress. Above all, intoxication prevents a person from remembering God. Early Muslims debated if drinking alcohol was considered a sin as it was very difficult for some of them to give up their addiction.

The verse does not deny that people may find some benefit in alcohol and gambling. In fact, there may be some health benefits of certain types of alcohol if taken in moderation. Furthermore, the production and sales of alcohol as well as the gambling industry contribute to the economy and provide employment. God acknowledges these benefits, but states that their harm outweighs the benefits.

And they ask you as to what they should spend. Say, 'All that is surplus.' This is a repetition of the question asked in verse 2:215 above:

> They ask you as to what they should spend. Say, 'Whatever wealth you spend, let it be for parents, relatives, orphans, the needy, and the traveler.' And whatever good that you may do, God indeed knows it.

God did not give a direct answer to the question in 2:215 and instead mentioned those who should receive the charity. Muslims insisted on an answer, so when they asked the question again, as recorded in this verse, God gives a direct answer which may not be pleasant for many. The answer is "all that is surplus"; certainly, this is not something that many believers can do. In order to spend "all that is surplus" one needs solid faith in God and absolute reliance on him, and detachment from worldly material riches.

Thus, does God clarify His communications for you so that you may reflect. There are important points to reflect upon in this verse. Firstly, when God legislates a law, believers are required to obey without question. He wants believers to understand the reasoning behind the legislation. In this way, he explains that although alcohol and gambling may have some benefit, the harms they cause are far worse. Secondly, for some of those who were addicted to alcohol and gambling, the verse still did not unequivocally state that both vices were forbidden. For them, the verse only compared their harms and benefits. Therefore, it is possible that even after the revelation of this verse, some of the early Muslims may have argued that these vices were not forbidden but it was only a recommendation. The general attitude of people who have weak faith and do not want to obey a ruling, is to look for loopholes and to evade the rules. By comparing the harms and benefits of alcohol and gambling, God requests the believers to reflect and understand *why* these two were prohibited. However, some continued with these vices and that is why Q. 5:90-91 was revealed later to express the prohibition explicitly and unequivocally:

> O you who have faith! Indeed, wine, gambling, idols and the divining arrows are abominations of Satan's doing, so avoid them, so that you may be felicitous. Indeed, Satan seeks to cast enmity and hatred among you through wine and gambling, and to hinder you from the remembrance of God and from prayer. Will you, then, relinquish?

فِي الدُّنْيَا وَالْآخِرَةِ ۗ وَيَسْأَلُونَكَ عَنِ الْيَتَامَىٰ ۖ قُلْ إِصْلَاحٌ لَّهُمْ خَيْرٌ ۖ وَإِن
تُخَالِطُوهُمْ فَإِخْوَانُكُمْ ۚ وَاللَّهُ يَعْلَمُ الْمُفْسِدَ مِنَ الْمُصْلِحِ ۚ وَلَوْ شَاءَ اللَّهُ
لَأَعْنَتَكُمْ ۚ إِنَّ اللَّهَ عَزِيزٌ حَكِيمٌ ﴿220﴾

About the world and the Hereafter. And they ask you concerning the orphans. Say, 'It is better to set right their affairs, and if you intermingle with them, they are of course your brothers: God knows the one who causes corruption from the one who brings about reform," and had God wished He would have put you to hardship.' Indeed, God is All-mighty, All-wise.

About the world and the Hereafter. This phrase seems to belong to the previous verse. Most of the verses in the Surah al-Baqarah end either with the letters *nun* or *mim;* that is the rhyme of the surah. If this section of the verse was placed at the end of verse 219, the verse would not have followed the same rhythmic pattern. Therefore, it was moved to the beginning of this verse.

The verse warns people of the harms of gambling and drinking alcohol. These have negative effects, not only in this world but in the Hereafter too. Therefore, when we think about certain deeds that have been prohibited in Islam, we should not only consider the harm they cause in this world, as this is only half the picture. Some deeds may seem to be harmless in this world, but in reality they affect a person's spiritually, thus they harm a person's status in the Hereafter. Therefore, when considering the harms and benefits of an act, we must think both about the world and the Hereafter.

Similarly, spending *all that is surplus* as suggested in the previous verse may not be logical according to worldly calculations. Yet, that act has considerable benefits in the Hereafter, especially if one believes in the words of God where He says, *He will replace whatever you may spend, and He is the best of providers.* (Q. 34:39)

And they ask you concerning the orphans. Say, 'It is better to set right their affairs, and if you intermingle with them, they are of course your brothers: Prior to Islam, the rights of orphans had been usually disregarded and their properties were considered booty by their surviving older relatives. Consequently, some of the harshest verses in the Quran were revealed for those who oppress the orphans; *Indeed those who consume the property of orphans wrongfully, only ingest fire into their bellies, and soon they will enter the Blaze.* (Q. 4:10)

Such harsh warnings caused some Muslims to take extreme measures to avoid orphans altogether, fearing that they may take the orphan's money by mistake or confuse the orphan's property with their own. This attitude left some orphans in difficult situations as it was hard for them to manage their own affairs. The verse addresses this unreasonable avoidance; it advises Muslims to attend to the needs of orphans. In the process of helping orphans, Muslims may use their own money to look after them and manage their affairs. However, they are also entitled to use the orphan's money for the interests of the orphans. So long as the money is spent for the benefit of the orphans, there is no harm in intermingling with them and their property.

وَلَا تَنكِحُوا الْمُشْرِكَاتِ حَتَّىٰ يُؤْمِنَّ ۚ وَلَأَمَةٌ مُّؤْمِنَةٌ خَيْرٌ مِّن مُّشْرِكَةٍ
وَلَوْ أَعْجَبَتْكُمْ ۗ وَلَا تُنكِحُوا الْمُشْرِكِينَ حَتَّىٰ يُؤْمِنُوا ۚ وَلَعَبْدٌ مُّؤْمِنٌ
خَيْرٌ مِّن مُّشْرِكٍ وَلَوْ أَعْجَبَكُمْ ۗ أُولَٰئِكَ يَدْعُونَ إِلَى النَّارِ ۖ وَاللَّهُ يَدْعُو
إِلَى الْجَنَّةِ وَالْمَغْفِرَةِ بِإِذْنِهِ ۖ وَيُبَيِّنُ آيَاتِهِ لِلنَّاسِ لَعَلَّهُمْ يَتَذَكَّرُونَ ﴿221﴾

Do not marry idolatresses until they embrace faith. A faithful slave girl is better than an idolatress, though she should impress you. And do not marry [your daughters] to idolaters until they embrace faith. A faithful slave is better than an idolater, though he should impress you. Those invite [others] to the Fire, but God invites to paradise and pardon, by His will, and He clarifies His signs for the people so that they may take admonition.

The verse clearly forbids Muslims to marry idolaters. Even in situations when Muslims are attracted to idolaters, they should always prefer believing men and women. The Quran uses the term attraction (*a'jaba*) instead of love for the feelings between a man and a woman. It is not a real love that people may have for their children and spouses which develops over time. If they convert to Islam, there is no problem in marrying them. The reason for such a strict rule is that there may be the possibility of those idolater spouses turning the hearts of believers away from faith. For Islam, faith is the most important asset the believers have, and they should not do anything that may potentially jeopardise it.

A faithful slave girl is better than an idolatress; as slavery is no longer relevant to the current society, there is no need to discuss the topic of marrying slaves. See the discussion above about Islam's attitude towards slavery.

وَيَسْأَلُونَكَ عَنِ الْمَحِيضِ قُلْ هُوَ أَذًى فَاعْتَزِلُوا النِّسَاءَ فِي الْمَحِيضِ وَلَا تَقْرَبُوهُنَّ حَتَّىٰ يَطْهُرْنَ فَإِذَا تَطَهَّرْنَ فَأْتُوهُنَّ مِنْ حَيْثُ أَمَرَكُمُ اللَّهُ إِنَّ اللَّهَ يُحِبُّ التَّوَّابِينَ وَيُحِبُّ الْمُتَطَهِّرِينَ ﴿222﴾

They ask you concerning [intercourse during] menses. Say, 'It is hurtful.' So, keep away from wives during the menses, and do not approach them till they are clean. And when they become clean, go into them as God has commanded you. Indeed, God loves the penitent and He loves those who keep clean.

Some would question the Prophet about specific issues, but their answers in the form of revelation did not descend immediately. God revealed verses according to a specific order and some of these questions were answered in bulk in a set of verses. This is why in the above set of verses there are unrelated questions and answers.

They ask you concerning [intercourse during] menses. The permissibility of intercourse during menstruation is another question which had been asked of the Prophet and this verse addresses the answer. As the verse was revealed in Medina, it may be possible that Muslims became aware of the strict Jewish laws regarding menstruation and wanted to know if Islam endorses these laws. According to the Old Testament (Leviticus: 22-24), menstruating women are considered impure; thus, they need to self-isolate for seven days and if men have intercourse with a menstruating woman, they will also need to self-isolate for seven days. Their bed also became impure for seven days, so they needed to sleep elsewhere.

Furthermore, the polytheists of Mecca did not have any ruling on the matter, and they continued to have intercourse with menstruating women. Between the two opposing attitudes, it is understandable that Muslims at the time were curious to know Islam's position on the matter, although some commentators believe that even the polytheists had strict rulings regarding menstruating women similar to that of the Jews.

Islam introduced a moderate approach which does not consider menstruating women to be impure. Instead, Islam only prohibits intercourse during menstruation on the grounds that it is painful for women. There is no isolation and no restriction on social activities of women during the period of menstruation.

and do not approach them till they are clean. There is a difference of opinion among commentators and jurisprudential schools about what the term "clean" (*yaṭhurna*) may mean here. Some commentators and jurists interpret it to mean the end of the menstruation cycle, as that is the point that women are clean from the menses. So, as soon as they stop bleeding the restrictions for intercourse are lifted. Others have interpreted this purity to occur after the ritual shower (*ghusl*) and hold that restrictions should be in place until the menstruating woman performs the *ghusl*.

And when they become clean, go into them as God has commanded you. According to the majority of commentators "as God has commanded you" means as God has commanded you not to have intercourse with them during their menses. So, when the menses is finished, you can have intercourse with them which was prohibited to you by command of God. Others have opined that it means go to them if you are in wedlock as God has commanded you not to have intercourse with women out of wedlock.[322]

نِسَاؤُكُمْ حَرْثٌ لَكُمْ فَأْتُوا حَرْثَكُمْ أَنَّىٰ شِئْتُمْ ۖ وَقَدِّمُوا
لِأَنْفُسِكُمْ ۚ وَاتَّقُوا اللَّهَ وَاعْلَمُوا أَنَّكُمْ مُلَاقُوهُ ۗ وَبَشِّرِ الْمُؤْمِنِينَ ﴿223﴾

"Your women are a tillage for you, so come to your tillage whenever (whichever way) you like, and send ahead for your souls, and be Godwary, and know that you will encounter Him; and give good news to the faithful."

Your women are a tillage for you, so come to your tillage; This verse is one of the most fascinating verses of the Quran concerning the treatment of women in a strongly male dominated society where women had previously been dealt with contempt and considered inferior beings. The verse warns men that they have been blessed with the companionship of such a great creation, who provide men with love, children and all kinds of support and companionship.

so come to your tillage whenever (whichever way) you like, and send ahead for your souls; Unfortunately, some commentators have interpreted the verse as permission for men to treat women whichever way they like. This interpretation is a product of the male dominant culture. Yet, in the context of the verse and in the light of the other verses of the Quran this meaning does not make any sense.

The following sentence "send ahead for yourselves", in this vein, further strengthens the argument that it is a warning for men rather than a warrant. The phrase, "send ahead for yourselves" further urges Muslims to treat their wives kindly and thus send good deeds to the Hereafter from which they would benefit. This is because good conduct in family has a great effect on a person's prosperity in the next life.

God warns men that he will be watching men's treatment over women and will hold them accountable for their mistreatment of women. There is a threatening tone to the verse which can be seen in similar verses, for example *Do whatever you wish, God certainly sees everything you do.* (Q. 41:40) God gives people time and opportunity to do whatever they want in this world but holds them accountable in the Hereafter. In the same manner, this verse warns men to be careful how they treat women; whichever way they treat women, they would be held accountable.

and be Godwary, and know that you will encounter Him; This statement further makes a case for the argument that the verse strongly urges believing men to treat their wives with dignity. Patriarchy had remained the dominant social system and, in this system, women had very little protection. They had been deprived of education, representation, and power; they were simply left to the mercy of men. Most men took advantage of this situation and treated women as their property. However, God urges Muslim men to stop such behaviour and treat women in a dignified manner. Failure to do so would have consequences in the Hereafter when they meet their Lord.

وَلَا تَجْعَلُوا اللَّهَ عُرْضَةً لِأَيْمَانِكُمْ أَنْ تَبَرُّوا وَتَتَّقُوا وَتُصْلِحُوا بَيْنَ
النَّاسِ وَاللَّهُ سَمِيعٌ عَلِيمٌ ﴿224﴾

And do not make God an obstacle, through your oaths, to do good deeds and be Godwary, and to bringing about concord between people. And God is All-hearing, All-knowing.

The verse continues with another aspect of spousal relationship. It apparently refers to a type of oath called *īlā'* which was a common practice in pre-Islamic Arabia. The oath used to be taken by husbands, often in a moment of anger, to refrain from sexual intercourse with their wives. This oath was a practice of physical separation between husbands and wives, and this would leave women under severe hardship. Women would lose their right to have intimacy with their husbands, but they would not be able to get a divorce. They would be in a suspended situation until either husband or wife dies. It seems that this tradition continued after the advent of Islam and some people swore by God to take such an oath to refrain from women. The verse condemns the oaths taken with the purpose of oppressing women and asks the believers to abstain from these practices.

Similarly, it was common amongst the people of Arabia that they would take oaths out of anger not to see their relatives, friends, or not to go to certain places, or not to mediate to amend hostilities among people. In these oaths, they would mention God's name to seal their oaths, however, the verse invalidates these oaths which prevents Muslims from good deeds. The believers are told not to use an oath to make an obstacle between good deeds and themselves.

لَّا يُؤَاخِذُكُمُ اللَّهُ بِاللَّغْوِ فِي أَيْمَانِكُمْ وَلَكِن يُؤَاخِذُكُم بِمَا كَسَبَتْ
قُلُوبُكُمْ وَاللَّهُ غَفُورٌ حَلِيمٌ ﴿225﴾

God shall not take you to task for what is unconsidered in your oaths, but He shall take you to task for what your hearts have incurred, and God is All-forgiving, All-forbearing.

This is following on from the previous verse that God forbids the believers to take on an oath of separation from their wives or an oath not *to bring concord between people*. God regards these oaths as "unconsidered" (*laghw*), meaning they have no effect in the eyes of God.

But He shall take you to task for what your hearts have incurred; If these oaths were something flowing on the tongue out of anger or ignorance or habit or the like, God would not take you to task, but he shall take you to task if your hearts are decided to carry them out and lead you to vices which are forbidden by God.

لِّلَّذِينَ يُؤْلُونَ مِن نِّسَائِهِمْ تَرَبُّصُ أَرْبَعَةِ أَشْهُرٍ فَإِنْ فَاءُوا فَإِنَّ اللَّهَ غَفُورٌ
رَّحِيمٌ ﴿226﴾

For those who forswear their wives shall be a waiting for four months. And if they recant, God is indeed All-forgiving, All-merciful.

God does not diminish the value of oaths completely, because oaths represent informal standards that hold social values together, such as honesty, integrity and honour. In the case of this verse, the husband has a period of four months to decide if he wishes to live with his wife or not. After four months he either must go back to his wife or he has to divorce her. He cannot leave her in a suspended situation to spite her.

And if they recant, God is indeed All-forgiving, All-merciful. This sentence explains that the husbands do not need to pay any atonement (*kaffāra*) for breaking their oaths and going back to their wives. God is forgiving and merciful in cases where they have to break their oaths because breaking these oaths leads to mercy and forgiveness of others.

وَإِنْ عَزَمُوا الطَّلَاقَ فَإِنَّ اللَّهَ سَمِيعٌ عَلِيمٌ ﴿227﴾

But if they resolve on divorce, God is indeed All-hearing, All-knowing.

The attributes used for God in this verse are very different from the attributes used in the previous verse. The previous verse attributes mercy and forgiveness to God in order to encourage the couples to re-join and to state that God will not punish the husband for breaking his oaths. However, in this verse where the option of divorce is chosen, the tone is different. Sometimes in cases of divorce the rights of women are infringed by taking the law lightly; God warns that he is All-hearing, All-knowing.

وَالْمُطَلَّقَاتُ يَتَرَبَّصْنَ بِأَنفُسِهِنَّ ثَلَاثَةَ قُرُوءٍ وَلَا يَحِلُّ لَهُنَّ أَن يَكْتُمْنَ مَا
خَلَقَ اللَّهُ فِي أَرْحَامِهِنَّ إِن كُنَّ يُؤْمِنَّ بِاللَّهِ وَالْيَوْمِ الْآخِرِ وَبُعُولَتُهُنَّ أَحَقُّ
بِرَدِّهِنَّ فِي ذَٰلِكَ إِنْ أَرَادُوا إِصْلَاحًا وَلَهُنَّ مِثْلُ الَّذِي عَلَيْهِنَّ بِالْمَعْرُوفِ
وَلِلرِّجَالِ عَلَيْهِنَّ دَرَجَةٌ وَاللَّهُ عَزِيزٌ حَكِيمٌ ﴿228﴾

Divorced women shall wait by themselves for three periods of purity [after menses], and it is not lawful for them to conceal what God has created in their wombs if they believe in God and the Last Day; and their husbands have a greater right to restore them during this [duration], if they desire reconcilement. The wives have rights similar to the obligations upon them, in accordance with honourable norms; and men have a degree above them, and God is All-mighty and All-wise.

The verse continues addressing spousal problems. In the previous verses, the Quran prohibited the practice of *īlā'* or the oath of separation, taken by the husband to leave his wife in limbo. He had a period of four months to decide to either go back to his wife or to divorce her. The verse at hand addresses the situation in case they decide to get a divorce.

Divorced women shall wait by themselves for three periods of purity [after menses]; Wives have to wait for three months before a divorce can take full effect and she can marry another person. This is to verify whether there is a possible pregnancy before the end of marriage. It also helps the couples to calm down and not to pursue a divorce out of anger. However, if the marriage was not consummated or if the wife has already been through menopause, then there is no need to wait. If the wife is pregnant their waiting period is until they give birth to their child as is mentioned in Q. 65:4:

> As for those of your wives who do not hope to have menses, should you have any doubts, their term shall be three months, and for those [as well] who do not have menses. As for those who are pregnant, their term shall be until they deliver. And whoever is wary of God, He shall grant him ease in his affairs.

and it is not lawful for them to conceal what God has created in their wombs if they believe in God and the Last Day; According to Islamic law the veracity of the testimony of a wife in the case of divorce in relation to the state of menses and pregnancy is taken for granted. They are not required to provide evidence for it. Therefore, the verse urges women to be truthful in these matters. They should not conceal their menses or their pregnancy to lengthen or shorten the waiting period.

and their husbands have a greater right to restore them during this [duration], if they desire reconcilement. The divorce does not take full effect until the end of the waiting period because during that time the husband can reverse his decision and stop the divorce. The verse states that, during the waiting period, he has the right to reconcile with his wife. Prospective grooms are not allowed to make advances to marry the wife during the waiting period. However, once the waiting period is complete, it is up to the woman to choose if she would like to remarry.

The wives have rights similar to the obligations upon them, in accordance with honourable norms; As discussed above, men have some rights over women, such as initiating the divorce proceedings, and the right to revoke the divorce during the waiting period. This section of the verse states that women's obligations are equivalent to their rights.

It also makes an important point of stating "in accordance with honourable norms". Thus, it places a stringent ethical mechanism to further strengthen the rights of women against men. The verse expects men to act within honourable norms in their dealing with women, including in the process of a divorce, and not to act on their self-interest alone. There are twelve verses in the Quran about divorce and in these verses, God Almighty repeats the word "honourable norms" (*bi-al-ma'rūf*) which demonstrates that in the eyes of God, it is of utmost importance to uphold these "honourable norms" in men's dealings with women.

However, throughout history, men have too often forgotten these warnings regarding holding up the "honourable norms" and solely focus on the literary interpretation of the law. Muslim scholars have often argued that the ethical issues or "honourable norms" are to be solved between men and women and that Islamic law can only deal with the legal aspect of the matter. This is why many of the current legal edicts go against the essence of the Quranic verses as they ignore the principle of "honourable norms". Given that God has put so much emphasis on the ethical aspect of the relationship between men and women, it may be prudent for Muslim legal scholars to revisit the matter and even go on to issue legal verdicts which are more favourable and fairer to women.

As the principle of "honourable norms" is so significant in spousal relations, it is important to discuss its exact meaning. The verses of the Quran do not elaborate on the meaning of this principle. However, Muhammad Abduh in *Tafsīr al-manār* observes that the meaning of "honourable norms" changes with the times; and must be determined according to the customs of every time.[323] The rights and obligations of a husband and wife may differ according to the requirements of the time and place in which they live. The existing values of society play a defining role in establishing these norms. In modern times, the fabric of society has evolved significantly from an agricultural society to an industrial society; where women are empowered with education and economic independence. Thus, the classical rulings which were based on the values of an agricultural society have become redundant. We do not know what the future may bring in terms of establishing the values or norms between men and women, but at this point it may be more prudent to revise existing rulings of Islamic law to be in tune with the spirit of "honourable norms".

and men have a degree above them, and God is All-mighty and All-wise. Quranic commentators have several varying views on the nature of the "degree" of men above women. Some commentators approached the verse from a purely legal aspect, whilst others looked at it from a creational aspect. Some views expressed have been so extreme as to be considered comical. Some have claimed that men are naturally endowed with better intellect than women as well as deeper and stronger faith, thereby concluding that this degree of superiority has been granted to men by God. This argument seems to stem from cultural biases that have been ingrained in the minds of men over the centuries and completely disregard the Islamic ethos. In Islam superiority comes from faith alone and not from any preordained biological characteristics. This a basic understanding of men and women's relationship may be comparable to Iblis's attitude towards Prophet Adam: "*I am better than him; You have created me of fire while You have created him (Adam) of clay.*" (Q. 7:12) The argument in favour of the superiority of men over women in creation is not acceptable in Islam. Men and women are different from each other, and they have been bestowed with different virtues. Therefore, they have a lot to offer to society in their own ways.

Those commentators who have explained the verse from a legal perspective have argued that the degree refers to men's share in inheritance as in Islam men have a greater share in inheritance. However, given that men have a responsibility to provide for women while women have no such duty, it cannot be considered as a degree above women. Some commentators have interpreted it as the position of leadership that men have in the family. Yet this position is given to men in order to regulate the matters of the family in relation to legal matters which does not give men a superior status in creation.

In conclusion, the 'degree' of men over women is neither creational nor intellectual. It only refers to some legal rights given to men for the management of the family. Of course, these rights come with responsibilities, and giving rights and responsibilities to men probably is based on their natural disposition. One of the greatest responsibilities of women is to give birth to children which makes them vulnerable in most societies. For this reason, they are relieved of many other responsibilities that God has tasked to the husband.

الطَّلَاقُ مَرَّتَانِ ۖ فَإِمْسَاكٌ بِمَعْرُوفٍ أَوْ تَسْرِيحٌ بِإِحْسَانٍ ۗ وَلَا يَحِلُّ لَكُمْ
أَنْ تَأْخُذُوا مِمَّا آتَيْتُمُوهُنَّ شَيْئًا إِلَّا أَنْ يَخَافَا أَلَّا يُقِيمَا حُدُودَ اللَّهِ ۖ فَإِنْ
خِفْتُمْ أَلَّا يُقِيمَا حُدُودَ اللَّهِ فَلَا جُنَاحَ عَلَيْهِمَا فِيمَا افْتَدَتْ بِهِ ۗ تِلْكَ حُدُودُ
اللَّهِ فَلَا تَعْتَدُوهَا ۚ وَمَنْ يَتَعَدَّ حُدُودَ اللَّهِ فَأُولَٰئِكَ هُمُ الظَّالِمُونَ ﴿229﴾

[Revocable] divorce may be only twice; then [let there be] either an honourable retention, or a kindly release. And it is not lawful for you to take back anything from what you have given them, unless the couple fear that they may not maintain God's bounds. So, if you fear they would not maintain God's bounds, there is no sin upon them in what she may give to secure her release. These are God's bounds, so do not transgress them, and whoever transgresses God's bounds —it is they who are the wrongdoers.

The Quran takes a clear position regarding the issue of divorce. Men should not take advantage of their position which has been given to them in accordance with their responsibilities. Unfortunately, men often try to take advantage in the divorce proceedings and oppress the women simply because they have the right of divorce.

[Revocable] divorce may be only twice; then [let there be] either an honourable retention, or a kindly release. This verse instructs men that divorce can only take place twice with the same wife. After the second divorce, if husband and wife reunite, men must maintain "an honourable retention" by living with her honourably, or "a kindly release" by divorcing her for the third time based on kindness and respect. According to Islam, it is not possible for husband and wife to remarry after the third divorce except under certain conditions, which will be explained in the next verse. Therefore, they must be certain whether they want to reunite or go their separate ways permanently. In either case, men must take an ethically just course of action and must not exploit their rights over women.

And it is not lawful for you to take back anything from what you have given them; Men are not allowed to take back anything from women, including their dowry *(mahr)* and whatever they have bought for them, when divorce occurs. However, in reality, men too often attempt to take back gifts and any other financial contributions that they had given to women. If husbands want to divorce their wives, wives have the right to keep everything that had been given to them whilst they were married. However, if it is the wife who wants to initiate the divorce, they may reach a settlement and the wife may choose to give up some of those things that the husband had previously gifted, including the dowry *(mahr)*.

Unless the couple fear that they may not maintain God's bounds. It is important to take note of this section of the verse. The majority of problems between a husband-and-wife stem from breaching "God's bounds" (*ḥudūd Allāh*). If they realise that it is not possible for them to restore these bounds, they would do better to part ways. Contrary to the formal and classical legal interpretation of this verse, another interpretation is that when it is apparent that no healthy relationship can continue between a husband and wife, the courts can give the right of divorce to both parties without seeking the husband's consent.

So, if you fear they would not maintain God's bounds, there is no sin upon them in what she may give to secure her release. In classical Islamic law, the husband holds the right of divorce, even after it becomes clear that a couple cannot remain married. However, this verse does not state "if the husband fears" rather it states "if you fear" so this may be interpreted to mean that it is the court which would decide on these matters and not the husband unilaterally. In those cases where marriage becomes intolerable, the wife is also able to initiate divorce proceedings before the courts. However, legal scholars should contemplate further upon this issue. Among the Shi'i jurists, Khomeini has taken this position. He explicitly stated that women have the right to claim divorce, even if the reason is that she simply dislikes her husband. Of course, according to Islamic law, cases of mistreatment, abuse and lack of financial support are also grounds for a wife to claim divorce. Whereas dislike of the husband is not considered valid grounds for a wife to claim a divorce and only Khomeini supports this view.

These are God's bounds, so do not transgress them, and whoever transgresses God's bounds —it is they who are the wrongdoers. The verse ends with an emphasis on "God's bounds" which is mentioned three times in this verse. This is an explicit reference to the ethical aspects of the relationship between a man and woman, and God strongly urges believers to take heed of these ethical values. According to Islam, the law alone is not sufficient to regulate gender relations and it is necessary that the ethical norms of the time and place must be taken into full consideration in regulating gender affairs. Gender affairs are more intimate and intricate than the scope of law; therefore, they must be based upon fear of God, having an awareness of the needs of each other and being kind. The combination of laws and the ethical norms of the society together provide a framework to regulate gender relations in Islam.

فَإِن طَلَّقَهَا فَلَا تَحِلُّ لَهُۥ مِنۢ بَعۡدُ حَتَّىٰ تَنكِحَ زَوۡجًا غَيۡرَهُۥۗ فَإِن طَلَّقَهَا فَلَا
جُنَاحَ عَلَيۡهِمَآ أَن يَتَرَاجَعَآ إِن ظَنَّآ أَن يُقِيمَا حُدُودَ ٱللَّهِۗ وَتِلۡكَ حُدُودُ ٱللَّهِ
يُبَيِّنُهَا لِقَوۡمٖ يَعۡلَمُونَ ﴿230﴾

And if he divorces her, she will not be lawful for him until she marries a husband other than him, and if he divorces her, there is no sin upon them to remarry if they think that they can maintain God's bounds. These are God's bounds, which He clarifies for a people who have knowledge.

According to Shi'i jurisprudence, if husband and wife have divorced on three separate occasions, they are not permitted to remarry again, unless she marries a different person and gets divorced. This differs from Sunni jurisprudence, where if a man divorces his wife by stating three times that he divorces her, on one occasion, he cannot remarry her again until she marries and divorces another man.

According to Shi'i jurisprudence, a marriage which would allow an ex-wife to return to her former husband after three separate divorces, must be a correct, permanent and consummated marriage. It cannot be a pretend marriage with the intention of cheating the legal ruling. The idea of impermissibility of marriage after three divorces is to deter the husband from making a mockery of the institution of marriage; therefore, there are strict rulings regarding reuniting following three divorces. What is notable again in this verse is the emphasis on "God's bounds" in all proceedings of divorce and marriage.

وَإِذَا طَلَّقْتُمُ النِّسَاءَ فَبَلَغْنَ أَجَلَهُنَّ فَأَمْسِكُوهُنَّ بِمَعْرُوفٍ أَوْ سَرِّحُوهُنَّ
بِمَعْرُوفٍ وَلَا تُمْسِكُوهُنَّ ضِرَارًا لِتَعْتَدُوا وَمَنْ يَفْعَلْ ذَٰلِكَ فَقَدْ ظَلَمَ
نَفْسَهُ وَلَا تَتَّخِذُوا آيَاتِ اللَّهِ هُزُوًا وَاذْكُرُوا نِعْمَتَ اللَّهِ عَلَيْكُمْ وَمَا
أَنْزَلَ عَلَيْكُمْ مِنَ الْكِتَابِ وَالْحِكْمَةِ يَعِظُكُمْ بِهِ وَاتَّقُوا اللَّهَ
وَاعْلَمُوا أَنَّ اللَّهَ بِكُلِّ شَيْءٍ عَلِيمٌ ﴿231﴾

When you divorce women and they complete their term, then either retain them honourably or release them honourably, and do not retain them maliciously in order that you may transgress; and whoever does that certainly wrongs himself. Do not take the communications of God in derision, and remember God's blessing upon you, and what He has sent down to you of the Book and wisdom, to advise you therewith. Be wary of God, and know that God has knowledge of all things.

The verse reinforces God's advice to pay attention to the spirit of the law instead of focusing only on the letter of the law in order to take advantage of it especially in the case of divorce. Here it is the husband who is the prime addressee of the warning, as they have been given a degree over their wife in the case of initiating a divorce.

And do not retain them maliciously in order that you may transgress; Husbands may decide to take advantage of their position by oppressing their wives, through focusing only on the letter of the law and completely disregarding the spirit of the law. For example, in order to refrain from paying the mandatory dowry or other financial compensations, they may mistreat their wives and force them to initiate the divorce so that they can avoid making any payments. Husbands should also be honourable in the process of divorce and afterwards; giving the wife her due rights, not to harass or annoy her. Furthermore, couples may try to cheat the ban regarding remarrying after three separate divorces by arranging fake marriages. The verse, therefore, strongly urges believers to avoid sham marriages. It is impossible to cheat God, and people would be held accountable for their misdeeds.

Their actions, therefore, must be in line with the spirit of the law not only with the letter of the law.

Do not take the communications of God in derision; This refers to attempts to find loopholes in the laws. Misusing the verses of the Quran to oppress women, rather than honouring them, treating them harshly rather kindly and by pressurising wives to give away a part or the whole of their dowry.

And remember God's blessing upon you, and what He has sent down to you of the Book and wisdom, to advise you therewith. The blessing of God may allude to the presence of the Prophet through whom they were guided to an honourable way of life. *Kitāb* may mean the Book as it is translated here, or it may refer to the law and what is prescribed to the believers as the legislation of God. This latter meaning is used frequently in the Quran like, *the prayer is indeed a timed prescription (kitāb) for the faithful.* This is a more fitting translation since the Book includes wisdom (*ḥikma*) as well. So, the meaning would be, "what he has sent down to you of legislation and wisdom." Certainly, the laws of God are always based on wisdom, and they must be practiced with wisdom.

وَإِذَا طَلَّقْتُمُ النِّسَاءَ فَبَلَغْنَ أَجَلَهُنَّ فَلَا تَعْضُلُوهُنَّ أَن يَنكِحْنَ أَزْوَاجَهُنَّ
إِذَا تَرَاضَوْا بَيْنَهُم بِالْمَعْرُوفِ ذَٰلِكَ يُوعَظُ بِهِ مَن كَانَ مِنكُمْ يُؤْمِنُ
بِاللَّهِ وَالْيَوْمِ الْآخِرِ ذَٰلِكُمْ أَزْكَىٰ لَكُمْ وَأَطْهَرُ وَاللَّهُ يَعْلَمُ وَأَنتُمْ لَا
تَعْلَمُونَ ﴿232﴾

When you divorce women and they complete their term, do not thwart them lest they should [re]marry their husbands, when they honourably reach mutual consent. Herewith are advised those of you who believe in God and the Last Day. That will be more decent and purer for you, and God knows, and you do not know.

According to the verse, once the waiting period of a woman is over, nobody should act to influence her, lest she marries out of coercion. Her family members have no right to influence her decision; the decision is entirely hers to choose whom she marries. She might remarry the ex-husband or find a new suitable husband. Based on this verse, some Shi'i scholars argue that even virgin females do not need to seek permission from their guardians to marry their husbands; they may marry someone of their own choosing. On the contrary other scholars, basing their rulings on traditions, argue that virgin females must seek permission from their guardians.

Herewith are advised those of you who believe in God and the Last Day. This part of the verse alludes to a very crucial matter. The law itself is not enough to stop injustice and violation of anyone's rights. Belief in God and the Last Day is needed for complete observance of these laws related to family and intimate relations. This is a day in which God gives full recompense of every action.

وَالْوَالِدَاتُ يُرْضِعْنَ أَوْلَادَهُنَّ حَوْلَيْنِ كَامِلَيْنِ ۖ لِمَنْ أَرَادَ أَنْ يُتِمَّ الرَّضَاعَةَ
وَعَلَى الْمَوْلُودِ لَهُ رِزْقُهُنَّ وَكِسْوَتُهُنَّ بِالْمَعْرُوفِ ۚ لَا تُكَلَّفُ نَفْسٌ إِلَّا
وُسْعَهَا ۚ لَا تُضَارَّ وَالِدَةٌ بِوَلَدِهَا وَلَا مَوْلُودٌ لَهُ بِوَلَدِهِ ۚ وَعَلَى الْوَارِثِ مِثْلُ
ذَٰلِكَ ۗ فَإِنْ أَرَادَا فِصَالًا عَنْ تَرَاضٍ مِنْهُمَا وَتَشَاوُرٍ فَلَا جُنَاحَ عَلَيْهِمَا ۗ وَإِنْ
أَرَدْتُمْ أَنْ تَسْتَرْضِعُوا أَوْلَادَكُمْ فَلَا جُنَاحَ عَلَيْكُمْ إِذَا سَلَّمْتُمْ مَا آتَيْتُمْ
بِالْمَعْرُوفِ ۗ وَاتَّقُوا اللَّهَ وَاعْلَمُوا أَنَّ اللَّهَ بِمَا تَعْمَلُونَ بَصِيرٌ ﴿233﴾

Mothers shall suckle their children for two full years, —that for such as desire to complete the suckling— and on the father shall be their maintenance and clothing, in accordance with honourable norms. No soul is to be tasked except according to its capacity: neither the mother shall be made to suffer harm on her child's account, nor the father on account of his child, and on the [father's] heir devolve [duties and rights] similar to that.

And if the couple desire to wean, with mutual consent and consultation, there will be no sin upon them. And if you want to have your children wet-nursed, there will be no sin upon you so long as you pay what you give in accordance with honourable norms, and be wary of God, and know that God sees best what you do.

Mothers shall suckle their children for two full years - that for such as desire to complete the suckling— and on the father shall be their maintenance and clothing; The Quran could have used the standard Arabic terms "*umm*" (mother) and "*abb*" (father), however, the specific words "*wālid*" (father) and "*wālida*" (mother) are used. This is because the standard terms may also be used for non-biological parents, or culturally it may be used to show great respect and affinity to a person. However, the terms "*wālid*" and "*wālida*" can only be used for biological parents. For example, Prophet Abraham's caretaker Āzar was referred to as "*abb*" to indicate that he was not the biological father of Prophet Abraham. (Q. 6:74) Otherwise, the verse would have used the word "*wālid*" as is the case in this verse. Interestingly, in another verse, Prophet Abraham prays for his parents and refers to them as "*wālid*" (Q.14:41). In this case he was referring to his biological parents.

The use of these specific words makes sense as the subject of the verse is suckling (by the biological mother), probably after the divorce takes place. The previous set of verses have mentioned the ethical and legal rulings of divorce and this verse deals with the issue of children in the case of divorce. According to Islamic law, if a mother wishes to suckle her infant after a divorce takes place, she has the right to have custody of them for two years. In this case, the ex-husband must make payments to the mother for the suckling, even if she is willing to do it as the mother of the infant. However, she may choose to forgo her right, in which case it would be the father's duty to find someone to suckle the infant and look after the child. After this period, there are different rulings for the custody of boys and girls.

in accordance with honourable norms; The expression "honourable norms" is used again in this verse to note that although it is the legal duty of the father to look after and provide for the children, ethical aspects of the process should be taken into consideration. These may include, maintaining the dignity and reputation of the mother as well as taking the financial situation of the father into consideration. Both parties should be pleased with the custody arrangements of their children.

وَالَّذِينَ يُتَوَفَّوْنَ مِنكُمْ وَيَذَرُونَ أَزْوَاجًا يَتَرَبَّصْنَ بِأَنفُسِهِنَّ أَرْبَعَةَ
أَشْهُرٍ وَعَشْرًا فَإِذَا بَلَغْنَ أَجَلَهُنَّ فَلَا جُنَاحَ عَلَيْكُمْ فِيمَا فَعَلْنَ فِي
أَنفُسِهِنَّ بِالْمَعْرُوفِ وَاللَّهُ بِمَا تَعْمَلُونَ خَبِيرٌ ﴿234﴾

As for those of you who die leaving wives, they shall wait by themselves four months and ten days, and when they complete their term, there will be no sin upon you in respect of what they may do with themselves in accordance with honourable norms. And God is well aware of what you do.

The verse discusses the waiting period for of widows. If a husband dies, the wife needs to wait for four months and ten days before remarrying, except if the wife is pregnant. Muslim legal schools issue different rulings in relation to a pregnant widow's waiting period. The Shi'i view indicates that she has to wait for the longer of the two periods: giving birth or waiting for four months and ten days.

After the waiting period, widows can do anything they wish; they may remarry a suitable groom or decide to live alone. The families and society have no right to pressure her towards a particular course of action. In Muslim societies, families often feel responsible for widows and impose some rigid norms upon them. These may include preventing them from remarrying within the first year or the second year or even for the rest of their lives following the death of the husband. If a widow acts contrary to these social norms, they may be considered shamed and outcasted. However, the verse removes this stigma and cultural norms against widowed women.

وَلَا جُنَاحَ عَلَيْكُمْ فِيمَا عَرَّضْتُم بِهِ مِنْ خِطْبَةِ النِّسَاءِ أَوْ أَكْنَنتُمْ فِي
أَنفُسِكُمْ عَلِمَ اللَّهُ أَنَّكُمْ سَتَذْكُرُونَهُنَّ وَلَٰكِن لَّا تُوَاعِدُوهُنَّ
سِرًّا إِلَّا أَن تَقُولُوا قَوْلًا مَّعْرُوفًا وَلَا تَعْزِمُوا عُقْدَةَ النِّكَاحِ حَتَّىٰ يَبْلُغَ
الْكِتَابُ أَجَلَهُ وَاعْلَمُوا أَنَّ اللَّهَ يَعْلَمُ مَا فِي أَنفُسِكُمْ فَاحْذَرُوهُ
وَاعْلَمُوا أَنَّ اللَّهَ غَفُورٌ حَلِيمٌ ﴿235﴾

There is no sin upon you in what you may hint in proposing to [recently widowed] women, or what you may secretly cherish within your hearts. God knows that you will be thinking of them, but do not make troth with them secretly, unless you say honourable words, and do not resolve on a marriage tie until the prescribed term is complete. Know that God knows what is in your hearts, so beware of Him; and know that God is All-forgiving, All-forbearing.

Potential suitors must wait until the end of a widow's waiting period before they are able to propose marriage to them. However, men are allowed to hint their interest to a widow during her waiting period. The condition of the waiting period is different from a recently divorced woman when it is not permissible for men to propose or even hint their interest to her during her waiting period if she is getting divorced. During the waiting period of divorce, a wife is still considered to be attached to her husband. In the case of a widowed woman, men may hint their interest in proposing after their waiting period is over.

This is a common issue within the society and therefore it is discussed in detail in the Quran. Marriage, divorce, death and conceiving babies are issues of life and death and happen on a daily basis in society, so regulation of these affairs is one of the priorities of the Quran. God wants to regulate family affairs in the best way so that society can function and focus on spiritual perfection and development.

لَّا جُنَاحَ عَلَيْكُمْ إِن طَلَّقْتُمُ النِّسَاءَ مَا لَمْ تَمَسُّوهُنَّ أَوْ تَفْرِضُوا
لَهُنَّ فَرِيضَةً ۚ وَمَتِّعُوهُنَّ عَلَى الْمُوسِعِ قَدَرُهُ وَعَلَى الْمُقْتِرِ قَدَرُهُ مَتَاعًا
بِالْمَعْرُوفِ ۖ حَقًّا عَلَى الْمُحْسِنِينَ ﴿236﴾

There is no sin upon you if you divorce women while you have not yet touched them or settled a dowry for them. Yet provide for them —the well-off according to his capacity, and the poorly-off according to his capacity— with a sustenance that is honourable, an obligation on the virtuous.

Verses 236 and 237 deal with the case in which divorce takes place before the marriage is consummated. There are two possible situations here. The first situation is when the couple have not yet agreed on a dowry or have not determined the amount of the dowry during the marriage ceremony. Verse 236 states that the husband must provide the wife with some amount of money which is determined according to the husband's financial situation, "the well-off according to his capacity, and the poorly-off according to his capacity." In both cases the amount should be based on the custom of the society (*'urf/ma'rūf*) and which would not diminish the social status of the wife.

وَإِن طَلَّقْتُمُوهُنَّ مِن قَبْلِ أَن تَمَسُّوهُنَّ وَقَدْ فَرَضْتُمْ لَهُنَّ فَرِيضَةً فَنِصْفُ مَا
فَرَضْتُمْ إِلَّا أَن يَعْفُونَ أَوْ يَعْفُوَ الَّذِي بِيَدِهِ عُقْدَةُ النِّكَاحِ ۚ وَأَن تَعْفُوا أَقْرَبُ
لِلتَّقْوَىٰ ۚ وَلَا تَنسَوُا الْفَضْلَ بَيْنَكُمْ ۚ إِنَّ اللَّهَ بِمَا تَعْمَلُونَ بَصِيرٌ ﴿237﴾

And if you divorce them before you touch them, and you have already settled a dowry for them, then [pay them] half of what you have settled, unless they forgo it, or someone in whose hand is the marriage tie forgoes it. And to forgo is nearer to Godwaryness; and do not forget graciousness among yourselves. Indeed, God sees best what you do.

Then [pay them] half of what you have settled, unless they forgo it; The second situation which is dealt with in this verse is when the amount of dowry has already been settled. The verses suggest that even if the marriage is not consummated, and even if the dowry is not fixed, the right of the wife regarding dowry would not be written off, although it would diminish.

unless they forgo it or someone in whose hand is the marriage tie forgoes it; The commentators have expressed two opinions regarding this part of the verse. Most commentators believe that "in whose hand is the marriage tie" refers to the guardian (*walī*) of the girl if she has not reached social maturity to defend her rights. Some others believe that this refers to the husband because he is the one who can decide to end the marriage. The first meaning suggests that "unless they forgo" refers to the wife and "someone in whose hand is the marriage tie forgoes" refers to her guardian. If on the other hand, "someone in whose hand is the marriage tie forgoes" refers to the husband, it means that the wife is liable to half of the dowry unless the husband forgoes and give her the full dowry.

And to forgo is nearer to Godwaryness, and do not forget graciousness among yourselves. This part of the verse suggests that it is a virtue for the ex-wife to refuse to take any amount of the dowry as this is closer to Godwaryness. On the other side, it is graciousness (*faḍl*) of the husband to pay the full amount so that he does not treat his ex-wife with any grudge or stinginess. The verse advises that it is a virtue for the ex-couple to show nobility, generosity and forgiveness and act upon the principle of "fair manner" and "benevolence". The overall tone and message of these verses illustrates that the real test for people comes through difficult situations such as these, where emotions such as anger, bitterness, disappointment and revenge are at their peak. Divorce is one of the most stressful situations that a person may go through and provides the perfect testing ground for the believers. A person must maintain the standards set by God and be gracious at all times. For the ex-husband this may include paying the full dowry even if the marriage was not consummated and for the ex-wife it may mean insisting on not accepting any amount. If the couple behave honourably, it is very probable that they may be successful in their tests.

حَافِظُوا عَلَى الصَّلَوَاتِ وَالصَّلَاةِ الْوُسْطَىٰ وَقُومُوا لِلَّهِ قَانِتِينَ ﴿238﴾

Be watchful of your prayers, and [especially] the middle prayer, and stand in obedience to God;

Be watchful of your prayers; This verse is intriguingly placed in the middle of a series of verses on the issue of divorce. The verse explains to the believers that the key to being able to maintain family relations and passing the tests and tribulations they experience, is to pay attention to their prayers and their relationship with God. If a person does not have harmonious relationships with others, it means that their relationship with God is also not harmonious. If believers do not treat others, including their spouses (and ex-spouses) and other family members, justly and kindly, it means that their relationship with God is troubled and superficial. One of the most important cures for family troubles and other relationship issues is to fill the heart with the fear and love of God and always treat others within the boundaries that have been set by God.

Prayer in general is instrumental in establishing the presence of fear and love of God, when it is done in accordance with the instruction provided by the Quran, the Prophet and the Imams. Prayer is not just a symbolic ritual; it is a means for believers to gain nearness to God by contemplating on his omnipresence, the Hereafter and the eternal destiny of human beings. Therefore, worshippers must observe all the conditions of establishing prayers including the time, cleanliness, presence of heart, humility and contemplation.

and [especially] the middle prayer; Commentators have expressed different opinions about which prayer is referred to as "the middle prayer". According to most Sunni scholars the middle prayer mentioned in the verse refers to the Afternoon Prayer (*Ṣalāt al-'Aṣr*). However, according to the majority of Shi'i scholars, based on numerous traditions attributed to the Imams, it refers to the Midday

Prayer (*Ṣalāt al-Dhur*), because it is in the middle of the day. It is at this time when people often fully engage in their daily affairs and forget about their spiritual matters. Therefore, it is of the utmost importance to escape from being occupied with our daily affairs in favour of the spiritual realm and to revitalise the soul through the remembrance of God.

and stand in obedience to God. The term used in the verse for obedience is *qānit*. *Qānit* has different meanings but the most common one is continuous obedience to God with humbleness and humility. According to the Quran, Prophet Abraham excelled in maintaining these qualities: *Surely Abraham was an example, devoutly obedient (qānit) to God and true in faith.* (Q. 16:120) This obedience was one of the foremost qualities of Prophet Abraham, and thus the believers are expected to work towards attaining the same quality in their prayers.

فَإِنْ خِفْتُمْ فَرِجَالًا أَوْ رُكْبَانًا فَإِذَا أَمِنتُمْ فَاذْكُرُوا اللَّهَ كَمَا عَلَّمَكُم مَّا لَمْ تَكُونُوا تَعْلَمُونَ ﴿239﴾

And should you fear [a danger], then [pray] on foot or mounted, and when you are safe, remember God, as He taught you what you did not know.

Prayer is the pillar of faith and cannot be abandoned under any circumstances. Even if believers face an enemy or if they are travelling with the threat of a potential attack from bandits, they should not abandon the prayer. They must pray whilst walking on foot or riding on their mounts. Of course, when the fear is removed and they are safe, they must pray as God has taught them to pray in Islam.

وَالَّذِينَ يُتَوَفَّوْنَ مِنكُمْ وَيَذَرُونَ أَزْوَاجًا وَصِيَّةً لِّأَزْوَاجِهِم مَّتَاعًا
إِلَى الْحَوْلِ غَيْرَ إِخْرَاجٍ فَإِنْ خَرَجْنَ فَلَا جُنَاحَ عَلَيْكُمْ فِي مَا فَعَلْنَ فِي
أَنفُسِهِنَّ مِن مَّعْرُوفٍ وَاللَّهُ عَزِيزٌ حَكِيمٌ ﴿240﴾

Those of you who die leaving wives shall bequeath for their wives providing for a year, without turning them out; but if they leave, there is no sin upon you in respect of what they may do with themselves observing honourable norms. And God is All-mighty, All-wise.

After the interlude of two verses on prayer, the chapter continues to discuss the issue of divorce and gender relations in Islam. The majority of commentators claim that this verse was abrogated by the verse Q. 2:234: *As for those of you who die leaving wives, they shall wait by themselves four months and ten days* as well as with Q. 4:12 regarding the inheritance shares. A closer look at the verse shows that this is not the case. According to the verse 240, husbands should make a will that widows should not be removed for a year when husbands die. Furthermore, the heirs should provide for the widow for a year. In its essence, the verse does not state anything contradictory to the two above mentioned verses. Rather, it makes an ethical recommendation husbands that they should take additional measures to safeguard their widows by extending the period of maintenance, after their death.

This is supported by the sequence of the verses that the waiting period of four months and ten days was mentioned before this verse, so it is untenable to suggest that the former verse abrogates the latter. If there is a case of abrogation, then this verse should abrogate the previous verse. However, there does not seem to be any sign of abrogation. It is a case of setting out an ethical norm by extending the waiting period of widows and giving them additional security. Verse 241 re-emphasises the importance of the spirit of the law taking precedence over the letter of the law and by advising the heirs of all husbands and widows to follow the conditions of affordability and preserving the dignity of widows.

وَلِلْمُطَلَّقَاتِ مَتَاعٌ بِالْمَعْرُوفِ ۖ حَقًّا عَلَى الْمُتَّقِينَ ﴿241﴾

For the divorced women there shall be a provision, in accordance with honourable norms —an obligation on the Godwary.

This verse emphasises the provision for the divorced women in the same way that the previous verse stressed the right of provision for the widows. Some commentators are of the view that this ordinance is similar to what was said in verse 236 about the women who are not appointed a dowry at the time of wedlock, and they are divorced before any the marriage is consummated. However, this view cannot be right, because firstly, the issue was mentioned just a few verses ago. Secondly, because it talks about all divorced women (*muṭṭalaqāt*) without specifying any group. Thirdly, the last sentence of the verse which makes this "an obligation on the Godwary" indicates that it is an additional provision that the Godwary person gives to their ex-wives voluntarily in addition to what was mentioned before.

كَذَٰلِكَ يُبَيِّنُ اللَّهُ لَكُمْ آيَاتِهِ لَعَلَّكُمْ تَعْقِلُونَ ﴿242﴾

Thus, does God clarify His signs to you so that you may apply reason.

This verse refers to the previous two verses, which were the final two statements mentioned in the chapter regarding divorce. It summarises the idea of focusing on the spirit of the law over the letter of the law. The verses on divorce set out the legal aspect of divorce and gender relations in Islam. However, there are ethical principles that should also be taken into consideration whilst dealing with these issues.

In the Quran, family laws are provided to regulate the affairs of the family in case of disputes, but believers need to do more than simply follow the letter of the law. They must consider the standards of noble behaviour, honourable treatment, graciousness, and forgiveness. They need to take advantage of these social issues to elevate their spiritual status. To achieve this, they need to always prioritise ethical norms over their legal rights and responsibilities. In the case of gender relations and divorce, men should always act graciously towards women and give them more than what they are legally entitled to. This is what God clarifies in these verses for the believers and urges them to contemplate and act upon the guidance provided for them.

أَلَمْ تَرَ إِلَى الَّذِينَ خَرَجُوا مِن دِيَارِهِمْ وَهُمْ أُلُوفٌ حَذَرَ الْمَوْتِ فَقَالَ لَهُمُ اللَّهُ مُوتُوا ثُمَّ أَحْيَاهُمْ إِنَّ اللَّهَ لَذُو فَضْلٍ عَلَى النَّاسِ وَلَٰكِنَّ أَكْثَرَ النَّاسِ لَا يَشْكُرُونَ ﴿243﴾

Have you not regarded those who left their homes in thousands, apprehensive of death, whereupon God said to them, 'Die,' then He revived them? Indeed, God is gracious to mankind, but most people do not give thanks.

وَقَاتِلُوا فِي سَبِيلِ اللَّهِ وَاعْلَمُوا أَنَّ اللَّهَ سَمِيعٌ عَلِيمٌ ﴿244﴾

Fight in the way of God, and know that God is All-hearing, All-knowing.

Surah al- Baqarah began with a new set of verses on the importance of *jihad*. This verse reminds the believers again, that they should not be afraid of participating in *jihad* or be frightened of death. Death is in the hands of God alone - regardless of whether people go to *jihad* or stay at home, they will all eventually die.

There are two types of *jihad* in Islam: *jihad* against vile human desires, or the lower self. This is called the greater *jihad* as it is a continuous battle of conscientious believers against anything which contradicts the instructions of God and universal human values. A

Godwary person is continuously engaged in this battle until the end of their life. The other type of *jihad* is fighting in the battlefield in the way of God, which is also called *qitāl* and the lesser *jihad*.

Like any other worldview, Islam warrants and encourages its followers to defend their lives and lands. There are many verses of the Quran calling believers to engage in defensive *jihad,* which is also part of the fight with the self. It would be healthier for Muslim scholars to denounce the violent ideologies attributed to Islam and recognise that they defended the idea of offensive *jihad* in Islam to legitimise the mistakes of the Umayyad and Abbasid rulers. Islam does not allow offensive *jihad,* and faith can never be spread with swords, guns and bombs. The idea of offensive *jihad* makes it legitimate for violent terrorist groups to exploit Islam. However, it is undeniable that Muslims are encouraged to take up arms to defend their lands and lives, which is also warranted by international laws.

This verse refers to a group of people who run away from defending their lives and property, possibly defying the orders of a prophet. To show them that death will always find them even if they run away from it, God makes them all die at once, and then revive them.

There is no information regarding who the verse is referring to, but there are two views regarding the reason for their exodus. Some believe that they were escaping from plague while others believe that they were escaping from jihad. Whatever the case, the overall message of the verse is to say that death is in the hands of God and there is no escaping from it. Whatever people choose to do in their lives, it would not change the fact that they will eventually die when the decree from God comes. Therefore, there is no need to attempt to escape from death, especially in the context of a justified war when there is a need to defend people against oppression.

مَّن ذَا الَّذِي يُقْرِضُ اللَّهَ قَرْضًا حَسَنًا فَيُضَاعِفَهُ لَهُ أَضْعَافًا كَثِيرَةً ۚ وَاللَّهُ
يَقْبِضُ وَيَبْسُطُ وَإِلَيْهِ تُرْجَعُونَ ﴿245﴾

Who is it that will lend God a good loan that He may multiply it for him several fold? And God tightens and expands [the means of life], and to Him you shall be brought back.

The verse continues to emphasise the importance of fighting in the way of God through supporting the financial needs of the army. The expression of "giving a loan to God" is a beautiful way of describing spending in the way of God. God takes any type of charity seriously, and so he uses this beautiful expression to show his appreciation. The use of the word "loan" indicates that God will certainly return the loan back to those who have lent it several fold, either in this world or the next.

God tightens and expands [the means of life]; This phrase reminds Muslims that it is God who is in control of the means of life. So, there is no need to worry about spending in the way of God. Regardless of what people spend, if God wishes, he may grant much more than what they spent. If God does not wish, he may withdraw his blessings in this world, but certainly, he would pay back the loan in many more ways than what we could even imagine.

أَلَمْ تَرَ إِلَى الْمَلَإِ مِن بَنِي إِسْرَائِيلَ مِن بَعْدِ مُوسَىٰ إِذْ قَالُوا لِنَبِيٍّ لَّهُمُ ابْعَثْ لَنَا مَلِكًا نُّقَاتِلْ فِي سَبِيلِ اللَّهِ قَالَ هَلْ عَسَيْتُمْ إِن كُتِبَ عَلَيْكُمُ الْقِتَالُ أَلَّا تُقَاتِلُوا قَالُوا وَمَا لَنَا أَلَّا نُقَاتِلَ فِي سَبِيلِ اللَّهِ وَقَدْ أُخْرِجْنَا مِن دِيَارِنَا وَأَبْنَائِنَا فَلَمَّا كُتِبَ عَلَيْهِمُ الْقِتَالُ تَوَلَّوْا إِلَّا قَلِيلًا مِّنْهُمْ وَاللَّهُ عَلِيمٌ بِالظَّالِمِينَ ﴿246﴾

Have you not regarded the elite of the Israelites after Moses, when they said to their Prophet, 'Appoint for us a king, that we may fight in the way of God.' He said, 'May it not be that you will not fight if fighting were prescribed for you?' They said, 'Why should we not fight in the way of God, when we have been expelled from our homes and [separated from] our children?' So, when fighting was prescribed for them, they turned back except a few of them, and God knows best the wrongdoers.

There does not seem to be an initial connection between this verse and the previous verses. On closer examination, however, this verse further emphasises the importance of *jihad* by using the example of the Israelites, who lived after the death of Prophet Moses and the attitude towards *jihad*.

The verse refers to a conversation between the elites of the Israelites with their Prophet appointed after Prophet Moses. This conversation may have been during the Period of Judges (circa 1150 BC—1025 BC) as referred to in the Bible. The verse at hand marks the end of this period, as in response to the request of the Jewish leaders, God appointed a king for the Jewish tribes to unite them and fight against the native Philistines, an ancient people who lived in Canaan. The Philistines had established military superiority over the Israelite tribes and defeated, plundered and enslaved them on many occasions. According to both Biblical and Muslim narrations, the prophet that the verse refers to is Prophet Samuel.

The dialogue between the Israelite leaders and Prophet Samuel is very interesting. The Jewish leaders ask Prophet Samuel to appoint a king so that they "may fight in the way of God" but when Prophet Samuel questions them further to understand their true intentions asking, "May it not be that you will not fight if fighting were prescribed for you?" They respond by saying that they would fight as "we have been expelled from our homes and [separated from] our children." In this way, they reveal that their true intentions were to return to their homes and save their children.

The dialogue reveals Prophet Samuel's doubts that the Israelites may not follow the appointed king to fight in the way of God, and instead they may try to pursue their own agenda. Prophet Samuel's fear was realised when a king was appointed, and fighting was prescribed upon the Israelites. Aside from a handful of sincere Israelites, many refused to go, and many others deserted their king in the battlefield.

As mentioned repeatedly in previous discussions, from the beginning of the study of the surah, all the examples about the Jews which are included in the Quran are also applicable to Muslims. The Quran does not demonise the Jews - rather it tells Muslims to take heed of the mistakes which the Jews made. Jews and Muslims are the same creation of God, both coming from the line of Prophet Abraham and having similar religions. They have the same inherent weaknesses, so therefore the Quran urges Muslims not to make the same mistakes as those who came before them.

However, when we look at the early history of Islam, despite all the warnings within the Quran, Muslims have committed many similar mistakes to those which the Jews had committed. Muslims disobeyed the Prophet, deserted him on the battlefield, refused to go to war when God commanded them to do so, and killed the grandchildren of the Prophet, when they believed it was politically justified.

People often lack true faith. In moments of comfort, they may reaffirm their faith and obedience to God, but when they are tested against their words they mostly fail. So, whenever the Jews are criticised in the Quran, we should consider it a criticism and point of reflection for Muslims too.

وَقَالَ لَهُمْ نَبِيُّهُمْ إِنَّ اللَّهَ قَدْ بَعَثَ لَكُمْ طَالُوتَ مَلِكًا ۚ قَالُوا أَنَّىٰ يَكُونُ لَهُ الْمُلْكُ عَلَيْنَا وَنَحْنُ أَحَقُّ بِالْمُلْكِ مِنْهُ وَلَمْ يُؤْتَ سَعَةً مِّنَ الْمَالِ ۚ قَالَ إِنَّ اللَّهَ اصْطَفَاهُ عَلَيْكُمْ وَزَادَهُ بَسْطَةً فِي الْعِلْمِ وَالْجِسْمِ ۖ وَاللَّهُ يُؤْتِي مُلْكَهُ مَن يَشَاءُ ۚ وَاللَّهُ وَاسِعٌ عَلِيمٌ ﴿247﴾

Their prophet said to them, 'God has appointed Saul as king for you.' They said, 'How can he have kingship over us, when we have a greater right to kingship than him, as he has not been given ample wealth?' He said, 'Indeed God has chosen him over you, and enhanced him vastly in knowledge and physique, and God gives His kingdom to whomever He wishes, and God is All-bounteous, All-knowing.'

Their prophet said to them, 'God has appointed Saul as king for you.' They said, 'How can he have kingship over us, when we have a greater right to kingship than him, as he has not been given ample wealth?' Saul was the first king of the Israelites after the Period of Judges, followed by King David and King Solomon. The appointment of Saul as king was a direct response to the request of the Israelites. But, as soon as God appointed Saul, they opposed his appointment on the grounds that he was neither rich nor one of the noblemen. The elites had expected Samuel to appoint one of them as their king. Although the Israelite elites asked Samuel to appoint a king; they did not ask God through Samuel. But Samuel knew that if he had appointed a king, they would have never followed him. Therefore, Samuel asked God to appoint a king to rule over the Israelites.

God's criterion for choosing a king differed from that of the elites. God does not judge people by wealth, lineage and power; even though people consider those to be the most important criteria. He chose Saul for his inner and outer qualities that the Israelite elites were too proud to notice. God had gifted Saul with knowledge and physical strength. The blessings that God had gifted to Saul shows that he was a friend of God, a man of great spiritual standing. God knew that he would lead the Israelites to a glorious victory.

Unfortunately, the Old Testament portrays a very disappointing image of figures such as Saul. Unlike the Quran, the Old Testament offers despicable depictions of some of the most respectable and honourable figures of faith. The case of Saul is one of the most damning examples. The Old Testament profiles Saul as a criminal and disobedient despot. Similar depictions also target David and Solomon in a similar manner.

Therefore, these misrepresentations provide important evidence for the distortion of the Old Testament. Otherwise, there is no other way to justify the inclusion of these nefarious attacks against noble figures. It may be that the culprits wanted to legitimise the misdeeds of those Israelite leaders who came after these noble figures. Their justification for committing evil deeds may have been made by claiming that Saul, David and Solomon also committed evil deeds, but still had a special status with God. Some of the stories included in the Old Testament portray the image of an unjust God who favours some figures regardless of what evil they have committed.

However, in the Quran, they are portrayed as exceptionally great people who have embodied both spiritual and worldly powers, yet show ultimate humility towards God and kindness to people and animals. They are presented as role models who people can aim to emulate to try to achieve a similar status to them by striving in the way of God.

God gives His kingdom to whomever He wishes; This statement provides an important insight into God's criteria for granting worldly power over his creation. He only grants this power to people of utmost spiritual strength and knowledge such as the Jewish prophet-kings and Prophet Muhammad. The Prophet never called himself a king, but he had all the powers of a king. Although kings and queens have ruled over many lands in this world, these would not be classified as God's Kingdom. It should be noted that "God gives His kingdom to whomever He wishes" should not be taken as a haphazard unwarranted choice. Rather, God's wish is based on wisdom, on *haqq* and justice.

The Israelites also challenged the Prophet by saying that he did not have any right over the spiritual kingdom because according to them only the descendants from the lineage of Jacob could be appointed as their king. However, the Quran objects to this line of argument *Or do they envy people for what God has given them of His blessing? But We had already given the family of Abraham the Scripture and wisdom and conferred upon them a great kingdom.* (Q 4:54) Therefore, anybody from the family of Prophet Abraham could have been blessed with that kingdom. Prophet Abraham was the first Imam of mankind, and in response to his exceptional spiritual elevation and prayer, God granted him the privilege of attaining the spiritual kingdom.

وَقَالَ لَهُمْ نَبِيُّهُمْ إِنَّ آيَةَ مُلْكِهِ أَن يَأْتِيَكُمُ التَّابُوتُ فِيهِ سَكِينَةٌ مِّن رَّبِّكُمْ وَبَقِيَّةٌ مِّمَّا تَرَكَ آلُ مُوسَىٰ وَآلُ هَارُونَ تَحْمِلُهُ الْمَلَائِكَةُ إِنَّ فِي ذَٰلِكَ لَآيَةً لَّكُمْ إِن كُنتُم مُّؤْمِنِينَ ﴿248﴾

Their prophet said to them, 'Indeed the sign of his kingship shall be that the Ark will come to you, bearing tranquility from your Lord and the relics left behind by the House of Moses and the House of Aaron, borne by the angels. There is indeed a sign in that for you, should you be faithful.'

Their prophet said to them, 'Indeed the sign of his kingship shall be that the Ark will come to you; God sent the Ark of the Covenant with Saul as evidence for his appointment over the Israelites when they refused Saul's kinship and demanded evidence from him. The Ark of the Covenant contained the stone tablets of the Ten Commandments that God revealed to Prophet Moses in writing.

According to the Bible, the Philistines had captured the Ark in the Battle of Shephelah. The Israelites considered the Ark of the Covenant as a representation of their identity, thus its capture was a source of great disappointment for the Israelites. Biblical accounts state that after they took it as war booty, the Philistines decided to return the Ark peacefully because different calamities befell them while they were in the possession of the Ark. This account does not make any sense as it would mean that the Philistines had believed in the spiritual status of the Ark and the divine status of Judaism, which was not the case. Rather, the Biblical accounts choose to ignore that the Ark was returned to the Israelites by God as a sign of Saul's kingship, probably because this information exposes the superficiality of faith of the Israelite leaders of the time.

"bearing tranquillity from your Lord", There are many narrations reported in Muslim sources on the meaning of tranquillity (*sakīna*) but these traditions seem to be under the influence of inaccurate legends, therefore there is no need to delve into them further.

A better way to understand the meaning of tranquillity is by looking to the Quran. In the Quran, tranquillity is a quality that comes to the heart which has already been conquered with faith: *It is Who sent down tranquillity (sakīna) into the hearts of the believers so that they may further enhance their faith.* (Q. 48:4) Therefore, it seems that that they received a feeling of fullness within their faith as a result of the tranquillity that they received. Jewish sources give further credence to this view that the Ark itself created this effect of tranquillity over the believers. They took it with them to battles so that it may give them tranquillity and courage to fight against their enemies. However, it is clear from the verse, that the Ark has this effect only on those hearts which already possessed firm faith. It would not have this effect on those hearts that have weak or superficial faith. Therefore, despite the existence of the Ark, the Israelites lost the battle against the Philistines.

the relics left behind by the House of Moses and the House of Aaron; According to Biblical sources, the Ark included the two stone tablets of the Ten Commandments and possibly the staff of Moses. As discussed previously, the Torah is the only Book of God, directly written by God and revealed as written tablets to Prophet Moses in Mount Sinai. It seems that the tablets were made of a special material such that Prophet Moses could easily carry them to his people. The Ark contained these original tablets and was very important to the Israelites. According to Shi'i narrations, the Ark still exists and is in the possession of the Twelfth Imam al-Mahdi.

فَلَمَّا فَصَلَ طَالُوتُ بِالْجُنُودِ قَالَ إِنَّ اللَّهَ مُبْتَلِيكُمْ بِنَهَرٍ فَمَنْ شَرِبَ مِنْهُ
فَلَيْسَ مِنِّي وَمَنْ لَمْ يَطْعَمْهُ فَإِنَّهُ مِنِّي إِلَّا مَنِ اغْتَرَفَ غُرْفَةً بِيَدِهِ فَشَرِبُوا
مِنْهُ إِلَّا قَلِيلًا مِنْهُمْ فَلَمَّا جَاوَزَهُ هُوَ وَالَّذِينَ آمَنُوا مَعَهُ قَالُوا لَا طَاقَةَ لَنَا
الْيَوْمَ بِجَالُوتَ وَجُنُودِهِ قَالَ الَّذِينَ يَظُنُّونَ أَنَّهُمْ مُلَاقُو اللَّهِ كَمْ مِنْ فِئَةٍ
قَلِيلَةٍ غَلَبَتْ فِئَةً كَثِيرَةً بِإِذْنِ اللَّهِ وَاللَّهُ مَعَ الصَّابِرِينَ ﴿249﴾

As Saul set out with the armies, he said, 'God will test you with a stream: anyone who drinks from it will not belong to me, but those who do not drink from it will belong to me, barring someone who draws a scoop with his hand.' But they drank from it, [all] except a few of them. So, when he crossed it along with the faithful who were with him, they said, 'We have no strength today against Goliath and his troops.' Those who were certain they will encounter God said, 'How many a small party has overcome a larger party by God's will! And God is with the patient.'

An important stylistic feature of the Quran is that it does not mention any irrelevant details of the stories it recounts, rather it focuses on the most important and relevant aspects. Similarly, here the verse omits the part of the story when the Israelite leaders eventually accepted Saul as their king. Saul then assembled his army to fight against the Philistines and they began to march towards the enemy lines.

As Saul set out with the armies; The Quran continues to narrate the event from this point. It is evident from the word "armies" that Saul raised a vast army. Every tribe of the Israelites dispatched their armies for this expedition. Despite the fact that the Israelites were given a divinely appointed king to lead them into the battle and witnessed the many signs supporting Saul, including the Ark, they began to disobey

Saul during this expedition. There are striking similarities between this event and some of the behaviour of the early Muslims when they disobeyed the Prophet at the Expedition of Tabuk (9/630). The hypocrites and those Muslims who had weak faith became comfortable with their gains, they abandoned their commitment to their faith and the Prophet. Instead of stating what was really in their hearts, they raised a number of excuses:

> Had there been a near gain, and an easy journey, certainly they would have followed you, but the distance was too far to them; yet they will swear by God: 'Had we been able, we would certainly have gone out with you', they destroy themselves. And God knows that verily they are liars. (Q. 9:42)

It is likely that the Israelites would have presented similar excuses. They were apathetic and simply wanted Saul to deliver a quick and miraculous victory without the Israelites having to confront the enemy and go through the trauma of fighting. However, in this world, God does not deliver quick victories; instead, he expects believers to exert their efforts and make sacrifices to achieve victory with the eventual support of God.

he said, 'God will test you with a stream: anyone who drinks from it will not belong to me, but those who do not drink from it will belong to me, barring someone who draws a scoop with his hand.' But they drank from it, [all] except a few of them. Saul understood that the majority of his army did not want to fight against the Philistines, and it would have been suicidal to start a fight with a disheartened army behind him. As a shrewd commander, he was after quality rather than the quantity. Therefore, he wanted to test his army in order to filter out the disloyal soldiers. Saul was aware that the support of God would only come to a fully committed army who was only fighting in the way of God. This was his only hope for victory as the Philistine army was much stronger than his army.

Therefore, he warned his army that they were approaching a stream and God would test them at the stream. Even though they were thirsty, the soldiers were not to drink from the stream. Those who were very thirsty were allowed to take a scoop of the water only with their hands. Those who drank water from the stream would be expelled from the army and Saul would continue with those who were obedient to his command.

Despite this warning from Saul, most of the army drank from the spring. Some took a scoop as they were permitted to do, and only a small number remained fully committed and did not drink at all. Saul expelled the disobedient majority from his army and continued with the remaining soldiers; those who did not drink at all and those who took a scoop. He was now aware that his army consisted of two ranks: the fully committed ones who would not waver in the battle and those he could not fully rely on.

So, when he crossed it along with the faithful who were with him, they said, 'We have no strength today against Goliath and his troops.' This statement was made by the ones who had drank a scoop with their hands, when they faced the army of Goliath. The reason Saul had taken this group with his army was to show the efficacy of God's test but also, by keeping this group in the army, Saul could give the appearance that he had a sizable army.

Those who were certain they will encounter God said, 'How many a small party has overcome a larger party by God's will! And God is with the patient.' On the other hand, those who were loyal to Saul reaffirmed their commitment. This is a very important event that demonstrates how the victory of God unfolds in the moment of need. It is all about sincerity and commitment; so long as believers fill their hearts with these two main elements and strive to fight in the way of God, victory is achieved eventually. However, if they lack commitment and sincerity, it is inevitable that they shall lose against superior forces.

وَلَمَّا بَرَزُوا لِجَالُوتَ وَجُنُودِهِ قَالُوا رَبَّنَا أَفْرِغْ عَلَيْنَا صَبْرًا وَثَبِّتْ أَقْدَامَنَا وَانصُرْنَا عَلَى الْقَوْمِ الْكَافِرِينَ ﴿250﴾

So, when they marched out for [encounter with] Goliath and his troops, they said, 'Our Lord, pour patience upon us, make our feet steady, and assist us against the faithless lot.'

The mindset of Saul and those Israelites of strong faith who did not drink any water from the stream is well described in this verse. They were firm in their pledge that they did not run away when faced with death. They were convinced that the support of God was with them against all odds and, most importantly, they understood the source of their strength came from God alone. This is a concise way of explaining the secret to success, for those who strive in the way of God to defeat their aggressors: absolute dedication, patience, humility and being aware of the fact that success only comes with the permission of God Almighty.

فَهَزَمُوهُم بِإِذْنِ اللَّهِ وَقَتَلَ دَاوُودُ جَالُوتَ وَآتَاهُ اللَّهُ الْمُلْكَ وَالْحِكْمَةَ وَعَلَّمَهُ مِمَّا يَشَاءُ وَلَوْلَا دَفْعُ اللَّهِ النَّاسَ بَعْضَهُم بِبَعْضٍ لَّفَسَدَتِ الْأَرْضُ وَلَٰكِنَّ اللَّهَ ذُو فَضْلٍ عَلَى الْعَالَمِينَ ﴿251﴾

Thus, they routed them with God's will, and David killed Goliath, and God gave him the kingdom and wisdom, and taught him whatever He liked. Were it not for God's repelling the people by means of one another, the earth would surely have been corrupted; but God is gracious to the people.

Thus, they routed them with God's will; According to the sources, the remaining loyal Israelites in the army of Saul were no more than a few hundred, yet they routed the massive army of Philistines with the support of God. It seemed that this small group was marching towards certain death, but God granted them success without even having to engage in a full-fledged war.

and David killed Goliath; David responded to Goliath's hand-in-hand combat challenge and killed him effortlessly. Goliath was a fearsome warrior and was a source of morale for the Philistinian army. David on the other hand was a young boy of around 14-15 years old who was there to bring food to his brother. He was not even old enough to be included in the army. But once he saw how Goliath boasted about his strength and bravery, and no one from Saul's army dared to meet him in the field, he took it upon himself to fight Goliath. When the Philistinian army witnessed how David defeated Goliath, they were demoralised and began to retreat.

and God gave him the kingdom and wisdom, and taught him whatever He liked. Several years after the victory against the Philistinians, Saul died, and God endowed David with the overarching rule over all the Israelites, which took place gradually. As mentioned above, Jewish sources provide an appalling depiction of Saul, including his "fear" of facing Goliath in a duel. They claim that David was braver than Saul, and for this reason, he deserved to be the king more than Saul. However, these arguments do not align with the reality of the battlefield. Saul was the commander of the army and commanders do not engage in duels. His mission was to unite and command his army on the battlefield and God granted the honour of defeating Goliath to David, thus paving the way for his appointment as the next king-prophet of the Jews.

This story is reminiscent of an event that occurred during the Battle of the Trench. The polytheist army besieged Medina but were stopped by the canal made around Medina by Muslims. The strongest man from the Arabs, 'Amr b. 'Abd Wudd crossed the trench and challenged the Muslims army to a duel. Like Goliath, he was the most fearsome warrior from the Quraysh and none of the Companions dared to face him in the battlefield. He repeated his challenge several times and mocked Muslims, but only Imam Ali responded to his call. The

Prophet did not face 'Amr b. 'Abd al-Wudd in the battlefield, because he was the commander of the army, thus was not meant to engage in a duel. Finally, the Quran praises Saul greatly and there is no reason to believe that the Biblical accounts of Saul are accurate.

Were it not for God's repelling the people by means of one another, the earth would surely have been corrupted; but God is gracious to the people. The commentators have provided different explanations regarding this statement. One explanation fits well with the context of the verse, while the others seem to be out of context. According to this explanation, God uses believers to prevent evil from overtaking the world. He encourages and supports believers to fight against evil in order to remove them from power so that the world can remain a suitable place for the spiritual growth of people. The idea is mentioned elsewhere in the Quran:

> Those who were expelled from their homes unjustly, only because they said, 'God is our Lord.' Had not God repulsed the people from one another, ruin would have befallen the monasteries, churches, synagogues and mosques in which God's Name is mentioned greatly. God will surely help those who help Him. Indeed, God is All-strong, All-mighty. (Q. 22:40)

Interestingly, this verse implies that God is not concerned about the places of worship such as monasteries, churches, synagogues and mosques as buildings. Rather, the factor that warrants God's concern is that these are places of worship. And he defends these places of worship through his support and encouragement of the faithful people.

The word "corruption" used here, most probably, alludes to the disappearance of faith. According to God, the most abhorrent corruption on the earth is the cessation of faith in God and the triumph of disbelief. Had Goliath succeeded, he would have uprooted the Jewish faith and disbelief would have become widespread. God wanted to prevent this with the help of Saul's army. This outlook goes against the idea of pacifism in religion. The Quran rejects complete pacifism and expects the believers to defend their lives, lands, and faith.

تِلْكَ آيَاتُ اللَّهِ نَتْلُوهَا عَلَيْكَ بِالْحَقِّ ۚ وَإِنَّكَ لَمِنَ الْمُرْسَلِينَ ﴿252﴾

These are the signs of God which We recite for you in truth, and you are indeed one of the apostles.

This verse ends the Quranic account of the episode of King Saul's encounter with Goliath. The incident is referred to as one of "the signs of God" in order to demonstrate how God appoints spiritually strong believers to overcome the prejudice of people and enemies of God. If God wishes, he could bestow special powers on selected people who have already achieved certain qualities to defeat the mightiest of armies against all odds. However, God's support only comes to sincere, committed and patient people; their spiritual strength attracts the support of God magnetically. Thus, with the help of God, they may achieve victory. This is the sign of God; that he supports people of high spiritual calibre.

One other important point to note is that although most of the Israelites were weak in their faith, the victory still came to them because of that committed minority.

تِلْكَ الرُّسُلُ فَضَّلْنَا بَعْضَهُمْ عَلَىٰ بَعْضٍ ۘ مِّنْهُم مَّن كَلَّمَ اللَّهُ ۖ وَرَفَعَ بَعْضَهُمْ دَرَجَاتٍ ۚ وَآتَيْنَا عِيسَى ابْنَ مَرْيَمَ الْبَيِّنَاتِ وَأَيَّدْنَاهُ بِرُوحِ الْقُدُسِ ۗ وَلَوْ شَاءَ اللَّهُ مَا اقْتَتَلَ الَّذِينَ مِن بَعْدِهِم مِّن بَعْدِ مَا جَاءَتْهُمُ الْبَيِّنَاتُ وَلَٰكِنِ اخْتَلَفُوا فَمِنْهُم مَّنْ آمَنَ وَمِنْهُم مَّن كَفَرَ ۚ وَلَوْ شَاءَ اللَّهُ مَا اقْتَتَلُوا وَلَٰكِنَّ اللَّهَ يَفْعَلُ مَا يُرِيدُ ﴿253﴾

These are the apostles, some of whom We gave an advantage over others: of them are those to whom God spoke, and some of them He raised in rank, and We gave Jesus, son of Mary, manifest proofs and strengthened him with the Holy Spirit. Had God wished, those who succeeded them would not have fought each other after the manifest proofs had come to them. But they differed. So, there were among them those who had faith and there were among them those who were faithless, and had God wished, they would not have fought one another; but God does whatever He wills.

These are the apostles, some of whom We gave an advantage over others; This verse mentions the "advantage" of some prophets over others and it is intriguingly placed straight after an episode in which Prophet David's name is mentioned. There is another example of this in the Quran where again the advantage of some prophets is mentioned together with Prophet David: *Your Lord is most knowing whoever is in the heavens and the earth. We gave an advantage to some prophets over others, and to David we gave the book [of Psalms].* (Q.17:55)

The advantage of prophets comes as a grace from God; it is not something earned by the prophets themselves. There are many blessings that have been given to people in this world as a direct result of the grace of God. For example, some people are more intelligent, or are more spiritual, or have more strength, or are better looking. These blessings are not earned, rather, they are gifts from God as a result of God's grace and wisdom. If God had created every creature equally, the world would be a very strange place. People are not equal in their capacity and spirituality. In the case of the prophets, it may be that these advantages were given to them for the benefit of the people around them, as these special advantages made it possible for people to be reminded of God and his bounties. For example, Prophet David had great courage to kill Goliath effortlessly. Furthermore, he was given many other advantages which made the Israelites accept his kingship without any overwhelming dispute.

Of them are those to whom God spoke, and some of them He raised in rank; God mentions the advantages of some prophets over others in the context of discussion between the Jews of Medina and Prophet Muhammad. A great portion of Surah al-Baqarah is dedicated to discussions and disputes that the Jews raised against the Prophet. In this verse God communicates his message, that Prophet Muhammad is given an advantage over other prophets. Like people, prophets are not created equally, and divine wisdom dictates the necessity of the advantages.

of them are those to whom God spoke, and some of them He raised in rank; God spoke to Prophet Moses without mediation of any angel; and he raised the rank of Prophet Muhammad, since the whole dispute is about the Prophets who came after Moses and were rejected by the Jews.

and We gave Jesus, son of Mary, manifest proofs and strengthened him with the Holy Spirit. Despite the manifest proofs given to Prophet Jesus, which included raising the dead, healing the blind and the leper and giving life to birds made of clay, most of the Jews rejected him and disputed over his case, in the same way as they disputed with Prophet Muhammad. Most commentators believe that the Holy Spirit referred to in this verse is Angel Gabriel. Here, Jesus is specifically mentioned to be supported by Angel Gabriel, even though all the prophets were supported by him, because he was supported by Gabriel from his cradle to his ascension in every way while other prophets only received revelation from Gabriel.

Had God wished, those who succeeded them would not have fought each other after the manifest proofs had come to them. But they differed. At this point, the verse explains why religious people and groups fight amongst themselves. The religion has come to remove differences which often lead to violence. Although the religion aims to bring justice and peace, some people have committed the most heinous crimes against humanity in the name of religion, including sectarian violence. Sectarian fighting within Judaism, Christianity and Islam has demonstrated throughout history that the followers of the Abrahamic religions have completely misunderstood and wrongly practised their religion. The acts of murdering and enslaving fellow believers completely go against the spirit and teachings of all the Abrahamic faiths.

This section of the verse details the overarching message that God Almighty had given the followers of the Abrahamic religion clear evidence through the prophets. Yet they still chose to dispute and fight despite the clear evidence and sometimes even about this evidence. The verse indicates that it was not ignorance or misunderstanding which led to these disputes. Rather, these fights were waged based on selfishness, greed and arrogance. Those who chose to disobey the teachings of the faith did not believe in the clear evidence of God, as the verse describes.

So, there were among them those who had faith and there were among them those who were faithless; These were not "faithless" in the sense that they did not believe in God, rather they did not have faith in the clear evidence that God had sent down about *who* should lead people in the name of religion. It is often the case that although people believed in the basic tenets of the faith and followed the rituals scrupulously, their opinion on the leadership differed. This is because leadership entails power and influence and people have an inherent propensity to love power. For this reason, they chose to follow those who empower them not based on their merit and the needs of the faith and the society but based upon mutual interest.

and had God wished, they would not have fought one another; God does not interfere directly in human affairs. He could have forced people to follow his instructions, but this would go against the idea of free will and most importantly, it would undermine the test that people must face in this world. When the great prophets of God arrived with great signs, including Moses, David, Solomon, Jesus and Muhammad, the people believed in them unequivocally. They produced such an overwhelming array of evidence and miracles that the people had no option but to follow them. However, when these prophets passed away, God tested the people to see if they would continue to follow the teachings of these prophets and their rightful successors. The environment at the time provided a great challenge for those followers who were not sincere and had not committed their faith deep within their hearts. Thus, they eventually faltered and are a lesson for us all to take heed of.

but God does whatever He wills. Certainly, God's will is based on wisdom - one can even say that it is wisdom itself. Adding this phrase to the end of the verse means that although God could have stopped them fighting and intervened in their decisions, this would have been against God's wisdom which is to give them free will to be tried and tested by their actions. *Had God wished, He would have brought them together on guidance. So do not be one of the ignorant.* (Q. 6:35)

يَا أَيُّهَا الَّذِينَ آمَنُوا أَنفِقُوا مِمَّا رَزَقْنَاكُم مِّن قَبْلِ أَن يَأْتِيَ يَوْمٌ لَّا بَيْعٌ فِيهِ
وَلَا خُلَّةٌ وَلَا شَفَاعَةٌ وَالْكَافِرُونَ هُمُ الظَّالِمُونَ ﴿254﴾

O you who have faith! Spend out of what We have provided you before there comes a day on which there will be no bargaining, neither friendship, nor intercession. And the faithless—they are the wrongdoers.

O you who have faith! Spend out of what We have provided you; The verse refers back to previous verses (244 and 245) on spending in the way of God, especially on matters related to *jihad*. The chapter then moves on to provide examples of previous nations who refused to participate in *jihad*, some of whom did not even want to provide financial support for it. This verse reinforces the importance of spending in the way of God, especially to defend the faith and faithful against aggressors.

before there comes a day on which there will be no bargaining, neither friendship, nor intercession. Some say "a day" here refers to the Day of Judgment, whilst others say it is the moment of death because that is the moment when no one can benefit from intercession. Both views may be correct, as when a person dies, they depart this world, therefore they have no opportunity to rectify their affairs nor would any friendship avail them and no one could intercede for them. In the same way, there will be no intercession on the Day of Judgment unless it is authorised by God. Other than that, no being is allowed to provide intercession independently. Some misguided people have claimed that due to their lineage or religious affiliation to a certain faith or sect they would be entitled to intercession, but as the verse elucidates, this is false.

And the faithless—they are the wrongdoers. This signifies that the most notorious wrongdoers among the people are the faithless. This is because they go against their nature and due to their unrestrained desires, they rebel against God and attempt to disrupt the balance that he has created in this world. Most importantly, they destroy the prospect of their spiritual advancement and lead themselves into eternal damnation.

اللَّهُ لَا إِلَٰهَ إِلَّا هُوَ الْحَيُّ الْقَيُّومُ لَا تَأْخُذُهُ سِنَةٌ وَلَا نَوْمٌ لَهُ مَا فِي السَّمَاوَاتِ
وَمَا فِي الْأَرْضِ مَنْ ذَا الَّذِي يَشْفَعُ عِنْدَهُ إِلَّا بِإِذْنِهِ يَعْلَمُ مَا بَيْنَ أَيْدِيهِمْ
وَمَا خَلْفَهُمْ وَلَا يُحِيطُونَ بِشَيْءٍ مِنْ عِلْمِهِ إِلَّا بِمَا شَاءَ وَسِعَ كُرْسِيُّهُ
السَّمَاوَاتِ وَالْأَرْضَ وَلَا يَئُودُهُ حِفْظُهُمَا وَهُوَ الْعَلِيُّ الْعَظِيمُ ﴿255﴾

Allah—there is no god except Him— is the Living One, the All-sustainer. Neither drowsiness befalls Him nor sleep. To Him belongs whatever is in the heavens and whatever is on the earth. Who is it that may intercede with Him except with His permission? He knows that which is before them and that which is behind them, and they do not comprehend anything of His knowledge except what He wishes. His seat embraces the heavens and the earth, and He is not wearied by their preservation, and He is the All-exalted, the All-supreme.

This verse is the well-known *Ayāt al-Kursī*. Both Sunni and Shi'i narrations hold the recitation of this verse in high esteem especially in moments of need and despair as well as for spiritual elevation. It was named *Ayāt al-Kursī* and referred to as such during the lifetime of the Prophet by the Prophet himself. This highlights its importance in being singled out from the rest of the surah. Many traditions refer to it as "the greatest verse in the Quran and the master (*sayyid*) of all verses of the Quran."

Allah—there is no god except Him—is the Living One, the All-sustainer. The introduction to the verse provides the most comprehensive description of God by using two of the most inclusive names of God – "the Living One, the All-sustainer". These are attributes of his essence and the attributes of his acts. That is why it is reported from Imam Ali that:

> I heard your Prophet atop these wooden planks [of the pulpit] saying, 'If one recites *Ayāt al-Kursī* after every obligatory (daily) prayer then nothing holds him back from entering Paradise except death; and none shall be able to persist in (doing) this except one who is sincere or one who is a (true) worshipper. And one who recites it when going to bed, God protects him, his neighbour, his neighbour's neighbour and [all] the houses that are around him.'[324]

In another report he said, "I heard the Messenger of God saying, 'O Ali there are fifty words in it, in each of which is fifty *baraka* (blessing, grace, abundant good).'"[325]

Allah—there is no god except Him— The name Allah appears in the Quran close to 1000 times. It is a name that refers to the sum total of his essence and attributes, including perfection, beauty, omniscience, omnipresence and omnipotence. The name Allah is like an acronym for all the attributes and beautiful names of God. It invokes that essence who is the most merciful (*al-Raḥīm*), the most powerful (*al-Qādir*), the most forgiving (*al-Ghafūr*), and the most wise (*al-Ḥakīm*). So, it means "the Being who concentrates in himself all the attributes of perfection." Therefore, although God can be considered through his different names and attributes (*asmā'* and *ṣifāt*) all of which refer to the same essence, when the name Allah is used it combines all of those attributes and beautiful names.

The word Allah is either derived from the verb *walaha* which means to confound and perplex, or, from the word *ilāh* which means the one who is yearned for, adored and worthy of worship. The definitive *al* (the) has been added to it to denote the only true being who is worthy of worship. Thus, the name Allah refers to that being about whom the creation is confounded and perplexed in understanding his reality and essence, yet all of creation yearns for him, adores him and worships him.

Allah has become a proper noun which refers to that absolute necessary existence who possesses all the attributes of perfection and is free from any type of deficiency. Although he is that being about whom all creation is perplexed, at the same time he is the most apparent existence. He is *the First and the Last, the Manifest and the Hidden, and He has knowledge of all things.* (Q. 57:3) Reflecting on the creation, the magnificence of the universe, and how its different components interact, leads us to a realisation of the uniqueness of the one who created it, and the astonishment, admiration and bewilderment that he invokes in the hearts and minds of all creation.

Is the Living One (*al-ḥayy*); God is the source of all life. The only originally living being. Anything that appears to be alive inherits its sense of "life" from his attribute of *al-Hayy*. He is ever-living or *al-ḥayy* not in the way his creation is alive but rather as the Being who never experiences death and who never had a birth. *Every soul will experience death* (Q. 29:57) except him. The verse is therefore driving the faithful to *put your trust in the Living One who dies not.* (Q. 25:58)

Al-Ḥayy along with *al-Qādir* (omnipotent) and *al-'Ālim* (omniscient) are the divine attributes of essence (*dhāt*), the primary attributes to which all other attributes of *dhāt* are subcategories.

the All-sustainer (*al-Qayyūm*). As *al-Ḥayy* is the mother of all attributes of essence (*dhāt*), al-*Qayyūm* is the mother of all divine attributes of acts (*fi'l*) such as *al-Khāliq* (the Creator), *al-Rāziq* (the Provider), *al-Muḥiyy* (the Giver of life), *al-Mumīt* (the Taker of life), *al-Mubdi'* (the Originator) and *al-Mu'īd* (the Resurrector). Together they describe God with all his attributes. *Al-Qayyūm* is from *qiyām* which literally means to stand on one's feet and, figuratively, it means to stand for a cause or to attend to something, upholding it, protecting it, managing it, and having power over it. *Is He who sustains every soul along with what it earns [comparable to the idols]? And yet they ascribe partners to God! Say, Name them!* (Q. 13:33)

If God were to stop maintaining and upholding the universe – whose existence is only as real as it is connected to him – then all besides him would simply vanish out of existence. *Indeed, God sustains the heavens and the earth lest they should fall apart, and if they were to fall apart there is none who can sustain them except Him.* (Q. 35:41) God does not simply create in detachment. He is constantly sustaining his creation and involved in their affairs, and they subsist through him alone. *Everyone in the heavens and the earth asks Him. Every day He is engaged in some work.* (Q. 55:29)

Knowing that there is only one true Lord of the universe and its dimensions gives tranquillity to the hearts of the believers. It reassures the believers that despite all the hostile forces and uncertainty in the universe, there is one creator who oversees everything, and whatever happens in this world shall become coherent in the end.

Neither drowsiness befalls him nor sleep. This phrase is mentioned as evidence for the attribute of the All-sustainer. It is also a statement to help man realise the fallacy of attempting to understand God in human terms. All the verses of the Quran warn us against falling into the trap of anthropomorphising God. To be able to sustain everything within the universe requires constant alertness for the needs of the sustained and that means that God is always alert. The whole of creation will fall apart if God takes away his attention even for one second.

"To Him belongs whatever is in the heavens and whatever is on the earth." God has created and sustained the universe, therefore of course everything belongs to him alone. This idea of ownership is different to the kind of ownership people have in this world. In this world people own things through convention, contract or inheritance, yet people have no control over sustaining their belongings; rather, their belongings exist independently of them. However, God's possession is an entirely different type of possession. It is absolute dependence of the possessed on the possessor at all times and for all things.

Who is it that may intercede with Him except with His permission? The system of intercession runs throughout nature as it runs in sentient interactions. The word 'who' (*man*) is used in the verse, which is usually only for sentient beings, because intercession with God is a universal phenomenon. Every cause intercedes with God for its effect.

Nothing works on its own accord and its own power in creation. Realising this truth, one might wonder about the system of causality in the world and the significance of the chain of causes and effects. The Asharite scholars like Ghazali negated the idea of causality. This verse explains that all causes are intermediaries. They just "intercede" by bringing about things -their effects- with the leave of God. The angels are intercessors who bring blessings to the world. The sun intercedes to bring the bounties of God to Earth. None of these causes can work except with his leave. God has set in place an order so that all things have a cause, and all matters occur only through cause-and-effect.

Ultimately, there is no authority except that of God and he is the only up-keeper (*al-qayyūm*) of all matters. That is why the Quran attributes events to God directly at times, and in other instances interchanges their attribution to their causes, emphasising that the ultimate power rests in him.

> Indeed, your Lord is God, who created the heavens and the earth in six days, and then settled on the Throne, directing the command.

> There is no intercessor, except by His leave. That is God, your Lord! So, worship Him. Will you not then take admonition? (Q. 10:3)

He knows that which is before them and that which is behind them; The expression "directing the command" in the above verse, (Q. 10:3) makes it clear that God is in charge of managing his creation. When God's mediums, such as angels, manage creation under the supervision of God, they may have some knowledge of what they are doing, but they cannot see the complete overall picture. Only God has the full picture and plan before him. He has the knowledge of the consequences of everything happening in the universe. Most importantly, only God knows the purpose of creation and neither the angels nor the prophets have the full knowledge of the direction of creation. No one aside from God knows where he is taking all of creation to.

In this sense, created beings are like infants - their parent may take them somewhere, but the infant cannot grasp what is really happening. God has given us some basic information about the purpose of creation, but he gives knowledge in accordance with the capacity of the person. Prophets, Imams and saints have greater comprehension to receive more knowledge in accordance with their capacity, whilst normal people receive less information again in accordance with their capacity- but none see the whole picture. No one knows what passed billions of years before them nor can they know what will go ahead in times yet to come.

and they do not comprehend anything of His knowledge except what He wishes. Knowledge is not independent of God. The knowledge that the intermediary causes have, especially those with life and intellect, is derived from his knowledge. Thus, none of them can proceed against the will and decree of God in any way, since they only know as much as he wishes them to know. Life, power, and knowledge belong to God alone, and he gives anyone as much or as little as he wishes.

A striking point about the superb eloquence of the verse is that the word "knowledge" (*'ilm*) in the preceding sentence ["He knows"] changes to the word "comprehension" (*iḥāṭa*) ["they do not comprehend"] in this sentence. This change highlights that they have no knowledge at all and do not "know" anything. They can only "encompass" and draw out from what God knows and his knowledge to the degree that he allows; "and they do not comprehend any of his knowledge" may also refer to the knowledge about God, of his essence and attributes. Therefore, no one can know anything about God except to the limit that he wishes.

His seat embraces the heavens and the earth; There is a difference between *'arsh* (*throne*) and seat (*kursī*). Although both may be used by a king, they are utilised for two different positions of authority or audience. Generally, a king's throne or seat represents his authority. Hence *'arsh* and *kursī* signify two different levels of the authority of God. Therefore, "his seat embraces the heavens and the earth" is a metaphoric reference to God's universal dominion, power, absolute control and authority. The *kursī* does not have a physical space somewhere in this universe; rather, it encompasses both the heavens and the earth, but is not within it. It is outside of space and time.

Some have imagined the "seat" and the "throne" of God in literal sense due to their anthropomorphic understanding of God. They have also understood it literally as a place where God sits. Razi explains that correct reports have stated that the *kursī* is a huge body under the *'arsh* and above the seventh heaven. Razi then goes on to offer other metaphoric meanings for the *kursī,* such as the authority (*sulṭān*), power (*qudra*) and dominion (*mulk*) of God or God's knowledge because it is the "seat" of the All-knowing. He then refers to the literal meaning and says, "ignoring the apparent meaning without proof is impermissible."[326] However, most Muslims, and the Imams of the Ahl al-Bayt in particular, have insisted that God has no physical form, nor can he be confined to a fixed place or ascribed any limitation, such as being bound by time and space. Imam Rida describes God as, "He is not in anything or above anything."[327]

The traditions from the Ahl al-Bayt tell us that the whole creation is in the *kursī* and the *kursī* is inside the *'arsh,* and the *'arsh* is carried by God. Furthermore, it is reported from the Prophet,

> 'The seven heavens and the seven earths in the Seat are but like a ring thrown in a vast open space.' Then he said, 'And surely the excellence of the Throne (*'arsh*) over the Seat (*kursī*) is like that of the open space over the ring.[328]

This hadith shows that "His seat embraces the heavens and the earth" means that it extends beyond them and encompasses them fully, rather than simply referring to how wide and vast they are in the physical sense. In another magnificent hadith, Hannān b. Sadīr asks Imam Jafar al-Sadiq about the throne and the seat. He replied,

> Indeed, the Throne has many diverse attributes. God uses in the Quran various adjectives to describe its various aspects. He says: '*and He is the Lord of the Great Throne.*' (Q. 9:129) It means, Lord of the great kingdom or authority. And He says: '*the All-beneficent, settled on the Throne.*' (Q. 20:5) It means that God is firm in his kingdom. It is the knowledge of the 'how' things. Also, the Throne is distinct from the Seat; and together they are two of the greatest doors of the unseen, and they both are unseen, and they are together in the unseen. The Seat is the manifest door of the unseen, from which appears creation and from which all the things come. Whilst the Throne is the concealed door of the unseen in which is found the knowledge of the states and conditions, and existence of measure and limits, [knowledge] of will and intention, as well as the knowledge of words, ac-

> tions and omissions, and the knowledge of the beginning and the return. Thus, the Seat and the Throne are two gates of knowledge joined together, because the dominion of the Throne is other than the dominion of the Seat, and its (the Throne's) knowledge is more hidden than the knowledge of the Seat.[329]

This narration is astonishing in the depth of knowledge that it conveys; something that cannot be found anywhere but with the Holy Family. The statement, "the Seat is the manifest door of the unseen" may be understood in the light of the Seat representing the level of the knowledge of measured things nearer to our material world, whereas the Throne represents infinite knowledge which has no limits. That is the realm of *There is not a thing but that its sources are with Us, and We do not send it down except in a known measure.* (Q. 15:21)

He is not wearied by their preservation; God is the only true independent reality and all else is constantly perishing unless preserved by him. The relationship of God to his creation is like that of a thinker to his thoughts or the sun to its rays and not that of a builder to a building. Creation cannot exist on its own without the *Rabb al-'ālamīn* - One who constantly sustains the Universe. "He is not wearied" is mentioned because man immediately tries to understand what he hears or reads in terms of his own experience. Constant preservation of a thing – even if it is just a thought – would tire and exhaust man. However, God does not rely on a physical body or any medium to preserve or maintain what he creates.

and He is the All-exalted, the All-supreme. The All-exalted (*al-'aliyy*) is translated as "the most high" but since God is not "above" or at any fixed location, its meaning is that God is too exalted and "high" to be comprehended by any of his creation. The All-supreme (*al-'aẓīm*), another of God's beautiful names, is also an exaltation of God as being too great and mighty to be fathomed by anyone or anything. His *'aẓama* (greatness) is known by the greatness of his creation.

لَا إِكْرَاهَ فِي الدِّينِ ۖ قَد تَّبَيَّنَ الرُّشْدُ مِنَ الْغَيِّ ۚ فَمَن يَكْفُرْ بِالطَّاغُوتِ وَيُؤْمِن
بِاللَّهِ فَقَدِ اسْتَمْسَكَ بِالْعُرْوَةِ الْوُثْقَىٰ لَا انفِصَامَ لَهَا ۗ وَاللَّهُ سَمِيعٌ عَلِيمٌ ﴿256﴾

There is no compulsion in religion: rectitude has become distinct from error. So, one who disavows the Rebels and has faith in God has held fast to the firmest handle for which there is no breaking; and God is All-hearing, All-knowing.

There is no compulsion in religion: Earlier commentators struggled to explain this phrase because they saw an apparent contradiction between this verse and the verses regarding *jihad*. This problem emerges due to a misunderstanding and misinterpretation of the concept of *jihad* in the Quran. As explained previously, *jihad* may only be warranted in cases of self-defence. However, some early Muslims relished waging war and thus pillaged, killed and enslaved many; thereby, leaving behind a troublesome legacy. That is why some Muslims commentators have claimed that this verse was abrogated by the verses about *jihad*. The earlier discussions have made it clear that faith is a matter of the heart and cannot be forced upon people by the sword.

There are numerous traditions in Islamic sources that collectively point out that this verse was revealed in response to some Muslim families who converted to Islam, but their children did not want to become Muslim. The traditions name different individuals, but overall it becomes clear that contextually the verse is addressing some Muslims in Medina who were worried about their children's reluctance to convert to Islam. These Muslims wanted to convert their children forcefully.

However, as the verse clearly indicates, it is never possible to force people to believe, even one's own children. Converting people by force goes against the fundamental ethos in Islam and may only create hypocrites who pretend to have faith. Hypocrisy is one of the most despised acts in the eyes of God and it would be an extremely vicious practice to make people hypocrites forcefully. Faith is an act of the heart, established through free will. The verses emphasis that by the revelation of Islam, the guidance has been established clearly and after this point if people decide to turn away from the faith, it is their own misjudgment to do so. They are free to choose in this world, but in the Hereafter, they would pay a hefty price for their misguided decisions. *And had your Lord wished, all those who are on earth would have believed. Would you then force people until they become faithful?* (Q. 10:99)

The verse states the obvious; that it is impossible to force people to embrace faith; they are created by God to make their own decisions. God is only responsible for conveying the evidence to people through his prophets. Although the prophets should represent the evidence of faith in the best possible manner, it is up to the people to decide. *The truth has been clarified by your Lord, so whoever wishes would believe and whoever wishes would reject.* (Q. 18:29)

So, one who disavows the Rebels and has faith in God has held fast to the firmest handle for which there is no breaking. Faith in God is not sufficient to become a true believer. Believers should first disavow those who are openly antagonistic to the authority of God (*Ṭāghūt*) and transgress against his will. If believers achieve this, they become true believers, and thus get the firm grip of "the firmest handle for which there is no breaking." So long as believers keep away from following *Ṭāghūt*, this grip remains firm.

اللَّهُ وَلِيُّ الَّذِينَ آمَنُوا يُخْرِجُهُم مِّنَ الظُّلُمَاتِ إِلَى النُّورِ ۖ وَالَّذِينَ كَفَرُوا
أَوْلِيَاؤُهُمُ الطَّاغُوتُ يُخْرِجُونَهُم مِّنَ النُّورِ إِلَى الظُّلُمَاتِ ۗ أُولَٰئِكَ
أَصْحَابُ النَّارِ ۖ هُمْ فِيهَا خَالِدُونَ ﴿257﴾

God is the Guardian of the faithful: He brings them out of darkness into light. As for the faithless, their patrons are the Rebels (Ṭāghūt), who drive them out of light into darkness. They shall be the inmates of the Fire, and they shall remain in it [forever].

The previous verse stated that God's guidance and misguidance has been clarified for people. The verse at hand then goes on to explain that for those who choose to have faith and disavow the *Ṭāghūt,* God becomes their guardian (*walī*). Those who choose to disbelieve and turn actively against God, the *Ṭāghūt* or the Rebels become their guardian. The verse explains a process which includes those who choose to embrace Islam and those who choose to turn away from Islam and openly fight against it. It also includes those who are born as faithful and who have been believers for a long period of time. God Almighty continuously takes them towards the light, and the deeper they go into the faith, the more God takes them into the light.

Conversely, those who choose to disbelieve and turn against God actively, their patron, *Ṭāghūt,* takes them further into darkness. *Ṭāghūt* drives disbelievers "out of light into darkness". However, as disbelievers they have never been in the light in a way that they could be taken out from it.

Commentators have expressed various opinions to explain this challenge, but Tabatabai presented the best clarification.[330] He says that when all people mature in their intellect, their intellect becomes their light. This is called the light of *fiṭra* or natural disposition. Human *fiṭra* has a natural propensity towards God, like a magnet constantly drawn towards its creator. At this state, people are also in darkness; although their *fiṭra* draws them towards the light and God, they do not know how to reach him due to lack of guidance and knowledge of the faith. The light of *fiṭra* is built within human nature, but there is also the darkness of obliviousness about the details of the faith, knowledge of God, and the right way to worship him.

By the virtue of true faith, God will take people out of the darkness of obliviousness and ignorance and carry them towards true light by showing them the ways of worship and self-purification. On the other hand, when people disbelieve in the guidance of God, *Ṭāghūt* would take them away from the light of *fiṭra* into absolute darkness. The next verses give three examples of how God takes people from darkness into light and how *Ṭāghūt* takes people from light into darkness.

أَلَمْ تَرَ إِلَى الَّذِي حَاجَّ إِبْرَاهِيمَ فِي رَبِّهِ أَنْ آتَاهُ اللَّهُ الْمُلْكَ إِذْ قَالَ إِبْرَاهِيمُ
رَبِّيَ الَّذِي يُحْيِي وَيُمِيتُ قَالَ أَنَا أُحْيِي وَأُمِيتُ قَالَ إِبْرَاهِيمُ فَإِنَّ اللَّهَ يَأْتِي
بِالشَّمْسِ مِنَ الْمَشْرِقِ فَأْتِ بِهَا مِنَ الْمَغْرِبِ فَبُهِتَ الَّذِي كَفَرَ وَاللَّهُ لَا
يَهْدِي الْقَوْمَ الظَّالِمِينَ ﴿258﴾

Have you not regarded him who argued with Abraham about his Lord, because God had given him kingdom? When Abraham said, 'My Lord is He who gives life and brings death,' he replied, 'I [too] give life and bring death.' Abraham said, 'Indeed, God brings the sun from the east; now you bring it from the west.' There at the faithless one was dumbfounded. And God does not guide the wrongdoing lot.

The first example shows how *Ṭāghūt* takes disbelievers from light into darkness. This verse details a debate between Prophet Abraham and a king, who from Biblical sources is understood to be Nimrud, the mighty king of Babylonia in today's Iraq. At the time, Babylonia was the strongest civilisation in the world. Prophet Abraham was a young man and would openly criticise the Babylonian religion. He had some sense of immunity due to his uncle Azar who was his caretaker and a very influential figure at the court of Nimrud. Prophet Abraham would openly defy his uncle and religious leaders, as it is mentioned elsewhere in the Quran:

> Certainly, We had given Abraham his rectitude before, and We had full knowledge of him. When he said to his father and his people, 'What are these images to which you keep on clinging?' They said, 'We found our fathers worshipping them.' He said, 'Certainly you and your fathers have been in manifest error.' They said, 'Are you telling the truth, or are you [just] kidding?' He said, 'Rather your Lord is the

> Lord of the heavens and the earth, who originated them, and I am a witness to this. By God, I will devise a stratagem against your idols after you have gone away.' So he broke them into pieces, —all except the biggest of them— so that they might come back to it. (Q. 21:51-57)

The following verses then inform about what happened when Prophet Abraham destroyed the idols. He was arrested and brought before King Nimrud. This demonstrates the high status of Azar in the court of the Nimrud, as he would not have been brought before the king if he had been a common man. When Prophet Abraham presented his arguments, Nimrud found them compelling. He wanted to argue with Prophet Abraham in order to defeat these arguments ideologically as they posed a grave threat to the very foundation of the system that ensured his power and domination. King Nimrud then intended to sentence Prophet Abraham to an exemplary punishment to deter others who may follow in his path. The debate between Prophet Abraham and Nimrud mentioned in the verse at hand took place just before he was thrown into fire.

Nimrud argued with Prophet Abraham about the concept of one God, refusing to accept this idea because the norm at the time was to believe in many gods, including Nimrud himself. Nimrud was being ungrateful just "because God had given him kingdom." He was openly rebelling against God's command and presenting himself as an equal to God. Because of his disbelief and ungratefulness, the *Ṭāghūt* took him into darkness.

because God had given him kingdom; This statement suggests that Nimrud's kingdom was given to him by God. This idea has puzzled some commentators because initially it seems strange that God would grant a kingdom to an oppressor like Nimrud. Tabatabai provides an excellent explanation for this question.[331] He contends that God grants all kinds of blessings in this world to his creations regardless of their beliefs and actions. He may give kingdoms or authority to some as people need to be ruled. The positive aspects of ruling over a kingdom are attached to God as he wants people to live in peace and harmony under a good authority. However, if those in authority choose to oppress or misguide people with their authority, their misdeeds are attached to them. It is like everything else in this world, in which their good aspects are attached to God whilst their negative aspects are attached to those who receive it.

When Abraham said, 'My Lord is He who gives life and brings death,' he replied, 'I [too] give life and bring death.' The Quran quotes the exchange between Prophet Abraham and King Nimrud. Nimrud challenged God's authority and claimed that he had the same power as God, but his arguments became twisted, and he attributed powers to himself that he lacked. To show that he had the same power as God in giving life and bringing death, he randomly killed an innocent person and freed a convict who was due to be executed. His arrogance blinded him completely, thus he did not realise the foolishness of his arguments. Tabatabai notes that at the time, Babylonia was at the peak of human civilization, many scientific discoveries were made which were so advanced for their time that the rest of the world have only caught up with them in the past few centuries.[332] Yet they were so simple-minded and backward in their understanding of religion. This demonstrates that there is no correlation between scientific advancement and a deeper understanding of faith. Nimrud made such ludicrous arguments, yet his subjects believed in him without question.

Abraham said, 'Indeed, God brings the sun from the east; you bring it from the west.' Prophet Abraham then challenged King Nimrud about something which was clearly beyond his power. He said, "God brings the sun from the east; you bring it from the west." At this point the faithless Nimrud was dumbfounded. The debate came to an end with a decisive victory for Prophet Abraham.

And God does not guide the wrongdoing lot. In the final sentence of this verse, God reaffirms the idea that he does not lead people to good or bad, rather, it is up to people to make the initial decision to follow their path. If they choose to follow the right path, God then guides them, but if they choose to follow the evil path, God withdraws his guidance. It is the human choice that triggers God's guidance and withdrawal of guidance.

أَوْ كَالَّذِي مَرَّ عَلَىٰ قَرْيَةٍ وَهِيَ خَاوِيَةٌ عَلَىٰ عُرُوشِهَا قَالَ أَنَّىٰ يُحْيِي هَٰذِهِ
اللَّهُ بَعْدَ مَوْتِهَا فَأَمَاتَهُ اللَّهُ مِائَةَ عَامٍ ثُمَّ بَعَثَهُ قَالَ كَمْ لَبِثْتَ قَالَ لَبِثْتُ يَوْمًا أَوْ
بَعْضَ يَوْمٍ قَالَ بَل لَّبِثْتَ مِائَةَ عَامٍ فَانظُرْ إِلَىٰ طَعَامِكَ وَشَرَابِكَ لَمْ يَتَسَنَّهْ
وَانظُرْ إِلَىٰ حِمَارِكَ وَلِنَجْعَلَكَ آيَةً لِّلنَّاسِ وَانظُرْ إِلَى الْعِظَامِ كَيْفَ نُنشِزُهَا
ثُمَّ نَكْسُوهَا لَحْمًا فَلَمَّا تَبَيَّنَ لَهُ قَالَ أَعْلَمُ أَنَّ اللَّهَ عَلَىٰ كُلِّ شَيْءٍ قَدِيرٌ ﴿259﴾

Or him who came upon a township as it lay fallen on its trellises. He said, 'How will God revive this after its death?!' So, God made him die for a hundred years, then He resurrected him. He said, 'How long have you remained?' Said he, 'I have remained a day or part of a day.' He said, 'Rather you have remained a hundred years. Now look at your food and drink which have not rotted! Then look at your donkey! [This was done] that We may make you a sign for mankind. And look at the bones, how We arrange them and then clothe them with flesh!' When it became evident to him, he said, 'I know that God has power over all things.'

This verse sets out the second example of how God takes the faithful from darkness into light. It also demonstrates the power of God in reviving the dead. There is also a subtle reference to what was mentioned in *Ayāt al-Kursī* that *they do not comprehend anything of His knowledge except what He wishes.*

Or him who came upon a township as it lay fallen on its trellises. Nearly all Muslim commentators agree that the person alluded to in this verse was Prophet Ezra, mentioned in the Quran as Uzayr. He was an honourable man in the eyes of God and when he asked God to show him how he would revive the dead his request was granted in a dramatic way to broaden the scope of his knowledge about life and death. Prophet Ezra is revered in Judaism due to his role in re-writing the Old Testament after it was destroyed by Nebuchadnezzar during the exile of the Jews to Babylon. When the Jews returned to Jerusalem, God granted Prophet Ezra the knowledge of the Old Testament so he could re-write it for the Jews.

The commentators have provided wild speculative guesses about the township referred to in this verse, however, none of these explanations are based on sound evidence. The verse tells us is that the town was "fallen on its trellises," indicating that the town was either attacked by an enemy who had destroyed the city or that they had fallen due to a destructive earthquake. It is probable that the city was a Jewish settlement which was raided by their enemies, so all the people were likely to have been either killed or enslaved in such a way that the town was deserted.

He said, 'How will God revive this after its death?! Prophet Ezra's question was certainly not out of disbelief since he was a prophet of God to whom the angels communicated including during this event. However, the scene was so dramatic, and the decomposition of bodies was so gruesome that it made him think about how these bodies would come back to life again. Not "how" in the sense of questioning the power of God, but "how" in the sense of seeking further knowledge about the omnipotence of God.

So God made him die for a hundred years, then He resurrected him. Due to his high spiritual status, and the honour he had with God, his request was granted and God taught him what he sought not by words but by a demonstration of the very act itself. He made Prophet Ezra die for 100 years along with his donkey, then God revived him.

He said, 'How long have you remained? Said he, 'I have remained a day or part of a day.'" The death felt like a deep sleep for Prophet Ezra, so he thought he had fallen asleep for a half day or a full day. Then God makes Prophet Ezra realise that he was not sleeping for a short period, rather he had died for a hundred years.

Now look at your food and drink which have not rotted! Then look at your ass. The flesh of the donkey that Prophet Ezra had been riding became rotten and only its bones had remained. However, his food and drink which, according to narrations contained milk and figs, were still fresh and intact. This contrast was to show him that no limit could be set on God's power. If God wills, he can keep the food and milk fresh for a hundred years just as he kept Prophet Ezra alive for that period, while his donkey had died and decomposed.

[This was done] that We may make you a sign for mankind. God performed this miracle to grant Ezra's request, but also to make this incident a sign and proof of the Resurrection for the people of his time and for posterity. In this sense, Prophet Ezra's story is similar to the story of the Seven Sleepers of the Cave (*Asḥāb al-kahf*) in which God's power was shown to them and to the people who knew their story.

And look at the bones, how We arrange them and then clothe them with flesh! God revived his donkey immediately, so that Prophet Ezra could witness the process of physical resurrection. The bones moved before his eyes and within swift motions they were clothed with flesh to show him the process of bodily resurrection. The incident clearly indicates that when people are resurrected, they would have a physical form, as the verse clearly demonstrates when God revives the donkey; the donkey has a physical form. Certainly, the physical form which is recreated in the afterlife would be suitable for the intense rewards and punishments of the Hereafter. In comparison to this world, people would be resurrected in the form of super-humans. It also indicates that on the Day of Judgment, even the animals would be revived alongside people.

When it became evident to him, he said, 'I know that God has power over all things.' Prophet Ezra is one of the fortunate people to have witnessed one of the most miraculous works of God. He directly witnessed God's power to resurrect people and animals. What he had faith in was shown to him as a factual event. In this way his faith and knowledge (*'ilm al-yaqīn*) was promoted to observing and witnessing (*'ayn al-yaqīn*). What he had already known had just occurred before his eyes. As it is said, seeing is very different to knowing in the mind alone.

وَإِذْ قَالَ إِبْرَاهِيمُ رَبِّ أَرِنِي كَيْفَ تُحْيِي الْمَوْتَىٰ ۖ قَالَ أَوَلَمْ تُؤْمِن ۖ قَالَ بَلَىٰ
وَلَٰكِن لِّيَطْمَئِنَّ قَلْبِي ۖ قَالَ فَخُذْ أَرْبَعَةً مِّنَ الطَّيْرِ فَصُرْهُنَّ إِلَيْكَ ثُمَّ اجْعَلْ
عَلَىٰ كُلِّ جَبَلٍ مِّنْهُنَّ جُزْءًا ثُمَّ ادْعُهُنَّ يَأْتِينَكَ سَعْيًا ۚ وَاعْلَمْ أَنَّ اللَّهَ عَزِيزٌ
حَكِيمٌ ﴿260﴾

And when Abraham said, 'My Lord! Show me how You revive the dead,' He said, 'Do you not believe?' He said, 'Yes indeed, but in order that my heart may be at rest.' He said, 'Take four of the birds. Then cut them into pieces, and place a part of them on every mountain, then call them; they will come to you hastening. And know that God is All-mighty and All-wise.'

The third example is of Prophet Abraham and his conversation with God. In a similar way to Prophet Ezra, Prophet Abraham knew that God has the power to revive the dead and he wishes to promote his knowledge (*'ilm al-yaqīn*) to witnessing (*'ayn al-yaqīn*).

And when Abraham said, 'My Lord! Show me how You revive the dead,' Prophet Abraham asked God to *show* him how he revives the dead. Although the requests of the two prophets are similar, there are two main differences between the verses 259 and 260. Firstly, the previous verse does not mention the name of the prophet; we can only surmise that he was Prophet Ezra based on certain evidenced outside the Quran, yet this verse mentions Prophet Abraham by name. Secondly, Prophet Ezra's question is different from Abraham's request: while Prophet Ezra asks *How will God revive this after its death?* Prophet Abraham wants to see God's power at work to add to his insight. God's response to Abraham is rhetorical and honours him greatly as God confirms Prophet Abraham's faith. He also takes Prophet Abraham further into the light by granting his request.

It seems the reason God does not mention Prophet Ezra's name in the verse is that not every prophet has the same status as Prophet Abraham in the eyes of God. Abraham received special treatment from God because of his extraordinary spiritual status. The difference is also clear from God's response to the two prophets. In the example of Prophet Ezra, God shows him the process of physical resurrection by putting him to deep sleep for a hundred years and waking him up intact. However, in the case of Prophet Abraham, God allows him to revive the bird *himself*:

He said, 'Take four of the birds. Then cut them into pieces, and place a part of them on every mountain, then call them; they will come to you hastening. This shows that God taught Prophet Abraham the knowledge by which he would revive the dead on the Day of Judgment. "Then call them" refers to this knowledge, and he asks Prophet Abraham to implement the knowledge.

مَّثَلُ الَّذِينَ يُنفِقُونَ أَمْوَالَهُمْ فِي سَبِيلِ اللَّهِ كَمَثَلِ حَبَّةٍ أَنبَتَتْ سَبْعَ سَنَابِلَ فِي كُلِّ سُنبُلَةٍ مِّائَةُ حَبَّةٍ وَاللَّهُ يُضَاعِفُ لِمَن يَشَاءُ وَاللَّهُ وَاسِعٌ عَلِيمٌ ﴿261﴾

The parable of those who spend their wealth in the way of God is that of a grain which grows seven ears, in every ear a hundred grains. God enhances several fold whomever He wishes, and God is All-bounteous, All-knowing.

Tusi contends that this verse is a continuation of verse 245 which is also about giving charity.[333] This is an example of the unique style of the Quran; a subject may be mentioned in a verse at some point, followed by a discussion into some related issues, but then the discussion comes full circle and returns to the main subject. This is because, when God addresses a subject, it may invoke other concepts which need to be addressed by God while the revelation descends. Therefore, the verses which are related to the secondary matter may come in between. The style of the Quran is similar to an oral dialogue and God addresses the Prophet, and through him the people, as God would speak with them.

Many orientalists have criticised the Quran, saying that it cannot be the word of God as it is too disjointed and erratic; yet this is simply because they have not understood the stylistic nature of the Quran and the context of its revelation.

It is important to remember that the Quran was not revealed as a written book and so it does not adhere to the conventions of a written book, such as having an introduction, main text and conclusion. The revelation of the Quran corresponds to the needs of its audience and was revealed in the form of speech and dialogue to have the greatest impact upon the hearts and minds of those who want to benefit from it. In conversation, it is natural to shift from one subject to another because the tone and style of the communication is defined based on the many other elements of the interaction.

The parable of those who spend their wealth in the way of God; Here, "in the way of God" refers to any charitable giving which pleases God, so the meaning of the verse becomes, "those who spend their wealth in any cause that pleases God." This may include feeding the poor, building mosques, schools or hospitals, providing finances for *jihad*, and many other instances of charity.

is that of a grain which grows seven ears, in every ear a hundred grains. The verse then draws a parable of grain that "grows seven ears, in every ear a hundred grains." It is not certain which exact grain God refers to in this parable. Rather, the main focus here is that it is spent in the way of God and will return to people in exponential growth in terms of the blessings of God. Of course, the numbers mentioned are symbolic and show God's power to give in numbers so it may be much more than seven hundred, as there is no limit to God's rewards.

الَّذِينَ يُنفِقُونَ أَمْوَالَهُمْ فِي سَبِيلِ اللَّهِ ثُمَّ لَا يُتْبِعُونَ مَا أَنفَقُوا مَنًّا وَلَا أَذًى لَّهُمْ أَجْرُهُمْ عِندَ رَبِّهِمْ وَلَا خَوْفٌ عَلَيْهِمْ وَلَا هُمْ يَحْزَنُونَ ﴿262﴾

Those who spend their wealth in the way of God, and then do not follow up what they have spent with reproaches and affronts, they shall have their reward near their Lord, and they will have no fear, nor will they grieve.

Sometimes people give charity but then make the goodness of their act void by mistreating those who receive their charity. They expect the needy to return their favour by being constantly grateful to them and always acknowledging the charity they have provided. This is indeed humiliating for the needy and a sign of a corrupt soul on the side of the giver. This is beautifully expressed in *Ṣaḥīfa Sajjādiyya*:

> Exalt me, but do not afflict me with pride! Make me worship You but do not let my worship become corrupted with self-admiration! Let good flow out from my hands to the people, but do not let it become corrupted by my making them feel obliged! Give me the highest moral traits but preserve me from vainglory.[334]

Furthermore, charity need not only be in a material form. Scholars dedicate their time and effort to educate their communities about the teachings of Islam. Their time and effort may be more valuable than a vast amount of material support. If they do not mistreat the community, and expect their reward from God alone, they would receive their rewards as well. If the charity givers do not misbehave, then "they shall have their reward near their Lord, and they will have no fear, nor will they grieve." They have deposited their good deeds in a very secure place, and they will certainly receive their reward, especially on the Day of Judgment when they will be in the most need of the utmost help. On that day, they will not regret what they have spent in the way of God as they will receive their reward exponentially.

God is not in need of people's charity. He can give people abundantly either material wealth or knowledge as much as he wishes and to whomever he wishes. However, the way God created the world is that people are connected to each other in one way or another. He likes people to form relations with each other through taking and giving, as this strengthen the community bonds. It is also a necessity of social life that people should have different potentials so that they could employ each other to collectively build society. This very important fact is mentioned in Q. 43:32:

> It is We who have dispensed among them their livelihood in the present life, and raised some of them above others in rank, so that some may take others into service, and your Lord's mercy is better than what they amass.

قَوْلٌ مَّعْرُوفٌ وَمَغْفِرَةٌ خَيْرٌ مِّن صَدَقَةٍ يَتْبَعُهَا أَذًى ۗ وَاللَّهُ غَنِيٌّ حَلِيمٌ ﴿263﴾

An honourable word with pardon is better than a charity followed by affront. God is All-sufficient, most forbearing.

Even if people are not able to give anything to the needy, they still need to be affable and kind to them and decline their request with kind words so that they are not offended. "Honourable word" here refers to this type of encounter. Q. 17:26 -28 advises:

> Give the relatives their [due] right, and the needy and the traveler [as well] ... and if you have to overlook them [for now], seeking the mercy of your Lord which you expect [in the future], speak to them gentle words.

Moreover, the verse adds something even more important than being kind and overlooking faults, and that is *maghfira*. *Maghfira* has been translated in the verse as pardon which makes it synonymous to *'afw*. Regarding the meaning of pardoning, the commentators have suggested that it means that the person should forgive the one who makes the request if he asks at a wrong time, or if he unduly insists, or if he uses bad language. However, none of these are implied by the verse. What should be considered in the verse is that there is a subtle difference between *'afw* which is to forgive and *maghfira* which is to cover. Therefore, the meaning would be, "an honourable word and preserving the honour and dignity of the requester by concealing his request and not letting others know about it is better than a charity followed by affront."

يَا أَيُّهَا الَّذِينَ آمَنُوا لَا تُبْطِلُوا صَدَقَاتِكُمْ بِالْمَنِّ وَالْأَذَىٰ كَالَّذِي يُنْفِقُ
مَالَهُ رِئَاءَ النَّاسِ وَلَا يُؤْمِنُ بِاللَّهِ وَالْيَوْمِ الْآخِرِ فَمَثَلُهُ كَمَثَلِ صَفْوَانٍ عَلَيْهِ
تُرَابٌ فَأَصَابَهُ وَابِلٌ فَتَرَكَهُ صَلْدًا لَا يَقْدِرُونَ عَلَىٰ شَيْءٍ مِمَّا كَسَبُوا وَاللَّهُ
لَا يَهْدِي الْقَوْمَ الْكَافِرِينَ ﴿264﴾

O you who have faith! Do not render your charities void by reproaches and affronts, like those who spend their wealth to be seen by people and have no faith in God and the Last Day. Their parable is that of a rock covered with soil: a downpour strikes it, leaving it bare. They have no power over anything of what they have earned, and God does not guide the faithless lot.

Charity should not be followed up by reproaches and affronts as it invalidates the act and destroys the reward. Nor should it be done to show off or be ostentatious. Rather, giving charity should be built upon the solid foundation of faith and sincerity. Those who give charity without these two conditions may receive the reward and the positive effects in this world, but they will not receive any benefit in the Hereafter.

To further elaborate on this important issue, and to mark the importance of the topic in this verse, God sets out a parable. Consider a piece of rock covered with a thin layer of soil. This is certainly not a good place to cultivate crops. The crop may initially grow due to the soil and fresh air and sunshine, but as soon as heavy rain pours down, it will be washed away, and the rock will be laid bare.

The Quran has likened hypocritical giving and charities followed by reproach and injury, to a rock covered with a thin layer of soil from which no benefit can be gained. The parable teaches us that if the charity is not given with the right intention and in the right form, it would be nullified as it is not established in fertile ground, a metaphor for faith and sincerity.

وَمَثَلُ الَّذِينَ يُنفِقُونَ أَمْوَالَهُمُ ابْتِغَاءَ مَرْضَاتِ اللَّهِ وَتَثْبِيتًا مِّنْ أَنفُسِهِمْ كَمَثَلِ جَنَّةٍ بِرَبْوَةٍ أَصَابَهَا وَابِلٌ فَآتَتْ أُكُلَهَا ضِعْفَيْنِ فَإِن لَّمْ يُصِبْهَا وَابِلٌ فَطَلٌّ وَاللَّهُ بِمَا تَعْمَلُونَ بَصِيرٌ ﴿265﴾

The parable of those who spend their wealth seeking God's pleasure and to confirm themselves, is that of a garden on a hillside: the downpour strikes it, whereupon it brings forth its fruit twofold; and if it is not a downpour that strikes it, then a shower, and God sees best what you do.

On the other hand, there are those who give charity for the sake of God and to confirm their faith and sincerity. This parable is to elaborate on the status of their hearts. There is no rocky field in this parable, rather their hearts are like a hillside garden where the soil is deep and fertile with ample amount of sunshine for the crop. When it is hit by a downpour of rain, due to its firm roots and fertile soil, there is only an increase in its abundance of fruit. The soil or the heart is so fertile that it does not even need a downpour of rain, even a scarce shower would be enough to make its fruit ripen.

أَيَوَدُّ أَحَدُكُمْ أَن تَكُونَ لَهُ جَنَّةٌ مِّن نَّخِيلٍ وَأَعْنَابٍ تَجْرِي مِن تَحْتِهَا
الْأَنْهَارُ لَهُ فِيهَا مِن كُلِّ الثَّمَرَاتِ وَأَصَابَهُ الْكِبَرُ وَلَهُ ذُرِّيَّةٌ ضُعَفَاءُ
فَأَصَابَهَا إِعْصَارٌ فِيهِ نَارٌ فَاحْتَرَقَتْ كَذَٰلِكَ يُبَيِّنُ اللَّهُ لَكُمُ الْآيَاتِ
لَعَلَّكُمْ تَتَفَكَّرُونَ ﴿266﴾

Would any of you like to have a garden of palm trees and vines, with streams running in it, with all kinds of fruit for him therein, and old age were to strike him while he has weakly offspring; whereupon a fiery hurricane were to hit it, whereat it lies burnt? Thus, does God clarify His signs for you so that you may reflect.

The verse further elaborates on the status of people who make their own acts of charity void. Their example is like an old man who enjoyed a comfortable life in a beautiful garden. In his old age, the garden is needed more than ever to look after his young and weak children or grandchildren, but at that moment of need, a hurricane destroys the garden. At this point, the old man comes to the desperate realisation that all the fruit of his life has gone. If he was just an old man without children to look after, he would not have cared as much. He would soon die himself, so he would not be in any need of the garden; it would not be as important for him. What makes the situation so dramatic is that these weak children will not survive without the garden in a good condition.

With this dramatic parable, the verse draws attention to the desperate situation of those who void their own charity and all good deeds. On the Day of Judgment, they will come to the realisation that they had ruined all the good that they had worked on. This is their true time of need, but they are deprived of their achievements due to their own misdeeds. People who have voided their good deeds and charities, will feel the same as this old man who is desperate.

يَا أَيُّهَا الَّذِينَ آمَنُوا أَنفِقُوا مِن طَيِّبَاتِ مَا كَسَبْتُمْ وَمِمَّا أَخْرَجْنَا لَكُم
مِّنَ الْأَرْضِ وَلَا تَيَمَّمُوا الْخَبِيثَ مِنْهُ تُنفِقُونَ وَلَسْتُم بِآخِذِيهِ إِلَّا أَن
تُغْمِضُوا فِيهِ وَاعْلَمُوا أَنَّ اللَّهَ غَنِيٌّ حَمِيدٌ ﴿267﴾

O you who have faith! Spend of the good things you have earned, and of what We bring forth for you from the earth, and do not be of the mind to give the bad part of it, for you yourselves would not take it, unless you overlook it. And know that God is All-sufficient, All-laudable.

The verse continues to develop the discussion of giving charity in the way of God. The focus of the verse is the *quality* of charity given. Whatever people donate in the way of God should be pure - in other words it should be earned through legitimate means. Also, the charity should be worthy and of good quality and should not be meagre. Often, people give away things which are of an inferior quality that they would not wear or eat themselves; this is a discouraged practice in Islam. It is a source of humiliation for the needy and therefore there is no need to give in this way as it would not be accepted. God only accepts that charity which is pure and of good quality.

الشَّيْطَانُ يَعِدُكُمُ الْفَقْرَ وَيَأْمُرُكُم بِالْفَحْشَاءِ ۖ وَاللَّهُ يَعِدُكُم مَّغْفِرَةً مِّنْهُ
وَفَضْلًا ۗ وَاللَّهُ وَاسِعٌ عَلِيمٌ ﴿268﴾

Satan frightens you of poverty and prompts you to [commit] indecent acts. But God promises you His forgiveness and grace, and God is All-bounteous, All-knowing.

This explains that people are disinclined to give freely because Satan whispers and frightens people with irrational worries to commit disobedience to God, especially in the case of giving charity to the needy. Satan always frightens people by the expectation of calamity, poverty and neediness. Unless a person has strong faith, it is difficult to escape the influence of such negative effects. While people sometimes see their future as bright and promising, at other times they see it as very dark and gloomy. The sources of these two effects come from two opposing corners: the feeling of hope and brightness comes from the angels and the darkness and gloominess comes from Satan. By urging people to give charity, God wants to shower people with his mercy both in this world and the Hereafter. He first washes away the sins of those who give charity and then compensates them for their spending both in this world and the Hereafter. God is vastly richer than whatever he gives, his treasure is never reduced. In essence, any thought which is disappointing, impedimental and short-sighted originates from a deviation from the natural disposition and is as a result of the whisperings of Satan. Conversely, any thought which is positive, instructive, and broad-sighted comes from the source of godly inspirations and the pure divine innate disposition.

But God promises you His forgiveness and grace; There is a tradition narrated in *Majma' al-bayān* from Imam Jafar al-Sadiq regarding this verse. He is reported to have said, "Two things are from God and two things are from Satan. Those two from God are forgiveness of sins and abundance in sustenance. And those two from Satan are promise to poverty and enjoinment to indecency."[335] Furthermore, it is reported from Imam Ali that "When you are confronted with poverty, bargain with God through charity,"[336] meaning to spend out in charity until you get free from poverty.

يُؤْتِي الْحِكْمَةَ مَنْ يَشَاءُ ۚ وَمَنْ يُؤْتَ الْحِكْمَةَ فَقَدْ أُوتِيَ خَيْرًا كَثِيرًا ۗ وَمَا
يَذَّكَّرُ إِلَّا أُولُو الْأَلْبَابِ ﴿269﴾

He gives wisdom to whomever He wishes, and he who is given wisdom, is certainly given an abundant good. But none takes admonition except those who possess intellect.

There is great wisdom in giving charity. Yet, people often see this as a financial burden, and they are either reluctant to give or they only give meagrely. God is clear that the more people give, the wiser it is for them. Firstly, it creates a bond between people and the family or society in which they live. Secondly, it maintains a fine financial balance between the rich and the poor and reduces the number of financial crimes. Thirdly, it provides an opportunity for the faithful to confirm their faith and wash away their sins.

The verse also informs believers that whatever wealth that has been given to people is not an indication of their prosperity in this world or in the next. But having wisdom is a decisive prosperity for people and they should make use of this prosperity through giving charity in abundance. Only those who can make use of their intellect can grasp this. Of course, every human being has intellect, and it is the most precious human faculty. However, not everyone uses it in the same way. Due to the effect of our whimsical desires, people may *think* that they are using their intellect, but in fact they are following their own base desires. Only those who have purified their intellect from worldly desires may use their intellect for the purpose it is designed for. People of wisdom recognise the difference between the Satanic temptations and godly inspirations, between truth and falsehood, and between passion and prudence.

وَمَا أَنفَقْتُم مِّن نَّفَقَةٍ أَوْ نَذَرْتُم مِّن نَّذْرٍ فَإِنَّ اللَّهَ يَعْلَمُهُ ۗ وَمَا لِلظَّالِمِينَ مِنْ أَنصَارٍ ﴿270﴾

Whatever charity you may give, or vows that you may vow, God indeed knows it, and the wrongdoers have no helpers.

or vows that you may vow; This refers to the charity people pledge to give on their own accord. It is not something that God has prescribed or recommended upon people. Sometimes people make a pledge that if their wish is granted by God, they will promise to feed a certain number of poor people or give a certain amount in charity. These kinds of charities are also valuable in the eyes of God. He reassures the believers that "God indeed knows it", he is aware of anything that is being done for his sake and he will grant them rewards.

and the wrongdoers have no helpers. The Arabic word used in the verse for wrongdoers is *ẓālimīn*. It is often translated as "wrongdoers", but this may not be an accurate translation for every instance *ẓālimīn* mentioned in the Quran. Sometimes the Quran even refers to Prophet Adam as *ẓālim* (sing. of *ẓālimīn*):

> We said, 'O Adam, dwell with your mate in Paradise, and eat thereof freely whencesoever you wish; but do not approach this tree, lest you should be among the wrongdoers (*ẓālimīn*).'
>
> Then Satan caused them to stumble from it, and he dislodged them from what they were in; and We said, 'Get down, being enemies of one another! On the earth shall be your abode and sustenance for a time.' (Q. 2:35-36)

Prophet Adam eventually succumbs to the deception of the Satan and becomes a *ẓālim,* but we also know that God never supports the *ẓālimīn:*

> And when his Lord tested Abraham with certain words, and he fulfilled them, He said, 'I am making you the Imam of mankind.' Said he, 'And from among my descendants?' He said, 'My pledge does not extend to the unjust.' (Q. 2:124)

Yet after his acknowledgement of his wrongdoing and his sincere repentance Prophet Adam received the grace and guidance of God:

> Then Adam received certain words from his Lord, and He turned to him clemently. Indeed, He is the All-clement, the All-merciful.
>
> We said, 'Get down from it, all together! Yet, should any guidance come to you from Me, those who follow My guidance shall have no fear, nor shall they grieve.' (Q. 2: 37-38)

This makes it clear that in the Quran, the word *ẓālim* has different meaning depending on the context in which it is used. At its most extreme usage *ẓālim* may refer to an "oppressor" (Q. 2:193) to indicate one who causes corruption on the earth by physically and spiritually harming others. Alternatively, in its mildest form it can refer to one wrong action that only harm the individual by way of being deprived of certain blessings, as Prophet Adam's remorseful communication with God after eating from the forbidden tree elucidates: *They said, 'Our Lord, we have wronged (ẓalamnā) ourselves! If You do not forgive us and have mercy upon us, we will surely be among the losers.'*

The context of the verse at hand is about those who give charity, but then invalidate it by affronts and reproaches. Therefore, those who behave this way are referred to as *ẓālimīn* in the sense that God would not reward them.

إِن تُبْدُوا الصَّدَقَاتِ فَنِعِمَّا هِيَ ۖ وَإِن تُخْفُوهَا وَتُؤْتُوهَا الْفُقَرَاءَ فَهُوَ خَيْرٌ لَّكُمْ ۚ وَيُكَفِّرُ عَنكُم مِّن سَيِّئَاتِكُمْ ۗ وَاللَّهُ بِمَا تَعْمَلُونَ خَبِيرٌ ﴿271﴾

If you disclose your charities, that is well, but if you hide them and give them to the poor, that is better for you, and it will atone for some of your misdeeds, and God is well aware of what you do.

If you disclose your charities, that is well; Sometimes, giving charity openly may provide a positive example and encourage others to do the same. If charity is always given privately and secretly, then people may assume that nobody gives charity anymore. Therefore, God states that both giving charity openly and discreetly is beneficial. It may be best that people give charity in both ways to take advantage of both rewards.

but if you hide them and give them to the poor, that is better for you, and it will atone for some of your misdeeds; Giving charity discreetly has a greater advantage over publicly announced charity. This is better because it preserves one's intention of doing good for God's sake alone and avoids the pitfalls of pride or showing off. It also preserves the honour and integrity of the recipient. Moreover, God promises that in addition to the reward that the charity will attract, hidden charity would lead to the atonement of sins and forgiveness from God. It is reported from the Holy Prophet that "Charity given in secret extinguishes the wrath of the Lord and extinguishes sins like water puts out fire; and it repels seventy doors of calamities."[337]

لَّيْسَ عَلَيْكَ هُدَاهُمْ وَلَٰكِنَّ اللَّهَ يَهْدِي مَن يَشَاءُ ۗ وَمَا تُنفِقُوا مِنْ خَيْرٍ
فَلِأَنفُسِكُمْ ۚ وَمَا تُنفِقُونَ إِلَّا ابْتِغَاءَ وَجْهِ اللَّهِ ۚ وَمَا تُنفِقُوا مِنْ خَيْرٍ
يُوَفَّ إِلَيْكُمْ وَأَنتُمْ لَا تُظْلَمُونَ ﴿272﴾

It is not up to you to guide them; rather it is God who guides whomever He wishes. And whatever wealth you spend, it is for your own benefit, as you do not spend but to seek God's pleasure, and whatever wealth you spend will be repaid to you in full, and you will not be wronged.

It is not up to you to guide them; rather it is God who guides whomever He wishes. Some commentators have been baffled by this seemingly irrelevant sentence placed in the middle of the discussion about giving charity. Considering the context, it is likely that this sentence is related to giving charity to those who are not guided and are in disbelief. So, the guidance mentioned in the verse is related to giving charity.

It is not immediately clear who the pronoun "them" refers to. Based on the views of many commentators and relevant traditions and the context of the verse, it is almost certain that "them" refers to the disbelievers who are in need of charity. So, the verse states that the Prophet and Muslims are not responsible for the guidance of the disbelievers - guidance comes from God alone. However, Muslims have a responsibility for the well-being of the disbelievers and they are responsible for taking care of them, whether in the form of giving charity or anything else. In terms of giving charity, the needy mentioned in the Quran have no religious priority, if certain people are needy, they qualify for charity regardless of their religious background.

And whatever wealth you spend, it is for your own benefit; This part of the verse is a reminder that in being charitable, a person is not helping others as much as they are helping themselves. It is also a reminder of God's self-sufficiency in helping his creation. What people give to the poor is no favour to God, nor does it help him provide for his creation. Rather, God blesses a person with the opportunity to become the means through which he aids other creatures. Further, they will reap the spiritual benefit of being charitable by receiving multiplied rewards in this world and in the Hereafter.

And you do not spend but to seek God's pleasure; This is a command in the form of a declaration, which makes it even more forceful. It implies that any charity given without seeking God's pleasure is in fact not charity at all. While, if an act of charity is done sincerely for God then, "whatever wealth you spend will be repaid to you in full, and you will not be wronged."

لِلْفُقَرَاءِ الَّذِينَ أُحْصِرُوا فِي سَبِيلِ اللَّهِ لَا يَسْتَطِيعُونَ ضَرْبًا فِي الْأَرْضِ
يَحْسَبُهُمُ الْجَاهِلُ أَغْنِيَاءَ مِنَ التَّعَفُّفِ تَعْرِفُهُمْ بِسِيمَاهُمْ لَا يَسْأَلُونَ النَّاسَ
إِلْحَافًا وَمَا تُنْفِقُوا مِنْ خَيْرٍ فَإِنَّ اللَّهَ بِهِ عَلِيمٌ ﴿273﴾

[The charities are] for the poor who are straitened in the way of God, not capable of moving about in the land [for trade]. The unaware suppose them to be well-off because of their reserve. You recognize them by their mark; they do not ask the people importunately. And whatever wealth you may spend, God indeed knows it.

[The charities are] for the poor who are straitened in the way of God, not capable of moving about in the land [for trade]. A verse in Surah Tawba details the cases in which charity should be spent:

> Charities are only for the poor and the needy, and those employed to collect them, and those whose hearts are to be reconciled, and for [the freedom of] the slaves and the debtors, and in the way of God, and for the traveler. [This is] an ordinance from God, and God is All-knowing, All-wise. (Q9:60)

This ordinance is about the obligatory charity or *zakat*. However, in this verse God talks about voluntary charities which should go to the poor and commends them because their poverty is due to the fact that they "are straitened in the way of God." This may be because of their migration with the Prophet leaving their property behind, or their preparation for *jihad*, or their eagerness to be with the Prophet all the time lest they miss any of his teachings. Contemporary examples could also be drawn from the above instances.

The unaware suppose them to be well-off because of their reserve. Anyone unaware of their condition would think that they are rich on account of their self-control and not displaying their poverty.

You recognize them by their mark; they do not ask the people importunately. They do not disclose their poverty except that which cannot be hidden in any way. These signs of poverty may include the effects of hunger on their faces, or old and torn clothes. These are the marks by which they are known.

They do not ask the people importunately. They never ask anyone to give them money in manipulative ways. Once a man becomes accustomed to begging for his needs, he may lose his restraint and soon begin to beg importunately and shamelessly. According to Tabatabai, more probably, the sentence does not negate discrete asking, but discourages importunity in asking. This may include asking for that which exceeds the limit of the necessary description of one's needs.[338]

الَّذِينَ يُنفِقُونَ أَمْوَالَهُم بِاللَّيْلِ وَالنَّهَارِ سِرًّا وَعَلَانِيَةً فَلَهُمْ أَجْرُهُمْ عِندَ رَبِّهِمْ وَلَا خَوْفٌ عَلَيْهِمْ وَلَا هُمْ يَحْزَنُونَ ﴿274﴾

Those who give their wealth by night and day, secretly and openly, they shall have their reward near their Lord, and they will have no fear, nor will they grieve.

This is the final verse which summarises the fourteen preceding verses that discuss charity. It is claimed that no other theme in the Quran has been discussed with such detail.

Those who give their wealth by night and day, secretly and openly; Tabatabai mentions that this verse covers all possible times (by night and by day) and conditions (secretly and openly) of spending; it shows how much those spenders were keen on obtaining the reward, and the depth of their desire to seek the pleasure of God.[339]

they shall have their reward near their Lord, and they will have no fear, nor will they grieve. As a result, God turns towards them with mercy and promises them a good promise in the language of kindness and grace. Most exegetes have noted that this verse was first revealed in praise of the Commander of the faithful, Imam Ali, who had only four silver coins on one occasion and he offered all of them in charity, one coin during the day and another at night, one more coin in public and the last in secret.[340] Praising his act, God generalises the sentence to make it an example for everyone to follow.

الَّذِينَ يَأْكُلُونَ الرِّبَا لَا يَقُومُونَ إِلَّا كَمَا يَقُومُ الَّذِي يَتَخَبَّطُهُ الشَّيْطَانُ مِنَ
الْمَسِّ ۚ ذَٰلِكَ بِأَنَّهُمْ قَالُوا إِنَّمَا الْبَيْعُ مِثْلُ الرِّبَا ۗ وَأَحَلَّ اللَّهُ الْبَيْعَ وَحَرَّمَ الرِّبَا ۚ
فَمَنْ جَاءَهُ مَوْعِظَةٌ مِنْ رَبِّهِ فَانْتَهَىٰ فَلَهُ مَا سَلَفَ وَأَمْرُهُ إِلَى اللَّهِ ۖ وَمَنْ عَادَ
فَأُولَٰئِكَ أَصْحَابُ النَّارِ ۖ هُمْ فِيهَا خَالِدُونَ ﴿275﴾

Those who exact usury will not stand but like one deranged by the Devil's touch. That is because they say, 'Trade is just like usury.' While God has allowed trade and forbidden usury. Whoever, on receiving advice from his Lord, relinquishes [usury], shall keep [the gains of] what is past, and his matter shall rest with God. As for those who resume, they shall be the inmates of the Fire and they shall remain in it [forever].

The attention of the chapter then shifts from charity to the harms of usury which is the exact opposite of charity, because it makes the poor poorer and the rich richer. This set of verses discuss the necessity of financial measures for the benefit of the individuals as well as the society as a whole. Financial stability is the backbone of spiritual advancement and social cohesion, and God wants Muslims to strive to create economically safe environments for people so that they can focus on their spiritual elevation. This verse discusses usury, but the language used here is not legislative, thus the verse does not wish to state that usury is unlawful.

The legislative aspect of usury had already been covered in Q. 3:130, so the verse at hand acts to emphasise its prohibition. The Prophet had already prohibited usury in the emergent Muslim society, but some Muslims continued to collect their usury for the money that they had lent before the revelation of Q. 3:130. Therefore, this verse was revealed to emphasise the evil effects of usury and to warn the believers that they must stop taking usury immediately. However, whatever they had gained prior to the revelation of the verse, could be kept.

The verse indicates that early Muslims were not scrupulously following the revelation, and therefore God made a second intervention to warn the early Muslims. The attitude of the early Muslims to Islam was not ideal; when the initial excitement of being a Muslim subsided, some Muslims continued with their old un-Islamic practices.

The verse points out that the usurer is not able to distinguish between right and wrong. This is the reason why some people argue that "business is transaction" and "usury is a type of transaction". Satan manipulated their desire and greed in a way that their desires overtook their intellect. Therefore, they are unable to see the destructive role of usury in society as a whole. Their selfish motivations make the poor in society poorer and the rich richer, and stunts the economic growth of the society. They only care and think about the unlawful profit they could make.

As for those who resume, they shall be the inmates of the Fire and they shall remain in it [forever]. The final sentence of the verse creates a theological problem for Muslims. According to Muslim theology, accepted by Asharites and Shi'is, Muslims will not remain in Hell forever. Once they have been purified from their vicious attributes, they will eventually come out of Hell. However, the verse at hand addresses all Muslims and states that those who continue to practice usury, "they shall be the inmates of the Fire and they shall remain in it forever." Mutazilite theologians argued that if God promises a group of people that they will remain in Hell forever, he will fulfil his promise. Using this verse, they argue that grave sinners who do not repent, even if they are Muslims, would remain in Hell forever.

Tabatabai provides a good analysis of the subject matter.[341] He argues that the criterion for remaining in Hell is the lack of submission to God. Even if people call themselves Muslims, but continue to commit sin due to their lack of submission to God, they may remain in Hell forever. Their constant disregard for God's command is an indication that their hearts lack true submission. However, if God wishes; once people are cleansed from their rebellious attributes, they may be released from Hell and allowed to enter Paradise. Rebellious people are not allowed to enter Paradise, because they would wreak havoc within it. Only pure and obedient people are allowed to enter Paradise. If people cannot shed their disobedient state, they risk remaining in Hell forever.

يَمْحَقُ اللَّهُ الرِّبَا وَيُرْبِي الصَّدَقَاتِ ۗ وَاللَّهُ لَا يُحِبُّ كُلَّ كَفَّارٍ أَثِيمٍ ﴿276﴾

God brings usury to naught, but He makes charities flourish. God does not like any sinful ingrate.

God compares the diminishing value of the wealth made from usury against the flourishing value of charities spent in the way of God. In this world, people assume that money made from usury increases in value whilst the money spent in charity is a loss. In the short term, this may seem true. However, investing in usury has two important effects: firstly, economic systems that favour usury create massive social and economic inequalities within society which then leads to social unrest and wars. Secondly, it destroys people's spirituality and takes them further into darkness. Therefore, it is destructive for both societies and individuals. Conversely, what is given in charity is valuable to society as well as to individuals, so in the long term, it is much more beneficial.

إِنَّ الَّذِينَ آمَنُوا وَعَمِلُوا الصَّالِحَاتِ وَأَقَامُوا الصَّلَاةَ وَآتَوُا الزَّكَاةَ لَهُمْ أَجْرُهُمْ عِندَ رَبِّهِمْ وَلَا خَوْفٌ عَلَيْهِمْ وَلَا هُمْ يَحْزَنُونَ﴿277﴾

Indeed, those who have faith, do righteous deeds, maintain the prayer and give the zakat, they shall have their reward near their Lord, and they will have no fear, nor will they grieve.

Zakat here is used in the general sense to refer to all forms of obligatory religious dues as well as voluntary giving such as interest-free loans and alms. There are many examples in the Quran, where after criticising a misdeed and those who commit them, the verses go on to praise the contrary position and detail the good deeds and the rewards of those who perform them. These verses are a good example of this style. It details the basic formula for gaining eternal bliss and avoiding a harsh treatment in the Hereafter.

يَا أَيُّهَا الَّذِينَ آمَنُوا اتَّقُوا اللَّهَ وَذَرُوا مَا بَقِيَ مِنَ الرِّبَا إِن كُنتُم مُّؤْمِنِينَ﴿278﴾

O you who have faith! Be wary of God, and abandon [all claims to] what remains of usury, should you be faithful.

The verse issues a strong warning for the believers who continue to receive usury from the loans that they had lent before the revelation of the verses prohibiting usury. Some reports specifically mention Khalid b. al-Walid, Uthman b. Affan and Abbas b. Abd al-Muttalib who asked the Prophet if they could at least claim the usury amount that was outstanding from people and it was then that this verse was revealed.[342] It may be the case that these believers justified taking usury by claiming that they had lent the money before the revelation of the prohibition verses even though the repayment became due after the revelation of the verses, thereby arguing that the prohibition did not affect them. Or it may be that some Muslims lent money to others when they were non-Muslims, but the repayment became due after they converted to Islam. Furthermore, they could have made the argument that if they had known about the prohibition, they would not have lent the money so if they do not receive the usury, they would incur financial losses. The verse clearly negates this argument and urges Muslims to abandon all forms of usury immediately.

فَإِن لَّمْ تَفْعَلُوا فَأْذَنُوا بِحَرْبٍ مِّنَ اللَّهِ وَرَسُولِهِ ۖ وَإِن تُبْتُمْ فَلَكُمْ رُءُوسُ
أَمْوَالِكُمْ لَا تَظْلِمُونَ وَلَا تُظْلَمُونَ ﴿279﴾

And if you do not, then be informed of a war from God and His apostle. And if you repent, then you will have your principal, neither harming others, nor suffering harm.

God then goes on to threaten those who still collect usury with open war. This is the strongest threat that has been issued against any sin in the Quran, thus illustrating the severity of the act. The verse is unequivocal that at this point God has instructed the Prophet to use force to stop usury in Medina.

God strongly despises usury due to its social implications and in this final warning he outlaws the practice altogether authorising the Prophet to enforce the prohibition by force if necessary. As such, the society in Medina had no choice but to abandon usury. One of the most striking aspects of the verse is that some of those who practiced usury were Muslims, so the verse orders the Prophet to fight against other Muslims if they do not give up collecting usury. The Prophet had the responsibility of removing oppressive vices from within society and usury is a form of oppression due to its role in creating and cementing social and financial inequalities.

In the modern world, the entire economic structure of the global economy has been built upon usury. The banking systems have normalised the use of usury and it is impossible to avoid it for people who live in Muslim and non-Muslim countries alike. There is a strong perception that lending money with some interest is a fair practice. However, this perception has emerged as a result of the scheme planned by those who stand to benefit the most from usury. It is indeed destructive for society as the examples above illustrate. The Credit Crunch in 2008 was a direct result of the malfunction of the usury-based economies and caused havoc to the lives of many people around the world. The cost of the economic crisis was $2.8tn in the western world and the public, mainly the poor, have been suffering the brunt of the blow and paying the greedy banks and global corporations. Muslims cannot do much to stop it, but they can try to avoid it as much as possible. Muslims may also contemplate the use of alternative financial systems to the usury-based economic system.

وَإِن كَانَ ذُو عُسْرَةٍ فَنَظِرَةٌ إِلَىٰ مَيْسَرَةٍ ۚ وَأَن تَصَدَّقُوا خَيْرٌ لَّكُمْ ۖ إِن كُنتُمْ
تَعْلَمُونَ ﴿280﴾

And if [the debtor] is in straits, let there be a respite until the time of ease; and if you remit [the debt] as charity, it will be better for you, should you know.

Financial legislation favours the debtors in Islam. It is forbidden for the lender to charge interest on the capital regardless of the situation. Furthermore, if the debtors are in financial hardship, the verse advises the lenders to give time to the debtors until they become able to repay their debts. The verse also encourages lenders to forsake the debt altogether for multitudinous rewards in the Hereafter.

This outlook on economics is fascinating and challenges the money-oriented capitalist economic philosophy. In this system, it is not the government's duty to enforce debt collection, rather the government's role is to help by paying the debt on behalf of the debtors who are in hardship. In the same era, elsewhere in the world, it was common practice that if the debtors could not pay their debts, they would have been forced into slavery. There is great wisdom in the Islamic economic system; it allows the economy to function and does not diminish people's purchasing power.

وَاتَّقُوا يَوْمًا تُرْجَعُونَ فِيهِ إِلَى اللَّهِ ثُمَّ تُوَفَّىٰ كُلُّ نَفْسٍ مَا كَسَبَتْ وَهُمْ لَا يُظْلَمُونَ ﴿281﴾

And beware of a day in which you will be brought back to God. Then every soul shall be recompensed fully for what it has earned, and they will not be wronged.

Among the commentators there is a consensus that this verse is one of the last verses to be revealed. The Quran issues yet another strong warning for those who continue to collect usury. The statement is harsh against those who after repeated warnings still continue to practice usury. This is because the usurers harm the entire society due to their greed and lack of care for others and for the greater good of the society. Their actions harm generations of people, and eventually pave the way for the destruction of societies.

And beware of a day in which you will be brought back to God. According to Muslim theology, people are always in the presence of God, yet this verse warns about a day when people will be brought back to God. Some commentators have suggested that it refers to the day on which people would be held accountable for what they have done, and they will be compensated for their actions; they will either receive reward or punishment on that day. However, the problem here is that the concept of return entails the idea that people are brought back to God after they had been there before in the past.

Razi provides an explanation for this problem.[343] He contends that human life consists of three stages: first is the period which people spend in the womb of their mothers. This is the stage where they are absolutely helpless; they are looked after by God completely. Then they come into this world where they have some influence over their lives as they grow into adults. However, when they die, they again move into the stage where they have no power over themselves and will be looked after by God alone. In this way, the return back to God means a return to the initial stage where people were absolutely dependent on God as they were in the womb of their mothers. Razi's position is unique in the explanation of this problem because none of the other commentators provide a definitive explanation for the "return". Their focus has been on being "present" before God which is different to what the verse states.

يَا أَيُّهَا الَّذِينَ آمَنُوا إِذَا تَدَايَنتُم بِدَيْنٍ إِلَىٰ أَجَلٍ مُّسَمًّى فَاكْتُبُوهُ ۚ وَلْيَكْتُب
بَّيْنَكُمْ كَاتِبٌ بِالْعَدْلِ ۚ وَلَا يَأْبَ كَاتِبٌ أَن يَكْتُبَ كَمَا عَلَّمَهُ اللَّهُ ۚ
فَلْيَكْتُبْ وَلْيُمْلِلِ الَّذِي عَلَيْهِ الْحَقُّ وَلْيَتَّقِ اللَّهَ رَبَّهُ وَلَا يَبْخَسْ مِنْهُ شَيْئًا ۚ
فَإِن كَانَ الَّذِي عَلَيْهِ الْحَقُّ سَفِيهًا أَوْ ضَعِيفًا أَوْ لَا يَسْتَطِيعُ أَن يُمِلَّ هُوَ
فَلْيُمْلِلْ وَلِيُّهُ بِالْعَدْلِ ۚ وَاسْتَشْهِدُوا شَهِيدَيْنِ مِن رِّجَالِكُمْ ۖ فَإِن لَّمْ
يَكُونَا رَجُلَيْنِ فَرَجُلٌ وَامْرَأَتَانِ مِمَّن تَرْضَوْنَ مِنَ الشُّهَدَاءِ أَن تَضِلَّ
إِحْدَاهُمَا فَتُذَكِّرَ إِحْدَاهُمَا الْأُخْرَىٰ ۚ وَلَا يَأْبَ الشُّهَدَاءُ إِذَا مَا دُعُوا ۚ وَلَا
تَسْأَمُوا أَن تَكْتُبُوهُ صَغِيرًا أَوْ كَبِيرًا إِلَىٰ أَجَلِهِ ۚ ذَٰلِكُمْ أَقْسَطُ عِندَ اللَّهِ
وَأَقْوَمُ لِلشَّهَادَةِ وَأَدْنَىٰ أَلَّا تَرْتَابُوا ۖ إِلَّا أَن تَكُونَ تِجَارَةً حَاضِرَةً تُدِيرُونَهَا
بَيْنَكُمْ فَلَيْسَ عَلَيْكُمْ جُنَاحٌ أَلَّا تَكْتُبُوهَا ۗ وَأَشْهِدُوا إِذَا تَبَايَعْتُمْ ۚ
وَلَا يُضَارَّ كَاتِبٌ وَلَا شَهِيدٌ ۚ وَإِن تَفْعَلُوا فَإِنَّهُ فُسُوقٌ بِكُمْ ۗ وَاتَّقُوا اللَّهَ ۖ
وَيُعَلِّمُكُمُ اللَّهُ ۗ وَاللَّهُ بِكُلِّ شَيْءٍ عَلِيمٌ ﴿282﴾

O, you who have faith! When you contract a loan for a specified term, write it down. Let a writer write between you with honesty, and let not the writer refuse to write as God has taught him. So, let him write, and let the one who incurs the debt dictate, and let him be wary of God, his Lord, and not diminish anything from it. But if the debtor be feeble-minded, or weak, or incapable of dictating himself, then let his guardian dictate with honesty, and take as witness two witnesses from your men, and if there are not two men, then a man and two women —from those whom you approve as witnesses so that if one of the two defaults the other will remind her. The witnesses must not refuse when they are called, and do not consider it wearisome to write it down, whether it be a big or a small sum, [as being lent] until its term. That is more just with God and more upright in respect to testimony, and the likeliest way to avoid doubt, unless it is an on the spot deal you transact between yourselves, in which case there is no sin upon you not to write it. Take witnesses when you make a deal, and let no harm be done to writer or witness, and if you did that, it would be sinful of you. Be wary of God and God shall teach you, and God has knowledge of all things.

This verse is by far the longest verse in the Quran and covers the technical issues about repaying a loan and drawing up contracts. The technical term used in the verse is *dayn,* and it refers to the duty of repayment which may be part of a transaction, lending or contract like the one which is made during marriage.

O, you who have faith! When you contract a loan for a specified term, write it down. The length of the verse is an indication of the importance of writing and registering social contracts to prevent disputes from arising. People are often inclined to forget the details of transactions after some time, or the parties fallout with each other as they may not want to pay back their debts. Writing a contract solves these issues and avoids major disputes between people in society.

It is clear that social interactions are important in the eyes of God and he encourages people to take measures to eliminate sources of conflict in society. Anything people can do to contribute to improved community relations and cohesion is highly appreciated by God and such efforts hold a religious value.

Let a writer write between you with honesty, and let not the writer refuse to write as God has taught him. In the early days of Islam, not everyone was able to read and write, so it may have been difficult to find reliable and honest scribes to record contracts. However, literate people are urged to not shun this responsibility because it is God who has enabled them to learn the skill of writing, so they need to be grateful for this gift by observing the command of God.

And let the one who incurs the debt dictate, and let him be wary of God, his Lord, and not diminish anything from it. The person who incurs the debt should dictate the terms and wording of the contract with the approval of the creditor. As discussed previously, the Quran always favours the rights of the debtor over the creditor. Therefore, the right of dictating the contract is given to the debtor, but the debtors are to be thankful to the creditors for entrusting them with what they need. Thankfulness entails honouring the contract. If the debtors are unable to dictate the contract, their guardians or agents should dictate on their behalf. Nowadays, solicitors or other specialists may carry out this task.

and take as witness two witnesses from your men, and if there are not two men, then a man and two women; The parties should also have two trustworthy witnesses to testify to the authenticity of the contract, so that neither of the parties can deny the contract. The witnesses should be two men or if two men are not available then one man and two women in replacement of the other man. The witness arrangement sounds unfair to women by equating one male witness to two women.

Before delving into this matter further, there is a distinction between "bearing testimony" and "providing testimony". Bearing testimony is related to drawing up the contract and it is clear from the verse that it requires two women in place of a man. However, if the matter is brought before a court, the issue then becomes providing testimony and it may not be the case that a judge would require two women to testify in place of one man. They may accept the testimony of a woman and a man only. This is a matter of dispute between different Muslim jurists. It is also important to consider that bearing testimony is a responsibility, not a right. Therefore, it may not be considered as depriving women of their rights. Rather, the responsibility is a burden and may result in nasty cases of prolonged litigation which may even lead to threats and bloody reprisals from ill-intentioned parties, unfortunately, this is the case in some Muslim majority societies.

According to the verse, two female witnesses needing to testify in place of one male witness seems to be related to forgetfulness associated with women. However, daily life shows us that it is not the case that women are more forgetful than men. In fact, in some cases they have a better memory for details than men. More contemporary commentators have moved away from the "forgetfulness" argument and often use the argument of women being "emotional". It may be accurate to say that women often express their emotions more than men. However, this does not mean women may deviate from the truth because of their emotions.

This understanding would be considered as biased against women and their ability to observe the boundaries of God. The Quran and Muslim history are full of pious, intelligent and wise women including the Queen of Sheba, Saint Mary, Lady Khadija, the wife of the Prophet, Lady Fatima, the daughter of the Prophet and Lady Zaynab, the granddaughter of the Prophet, who have acclaimed much praised by God and by people. The Queen of Sheba was neither forgetful nor emotional when she received Solomon's letter. Instead of acting impulsively as many men in her court would have done if they were in her place, she consults with her advisers: *She said, 'O eminent ones, advise me in my affair. I would not decide a matter until you witness [for] me.'* (Q. 27:32) As a matter of fact, whilst her advisers were defiant to Solomon's request and *They said, 'We are men of strength and of great military might,'* (Q. 27:33) she was the most rational and circumspect amongst them: *She said, 'indeed kings - when they enter a city, they ruin it and render the honoured of its people humbled. And thus, so they do.'* (Q. 27:34) She was also not forgetful of the destructive effects of an All-out war with powerful adversaries. So, the Quran refutes the feasibility of these arguments.

Therefore, there must be another explanation for this ruling. The ruling does not mean that God allowed a gross infringement of women's rights, as bearing witness was considered a responsibility rather than a right. In fact, God strikes a balance between societal actualities and the rights of women. Anything more or less could disrupt the delicate balance within the society.

Within this framework a further argument can be made that in male dominated societies, women could be more susceptible to be influenced by men in the event of their need to testify. This external influence on women may be the cause of the deviation (*taḍillu*) that the verse refers to. Unfortunately, within many eastern societies, direct male domination still continues, which provides women with little room to exercise their rights and responsibilities. Having said that, in western societies it appears that there is no more male domination, but in reality, it still continues covertly. Media, politics and wealth are largely controlled by men, and they are the ones who impose the values and behaviours on society, including women.

وَإِن كُنتُمْ عَلَىٰ سَفَرٍ وَلَمْ تَجِدُوا كَاتِبًا فَرِهَانٌ مَّقْبُوضَةٌ فَإِنْ أَمِنَ
بَعْضُكُم بَعْضًا فَلْيُؤَدِّ الَّذِي اؤْتُمِنَ أَمَانَتَهُ وَلْيَتَّقِ اللَّهَ رَبَّهُ وَلَا تَكْتُمُوا
الشَّهَادَةَ وَمَن يَكْتُمْهَا فَإِنَّهُ آثِمٌ قَلْبُهُ وَاللَّهُ بِمَا تَعْمَلُونَ عَلِيمٌ ﴿283﴾

If you are on a journey and cannot find a writer, then a retained pledge [shall suffice]. And if one of you entrusts to another, let him who is trusted deliver his trust, and let him be wary of God, his Lord. And do not conceal testimony; anyone who conceals it, his heart will indeed be sinful. And God knows best what you do.

This verse concludes the discussion in the previous verse. It recommends that if parties are not able to find scribes to record the contract, due to the fact that they are travelling, then they should agree on a retainer and the buyer should provide a deposit and make the contract secure. However, if there is absolute trust between the parties, they may forgo these formalities and proceed with the transaction without writing it down or the need for a deposit.

The verses clearly state that those who are trusted must fulfil their trust. Honouring pledges is not only related to transactions; believers must fulfil their pledges under all circumstances - it is one of the most important and crucial tenets of faith. The vital importance of truthfulness is strongly emphasised elsewhere in the Quran: *Indeed, God commands you to deliver the trusts to their [rightful] owners, and, when you judge between people, to judge with fairness.* (Q. 4:58)

A very important narration attributed to the Holy Prophet further elaborates on the importance of truthfulness:

> Do not judge [the true character of] people based on their prayer, fasting, pilgrimage, charity or their broken voice [in tears] in the night prayers. But judge their true character based on their honesty and not betraying the trust.

In this tradition, the Prophet emphasises that if people perform all their obligatory and recommended acts, yet fail to fulfil their promises, then they do not have the good character of a believer.

لِلَّهِ مَا فِي السَّمَاوَاتِ وَمَا فِي الْأَرْضِ ۗ وَإِن تُبْدُوا مَا فِي أَنفُسِكُمْ أَوْ تُخْفُوهُ يُحَاسِبْكُم بِهِ اللَّهُ ۖ فَيَغْفِرُ لِمَن يَشَاءُ وَيُعَذِّبُ مَن يَشَاءُ ۗ وَاللَّهُ عَلَىٰ كُلِّ شَيْءٍ قَدِيرٌ ﴿284﴾

To God belongs whatever is in the heavens and whatever is in the earth; and whether you disclose what is in your hearts or hide it, God will bring you to account for it. Then He will forgive whomever He wishes and punish whomever He wishes, and God has power over all things.

This verse finalises all the decrees which have been mentioned in this chapter. Surah al-Baqarah includes numerous commands, covering various aspects of human interactions. Along with the following two verses, the verse seals the chapter.

To God belongs whatever is in the heavens and whatever is in the earth; God has the true ownership of the heavens and the earth and whatever is in them. He is the absolute and only true owner of all that exists. His ownership is real ownership rather than conventional ownership. In real ownership that which is owned has no independent existence without the owner. This is unlike the conventional ownership in which that which is owned has independent existence. God's ownership infuses the heart of the faithful with absolute reliance on God and brings forth a realisation that all are subservient to him and come to him utterly poor. Such a person has also no reason to hoard, usurp, oppress, colonise or transgress the rights of others. He sees himself as only a temporary custodian of all that he possesses and it becomes meaningless to be stingy, greedy, selfish or even fearful and anxious of their future.

And whether you disclose what is in your hearts or hide it, God will bring you to account for it. Since God has created everything and rules over everything, he is aware of everything that takes place within his kingdom. He is aware of the true inner qualities of his creation, and whatever people show in action. If we had truly contemplated this, we would have humbled ourselves before God. Humanity lives on absolute reliance on God - without his support and guidance, we cannot sustain, survive or achieve anything. We would have ceased to exist instantaneously.

Muslim theology maintains that people are only accountable for the actions they commit. They are not accountable for what they keep in their hearts. For example, aside from the pure ones, to some extent all people have jealousy in their hearts. But unless they act upon it, they would not be held accountable for it, otherwise all people would need to be punished. Yet the verse makes reference to "whether you disclose what is in your hearts or hide it, God will bring you to account for it." There seems to be a contradiction here.

The best explanation for this problem is provided by Razi, Kashani and Tabatabai.[344] According to them, this statement refers to what has been established in the heart as a quality. If people are too focused on certain things in their mind, it becomes part of their personality or inner quality that they carry with them to the Hereafter. They may not have found an opportunity to manifest this quality, yet this quality is engraved on their heart; therefore, they would be held accountable for the established hidden mischief in their hearts. On the other hand, if people have momentarily uncontrolled thoughts of sin in their minds, it would not be part of their inner quality, thus they would not be held accountable for them.

Then He will forgive whomever He wishes and punish whomever He wishes; Certainly, God does not do this indiscriminately. God's wish is not like human wish which is based on human desires. Rather, God's will is based on wisdom and truth. So, the statement means that he is able to forgive and punish whomever he pleases, and it is not for others to judge whom God should never forgive or whom God can never punish. And nor can anyone withhold or restrict God from recompensing his creatures as they deserve.

آمَنَ الرَّسُولُ بِمَا أُنزِلَ إِلَيْهِ مِن رَّبِّهِ وَالْمُؤْمِنُونَ كُلٌّ آمَنَ بِاللَّهِ وَمَلَائِكَتِهِ
وَكُتُبِهِ وَرُسُلِهِ لَا نُفَرِّقُ بَيْنَ أَحَدٍ مِّن رُّسُلِهِ وَقَالُوا سَمِعْنَا وَأَطَعْنَا غُفْرَانَكَ
رَبَّنَا وَإِلَيْكَ الْمَصِيرُ ﴿285﴾

The Apostle has faith in what has been sent down to him from his Lord, and all the faithful. Each [of them] has faith in God, His angels, His scriptures and His apostles. [They declare,] 'We make no distinction between any of His apostles.' And they say, 'We hear and obey. Our Lord, forgive us, and toward You is the return.'

The Apostle has faith in what has been sent down to him from his Lord, and all the faithful. This verse brings the chapter to a close and reaffirms the Prophet's and believer's faith in the Almighty. It mentions the Prophet and the faithful separately to distinguish between their levels of faith. The Prophet's faith was very different to that of his followers; it was much deeper and stronger, and based on more knowledge and insight. Hence the Prophet was totally absorbed in his submission to God. This is while the believers were still struggling with some of the fundamental aspects of faith.

Each [of them] has faith in God, His angels, His scriptures and His apostles. At the very beginning of this chapter God described the pious as those who believe in the unseen. Believing in angels is an important aspect of believing in the unseen since they are not perceivable by our senses. Obviously, it is absurd to consider the sensual faculties as the criterion to determine what exists and what does not or to think that whatever the senses cannot capture does not exist. In the Quran, and in all heavenly Books, God insists on the belief in the angels because they are part of the reality of creation, and because they have a great bearing on human life in this world and the next. Therefore, believing in angels is crucial to having correct faith. Furthermore, believing in angels affirms that the creation of God is not limited to this world.

[They declare,] 'We make no distinction between any of His apostles.' The last verses of Surah al-Baqarah are perhaps some of the last verses to be revealed. The entire chapter was revealed in Medina and by the time it was completed, the ministry of the Prophet was coming to its end. It is striking that at this point, when the Quran was almost completed, the believers were still expected to believe not only in the Quran, but also in the other divine scriptures. Similarly, God expects the believers to believe in not only Prophet Muhammad but also all other prophets. Muslims are not allowed to discriminate between God's prophets and scriptures. They cannot say that a certain prophet or nation received better guidance than the others or one Book of God is holier than the others. The Quran does not speak in racist terms as many people may think. Some Muslims ridicule the Jews based on their rejection and disobedience to God and his messengers, but the Quran criticises the early Muslims in the same way as it criticised the Jews. The Quran also praises some of the sincere Jews and Christians as it also praises some Muslims. Readers of the Quran must bear in mind that God never discriminates against his creation. He loves and cares about them all and his ultimate objective is the salvation of his creation regardless of their gender, race and colour.

لَا يُكَلِّفُ اللَّهُ نَفْسًا إِلَّا وُسْعَهَا ۚ لَهَا مَا كَسَبَتْ وَعَلَيْهَا مَا اكْتَسَبَتْ ۗ رَبَّنَا لَا
تُؤَاخِذْنَا إِن نَّسِينَا أَوْ أَخْطَأْنَا ۚ رَبَّنَا وَلَا تَحْمِلْ عَلَيْنَا إِصْرًا كَمَا حَمَلْتَهُ عَلَى
الَّذِينَ مِن قَبْلِنَا ۚ رَبَّنَا وَلَا تُحَمِّلْنَا مَا لَا طَاقَةَ لَنَا بِهِ ۖ وَاعْفُ عَنَّا وَاغْفِرْ لَنَا
وَارْحَمْنَا ۚ أَنتَ مَوْلَانَا فَانصُرْنَا عَلَى الْقَوْمِ الْكَافِرِينَ ﴿286﴾

God does not task any soul beyond its ease. Whatever [good] it earns is to its benefit, and whatever [evil] it incurs is to its harm. 'Our Lord! Take us not to task if we forget or make mistakes! Our Lord! Place not upon us a burden as You placed on those who were before us! Our Lord! Lay not upon us what we have no strength to bear! Excuse us and forgive us, and be merciful to us! You are our Master, so help us against the faithless lot!'

God does not task any soul beyond its ease. This means that whatever God has commanded is within a person's power to do. The term "*wus'*" is often translated as one's capacity but it has the meaning of less than one's capacity. That means God would never test a person to the very brink of their capacity. The limit of a person's capacity is not the five daily prayers or going to pilgrimage once in a lifetime. But God tasks people with less than their capacity to make things easy for them. Of course, God has tasked some special people including the great prophets to a higher degree but even for them the task did not reach the limit of their capacity.

The entirety of Islamic legislation must be understood in the light of this very verse; if an obligation is deemed to be beyond one's *wus'* then that legislation is a misunderstanding of the jurists.

Whatever [good] it earns is to its benefit, and whatever [evil] it incurs is to its harm. After reassuring the believers that whatever God instructs them to do is well within the limits of their capacity, this statement informs the believers of their responsibilities and the result of their own actions. It rejects the delusions of determinism, chance and discrimination. Instead, it is a reminder that whatever God commands people to do is for their own sake, and whatever people have earned in this world, they would receive the benefit of it in the Hereafter. They would also receive the consequences of whatever evil they have earned.

'Our Lord! Take us not to task if we forget or make mistakes!' Juxtaposed to the two essential principles, that man's duty is well within the limits of his capacity, and that everyone is responsible for their own deeds, God teaches his servants to request seven things from him to further ease the burden of responsibility on them. When God puts a supplication in the mouth of his servants, it means that he is determined to fulfil it.

Of course, God would not punish people for the misdeeds they do out of forgetfulness and error. However, there are instances of forgetfulness and error which result from carelessness. These errors are punishable, but God alleviates this by teaching the believers to ask for forgiveness even for these errors. Since they know that they are punishable for their own actions, they call *God* as their Lord (*rabbanā*), the one who has created them and is sustaining them with his special grace. The believers should utter these words with a repentant heart to express their submission and humility to God. Moreover, for the believers, this request is another way of acknowledging their shortcomings and weaknesses, as well as God's mercy because of which their unintentional sins and mistakes are forgiven.

'Our Lord! Place not upon us a burden as You placed on those who were before us!' There are some instances in the Quran that suggest that God may lay heavy burdens on some people. As described in the early verses of this surah, the Israelites worshipped the Golden Calf when Moses left them to go to God's tryst. When Moses returned, God forgave them on the condition that those who worshipped the Golden Calf must be killed. This was indeed a very heavy burden for the Israelites as a result of their flagrant violation of God's commands. The verse uses the word *iṣr* (which alludes to a very heavy burden) for this kind of responsibility and encourages the believers to ask God not to task them with such heavy burdens.

'Excuse us and forgive us, and be merciful to us!' The final point in this verse is about the remission of sins. When a person commits a sin, the consequence of the sin would follow them in this world as well as the Hereafter. This is how God has established the system of the universe; every action has a consequence and the consequence remains with the perpetrator both in this world and in the next. "Excuse us!" is a plea to remove the consequences of the sin.

Furthermore, even if the consequences of the sins are removed, the scars of the sins would remain on the soul, which would make the soul defective. Therefore, believers should ask God to heal the defective state of their souls, and to cover their defects and shortcomings. This is the meaning of "forgive us." The Arabic word used for excusing is *'afw,* while the Arabic word used for forgiveness is *maghfira*. The difference between *'afw* and *maghfira* has been explained previously. All these must be accompanied with the All-embracing mercy of God which enables believers to enter Paradise - the ultimate mercy.

'You are our Master, so help us against the faithless lot!' Lastly, God makes it clear that if believers ask God to help them in their struggle against disbelievers, whilst having the right intention and using the correct logic and argument, he will of course help them.

This extremely beautiful supplication brings the chapter to an end. After all the legislation, instructions, historical anecdotes, eye-opening parables, and thought-provoking concepts, this ending is certainly the most promising and the most hope-giving conclusion to the chapter.

Our supplication at the end of this book is to ask for the fulfilment of this prayer for all our dear readers:

"'Our Lord! Take us not to task if we forget or make mistakes!
Our Lord! Place not upon us a burden
as You placed on those who were before us!
Our Lord! Lay not upon us what we have no strength to bear!
Excuse us and forgive us, and be merciful to us!
You are our Master, so help us against the faithless lot!'"

Endnotes

1. Seyfeddin Kara, *In Search of Ali Ibn Abi Talib's Codex: History and Traditions of the Earliest Copy of the Qur'an* (Berlin: Gerlach Press, 2018).

2. Mohammad Hossein Ṭabāṭabā'ī, *al-Mizān fī tafsīr al-qur'ān*, vol. 1 (Qom: Ismā'īlīyān, 1985), 12.

3. Mohammad Hossein Ṭabāṭabā'ī, *The Qur'an in Islam* (London, 1987), 53.

4. For an analysis of Ṭabāṭabā'ī method see, Seyfeddin Kara, 'Rational-Analytical Tafsīr in Modern Iran: The Influence of the Uṣūlī School of Jurisprudence on the Interpretation of the Qur'an', in *Approaches to the Qur'an in Contemporary Iran*, ed. Alessandro Cancian (London: Oxford University Press, 2019), 19–39.

5. Ali Quli Qara'i, *The Qur'ān: With a Phrase-by-Phrase English Translation*, Second Edition (London: ICAS Press, 2005).

6. al-Faḍl b. al-Ḥasan b. al-Faḍl Ṭabrisī, *Majma' al-bayān fī tafsīr al-qur'ān*, vol. 1 of 10 vols. (Beirut: Dār al-'Ulūm, 2005), 118.

7. Muḥammad b. Murtaḍā Fayḍ Kāshānī, *Tafsīr al-ṣāfī*, vol.1 of 7 vols. (Tehran: Dār al-Kutub, 2007), 91.

8. Mohammad Hossein Ṭabāṭabā'ī, *al-Mizān,* 1:34–35.

9. Shaykh al-Ṭūsī, *al-Tibyānfī tafsīr al-Qur'ān*, vol.1 of 10 vols. (Beirut: Dār al-Iḥyā al-Turāth al-'Arabī, 1971), 56.

10. *Nahj al-balāgha*, sermon 179.

11. Fakhr al-Dīn Rāzī, *Mafātīḥ al-ghayb*, vol. 2 of 32 vols. (Damascus: Dār al-Fikr, 1981), 274.

12. al-Fayḍ Kāshānī, *Tafsīr al-ṣāfī*, vol. 1 (Qom: Markaz al-Abḥāth wa-al-Dirarāsāt al-Islāmiyya, 1997), 92.

13. Ṭabāṭabā'ī, *al-Mīzān fī tafsīr al-qur'ān*, vol 1 of 22 vols. (Beirut: Mu'assasat al-A'lamī, 1973), 55-56.

14. Jalāl al-Dīn al-Khuḍayrī al-Suyūṭī, *Tafsīr al-jalālayn*, vol. 1 of 8 vols. (Beirut: Dār al-Kutub al-'Ilmiyya, 1996).

15. al-Shaykh al-Ṣadūq, *'Uyūn akhbār al-riḍā*, ed. Ḥusayn al-A'lamī, vol. 2 (Beirut: Muassasa al-A'lāmī, 1984), 115.

16. Kāshānī, *Tafsīr al-ṣāfī*, 1:98.

17. These words are mentioned in Q. 6:98.

18. *Nahj al-balāgha*, Sermon 189.

19. Matthew: 13: 1-23; Mark 4: 1-20; Luke 8: 4-15, New King James Version (NKJV).

20. Matthew 13, (NKJV).

21. C. W. F. Smith, *The Jesus of the Parables* (Philadelphia: Westminster Press, 1948), 17.

22. Which may be translated as *The Subtle Allusions*. This is probably a name borrowed from a hadith of Imam Jafar al-Sadiq mentioned in *Miṣbāḥ al-sharī'a*, a book of ethical science attributed to Imam Jafar al-Sadiq.

23. 'Abd al-Karīm b. Hūzān Abū al-Qāsim al-Qushayrī, *Laṭā'if al-isharat bi-tafsīr al-qur'ān*, vol. 1 of 3 vols. (al-Hay'a al-Miṣriyya al-'Āmma lil-Kitāb, 2000), 66.

24. al-Ḥasan al-'Askarī, *Tafsīr al-imām al-'askarī* (Madrasa al-Imām Mahdī, 1989), 135–36.

25. Nasir Makarim Shirazi, *Tafsīr-i nimūna*, vol. 1 of 27 vols. (Tehran: Dār al-Kitāb, 2008), 157.

26. See Q. 42:4

27. Ṭabrisī, *Majma' al-bayān*, vol. 8:194.

28. Some commentators believe that the sudden revelation was the

descent of the totality of the Quran without words to the heart of the Prophet. See Ṭabāṭabā'ī *al-Mīzān*, 5:126.

29. Q. 6:7.

30. Q. 6:36.

31. Ṭabāṭabā'ī, *al-Mīzān,* 1:60.

32. Ibid., 1:91–92.

33. al-Qushayrī, *Laṭā'if al-ishārāt*, 1:69.

34. Ṭabrisī, *Majma' al-bayān*, 1:162.

35. Ibid.

36. Ibid.

37. There are two types of restriction in experiencing God: The first is restriction of our existence, but this will diminish over time, as we continue our journey towards God in the Hereafter. This view is reinforced by the verse of Quran: "and purify you with a purification" (Q. 33:33), as it states the Members of the Household of the Prophet will be continuously purified and thus refers to expansion in their existence. This is also the case for normal people. The second restriction comes from our evil deeds which restrict us from God Almighty – therefore, so long as we commit evil deeds it will be a restriction in experiencing God.

38. Q. 22:73.

39. Q. 29:41.

40. Ṭabrisī, *Majma' al-bayan*, 1:165.

41. Ibid., 1:170.

42. *Nahj al-balāgha*, Sermon 1.

43. Kāshānī, *Tafsīr al-ṣāfī,* 1:105.

44. Ibid., 106.

45. See Ṭabrisī, *Majma' al-bayān*, 1:172.

46. Muḥammad Jamāl al-Dīn al-Qāsimī, *Maḥāsin al-ta'wīl*, vol. 1 of 9

vols. (Beirut: Dār al-Kutub al-'Ilmiyya, 2002), 282.

47. Ibid.

48. Ibid.

49. Ṭabāṭabā'ī, *al-Mīzān*, 17:370.

50. Rāzī, Mafātīḥ al-ghayb, 2:388.

51. See Bart D. Ehrman, *How Jesus Became God: The Exaltation of a Jewish Preacher from Galilee* (USA: HarperOne, 2014).

52. al-Shaykh al-Ṣadūq, *'Ilal al-sharā'i*, vol. 1 (Qum: Nashr-e Dāvari, 2006), 104.

53. Kāshānī, *Tafsīr al-ṣāfi*, 1:106.

54. 'Alī b. Ibrāhīm Qummī, *Tafsīr qummī*, vol. 1 of 2 vols. (Beirut: Dār al-Kutub, 1983), 36.

55. Kāshānī, *Tafsīr al-ṣāfi*, 1:108.

56. Muḥammad b. Muḥammad b. Nu'mān Shaykh al-Mufīd, *Awā'il al-maqālāt* (Beirut: Dār al-Mufīd, 1994).

57. The most well-known Sunni *Tafsīr* work, written first by Jalāladdīn al-Maḥallī (d. 864/1469) and then his student Jalāladdīn al-Suyūṭī.

58. Jalāladdīn al-Maḥallī and Jalāladdīn al-Suyūṭī, *Tafsīr al-jalālayn* (Beirut: Dār al-Ma'rifa, 1971), 9.

59. Rāzī, *Mafātīḥ al-ghayb*, 2:424–27.

60. Ibid.

61. Ṭabāṭabā'ī, *al-Mizān fi Tafsīr al-qur'ān*, 1:114–21.

62. Ibid.

63. See Rāzī , *Tafsīr al-kabīr*, 2:427–48.

64. Ṭūsī, *al-Tibyān,* 1:156.

65. Rāzī , *Mafātīḥ al-ghayb,* 3:452.

66. Ibid.

67. Ṭūsī, *al-Tibyān,* 1:158.

68. Ibid.

69. Ibid. 1:159.

70. The famous student of Ibn Abbas, who was the one who inspired the rational Mutazilite tafsir.

71. Ṭūsī, *al-Tibyān* 1:169.

72. Ṭabarsī, *Majma' al-bayān* 1:200.

73. Kāshānī, *Tafsīr al-ṣāfi*, 1:120.

74. Ibid., 1:122.

75. Ṭūsī, *al-Tibyān,* 1:177.

76. Ibid., 178.

77. Rāzī, *Mafātīḥ al-ghayb*, 3:474.

78. Ṭabrisī, *Majma' al-bayān* 1:208; Ṭūsī, *al-Tibyān*, 1:183.

79. Rāzī, *Mafātīḥ al-ghayb,* 3:484.

80. Kāshānī, *Tafsīr al-ṣāfi,* 1:124.

81. Ṭūsī, *al-Tibyān,* 1:186.

82. For example, "Jesus left there and went to his hometown, accompanied by his disciples. 2 When the Sabbath came, he began to teach in the synagogue, and many who heard him were amazed. "Where did this man get these things?" they asked. "What's this wisdom that has been given him? What are these remarkable miracles he is performing? 3 Isn't this the carpenter? Isn't this Mary's son and the brother of James, Joseph, [a] Judas and Simon? Aren't his sisters here with us?" And they took offense at him. 4 Jesus said to them, "A prophet is not without honor except in his own town, among his relatives and in his own home." 5 He could not do any miracles there, except lay his hands on a few sick people and heal them. 6 He was amazed at their lack of faith." (Mark 6:1-6, New International Version).

83. *Nahj al-balāgha*, Sermon 50.

84. *Nahj al-balāgha*, Sermon 175.

85. See Kāshānī, *Tafsīr al-ṣāfi,* 1:126.

86. Ibid.

87. Ibid.

88. For example, Q. 10:3, 34:23, 20:109, 19:87.

89. Kāshānī, *Tafsīr al-ṣāfī*, 1:127.

90. al-Qāsimī, *Maḥāsin al-ta'wīl,* 1:303.

91. Ṭūsī, *al-Tibyān,* 1:213.

92. See Richard H. Wilkinson, *The Complete Gods and Goddesses of Ancient Egypt* (London: Thames & Hudson, 2003).

93. Exodus: 32:29, NIV.

94. 'Alī Akbar Qurashī, *Aḥsan al-ḥadīth*, vol. 1, (Tehran: Vāḥid-i Taḥqīqāt-i Islāmī-i Bunyād-i Bi'sa, 1987), 128.

95. Ibid.

96. *Mafātīḥ al-ghayb,* 3:519.

97. This number is mentioned in Q. 7:155. The same number is stated in the Old Testament as 'seventy of the elders of Israel' (Exodus, 24:1).

98. In order to solve this obvious contradiction between the verses of the Old Testament, Rabbis interpreted Exodus, 24:9-10 that Moses and the seventy Jewish leaders saw the second deity or god; not the Almighty God. Therefore, they complicated the matter further as such interpretation compromised the monotheistic nature of Jewish Scriptures and faith. See, Ehrman, *How Jesus Became God.*

99. Kāshānī, *Tafsīr al-ṣāfī,* 1:134.

100. Ibid., 1:133.

101. Rāzī, *Mafātīḥ al-ghayb*, 3:1.

102. Qurashī, *Aḥsan al-ḥadīth,* 1:132.

103. al-Zamakhsharī, *al-Kashshāf,* 1:142.

104. Ṭabrisī, *Majma' al-bayān*, 1:247.

105. al-Zamakhsharī, *al-Kashshāf,* 1:142.

106. Mahmud Taleghani, *Partovi az qur'an*, vol. 1 (Tehran: Shirkat-i Sehami-i Intishār,1983), 166.

107. Rāzī, *Mafātīḥ al-ghayb*, 3:525.

108. Ibid.

109. Qurashī, *Aḥsan al-ḥadīth*, 1:143.

110. Ṭabrisī, *Tibyān,* 1:268.

111. Rāzī, *Mafātīḥ al-ghayb*, 3:525.

112. According to the Old Testament, Prophet Jacob, who was later given the name of Israel, is the founder of Israelites. He had twelve sons who were the ancestors of the twelve Israelite tribes.

113. Rāzī, *Mafātīḥ al-ghayb*, 3:530.

114. Ibid.

115. New International Version

116. Ṭabrisī, *Majma' al-bayān*, 1:256.

117. Nation is not used in its modern meaning.

118. Qurashī, *Aḥsan al-ḥadīth*, 1:146.

119. Muḥammad Bāqir Majlisī, *Biḥār al-anwār*, vol. 2 of 111 vols. (Beirut: Dār Iḥyā' al-Turāth al-'Arabī, 1983), 22.

120. Muḥammad b. al-Ḥasan al-Ṣaffār, *Baṣā'ir al-darajāt*, vol. 1 (Qom: Āyatullāh Mar'ashī Najafī Library, 1983), 29.

121. Rāzī, *Mafātīḥ al-ghayb*, 3:536.

122. Ṭūsī, *al-Tibyān,* 1:283.

123. Qummī, *Tafsīr qummī*, 1:48.

124. Ṭūsī, *al-Tibyān,* 1:283.

125. Muḥīṭ Ṭabāṭabā'ī, "Ṣābi'īn ahle itāband," in *Yādnāmeh ustād motahari,* ed. by Abdolkarim Soroush (Tehran: Ṣāzimāne Tablīghāte Islami, 1984), 43-60

126. Shab. 88a

127. Ṭabāṭabā'ī, *al-Mizān*, 1:198

128. ʿAbd al-Karīm al-Qushayrī, *Laṭāʾif al-ishārāt: Subtle Allusions*, trans. Kristin Zahra Sands (USA: Fons Vitae, 2017), 77.

129. A leading Shāfiʿī scholar of various Islamic fields including exegesis. He was a student of Ṭabarī and spread the Shāfiʿī legal school in Transoxiana. For his great erudition and influence, he was given the title of al-Qaffāl al-Kabīr (al-Qaffāl the Great). Razi often quotes from al-Qaffāl to support his arguments.

130. Rāzī, *Mafātīḥ al-ghayb*, 4:539.

131. Rāghib, *s-b-t*

132. See for example, Rāzi, vol. 3:542.

133. Aḥmad b. Muṣṭafa al-Marāghī, *Tafsīr al-marāghī*, vol. 1 of 30 vols. (Egypt: Shirkat Maktaba wa-Maṭbuʿa, 1946), 133.

134. al-Qushayrī, *Laṭāʾif al-ishārāt: Subtle Allusions*, 77.

135. Rāzī , *Mafātīḥ al-ghayb*, 4:542; Abū Isḥāk al-Thaʿlabī, *Tafsīr al-thaʿlabī*, ed. Ibn ʿĀshūr Abū Muḥammad, vol. 1 of 10 vols. (Beirut: Dār Iḥyā, 2002), 213.

136. Ṭabrisī, *Majmaʿ al-bayān*, 1:265.

137. Ibid

138. Sources of Emulation, the Highest Religious Authorities in Shiʿi faith.

139. Muḥammad Javād Balāghī, *Ālāʾ al-raḥmān fi tafsīr al-qurʾān*, vol. 1of 2 vols. (Qom: Maktabat al-Wijdān, 1971), 101.

140. Rāzī , *Mafātīḥ al-ghayb*, 3:549.

141. Qummī, *Tafsīr al-qummi*, 1:49.

142. Rāzī , *Mafātiḥ al-ghayb*, 3:552.

143. Ibid.

144. Ṭabarsī, *Majmaʿ al-bayān*, 1:278.

145. Kāshānī, *Tafsīr al-ṣāfi*, 1:144.

146. al-Qushayrī, *Laṭā'if al-Ishārāt*, 1:99.

147. Ibid.

148. Ibid.

149. Kāshānī, *Tafsīr al-ṣāfī*, 4:319.

150. Jalāl al-Dīn al-Suyūṭī, *al-Durr al-manthūr fī al-tafsīr bi-al-ma'thūr*, vol. 5 of 8 vols. (Qom: al-Najafī, 1982), 325.

151. Majlisī, *Biḥār al-anwār*, 95:63.

152. Qurashī, *Aḥsan al-ḥadīth*, 1:161.

153. See also Q. 21:79 and 34:10.

154. Ṭūsī, *al-Tibyān*, 1:313.

155. Ibid.

156. Ṭabrisī, *Majma' al-bayān*, 1:285.

157. Mohammad Saeed Bahmanpour, "Review of Revelation and Falsification: The Kitāb al-Qira'at of Ahmad b. Muhammad," *Journal of Shi'a Islamic Studies* 3:2 (2010), 231–33.

158. Ibn Hishām, *Sīra al-nabawī*, ed. 'Umar 'Abd al-Salām Tadmurī, (Beirut: Dār al-Kitāb al-'Arabī, 1990).

159. Ṭūsī, *al-Tibyān*, 1:318.

160. It is ironic that nowadays some Muslims have the same mindset that they assume they are entitled to do anything they wish to non-Muslims or who they perceive to be non-Muslims. Therefore, it is not about being part of a specific religion, thus we cannot attribute these qualities to the members of a specific religion. It is about having an arrogant and deceitful mindset that de-humanises others to legitimise its unjust deeds. Whether they are Jews or Muslims, God categorically condemns such a twisted mindset.

161. Kāshānī, *Tafsīr al-ṣāfī*, 1:147.

162. Imam Hasan Askari, *Tafseer Imam Hasan Askari*, trans. S. H. Rizvi, Online (Qom: Ansariyan Publications, 2009), (https://www.al-islam.org/tafseer-imam-hasan-askari/exegesis-surah-baqarah-verses-

63-92#exegesis-surah-baqarah-verse-278-79).

163. Rāzī, *Mafātiḥ al-ghayb*, 3:565.

164. Kāshānī, *Tafsīr al-ṣāfī*,1:148.

165. Rāzī, *Mafātīḥ al-ghayb*, 3:568.

166. Ibid.

167. Majlisī, *Biḥār al-anwār*, 6:241-61.

168. Exodus 20, New International Version.

169. For examples see, Jeffrey P. Greenman and Timothy Larsen, eds., *The Decalogue Through the Centuries: From the Hebrew Scriptures to Benedict XVI* (Louisville, Kentucky: Presbyterian Publishing Corporation, 2012); William P. Brown, ed., *The Ten Commandments: The Reciprocity of Faithfulness* (Louisville, London: Presbyterian Publishing Corporation, 2004).

170. Rāzī , *Mafātiḥ al-ghayb*, 3:586.

171. Muḥammad b. Ya'qūb b. Isḥāq Kulaynī, *al-Kāfī fī 'ilm al-dīn*, ed. Muḥammad Ghafārī 'Alī Akbar Akhūndī vol. 2 of 15 vols. (Tehran: Dār al-Kutub al-Islāmiyya, 1986), 426.

172. Kāshānī, *Tafsīr al-ṣāfī*, 1:150.

173. Ibid.

174. Ibid.

175. Ṭūsī, *al-Tibyān*, 1:331.

176. Ḥusayn b. Mas'ūd al-Baghawī, *Ma'ālim al-tanzīl*, vol. 1 (Beirut: Dār al-Kutub al-'Ilmiyya, 1971), 140.

177. Ibid.

178. Kāshānī, *Tafsīr al-ṣāfī*, 1:157.

179. Ibid., 1:154.

180. See Rāzī , *Mafātiḥ al-ghayb*, 3:596.

181. Rāzī , *Mafātīḥ al-ghayb*, 3:597.

182. Ṭabāṭabā'ī, *al-Mīzān*, 5:132.

183. Rāzī , *Mafātīḥ al-ghayb*, 3:597.

184. This issue is discussed further in reference to verse 89.

185. Kāshānī, *Tafsīr al-ṣāfi*, 1:158.

186. Muḥammad b. Mas'ūd 'Ayyāshī, *Tafsīr al-'ayyāshī*, ed. Sayyid Hāshim Rasūlī Maḥlātī, vol. 1 of 2 vols. (Tehran: al-Maṭba'a al-'Alamiyya, 1961), 49–50.

187. For a detailed study on the origins of Medinan Jews, see Moshe Gil, *Jews in Islamic Countries in the Middle Ages*, trans. David Strassler (Leiden: Brill, 2004).

188. Rāzī, *Mafātīḥ al-Ghaib*, 3:599.

189. Abū Ḥāmid Ghazālī, *Iḥyā' 'ulūm al-dīn*, Persian translation, vol 3 (Tehran: no publisher, 1955), 125.

190. A derogatory term to refer Shi'is.

191. Abu al-Qasim Khoei, *Miṣbāḥ al-fuqāha*, vol. 3 of 7 vols. (Qom: 1958), 436

192. *Nahj al-balāgha*, Wisdom 456.

193. Ṭabāṭabā'ī, *al-Mīzān*, 1:222.

194. Rāzī , *Mafātīḥ al-ghayb*, 3:602.

195. Kāshānī, *Tafsīr al-ṣāfi*, 1:163.

196. Muqātil b. Sulaymān, *Tafsīr*, vol. 1 of 8 vols. (Beirut: Dār al-Kutub al-'Ilmiyya, 2003), 124.

197. Muḥammad b. Jarīr Ṭabarī, *Jāmi' al-bayān 'an ta'wīl āya al-qur'ān*, vol. 2 of 25 vols. (Cairo: Dār Hijr, 2008) 262-63

198. Ibid.

199. Mullā Fatḥullāh Kāshānī, *Manhaj al-ṣādigīn*, vol. 1 (Qom: Būstān-i Kitāb, 2011), 237.

200. Muqātil b. Sulaymān, *Tafsīr*, 1:124.

201. Ṭabrisī, *Majma' al-Bayān*, 1:318.

202. Kāshānī, *Tafsīr al-ṣāfī,* 1:164.

203. Sayyid Qutb, *Fī ẓilāl al-qur'ān*, vol. 1 (Beirut: Dār al-Shurūq, 1977), 91.

204. Ṭabrisī, *Majma' al-bayān*, 1:319.

205. Sayyid Qutb, *In the Shade of the Qur'an* (*Fī ẓilāl al-qur'ān*), vols 1-2 (no publication details), 101. [https://tafsirzilal.files.wordpress.com/2012/06/al-baqarah-eng.pdf]

206. Ṭabrisī, *Majma' al-bayān*, 1:319.

207. Rāzī , *Mafātīḥ al-ghayb*, 3:606.

208. Ṭabarsī, *Majma' al-bayān*, 1:320.

209. Ṭabāṭabā'ī, *al-Mīzān,* 1:228.

210. Qutb, *Fī ẓilāl al-qur'ān,* 1-2:104.

211. Rāzī , *Mafātīḥ al-ghayb*, 3:610.

212. Ibid.

213. Ya'qūb Ja'farī, *Tafsīr kawthar*, vol. 1 of 6 vols. (Qom: Muassasa-i Intishārāt-i Hijrat, 1997), 296.

214. Qutb, *Fī ẓilāl al-qur'ān,* 1-2:103.

215. Ṭabāṭabā'ī, *al-Mīzān*, 1:229.

216. According to Islamic theology, angels do have free will, but they do not have desires like human beings. Archangel Gabriel has no free will in conveying the message of God; he must deliver God's message to his prophets. In the same manner, prophets also have no free will in conveying God's message to human beings. Once they accept their mission, they have no choice but to deliver the message as it is.

217. Qutb, *Fī ẓilāl al-qur'ān*, 1-2:105.

218. He was the Vizier of Solomon who was implicitly mentioned in the Quran as the human who transferred the throne of the Queen of Sheba to the court of Solomon in the blink of an eye. See Q. 27:38-42.

219. Qummī, *Tafsīr qummī*, 1:55.

220. Ṭabāṭabā'ī, *al-Mīzān*, 1:237.

221. Kāshānī, *Tafsīr al-ṣāfī*, 1:171.

222. Ibid., 172.

223. 'Ayyāshī, *Tafsīr al-'ayyāshī*, 1:52.

224. Ibid., 1:52–54.

225. See also al-Suyūṭī, *al-Durr al-manthūr*, 1: 97.

226. Ṭabāṭabā'ī, *al-Mīzān*, 1:233-39

227. Ibid., 237.

228. In Arabic, the word *unẓurnā* means "be patient with us" so it has the same meaning as the word *ra'inā*.

229. Qutb, *Fī ẓilāl al-qur'ān*, 1-2:115.

230. Ṭabāṭabā'ī, *al-Mīzān*, 1:249.

231. 'Abbās b. Muḥammad Riḍā Qummī, *Mafātīḥ al-jinān*, the common follow ups (*ta'qībāt*) of prayer.

232. Abu Ammaar Yasir Qadhi, *An Introduction to the Sciences of the Qur'an* (UK: Al-Hidaayah Publishing & Distribution, 1999), 235.

233. Abū Ja'far al-Naḥḥās, *al-Nasikh wa-al-mansūkh* (Riyadh: Markaz al-Turāth, 2013).

234. Abū al-Qāsim b.'Alī Akbar Khū'ī, *Prolegomena to the Qur'an* (New York: Oxford University Press, 1998), 192.

235. Ismail Ragi al-Faruqi, "Towards a New Methodology for Qur'anic Exegesis," *Islamic Studies* 1/1 (1962), 44.

236. 'Abd al-'Aẓīm al-Zurqānī, *Manāhil al-'irfān fī 'ulūm al-qur'ān* (Beirut: Dār al-Kutub al-'Ilmīya, 1996).

237. Muḥammad b. Idrīs al-Shāfi'ī, *Treatise on the Foundations of Islamic Jurisprudence – Al Shafi'i's Risala*, trans. Majid Khadduri (Turkey: Fons Vitae Publishing, 2008).

238. al-Suyūṭī, *al-Durr al-manthūr*, 6:185.

239. Ṭabrisī, *Majma' al-bayān*, 1:345.

240. Ṭūsī, *al-Tibyān*, 1:395; Qurashī, *Aḥsan al-ḥadīth*, 1:210.

241. Muḥammad al-Bukhārī, *Ṣaḥīḥ al-bukhārī*, vol. 8 of 9 vols. (Beirut: Dār Ṭawq al-Najāt, 2001), 208-211; Ibn al-Ḥajjāj Muslim, *Ṣaḥīḥ muslim*, vol. 4 of 5 vols. (Beirut: Dār Iḥyā' al-Turāth al-'Arabī, 2010), 167.

242. Mālik b. Anas, *Muwaṭṭā'*, vol. 1 (Beirut: Dār Iḥyā', 1994), 456.

243. John Burton provides a detailed analysis of these tradtion, see John Burton, *The Collection of the Qur'an*, First Edition (UK: Cambridge University Press, 1977).

244. Ṭūsī, *al-Tibyān*, 1:402.

245. Ṭabarsī, *Majma' al-bayān*, 1:353.

246. Ḥuyayy b. Akhṭab's daughter Ṣafiyya (d. 50/670) was captured in the Battle of Khaybar after her husband was killed. She embraced Islam and was married to the Prophet. She was highly revered in Muslim sources as a noble and virtuous woman. She was the last wife of the Prophet who died in Medina.

247. Ṭabarsī, *Majma' al-bayān*, 1:354.

248. Ibid.

249. Qurashī, *Aḥsan al-ḥadith,* vol. 1, p. 216.

250. Rāzī , *Mafātīḥ al-ghayb,* 4:9.

251. Tūsī, *al-Tibyān* 2:414.

252. al-'Askarī, *Tafsīr al-imām al-'askarī*, 544–45.

253. For example, "Certainly We gave the Children of Israel the Book, judgment and prophethood and We provided them with all the good things, and We gave them an advantage over all the nations, and We gave them manifest precepts. But they did not differ except after knowledge had come to them..." (Q. 45:16-17)

254. Rāzī , *Mafātīḥ al-ghayb,* 4:10–18.

255. Ibid.

256. Ibid.

257. 'Ayyāshī, *Tafsīr al-'ayyāshī*, 1:178–80.

258. Kāshānī, *Tafsīr al-ṣāfī*, 1:181–82.

259. Tūsī, *al-Tibyān*, 2:419.

260. Ibid., 2:424.

261. Ibid., 2:223–24.

262. Muḥammad Bāqir Majlisī, *Biḥār al-anwār*, vol. 24 of 104 vols. (Muassasa al-Wafā', 1983), 303.

263. It is a compilation of traditions about the topics of unity of God and other theological issues about the nature of God.

264. Ehrman, *How Jesus Became God: The Exaltation of a Jewish Preacher from Galilee.*

265. Kāshānī, *Tafsīr al-ṣāfī*, 1:184–85; 'Ayyāshī, *Tafsīr al-'ayyāshī*, 1:57.

266. Kulaynī, *al-Kāfī*, 1:202–5.

267. Ṭabrisī, *Majma' al-bayān*, 1:380.

268. Ibid., 1:380-81.

269. Kulaynī, *al-Kāfī*, 4:541.

270. Ṭabāṭabā'ī, *al-Mizān*, 1:296.

271. Ibid., 1:297.

272. Ṭabrisī, *Majma' al-bayān*, 1:399.

273. Ṭabāṭabā'ī, *al-Mizān*, 1:300–305.

274. Tūsī, *al-Tibyān*, 2:485–86.

275. Ṭabrisī, *Majma' al-bayān*, 1:407.

276. Ibid., 1:432–33.

277. Tūsī, *al-Tibyān*, 2:2–5.

278. Ibid., 2:201–2.

279. *Nahj al-balāgha*, Wisdom 95.

280. Ṭabrisī, *Majma' al-bayān* 1:468.

281. Ibid.,

282. Ibid., 1:445–46.

283. Ṭabāṭabā'ī, *al-Mizān,* 1:408–16.

284. Ṭabrisī, *Majma' al-bayān,* 1:457.

285. Akhbārīs are a group of Twelver Shi'i jurists who take the only source of fiqh to be narrations and hadiths by the Prophet and Imams.

286. Kāshānī, *Tafsīr al-ṣāfī*, 1:211.

287. Ṭabrisī, *Majma' al-bayān,* 1:465–66.

288. Muḥammad b. 'Alī Ibn Bābūya, *Man lā yaḥḍuruhu al-faqīh*, ed. 'Alī Akbar al-Ghaffārī, vol. 3 of 4 vols. (Qom: Daftar-i Intishārāt-i Islamī, 1993), 345.

289. Ibn Bābūya, *Man lā yaḥḍuruhu al-faqīh*, 3:345.

290. Of course, everyone may commit minor sins, those who avoid committing major sins will be addressed by God Almighty.

291. 'Ayyāshī, *Tafsīr al-'ayyāshī*, 1:75.

292. *Khums* is a jurisprudential term meaning to pay one fifth of the annual surplus income, or of mine and treasure, taking into account the required conditions in jurisprudence.

293. Maḥmūd b. 'Umar al-Zamakhsharī, *al-Kashshāf 'an ḥaqā'iq al-tanzīl wa 'uyūn*, vol. 1 (Beirut: Dār al-Kitāb al-'Arabī, 1987), 208.

294. Tūsī, *al-Tibyān,* 2:97.

295. *Nahj al-balāgha*, Wisdom 372.

296. Tūsī, *al-Tibyān,* 2:99; Ṭabrisī, *Majma' al-bayān,* 1975, 1:478.

297. Tūsī, *al-Tibyān,* 2:107–9.

298. Ṭabrisī, *Majma' al-bayān,* 2:490.

299. Tūsī, *al-Tibyān,* 2:117.

300. Ibid., 2:120–23.

301. Kāshānī, *Tafsīr al-ṣāfī*, 1:315.

302. Ṭabrisī, *Majma' al-bayān,* 2:500.

303. Tūsī, *al-Tibyān,* 2:130.

304. Ibid., 2:130–31.

305. Kāshānī, *Tafsīr al-ṣāfi,* 1:222–24.

306. Ṭabrisī, *Majma' al-bayān,* 2:504–5.

307. Kāshānī, *Tafsīr al-ṣāfi,* 1:228.

308. Rāzī , *Mafātīḥ al-ghayb,* 5:287–89.

309. Burton, *The Collection of the Quran*

310. Ṭabāṭabā'ī, *al-Mizān* 2:60–63.

311. Singular *takbīr,* refers to the Arabic phrase for magnification of God.

312. al-Qushayrī, *Laṭā'if al-ishārāt,* 1:168.

313. Mahdī Bahr al-'Ulūm, *Risāla al-sayr wa-al-sulūk* (Tehran: Intisharāt-e Hikmat, 1982).

314. Ṭabāṭabā'ī, *al-Mizān* , 2:102–3.

315. 'Ayyāshī, *Tafsīr al-'ayyāshī,* 1:104.

316. Ṭabāṭabā'ī, *al-Mizān* 2:123–24.

317. Ṭabrisī, *Majma' al-bayān,* 2:546.

318. Ṭabāṭabā'ī, *al-Mizān* 2:124–27.

319. al-Shaykh al-Mufid, *Awā'il al-maqālāt fi al-madhāhib wa-al-mukhtārāt,* (Beirut: Dār al-Mufīd, 1993).

320. Ibid., 83.

321. al-Mufid, *Awā'il al-maqālāt,* 83.

322. Tūsī, *al-Tibyān,* 2:222.

323. Muhammad Abduh, *Tafsīr Al-Manār,* ed. Rashid Rida, vol. 2 of 12 vols. (Cairo: Dār al-Manār, 1947), 375–76.

324. Ṭabrisī, *Majma' al-bayān,* 2:626; 'Ayyāshī, *Tafsīr al-'ayyāshī,* 1:283.

325. Ṭabrisī, *Majma' al-bayān,* 2:626.

326. Rāzī , *Mafātīḥ al-ghayb,* vol. 7:14.

327. Majlisī, *Biḥār al-anwār*, 10:319.

328. 'Ayyāshī, *Tafsīr al-'ayyāshī*, 1:137.

329. Al-Shaykh al-Sadūq, *Ma'ani al-akhbar*, pp. 321-323.

330. Ṭabāṭabā'ī, *al-Mizān,* 2:359–60.

331. Ibid., 2:351–52.

332. Ibid., 2:353–54.

333. Tūsī, *al-Tibyān,* 2:231.

334. Imam Ali Zayn al-Abidin, *The Psalms of Islam (Sahifa Sajjadiya),* trans. William C. Chittick, online version (Muhammadi Trust, 1988), 197, [https://www.al-islam.org/sahifa-al-kamilah-al-sajjadiyya-imam-ali-zayn-al-abidin.]

335. Ṭabrisī, *Majma' al-bayān,* 2:381.

336. *Nahjul-balāgha*, Saying 258.

337. al-Tha'labī, *Tafsīr al-tha'labī*, 7:62.

338. Ṭabāṭabā'ī, *al-Mizān* 2:388.

339. Ibid., 2:400.

340. Kāshānī, *Tafsīr al-ṣāfī*, 1:301; Ṭabrisī, 2:667.

341. Ṭabāṭabā'ī, *al-Mizān* 2:418–20.

342. Qummī, *Tafsīr al-qummī*, 1:93; Ṭabrisī, *Majma' al-bayān,* 2:673; al-Tha'labī, *Tafsīr al-tha'labī*, 2:284.

343. Rāzī , *Mafātīḥ al-ghayb,* 7:7–9.

344. Abduh, *Tafsīr al-manār*. vol. 2

BIBLIOGRAPHY

Abduh, Muhammad. *Tafsīr al-manār*. Edited by Rashid Rida. Vol. 2. 12 vols. Cairo: Dār al-Manār, 1947.

Askari, Imam Hasan. *Tafseer Imam Hasan Askari*. Translated by S. H. Rizvi. Online. Qom: Ansariyan Publications, 2009. [https://www.al-islam.org/tafseer-imam-hasan-askari/exegesis-surah-baqarah-verses-63-92#exegesis-surah-baqarah-verse-278-79.]

———. *Tafsīr al-imām al-ʿaskarī*. Madrasa al-Imām Mahdī, 1989.

ʿAyyāshī, Muḥammad b. Masʿūd. *Tafsīr al-ʿayyāshī*. Edited by Sayyid Hāshim Rasūlī Maḥlātī. Vol. 1. 2 vols. Tehran: al-Maṭbaʿa al-ʿAlamiyya, 1961

al-Baghawī, Ḥusayn b. Masʿūd. *Maʿālim al-tanzīl*. Vol. 1. Beirut: Dār al-Kutub al-ʿIlmiyya, 1971.

Bahmanpour, Mohammad Saeed. 'Book Review of Revelation and Falsification The Kitab Al-Qira'at of Ahmad b Muhammad'. *Journal of Shi'a Islamic Studies* 3/2 (2010): 231–33.

———. *The Idols Will Fall*. London: ICAS Press, 2009.

Baḥr al-ʿUlūm, Mahdī. *Risāla al-Sayr wa-al-sulūk*. Tehran: Intisharāt-e Hikmat, 1982.

Balāghī, Muḥammad Javād. *Ālā' al-raḥmān fī tafsīr al-qur'ān*. Vol. 1. 2 vols. Qom: Maktabat al-Wijdān, 1971.

Brown, William P., ed. *The Ten Commandments: The Reciprocity of*

Faithfulness. Louisville, London: Presbyterian Publishing Corporation, 2004.

al-Bukhārī, Muḥammad. *Ṣaḥīḥ al-bukhārī.* Vol. 8. 9 vols. Beirut: Dār Ṭawq al-Najāt, 2001.

Burton, John. *The Collection of the Qur'an*. First Edition. Cambridge University Press, 1977.

Ehrman, Bart D. *How Jesus Became God: The Exaltation of a Jewish Preacher from Galilee.* USA: HarperOne, 2014.

al-Faruqi, Ismail Ragi. 'Towards a New Methodology for Qur'anic Exegesis,' *Islamic Studies* 1/1 (1962).

Ghazālī, Abū Ḥāmid. *Iḥyā' ʿulūm al-dīn.* Persian translation. Vol 3. Tehran: no publisher, 1955.

Gil, Moshe. *Jews in Islamic Countries in the Middle Ages.* Translated by David Strassler. Leiden: Brill, 2004.

Greenman, Jeffrey P., and Timothy Larsen, eds. *The Decalogue Through the Centuries: From the Hebrew Scriptures to Benedict XVI.* Louisville, Kentucky: Presbyterian Publishing Corporation, 2012.

Ibn Anas, Mālik. *Muwaṭṭā'.* Vol. 1. Beirut: Dār Iḥyā', 1994.

Ibn Bābūya, Muḥammad b. ʿAlī. *Man lā yaḥḍuruhu al-faqīh.* Edited by ʿAlī Akbar al-Ghaffārī. Vol. 3. 4 vols. Qom: Daftar-i Intishārāt-i Islamī, 1993.

Ibn Hishām. *Sīra al-nabawī.* Edited by ʿUmar ʿAbd al-Salām Tadmurī. Vol. 2. Beirut: Dār al-Kitāb al-ʿArabī, 1990.

Ibn Sulaymān, Muqātil. *Tafsīr*. Vol. 1. 8 vols. Beirut: Dār al-Kutub al-ʿIlmiyya, 2003.

Jaʿfarī, Yaʿqūb. *Tafsīr kawthar.* Vol. 1. 6 vols. Qom: Muassasa-i Intishārāt-i Hijrat, 1997.

Kara, Seyfeddin. *In Search of Ali Ibn Abi Talib's Codex: History and Traditions of the Earliest Copy of the Qur'an.* Berlin: Gerlach Press, 2018.

———. 'Rational-Analytical Tafsīr in Modern Iran: The Influence of the Uṣūlī School of Jurisprudence on the Interpretation of the Qur'an.' In *Approaches to the Qur'an in Contemporary Iran*, edited by Alessandro Cancian, 19–39. London: Oxford University Press, 2019.

Kāshānī, Fayḍ. *Tafsīr al-ṣāfī.* Vol. 1. 2 vols. Qom: Markaz al-Abḥāth wa-al-Dirarāsāt al-Islāmiyya, 1997.

———. *Tafsīr al-ṣāfī.* Vol. 1. 7 vols. Tehran: Dār al-Kutub, 2007.

Kāshānī, Mullā Fatḥullāh. *Manhaj al-ṣādigīn.* Qom: Būstān-i Kitāb, 2011.

Khoei, Abu al-Qasim. *Miṣbāḥ al-fuqāha.* Vol. 3. 7 vols. Qom: 1958.

———. *Prolegomena to the Qur'an.* New York: Oxford University Press, 1998.

Kulaynī, Muḥammad b. Ya'qūb b. Isḥāq. *Al-kāfī fī 'ilm al-dīn.* Edited by Muḥammad Ghafārī 'Alī Akbar Akhūndī. Vol. 1-2. 15 vols. Tehran: Dār al-Kutub al-Islāmiyya, 1986.

Makarim Shirazi, Nasir. *Tafsīr-i nimūna.* Vol. 1. 27 vols. Tehran: Dār al-Kitāb, 2008.

al-Maḥallī, Jalāladdīn, and Jalāladdīn al-Suyūṭī. *Tafsīr al-jalālayn.* Vol. 1. Beirut: Dār al-Ma'rifa, 1971.

———. *Tafsīr al-jalālayn.* Vol. 1. 8 vols. Beirut: Dār al-Kutub al-'Ilmiyya, 1996.

———. *al-Durr al-manthūr fī al-tafsīr bi-al-ma'thūr.* Vol. 5. 8 vols. Qom: al-Najafī, 1982.

Majlisī, Muḥammad Bāqir. *Biḥār al-anwār.* Vol. 24. 104 vols.

Muassasa al-Wafā', 1983.

———. *Biḥār al-anwār.* Vol. 2,10. 111 vols. Beirut: Dār Iḥyā' al-Turāth al-'Arabī, 1983.

al-Marāghī, Aḥmad b. Muṣṭafā. *Tafsīr al-marāghī.* Vol. 1. 30 vols. Egypt: Shirkat Maktaba wa-Maṭbu'a, 1946.

al-Mufīd, al-Shaykh. *Awā'il al-maqālāt fī al-madhāhib wa-al-kukhtārāt.* Beirut: Dār al-Mufīd, 1993.

Muslim, Ibn al-Ḥajjāj. *Ṣaḥīḥ muslim.* Vol. 4. 5 vols. Beirut: Dār Iḥyā' al-Turāth al-'Arabī, 2010.

al-Naḥḥās, Abū Ja'far. *Al-nasikh wa-al-mansūkh.* Riyadh: Markaz al-Turāth, 2013.

Qadhi, Abu Ammaar Yasir. *An Introduction to the Sciences of the Qur'an.* UK: Al-Hidaayah Publishing & Distribution, 1999.

Qara'i, Ali Quli. *The Qur'ān: With a Phrase-by-Phrase English Translation.* Second Edition. London: ICAS Press, 2005.

al-Qāsimī, Muḥammad Jamāl al-Dīn. *Maḥāsin al-ta'wīl.* Vol. 1. 9 vols. Beirut: Dār al-Kutub al-'Ilmiyya, 2002.

al-Qushayrī, Abū al-Qāsim 'Abd al-Karīm. *Laṭā'if al-ishārāt: Subtle Allusions.* Translated by Kristin Zahra Sands. USA: Fons Vitae, 2017.

———. *Laṭā'if al-ishārāt bi-tafsīr al-qur'ān.* Vol. 1. 3 vols. Cairo: Al-Hay'a al-Miṣriyya al-'Āmma lil-Kitāb, 2000.

Qummī, 'Alī b. Ibrāhīm. *Tafsīr Qummī.* Edited by Ṭayyib Mūsāwī Jazāirī. Vol. 1. 2 vols. Qom: Dār al-Kutub, 1983.

Qurashī, 'Alī Akbar. *Aḥsan al-ḥadīth.* Vol. 1. Tehran: Vāhid-i Tahqīqāt-i Islāmī-i Bunyād-i Bi'sa, 1987.

Qutb, Sayyid. *Fī ẓilāl al-qur'ān*. Vol. 1. 6 vols. Beirut: Dār al-Shurūq, 1977.

———. *In the Shade of the Qur'an (Fī ẓilāl al-qur'ān)*. Vols 1-2 (no publication details). [https://tafsirzilal.files.wordpress.com/2012/06/al-baqarah-eng.pdf]

Rāzī, Fakhr al-Dīn. *Mafātīḥ al-ghayb*. Vol. 1, 2, 3, 4, 5, 7. 32 vols. Damascus: Dār al-Fikr, 1981.

al-Ṣadūq, al-Shaykh. *ʿUyūn akhbār al-riḍā*. Edited by Ḥusayn al-Aʿlamī. Vol. 2. 2 vols. Beirut: Muassasa al-Aʿlāmī, 1984.

———. *ʿIlal al-sharāʾi*. Qum: Nashr-e Dāvari, 2006.

al-Ṣaffār, Muḥammad b. al-Ḥasan. *Baṣāʾir al-darajāt*. Qom: Āyatollāh Marʿashī Najafī Library, 1983.

al-Shāfiʿī, Muḥammad b. Idrīs. *Treatise on the Foundations of Islamic Jurisprudence – Al Shafi'i's Risala*. Translated by Majid Khadduri. Turkey: Fons Vitae Publishing, 2008.

Smith, C. W. F. *The Jesus of the Parables*. Philadelphia: Westminster Press, 1948.

Ṭabāṭabā'ī, Mohammad Hossein. *Al-mizān fi tafsīr al-qur'ān*. Vol. 1-2. 20 vols. Qom: Ismāʿīlīyān, 1985.

———. *Al-mīzān fi tafsīr al-qur'ān*. Vol. 1. 22 vols. Beirut: Muassasa al-Aʿlāmī lil-Maṭbūʿāt, 1997.

———. *The Qur'an in Islam*. London: Zahra Publications, 1987.

Ṭabāṭabā'ī, Muḥīṭ. 'Ṣābi'īn ahle itāband.' In *Yādnāme ustād Motahhari*, ed. by Abdolkarim Soroush. Tehran: Ṣāzimān-e Tablīghāt-e Islami, 1984.

Ṭabarī, Muḥammad b. Jarīr. *Jāmiʿ al-bayān ʿan taʾwīl āya al-qurān*. Vol. 2. 25 vols. Cairo: Dār Hijr, 2008.

Ṭabrisī, Abū ʿAlī. *Majmaʿ al-bayān fī tafsīr al-qurʾān*. Vol. 1. 10 vols. Beirut: Dār al-Maʿrifa, 1975.

———. *Majmaʿ Al-bayān fī tafsīr al-qurʾān*. Vol. 2. 10 vols. Beirut: Dār al-Maʿrifa, 1975.

Taleghani, Mahmoud. *Partovi az qurʾan*. Vol. 1. Tehran: Shirkat-i Sehami-i Intishār,1983.

al-Thaʿlabī, Abū Isḥāk. *Tafsīr al-thaʿlabī*. Edited by Ibn ʿĀshūr Abū Muḥammad. Vol. 1. 10 vols. Beirut: Dār Iḥyā, 2002.

———. *Tafsīr al-thaʿlabī*. Edited by Ibn ʿĀshūr Abū Muḥammad. Vol. 2. 10 vols. Beirut: Dār Iḥyā, 2002.

Tūsī, Shaykh. *Al-tibyān fī tafsīr al-qurʾān*. Vol. 1-2. 10 vols. Beirut: Dār al-Iḥyā al-Turāth al-ʿArabī, 1971.

Wilkinson, Richard H. T*he Complete Gods and Goddesses of Ancient Egypt*. London: Thames & Hudson, 2003.

Zamakhsharī, Maḥmūd b. ʿUmar. *Al-kashshāf ʿan ḥaqāʿiq al-tanzīl wa- ʿuyūn*. Vol. 1. 4 vols. Beirut: Dār al-Kitāb al-ʿArabī, 1987.

Zayn al-Abidin, Imam Ali. *The Psalms of Islam (Sahifa Sajjadiya)*. Translated by William C. Chittick. Online Version. Muhammadi Trust, 1988. [https://www.al-islam.org/sahifa-al-kamilah-al-sajjadiyya-imam-ali-zayn-al-abidin.]

al-Zurqānī, ʿAbd al-ʿAẓīm. *Manāhil al- ʿirfān fī ʿulūm al-qurʾān*. Beirut: Dār al-Kutub al-ʿIlmīya, 1996.

www.ingramcontent.com/pod-product-compliance
Lightning Source LLC
Chambersburg PA
CBHW021426080526
44588CB00009B/442